Mastering Regular Expressions

Mastering Regular Expressions

Second Edition

Jeffrey E. F. Friedl

O'REILLY®

Beijing · Cambridge · Farnham · Köln · Paris · Sebastopol · Taipei · Tokyo

Mastering Regular Expressions, Second Edition
by Jeffrey E. F. Friedl

Copyright © 2002, 1997 O'Reilly & Associates, Inc. All rights reserved.
Printed in the United States of America.

Published by O'Reilly & Associates, Inc., 1005 Gravenstein Highway North, Sebastopol, CA 95472.

O'Reilly & Associates books may be purchased for educational, business, or sales promotional use. Online editions are also available for most titles (*safari.oreilly.com*). For more information contact our corporate/institutional sales department: 800-998-9938 or *corporate@oreilly.com*.

Editor: Andy Oram

Production Editor: Jeffrey E. F. Friedl

Cover Designer: Edie Freedman

Printing History:

January 1997:	First Edition.
July 2002:	Second Edition.

ISBN: 0-596-00289-0

[M]

FOR 文枝 (Fumie)

For putting up with me.

And for the years I worked on this book,
for putting up without me.

Table of Contents

Preface

This book is about a powerful tool called "regular expressions". It teaches you how to use regular expressions to solve problems and get the most out of tools and languages that provide them. Most documentation that mentions regular expressions doesn't even begin to hint at their power, but this book is about *mastering* regular expressions.

Regular expressions are available in many types of tools (editors, word processors, system tools, database engines, and such), but their power is most fully exposed when available as part of a programming language. Examples include Java and JScript, Visual Basic and VBScript, JavaScript and ECMAScript, C, C++, C#, elisp, Perl, Python, Tcl, Ruby, PHP, sed, and awk. In fact, regular expressions are the very heart of many programs written in some of these languages.

There's a good reason that regular expressions are found in so many diverse languages and applications: they are extremely powerful. At a low level, a regular expression describes a chunk of text. You might use it to verify a user's input, or perhaps to sift through large amounts of data. On a higher level, regular expressions allow you to master your data. Control it. Put it to work for you. To master regular expressions is to master your data.

The Need for This Book

I finished the first edition of this book in late 1996, and wrote it simply because there was a need. Good documentation on regular expressions just wasn't available, so most of their power went untapped. Regular-expression documentation was available, but it centered on the "low-level view." It seemed to me that they were analogous to showing someone the alphabet and expecting them to learn to speak.

Why I've Written the Second Edition

In the five and a half years since the first edition of this book was published, the world of regular expressions expanded considerably. The regular expressions of almost every tool and language became more powerful and expressive. Perl, Python, Tcl, Java, and Visual Basic all got new regular-expression backends. New languages with regular expression support, like Ruby, PHP, and C#, were developed and became popular. During all this time, the basic core of the book — how to truly understand regular expressions and how to get the most from them — maintained as important and relevant as ever.

Gradually, the first edition started to show its age. It needed updating to reflect the new languages and features, as well as the expanding role that regular expressions play in today's Internet world. When I decided to update the first edition, it was with a promise to my wife that it would take no more than three months. Two years later, luckily still married, almost the entire book has been rewritten from scratch. It's good, though, that it took so long, for it brought me into 2002, a particularly active year for regular expressions. In early 2002, both Java 1.4 (with `java.util.regex`) and Microsoft's .NET were released, and Perl 5.8 was released that summer. They are all covered fully in this book.

Intended Audience

This book will interest anyone who has an opportunity to use regular expressions. If you don't yet understand the power that regular expressions can provide, you should benefit greatly as a whole new world is opened up to you. This book should expand your understanding, even if you consider yourself an accomplished regular-expression expert. After the first edition, it wasn't uncommon for me to receive an email that started "I *thought* I knew regular expressions until I read *Mastering Regular Expressions. Now* I do."

Programmers working on text-related tasks, such as web programming, will find an absolute gold mine of detail, hints, tips, and *understanding* that can be put to immediate use. The detail and thoroughness is simply not found anywhere else.

Regular expressions are an idea — one that is implemented in various ways by various utilities (many, many more than are specifically presented in this book). If you master the general concept of regular expressions, it's a short step to mastering a particular implementation. This book concentrates on that idea, so most of the knowledge presented here transcends the utilities and languages used to present the examples.

How to Read This Book

This book is part tutorial, part reference manual, and part story, depending on when you use it. Readers familiar with regular expressions might feel that they can immediately begin using this book as a detailed reference, flipping directly to the section on their favorite utility. I would like to discourage that.

To get the most out of this book, read the first six chapters as a story. I have found that certain habits and ways of thinking can be a great help to reaching a full understanding, but such things are absorbed over pages, not merely memorized from a list.

This book tells a story, but one with many details. Once you've read the story to get the overall picture, this book is also useful as a reference. The last three chapters (covering specifics of Perl, Java, and .NET) rely heavily on your having read the first six chapters. To help you get the most from each part, I've used cross references liberally, and I've worked hard to make the index as useful as possible. (Cross references are often presented as "☞" followed by a page number.)

Until you read the full story, this book's use as a reference makes little sense. Before reading the story, you might look at one of the tables, such as the chart on page 91, and think it presents all the relevant information you need to know. But a great deal of background information does not appear in the charts themselves, but rather in the associated story. Once you've read the story, you'll have an appreciation for the issues, what you can remember off the top of your head, and what is important to check up on.

Organization

The nine chapters of this book can be logically divided into roughly three parts. Here's a quick overview:

The Introduction
Chapter 1 introduces the concept of regular expressions.
Chapter 2 takes a look at text processing with regular expressions.
Chapter 3 provides an overview of features and utilities, plus a bit of history.

The Details
Chapter 4 explains the details of how regular expressions work.
Chapter 5 works through examples, using the knowledge from Chapter 4.
Chapter 6 discusses efficiency in detail.

Tool-Specific Information
Chapter 7 covers Perl regular expressions in detail.
Chapter 8 looks at regular-expression packages for Java.
Chapter 9 looks at .NET's language-neutral regular-expression package.

The Introduction

The introduction elevates the absolute novice to "issue-aware" novice. Readers with a fair amount of experience can feel free to skim the early chapters, but I particularly recommend Chapter 3 even for the grizzled expert.

* Chapter 1, *Introduction to Regular Expressions*, is geared toward the complete novice. I introduce the concept of regular expressions using the widely available program *egrep*, and offer my perspective on how to *think* regular expressions, instilling a solid foundation for the advanced concepts presented in later chapters. Even readers with former experience would do well to skim this first chapter.

* Chapter 2, *Extended Introductory Examples*, looks at real text processing in a programming language that has regular-expression support. The additional examples provide a basis for the detailed discussions of later chapters, and show additional important thought processes behind crafting advanced regular expressions. To provide a feel for how to "speak in regular expressions," this chapter takes a problem requiring an advanced solution and shows ways to solve it using two unrelated regular-expression–wielding tools.

* Chapter 3, *Overview of Regular Expression Features and Flavors*, provides an overview of the wide range of regular expressions commonly found in tools today. Due to their turbulent history, current commonly-used regular-expression flavors can differ greatly. This chapter also takes a look at a bit of the history and evolution of regular expressions and the programs that use them. The end of this chapter also contains the "Guide to the Advanced Chapters." This guide is your road map to getting the most out of the advanced material that follows.

The Details

Once you have the basics down, it's time to investigate the *how* and the *why*. Like the "teach a man to fish" parable, truly understanding the issues will allow you to apply that knowledge whenever and wherever regular expressions are found.

* Chapter 4, *The Mechanics of Expression Processing*, ratchets up the pace several notches and begins the central core of this book. It looks at the important inner workings of how regular expression engines really work from a *practical* point of view. Understanding the details of how a regular expressions are handled goes a very long way toward allowing you to master them.

* Chapter 5, *Practical Regex Techniques*, then puts that knowledge to high-level, practical use. Common (but complex) problems are explored in detail, all with the aim of expanding and deepening your regular-expression experience.

- Chapter 6, *Crafting an Efficient Expression*, looks at the real-life efficiency ramifications of the regular expressions available to most programming languages. This chapter puts information detailed in Chapters 4 and 5 to use for exploiting an engine's strengths and stepping around its weaknesses.

Tool-Specific Information

Once the lessons of Chapters 4, 5, and 6 are under your belt, there is usually little to say about specific implementations. However, I've devoted an entire chapter to each of three popular systems:

- Chapter 7, *Perl*, closely examines regular expressions in Perl, arguably the most popular regular-expression–laden programming language in use today. It has only four operators related to regular expressions, but their myriad of options and special situations provides an extremely rich set of programming options — and pitfalls. The very richness that allows the programmer to move quickly from concept to program can be a minefield for the uninitiated. This detailed chapter clears a path.

- Chapter 8, *Java*, surveys the landscape of regular-expression packages available for Java. Points of comparison are discussed, and two packages with notable strengths are covered in more detail.

- Chapter 9, *.NET*, is the documentation for the .NET regular-expression library that Microsoft neglected to provide. Whether using VB.NET, C#, C++, JScript, VBscript, ECMAScript, or any of the other languages that use .NET components, this chapter provides the details you need to employ .NET regular-expressions to the fullest.

Typographical Conventions

When doing (or talking about) detailed and complex text processing, being precise is important. The mere addition or subtraction of a space can make a world of difference, so I've used the following special conventions in typesetting this book:

- A regular expression generally appears like ⌈this⌋. Notice the thin corners which flag "this is a regular expression." Literal text (such as that being searched) generally appears like 'this'. At times, I'll leave off the thin corners or quotes when obviously unambiguous. Also, code snippets and screen shots are always presented in their natural state, so the quotes and corners are not used in such cases.

- I use visually distinct ellipses within literal text and regular expressions. For example [⋯] represents a set of square brackets with unspecified contents, while [. . .] would be a set containing three periods.

- Without special presentation, it is virtually impossible to know how many spaces are between the letters in "a   b", so when spaces appear in regular expressions and selected literal text, they are presented with the '␣' symbol. This way, it will be clear that there are exactly four spaces in 'a␣␣␣␣b'.

  I also use visual tab, newline, and carriage-return characters. Here's a summary of the four:

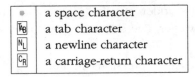

␣	a space character
ᵀᴀᴮ	a tab character
ᴺʟ	a newline character
ᶜʀ	a carriage-return character

- At times, I use underlining or shade the background to highlight parts of literal text or a regular expression. In this example the underline shows where in the text the expression actually matches:

  Because ⌈cat⌋ matches 'It␣indicates␣your␣cat␣is␣⋯' instead of the word 'cat', we realize . . .

  In this example the underlines highlight what has just been added to an expression under discussion:

  To make this useful, we can wrap ⌈Subject|Date⌋ with parentheses, and append a colon and a space. This yields ⌈(Subject|Date):␣⌋.

- This book is full of details and examples, so to help you get the most out of it, I've provided an extensive set of cross references. They often appear in the text in a "☞123" notation, which means "see page 123." For example, it might appear like " . . . is described in Table 8-1 (☞ 373)."

Exercises

Occasionally, and particularly in the early chapters, I'll pose a question to highlight the importance of the concept under discussion. They're not there just to take up space; I really do want you to try them before continuing. Please. So as not to dilute their importance, I've sprinkled only a few throughout the entire book. They also serve as checkpoints: if they take more than a few moments, it's probably best to go over the relevant section again before continuing on.

To help entice you to actually think about these questions as you read them, I've made checking the answers a breeze: just turn the page. Answers to questions marked with ❖ are always found by turning just one page. This way, they're out of sight while you think about the answer, but are within easy reach.

Links, Code, Errata, and Contacts

I learned the hard way with the first edition that URLs change more quickly than a printed book can be updated, so rather than providing an appendix of URLs, I'll provide just one:

```
http://regex.info/
```

There you can find regular-expression links, many of the code snippets from this book, a searchable index, and much more. In the unlikely event this book contains an error :-), the errata will be available as well.

If you find an error in this book, or just want to drop me a note, you can contact me at jfriedl@regex.info.

The publisher can be contacted at:

O'Reilly & Associates, Inc.
1005 Gravenstein Highway North
Sebastopol, CA 95472
(800) 998-9938 (in the United States or Canada)
(707) 829-0515 (international/local)
(707) 829-0104 (fax)
bookquestions@oreilly.com

For more information about books, conferences, Resource Centers, and the O'Reilly Network, see the O'Reilly web site at:

```
http://www.oreilly.com
```

Personal Comments and Acknowledgments

Writing the first edition of this book was a grueling task that took two and a half years and the help of many people. After the toll it took on my health and sanity, I promised that I'd never put myself through such an experience again.

I've many people to thank for helping me break that promise. Foremost is my wife, Fumie. If you find this book useful, thank her; without her support and understanding, I would have never had the sanity to make it through what turned out to be almost a two year complete rewrite.

I also appreciate the support of Yahoo! Inc., where I have enjoyed slinging regular expressions for five years, and my manager Mike Bennett. His flexibility and understanding allowed this project to happen.

While researching and writing this book, many people helped educate me on languages or systems I didn't know, and more still reviewed and corrected drafts as the manuscript developed. In particular, I'd like to thank my brother, Stephen Friedl, for his meticulous and detailed reviews of the manuscript. The book is much better because of them.

I'd also like to thank William F. Maton, Dean Wilson, Derek Balling, Jarkko Hietaniemi, Jeremy Zawodny, Ethan Nicholas, Kasia Trapszo, Jeffrey Papen, Dr. Yadong Li, Daniel F. Savarese, David Flanagan, Kristine Rudkin, Shawn Purcell, Josh Woodward, Ray Goldberger, and my editor, Andy Oram. Also thanks to O'Reilly's Linda Mui for navigating this book through the pre-publication minefield and keeping the troops rallied, and Jessamyn Reed for creating the new figures this edition required.

Special thanks for providing an insider's look at Java go to Mike "madbot" McCloskey, Mark Reinhold, and Dr. Cliff Click, all of Sun Microsystems. For .NET insight, I'd like to thank David Gutierrez and Kit George, of Microsoft.

I'd like to thank Dr. Ken Lunde of Adobe Systems, who created custom characters and fonts for a number of the typographical aspects of this book. The Japanese characters are from Adobe Systems' *Heisei Mincho W3* typeface, while the Korean is from the Korean Ministry of Culture and Sports *Munhwa* typeface. It's also Ken who originally gave me the guiding principle that governs my writing: "you do the research so your readers don't have to."

For help in setting up the server for `http://regex.info`, I'd like to thank Jeffrey Papen and Peak Web Hosting (`http://www.PeakWebhosting.com/`).

1

Introduction to Regular Expressions

Here's the scenario: you're given the job of checking the pages on a web server for doubled words (such as "this this"), a common problem with documents subject to heavy editing. Your job is to create a solution that will:

- Accept any number of files to check, report each line of each file that has doubled words, highlight (using standard ANSI escape sequences) each doubled word, and ensure that the source filename appears with each line in the report.

- Work across lines, even finding situations where a word at the end of one line is repeated at the beginning of the next.

- Find doubled words despite capitalization differences, such as with 'The the ', as well as allow differing amounts of *whitespace* (spaces, tabs, newlines, and the like) to lie between the words.

- Find doubled words even when separated by HTML tags. HTML tags are for marking up text on World Wide Web pages, for example, to make a word bold: '···it is <B>very</B> very important···'.

That's certainly a tall order! But, it's a real problem that needs to be solved. At one point while working on the manuscript for this book, I ran such a tool on what I'd written so far and was surprised at the way numerous doubled words had crept in. There are many programming languages one could use to solve the problem, but one with regular expression support can make the job substantially easier.

Regular expressions are the key to powerful, flexible, and efficient text processing. Regular expressions themselves, with a general pattern notation almost like a mini programming language, allow you to describe and parse text. With additional support provided by the particular tool being used, regular expressions can add, remove, isolate, and generally fold, spindle, and mutilate all kinds of text and data.

It might be as simple as a text editor's search command or as powerful as a full text processing language. This book shows you the many ways regular expressions can increase your productivity. It teaches you how to *think* regular expressions so that you can master them, taking advantage of the full magnitude of their power.

A full program that solves the doubled-word problem can be implemented in just a few lines of many of today's popular languages. With a single regular-expression search-and-replace command, you can find and highlight doubled words in the document. With another, you can remove all lines without doubled words (leaving only the lines of interest left to report). Finally, with a third, you can ensure that each line to be displayed begins with the name of the file the line came from. We'll see examples in Perl and Java in the next chapter.

The host language (Perl, Java, VB.NET, or whatever) provides the peripheral processing support, but the real power comes from regular expressions. In harnessing this power for your own needs, you learn how to write regular expressions to identify text you want, while bypassing text you don't. You can then combine your expressions with the language's support constructs to actually do something with the text (add appropriate highlighting codes, remove the text, change the text, and so on).

Solving Real Problems

Knowing how to wield regular expressions unleashes processing powers you might not even know were available. Numerous times in any given day, regular expressions help me solve problems both large and small (and quite often, ones that are small but would be large if not for regular expressions).

Showing an example that provides the key to solving a large and important problem illustrates the benefit of regular expressions clearly, but perhaps not so obvious is the way regular expressions can be used throughout the day to solve rather "uninteresting" problems. I use "uninteresting" in the sense that such problems are not often the subject of bar-room war stories, but quite interesting in that until they're solved, you can't get on with your real work.

As a simple example, I needed to check a lot of files (the 70 or so files comprising the source for this book, actually) to confirm that each file contained 'SetSize' exactly as often (or as rarely) as it contained 'ResetSize'. To complicate matters, I needed to disregard capitalization (such that, for example, 'setSIZE' would be counted just the same as 'SetSize'). Inspecting the 32,000 lines of text by hand certainly wasn't practical.

Even using the normal "find this word" search in an editor would have been arduous, especially with all the files and all the possible capitalization differences.

Regular expressions to the rescue! Typing just a *single,* short command, I was able to check all files and confirm what I needed to know. Total elapsed time: perhaps 15 seconds to type the command, and another 2 seconds for the actual check of all the data. Wow! (If you're interested to see what I actually used, peek ahead to page 36.)

As another example, I was once helping a friend with some email problems on a remote machine, and he wanted me to send a listing of messages in his mailbox file. I could have loaded a copy of the whole file into a text editor and manually removed all but the few header lines from each message, leaving a sort of table of contents. Even if the file wasn't as huge as it was, and even if I wasn't connected via a slow dial-up line, the task would have been slow and monotonous. Also, I would have been placed in the uncomfortable position of actually seeing the text of his personal mail.

Regular expressions to the rescue again! I gave a simple command (using the common search tool *egrep* described later in this chapter) to display the `From:` and `Subject:` line from each message. To tell *egrep* exactly which kinds of lines I wanted to see, I used the regular expression `^(From|Subject):`.

Once he got his list, he asked me to send a particular (5,000-line!) message. Again, using a text editor or the mail system itself to extract just the one message would have taken a long time. Rather, I used another tool (one called *sed*) and again used regular expressions to describe exactly the text in the file I wanted. This way, I could extract and send the desired message quickly and easily.

Saving both of us a lot of time and aggravation by using the regular expression was not "exciting," but surely much more exciting than wasting an hour in the text editor. Had I not known regular expressions, I would have never considered that there was an alternative. So, to a fair extent, this story is representative of how regular expressions and associated tools can empower you to do things you might have never thought you wanted to do.

Once you learn regular expressions, you'll realize that they're an invaluable part of your toolkit, and you'll wonder how you could ever have gotten by without them.[†]

A full command of regular expressions is an invaluable skill. This book provides the information needed to acquire that skill, and it is my hope that it provides the motivation to do so, as well.

---

† If you have a TiVo, you already know the feeling!

Regular Expressions as a Language

Unless you've had some experience with regular expressions, you won't understand the regular expression ⌜^(From|Subject):⌟ from the last example, but there's nothing magic about it. For that matter, there is nothing magic about magic. The magician merely understands something simple which doesn't *appear* to be simple or natural to the untrained audience. Once you learn how to hold a card while making your hand look empty, you only need practice before you, too, can "do magic." Like a foreign language — once you learn it, it stops sounding like gibberish.

The Filename Analogy

Since you have decided to use this book, you probably have at least some idea of just what a "regular expression" is. Even if you don't, you are almost certainly already familiar with the basic concept.

You know that *report.txt* is a specific filename, but if you have had any experience with Unix or DOS/Windows, you also know that the pattern "*.txt" can be used to select multiple files. With filename patterns like this (called *file globs* or *wildcards*), a few characters have special meaning. The star means "match anything," and a question mark means "match any one character." So, with the file glob "*.txt", we start with a match-anything ⌜*⌟ and end with the literal ⌜.txt⌟, so we end up with a pattern that means "select the files whose names start with anything and end with .txt".

Most systems provide a few additional special characters, but, in general, these filename patterns are limited in expressive power. This is not much of a shortcoming because the scope of the problem (to provide convenient ways to specify groups of files) is limited, well, simply to filenames.

On the other hand, dealing with general text is a much larger problem. Prose and poetry, program listings, reports, HTML, code tables, word lists... you name it, if a particular need is specific enough, such as "selecting files," you can develop some kind of specialized scheme or tool to help you accomplish it. However, over the years, a *generalized pattern language* has developed, which is powerful and expressive for a wide variety of uses. Each program implements and uses them differently, but in general, **this powerful pattern language and the patterns themselves are called** *regular expressions*.

The Language Analogy

Full regular expressions are composed of two types of characters. The special characters (like the ∗ from the filename analogy) are called *metacharacters*, while the rest are called *literal*, or normal text characters. What sets regular expressions apart from filename patterns are the advanced expressive powers that their metacharacters provide. Filename patterns provide limited metacharacters for limited needs, but a regular expression "language" provides rich and expressive metacharacters for advanced uses.

It might help to consider regular expressions as their own language, with literal text acting as the words and metacharacters as the grammar. The words are combined with grammar according to a set of rules to create an expression that communicates an idea. In the email example, the expression I used to find lines beginning with 'From:' or 'Subject:' was `^(From|Subject):`. The metacharacters are underlined; we'll get to their interpretation soon.

As with learning any other language, regular expressions might seem intimidating at first. This is why it seems like magic to those with only a superficial understanding, and perhaps completely unapproachable to those who have never seen it at all. But, just as 正規表現は簡単だよ!† would soon become clear to a student of Japanese, the regular expression in

```
s!<emphasis>([0-9]+(\.[0-9]+){3})</emphasis>!<inet>$1</inet>!
```

will soon become crystal clear to you, too.

This example is from a Perl language script that my editor used to modify a manuscript. The author had mistakenly used the typesetting tag <emphasis> to mark Internet IP addresses (which are sets of periods and numbers that look like 209.204.146.22). The incantation uses Perl's text-substitution command with the regular expression

```
<emphasis>([0-9]+(\.[0-9]+){3})</emphasis>
```

to replace such tags with the appropriate <inet> tag, while leaving other uses of <emphasis> alone. In later chapters, you'll learn all the details of exactly how this type of incantation is constructed, so you'll be able to apply the techniques to your own needs, with your own application or programming language.

---

† "Regular expressions are easy!" A somewhat humorous comment about this: as Chapter 3 explains, the term *regular expression* originally comes from formal algebra. When people ask me what my book is about, the answer "regular expressions" draws a blank face if they are not already familiar with the concept. The Japanese word for regular expression, 正規表現, means as little to the average Japanese as its English counterpart, but my reply in Japanese usually draws a bit more than a blank stare. You see, the "regular" part is unfortunately pronounced identically to a much more common word, a medical term for "reproductive organs." You can only imagine what flashes through their minds until I explain!

The goal of this book

The chance that *you* will ever want to replace `<emphasis>` tags with `<inet>` tags is small, but it is very likely that you will run into similar "replace *this* with *that*" problems. The goal of this book is not to teach solutions to specific problems, but rather to teach you how to *think* regular expressions so that you will be able to conquer whatever problem you may face.

The Regular-Expression Frame of Mind

As we'll soon see, complete regular expressions are built up from small building-block units. Each individual building block is quite simple, but since they can be combined in an infinite number of ways, knowing how to combine them to achieve a particular goal takes some experience. So, this chapter provides a quick overview of some regular-expression concepts. It doesn't go into much depth, but provides a basis for the rest of this book to build on, and sets the stage for important side issues that are best discussed before we delve too deeply into the regular expressions themselves.

While some examples may seem silly (because some *are* silly), they represent the kind of tasks that you will want to do—you just might not realize it yet. If each point doesn't seem to make sense, don't worry too much. Just let the gist of the lessons sink in. That's the goal of this chapter.

If You Have Some Regular-Expression Experience

If you're already familiar with regular expressions, much of this overview will not be new, but please be sure to at least glance over it anyway. Although you may be aware of the basic meaning of certain metacharacters, perhaps some of the ways of thinking about and looking at regular expressions will be new.

Just as there is a difference between playing a musical piece well and *making music*, there is a difference between knowing about regular expressions and *really understanding* them. Some of the lessons present the same information that you are already familiar with, but in ways that may be new and which are the first steps to *really understanding*.

Searching Text Files: Egrep

Finding text is one of the simplest uses of regular expressions—many text editors and word processors allow you to search a document using a regular-expression pattern. Even simpler is the utility *egrep*. Give *egrep* a regular expression and some files to search, and it attempts to match the regular expression to each line of each file, displaying only those lines in which a match is found. *egrep* is freely available for many systems, including DOS, MacOS, Windows, Unix, and so on. See this book's web site, `http://regex.info`, for links on how to obtain a copy of *egrep* for your system.

Returning to the email example from page 3, the command I actually used to generate a makeshift table of contents from the email file is shown in Figure 1-1. *egrep* interprets the first command-line argument as a regular expression, and any remaining arguments as the file(s) to search. Note, however, that the single quotes shown in Figure 1-1 are *not* part of the regular expression, but are needed by my command shell.[†] When using *egrep*, I usually wrap the regular expression with single quotes. Exactly which characters are special, in what contexts, to whom (to the regular-expression, or to the tool), and in what order they are interpreted are all issues that grow in importance when you move to regular-expression use in full-fledged programming languages—something we'll see starting in the next chapter.

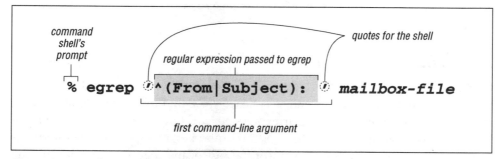

Figure 1-1: Invoking egrep from the command line

We'll start to analyze just what the various parts of the regex mean in a moment, but you can probably already guess just by looking that some of the characters have special meanings. In this case, the parentheses, the ⌜^⌟, and the ⌜|⌟ characters are regular-expression metacharacters, and combine with the other characters to generate the result I want.

On the other hand, if your regular expression doesn't use any of the dozen or so metacharacters that *egrep* understands, it effectively becomes a simple "plain text" search. For example, searching for ⌜cat⌟ in a file finds and displays all lines with the three letters c·a·t in a row. This includes, for example, any line containing vac<u>at</u>ion.

---

† The command shell is the part of the system that accepts your typed commands and actually executes the programs you request. With the shell I use, the single quotes serve to group the command argument, telling the shell not to pay too much attention to what's inside. If I didn't use them, the shell might think, for example, a '∗' that I intended to be part of the regular expression was really part of a filename pattern that *it* should interpret. I don't want that to happen, so I use the quotes to "hide" the metacharacters from the shell. Windows users of COMMAND.COM or CMD.EXE should probably use double quotes instead.

Even though the line might not have the *word* cat, the c·a·t sequence in vacation is still enough to be matched. Since it's there, *egrep* goes ahead and displays the whole line. The key point is that regular-expression searching is not done on a "word" basis—*egrep* can understand the concept of bytes and lines in a file, but it generally has no idea of English's (or any other language's) words, sentences, paragraphs, or other high-level concepts.

Egrep Metacharacters

Let's start to explore some of the *egrep* metacharacters that supply its regular-expression power. I'll go over them quickly with a few examples, leaving the detailed examples and descriptions for later chapters.

Typographical Conventions   Before we begin, please make sure to review the typographical conventions explained in the preface, on page *xix*. This book forges a bit of new ground in the area of typesetting, so some of my notations may be unfamiliar at first.

Start and End of the Line

Probably the easiest metacharacters to understand are ⌜^⌟ (*caret*) and ⌜$⌟ (*dollar*), which represent the start and end, respectively, of the line of text as it is being checked. As we've seen, the regular expression ⌜cat⌟ finds c·a·t anywhere on the line, but ⌜^cat⌟ matches only if the c·a·t is at the beginning of the line—the ⌜^⌟ is used to effectively *anchor* the match (of the rest of the regular expression) to the start of the line. Similarly, ⌜cat$⌟ finds c·a·t only at the end of the line, such as a line ending with scat.

It's best to get into the habit of interpreting regular expressions in a rather literal way. For example, don't think
　　⌜^cat⌟ matches a line with cat at the beginning
but rather:
　　⌜^cat⌟ matches if you have the beginning of a line, followed immediately
　　by c, followed immediately by a, followed immediately by t.

They both end up meaning the same thing, but reading it the more literal way allows you to intrinsically understand a new expression when you see it. How would *egrep* interpret ⌜^cat$⌟, ⌜^$⌟, or even simply ⌜^⌟ alone? ❖ Turn the page to check your interpretations.

The caret and dollar are special in that they match a *position* in the line rather than any actual text characters themselves. Of course, there are various ways to actually match real text. Besides providing literal characters like ⌜cat⌟ in your regular expression, you can also use some of the items discussed in the next few sections.

Character Classes

Matching any one of several characters

Let's say you want to search for "grey," but also want to find it if it were spelled "gray." The regular-expression construct ⌈[⋯]⌋, usually called a *character class*, lets you list the characters you want to allow at that point in the match. While ⌈e⌋ matches just an e, and ⌈a⌋ matches just an a, the regular expression ⌈[ea]⌋ matches either. So, then, consider ⌈gr[ea]y⌋: this means to find " g, followed by r, followed by either an e or an a, all followed by y." Because I'm a really poor speller, I'm always using regular expressions like this against a huge list of English words to figure out proper spellings. One I use often is ⌈sep[ea]r[ea]te⌋, because I can never remember whether the word is spelled "seperate," "separate," "separete," or what. The one that pops up in the list is the proper spelling; regular expressions to the rescue.

Notice how outside of a class, literal characters (like the ⌈g⌋ and ⌈r⌋ of ⌈gr[ae]y⌋) have an implied "and then" between them — "match ⌈g⌋ **and then** match ⌈r⌋..." It's completely opposite inside a character class. The contents of a class is a list of characters that can match at that point, so the implication is "or."

As another example, maybe you want to allow capitalization of a word's first letter, such as with ⌈[Ss]mith⌋. Remember that this still matches lines that contain smith (or Smith) embedded within another word, such as with blacksmith. I don't want to harp on this throughout the overview, but this issue does seem to be the source of problems among some new users. I'll touch on some ways to handle this embedded-word problem after we examine a few more metacharacters.

You can list in the class as many characters as you like. For example, ⌈[123456]⌋ matches any of the listed digits. This particular class might be useful as part of ⌈<H[123456]>⌋, which matches <H1>, <H2>, <H3>, etc. This can be useful when searching for HTML headers.

Within a character class, the *character-class metacharacter* '-' (*dash*) indicates a range of characters: ⌈<H[1-6]>⌋ is identical to the previous example. ⌈[0-9]⌋ and ⌈[a-z]⌋ are common shorthands for classes to match digits and English lowercase letters, respectively. Multiple ranges are fine, so ⌈[0123456789abcdefABCDEF]⌋ can be written as ⌈[0-9a-f A-F]⌋ (or, perhaps, ⌈[A-Fa-f0-9]⌋, since the order in which ranges are given doesn't matter). These last three examples can be useful when processing hexadecimal numbers. You can freely combine ranges with literal characters: ⌈[0-9A-Z_!.?]⌋ matches a digit, uppercase letter, underscore, exclamation point, period, or a question mark.

Note that a dash is a metacharacter only within a character class — otherwise it matches the normal dash character. In fact, it is not even always a metacharacter within a character class. If it is the first character listed in the class, it can't possibly

---

Reading ⌜^cat$⌟, ⌜^$⌟, *and* ⌜^⌟

❖ *Answers to the questions on page 8.*

⌜^cat$⌟ **Literally means**: matches if the line has a beginning-of-line (which, of course, all lines have), followed immediately by c·a·t, and then followed immediately by the end of the line.

Effectively means: a line that consists of only cat — no extra words, spaces, punctuation...just 'cat'.

⌜^$⌟ **Literally means**: matches if the line has a beginning-of-line, followed immediately by the end of the line.

Effectively means: an empty line (with nothing in it, not even spaces).

⌜^⌟ **Literally means**: matches if the line has a beginning-of-line.

Effectively *meaningless*! Since every line has a beginning, every line will match—even lines that are empty!

---

indicate a range, so it is not considered a metacharacter. Along the same lines, the question mark and period at the end of the class are usually regular-expression metacharacters, but only when *not* within a class (so, to be clear, the only special characters within the class in ⌜[0-9A-Z_!.?]⌟ are the two dashes).

> Consider character classes as their own mini language. The rules regarding which metacharacters are supported (and what they do) are completely different inside and outside of character classes.

We'll see more examples of this shortly.

Negated character classes

If you use ⌜[^···]⌟ instead of ⌜[···]⌟, the class matches any character that *isn't* listed. For example, ⌜[^1-6]⌟ matches a character that's *not* 1 through 6. The leading ^ in the class "negates" the list, so rather than listing the characters you want to include in the class, you list the characters you don't want to be included.

You might have noticed that the ^ used here is the same as the start-of-line caret introduced on page 8. The character is the same, but the meaning is completely different. Just as the English word "wind" can mean different things depending on the context (sometimes a strong breeze, sometimes what you do to a clock), so can a metacharacter. We've already seen one example, the range-building dash. It is valid only inside a character class (and at that, only when not first inside the class). ^ is a line anchor outside a class, but a class metacharacter inside a class (but, only when it is immediately after the class's opening bracket; otherwise, it's not special inside a class). Don't fear—these are the most complex special cases; others we'll see later aren't so bad.

As another example, let's search that list of English words for odd words that have q followed by something other than u. Translating that into a regular expression, it becomes ⌈q[^u]⌋. I tried it on the list I have, and there certainly weren't many. I did find a few, including a number of words that I didn't even know were English.

Here's what happened. (What I typed is in bold.)

```
% egrep 'q[^u]' word.list
Iraqi
Iraqian
miqra
qasida
qintar
qoph
zaqqum%
```

Two notable words not listed are "Qantas", the Australian airline, and "Iraq". Although both words are in the *word.list* file, neither were displayed by my *egrep* command. Why? ❖ Think about it for a bit, and then turn the page to check your reasoning.

Remember, a negated character class means "match a character that's not listed" and not "don't match what is listed." These might seem the same, but the Iraq example shows the subtle difference. A convenient way to view a negated class is that it is simply a shorthand for a normal class that includes all possible characters *except* those that are listed.

Matching Any Character with Dot

The metacharacter ⌈.⌋ (usually called *dot* or *point*) is a shorthand for a character class that matches any character. It can be convenient when you want to have an "any character here" placeholder in your expression. For example, if you want to search for a date such as 03/19/76, 03-19-76, or even 03.19.76, you could go to the trouble to construct a regular expression that uses character classes to explicitly allow '/', '-', or '.' between each number, such as ⌈03[-./]19[-./]76⌋. However, you might also try simply using ⌈03.19.76⌋.

Quite a few things are going on with this example that might be unclear at first. In ⌈03[-./]19[-./]76⌋, the dots are *not* metacharacters because they are within a character class. (Remember, the list of metacharacters and their meanings are different inside and outside of character classes.) The dashes are also not class metacharacters *in this case* because each is the first thing after [or [^. Had they not been first, as with ⌈[.-/]⌋, it they would be the class range metacharacter, which would be a mistake in this situation.

Quiz Answer

❖ *Answer to the question on page 11.*

Why doesn't ⌈q[^u]⌋ match 'Qantas' or 'Iraq'?

Qantas didn't match because the regular expression called for a lowercase q, whereas the Q in Qantas is uppercase. Had we used ⌈Q[^u]⌋ instead, we would have found it, but not the others, since they don't have an uppercase Q. The expression ⌈[Qq][^u]⌋ would have found them all.

The Iraq example is somewhat of a trick question. The regular expression calls for q *followed by a character* that's not u, which precludes matching q *at the end of the line*. Lines generally have newline characters at the very end, but a little fact I neglected to mention (sorry!) is that *egrep* strips those before checking with the regular expression, so after a line-ending q, there's no non-u to be matched.

Don't feel too bad because of the trick question.[†] Let me assure you that had *egrep* not automatically stripped the newlines (many other tools don't strip them), or had Iraq been followed by spaces or other words or whatnot, the line would have matched. It is important to eventually understand the little details of each tool, but at this point what I'd like you to come away with from this exercise is that *a character class, even negated, still requires a character to match*.

With ⌈03.19.76⌋, the dots *are* metacharacters — ones that match any character (including the dash, period, and slash that we are expecting). However, it is important to know that each dot can match any character at all, so it can match, say, 'lottery numbers: 19 203319 7639'.

So, ⌈03[-./]19[-./]76⌋ is more precise, but it's more difficult to read and write. ⌈03.19.76⌋ is easy to understand, but vague. Which should we use? It all depends upon what you know about the data being searched, and just how specific you feel you need to be. One important, recurring issue has to do with balancing your knowledge of the text being searched against the need to always be exact when writing an expression. For example, if you know that with your data it would be highly unlikely for ⌈03.19.76⌋ to match in an unwanted place, it would certainly be reasonable to use it. Knowing the target text well is an important part of wielding regular expressions effectively.

---

† Once, in fourth grade, I was leading the spelling bee when I was asked to spell "miss." My answer was "m·i·s·s." Miss Smith relished in telling me that no, it was "M·i·s·s" with a capital M, that I should have asked for an example sentence, and that I was out. It was a traumatic moment in a young boy's life. After that, I never liked Miss Smith, and have since been a very poor speler.

Alternation

Matching any one of several subexpressions

A very convenient metacharacter is ⌈|⌋, which means "or." It allows you to combine multiple expressions into a single expression that matches any of the individual ones. For example, ⌈Bob⌋ and ⌈Robert⌋ are separate expressions, but ⌈Bob|Robert⌋ is one expression that matches either. When combined this way, the subexpressions are called *alternatives*.

Looking back to our ⌈gr[ea]y⌋ example, it is interesting to realize that it can be written as ⌈grey|gray⌋, and even ⌈gr(a|e)y⌋. The latter case uses parentheses to constrain the alternation. (For the record, parentheses are metacharacters too.) Note that something like ⌈gr[a|e]y⌋ is *not* what we want — within a class, the '|' character is just a normal character, like ⌈a⌋ and ⌈e⌋.

With ⌈gr(a|e)y⌋, the parentheses are required because without them, ⌈gra|ey⌋ means "⌈gra⌋ or ⌈ey⌋," which is not what we want here. Alternation reaches far, but not beyond parentheses. Another example is ⌈(First|1st)·[Ss]treet⌋.[†] Actually, since both ⌈First⌋ and ⌈1st⌋ end with ⌈st⌋, the combination can be shortened to ⌈(Fir|1)st·[Ss]treet⌋. That's not necessarily quite as easy to read, but be sure to understand that ⌈(first|1st)⌋ and ⌈(fir|1)st⌋ effectively mean the same thing.

Here's an example involving an alternate spelling of my name. Compare and contrast the following three expressions, which are all effectively the same:

    ⌈Jeffrey|Jeffery⌋
    ⌈Jeff(rey|ery)⌋
    ⌈Jeff(re|er)y⌋

To have them match the British spellings as well, they could be:

    ⌈(Geoff|Jeff)(rey|ery)⌋
    ⌈(Geo|Je)ff(rey|ery)⌋
    ⌈(Geo|Je)ff(re|er)y⌋

Finally, note that these three match effectively the same as the longer (but simpler) ⌈Jeffrey|Geoffery|Jeffery|Geoffrey⌋. They're all different ways to specify the same desired matches.

Although the ⌈gr[ea]y⌋ versus ⌈gr(a|e)y⌋ examples might blur the distinction, be careful not to confuse the concept of alternation with that of a character class. A character class can match just a *single character* in the target text. With alternation, since each alternative can be a full-fledged regular expression in and of itself, each

---

[†] Recall from the typographical conventions on page *xx* that "·" is how I sometimes show a space character so it can be seen easily.

alternative can match an arbitrary amount of text. Character classes are almost like their own special mini-language (with their own ideas about metacharacters, for example), while alternation is part of the "main" regular expression language. You'll find both to be extremely useful.

Also, take care when using caret or dollar in an expression that has alternation. Compare ⌈^From|Subject|Date:␣⌋ with ⌈^(From|Subject|Date):␣⌋. Both appear similar to our earlier email example, but what each matches (and therefore how useful it is) differs greatly. The first is composed of three alternatives, so it matches "⌈^From⌋ or ⌈Subject⌋ or ⌈Date:␣⌋," which is not particularly useful. We want the leading caret and trailing ⌈:␣⌋ to apply to each alternative. We can accomplish this by using parentheses to "constrain" the alternation:

  ⌈^(From|Subject|Date):␣⌋

The alternation is constrained by the parentheses, so literally, this regex means "match the start of the line, then one of ⌈From⌋, ⌈Subject⌋, or ⌈Date⌋, and then match ⌈:␣⌋." Effectively, it matches:

  1) start-of-line, followed by F·r·o·m, followed by ':␣'
  or 2) start-of-line, followed by S·u·b·j·e·c·t, followed by ':␣'
  or 3) start-of-line, followed by D·a·t·e, followed by ':␣'

Putting it less literally, it matches lines beginning with 'From:␣', 'Subject:␣', or 'Date:␣', which is quite useful for listing the messages in an email file.

Here's an example:

```
% egrep '^(From|Subject|Date): '  mailbox
From: elvis@tabloid.org (The King)
Subject: be seein' ya around
Date: Thu, 22 Aug 2002 11:04:13
From: The Prez <president@whitehouse.gov>
Date: Tue, 27 Aug 2002 8:36:24
Subject: now, about your vote⋯
    ⋮
```

Ignoring Differences in Capitalization

This email header example provides a good opportunity to introduce the concept of a *case-insensitive* match. The field types in an email header usually appear with leading capitalization, such as "Subject" and "From," but the email standard actually allows mixed capitalization, so things like "DATE" and "from" are also allowed. Unfortunately, the regular expression in the previous section doesn't match those.

One approach is to replace ⌈From⌋ with ⌈[Ff][Rr][Oo][Mm]⌋ to match any form of "from," but this is quite cumbersome, to say the least. Fortunately, there is a way to tell *egrep* to ignore case when doing comparisons, i.e., to perform the match in a *case insensitive* manner in which capitalization differences are simply ignored. It is not a part of the regular-expression language, but is a related useful feature many tools provide. *egrep*'s command-line option "-i" tells it to do a case-insensitive match. Place -i on the command line before the regular expression:

```
% egrep -i '^(From|Subject|Date): ' mailbox
```

This brings up all the lines we matched before, but also includes lines such as:

```
SUBJECT: MAKE MONEY FAST
```

I find myself using the -i option quite frequently (perhaps related to the footnote on page 12!) so I recommend keeping it in mind. We'll see other convenient support features like this in later chapters.

Word Boundaries

A common problem is that a regular expression that matches the word you want can often also match where the "word" is embedded within a larger word. I mentioned this briefly in the cat, gray, and Smith examples. It turns out, though, that some versions of *egrep* offer limited support for word recognition: namely the ability to match the boundary of a word (where a word begins or ends).

You can use the (perhaps odd looking) *metasequences* ⌈\<⌉ and ⌈\>⌉ if your version happens to support them (not all versions of *egrep* do). You can think of them as word-based versions of ⌈^⌉ and ⌈$⌉ that match the *position* at the start and end of a word, respectively. Like the line anchors caret and dollar, they anchor other parts of the regular expression but don't actually consume any characters during a match. The expression ⌈\<cat\>⌉ literally means " match if we can find a start-of-word position, followed immediately by c·a·t, followed immediately by an end-of-word position." More naturally, it means "find the word cat." If you wanted, you could use ⌈\<cat⌉ or ⌈cat\>⌉ to find words starting and ending with cat.

Note that ⌈<⌉ and ⌈>⌉ alone are not metacharacters — when combined with a back-slash, the *sequences* become special. This is why I called them "metasequences." It's their special interpretation that's important, not the number of characters, so for the most part I use these two meta-words interchangeably.

Remember, not all versions of *egrep* support these word-boundary metacharacters, and those that do don't magically understand the English language. The "start of a word" is simply the position where a sequence of alphanumeric characters begins; "end of word" is where such a sequence ends. Figure 1-2 on the next page shows a sample line with these positions marked.

The word-starts (as *egrep* recognizes them) are marked with up arrows, the word-ends with down arrows. As you can see, "start and end of word" is better phrased as "start and end of an alphanumeric sequence," but perhaps that's too much of a mouthful.

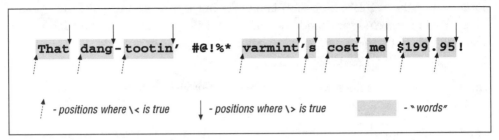

Figure 1-2: Start and end of "word" positions

In a Nutshell

Table 1-1 summarizes the metacharacters we have seen so far.

Table 1-1: Summary of Metacharacters Seen So Far

Metacharacter	Name	Matches
.	*dot*	any one character
[···]	*character class*	any character listed
[^···]	*negated character class*	any character not listed
^	*caret*	the position at the start of the line
$	*dollar*	the position at the end of the line
\<	*backslash less-than*	[†]the position at the start of a word
\>	*backslash greater-than*	[†]the position at the end of a word
		[†]*not supported by all versions of egrep*
|	*or, bar*	matches either expression it separates
(···)	*parentheses*	used to limit scope of ⌈|⌋, plus additional uses yet to be discussed

In addition to the table, important points to remember include:

- The rules about which characters are and aren't metacharacters (and exactly what they mean) are different inside a character class. For example, dot is a metacharacter outside of a class, but not within one. Conversely, a dash is a metacharacter within a class (usually), but not outside. Moreover, a caret has one meaning outside, another if specified inside a class immediately after the opening [, and a third if given elsewhere in the class.

- Don't confuse alternation with a character class. The class ⌈[abc]⌋ and the alternation ⌈(a|b|c)⌋ effectively mean the same thing, but the similarity in this example does not extend to the general case. A character class can match exactly one character, and that's true no matter how long or short the specified list of acceptable characters might be.

Alternation, on the other hand, can have arbitrarily long alternatives, each textually unrelated to the other: ⌜\<(1,000,000|million|thousand•thou)\>⌟. However, alternation can't be negated like a character class.

- A negated character class is simply a notational convenience for a normal character class that matches everything not listed. Thus, ⌜[^x]⌟ doesn't mean "match unless there is an x," but rather "match if there is something that is not x." The difference is subtle, but important. The first concept matches a blank line, for example, while ⌜[^x]⌟ does not.

- The useful -i option discounts capitalization during a match (☞ 15).[†]

What we have seen so far can be quite useful, but the real power comes from *optional* and *counting* elements, which we'll look at next.

Optional Items

Let's look at matching color or colour. Since they are the same except that one has a u and the other doesn't, we can use ⌜colou?r⌟ to match either. The metacharacter ⌜?⌟ (*question mark*) means *optional*. It is placed after the character that is allowed to appear at that point in the expression, but whose existence isn't actually required to still be considered a successful match.

Unlike other metacharacters we have seen so far, the question mark attaches only to the immediately-preceding item. Thus, ⌜colou?r⌟ is interpreted as "⌜c⌟ then ⌜o⌟ then ⌜l⌟ then ⌜o⌟ then ⌜u?⌟ then ⌜r⌟."

The ⌜u?⌟ part is always successful: sometimes it matches a u in the text, while other times it doesn't. The whole point of the ?-optional part is that it's successful either way. This isn't to say that any regular expression that contains ? is always successful. For example, against 'semicolon', both ⌜colo⌟ and ⌜u?⌟ are successful (matching colo and nothing, respectively). However, the final ⌜r⌟ fails, and that's what disallows semicolon, in the end, from being matched by ⌜colou?r⌟.

As another example, consider matching a date that represents July fourth, with the "July" part being either July or Jul, and the "fourth" part being fourth, 4th, or simply 4. Of course, we could just use ⌜(July|Jul)•(fourth|4th|4)⌟, but let's explore other ways to express the same thing.

First, we can shorten the ⌜(July|Jul)⌟ to ⌜(July?)⌟. Do you see how they are effectively the same? The removal of the ⌜|⌟ means that the parentheses are no longer really needed. Leaving the parentheses doesn't hurt, but with them removed, ⌜July?⌟ is a bit less cluttered. This leaves us with ⌜July?•(fourth|4th|4)⌟.

[†] Recall from the typographical conventions (page *xx*) that something like "☞ 15" is a shorthand for a reference to another page of this book.

Moving now to the second half, we can simplify the ⌜4th|4⌝ to ⌜4(th)?⌝. As you can see, ⌜?⌝ can attach to a parenthesized expression. Inside the parentheses can be as complex a subexpression as you like, but "from the outside" it is considered a single unit. Grouping for ⌜?⌝ (and other similar metacharacters which I'll introduce momentarily) is one of the main uses of parentheses.

Our expression now looks like ⌜July?•(fourth|4(th)?)⌝. Although there are a fair number of metacharacters, and even nested parentheses, it is not that difficult to decipher and understand. This discussion of two essentially simple examples has been rather long, but in the meantime we have covered tangential topics that add a lot, if perhaps only subconsciously, to our understanding of regular expressions. Also, it's given us some experience in taking different approaches toward the same goal. As we advance through this book (and through to a better understanding), you'll find many opportunities for creative juices to flow while trying to find the optimal way to solve a complex problem. Far from being some stuffy science, writing regular expressions is closer to an art.

Other Quantifiers: Repetition

Similar to the question mark are ⌜+⌝ (*plus*) and ⌜*⌝ (an asterisk, but as a regular-expression metacharacter, I prefer the term *star*). The metacharacter ⌜+⌝ means "one or more of the immediately-preceding item," and ⌜*⌝ means "any number, including none, of the item." Phrased differently, ⌜···*⌝ means "try to match it as many times as possible, but it's okay to settle for nothing if need be." The construct with plus, ⌜···+⌝, is similar in that it also tries to match as many times as possible, but different in that it fails if it can't match at least once. These three metacharacters, question mark, plus, and star, are called *quantifiers* because they influence the quantity of what they govern.

Like ⌜···?⌝, the ⌜···*⌝ part of a regular expression always succeeds, with the only issue being what text (if any) is matched. Contrast this to ⌜···+⌝, which fails unless the item matches at least once.

For example, ⌜•?⌝ allows a single optional space, but ⌜•*⌝ allows *any number* of optional spaces. We can use this to make page 9's <H[1-6]> example flexible. The HTML specification[†] says that spaces are allowed immediately before the closing >, such as with <H3•> and <H4•••>. Inserting ⌜•*⌝ into our regular expression where we want to allow (but not require) spaces, we get ⌜<H[1-6]•*>⌝. This still matches <H1>, as no spaces are required, but it also flexibly picks up the other versions.

---

† If you are not familiar with HTML, never fear. I use these as real-world examples, but I provide all the details needed to understand the points being made. Those familiar with parsing HTML tags will likely recognize important considerations I don't address at this point in the book.

Exploring further, let's search for an HTML tag such as `<HR SIZE=14>`, which indicates that a line (a Horizontal Rule) 14 pixels thick should be drawn across the screen. Like the `<H3>` example, optional spaces are allowed before the closing angle bracket. Additionally, they are allowed on either side of the equal sign. Finally, one space is required between the `HR` and `SIZE`, although more are allowed. To allow more, we could just add ⌜•*⌟ to the ⌜•⌟ already there, but instead let's change it to ⌜•+⌟. The plus allows extra spaces while still requiring at least one, so it's effectively the same as ⌜••*⌟, but more concise. All these changes leave us with ⌜`<HR •+ SIZE •* = •* 14 •*>`⌟.

Although flexible with respect to spaces, our expression is still inflexible with respect to the size given in the tag. Rather than find tags with only one particular size such as `14`, we want to find them all. To accomplish this, we replace the ⌜14⌟ with an expression to find a general number. Well, in this case, a "number" is one or more digits. A digit is ⌜`[0-9]`⌟, and "one or more" adds a plus, so we end up replacing ⌜14⌟ by ⌜`[0-9]+`⌟. (A character class is one "unit," so can be subject directly to plus, question mark, and so on, without the need for parentheses.)

This leaves us with ⌜`<HR •+ SIZE •* = •* [0-9]+ •*>`⌟, which is certainly a mouthful even though I've presented it with the metacharacters bold, added a bit of spacing to make the groupings more apparent, and am using the "visible space" symbol '•' for clarity. (Luckily, *egrep* has the `-i` case-insensitive option, ☞ 15, which means I don't have to use ⌜`[Hh][Rr]`⌟ instead of ⌜HR⌟.) The unadorned regular expression ⌜`<HR +SIZE *= *[0-9]+ *>`⌟ likely appears even more confusing. This example looks particularly odd because the subjects of most of the stars and pluses are space characters, and our eye has always been trained to treat spaces specially. That's a habit you will have to break when reading regular expressions, because the space character is a normal character, no different from, say, `j` or `4`. (In later chapters, we'll see that some other tools support a special mode in which whitespace is ignored, but *egrep* has no such mode.)

Continuing to exploit a good example, let's consider that the size attribute is optional, so you can simply use `<HR>` if the default size is wanted. (Extra spaces are allowed before the `>`, as always.) How can we modify our regular expression so that it matches either type? The key is realizing that the size part is *optional* (that's a hint). ❖ Turn the page to check your answer.

Take a good look at our latest expression (in the answer box) to appreciate the differences among the question mark, star, and plus, and what they really mean in practice. Table 1-2 on the next page summarizes their meanings.

Note that each quantifier has some minimum number of matches required to succeed, and a maximum number of matches that it will ever attempt. With some, the minimum number is zero; with some, the maximum number is unlimited.

Making a Subexpression Optional

❖ *Answer to the question on page 19.*

In this case, "optional" means that it is allowed once, but is not required. That means using ⌜?⌟. Since the thing that's optional is larger than one character, we must use parentheses: ⌜(⋯)?⌟. Inserting into our expression, we get:

   ⌜<HR(␣+SIZE␣*=␣*[0-9]+)?␣*>⌟

Note that the ending ⌜␣*⌟ is kept outside of the ⌜(⋯)?⌟. This still allows something such as <HR␣>. Had we included it within the parentheses, ending spaces would have been allowed only when the size component was present.

Similarly, notice that the ⌜␣+⌟ before SIZE *is* included within the parentheses. Were it left outside them, a space would have been required after the HR, even when the SIZE part wasn't there. This would cause '<HR>' to not match.

Table 1-2: Summary of Quantifier "Repetition Metacharacters"

	Minimum Required	Maximum to Try	Meaning
?	none	1	one allowed; none required ("*one optional*")
*	none	no limit	unlimited allowed; none required ("*any amount okay*")
+	1	no limit	unlimited allowed; one required ("*at least one*")

Defined range of matches: intervals

Some versions of *egrep* support a metasequence for providing your own minimum and maximum: ⌜⋯{*min,max*}⌟. This is called the *interval* quantifier. For example, ⌜⋯{3,12}⌟ matches up to 12 times if possible, but settles for three. One might use ⌜[a-zA-Z]{1,5}⌟ to match a US stock ticker (from one to five letters). Using this notation, {0,1} is the same as a question mark.

Not many versions of *egrep* support this notation yet, but many other tools do, so it's covered in Chapter 3 when we look in detail at the broad spectrum of metacharacters in common use today.

Parentheses and Backreferences

So far, we have seen two uses for parentheses: to limit the scope of alternation, ⌜|⌟, and to group multiple characters into larger units to which you can apply quantifiers like question mark and star. I'd like to discuss another specialized use that's not common in *egrep* (although GNU's popular version does support it), but which is commonly found in many other tools.

In many regular-expression flavors, parentheses can "remember" text matched by the subexpression they enclose. We'll use this in a partial solution to the doubled-word problem at the beginning of this chapter. If you knew the the specific doubled word to find (such as "the" earlier in this sentence — did you catch it?), you could search for it explicitly, such as with ⌈the•the⌋. In this case, you would also find items such as <u>the•theory</u>, but you could easily get around that problem if your *egrep* supports the word-boundary metasequences ⌈\<···\>⌋ mentioned on page 15: ⌈\<the•the\>⌋. We could use ⌈•+⌋ for the space for even more flexibility.

However, having to check for every possible pair of words would be an impossible task. Wouldn't it be nice if we could match one generic word, and then say "now match the same thing again"? If your *egrep* supports *backreferencing*, you can. Backreferencing is a regular-expression feature that allows you to match new text that is the same as some text matched earlier in the expression.

We start with ⌈\<the•+the\>⌋ and replace the initial ⌈the⌋ with a regular expression to match a general word, say ⌈[A-Za-z]+⌋. Then, for reasons that will become clear in the next paragraph, let's put parentheses around it. Finally, we replace the second 'the' by the special metasequence ⌈\1⌋. This yields ⌈\<([A-Za-z]+)•+\1\>⌋.

With tools that support backreferencing, parentheses "remember" the text that the subexpression inside them matches, and the special metasequence ⌈\1⌋ represents that text later in the regular expression, whatever it happens to be at the time.

Of course, you can have more than one set of parentheses in a regular expression. Use ⌈\1⌋, ⌈\2⌋, ⌈\3⌋, etc., to refer to the first, second, third, etc. sets. Pairs of parentheses are numbered by counting opening parentheses from the left, so with ⌈([a-z])([0-9])\1\2⌋, the ⌈\1⌋ refers to the text matched by ⌈[a-z]⌋, and ⌈\2⌋ refers to the text matched by ⌈[0-9]⌋.

With our 'the•the' example, ⌈[A-Za-z]+⌋ matches the first 'the'. It is within the first set of parentheses, so the 'the' matched becomes available via ⌈\1⌋. If the following ⌈•+⌋ matches, the subsequent ⌈\1⌋ will require another 'the'. If ⌈\1⌋ is successful, then ⌈\>⌋ makes sure that we are now at an end-of-word boundary (which we wouldn't be were the text 'the•theft'). If successful, we've found a repeated word. It's not always the case that that is an error (such as with "that" in this sentence), but that's for you to decide once the suspect lines are shown.

When I decided to include this example, I actually tried it on what I had written so far. (I used a version of *egrep* that supports both ⌈\<···\>⌋ and backreferencing.) To make it more useful, so that 'The•the' would also be found, I used the case-insensitive -i option mentioned on page 15.[†]

---

† Be aware that the popular GNU version of *egrep* has a bug with its -i option such that it doesn't apply to backreferences. Thus, it finds "the the" but *not* "The the."

Here's the command I ran:

```
% egrep -i '\<([a-z]+) +\1\>' files
```

I was surprised to find fourteen sets of mistakenly 'doubled doubled' words! I
corrected them, and since then have built this type of regular-expression check
into the tools that I use to produce the final output of this book, to ensure none
creep back in.

As useful as this regular expression is, it is important to understand its limitations.
Since *egrep* considers each line in isolation, it isn't able to find when the ending
word of one line is repeated at the beginning of the next. For this, a more flexible
tool is needed, and we will see some examples in the next chapter.

The Great Escape

One important thing I haven't mentioned yet is how to actually match a character
that a regular expression would normally interpret as a metacharacter. For example, if I searched for the Internet hostname ega.att.com using ⌈ega.att.com⌋, it
could end up matching something like megawatt computing. Remember, ⌈.⌋ is a
metacharacter that matches any character, including a space.

The metasequence to match an actual period is a period preceded by a backslash:
⌈ega\.att\.com⌋. The sequence ⌈\.⌋ is described as an *escaped period* or *escaped
dot,* and you can do this with all the normal metacharacters, except in a character-
class.[†]

A backslash used in this way is called an "escape" — when a metacharacter is
escaped, it loses its special meaning and becomes a literal character. If you like,
you can consider the sequence to be a special metasequence to match the literal
character. It's all the same.

As another example, you could use ⌈\([a-zA-Z]+\)⌋ to match a word within
parentheses, such as '(very)'. The backslashes in the ⌈\(⌋ and ⌈\)⌋ sequences
remove the special interpretation of the parentheses, leaving them as literals to
match parentheses in the text.

When used before a non-metacharacter, a backslash can have different meanings
depending upon the version of the program. For example, we have already seen
how some versions treat ⌈\<⌋, ⌈\>⌋, ⌈\1⌋, etc. as metasequences. We will see many
more examples in later chapters.

---

† Most programming languages and tools allow you to escape characters within a character class as
  well, but most versions of *egrep* do not, instead treating '\' within a class as a literal backslash to be
  included in the list of characters.

Expanding the Foundation

I hope the examples and explanations so far have helped to establish the basis for a solid understanding of regular expressions, but please realize that what I've provided so far lacks depth. There's so much more out there.

Linguistic Diversification

I mentioned a number of regular expression features that most versions of *egrep* support. There are other features, some of which are not supported by all versions, which I'll leave for later chapters.

Unfortunately, the regular expression language is no different from any other in that it has various dialects and accents. It seems each new program employing regular expressions devises its own "improvements." The state of the art continually moves forward, but changes over the years have resulted in a wide variety of regular expression "flavors." We'll see many examples in the following chapters.

The Goal of a Regular Expression

From the broadest top-down view, a regular expression either matches within a lump of text (with *egrep*, each line) or it doesn't. When crafting a regular expression, you must consider the ongoing tug-of-war between having your expression match the lines you want, yet still not matching lines you don't want.

Also, while *egrep* doesn't care where in the line the match occurs, this concern is important for many other regular-expression uses. If your text is something such as

```
 ···zip is 44272. If you write, send $4.95 to cover postage and···
```
and you merely want to find lines matching `[0-9]+`, you don't care which numbers are matched. However, if your intent is to *do something* with the number (such as save to a file, add, replace, and such — we will see examples of this kind of processing in the next chapter), you'll care very much exactly *which* numbers are matched.

A Few More Examples

As with any language, experience is *a very good thing*, so I'm including a few more examples of regular expressions to match some common constructs.

Half the battle when writing regular expressions is getting successful matches when and where you want them. The other half is to *not* match when and where you don't want. In practice, both are important, but for the moment, I would like to concentrate on the "getting successful matches" aspect. Even though I don't take these examples to their fullest depths, they still provide useful insight.

Variable names

Many programming languages have identifiers (variable names and such) that are allowed to contain only alphanumeric characters and underscores, but which may not begin with a digit. They are matched by ⌜[a-zA-Z_][a-zA-Z_0-9]*⌟. The first character class matches what the first character can be, the second (with its accompanying star) allows the rest of the identifier. If there is a limit on the length of an identifier, say 32 characters, you might replace the star with ⌜{0,31}⌟ if the ⌜{*min*,*max*}⌟ notation is supported. (This construct, the interval quantifier, was briefly mentioned on page 20.)

A string within double quotes

A simple solution to matching a string within double quotes might be: ⌜"[^"]*"⌟

The double quotes at either end are to match the opening and closing double quotes of the string. Between them, we can have anything... except another double quote! So, we use ⌜[^"]⌟ to match all characters except a double quote, and apply using a star to indicate we can have any number of such non double-quote characters.

A more useful (but more complex) definition of a double-quoted string allows double quotes within the string if they are escaped with a backslash, such as in `"nail␣the␣2\"x4\"␣plank"`. We'll see this example several times in future chapters while covering the many details of how a match is actually carried out.

Dollar amount (with optional cents)

One approach to matching a dollar amount is: ⌜\$[0-9]+(\.[0-9][0-9])?⌟

From a top-level perspective, this is a simple regular expression with three parts: ⌜\$⌟ and ⌜···+⌟ and ⌜(···)?⌟, which might be loosely paraphrased as "a literal dollar sign, a bunch of one thing, and finally perhaps another thing." In this case, the "one thing" is a digit (with a bunch of them being a number), and "another thing" is the combination of a decimal point followed by two digits.

This example is a bit naïve for several reasons. For example, it considers dollar amounts like $1000, but not $1,000. It does allow for optional cents, but frankly, that's not really very useful when applied with *egrep*. *egrep* never cares exactly *how much* is matched, but merely *whether* there is a match. Allowing something optional at the end never changes whether there's an overall match to begin with.

But, if you need to find lines that contain *just* a price, and nothing else, you can wrap the expression with ⌜^···$⌟. In this case, the optional cents part becomes important since it might or might not come between the dollar amount and the end of the line, and allowing or disallowing it makes the difference in achieving an overall match.

One type of value our expression doesn't match is '$.49'. To solve this, you might be tempted to change the plus to a star, but that doesn't work. As to why, I'll leave it as a teaser until we look at this example again in Chapter 5 (☞ 194).

An HTTP/HTML URL

The format of web URLs can be complex, so constructing a regular expression to match any possible URL can be equally complex. However, relaxing your standards slightly can allow you to match most common URLs with a fairly simple expression. One common reason I might do this, for example, would be to search my email archive for a URL that I vaguely remember having received, but which I think I might recognize when I see it.

The general form of a common HTTP/HTML URL is along the lines of

```
http://hostname/path.html
```

although ending with .htm is common as well.

The rules about what can and can't be a *hostname* (computer name, such as www.yahoo.com) are complex, but for our needs we can realize that if it follows 'http://', it's probably a hostname, so we can make do with something simple, such as ⌈[-a-z0-9_.]+⌋. The *path* part can be even more varied, so we'll use ⌈[-a-z0-9_:@&?=+,.!/~*'%$]*⌋ for that. Notice that these classes have the dash first, to ensure that it's taken as a literal character and included in the list, as opposed to part of a range (☞ 9).

Putting these all together, we might use as our first attempt something like:

```
% egrep -i '\<http://[-a-z0-9_.:]+/[-a-z0-9_:@&?=+,.!/~*'%$]*\.html?\>' files
```

Again, since we've taken liberties and relaxed what we'll match, we could well match something such as 'http://..../foo.html', which is certainly not a valid URL. Do we care about this? It all depends on what you're trying to do. For my scan of my email archive, it doesn't really matter if I get a few false matches. Heck, I could probably get away with even something as simple as:

```
% egrep -i '\<http://[^ ]*\.html?\>' files...
```

As we'll learn when getting deeper into how to craft an expression, knowing the data you'll be searching is an important aspect of finding the balance between complexity and completeness. We'll visit this example again, in more detail, in the next chapter.

An HTML tag

With a tool like *egrep*, it doesn't seem particularly common or useful to simply match lines with HTML tags. But, exploring a regular expression that matches HTML tags exactly can be quite fruitful, especially when we delve into more advanced tools in the next chapter.

Looking at simple cases like '`<TITLE>`' and '`<HR>`', we might think to try ⌜`<.*>`⌟. This simplistic approach is a frequent first thought, but it's certainly incorrect. Converting ⌜`<.*>`⌟ into English reads "match a '`<`', followed by as much of anything as can be matched, followed by '`>`'." Well, when phrased that way, it shouldn't be surprising that it can match more than just one tag, such as the marked portion of '`this `<u>`<I>short</I>`</u>` example`'.

This might have been a bit surprising, but we're still in the first chapter, and our understanding at this point is only superficial. I have this example here to highlight that regular expressions are not a difficult subject, but they can be tricky if you don't truly understand them. Over the next few chapters, we'll look at all the details required to understand and solve this problem.

Time of day, such as "9:17 am" or "12:30 pm"

Matching a time can be taken to varying levels of strictness. Something such as

   ⌜`[0-9]?[0-9]:[0-9][0-9] (am|pm)`⌟

picks up both `9:17 am` and `12:30 pm`, but also allows something nonsensical like `99:99 pm`.

Looking at the hour, we realize that if it is a two-digit number, the first digit must be a one. But, ⌜`1?[0-9]`⌟ still allows an hour of `19` (and also an hour of `0`), so maybe it is better to break the hour part into two possibilities: ⌜`1[012]`⌟ for two-digit hours and ⌜`[1-9]`⌟ for single-digit hours. The result is ⌜`(1[012]|[1-9])`⌟.

The minute part is easier. The first digit should be ⌜`[0-5]`⌟. For the second, we can stick with the current ⌜`[0-9]`⌟. This gives ⌜`(1[012]|[1-9]):[0-5][0-9] (am|pm)`⌟ when we put it all together.

Using the same logic, can you extend this to handle 24-hour time with hours from `0` through `23`? As a challenge, allow for a leading zero, at least through to `09:59`. ❖ Try building your solution, and then turn the page to check mine.

Regular Expression Nomenclature

Regex

As you might guess, using the full phrase "regular expression" can get a bit tiring, particularly in writing. Instead, I normally use "regex." It just rolls right off the tongue (it rhymes with "FedEx," with a hard *g* sound like "regular" and not a soft one like in "Regina") and it is amenable to a variety of uses like "when you regex...," "budding regexers," and even "regexification."[†] I use the phrase "regex engine" to refer to the part of a program that actually does the work of carrying out a match attempt.

Matching

When I say a regex "matches" a string, I really mean that it matches *in* a string. Technically, the regex ⌈a⌋ doesn't *match* cat, but matches the a *in* cat. It's not something that people tend to confuse, but it's still worthy of mention.

Metacharacter

Whether a character is a metacharacter (or "metasequence"—I use the words interchangeably) depends on exactly where in the regex it's used. For example, ⌈*⌋ is a metacharacter, but only when it's not within a character class and when not escaped. "Escaped" means that it has a backslash in front of it—usually. The star is escaped in ⌈*⌋, but not in ⌈*⌋ (where the first backslash escapes the second), although the star "has a backslash in front of it" in both examples.

Depending upon the regex flavor, there are various situations when certain characters are and aren't metacharacters. Chapter 3 discusses this in more detail.

Flavor

As I've hinted, different tools use regular expressions for many different things, and the set of metacharacters and other features that each support can differ. Let's look at word boundaries again as an example. Some versions of *egrep* support the \<···\> notation we've seen. However, some do not support the separate word-start and word-end, but one catch-all ⌈\b⌋ metacharacter (which we haven't seen yet — we'll see it in the next chapter). Still others support both, and many others support neither.

I use the term "flavor" to describe the sum total of all these little implementation decisions. In the language analogy, it's the same as a dialect of an individual speaker. Superficially, this concept refers to which metacharacters are and aren't

---

[†] You might also come across the decidedly unsightly "regexp." I'm not sure how one would pronounce that, but those with a lisp might find it a bit easier.

Extending the Time Regex to Handle a 24-Hour Clock

❖ *Answer to the question on page 26.*

There are various solutions, but we can use similar logic as before. This time, I'll break the task into three groups: one for the morning (hours 00 through 09, with the leading zero being optional), one for the daytime (hours 10 through 19), and one for the evening (hours 20 through 23). This can be rendered in a pretty straightforward way: ⌈0?[0-9]|1[0-9]|2[0-3]⌋.

Actually, we can combine the first two alternatives, resulting in the shorter ⌈[01]?[0-9]|2[0-3]⌋. You might need to think about it a bit to convince yourself that they'll really match exactly the same text, but they do. The figure below might help, and it shows another approach as well. The shaded groups represent numbers that can be matched by a single alternative.

⌈ `[01]?[0-9]|2[0-3]` ⌋   ⌈ `[01]?[4-9]|[012]?[0-3]` ⌋

0	1	2	3	4	5	6	7	8	9

00	01	02	03	04	05	06	07	08	09
10	11	12	13	14	15	16	17	18	19
20	21	22	23						

0	1	2	3	4	5	6	7	8	9

00	01	02	03	04	05	06	07	08	09
10	11	12	13	14	15	16	17	18	19
20	21	22	23						

supported, but there's much more to it. Even if two programs both support ⌈\<···\>⌋, they might disagree on exactly what they do and don't consider to be a word. This concern is important when you *use* the tool.

Don't confuse "flavor" with "tool." Just as two people can speak the same dialect, two completely different programs can support exactly the same regex flavor. Also, two programs with the same name (and built to do the same task) often have slightly (and sometimes not-so-slightly) different flavors. Among the various programs called *egrep*, there is a wide variety of regex flavors supported.

In the late 1990s, the particularly expressive flavor offered by the Perl programming language was widely recognized for its power, and soon other languages were offering Perl-inspired regular expressions (many even acknowledging the inspirational source by labeling themselves "Perl-compatible"). The adopters include Python, many Java regex package, Microsoft's .NET Framework, Tcl, and a variety of C libraries, to name a few. Yet, all are different in important respects. On top of this, Perl's regular expressions themselves are evolving and growing (sometimes, now, in response to advances seen with other tools). As always, the overall landscape continues to become more varied and confusing.

Subexpression

The term "subexpression" simply refers to part of a larger expression, although it often refers to some part of an expression within parentheses, or to an alternative of ⌜|⌟. For example, with ⌜^(Subject|Date):⌟, the ⌜Subject|Date⌟ is usually referred to as a subexpression. Within that, the alternatives ⌜Subject⌟ and ⌜Date⌟ are each referred to as subexpressions as well. But technically, ⌜S⌟ is a subexpression, as is ⌜u⌟, and ⌜b⌟, and ⌜j⌟, . . .

Something such as 1-6 isn't considered a subexpression of ⌜H[1-6]•*⌟, since the '1-6' is part of an unbreakable "unit," the character class. But, ⌜H⌟, ⌜[1-6]⌟, and ⌜•*⌟ are all subexpressions of ⌜H[1-6]•*⌟.

Unlike alternation, quantifiers (star, plus, and question mark) always work with the smallest immediately-preceding subexpression. This is why with ⌜mis+pell⌟, the + governs the ⌜s⌟, not the ⌜mis⌟ or ⌜is⌟. Of course, when what immediately precedes a quantifier is a parenthesized subexpression, the entire subexpression (no matter how complex) is taken as one unit.

Character

The word "character" can be a loaded term in computing. The character that a byte represents is merely a matter of interpretation. A byte with such-and-such a value has that same value in any context in which you might wish to consider it, but which *character* that value *represents* depends on the encoding in which it's viewed. As a concrete example, two bytes with decimal values 64 and 53 represent the characters "@" and "5" respectively, if considered in the ASCII encoding, yet on the other hand are completely different if considered in the EBCDIC encoding (they are a space and some kind of a control character).

On the third hand, if those two bytes are considered in one of the popular encodings for Japanese characters, together they represent the single character 正. Yet, to represent this same character in another of the Japanese encodings requires two completely different bytes. Those two different bytes, by the way, yield the two characters "Àµ" in the popular *Latin-1* encoding, but yield the one Korean character 삵 in one of the Unicode encodings.[†] The point is this: how bytes are to be interpreted is a matter of perspective (called an *encoding*), and to be successful, you've got to make sure that your perspective agrees with the perspective taken by the tool you're using.

[†] The definitive book on multiple-byte encodings is Ken Lunde's *CJKV Information Processing*, also published by O'Reilly & Associates. The CJKV stands for *Chinese, Japanese, Korean,* and *Vietnamese,* which are languages that tend to require multiple-byte encodings. Ken and Adobe kindly provided many of the special fonts used in this book.

Until recently, text-processing tools generally treated their data as a bunch of ASCII bytes, without regard to the encoding you might be intending. Recently, however, more and more systems are using some form of Unicode to process data internally (Chapter 3 includes an introduction to Unicode ☞ 105). On such systems, if the regular-expression subsystem has been implemented properly, the user doesn't normally have to pay much attention to these issues. That's a big "if," which is why Chapter 3 looks at this issue in depth.

Improving on the Status Quo

When it comes down to it, regular expressions are not difficult. But, if you talk to the average user of a program or language that supports them, you will likely find someone that understands them "a bit," but does not feel secure enough to really use them for anything complex or with any tool but those they use most often.

Traditionally, regular expression documentation tends to be limited to a short and incomplete description of one or two metacharacters, followed by a table of the rest. Examples often use meaningless regular expressions like ⌈a*((ab)*|b*)⌋, and text like 'a·xxx·ce·xxxxxx·ci·xxx·d'. They also tend to completely ignore subtle but important points, and often claim that their flavor is the same as some other well-known tool, almost always forgetting to mention the exceptions where they inevitably differ. The state of regex documentation needs help.

Now, I don't mean to imply that this chapter fills the gap for all regular expressions, or even for *egrep* regular expressions. Rather, this chapter merely provides the foundation upon which the rest of this book is built. It may be ambitious, but I hope this book does fill the gaps for you. I received many gratifying responses to the first edition, and have worked very hard to make this one even better, both in breadth and in depth.

Perhaps because regular-expression documentation has traditionally been so lacking, I feel the need to make the extra effort to make things particularly clear. Because I want to make sure you can use regular expressions to their fullest potential, I want to make sure you really, *really* understand them.

This is both good and bad.

It is good because you will learn how to *think* regular expressions. You will learn which differences and peculiarities to watch out for when faced with a new tool with a different flavor. You will know how to express yourself even with a weak, stripped-down regular expression flavor. You will understand what makes one expression more efficient than another, and will be able to balance tradeoffs among complexity, efficiency, and match results. When faced with a particularly complex task, you will know how to work through an expression the way the program would, constructing it as you go. In short, you will be comfortable using regular expressions to their fullest.

The problem is that the learning curve of this method can be rather steep, with three separate issues to tackle:

- **How regular expressions are used**   Most programs use regular expressions in ways that are more complex than *egrep*. Before we can discuss in detail how to write a really useful expression, we need to look at the ways regular expressions can be used. We start in the next chapter.

- **Regular expression features**   Selecting the proper tool to use when faced with a problem seems to be half the battle, so I don't want to limit myself to only using one utility throughout this book. Different programs, and often even different versions of the same program, provide different features and metacharacters. We must survey the field before getting into the details of using them. This is the subject of Chapter 3.

- **How regular expressions really work**   Before we can learn from useful (but often complex) examples, we need to "look under the hood" to understand just how a regular expression search is conducted. As we'll see, the order in which certain metacharacters are checked can be very important. In fact, regular expression engines can be implemented in different ways, so different programs sometimes do different things with the same expression. We examine this meaty subject in Chapters 4, 5, and 6.

This last point is the most important and the most difficult to address. The discussion is unfortunately sometimes a bit dry, with the reader chomping at the bit to get to the fun part — tackling real problems. However, understanding how the regex engine really works is the key to *really understanding*.

You might argue that you don't want to be taught how a car works when you simply want to know how to drive. But, learning to drive a car is a poor analogy for learning about regular expressions. My goal is to teach you how to solve problems with regular expressions, and that means constructing regular expressions. The better analogy is not how to drive a car, but how to build one. Before you can build a car, you have to know how it works.

Chapter 2 gives more experience with driving. Chapter 3 takes a short look at the history of driving, and a detailed look at the bodywork of a regex flavor. Chapter 4 looks at the all-important engine of a regex flavor. Chapter 5 shows some extended examples, Chapter 6 shows you how to tune up certain kinds of engines, and the chapters after that examine some specific makes and models. Particularly in Chapters 4, 5, and 6, we'll spend a lot of time under the hood, so make sure to have your coveralls and shop rags handy.

Summary

Table 1-3 summarizes the *egrep* metacharacters we've looked at in this chapter.

Table 1-3: Egrep Metacharacter Summary

Items to Match a Single Character		
Metacharacter		**Matches**
.	*dot*	Matches any one character
[···]	*character class*	Matches any one character listed
[^···]	*negated character class*	Matches any one character not listed
\char	*escaped character*	When *char* is a metacharacter, or the escaped combination is not otherwise special, matches the literal *char*
Items Appended to Provide "Counting" : The Quantifiers		
?	*question*	One allowed, but it is optional
*	*star*	Any number allowed, but all are optional
+	*plus*	At least one required; additional are optional
{min,max}	*specified range*†	*Min* required, *max* allowed
Items That Match a Position		
^	*caret*	Matches the position at the start of the line
$	*dollar*	Matches the position at the end of the line
\<	*word boundary*†	Matches the position at the start of a word
\>	*word boundary*†	Matches the position at the end of a word
Other		
|	*alternation*	Matches either expression it separates
(···)	*parentheses*	Limits scope of alternation, provides grouping for the quantifiers, and "captures" for backreferences
\1, \2, ...	*backreference*†	Matches text previously matched within first, second, etc., set of parentheses.
		†*not supported by all versions of egrep*

In addition, be sure that you understand the following points:

- Not all *egrep* programs are the same. The metacharacters supported, as well as their exact meanings, are often different — see your local documentation (☞ 23).

- Three reasons for using parentheses are constraining alternation (☞ 13), grouping (☞ 14), and capturing (☞ 21).

- Character classes are special, and have their own set of metacharacters totally distinct from the "main" regex language (☞ 10).

- Alternation and character classes are fundamentally different, providing unrelated services that appear, in only one limited situation, to overlap (☞ 13).

- A negated character class is still a "positive assertion" — even negated, a character class must match a character to be successful. Because the listing of characters to match is negated, the matched character must be one of those *not* listed in the class (☞ 12).

- The useful -i option discounts capitalization during a match (☞ 15).

- There are three types of escaped items:
    1. The pairing of ⌐\⌐ and a metacharacter is a metasequence to match the literal character (for example, ⌐*⌐ matches a literal asterisk).
    2. The pairing of ⌐\⌐ and selected non-metacharacters becomes a metasequence with an implementation-defined meaning (for example, ⌐\<⌐ often means "start of word").
    3. The pairing of ⌐\⌐ and any other character defaults to simply matching the character (that is, the backslash is ignored).

    Remember, though, that a backslash within a character class is not special at all with most versions of *egrep*, so it provides no "escape services" in such a situation.

- Items governed by a question mark or star don't need to actually match any characters to "match successfully." They are *always* successful, even if they don't match anything (☞ 17).

Personal Glimpses

The doubled-word task at the start of this chapter might seem daunting, yet regular expressions are so powerful that we could solve much of the problem with a tool as limited as *egrep*, right here in the first chapter. I'd like to fill this chapter with flashy examples, but because I've concentrated on the solid foundation for the later chapters, I fear that someone completely new to regular expressions might read this chapter, complete with all the warnings and cautions and rules and such, and feel "why bother?"

Recently, my brothers were teaching some friends how to play *schaffkopf*, a card game that's been in my family for generations. It is much more exciting than it appears at first glance, but has a rather steep learning curve. After about half an hour, my sister-in-law Liz, normally the quintessence of patience, got frustrated with the seemingly complex rules and said "Can't we just play rummy?" Yet, as it turned out, they ended up playing late into the night. Once they were able to get over the initial hump of the learning curve, a first-hand taste of the excitement was all it took to hook them. My brothers knew it would, but it took some time and work to get to the point where Liz and the others new to the game could appreciate what they were getting into.

It might take some time to become acclimated to regular expressions, so until you get a real taste of the excitement by using them to solve *your* problems, it might all feel just a bit too academic. If so, I hope you will resist the desire to "play rummy." Once you understand the power that regular expressions provide, the small amount of work spent learning them will feel trivial indeed.

2

Extended Introductory Examples

Remember the doubled-word problem from the first chapter? I said that a full solution could be written in just a few lines in a language like Perl. Such a solution might look like:

```
$/ = ".\n";
while (<>) {
    next if !s/\b([a-z]+)((?:\s|<[^>]+>)+)(\1\b)/\e[7m$1\e[m$2\e[7m$3\e[m/ig;
    s/^(?:[^\e]*\n)+//mg;        # Remove any unmarked lines.
    s/^/$ARGV: /mg;             # Ensure lines begin with filename.
    print;
}
```

Yup, that's the *whole* program.

Even if you're familiar with Perl, I don't expect you to understand it (*yet!*). Rather, I wanted to show an example beyond what *egrep* can allow, and to whet your appetite for the real power of regular expressions.

Most of this program's work revolves around its three regular expressions:

- ⌜\b([a-z]+)((?:\s|<[^>]+>)+)(\1\b)⌟
- ⌜^(?:[^\e]*\n)+⌟
- ⌜^⌟

Though this is a Perl example, these three regular expressions can be used verbatim (or with only a few changes) in many other languages, including Python, Java, Visual Basic .NET, Tcl, and more.

Now, looking at these, that last ⌜^⌟ is certainly recognizable, but the other expressions have items unfamiliar to our *egrep*-only experience. This is because Perl's regex flavor is not the same as *egrep*'s. Some of the notations are different, and Perl (as well as most modern tools) tend to provide a much richer set of metacharacters than *egrep*. We'll see many examples throughout this chapter.

About the Examples

This chapter takes a few sample problems — validating user input; working with email headers; converting plain text to HTML — and wanders through the regular expression landscape with them. As I develop them, I'll "think out loud" to offer a few insights into the thought processes that go into crafting a regex. During our journey, we'll see some constructs and features that *egrep* doesn't have, and we'll take plenty of side trips to look at other important concepts as well.

Toward the end of this chapter, and in subsequent chapters, I'll show examples in a variety of languages including Java and Visual Basic .NET, but the examples throughout most of this chapter are in Perl. Any of these languages, and most others for that matter, allow you to employ regular expressions in much more complex ways than *egrep*, so using any of them for the examples would allow us to see interesting things. I choose to start with Perl primarily because it has the most ingrained, easily accessible regex support among the popular languages. Also, Perl provides many other concise data-handling constructs that alleviate much of the "dirty work" of our example tasks, letting us concentrate on regular expressions.

Just to quickly demonstrate some of these powers, recall the file-check example from page 2, where I needed to ensure that each file contained 'ResetSize' exactly as many times as 'SetSize'. The utility I used was Perl, and the command was:

```
% perl -0ne 'print "$ARGV\n" if s/ResetSize//ig != s/SetSize//ig' *
```

(I don't expect that you understand this yet — I hope merely that you'll be impressed with the brevity of the solution.)

I like Perl, but it's important not to get too caught up in its trappings here. Remember, this chapter concentrates on *regular expressions*. As an analogy, consider the words of a computer science professor in a first-year course: "You're going to learn computer-science concepts here, but we'll use Pascal to show you."[†]

Since this chapter doesn't assume that you know Perl, I'll be sure to introduce enough to make the examples understandable. (Chapter 7, which looks at all the nitty-gritty details of Perl, does assume some basic knowledge.) Even if you have experience with a variety of programming languages, normal Perl may seem quite odd at first glance because its syntax is very compact and its semantics thick. In the interest of clarity, I won't take advantage of much that Perl has to offer, instead presenting programs in a more generic, almost pseudo-code style. While not "bad," the examples are not the best models of The Perl Way of programming. But, we *will* see some great uses of regular expressions.

---

† Pascal is a traditional programming language originally designed for teaching. Thanks to William F. Maton, and his professor, for the analogy.

A Short Introduction to Perl

Perl is a powerful scripting language first developed in the late 1980s, drawing ideas from many other programming languages and tools. Many of its concepts of text handling and regular expressions are derived from two specialized languages called awk and sed, both of which are quite different from a "traditional" language such as C or Pascal.

Perl is available for many platforms, including DOS/Windows, MacOS, OS/2, VMS, and Unix. It has a powerful bent toward text handling, and is a particularly common tool used for Web-related processing. See `www.perl.com` for information on how to get a copy of Perl for your system.

This book addresses the Perl language as of Version 5.8, but the examples in this chapter are written to work with versions as early as Version 5.005.

Let's look at a simple example:

```
$celsius = 30;
$fahrenheit = ($celsius * 9 / 5) + 32;   # calculate Fahrenheit
print "$celsius C is $fahrenheit F.\n";  # report both temperatures
```

When executed, this produces:

```
30 C is 86 F.
```

Simple variables, such as $fahrenheit and $celsius, always begin with a dollar sign, and can hold a number or any amount of text. (In this example, only numbers are used.) Comments begin with # and continue for the rest of the line.

If you're used to languages such as C, C#, Java, or VB.NET, perhaps most surprising is that in Perl, variables can appear within a double-quoted string. With the string `"$celsius C is $fahrenheit F.\n"`, each variable is replaced by its value. In this case, the resulting string is then printed. (The \n represents a newline.)

Perl offers control structures similar to other popular languages:

```
$celsius = 20;
while ($celsius <= 45)
{
  $fahrenheit = ($celsius * 9 / 5) + 32; # calculate Fahrenheit
  print "$celsius C is $fahrenheit F.\n";
  $celsius = $celsius + 5;
}
```

The body of the code controlled by the `while` loop is executed repeatedly so long as the condition (the **$celsius <= 45** in this case) is true. Putting this into a file, say *temps*, we can run it directly from the command line.

Here's how a run looks:

```
% perl -w temps
20 C is 68 F.
25 C is 77 F.
30 C is 86 F.
35 C is 95 F.
40 C is 104 F.
45 C is 113 F.
```

The -w option is neither necessary nor has anything directly to do with regular expressions. It tells Perl to check your program more carefully and issue warnings about items it thinks to be dubious, (such as using uninitialized variables and the like — variables do not normally need to be predeclared in Perl). I use it here merely because it is good practice to always do so.

Well, that's it for the general introduction to Perl. We'll move on now to see how Perl allows us to use regular expressions.

Matching Text with Regular Expressions

Perl uses regular expressions in many ways, the simplest being to check if a regex matches text (or some part thereof) held in a variable. This snippet checks the string held in variable $reply and reports whether it contains only digits:

```
if ($reply =~ m/^[0-9]+$/) {
    print "only digits\n";
} else {
    print "not only digits\n";
}
```

The mechanics of the first line might seem a bit strange: the regular expression is ⌈^[0-9]+$⌋, while the surrounding **m/**⋯**/** tells Perl what to do with it. The **m** means to attempt a *regular expression match*, while the slashes delimit the regex itself.[†] The preceding =~ links m/⋯/ with the string to be searched, in this case the contents of the variable $reply.

Don't confuse =~ with = or ==. The operator == tests whether two numbers are the same. (The operator **eq**, as we will soon see, is used to test whether two *strings* are the same.) The = operator is used to assign a value to a variable, as with **$celsius = 20**. Finally, =~ links a regex search with the target string to be searched. In the example, the search is m/^[0-9]+$/ and the target is $reply. Other languages approach this differently, and we'll see examples in the next chapter.

---

† In many situations, the m is optional. This example can also appear as **$reply =~ /^[0-9]+$/**, which some readers with past Perl experience may find to be more natural. Personally, I feel the m is descriptive, so I tend to use it.

It might be convenient to read `=~` as "matches," such that

```
if ($reply =~ m/^[0-9]+$/)
```

becomes:

> if the text contained in the variable `$reply` *matches* the regex ⌈^[0-9]+$⌋, then ...

The whole result of **`$reply =~ m/^[0-9]+$/`** is a *true* value if the ⌈^[0-9]+$⌋ matches the string held in `$reply`, a *false* value otherwise. The `if` uses this true or false value to decide which message to print.

Note that a test such as **`$reply =~ m/[0-9]+/`** (the same as before except the wrapping caret and dollar have been removed) would be true if `$reply` contained at least one digit *anywhere*. The surrounding ⌈^···$⌋ ensures that the entire `$reply` contains *only* digits.

Let's combine the last two examples. We'll prompt the user to enter a value, accept that value, and then verify it with a regular expression to make sure it's a number. If it is, we calculate and display the Fahrenheit equivalent. Otherwise, we issue a warning message:

```
print "Enter a temperature in Celsius:\n";
$celsius = <STDIN>;  # this reads one line from the user
chomp($celsius);     # this removes the ending newline from $celsius

if ($celsius =~ m/^[0-9]+$/) {
    $fahrenheit = ($celsius * 9 / 5) + 32; # calculate Fahrenheit
    print "$celsius C is $fahrenheit F\n";
} else {
    print "Expecting a number, so I don't understand \"$celsius\".\n";
}
```

Notice in the last `print` how we escaped the quotes to be printed, to distinguish them from the quotes that delimit the string? As with literal strings in most languages, there are occasions to escape some items, and this is very similar to escaping a metacharacter in a regex. The relationship between a string and a regex isn't quite as important with Perl, but is extremely important with languages like Java, Python, and the like. The section "A short aside — metacharacters galore" (☞ 44) discusses this in a bit more detail. (One notable exception is VB.NET, which requires '""' rather than '\"' to get a double quote into a string literal.)

If we put this program into the file *c2f,* we might run it and see:

```
% perl -w c2f
Enter a temperature in Celsius:
22
22 C is 71.599999999999994316 F
```

Oops. As it turns out, Perl's simple `print` isn't so good when it comes to floating-point numbers.

I don't want to get bogged down describing all the details of Perl in this chapter, so I'll just say without further comment that you can use `printf` ("print formatted") to make this look better:

```
printf "%.2f C is %.2f F\n", $celsius, $fahrenheit;
```

The `printf` function is similar to the C language's `printf`, or the `format` of Pascal, Tcl, *elisp*, and Python. It doesn't change the values of the variables, but merely how they are displayed. The result are now much nicer:

```
Enter a temperature in Celsius:
22
22.00 C is 71.60 F
```

Toward a More Real-World Example

Let's extend this example to allow negative and fractional temperature values. The math part of the program is fine — Perl normally makes no distinction between integers and floating-point numbers. We do, however, need to modify the regex to let negative and floating-point values pass. We can insert a leading ⌜-?⌟ to allow a leading minus sign. In fact, we may as well make that ⌜[-+]?⌟ to allow a leading plus sign, too.

To allow an optional decimal part, we add ⌜(\.[0-9]*)?⌟. The escaped dot matches a literal period, so ⌜\.[0-9]*⌟ is used to match a period followed by any number of optional digits. Since ⌜\.[0-9]*⌟ is enclosed by ⌜(⋯)?⌟, the whole subexpression becomes optional. (Realize that this is very different from ⌜\.?[0-9]*⌟, which incorrectly allows additional digits to match even if ⌜\.⌟ does not match.)

Putting this all together, we get

```
if ($celsius =~ m/^[-+]?[0-9]+(\.[0-9]*)?$/)   {
```

as our check line. It allows numbers such as `32`, `-3.723`, and `+98.6`. It is actually not quite perfect: it doesn't allow a number that begins with a decimal point (such as `.357`). Of course, the user can just add a leading zero to allow it to match (e.g., `0.357`), so I don't consider it a major shortcoming. This floating-point problem can have some interesting twists, and I look at it in detail in Chapter 5 (☞ 194).

Side Effects of a Successful Match

Let's extend the example further to allow someone to enter a value in either Fahrenheit or Celsius. We'll have the user append a `C` or `F` to the temperature entered. To let this pass our regular expression, we can simply add ⌜[CF]⌟ after the expression to match a number, but we still need to change the rest of the program to recognize which kind of temperature was entered, and to compute the other.

In Chapter 1, we saw how some versions of *egrep* support ⌜\1⌟, ⌜\2⌟, ⌜\3⌟, etc. as metacharacters to refer to the text matched by parenthesized subexpressions earlier within the regex (☞ 21). Perl and most other modern regex-endowed languages support these as well, but also provide a way to refer to the text matched by parenthesized subexpressions from code *outside* of the regular expression, after a match has been successfully completed.

We'll see examples of how other languages do this in the next chapter (☞ 135), but Perl provides the access via the variables $1, $2, $3, etc., which refer to the text matched by the first, second, third, etc., parenthesized subexpression. As odd as it might seem, these *are* variables. The variable names just happen to be numbers. Perl sets them every time the application of a regex is successful.

To summarize, use the metacharacter ⌈\1⌋ within the regular expression to refer to some text matched earlier during the same match attempt, and use the variable $1 in subsequent code to refer to that same text after the match has been successfully completed.

To keep the example uncluttered and focus on what's new, I'll remove the fractional-value part of the regex for now, but we'll return to it again soon. So, to see $1 in action, compare:

```
$celsius =~ m/^[-+]?[0-9]+[CF]$/
$celsius =~ m/^([-+]?[0-9]+)([CF])$/
```

Do the added parentheses change the meaning of the expression? Well, to answer that, we need to know whether they provide grouping for star or other quantifiers, or provide an enclosure for ⌈|⌋. The answer is no on both counts, so what matches remains unchanged. However, they do enclose two subexpressions that match "interesting" parts of the string we are checking. As Figure 2-1 illustrates, $1 will receive the number entered, and $2 will receive the C or F entered. Referring to the flowchart in Figure 2-2 on the next page, we see that this allows us to easily decide how to proceed after the match.

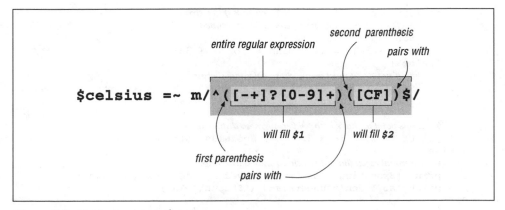

Figure 2-1: Capturing parentheses

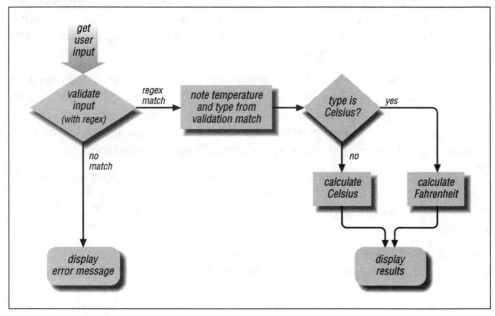

Figure 2-2: Temperature-conversion program's logic flow

Temperature-conversion program

```
print "Enter a temperature (e.g., 32F, 100C):\n";
$input = <STDIN>; # This reads one line from the user.
chomp($input);     # This removes the ending newline from $input.

if ($input =~ m/^([-+]?[0-9]+)([CF])$/)
{
    # If we get in here, we had a match. $1 is the number, $2 is "C" or "F".
    $InputNum = $1;  # Save to named variables to make the ...
    $type     = $2;  # ... rest of the program easier to read.

    if ($type eq "C") {        # 'eq' tests if two strings are equal
        # The input was Celsius, so calculate Fahrenheit
        $celsius = $InputNum;
        $fahrenheit = ($celsius * 9 / 5) + 32;
    } else {
        # If not "C", it must be an "F", so calculate Celsius
        $fahrenheit = $InputNum;
        $celsius = ($fahrenheit - 32) * 5 / 9;
    }
    # At this point we have both temperatures, so display the results:
    printf "%.2f C is %.2f F\n", $celsius, $fahrenheit;
} else {
    # The initial regex did not match, so issue a warning.
    print "Expecting a number followed by \"C\" or \"F\",\n";
    print "so I don't understand \"$input\".\n";
}
```

If the program shown on the facing page is named *convert*, we can use it like this:

```
% perl -w convert
Enter a temperature (e.g., 32F, 100C):
39F
3.89 C is 39.00 F
% perl -w convert
Enter a temperature (e.g., 32F, 100C):
39C
39.00 C is 102.20 F
% perl -w convert
Enter a temperature (e.g., 32F, 100C):
oops
Expecting a number followed by "C" or "F",
so I don't understand "oops".
```

Intertwined Regular Expressions

With advanced programming languages like Perl, regex use can become quite intertwined with the logic of the rest of the program. For example, let's make three useful changes to our program: allow floating-point numbers as we did earlier, allow for the f or c entered to be lowercase, and allow spaces between the number and letter. Once all these changes are done, input such as '98.6 f' will be allowed.

Earlier, we saw how we can allow floating-point numbers by adding ⌈(\.[0-9]*)?⌉ to the expression:

```
if ($input =~ m/^([-+]?[0-9]+(\.[0-9]*)?)([CF])$/)
```

Notice that it is added *inside* the first set of parentheses. Since we use that first set to capture the number to compute, we want to make sure that they capture the fractional portion as well. However, the added set of parentheses, even though ostensibly used only to group for the question mark, also has the side effect of capturing into a variable. Since the opening parenthesis of the pair is the second (from the left), it captures into $2. This is illustrated in Figure 2-3.

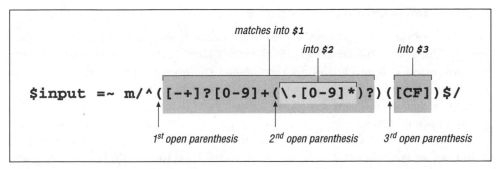

Figure 2-3: Nesting parentheses

Figure 2-3 illustrates how closing parentheses nest with opening ones. Adding a set of parentheses earlier in the expression doesn't influence the meaning of ⌜[CF]⌟ directly, but it does so indirectly because the parentheses surrounding it have now become the third pair. Becoming the third pair means that we need to change the assignment to $type to refer to $3 instead of $2 (but see the sidebar on the facing page for an alternative approach).

Next, allowing spaces between the number and letter is easier. We know that an unadorned space in a regex requires exactly one space in the matched text, so ⌜•*⌟ can be used to allow any number of spaces (but still not require any):

```
if ($input =~ m/^([-+]?[0-9]+(\.[0-9]*)?)_*([CF])$/)
```

This does give a limited amount of flexibility to the user of our program, but since we are trying to make something useful in the real world, let's construct the regex to also allow for other kinds of *whitespace* as well. Tabs, for instance, are quite common. Writing ⌜▨*⌟, of course, doesn't allow for spaces, so we need to construct a character class to match either one: ⌜[•▨]*⌟.

Compare that with ⌜(•*|▨*)⌟ and see if you can recognize how they are fundamentally different? ❖ After considering this, turn the page to check your thoughts.

In this book, spaces and tabs are easy to notice because of the • and ▨ typesetting conventions I've used. Unfortunately, it is not so on-screen. If you see something like [   ]*, you can guess that it is probably a space and a tab, but you can't be sure until you check. For convenience, Perl regular expressions provide the ⌜\t⌟ metacharacter. It simply matches a tab—its only benefit over a literal tab is that it is visually apparent, so I use it in my expressions. Thus, ⌜[•▨]*⌟ becomes ⌜[•\t]*⌟.

Some other Perl convenience metacharacters are ⌜\n⌟ (newline), ⌜\f⌟ (ASCII form-feed), and ⌜\b⌟ (backspace). Well, actually, ⌜\b⌟ is a backspace in some situations, but in others, it matches a word boundary. How can it be both? The next section tells us.

A short aside—metacharacters galore

We saw \n in earlier examples, but in those cases, it was in a string, not a regular expression. Like most languages, Perl *strings* have metacharacters of their own, and these are completely distinct from *regular expression* metacharacters. It is a common mistake for new programmers to get them confused. (VB.NET is a notable language that has very few string metacharacters.) Some of these string metacharacters conveniently look exactly the same as some comparable regex metacharacters. You can use the string metacharacter \t to get a tab into your string, while you can use the regex metacharacter ⌜\t⌟ to insert a tab-matching element into your regex.

Non-Capturing Parentheses: ⌜*(?:* ⋯ *)*⌟

In Figure 2-3, we use the parentheses of the ⌜(\.[0-9]*)?⌟ part for their grouping property, so we could apply a question mark to the whole of ⌜\.[0-9]*⌟ and make it optional. Still, as a side effect, text matched within these parentheses is captured and saved to $2, which we don't use. Wouldn't it be better if there were a type of parentheses that we could use for grouping which didn't involve the overhead (and possible confusion) of capturing and saving text to a variable that we never intend to use?

Perl, and recently some other regex flavors, do provide a way to do this. Rather than using ⌜(⋯)⌟, which group and capture, you can use the special notation ⌜(?:⋯)⌟, which group *but do not capture*. With this notation, the "opening parentheses" is the three-character sequence (?:, which certainly looks odd. This use of '?' has no relation to the "optional" ⌜?⌟ metacharacter. (Peek ahead to page 90 for a note about why this odd notation was chosen.)

So, the whole expression becomes:

```
if ($input =~ m/^([-+]?[0-9]+(?:\.[0-9]*)?)([CF])$/)
```

Now, even though the parentheses surrounding ⌜[CF]⌟ are ostensibly the third set, the text they match goes to $2 since, for counting purposes, the ⌜(?:⋯)⌟ set doesn't, well, count.

The benefits of this are twofold. One is that by avoiding the unnecessary capturing, the match process is more efficient (efficiency is something we'll look at in great detail in Chapter 6). Another is that, overall, using exactly the type of parentheses needed for each situation may be less confusing later to someone reading the code who might otherwise be left wondering about the exact nature of each set of parentheses.

On the other hand, the ⌜(?:⋯)⌟ notation *is* somewhat unsightly, and perhaps makes the expression more difficult to grasp at a glance. Are the benefits worth it? Well, personally, I tend to use exactly the kind of parentheses I need, but in this particular case, it's probably not worth the confusion. For example, efficiency isn't really an issue since the match is done just once (as opposed to being done repeatedly in a loop).

Throughout this chapter, I'll tend to use ⌜(⋯)⌟ even when I don't need their capturing, just for their visual clarity.

The similarity is convenient, but I can't stress enough how important it is to maintain the distinction between the different types of metacharacters. It may not seem important for such a simple example as \t, but as we'll later see when looking at numerous different languages and tools, knowing which metacharacters are being used in each situation is extremely important.

Quiz Answer

❖ *Answer to the question on page 44.*

How do ⌈[⬚ ⬚]*⌋ and ⌈ ⬚*|⬚*⌋ compare?

⌈(⬚*|⬚*)⌋ allows either ⌈ ⬚*⌋ or ⬚*⌋ to match, which allows either some spaces (or nothing) or some tabs (or nothing). It doesn't, however, allow a *combination* of spaces and tabs.

On the other hand, ⌈[⬚ ⬚]*⌋ matches ⌈[⬚ ⬚]⌋ any number of times. With a string such as '⬚ ⬚ ⬚' it matches three times, a tab the first time and spaces the rest.

⌈[⬚ ⬚]*⌋ is logically equivalent to ⌈(⬚|⬚)*⌋, although for reasons shown in Chapter 4, a character class is often much more efficient.

We have already seen multiple sets of metacharacters conflict. In Chapter 1, while working with *egrep*, we generally wrapped our regular expressions in single quotes. The whole *egrep* command line is written at the command-shell prompt, and the shell recognizes several of its own metacharacters. For example, to the shell, the space is a metacharacter that separates the command from the arguments and the arguments from each other. With many shells, single quotes are metacharacters that tell the shell to not recognize other shell metacharacters in the text between the quotes. (DOS uses double quotes.)

Using the quotes for the shell allows us to use spaces in our regular expression. Without the quotes, the shell would interpret the spaces in its own way instead of passing them through to *egrep* to interpret in *its* way. Many shells also recognize metacharacters such as $, *, ?, and so on—characters that we are likely to want to use in a regex.

Now, all this talk about other shell metacharacters and Perl's string metacharacters has nothing to do with regular expressions themselves, but it has everything to do with *using* regular expressions in real situations. As we move through this book, we'll see numerous (sometimes complex) situations where we need to take advantage of multiple levels of simultaneously interacting metacharacters.

And what about this ⌈\b⌋ business? This *is* a regex thing: in Perl regular expressions, ⌈\b⌋ normally matches a word boundary, but within a character class, it matches a backspace. A word boundary would make no sense as part of a class, so Perl is free to let it mean something else. The warnings in the first chapter about how a character class's "sub language" is different from the main regex language certainly apply to Perl (and every other regex flavor as well).

Generic "whitespace" with \s

While discussing whitespace, we left off with ⌜[●\t]*⌟. This is fine, but many regex flavors provide a useful shorthand: ⌜\s⌟. While it looks similar to something like ⌜\t⌟ which simply represents a literal tab, the metacharacter ⌜\s⌟ is a shorthand for a whole character class that matches any "whitespace character." This includes (among others) space, tab, newline, and carriage return. With our example, the newline and carriage return don't really matter one way or the other, but typing ⌜\s*⌟ is easier than ⌜[●\t]*⌟. After a while, you get used to seeing it, and ⌜\s*⌟ becomes easy to read even in complex regular expressions.

Our test now looks like:

```
$input =~ m/^([-+]?[0-9]+(\.[0-9]*)?)\s*([CF])$/
```

Lastly, we want to allow a lowercase letter as well as uppercase. This is as easy as adding the lowercase letters to the class: ⌜[CFcf]⌟. However, I'd like to show another way as well:

```
$input =~ m/^([-+]?[0-9]+(\.[0-9]*)?)\s*([CF])$/i
```

The added i is called a *modifier,* and placing it after the m/···/ instructs Perl to do the match in a case-insensitive manner. It's not actually part of the regex, but part of the m/···/ syntactic packaging that tells Perl what you want to do (apply a regex), and which regex to do it with (the one between the slashes). We've seen this type of thing before, with *egrep*'s -i option (☞ 15).

It's a bit too cumbersome to say "the i modifier" all the time, so normally "/i" is used even though you don't add an extra / when actually using it. This /i notation is one way to specify modifiers in Perl — in the next chapter, we'll see other ways to do it in Perl, and also how other languages allow for the same functionality. We'll also see other modifiers as we move along, including /g ("global match") and /x ("free-form expressions") later in this chapter.

Well, we've made a lot of changes. Let's try the new program:

```
% perl -w convert
Enter a temperature (e.g., 32F, 100C):
32 f
0.00 C is 32.00 F
% perl -w convert
Enter a temperature (e.g., 32F, 100C):
50 c
10.00 C is 50.00 F
```

Oops! Did you notice that in the second try we thought we were entering 50° Celsius, yet it was interpreted as 50° Fahrenheit? Looking at the program's logic, do you see why?

Let's look at that part of the program again:

```
if ($input =~ m/^([-+]?[0-9]+(\.[0-9]*)?)\s*([CF])$/i)
{
    ⋮
    $type = $3;   # save to a named variable to make rest of program more readable

    if ($type eq "C") { # 'eq' tests if two strings are equal
    ⋮
    } else {
    ⋮
```

Although we modified the regex to allow a lowercase f, we neglected to update the rest of the program appropriately. As it is now, if $type isn't exactly 'c', we assume the user entered Fahrenheit. Since we now also allow 'c' to mean Celsius, we need to update the $type test:

```
if ($type eq "C" or $type eq "c") {
```

Actually, since this is a book on regular expressions, perhaps I should use:

```
if ($type =~ m/c/i) {
```

In either case, it now works as we want. The final program is shown below. These examples show how the use of regular expressions can become intertwined with the rest of the program.

Temperature-conversion program – final listing

```
print "Enter a temperature (e.g., 32F, 100C):\n";
$input = <STDIN>; # This reads one line from the user.
chomp($input);       # This removes the ending newline from $input.

if ($input =~ m/^([-+]?[0-9]+(\.[0-9]*)?)\s*([CF])$/i)
{
    # If we get in here, we had a match. $1 is the number, $3 is "C" or "F".
    $InputNum = $1;   # Save to named variables to make the ...
    $type     = $3;   # ... rest of the program easier to read.

    if ($type =~ m/c/i) {      # Is it "c" or "C"?
        # The input was Celsius, so calculate Fahrenheit
        $celsius = $InputNum;
        $fahrenheit = ($celsius * 9 / 5) + 32;
    } else {
        # If not "C", it must be an "F", so calculate Celsius
        $fahrenheit = $InputNum;
        $celsius = ($fahrenheit - 32) * 5 / 9;
    }
    # At this point we have both temperatures, so display the results:
    printf "%.2f C is %.2f F\n", $celsius, $fahrenheit;
} else {
    # The initial regex did not match, so issue a warning.
    print "Expecting a number followed by \"C\" or \"F\",\n";
    print "so I don't understand \"$input\".\n";
}
```

Intermission

Although we have spent much of this chapter coming up to speed with Perl, we've encountered a lot of new information about regexes:

1. Most tools have their own particular flavor of regular expressions. Perl's appear to be of the same general type as *egrep*'s, but has a richer set of meta-characters. Many other languages, such as Java, Python, the .NET languages, and Tcl, have flavors similar to Perl's.

2. Perl can check a string in a variable against a regex using the construct **$variable =~ m/***regex***/**. The m indicates that a *match* is requested, while the slashes delimit (and are not part of) the regular expression. The whole test, as a unit, is either true or false.

3. The concept of metacharacters — characters with special interpretations — is not unique to regular expressions. As discussed earlier about shells and double-quoted strings, multiple contexts often vie for interpretation. Knowing the various contexts (shell, regex, and string, among others), their metacharacters, and how they can interact becomes more important as you learn and use Perl, Java, Tcl, GNU Emacs, awk, Python, or other advanced languages. (And of course, within regular expressions, character classes have their own mini language with a distinct set of metacharacters.)

4. Among the more useful shorthands that Perl and many other flavors of regex provide (some of which we haven't seen yet) are:

\t	a tab character
\n	a newline character
\r	a carriage-return character
\s	matches any "whitespace" character (space, tab, newline, formfeed, and such)
\S	anything not ⌈\s⌋
\w	⌈[a-zA-Z0-9_]⌋ (useful as in ⌈\w+⌋, ostensibly to match a word)
\W	anything not ⌈\w⌋, i.e., ⌈[^a-zA-Z0-9_]⌋
\d	⌈[0-9]⌋, i.e., a digit
\D	anything not ⌈\d⌋, i.e., ⌈[^0-9]⌋

5. The /i modifier makes the test case-insensitive. Although written in prose as "/i", only "i" is actually appended after the match operator's closing delimiter.

6. The somewhat unsightly ⌈(?:···)⌋ non-capturing parentheses can be used for grouping without capturing.

7. After a successful match, Perl provides the variables $1, $2, $3, etc., which hold the text matched by their respective ⌈(···)⌋ parenthesized subexpressions in the regex. In concert with these variables, you can use a regex to pluck information from a string. (Other languages provide the same type of information in other ways; we'll see many examples in the next chapter.)

Subexpressions are numbered by counting open parentheses from the left, starting with one. Subexpressions can be nested, as in ⌜(Washington(·DC)?)⌟. Raw ⌜(···)⌟ parentheses can be intended for grouping only, but as a byproduct, they still capture into one of the special variables.

Modifying Text with Regular Expressions

So far, the examples have centered on finding, and at times, "plucking out" information from a string. Now we look at *substitution* (also called *search and replace*), a regex feature that Perl and many tools offer.

As we have seen, **$var =~ m/*regex*/** attempts to match the given regular expression to the text in the given variable, and returns true or false appropriately. The similar construct **$var =~ s/*regex*/*replacement*/** takes it a step further: if the regex is able to match somewhere in the string held by $var, the text actually matched is replaced by *replacement*. The regex is the same as with m/···/, but the replacement (between the middle and final slash) is treated as a double-quoted string. This means that you can include references to variables, including $1, $2, and so on to refer to parts of what was just matched.

Thus, with **$var =~ s/···/···/** the value of the variable is actually changed. (If there is no match to begin with, no replacement is made and the variable is left unchanged.) For example, if $var contained Jeff·Friedl and we ran

```
$var =~ s/Jeff/Jeffrey/;
```

$var would end up with Jeffrey·Friedl. And if we did that again, it would end up with Jeffreyrey·Friedl. To avoid that, perhaps we should use a word-boundary metacharacter. As mentioned in the first chapter, some versions of *egrep* support ⌜\<⌟ and ⌜\>⌟ for their *start-of-word* and *end-of-word* metacharacters. Perl, however, provides the catch-all ⌜\b⌟, which matches either:

```
$var =~ s/\bJeff\b/Jeffrey/;
```

Here's a slightly tricky quiz: like m/···/, the s/···/···/ operation can use modifiers, such as the /i from page 47. (The modifier goes after the replacement.) Practically speaking, what does

```
$var =~ s/\bJeff\b/Jeff/i;
```

accomplish? ❖ Flip the page to check your answer.

Example: Form Letter

Let's look at a rather humorous example that shows the use of a variable in the replacement string. I can imagine a form-letter system that might use a letter template with markers for the parts that must be customized for each letter.

Here's an example:

```
Dear =FIRST=,
You have been chosen to win a brand new =TRINKET=! Free!
Could you use another =TRINKET= in the =FAMILY= household?
Yes =SUCKER=, I bet you could! Just respond by.....
```

To process this for a particular recipient, you might have the program load:

```
$given = "Tom";
$family = "Cruise";
$wunderprize = "100% genuine faux diamond";
```

Once prepared, you could then "fill out the form" with:

```
$letter =~ s/=FIRST=/$given/g;
$letter =~ s/=FAMILY=/$family/g;
$letter =~ s/=SUCKER=/$given $family/g;
$letter =~ s/=TRINKET=/fabulous $wunderprize/g;
```

Each substitution's regex looks for a simple marker, and when found, replaces it with the text wanted in the final message. The replacement part is actually a Perl string in its own right, so it can reference variables, as each of these do. For example, the marked portion of s/=TRINKET=/fabulous $wunderprize/g is interpreted just like the string "fabulous $wunderprize". If you just had the one letter to generate, you could forego using variables in the replacement string altogether, and just put the desired text directly. But, using this method makes automation possible, such as when reading names from a list.

We haven't seen the /g "global replacement" modifier yet. It instructs the s/⋯/⋯/ to continue trying to find more matches, and make more replacements, after (and from where) the first substitution completes. This is needed if each string we check could contain multiple instances of the text to be replaced, and we want each substitution to replacements them all, not just one.

The results are predictable, but rather humorous:

Dear Tom,
You have been chosen to win a brand new fabulous 100% genuine faux diamond! Free!
Could you use another fabulous 100% genuine faux diamond in the Cruise household?
Yes Tom Cruise, I bet you could! Just respond by . . . . .

Example: Prettifying a Stock Price

As another example, consider a problem I faced while working on some stock-pricing software with Perl. I was getting prices that looked like "9.0500000037272". The price was obviously 9.05, but because of how a computer represents the number internally, Perl sometimes prints them this way unless special formatting is used. Normally, I would just use printf to display the price with exactly two decimal digits as I did in the temperature-conversion example, but that was not

---

Quiz Answer

❖ *Answer to the question on page 50.*

Just what does   `$var =˜ s/\bJeff\b/Jeff/i`   do?

It might be tricky because of the way I posed it. Had I used ⌈`\bJEFF\b`⌋ or ⌈`\bjeff\b`⌋ or perhaps ⌈`\bjEfF\b`⌋ as the regex, the intent might have been more obvious. Because of `/i`, the word "Jeff" will be found without regard to capitalization. It will then be replaced by 'Jeff', which has exactly the capitalization you see. (`/i` has no effect on the replacement text, although there are other modifiers examined in Chapter 7 that do.)

The end result is that "`jeff`", in any capitalization, is replaced by exactly 'Jeff'.

---

appropriate in this case. At the time, stock prices were still given as fractions, and a price that ended with, say, $1/8$, should be shown with three decimals (".125"), not two.

I boiled down my needs to "always take the first two digits after the decimal point, and take the third digit only if it is not zero. Then, remove any other digits." The result is that 12.3750000000392 or the already correct 12.375 is returned as "12.375", yet 37.500 is reduced to "37.50". Just what I wanted.

So, how would we implement this? The variable `$price` contains the string in question, so let's use:

```
$price =˜ s/(\.\d\d[1-9]?)\d*/$1/
```

(Reminder: ⌈`\d`⌋ was introduced on page 49, and matches a digit.)

The initial ⌈`\.`⌋ causes the match to start at the decimal point. The subsequent ⌈`\d\d`⌋ then matches the first two digits that follow. The ⌈`[1-9]?`⌋ matches an additional non-zero digit if that's what follows the first two. Anything matched so far is what we want to *keep*, so we wrap it in parentheses to capture to `$1`. We can then use `$1` in the replacement string. If this is the only thing that matches, we replace exactly what was matched with itself — not very useful. However, we go on to match other items outside the `$1` parentheses. They don't find their way to the replacement string, so the effect is that they're removed. In this case, the "to be removed" text is any extra digits, the ⌈`\d*`⌋ at the end of the regex.

Keep this example in mind, as we'll come back to it in Chapter 4 when looking at the important mechanics of just what goes on behind the scenes during a match. Some very interesting lessons can be learned by playing with this example.

Automated Editing

I encountered another simple yet real-world example while working on this chapter. I was logged in to a machine across the Pacific, but the network was particularly slow. Just getting a response from hitting RETURN took more than a minute, but I needed to make a few small changes to a file to get an important program going. In fact, all I wanted to do was change every occurrence of `sysread` to `read`. There were only a few such changes to make, but with the slow response, the idea of starting up a full-screen editor was impractical.

Here's all I did to make all the changes I needed:

```
% perl -p -i -e 's/sysread/read/g' file
```

This runs the Perl program **s/sysread/read/g**. (Yes, that's the whole program — the -e flag indicates that the entire program follows right there on the command line.) The -p flag results in the substitution being done for every line of the named file, and the -i flag causes any changes to be written back to the file when done.

Note that there is no explicit target string for the substitute command to work on (that is, no **$var =~** ⋯) because conveniently, the -p flag implicitly applies the program, in turn, to each line of the file. Also, because I used the /g modifier, I'm sure to replace multiple occurrences that might be in a line.

Although I applied this to only one file, I could have easily listed multiple files on the command line and Perl would have applied my substitution to each line of each file. This way, I can do mass editing across a huge set of files, all with one simple command. The particular mechanics with which this was done are unique to Perl, but the moral of the story is that regular expressions as part of a scripting language can be very powerful, even in small doses.

A Small Mail Utility

Let's work on another example tool. Let's say we have an email message in a file, and we want to prepare a file for a reply. During the preparation, we want to quote the original message so we can easily insert our own reply to each part. We also want to remove unwanted lines from the header of the original message, as well as prepare the header of our own reply.

The sidebar on the next page shows an example. The header has interesting fields —date, subject, and so on—but also much that we are not interested in that we'll want to remove. If the script we're about to write is called *mkreply*, and the original message is in the file *king.in*, we would make the reply template with:

```
% perl -w mkreply king.in > king.out
```

(In case you've forgotten, the -w option enables extra Perl warnings ☞ 38.)

A Sample Email Message

```
From elvis Fri Feb 29 11:15 2002
Received: from elvis@localhost by tabloid.org (8.11.3) id KA8CMY
Received: from tabloid.org by gateway.net (8.12.5/2) id N8XBK
To: jfriedl@regex.info (Jeffrey Friedl)
From: elvis@tabloid.org (The King)
Date: Fri, Feb 29 2002 11:15
Message-Id: <2002022939939.KA8CMY@tabloid.org>
Subject: Be seein' ya around
Reply-To: elvis@hh.tabloid.org
X-Mailer: Madam Zelda's Psychic Orb [version 3.7 PL92]

Sorry I haven't been around lately. A few years back I checked
into that ole heartbreak hotel in the sky, ifyaknowwhatImean.
The Duke says "hi".
        Elvis
```

We want the resulting file, *king.out*, to contain something like:

```
To: elvis@hh.tabloid.org (The King)
From: jfriedl@regex.info (Jeffrey Friedl)
Subject: Re: Be seein' ya around

On Fri, Feb 29 2002 11:15 The King wrote:
|> Sorry I haven't been around lately. A few years back I checked
|> into that ole heartbreak hotel in the sky, ifyaknowwhatImean.
|> The Duke says "hi".
|>          Elvis
```

Let's analyze this. To print out our new header, we need to know the destination address (in this case elvis@hh.tabloid.org, derived from the Reply-To field of the original), the recipient's real name (The King), our own address and name, as well as the subject. Additionally, to print out the introductory line for the message body, we need to know the message date.

The work can be split into three phases:

1. Extract information from the message header
2. Print out the reply header
3. Print out the original message, indented by '|> '

I'm getting a bit ahead of myself—we can't worry about processing the data until we determine how to read the data into the program. Fortunately, Perl makes this a breeze with the magic "<>" operator. This funny-looking construct gives you the next line of input when you assign from it to a normal $variable, as with "$variable = <>". The input comes from files listed after the Perl script on the command line (from *king.in* in the previous example).

Don't confuse the two-character operator <> with the shell's "> *filename*" redirection or Perl's greater-than/less-than operators. It is just Perl's funny way to express a kind of a getline() function.

Once all the input has been read, `<>` conveniently returns an undefined value (which is interpreted as a Boolean false), so an entire file can be processed with:

```
while ($line = <>) {
    ... work with $line here ...
}
```

We'll use something similar for our email processing, but the nature of email means we need to process the header specially. The header includes everything before the first blank line; the body of the message follows. To read only the header, we might use:

```
# Process the header
while ($line = <>) {
    if ($line =~ m/^\s*$/) {
        last;  # stop processing within this while loop, continue below
    }
    ... process header line here ...
}
... processing for the rest of the message follows ...
    ⋮
```

We check for the header-ending blank line with the expression ⌜`^\s*$`⌟. It checks to see whether the target string has a beginning (as all do), followed by any number of whitespace characters (although we aren't really expecting any except the newline character that ends each line), followed by the end of the string.[†] The keyword `last` breaks out of the enclosing `while` loop, stopping the header-line processing.

So, inside the loop, after the blank-line check, we can do whatever work we like with each header line. In this case, we need to extract information, such as the subject and date of the message.

To pull out the subject, we can employ a popular technique we'll use often:

```
if ($line =~ m/^Subject: (.*)/i) {
    $subject = $1;
}
```

This attempts to match a string beginning with '`Subject:␣`', having any capitalization. Once that much of the regex matches, the subsequent ⌜`.*`⌟ matches whatever else is on the rest of the line. Since the ⌜`.*`⌟ is within parentheses, we can later use `$1` to access the text of the subject. In our case, we just save it to the variable `$subject`. Of course, if the regex doesn't match the string (as it won't with most), the result for the `if` is false and `$subject` isn't set for that line.

---

† I use the word "string" instead of "line" because, although it's not really an issue with this particular example, regular expressions can be applied to a string that contains a multiline chunk of text. The caret and dollar anchors (normally) match only at the start and end of the string as a whole (we'll see a counter example later in this chapter). In any case, the distinction is not vital here because, due to the nature of our algorithm, we *know* that `$line` never has more than one logical line.

A Warning About ⌈ . *⌋

The expression ⌈ . *⌋ is often used to mean "a bunch of anything," since dot can match anything (with some tools, anything except newlines) and star means that any amount is allowed, but none required. This can be quite useful.

However, some hidden "gotchas" can bite the user who doesn't fully understand the implications of how it works when used as part of a larger expression. We've already seen one example (☞ 26), and will see many more in Chapter 4 when this topic is discussed in depth (☞ 164).

Similarly, we can look for the `Date` and `Reply-To` fields:

```
if ($line =~ m/^Date: (.*)/i) {
    $date = $1;
}
if ($line =~ m/^Reply-To: (.*)/i) {
    $reply_address = $1;
}
```

The `From:` line involves a bit more work. First, we want the one that begins with 'From:', not the more cryptic first line that begins with 'From␣'. We want:

```
From: elvis@tabloid.org (The King)
```

It has the originating address, as well as the name of the sender in parentheses; our goal is to extract the name.

To match up through the address, we can use ⌈^From:␣(\S+)⌋. As you might guess, ⌈\S⌋ matches anything that's *not* whitespace (☞ 49), so ⌈\S+⌋ matches up until the first whitespace (or until the end of the target text). In this case, that's the originating address. Once that's matched, we want to match whatever is in parentheses. Of course, we also need to match the parentheses themselves. This is done using ⌈\(⌋ and ⌈\)⌋, escaping the parentheses to remove their special metacharacter meaning. Inside the parentheses, we want to match anything—anything except another parenthesis! That's accomplished with ⌈[^()]*⌋. Remember, the character-class metacharacters are different from the "normal" regex metacharacters; inside a character class, parentheses are not special and do not need to be escaped.

So, putting this all together we get:

⌈^From:␣(\S+)␣\(([^()]*)\)⌋.

At first it might be a tad confusing with all those parentheses, so Figure 2-4 on the facing page shows it more clearly.

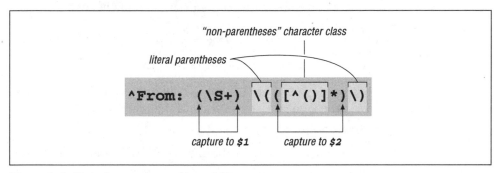

Figure 2-4: Nested parentheses; $1 and $2

When the regex from Figure 2-4 matches, we can access the sender's name as $2, and also have $1 as a possible return address:

```
if ($line =~ m/^From: (\S+) \(([^()]*)\)/i) {
    $reply_address = $1;
    $from_name = $2;
}
```

Since not all email messages come with a Reply-To header line, we use $1 as a provisional return address. If there turns out to be a Reply-To field later in the header, we'll overwrite $reply_address at that point. Putting this all together, we end up with:

```
while ($line = <>)
{
    if ($line =~ m/^\s*$/ ) { # If we have an empty line...
        last; # this immediately ends the 'while' loop.
    }

    if ($line =~ m/^Subject: (.*)/i) {
        $subject = $1;
    }

    if ($line =~ m/^Date: (.*)/i) {
        $date = $1;
    }

    if ($line =~ m/^Reply-To: (\S+)/i) {
        $reply_address = $1;
    }

    if ($line =~ m/^From: (\S+) \(([^()]*)\)/i) {
        $reply_address = $1;
        $from_name = $2;
    }
}
```

Each line of the header is checked against all the regular expressions, and if it matches one, some appropriate variable is set. Many header lines won't be matched by any of the regular expressions, and so end up being ignored.

Once the `while` loop is done, we are ready to print out the reply header:[†]

```
print "To: $reply_address ($from_name)\n";
print "From: Jeffrey Friedl <jfriedl\@regex.info>\n";
print "Subject: Re: $subject\n";
print "\n" ; # blank line to separate the header from message body.
```

Notice how we add the `Re:` to the subject to informally indicate that it is a reply. Finally, after the header, we can introduce the body of the reply with:

```
print "On $date $from_name wrote:\n";
```

Now, for the rest of the input (the body of the message), we want to print each line with '`|>␣`' prepended:

```
while ($line = <>) {
    print "|> $line";
}
```

Here, we don't need to provide a newline because we know that `$line` contains one from the input.

It is interesting to see that we can rewrite the code to prepend the quoting marker using a regex construct:

```
$line =~ s/^/|> /;
print $line;
```

The substitute searches for ⌜^⌟, which of course immediately matches at the beginning of the string. It doesn't actually match any characters, though, so the substitute "replaces" the "nothingness" at the beginning of the string with '`|>␣`'. In effect, it inserts '`|>␣`' at the beginning of the string. It's a novel use of a regular expression that is gross overkill in this particular case, but we'll see similar (but much more useful) examples later in this chapter.

Real-world problems, real-world solutions

It's hard to present a real-world example without pointing out its real-world shortcomings. First, as I have commented, the goal of these examples is to show regular expressions in action, and the use of Perl is simply a vehicle to do so. The Perl code I've used here is not necessarily the most efficient or even the best approach, but, hopefully, it clearly shows the regular expressions at work.

Also, real-world email messages are far more complex than indicated by the simple problem addressed here. A `From:` line can appear in various different formats, only one of which our program can handle. If it doesn't match our pattern exactly, the `$from_name` variable never gets set, and so remains undefined (which is a kind of "no value" value) when we attempt to use it. The ideal fix would be to update the regex to handle all the different address/name formats, but as a first

---

† In Perl regular expressions and double-quoted strings, most '@' must be escaped (☞ 77).

step, after checking the original message (and before printing the reply template), we can put:

```
if (    not defined($reply_address)
    or not defined($from_name)
    or not defined($subject)
    or not defined($date) )
{
    die "couldn't glean the required information!";
}
```

Perl's `defined` function indicates whether the variable has a value, while the `die` function issues an error message and exits the program.

Another consideration is that our program assumes that the `From:` line appears before any `Reply-To:` line. If the `From:` line comes later, it overwrites the `$reply_address` we took from the `Reply-To:` line.

The "real" real world

Email is produced by many different types of programs, each following their own idea of what they think the standard is, so email can be tricky to handle. As I discovered once while attempting to write some code in Pascal, it can be *extremely* difficult without regular expressions. So much so, in fact, that I found it easier to write a Perl-like regex package in Pascal than attempt to do everything in raw Pascal! I had taken the power and flexibility of regular expressions for granted until I entered a world without them. I certainly didn't want to stay in that world long.

Adding Commas to a Number with Lookaround

Presenting large numbers with commas often makes reports more readable. Something like

```
print "The US population is $pop\n";
```

might print out "The US population is 281421906," but it would look more natural to most English speakers to use "281,421,906" instead. How might we use a regular expression to help?

Well, when we insert commas mentally, we count sets of digits by threes from the right, and insert commas at each point where there are still digits to the left. It'd be nice if we could apply this natural process directly with a regular expression, but regular expressions generally work left-to-right. However, if we distill the idea of where commas should be inserted as "locations having digits on the right in exact sets of three, and at least some digits on the left," we can solve this problem easily using a set of relatively new regex features collectively called *lookaround.*

Lookaround constructs are similar to word-boundary metacharacters like ⌜\b⌝ or the anchors ⌜^⌝ and ⌜$⌝ in that they don't match text, but rather match *positions* within the text. But, lookaround is a much more general construct than the special-case word boundary and anchors.

One type of lookaround, called *lookahead*, peeks forward in the text (toward the right) to see if its subexpression can match, and is successful as a regex component if it can. Positive lookahead is specified with the special sequence ⌜(?=⋯)⌟, such as with ⌜(?=\d)⌟, which is successful at positions where a digit comes next. Another type of lookaround is *lookbehind*, which looks back (toward the left). It's given with the special sequence ⌜(?<=⋯)⌟, such as ⌜(?<=\d)⌟, which is successful at positions with a digit to the left (i.e., at positions after a digit).

Lookaround doesn't "consume" text

An important thing to understand about lookahead and other lookaround constructs is that although they go through the motions to see if their subexpression is able to match, they don't actually "consume" any text. That may be a bit confusing, so let me give an example. The regex ⌜Jeffrey⌟ matches

       by Jeffrey Friedl.

but the same regex within lookahead, ⌜(?=Jeffrey)⌟, matches only the marked location in:

       by ⌞Jeffrey Friedl.

Lookahead uses its subexpression to check the text, but only to find a *location* in the text at which it can be matched, not the actual *text* it matches. But, combining it with something that does match text, such as ⌞Jeff⌟, allows us to be more specific than ⌞Jeff⌟ alone. The combined expression, ⌜**(?=Jeffrey)**Jeff⌟, illustrated in the figure on the facing page, effectively matches "Jeff" only if it is part of "Jeffrey." It does match:

       by Jeffrey Friedl.

just like ⌞Jeff⌟ alone would, but it *doesn't* match on this line:

       by Thomas Jefferson

By itself, ⌞Jeff⌟ would easily match this line as well, but since there's no position at which ⌜(?=Jeffrey)⌟ can match, they fail as a pair. Don't worry too much if the benefit of this doesn't seem obvious at this point. Concentrate now on the mechanics of what lookahead means—we'll soon see realistic examples that illustrate their benefit more clearly.

It might be insightful to realize that ⌜**(?=Jeffrey)**Jeff⌟ is effectively the same as ⌞Jeff**(?=rey)**⌟. Both match "Jeff" only if it is part of "Jeffrey."

It's also interesting to realize that the order in which they're combined is very important. ⌞Jeff**(?=Jeffrey)**⌟ doesn't match any of these examples, but rather matches "Jeff" only if followed immediately by "Jeffrey."

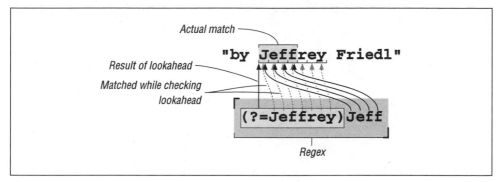

Figure 2-5: How ⌈(?=Jeffrey)Jeff⌋ is applied

Another important thing to realize about lookaround constructs concerns their somewhat ungainly notation. Like the non-capturing parentheses "(?:⋯)" introduced on page 45, these constructs use special sequences of characters as their "open parenthesis." There are a number of such special "open parenthesis" sequences, but they all begin with the two-character sequence "(?". The character following the question mark tells what special function they perform. We've already seen the group-but-don't-capture "(?:⋯)", lookahead "(?=⋯)", and lookbehind "(?<=⋯)" constructs, and we will see more as we go along.

A few more lookahead examples

We'll get to adding commas to numbers soon, but first let's see a few more examples of lookaround. We'll start by making occurrences of "Jeffs" possessive by replacing them with "Jeff's". This is easy to solve without any kind of lookaround, with **s/Jeffs/Jeff's/g**. (Remember, the /g is for "global replacement" ☞ 51.) Better yet, we can add word-boundary anchors: **s/\bJeffs\b/Jeff's/g**.

We might even use something fancy like **s/\b(Jeff)(s)\b/$1'$2/g**, but this seems gratuitously complex for such a simple task, so for the moment we'll stick with **s/\bJeffs\b/Jeff's/g**. Now, compare this with:

```
s/\bJeff(?=s\b)/Jeff'/g
```

The only change to the regular expression is that the trailing ⌈s\b⌋ is now within lookahead. Figure 2-6 on the next page illustrates how this regex matches. Corresponding to the change in the regex, the 's' has been removed from the replacement string.

After ⌈Jeff⌋ matches, the lookahead is attempted. It is successful only if ⌈s\b⌋ can match at that point (i.e., if 's' and a word boundary is what follows 'Jeff'). But, because the ⌈s\b⌋ is part of a lookahead subexpression, the 's' it matches isn't actually considered part of the final match. Remember, while ⌈Jeff⌋ selects text, the lookahead part merely "selects" a position. The only benefit, then, to having the

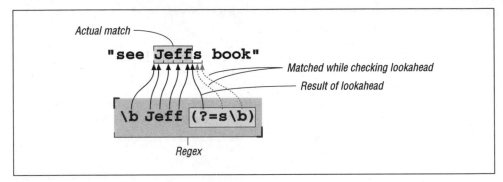

Figure 2-6: How ⌈`\bJeff(?=s\b)`⌋ *is applied*

lookahead in this situation is that it can cause the whole regex to fail in some
cases where it otherwise wouldn't. Or, another way to look at it, it allows us to
check the entire ⌈Jeffs⌋ while pretending to match only ⌈Jeff⌋.

Why would we want to pretend to match less than we really did? In many cases,
it's because we want to recheck that same text by some later part of the regex, or
by some later application of the regex. We see this in action in a few pages when
we finally get to the number commafication example. The current example has a
different reason: we want to check the whole of ⌈Jeffs⌋ because that's the situation where we want to add an apostrophe, but if we actually match only 'Jeff',
that allows the replacement string to be smaller. Since the 's' is no longer part of
the match, it no longer needs to be part of what is replaced. That's why it's been
removed from the replacement string.

So, while both the regular expressions and the replacement string of each example
are different, in the end their results are the same. So far, these regex acrobatics
may seem a bit academic, but I'm working toward a goal. Let's take the next step.

When moving from the first example to the second, the trailing ⌈s⌋ was moved from
the "main" regex to lookahead. What if we did something similar with the leading
⌈Jeff⌋, putting it into look*behind*? That would be ⌈`(?<=\bJeff)(?=s\b)`⌋, which
reads as "find a spot where we can look behind to find 'Jeff', and also look
ahead to find 's'." It exactly describes where we want to insert the apostrophe. So,
using this in our substitution gives:

> **`s/(?<=\bJeff)(?=s\b)/'/g`**

Well, this is getting interesting. The regex doesn't actually match any text, but
rather matches *at a position* where we wish to insert an apostrophe. At such locations, we then "replace" the nothingness we just matched with an apostrophe. Figure 2-7 illustrates this. We saw this exact type of thing just a few pages ago with
the **`s/^/|>•/`** used to prepend '|>•' to the line.

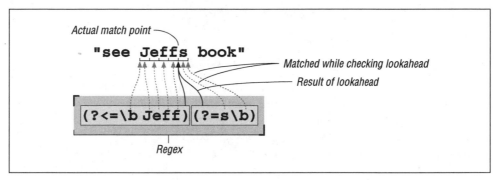

Figure 2-7: How⌐(?<=\bJeff)(?=s\b)⌐ is applied

Would the meaning of the expression change if the order of the two lookaround constructs was switched? That is, what does **s/(?=s\b)(?<=\bJeff)/'/g** do? ❖ Turn the page to check your answer.

"Jeffs" summary   Table 2-1 summarizes the various approaches we've seen to replacing Jeffs with Jeff's.

Table 2-1: Approaches to the "Jeffs" Problem

Solution	Comments
s/\bJeffs\b/Jeff's/g	The simplest, most straightforward, and efficient solution; the one I'd use if I weren't trying to show other interesting ways to approach the same problem. Without lookaround, the regex "consumes" the entire 'Jeffs'.
s/\b(Jeff)(s)\b/$1'$2/g	Complex without benefit. Still consumes entire 'Jeffs'.
s/\bJeff(?=s\b)/Jeff'/g	Doesn't actually consume the 's', but this not of much practical value here except to illustrate lookahead.
s/(?<=\bJeff)(?=s\b)/'/g	This regex doesn't actually "consume" any text. It uses both lookahead and lookbehind to match *positions* of interest, at which a comma is inserted. Very useful to illustrate lookaround.
s/(?=s\b)(?<=\bJeff)/'/g	This is exactly the same as the one above, but the two lookaround tests are reversed. Because the tests don't consume text, the order in which they're applied makes no difference to whether there's a match.

Before moving back to the adding-commas-to-numbers example, let me ask one question about these expressions. If I wanted to find "Jeffs" in a case-insensitive manner, but preserve the original case after the conversion, which of the expressions could I add /i to and have it work properly? I'll give you a hint: it won't

---

Quiz Answer

❖ *Answer to the question on page 63.*

What does `s/(?=s\b)(?<=\bJeff)//g` **do?**

In this case, it doesn't matter which order ⌜`(?=s\b)`⌟ and ⌜`(?<=\bJeff)`⌟ are arranged. Whether "checking on the right, then the left" or the other way around, the key is that both checks must succeed at the same position for the combination of the two checks to succeed. For example, in the string 'Thomas Jefferson', both ⌜`(?=s\b)`⌟ and ⌜`(?<=\bJeff)`⌟ can match (at the two locations marked), but since there is no one position where both can be successful, the combination of the two cannot match.

It's fine for now to use the somewhat vague phrase "combination of the two" to talk about this, as the meaning is fairly intuitive in this case. There are times, however, when exactly *how* a regex engine goes about applying a regex may not necessarily be quite so intuitive. Since how it works has immediate practical effects on what our regular expressions really mean, Chapter 4 discusses this in explicit detail.

---

work properly with two of them. ❖ Think about which ones would work, and why, and then turn the page to check your answer.

Back to the comma example...

You've probably already realized that the connection between the "Jeffs" example and the comma example lies in our wanting to insert something at a *location* that we can describe with a regular expression.

Earlier, we realized that we wanted to insert commas at "locations having digits on the right in exact sets of three, and at least some digits on the left." The second requirement is simple enough with lookbehind. One digit on the left is enough to fulfill the "some digits on the left" requirement, and that's ⌜`(?<=\d)`⌟.

Now for "locations having digits on the right in exact sets of three." An exact set of three digits is ⌜`\d\d\d`⌟, of course. We can wrap it with ⌜`(···)+`⌟ to allow more than one (the "sets" of our requirement), and append ⌜`$`⌟ to ensure that nothing follows (the "exact" of our requirement). Alone, ⌜`(\d\d\d)+$`⌟ matches sets of triple digits to the end of the string, but when inserted into the ⌜`(?=···)`⌟ lookahead construct, it matches at *locations* that are even sets of triple digits from the end of the string, such as at the marked locations in '123456789'. That's actually more than we want —we don't want to put a comma before the first digit—so we add ⌜`(?<=\d)`⌟ to further limit the match locations.

This snippet:

```
$pop =~ s/(?<=\d)(?=(\d\d\d)+$)/,/g;
print "The US population is $pop\n";
```

indeed prints "The US population is 281,421,906" as we desire. It might, however, seem a bit odd that the parentheses surrounding ⌈\d\d\d⌉ are capturing parentheses. Here, we use them only for grouping, to apply the plus to the set of three digits, and so don't need their capture-to-$1 functionality.

I could have used ⌈(?:···)⌉, the non-capturing parentheses introduced in the sidebar on page 45. This would leave the regex as ⌈(?<=\d)(?=(?:\d\d\d)+$)⌉. This is "better" in that it's more specific—someone reading this later won't have to wonder if or where the $1 associated with capturing parentheses might be used. It's also just a bit more efficient, since the engine doesn't have to bother remembering the captured text. On the other hand, even with ⌈(···)⌉ the expression can be a bit confusing to read, and with ⌈(?:···)⌉ even more so, so I chose the clearer presentation this time. These are common tradeoffs one faces when writing regular expressions. Personally, I like to use ⌈(?:···)⌉ everywhere it naturally applies (such as this example), but opt for clarity when trying to illustrate other points (as is usually the case in this book).

Word boundaries and negative lookaround

Let's say that we wanted to extend the use of this expression to commafying numbers that might be included within a larger string. For example:

```
$text = "The population of 281421906 is growing";
    ⋮
$text =~ s/(?<=\d)(?=(\d\d\d)+$)/,/g;
print "$text\n";
```

As it stands, this doesn't work because the ⌈$⌉ requires that the sets of three digits line up with the end of the string. We can't just remove it, since that would have it insert a comma everywhere that there was a digit on the left, and at least three digits on the right—we'd end up with "... of 2,8,1,4,2,1,906 is..."!

It might seem odd at first, but we could replace ⌈$⌉ with something to match a word boundary, ⌈\b⌉. Even though we're dealing with numbers only, Perl's concept of "words" helps us out. As indicated by ⌈\w⌉ (☞ 49), Perl and most other programs consider alphanumerics and underscore to be part of a word. Thus, any location with those on one side (such as our number) and not those on the other side (e.g., the end of the line, or the space after a number) is a word boundary.

This "such-and-such on one side, and this-and-that on the other" certainly sounds familiar, doesn't it? It's exactly what we did in the "Jeffs" example. One difference here is that one side must *not* match something. It turns out that what we've so far been called lookahead and lookbehind should really be called *positive lookahead*

Quiz Answer

❖ *Answer to the question on page 64.*

Which "Jeffs" solutions would preserve case when applied with /i?

To preserve case, you've got to either replace the exact characters consumed (rather than just always inserting 'Jeff's'), or not consume any letters. The second solution listed in Table 2-1 takes the first approach, capturing what is consumed and using $1 and $2 to put it back. The last two solutions in the table take the "don't consume anything" approach. Since they don't consume text, they have nothing to preserve.

The first and third solutions hard-code the replacement string. If applied with /i, they don't preserve case. They end up incorrectly replacing JEFFS with Jeff's and JEFF's, respectively.

---

and *positive lookbehind*, since they are successful at positions where their subexpression is able to match. As Table 2-2 shows, their converse, *negative lookahead* and *negative lookbehind*, are also available. As their name implies, they are successful as positions where their subexpression is not able to match.

Table 2-2: Four Types of Lookaround

Type	Regex	Successful if the enclosed subexpression . . .
Positive Lookbehind	(?<=......)	successful if *can* match to the *left*
Negative Lookbehind	(?<!......)	successful if *can not* match to the *left*
Positive Lookahead	(?=......)	successful if *can* match to the *right*
Negative Lookahead	(?!......)	successful if *can not* match to the *right*

So, if a word boundary is a position with ⌈\w⌋ on one side and not ⌈\w⌋ on the other, we can use ⌈(?<!\w)(?=\w)⌋ as a start-of-word boundary, and its compliment ⌈(?<=\w)(?!\w)⌋ as an end-of-word boundary. Putting them together, we could use ⌈(?<!\w)(?=\w)|(?<=\w)(?!\w)⌋ as a replacement for ⌈\b⌋. In practice, it would be silly to do this for languages that natively support \b (\b is much more direct and efficient), but the individual alternatives may indeed be useful (☞ 132).

For our comma problem, though, we really need only ⌈(?!\d)⌋ to cap our sets of three digits. We use that instead of ⌈\b⌋ or ⌈$⌋, which leaves us with:

```
$text =~ s/(?<=\d)(?=(\d\d\d)+(?!\d))/,/g;
```

This now works on text like "...tone of 12345Hz," which is good, but unfortunately it also matches the year in "... the 1970s ..." Actually, any of these match "... in 1970 ...," which is not good. There's no substitute for knowing the data you intend to apply a regex to, and knowing when that application is appropriate (and if your data has year numbers, this regex is probably not appropriate).

Throughout this discussion of boundaries and what we don't want to match, we used negative lookahead, ⌜(?!\w)⌝ or ⌜(?!\d)⌝. You might remember the "something not a digit" metacharacter ⌜\D⌝ from page 49 and think that perhaps this could be used instead of ⌜(?!\d)⌝. That would be a mistake. Remember, in ⌜\D⌝'s meaning of "something not a digit," *something* is required, just something that's not a digit. If there's *nothing* in the text being searched after the digit, ⌜\D⌝ can't match. (We saw something similar to this back in the sidebar on page 12.)

Commafication without lookbehind

Lookbehind is not as widely supported (nor as widely used) as lookahead. Lookahead support was introduced to the world of regular expressions years before lookbehind, and though Perl now has both, this is not yet true for many languages. Therefore, it might be instructive to consider how to solve the commafication problem without lookbehind. Consider:

```
$text =~ s/(\d)(?=(\d\d\d)+(?!\d))/$1,/g;
```

The change from the previous example is that the positive lookbehind that had been wrapped around the leading ⌜\d⌝ has been replaced by capturing parentheses, and the corresponding $1 has been inserted into the replacement string, just before the comma.

What about if we don't have lookahead either? We can put the ⌜\b⌝ back for the ⌜(?!\d)⌝, but does the technique used to eliminate the lookbehind also work for the remaining lookahead? That is, does the following work?

```
$text =~ s/(\d)((\d\d\d)+\b)/$1,$2/g;
```

❖ Turn the page to check your answer.

Text-to-HTML Conversion

Let's write a little tool to convert plain text to HTML. It's difficult to write a general tool that's useful for every situation, so for this section we'll just write a simple tool whose main goal is to be a teaching vehicle.

In all our examples to this point, we've applied regular expressions to variables containing exactly one line of text. For this project, it is easier (and more interesting) if we have the entire text we wish to convert available as one big string. In Perl, we can easily do this with:

```
undef $/;       # Enter "file-slurp" mode.
$text = <>;     # Slurp up the first file given on the command line.
```

Quiz Answer

❖ *Answer to the question on page 67.*

Does `$text =~ s/(\d)((\d\d\d)+\b)/$1,$2/g` "commaify" a number?

This won't work the way we want. It leaves results such as "281,421906." This is because the digits matched by ⌈`(\d\d\d)+`⌋ are now actually part of the final match, and so are not left "unmatched" and available to the next iteration of the regex via the `/g`.

When one iteration ends, the next picks up the inspection of the text at the point where the previous match ended. We'd like that to be the point where the comma was inserted so we can go ahead and check to see whether additional commas need to be inserted later in the same number. But, in this case, that restarting point is at the end of all the digits. The whole point of using lookahead was to get the positional check without actually having the inspected text check count toward the final "string that matched."

Actually, this expression can still be used to solve this problem. If the expression is applied repeatedly by the host language, such as via a while loop, the newly-modified text is completely revisited each time. With each such application, one more comma is added (to each number in the target string, due to the `/g` modifier). Here's an example:

```
while ( $text =~ s/(\d)((\d\d\d)+\b)/$1,$2/g ) {
    # Nothing to do inside the body of the while -- we merely want to reapply the regex until it fails
}
```

If our sample file contains the three short lines

```
This is a sample file.
It has three lines.
That's all
```

the variable `$text` will then contain

This is a sample file.◻It has three lines.◻That's all◻

although depending on the system, it could instead be

This is a sample file.◻◻It has three lines.◻◻That's all◻◻

since most systems use a newline to end lines, but some (most notably Windows) use a carriage-return/newline combination. We'll be sure that our simple tool works with either.

Cooking special characters

Our first step is to make any '&', '<', and '>' characters in the original text "safe" by converting them to their proper HTML encodings, '&', '<', and '>' respectively. Those characters are special to HTML, and not encoding them properly can cause display problems. I call this simple conversion "cooking the text for HTML," and it's fairly simple:

```
$text =~ s/&/&amp;/g;   # Make the basic HTML ...
$text =~ s/</&lt;/g;    # ... characters &, <, and > ...
$text =~ s/>/&gt;/g;    # ... HTML safe.
```

Here again, we're using /g so that all of target characters will be converted (as opposed to just the first of each in the string if we didn't use /g). It's important to convert **&** first, since all three have '&' in the replacement.

Separating paragraphs

Next, we'll mark paragraphs by separating them with the <p> paragraph-separator HTML tag. An easy way to identify paragraphs is to consider them separated by blank lines. There are a number of ways that we might try to identify a blank line. At first you might be tempted to use

```
$text =~ s/^$/<p>/g;
```

to match a "start-of-line position followed immediately by an end-of-line position." Indeed, as we saw in the answer on page 10, this would work in a tool like *egrep* where the text being searched is always considered in chunks containing a single logical line. It would also work in Perl in the context of the earlier email example where we knew that each string contained exactly one logical line.

But, as I mentioned in the footnote on page 55, ⌜^⌟ and ⌜$⌟ normally refer not to logical *line* positions, but to the absolute start- and end-of-*string* positions.[†] So, now that we have multiple logical lines embedded within our target string, we need to do something different.

Luckily, most regex-endowed languages give us an easy solution, an *enhanced line anchor* match mode in which the meaning of ⌜^⌟ and ⌜$⌟ to change from *string* related to the *logical-line* related meaning we need for this example. With Perl, this mode is specified with the /m modifier:

```
$text =~ s/^$/<p>/mg;
```

Notice how /m and /g have been combined. (When using multiple modifiers, you can combine them in any order.) We'll see how other languages handle modifiers in the next chapter.

Thus, if we start with '···chapter.◫◫Thus···' in $text, we will end up with '···chapter.◫<p>◫Thus···' as we want.

It won't work, however, if there are spaces or other whitespace on the "blank" line. To allow for spaces, we can use ⌜^ *$⌟, or perhaps ⌜^[\t\r]*$⌟ to allow for

---

† Actually, ⌜$⌟ is often a bit more complex than simply "end of string," although that's not important to us for this example. For details, see the discussion of end-of-line anchors on page 127.

spaces, tabs, and the carriage return that some systems have before the line-ending newline. These are fundamentally different from ⌜^$⌟ alone in that these now match actual *characters*, while ⌜^$⌟ matches only a *position*. But, since we don't need those spaces, tabs, and carriage returns in this case, it's fine to match them (and then replace them with our paragraph tag).

If you remember ⌜\s⌟ from page 47, you might be inclined to use ⌜^\s*$⌟, just as we did in the email example on page 55. If we use ⌜\s⌟ instead of ⌜[\t\r]⌟, the fact that ⌜\s⌟ can match a newline means that the overall meaning changes from "find *lines* that are blank except for whitespace" to "find *spans of lines* that are blank except for whitespace." This means that if we have several blank lines in a row, ⌜^\s*$⌟ is able to match them all in one shot. The fortunate result is that the replacement leaves just one <p> instead of the several in a row we would otherwise end up with.

Therefore, if we have the string

      ⋯ with.▨▨▨▨·▨Therefore ⋯

in the variable $text, and we use

      $text =~ **s/^[\t\r]*$/<p>/mg**;

we'll end up with:

      ⋯ with.▨<p><p><p>▨Therefore ⋯

But, if we use

      $text =~ **s/^\s*$/<p>/mg**;

we'll end up instead with the more desirable:

      ⋯ with.▨<p>▨Therefore ⋯

So, we'll stick with ⌜^\s*$⌟ in our final program.

"Linkizing" an email address

The next step in our text-to-HTML converter is to recognize an email address, and turn it into a "mailto" link. This would convert something like "jfriedl@oreilly.com" to <a·href="mailto:jfriedl@oreilly.com">jfriedl@oreilly.com</a>.

It's a common desire to match or validate an email address with a regular expression. The official address specification is quite complex, so do to it exactly is difficult, but we can use something less complex that works for most email addresses we might run into. The basic form of an email address is *"username@hostname"*. Before looking at just what regular expression to use for each of those parts, let's look at the context we'll use them in:

      $text =~ **s/\b(***username regex***\@***hostname regex***)\b/<a href="mailto:$1">$1<\/a>/g**;

The first things to notice are the two marked backslash characters, one in the regex ('\@') and one toward the end of the replacement string. Each is there for a different reason. I'll defer the discussion of \@ until a bit later (☞ 77), for the moment merely saying that Perl requires @ symbols to be escaped when used in a regex literal.

The backslash before the '/' in the replacement string is a bit more useful to talk about at the moment. We've seen that the basic form of a Perl search-and-replace is s/*regex*/*replacement*/*modifiers*, with the forward slashes delimiting the parts. Now, if we wish to include a forward slash within one of the parts, Perl requires us to escape it to indicate that it should not be taken as a delimiter, but rather included as part of the regex or replacement string. This means that we would need to use <\/a> if we wish to get </a> into the replacement string, which is just what we did here.

This works, but it's a little ugly, so Perl allows us to pick our own delimiters. For instance, s!*regex*!*string*!*modifiers* or s{*regex*}{*string*}*modifiers*. With either, since the slash in the replacement string no longer conflicts with the delimiter, it no longer needs to be escaped. The delimiters for the regex and string parts pair up nicely in the second example, so I'll use that form from now on.

Returning to the code snippet, notice how the entire address part is wrapped in ⌜\b…\b⌟. Adding these word boundaries help to avoid an embedded match like in 'jfriedl@oreilly.compiler'. Although running into a nonsensical string like that is probably rare, it's simple enough to use the word boundaries to guard against matching it when we do, so I use them. Notice also that the entire address part is wrapped in parentheses. These are to capture the matched address, making it available to the replacement string '<a href="mailto:$1">$1</a>'.

Matching the username and hostname

Now we turn our attention to actually matching an email address by building those *username* and *hostname* regular expressions. Hostnames, like regex.info and www.oreilly.com, consist of dot-separated parts ending with 'com', 'edu', 'info', 'uk', or other selected sequences. A simplistic approach to matching an email address could be ⌜\w+\@\w+(\.\w+)+⌟, which allows ⌜\w+⌟ for the username and the same for each part of the hostname. In practice, though, you'll need something a little more specific. For usernames, you'll run into some with periods and dashes in them (although rarely does a username start with one of these). So, rather than ⌜\w+⌟, we'll try ⌜\w[-.\w]*⌟. This requires the name to start with a ⌜\w⌟ character, but then allows periods and dashes as well. (Notice how we are sure to put the dash first in the class, to ensure that it's taken as a literal dash, and not the part of an a-z type of range? A range like .-\w is almost certainly wrong, yielding a fairly random set of letters, numbers, and punctuation that's dependent on the program and the computer's native character encoding.)

The hostname part is a bit more complex in that the dots are strictly separators, which means that there must be something in between for them to separate. This is why even in the simplistic version earlier, the hostname part uses ⌈\w+(\.\w+)+⌋ instead of ⌈[\w.]+⌋. The latter incorrectly matches '..x..'. But, even the former matches in 'Artichokes 4@1.00', so we still need to be more specific.

One approach is to specifically list what the last component can be, along the lines of ⌈\w+(\.\w+)*\.(com|edu|info)⌋. (That list of alternatives really should be `com|edu|gov|int|mil|net|org|biz|info|name|museum|coop|aero|[a-z][a-z]`, but I'll use the shorter list to keep the example uncluttered.) This allows a leading ⌈\w+⌋ part, along with optional additional ⌈\.\w+⌋ parts, finally followed by one of the specific ending parts we've listed.

Actually, ⌈\w⌋ is not quite appropriate. It allows ASCII letters and digits, which is good, but with some systems may allow non-ASCII letters such as à, ç, Ξ, Æ, and with most flavors, an underscore as well. None of these extra characters are allowed in a hostname. So, we probably should use ⌈[a-zA-Z0-9]⌋, or perhaps ⌈[a-z0-9]⌋ with the /i modifier (for a case-insensitive match). Hostnames can also have a dash as well, so we'll use ⌈[-a-z0-9]⌋ (again, being careful to put the dash first). This leaves us with ⌈[-a-z0-9]+(\.[-a-z0-9]+)*\.(com|edu|info)⌋ for the hostname part.

As with all regex examples, it's important to remember the context in which they will be used. By itself, ⌈[-a-z0-9]+(\.[-a-z0-9]+)*\.(com|edu|info)⌋ could match, say 'run C:\\startup.command at startup', but once we drop it into the context of our program, we'll be sure that it matches where we want, and not where we don't. In fact, I'd like to drop it right into the

```
$text =~ s{\b(username regex\@hostname regex)\b}{<a href="mailto:$1">$1</a>}gi;
```

form mentioned earlier (updated here with the s{⋯}{⋯} delimiters, and the /i modifier), but there's no way I could get it to fit onto the page. Perl, of course, doesn't care if it fits nicely or looks pretty, but I do. That's why I'll now introduce the /x modifier, which allows us to rewrite that regex as:

```
$text =~ s{
    \b
    # Capture the address to $1 . . .
    (
    username regex
    \@
    hostname regex
    )
    \b
}{<a href="mailto:$1">$1</a>}gix;
```

Wow, that's different! The /x modifier appears at the end of that snippet (along with the /g and /i modifiers), and does two simple but powerful things for the regular expression. First, it causes most whitespace to be ignored, so you can "free-format" the expression for readability. Secondly, it allows comments with a leading #.

Specifically, /x turns whitespace into an "ignore me" metacharacter, and # into an "ignore me, and everything else up to the next newline" metacharacter. They aren't taken as metacharacters within a character class (which means that classes are *not* free-format, even with /x), and as with other metacharacters, you can escape whitespace and # that you want to be taken literally. Of course, you can always use ⌜\s⌟ to match whitespace, as in **m/<a \s+ href=···>/x**.

Realize that /x applies only to the regular expression, and not to the replacement string. Also, even though we've now switched to using the s{···}{···} form, where the modifiers come after the final '}' (e.g., '}x'), in conversation we still refer to "the x modifier" as "/x".

Putting it together

Well, now we can drop in our username and hostname parts, combined with what we developed earlier, to leave us with the program so far:

```
undef $/;      # Enter "file-slurp" mode.
$text = <>;    # Slurp up the first file given on the command line.

$text =~ s/&/&amp;/g;      # Make the basic HTML . . .
$text =~ s/</&lt;/g;       # . . . characters &, <, and > . . .
$text =~ s/>/&gt;/g;       # . . . HTML safe.

$text =~ s/^\s*$/<p>/mg;   # Separate paragraphs.

# Turn email addresses into links . . .
$text =~ s{
    \b
    # Capture the address to $1 . . .
    (
      \w[-.\w]*                                 # username
      \@
      [-a-z0-9]+(\.[-a-z0-9]+)*\.(com|edu|info) # hostname
    )
    \b
}{<a href="mailto:$1">$1</a>}gix;

print $text;   # Finally, display the HTML-ized text.
```

All the regular expressions work with the same multiline string, but notice that only the expression to separate paragraphs requires the /m modifier, since only that expression has ⌜^⌟ or ⌜$⌟. Using /m on the others wouldn't hurt (well, except to make the reader wonder why it was there).

"Linkizing" an HTTP URL

Finally, let's turn our attention to recognizing a normal HTTP URL, turning it into a link to itself. This would convert something like "http://www.yahoo.com/" to `<a href="http://www.yahoo.com/">http://www.yahoo.com/</a>`.

The basic form of an HTTP URL is "`http://`*hostname*/*path*", where the */path* part is optional. This gives us a form of:

```
$text =~ s{
    \b
    # Capture the URL to $1 . . .
    (
        http:// hostname
        (
            / path
        )?
    )
}{<a href="$1">$1</a>}gix;
```

For the hostname part, we can use the same subexpression we used for the email address. The path part of a URL can consist of a variety of characters, and in the previous chapter we used ⌈`[-a-z0-9_:@&?=+,.!/~*'%$]*`⌉ (☞ 25), which is most ASCII characters except whitespace, control characters, and things like `< > ( ) { }`.

There's one other thing we must do before using it with Perl, and that's escape the `@` and `$` characters. Again, I'll defer on the explanation until a bit later (☞ 77). Now, let's plug in our hostname and path parts:

```
$text =~ s{
    \b
    # Capture the URL to $1 . . .
    (
        http:// [-a-z0-9]+(\.[-a-z0-9]+)*\.(com|edu|info) \b # hostname
        (
            / [-a-z0-9_:\@&?=+,.!/~*'%\$]*   # optional path
        )?
    )
}{<a href="$1">$1</a>}gix;
```

You'll notice that there's no ⌈`\b`⌉ after the path, since it's perfectly allowable for a URL to end with punctuation, such as the URL for O'Reilly's page on this book:

```
http://www.oreilly.com/catalog/regex2/.
```

Using at the end ⌈`\b`⌉ would disallow a URL ending this way.

That being said, in practice we probably want to put some artificial restrictions on what the URL can end with. Consider the following text:

```
Read "odd" news at http://dailynews.yahoo.com/h/od, and
maybe some tech stuff at http://www.slashdot.com!
```

Our current regex matches the marked text, although it's obvious that the trailing punctuation in each really shouldn't be part of the URL. When trying to match URLs embedded in English text, it seems to make sense to not include an ending 「., ?!」 as part of the URL. (This isn't part of any standard, but just a heuristic I've come up with that seems to work most of the time.) Well, that's as easy as adding a "can't be any of 「[., ?!]」" negative lookbehind, 「(?<![.,?!])」, to the end of the path part. The effect is that after we've matched what we intend to take as the URL, the lookbehind peeks back to ensure that the last character is appropriate. If not, the engine must reevaluate what's taken as the URL so that this final condition is fulfilled. That means it's forced to leave off the offending punctuation so the final lookbehind can match. (We'll see a different way to solve this problem in Chapter 5 ☞ 205.)

Inserting this, we can now try the full program:

```
undef $/;      # Enter "file-slurp" mode
$text = <>;    # Slurp up the first file given on the command line.

$text =~ s/&/&amp;/g;      # Make the basic HTML . . .
$text =~ s/</&lt;/g;       # . . . characters &, <, and > . . .
$text =~ s/>/&gt;/g;       # . . . HTML safe.

$text =~ s/^\s*$/<p>/mg;   # Separate paragraphs.

# Turn email addresses into links . . .
$text =~ s{
    \b
    # Capture the address to $1 . . .
    (
      \w[-.\w]*                                    # username
      \@
      [-a-z0-9]+(\.[-a-z0-9]+)*\.(com|edu|info)    # hostname
    )
    \b
}{<a href="mailto:$1">$1</a>}gix;

# Turn HTTP URLs into links . . .
$text =~ s{
    \b
    # Capture the URL to $1 . . .
    (
      http:// [-a-z0-9]+(\.[-a-z0-9]+)*\.(com|edu|info) \b    # hostname
      (
          / [-a-z0-9_:\@&?=+,.!/~*'%\$]*    # Optional path
          (?<![.,?!])                        # Not allowed to end with [.,?!]
      )?
    )
}{<a href="$1">$1</a>}gix;

print $text;  # Finally, display the HTML-ized text.
```

Building a regex library

Note that the same expression is used for each of the two hostnames, which means that if we ever update one, we have to be sure to update the other. Rather than keeping that potential source of confusion, consider the three instances of $HostnameRegex in this modified snippet from our program:

```
$HostnameRegex = qr/[-a-z0-9]+(\.[-a-z0-9]+)*\.(com|edu|info)/i;

# Turn email addresses into links . . .
$text =~ s{
    \b
    # Capture the address to $1 . . .
    (
      \w[-.\w]*                               # username
      \@
      $HostnameRegex                          # hostname
    )
    \b
}{<a href="mailto:$1">$1</a>}gix;

# Turn HTTP URLs into links . . .
$text =~ s{
    \b
    # Capture the URL to $1 . . .
    (
        http:// $HostnameRegex \b             # hostname
        (
            / [-a-z0-9_:\@&?=+,.!/~*'%\$]*     # Optional path
            (?<![.,?!])                        # not allowed to end with [.,?!]
        )?
    )
}{<a href="$1">$1</a>}gix;
```

The first line introduces Perl's qr operator. It's similar to the m and s operators in that it takes a regular expression (i.e., used as qr/⋯/, just like m/⋯/ and s/⋯/⋯/), but rather than immediately applying it to some text in search of a match, it converts the regex provided into a *regex object*, which you can save to a variable. Later, you can use that object in place of a regular expression, or even as subexpression of some other regex (as we've done here, using the regex object assigned to $HostnameRegex as part of the regex of the two substitutions). This is very convenient because it makes things clearer. As a bonus, we then need only one "master source" to specify the regex to match a hostname, which we can then use as often as we like. There are additional examples of building this type of "regex library" in Chapter 6 (☞ 277), and a detailed discussion in Chapter 7 (☞ 303).

Other languages offer ways to create their own regex objects; several languages are explored briefly in the next chapter, with Java packages an .NET discussed in detail in Chapters 8 and 9.

Why '$' and '@' sometimes need to be escaped

You'll notice that the same '$' is used as both the end-of-string metacharacter, and to request interpolation (inclusion) of a variable. Normally, there's no ambiguity to what '$' means, but within a character class it gets a bit tricky. Since it can't possibly mean end-of-string within a class, in that situation Perl considers it a request to interpolate (include from) a variable, unless it's escaped. If escaped, the '$' is just included as a member of the class. That's what we want this time, so that's why we have to escape the dollar sign in the path part of the URL-matching regex.

It's somewhat similar for @. Perl uses @ at the beginning of array names, and Perl string or regex literals allow arrays to be interpolated. If we wish a literal @ to be part of a regex, we must escape it so that it's not taken as an array interpolation.

Some languages don't allow variable interpolation (Java, VB.NET, C, C#, Emacs, and awk, for instance). Some do allow variable interpolation (including Perl, PHP, Python, Ruby, and Tcl), but each has their own way to do it. This is discussed further in the next chapter (☞ 101).

That Doubled-Word Thing

The doubled-word problem in Chapter 1 hopefully whetted your appetite for the power of regular expressions. I teased you at the start of this chapter with a cryptic bunch of symbols I called a solution:

```
$/ = ".\n";
while (<>) {
  next if !s/\b([a-z]+)((?:\s|<[^>]+>)+)(\1\b)/\e[7m$1\e[m$2\e[7m$3\e[m/ig;
  s/^(?:[^\e]*\n)+//mg;      # Remove any unmarked lines.
  s/^/$ARGV: /mg;           # Ensure lines begin with filename.
  print;
}
```

Now that you've seen a bit of Perl, you hopefully understand at least the general form — the < >, the three s/···/···/, and the print. Still, it's rather heady stuff! If this chapter has been your only exposure to Perl (and these chapters your only exposure to regular expressions), this example is probably a bit beyond what you want to be getting into at this point.

However, when it comes down to it, I don't think the regex is really so difficult. Before looking at the program again, it might be good to review the specification found on page 1, and to see a sample run:

```
% perl -w FindDbl ch01.txt
ch01.txt: check for doubled words (such as this this), a common problem with
ch01.txt: * Find doubled words despite capitalization differences, such as with 'The
ch01.txt: the ', as well as allow differing amounts of whitespace (space, tabs,
ch01.txt: /\<(1,000,000|million|thousand thousand)/. But alternation can't be
ch01.txt: of this chapter. If you knew the the specific doubled word to find (such
    ⋮
```

Let's look at the program now, first in Perl. We'll then briefly look at a solution in Java to see a different approach for working with regular expressions. This time, the listing below uses the s{*regex*}{*replacement*}*modifiers* form of the substitution. It also uses the /x modifier to make the listing clearer (and with the extra room, now uses the more readable 'next unless' instead of 'next if !'). Otherwise, it is identical to the short version at the start of this chapter.

Double-word example in Perl

```
$/ = ".\n";    ❶ # Sets a special "chunk-mode"; chunks end with a period-newline combination

while (<>)   ❷
{
    next unless s{ ❸ # (regex starts here)
            ### Need to match one word:
            \b              # Start of word . . . .
            ( [a-z]+ )      # Grab word, filling $1 (and \1).

            ### Now need to allow any number of spaces and/or <TAGS>
            (               # Save what intervenes to $2.
                (?:         # (Non-capturing parens for grouping the alternation)
                    \s          # Whitespace (includes newline, which is good).
                    |           # -or-
                    <[^>]+>     # Item like <TAG>.
                )+          # Need at least one of the above, but allow more.
            )

            ### Now match the first word again:
            (\1\b)          # \b ensures not embedded. This copy saved to $3.
        #(regex ends here)
    }
    # Above is the regex. The replacement string is below, followed by the modifiers, /i, /g, and /x
    {\e[7m$1\e[m$2\e[7m$3\e[m}igx;   ❹

    s/^(?:[^\e]*\n)+//mg;    ❺   # Remove any unmarked lines.
    s/^/$ARGV: /mg;          ❻   # Ensure lines begin with filename.
    print;
}
```

This short program does use a fair number of things we haven't seen yet. Let me briefly explain it and some of the logic behind it, but I direct you to the Perl man page for details (or, if regex-related, to Chapter 7). In the description that follows, "magic" means "because of a feature of Perl that you may not be familiar with yet."

❶ Because the doubled-word problem must work even when the doubled words are split across lines, I can't use the normal line-by-line processing I used with the mail utility example. Setting the special variable $/ (yes, that's a variable) as shown puts the subsequent <> into a magic mode such that it returns not single lines, but more-or-less paragraph-sized chunks. The value returned is just one string, but a string that could potentially contain many of what we would consider to be logical lines.

❷   Did you notice that I don't assign the value from < > to anything? When used as the conditional of a `while` like this, < > magically assigns the string to a special default variable.[†] That same variable holds the default string that `s/···/···/` works on, and that `print` displays. Using these defaults makes the program less cluttered, but also less understandable to someone new to the language, so I recommend using explicit operands until you're comfortable.

❸   The **next unless** before the substitute command has Perl abort processing on the current string (to continue with the next) if the substitution doesn't actually do anything. There's no need to continue working on a string in which no doubled words are found.

❹   The replacement string is really just `"$1 $2 $3"` with intervening ANSI escape sequences that provide highlighting to the two doubled words, but not to whatever separates them. These escape sequences are `\e[7m` to begin highlighting, and `\e[m` to end it. (`\e` is Perl's regex and string shorthand for the ASCII escape character, which begins these ANSI escape sequences.)

Looking at how the parentheses in the regex are laid out, you'll realize that `"$1$2$3"` represents exactly what was matched in the first place. So, other than adding in the escape sequences, this whole substitute command is essentially a (slow) no-op.

We know that `$1` and `$3` represent matches of the same word (the whole point of the program!), so I could probably get by with using just one or the other in the replacement. However, since they might differ in capitalization, I use both variables explicitly.

❺   The string may contain many logical lines, but once the substitution has marked all the doubled words, we want keep only logical lines that have an escape character. Removing those that don't leaves only the lines of interest in the string. Since we used the enhanced line anchor match mode (the `/m` modifier) with this substitution, the regex ⌈`^([^\e]*\n)+`⌋ can find logical lines of non-escapes. Use of this regex in the substitute causes those sequences to be removed. The result is that only logical lines that have an escape remain, which means that only logical lines that have doubled words in them remain.[‡]

❻   The variable `$ARGV` magically provides the name of the input file. Combined with `/m` and `/g`, this substitution tacks the input filename to the beginning of each logical line remaining in the string. Cool!

---

† The default variable is `$_` (yes, that's a variable too). It's used as the default operand for many functions and operators.

‡ This logic assumes that the input file doesn't have an ASCII escape character itself. If it did, this program could report lines in error.

Finally, the `print` spits out what's left of the string, escapes and all. The `while` loop repeats the same processing for all the strings (paragraph-sized chunks of text) that are read from the input.

Moving bits around: operators, functions, and objects

As I emphasized earlier, I use Perl in this chapter as a tool to show the concepts. It happens to be a very useful tool, but I again want to stress that this problem can be easily solved with regular expressions in many other languages.

Still, the task of showing the concepts is made a bit easier due to a unique feature of Perl among advanced languages that regular expressions are a "first class," low-level feature of the language. This means that there are basic operators that work with regular expressions in the same way that + and – work with numbers. This reduces the amount of "syntactic baggage" needed to wield regular expressions.

Most languages do not provide this. For reasons that are discussed in Chapter 3 (☞ 93), many modern languages instead provide functions or objects for manipulating and applying regular expressions. There might be a function, for example, that accepts a string to be interpreted as a regular expression, as well as text to be searched, and returns a true or false depending on whether the regular expression matches the text. More commonly, though, these two tasks (first, interpreting a string as a regular expression, and second, applying the regular expression to text) are broken up into two or more separate functions, as seen in the Java listing on the facing page. The code uses the `java.util.regex` package that comes standard as of Java 1.4.

You can see near the top the same three regular expressions we used in the Perl example, passed as strings to the three `Pattern.compile` routines. A direct comparison shows that the Java version has a few extra backslashes, but that's just a side effect of Java's requirement that regular expressions be provided as strings. Backslashes intended for the regular expression must be escaped to prevent Java's string parser from interpreting the backslashes in its own way (☞ 44).

You'll also notice that the regular expressions are located not in the main text-processing part of the program, but at the start, in the initialization section. The `Pattern.compile` function merely analyzes the string as a regular expression, and builds an internal "compiled version" that is assigned to a `Pattern` variable (`regex1`, etc.). Then, in the main text-processing part of the program, that compiled version is applied to text with `regex1.matcher(text)`, the result of which is used to do the replacement. Again, we'll get into the details in the next chapter, but the point here is that when learning any regex-enabled language, there are two parts to the story: the regex flavor itself, and how the language lets you wield the regular expressions.

Double-word example in Java

```java
import java.io.*;
import java.util.regex.Pattern;
import java.util.regex.Matcher;

public class TwoWord
{
 public static void main(String [] args)
 {
    Pattern regex1 = Pattern.compile(
        "\\b([a-z]+)((?:\\s|\\<[^>]+\\>)+)(\\1\\b)",
        Pattern.CASE_INSENSITIVE);
    String replace1 = "\033[7m$1\033[m$2\033[7m$3\033[m";
    Pattern regex2 = Pattern.compile("^(?:[^\\e]*\\n)+", Pattern.MULTILINE);
    Pattern regex3 = Pattern.compile("^([^\\n]+)", Pattern.MULTILINE);

    // For each command-line argument....
    for (int i = 0; i < args.length; i++)
    {
      try {
        BufferedReader in = new BufferedReader(new FileReader(args[i]));
        String text;

        // For each paragraph of each file.....
        while ((text = getPara(in)) != null)
        {
            // Apply the three substitutions
            text = regex1.matcher(text).replaceAll(replace1);
            text = regex2.matcher(text).replaceAll("");
            text = regex3.matcher(text).replaceAll(args[i] + ": $1");

            // Display results
            System.out.print(text);
        }
      } catch (IOException e) {
        System.err.println("can't read ["+args[i]+"]: " + e.getMessage());
      }
    }
 }

 // Routine to read next "paragraph" and return as a string
 static String getPara(BufferedReader in) throws java.io.IOException
 {
    StringBuffer buf = new StringBuffer();
    String line;

    while ((line = in.readLine()) != null &&
           (buf.length() == 0 || line.length() != 0))
    {
        buf.append(line + "\n");
    }
    return  buf.length() == 0 ? null : buf.toString();
 }
}
```

3

Overview of Regular Expression Features and Flavors

Now that you have a feel for regular expressions and a few diverse tools that use them, you might think we're ready to dive into using them wherever they're found. But even a simple comparison among the *egrep* versions of the first chapter and the Perl and Java in the previous chapter shows that regular expressions and the way they're used can vary wildly from tool to tool.

When looking at regular expressions in the context of their host language or tool, there are three broad issues to consider:

- What metacharacters are supported, and their meaning. Often called the regex "flavor."

- How regular expressions "interface" with the language or tool, such as how to specify regular-expression operations, what operations are allowed, and what text they operate on.

- How the regular-expression engine actually goes about applying a regular expression to some text. The method that the language or tool designer uses to implement the regular-expression engine has a strong influence on the results one might expect from any given regular expression.

Regular Expressions and Cars

The considerations just listed parallel the way one might think while shopping for a car. With regular expressions, the metacharacters are the first thing you notice, just as with a car it's the body shape, shine, and nifty features like a CD player and leather seats. These are the types of things you'll find splashed across the pages of a glossy brochure, and a list of metacharacters like the one on page 32 is the regular-expression equivalent. It's important information, but only part of the story.

How regular expressions interface with their host program is also important. The interface is partly cosmetic, as in the syntax of how to actually provide a regular expression to the program. Other parts of the interface are more functional, defining what operations are supported, and how convenient they are to use. In our car comparison, this would be how the car "interfaces" with us and our lives. Some issues might be cosmetic, such as what side of the car you put gas in, or whether the windows are powered. Others might be a bit more important, such as if it has an automatic or manual transmission. Still others deal with functionality: can you fit the thing in your garage? Can you transport a king-size mattress? Skis? Five adults? (And how easy is it for those five adults to get in and out of the car—easier with four doors than with two.) Many of these issues are also mentioned in the glossy brochure, although you might have to read the small print in the back to get all the details.

The final concern is about the engine, and how it goes about its work to turn the wheels. Here is where the analogy ends, because with cars, people tend to understand at least the minimum required about an engine to use it well: if it's a gasoline engine, they won't put diesel fuel into it. And if it has a manual transmission, they won't forget to use the clutch. But, in the regular-expression world, even the most minute details about how the regex engine goes about its work, and how that influences how expressions should be crafted and used, are usually absent from the documentation. However, these details are so important to the practical use of regular expressions that the entire next chapter is devoted to it.

In This Chapter

As the title might suggest, this chapter provides an overview of regular expression features and flavors. It looks at the types of metacharacters commonly available, and some of the ways regular expressions interface with the tools they're part of. These are the first two points mentioned at the chapter's opening. The third point —how a regex engine goes about its work, and what that means to us in a practical sense—is covered in the next few chapters.

One thing I should say about this chapter is that it does not try to provide a reference for any particular tool's regex features, nor does it teach how to use regexes in any of the various tools and languages mentioned as examples. Rather, it attempts to provide a global perspective on regular expressions and the tools that implement them. If you lived in a cave using only one particular tool, you could live your life without caring about how other tools (or other versions of the same tool) might act differently. Since that's not the case, knowing something about your utility's computational pedigree adds interesting and valuable insight.

A Casual Stroll Across the Regex Landscape

I'd like to start with the story about the evolution of some regular expression flavors and their associated programs. So, grab a hot cup (or frosty mug) of your
favorite brewed beverage and relax as we look at the sometimes wacky history
behind the regular expressions we have today. The idea is to add color to our
regex understanding, and to develop a feeling as to why "the way things are" are
the way things are. There are some footnotes for those that are interested, but for
the most part, this should be read as a light story for enjoyment.

The Origins of Regular Expressions

The seeds of regular expressions were planted in the early 1940s by two neuro-
physiologists, Warren McCulloch and Walter Pitts, who developed models of how
they believed the nervous system worked at the neuron level.[†] Regular expressions
became a reality several years later when mathematician Stephen Kleene formally
described these models in an algebra he called *regular sets*. He devised a simple
notation to express these regular sets, and called them *regular expressions*.

Through the 1950s and 1960s, regular expressions enjoyed a rich study in theoretical mathematics circles. Robert Constable has written a good summary[‡] for the
mathematically inclined.

Although there is evidence of earlier work, the first published computational use
of regular expressions I have actually been able to find is Ken Thompson's 1968
article *Regular Expression Search Algorithm*[§] in which he describes a regular-
expression compiler that produced IBM 7094 object code. This led to his work on
qed, an editor that formed the basis for the Unix editor *ed*.

ed's regular expressions were not as advanced as those in *qed*, but they were the
first to gain widespread use in non-technical fields. *ed* had a command to display
lines of the edited file that matched a given regular expression. The command,
"g/*Regular Expression*/p", was read "Global Regular Expression Print." This particular function was so useful that it was made into its own utility, *grep* (after which
egrep—extended *grep*—was later modeled).

[†] "A logical calculus of the ideas imminent in nervous activity," first published in *Bulletin of Math. Bio-
physics* 5 (1943) and later reprinted in *Embodiments of Mind* (MIT Press, 1965). The article begins
with an interesting summary of how neurons behave (did you know that intra-neuron impulse
speeds can range from 1 all the way to 150 meters per second?), and then descends into a pit of for-
mulae that is, literally, all Greek to me.

[‡] Robert L. Constable, "The Role of Finite Automata in the Development of Modern Computing Theory," in *The Kleene Symposium*, Eds. Barwise, Keisler, and Kunen (North-Holland Publishing Company, 1980), 61–83.

[§] *Communications of the ACM*, Vol.11, No. 6, June 1968.

Grep's metacharacters

The regular expressions supported by *grep* and other early tools were quite limited when compared to *egrep*'s. The metacharacter * was supported, but + and ? were not (the latter's absence being a particularly strong drawback). *grep*'s capturing metacharacters were \(···\), with *un*escaped parentheses representing literal text.[†] *grep* supported line anchors, but in a limited way. If ^ appeared at the beginning of the regex, it was a metacharacter matching the beginning of the line. Otherwise, it wasn't a metacharacter at all and just matched a literal circumflex (also called a "caret"). Similarly, $ was the end-of-line metacharacter only at the end of the regex. The upshot was that you couldn't do something like ⌈end$|^start⌋. But that's okay, since alternation wasn't supported either!

The way metacharacters interact is also important. For example, perhaps *grep*'s largest shortcoming was that star could not be applied to a parenthesized expression, but only to a literal character, a character class, or dot. So, in *grep*, parentheses were useful only for capturing matched text, and not for general grouping. In fact, some early versions of *grep* didn't even allow nested parentheses.

Grep evolves

Although many systems have *grep* today, you'll note that I've been using past tense. The past tense refers to the flavor of the old versions, now upwards of 30 years old. Over time, as technology advances, older programs are sometimes retrofitted with additional features, and *grep* has been no exception.

Along the way, AT&T Bell Labs added some new features, such as incorporating the \{*min,max*\} notation from the program *lex*. They also fixed the -y option, which in early versions was supposed to allow case-insensitive matches but worked only sporadically. Around the same time, people at Berkeley added start- and end-of-word metacharacters and renamed -y to -i. Unfortunately, you still couldn't apply star or the other quantifiers to a parenthesized expression.

Egrep evolves

By this time, Alfred Aho (also at AT&T Bell Labs) had written *egrep*, which provided most of the richer set of metacharacters described in Chapter 1. More importantly, he implemented them in a completely different (and generally better) way. Not only were ⌈+⌋ and ⌈?⌋ added, but they could be applied to parenthesized expressions, greatly increasing *egrep* expressive power.

---

† Historical trivia: *ed* (and hence *grep*) used escaped parentheses rather than unadorned parentheses as delimiters because Ken Thompson felt regular expressions would be used to work primarily with C code, where needing to match raw parentheses would be more common than backreferencing.

Alternation was added as well, and the line anchors were upgraded to "first-class" status so that you could use them almost anywhere in your regex. However, *egrep* had problems as well—sometimes it would find a match but not display the result, and it didn't have some useful features that are now popular. Nevertheless, it was a vastly more useful tool.

Other species evolve

At the same time, other programs such as awk, *lex*, and sed, were growing and changing at their own pace. Often, developers who liked a feature from one program tried to add it to another. Sometimes, the result wasn't pretty. For example, if support for plus was added to *grep*, + by itself couldn't be used because *grep* had a long history of a raw '+' not being a metacharacter, and suddenly making it one would have surprised users. Since '\+' was probably not something a *grep* user would have otherwise normally typed, it could safely be subsumed as the "one or more" metacharacter.

Sometimes new bugs were introduced as features were added. Other times, added features were later removed. There was little to no documentation for the many subtle points that round out a tool's flavor, so new tools either made up their own style, or attempted to mimic "what seemed to work" with other tools.

Multiply that by the passage of time and numerous programmers, and the result is general confusion (particularly when you try to deal with everything at once).[†]

POSIX—An attempt at standardization

POSIX, short for Portable Operating System Interface, is a wide-ranging standard put forth in 1986 to ensure portability across operating systems. Several parts of this standard deal with regular expressions and the traditional tools that use them, so it's of some interest to us. None of the flavors covered in this book, however, strictly adhere to all the relevant parts. In an effort to reorganize the mess that regular expressions had become, POSIX distills the various common flavors into just two classes of regex flavor, *Basic Regular Expressions* (BREs), and *Extended Regular Expressions* (EREs). POSIX programs then support one flavor or the other. Table 3-1 on the next page summarizes the metacharacters in the two flavors.

One important feature of the POSIX standard is the notion of a *locale*, a collection of settings that describe language and cultural conventions for such things as the display of dates, times, and monetary values, the interpretation of characters in the active encoding, and so on. Locales aim to allow programs to be internationalized. Thy are not regex-specific concept, although they can affect regular-expression use. For example, when working with a locale that describes the *Latin-1*

---

† Such as when writing a book about regular expressions—ask me, I know!

Table 3-1: Overview of POSIX Regex Flavors

Regex feature	BREs	EREs
dot, ^, $, [⋯], [^⋯]	✓	✓
"any number" quantifier	*	*
+ and ? quantifiers		+ ?
range quantifier	\{*min,max*\}	{*min,max*}
grouping	\(⋯\)	(⋯)
can apply quantifiers to parentheses	✓	✓
backreferences	\1 through \9	
alternation		✓

(ISO-8859-1) encoding, à and À (characters with ordinal values 224 and 160, respectively) are considered "letters," and any application of a regex that ignores capitalization would know to treat them as identical.

Another example is ⌜\w⌟, commonly provided as a shorthand for a "word-con-stituent character" (ostensibly, the same as ⌜[a-zA-Z0-9_]⌟ in many flavors). This feature is not required by POSIX, but it is allowed. If supported, ⌜\w⌟ would know to allow all letters and digits defined in the locale, not just those in ASCII.

Note, however, that the need for this aspect of locales is mostly alleviated when working with tools that support Unicode. Unicode is discussed further beginning on page 106.

Henry Spencer's regex package

Also first appearing in 1986, and perhaps of more importance, was the release by Henry Spencer of a regex package, written in C, which could be freely incorporate by others into their own programs — a first at the time. Every program that used Henry's package — and there were many — provided the same consistent regex fla-vor unless the program's author went to the explicit trouble to change it.

Perl evolves

At about the same time, Larry Wall started developing a tool that would later become the language Perl. He had already greatly enhanced distributed software development with his *patch* program, but Perl was destined to have a truly monu-mental impact.

Larry released Perl Version 1 in December 1987. Perl was an immediate hit because it blended so many useful features of other languages, and combined them with the explicit goal of being, in a day-to-day practical sense, *useful*.

One immediately notable feature was a set of regular expression operators in the tradition of the specialty tools sed and awk — a first for a general scripting language. For the regular expression engine, Larry borrowed code from an earlier project, his news reader *rn* (which based its regular expression code on that in James Gosling's Emacs).[†] The regex flavor was considered powerful by the day's standards, but was not nearly as full-featured as it is today. Its major drawbacks were that it supported at most nine sets of parentheses, and at most nine alternatives with ⌜|⌟, and worst of all, ⌜|⌟ was not allowed within parentheses. It did not support case-insensitive matching, nor allow ⌜\w⌟ within a class (it didn't support ⌜\s⌟ or ⌜\d⌟ anywhere). It didn't support the ⌜{*min*,*max*}⌟ range quantifier.

Perl 2 was released in June 1988. Larry had replaced the regex code entirely, this time using a greatly enhanced version of the Henry Spencer package mentioned in the previous section. You could still have at most nine sets of parentheses, but now you could use ⌜|⌟ inside them. Support for ⌜\d⌟ and ⌜\s⌟ was added, and support for ⌜\w⌟ was changed to include an underscore, since then it would match what characters were allowed in a Perl variable name. Furthermore, these metacharacters were now allowed inside classes. (Their opposites, ⌜\D⌟, ⌜\W⌟, and ⌜\S⌟, were also newly supported, but *weren't* allowed within a class, and in any case sometimes didn't work correctly.) Importantly, the /i modifier was added, so you could now do case-insensitive matching.

Perl 3 came out more than a year later, in October 1989. It added the /e modifier, which greatly increased the power of the replacement operator, and fixed some backreference-related bugs from the previous version. It added the ⌜{*min*,*max*}⌟ range quantifiers, although unfortunately, they didn't always work quite right. Worse still, with Version 3, the regular expression engine couldn't always work with 8-bit data, yielding unpredictable results with non-ASCII input.

Perl 4 was released half a year later, in March 1991, and over the next two years, it was improved until its last update in February 1993. By this time, the bugs were fixed and restrictions expanded (you could use ⌜\D⌟ and such within character classes, and a regular expression could have virtually unlimited sets of parentheses). Work also went into optimizing how the regex engine went about its task, but the real breakthrough wouldn't happen until 1994.

Perl 5 was officially released in October 1994. Overall, Perl had undergone a massive overhaul, and the result was a vastly superior language in every respect. On the regular-expression side, it had more internal optimizations, and a few metacharacters were added (including ⌜\G⌟, which increased the power of iterative

---

† James Gosling would later go on to develop his own language, Java, which somewhat ironically does not natively support regular expressions. Java 1.4 however, does include a wonderful regular expression package, covered in depth in Chapter 8.

matches ☞ 128), non-capturing parentheses (☞ 45), lazy quantifiers (☞ 140), look-ahead (☞ 60), and the /x modifier[†] (☞ 72).

More important than just for their raw functionality, these "outside the box" modifications made it clear that regular expressions could really be a powerful programming language unto themselves, and were still ripe for further development.

The newly-added non-capturing parentheses and lookahead constructs required a way to be expressed. None of the grouping pairs — (···), [···], <···>, or {···} — were available to be used for these new features, so Larry came up with the various '(?' notations we use today. He chose this unsightly sequence because it previously would have been an illegal combination in a Perl regex, so he was free to give it meaning. One important consideration Larry had the foresight to recognize was that there would likely be additional functionality in the future, so by restricting what was allowed after the '(?' sequences, he was able to reserve them for future enhancements.

Subsequent versions of Perl grew more robust, with fewer bugs, more internal optimizations, and new features. I like to believe that the first edition of this book played some small part in this, for as I researched and tested regex-related features, I would send my results to Larry and the Perl Porters group, which helped give some direction as to where improvements might be made.

New regex features added over the years include limited lookbehind (☞ 60), "atomic" grouping (☞ 137), and Unicode support. Regular expressions were brought to the next level by the addition of conditional constructs (☞ 138), allowing you to make if-then-else decisions right there as part of the regular expression. And if that wasn't enough, there are now constructs that allow you to intermingle Perl code within a regular expression, which takes things full circle (☞ 327). The version of Perl covered in this book is 5.8.

A partial consolidation of flavors

The advances seen in Perl 5 were perfectly timed for the World Wide Web revolution. Perl was built for text processing, and the building of web pages is just that, so Perl quickly became *the* language for web development. Perl became vastly more popular, and with it, its powerful regular expression flavor did as well.

Developers of other languages were not blind to this power, and eventually regular expression packages that were "Perl compatible" to one extent or another were created. Among these were packages for Tcl, Python, Microsoft's .NET suite of languages, Ruby, PHP, C/C++, and many packages for Java.

[†] My claim to fame is that Larry added the /x modifier after seeing a note from me discussing a long and complex regex. In the note, I had "pretty printed" the regular expression for clarity. Upon seeing it, he thought that it would be convenient to do so in Perl code as well, so he added /x.

Versions as of this book

Table 3-2 shows a few of the version numbers for programs and libraries that I talk about in the book. Older versions may well have fewer features and more bugs, while newer versions may have additional features and bug fixes (and new bugs of their own).

Because Java did not originally come with regex support, numerous regex libraries have been developed over the years, so anyone wishing to use regular expressions in Java needed to find them, evaluate them, and ultimately select one to use. Chapter 6 looks at seven such packages, and ways to evaluate them. For reasons discussed there, the regex package that Sun eventually came up with (their `java.util.regex`, now standard as of Java 1.4) is what I use for most of the Java examples in this book.

Table 3-2: Versions of Some Tools Mentioned in This Book

GNU awk 3.1	MySQL 3.23.49	Procmail 3.22
GNU *egrep/grep* 2.4.2	.NET Framework 2002 (1.0.3705)	Python 2.2.1
GNU Emacs 21.2.1	PCRE 3.8	Ruby 1.6.7
flex 2.5.4	Perl 5.8	GNU sed 3.02
`java.util.regex` (Java 1.4.0)	PHP (`preg` routines) 4.0.6	Tcl 8.4

At a Glance

A chart showing just a few aspects of some common tools gives a good clue to how different things still are. Table 3-3 provides a very superficial look at a few aspects of the regex flavors of a few tools.

Table 3-3: A (Very) Superficial Look at the Flavor of a Few Common Tools

Feature	Modern *grep*	Modern *egrep*	GNU Emacs	Tcl	Perl	.NET	Sun's Java package
`*`, `^`, `$`, `[⋯]`	✓	✓	✓	✓	✓	✓	✓
`?` `+` `|`	`\?` `\+` `\\|`	`?` `+` `|`	`?` `+` `\\|`	`?` `+` `|`	`?` `+` `|`	`?` `+` `|`	`?` `+` `|`
grouping	`\(⋯\)`	`(⋯)`	`\(⋯\)`	`(⋯)`	`(⋯)`	`(⋯)`	`(⋯)`
`(?:⋯)`					✓	✓	✓
word boundary		`\<` `\>`	`\<` `\>` `\b,\B`	`\m, \M, \y`	`\b,\B`	`\b,\B`	`\b,\B`
`\w`, `\W`		✓	✓	✓	✓	✓	✓
backreferences	✓		✓	✓	✓	✓	✓
						✓ supported	

A chart like Table 3-3 is often found in other books to show the differences among tools. But, this chart is only the tip of the iceberg—for every feature shown, there are a dozen important issues that are overlooked.

Foremost is that programs change over time. For example, Tcl used to not support backreferences and word boundaries, but now does. It first supported word boundaries with the ungainly-looking ⌈[:<:]⌋ and ⌈[:>:]⌋, and still does, although such use is deprecated in favor of its more-recently supported ⌈\m⌋, ⌈\M⌋, and ⌈\y⌋ (start of word boundary, end of word boundary, or either).

Along the same lines, programs such as *grep* and *egrep*, which aren't from a single provider but rather can be provided by anyone who wants to create them, can have whatever flavor the individual author of the program wishes. Human nature being what is, each tends to have its own features and peculiarities. (The GNU versions of many common tools, for example, are often more powerful and robust than other versions.)

And perhaps as important as the easily visible features are the many subtle (and some not-so-subtle) differences among flavors. Looking at the table, one might think that regular expressions are exactly the same in Perl, .NET, and Java, which is certainly not true. Just a few of the questions one might ask when looking at something like Table 3-3 are:

- Are star and friends allowed to quantify something wrapped in parentheses?

- Does dot match a newline? Do negated character classes match it? Do either match the null character?

- Are the line anchors really *line* anchors (i.e., do they recognize newlines that might be embedded within the target string)? Are they first-class metacharacters, or are they valid only in certain parts of the regex?

- Are escapes recognized in character classes? What else is or isn't allowed within character classes?

- Are parentheses allowed to be nested? If so, how deeply (and how many parentheses are even allowed in the first place)?

- If backreferences are allowed, when a case-insensitive match is requested, do backreferences match appropriately? Do backreferences "behave" reasonably in fringe situations?

- Are octal escapes such as ⌈\123⌋ allowed? If so, how do they reconcile the syntactic conflict with backreferences? What about hexadecimal escapes? Is it *really* the regex engine that supports octal and hexadecimal escapes, or is it some other part of the utility?

- Does ⌈\w⌋ match only alphanumerics, or additional characters as well? (Among the programs shown supporting \w in Table 3-3, there are several different interpretations). Does ⌈\w⌋ agree with the various word-boundary metacharacters on what does and doesn't constitute a "word character"? Do they respect the locale, or understand Unicode?

Many issues must be kept in mind, even with a tidy little summary like Table 3-3 as a superficial guide. (As another example, peek ahead to Table 8-1 on page 373 for a look at a chart showing some differences among Java packages.) If you realize that there's a lot of dirty laundry behind that nice façade, it's not too difficult to keep your wits about you and deal with it.

As mentioned at the start of the chapter, much of this is just superficial syntax, but many issues go deeper. For example, once you understand that something such as ⌈(Jul|July)⌋ in *egrep* needs to be written as ⌈\(Jul\|July\)⌋ for GNU Emacs, you might think that everything is the same from there, but that's not always the case. The differences in the semantics of how a match is attempted (or, at least, how it appears to be attempted) is an extremely important issue that is often overlooked, yet it explains why these two apparently identical examples would actually end up matching differently: one always matches 'Jul', even when applied to 'July'. Those very same semantics also explain why the opposite, ⌈(July|Jul)⌋ and ⌈\(July\|Jul\)⌋, do match the same text. Again, the entire next chapter is devoted to understanding this.

Of course, what a tool can *do* with a regular expression is often more important than the flavor of its regular expressions. For example, even if Perl's expressions were less powerful than *egrep*'s, Perl's flexible use of regexes provides for more raw usefulness. We'll look at a lot of individual features in this chapter, and in depth at a few languages in later chapters.

Care and Handling of Regular Expressions

The second concern outlined at the start of the chapter is the syntactic packaging that tells an application "Hey, here's a regex, and this is what I want you to do with it." *egrep* is a simple example because the regular expression is expected as an argument on the command line. Any extra syntactic sugar, such as the single quotes I used throughout the first chapter, are needed only to satisfy the command shell, not *egrep*. Complex systems, such as regular expressions in programming languages, require more complex packaging to inform the system exactly what the regex is and how it should be used.

The next step, then, is to look at what you can do with the results of a match. Again, *egrep* is simple in that it pretty much always does the same thing (displays lines that contain a match), but as the previous chapter began to show, the real power is in doing much more interesting things. The two basic actions behind those interesting things are *match* (to check if a regex matches in a string, and to perhaps pluck information from the string), and *search-and-replace*, to modify a string based upon a match. There are many variations of these actions, and many variations on how individual languages let you perform them.

In general, a programming language can take one of three approaches to regular expressions: integrated, procedural, and object-oriented. With the first, regular expression operators are built directly into the language, as with Perl. In the other two, regular expressions are not part of the low-level syntax of the language. Rather, normal strings are passed as arguments to normal functions, which then interpret the strings as regular expressions. Depending on the function, one or more regex-related actions are then performed. One derivative or another of this style is use by most (non-Perl) languages, including Java, the .NET languages, Tcl, Python, PHP, Emacs lisp, and Ruby.

Integrated Handling

We've already seen a bit of Perl's integrated approach, such as this example from page 55:

```
if ($line =~ m/^Subject: (.*)/i) {
    $subject = $1;
}
```

Here, for clarity, variable names I've chosen are in italic, while the regex-related items are bold, and the regular expression itself is underlined. We know that Perl applies the regular expression ⌈^Subject: (.*)⌋ to the text held in $line, and if a match is found, executes the block of code that follows. In that block, the variable $1 represents the text matched within the regular expression's parentheses, and this gets assigned to the variable $subject.

Another example of an integrated approach is when regular expressions are part of a configuration file, such as for *procmail* (a Unix mail-processing utility.) In the configuration file, regular expressions are used to route mail messages to the sections that actually process them. It's even simpler than with Perl, since the operands (the mail messages) are implicit.

What goes on behind the scenes is quite a bit more complex than these examples show. An integrated approach simplifies things to the programmer because it hides in the background some of mechanics of preparing the regular expression, setting up for the match, applying the regular expression, and deriving results from that application. Hiding these steps makes the normal case very easy to work with, but as we'll see later, it can make some cases less efficient or clumsier to work with.

But, before getting into those details, let's uncover the hidden steps by looking at the other methods.

Procedural and Object-Oriented Handling

Procedural and object-oriented handling are fairly similar. In either case, regex functionality is provided not by built-in regular-expression operators, but by normal functions (procedural) or constructors and methods (object-oriented). In this case, there are no true regular-expression operands, but rather normal string arguments that the functions, constructors, or methods choose to interpret as regular expressions.

The next sections show examples in Java, VB.NET, and Python.

Regex handling in Java

Let's look at the equivalent of the "Subject" example in Java, using Sun's `java.util.regex` package. (Java is covered in depth in Chapter 8.)

```
          import java.util.regex.*;  // Make regex classes easily available
            ⋮
❶  Pattern r = Pattern.compile("^Subject: (.*)", Pattern.CASE_INSENSITIVE);
❷  Matcher m = r.matcher(line);
❸  if (m.find()) {
❹      subject = m.group(1);
   }
```

Variable names I've chosen are again in italic, the regex-related items are bold, and the regular expression itself is underlined. Well, to be precise, what's underlined is a normal string literal *to be interpreted* as a regular expression.

This example shows an object-oriented approach with regex functionality supplied by two classes in Sun's `java.util.regex` package: `Pattern` and `Matcher`. The actions performed are:

❶ Inspect the regular expression and compile it into an internal form that matches in a case-insensitive manner, yielding a "`Pattern`" object.

❷ Associate it with some text to be inspected, yielding a "`Matcher`" object.

❸ Actually apply the regex to see if there is a match in the previously-associated text, and let us know the result.

❹ If there is a match, make available the text matched within the first set of capturing parentheses.

Actions similar to these are required, explicitly or implicitly, by any program wishing to use regular expressions. Perl hides most of these details, and this Java implementation usually exposes them.

A procedural example. Sun's Java regex package does, however, provide a few procedural-approach "convenience functions" that hide much of the work. Rather than require you to first create a regex object, then use that object's methods to apply it, these static functions create a temporary object for you, throwing it away once done. Here's an example showing the `Pattern.matches(⋯)` function:

```
if (! Pattern.matches("\\s*", line))
{
      // ... line is not blank ...
}
```

This function wraps an implicit ⌈^⋯$⌋ around the regex, and returns a Boolean indicating whether it can match the input string. It's common for a package to provide both procedural and object-oriented interfaces, just as Sun did here. The differences between them often involve convenience (a procedural interface can be easier to work with for simple tasks, but more cumbersome for complex tasks), functionality (procedural interfaces generally have less functionality and options than their object-oriented counterparts), and efficiency (in any given situation, one is likely to be more efficient than the other — a subject covered in detail in Chapter 6).

There are many regex packages for Java (half a dozen are discussed in Chapter 8), but Sun is in a position to integrate theirs with the language more than anyone else. For example, they've integrated it with the string class; the previous example can actually be written as:

```
if (! line.matches("\\s*", ))
{
      // ... line is not blank ...
}
```

Again, this is not as efficient as a properly-applied object-oriented approach, and so is not appropriate for use in a time-critical loop, but it's quite convenient for "casual" use.

Regex handling in VB and other .NET languages

Although all regex engines perform essentially the same basic tasks, they differ in how those tasks and services are exposed to the programmer, even among implementations sharing the same approach. Here's the "Subject" example in VB.NET (.NET is covered in detail in Chapter 9):

```
Imports System.Text.RegularExpressions    ' Make regex classes easily available
    ⋮
Dim R as Regex = New Regex("^Subject: (.*)", RegexOptions.IgnoreCase)
Dim M as Match = R.Match(line)
If M.Success
    subject = M.Groups(1).Value
End If
```

Overall, this is generally similar to the Java example, except that .NET combines steps ❷ and ❸, and requires an extra `Value` in ❹. Why the differences? One is not inherently better or worse—each was just chosen by the developers who happened to have thought was the best approach at the time. (More on this in a bit.)

.NET also provides a few procedural-approach functions. Here's one to check for a blank line:

```
If Not Regex.IsMatch(Line, "^\s*$") Then
    '  ... line is not blank ...
End If
```

Unlike Sun's `Pattern.matches` function, which adds an implicit ⌜^ ... $⌝ around the regex, Microsoft chose to offer this more general function. It's just a simple wrapper around the core objects, but it involves less typing and variable corralling for the programmer, at only a small efficiency expense.

Regex handling in Python

As a final example, let's look at the ⌜Subject⌝ example in Python:

```
import re;
    ⋮
R = re.compile("^Subject: (.*)", re.IGNORECASE);
M = R.search(line)
if M:
    subject = M.group(1)
```

Again, this looks very similar to what we've seen before.

Why do approaches differ?

Why does one language do it one way, and another language another? There may be language-specific reasons, but it mostly depends on the whim and skills of the engineers that develop each package. In fact, there are many unrelated regular-expression packages for Java (see Chapter 8), each written by someone who wanted the functionality that Sun didn't originally provide. Each has its own strengths and weaknesses, but it's interesting to note that they all provide their functionality in quite different ways from each other, and from what Sun eventually decided to implement themselves.

A Search-and-Replace Example

The "Subject" example is pretty simple, so the various approaches really don't have an opportunity to show how different they really are. In this section, we'll look at a somewhat more complex example, further highlighting the different designs.

In the previous chapter (☞ 73), we saw this Perl search-and-replace to "linkize" an email address:

```
$text =~ s{
   \b
   # Capture the address to $1 . . .
   (
     \w[-.\w]*                                    # username
     @
     [-\w]+(\.[-\w]+)*\.(com|edu|info)   # hostname
   )
   \b
}{<a href="mailto:$1">$1</a>}gix;
```

Let's see how this is done in other languages.

Search-and-replace in Java

Here's the search-and-replace example with Sun's `java.util.regex` package:

```
import java.util.regex.*;  // Make regex classes easily available
   ⋮
Pattern r = Pattern.compile(
   "\\b                                               \n"+
   "# Capture the address to $1 . . .                 \n"+
   "(                                                 \n"+
   "  \\w[-.\\w]*                         # username  \n"+
   "  @                                               \n"+
   "  [-\\w]+(\\.[-\\w]+)*\\.(com|edu|info)  # hostname  \n"+
   ")                                                 \n"+
   "\\b                                               \n",
   Pattern.CASE_INSENSITIVE|Pattern.COMMENTS);

Matcher m = r.matcher(text);
String result = m.replaceAll("<a href=\"mailto:$(1)\">$(1)</a>");
System.out.println(result);
```

There are a number of things to note. Perhaps the most important is that each '\' wanted in the regular expression requires '\\' in the string literal. Thus, using '\\w' in the string literal results in '\w' in the regular expression. This is because regular expressions are provided as normal Java string literals, which as we've seen before (☞ 44), require special handling. For debugging, it might be useful to use

```
System.out.println(P.pattern());
```

to display the regular expression as the regex function actually received it. One reason that I include newlines in the regex is so that it displays nicely when printed this way. Another reason is that each '#' introduces a comment that goes until the next newline; so, at least some of the newlines are required to restrain the comments.

Perl uses notations like /g, /i, and /x to signify special conditions (these are the modifiers for *replace all*, *case-insensitivity*, and *free formatting* modes ☞ 133), but `java.util.regex` uses either different functions (`replaceAll` *vs.* `replace`) or flag arguments passed to the function (e.g., `Pattern.CASE_INSENSITIVE` and `Pattern.COMMENTS`).

Search-and-replace in VB.NET

The general approach in VB.NET is similar:

```
Dim R As Regex = New Regex _
("\b                                                 " & _
 "(?# Capture the address to $1 ...)                 " & _
 "(                                                  " & _
 "  \w[-.\w]*                        (?# username)   " & _
 "  @                                                " & _
 "  [-\w]+(\.[-\w]+)*\.(com|edu|info) (?# hostname)  " & _
 ")                                                  " & _
 "\b                                                 ", _
 RegexOptions.IgnoreCase Or RegexOptions.IgnorePatternWhitespace)

Dim Copy As String = R.Replace(text, "<a href=""mailto:${1}"">${1}</a>")
Console.WriteLine(Copy)
```

Due to the inflexibility of VB.NET string literals (they can't span lines, and it's difficult to get newline characters into them), longer regular expressions are not as convenient to work with as in some other languages. On the other hand, because '\' is not a string metacharacter in VB.NET, the expression can be less visually cluttered. A double quote *is* a metacharacter in VB.NET string literals: to get one double quote into the string's value, you need two double quotes in the string literal.

Search and Replace in Other Languages

Let's quickly look at a few examples from other traditional tools and languages.

Awk

Awk uses an integrated approach, **/regex/**, to perform a match on the current input line, and uses "**var ~** ···" to perform a match on other data. You can see where Perl got its notation for matching. (Perl's substitution operator, however, is modeled after sed's.) The early versions of awk didn't support a regex substitution, but modern versions have the `sub(···)` operator:

```
sub(/mizpel/, "misspell")
```

This applies the regex `mizpel` to the current line, replacing the first match with `misspell`. Note how this compares to Perl's (and sed's) **s/mizpel/misspell/**.

To replace all matches within the line, awk does not use any kind of `/g` modifier, but a different operator altogether: **gsub(/mizpel/, "misspell")**.

Tcl

Tcl takes a procedural approach that might look confusing if you're not familiar with Tcl's quoting conventions. To correct our misspellings with Tcl, we might use:

```
regsub mizpel $var misspell newvar
```

This checks the string in the variable var, and replaces the first match of ⌈mizpel⌋ with misspell, putting the now possibly-changed version of the original string into the variable newvar (which is *not* written with a dollar sign in this case). Tcl expects the regular expression first, the target string to look at second, the replacement string third, and the name of the target variable fourth. Tcl also allows optional flags to its regsub, such as -all to replace all occurrences of the match instead of just the first:

```
regsub -all mizpel $var misspell newvar
```

Also, the -nocase option causes the regex engine to ignore the difference between uppercase and lowercase characters (just like *egrep*'s -i flag, or Perl's /i modifier).

GNU Emacs

The powerful text editor GNU Emacs (just "Emacs" from here on) supports *elisp* (Emacs lisp) as a built-in programming language. It provides a procedural regex interface with numerous functions providing various services. One of the main ones is re-search-forward, which accepts a normal string as an argument and interprets it as a regular expression. It then starts searching the text from the "current position," stopping at the first match, or aborting if no match is found. (This function is invoked when one invokes a "regexp search" while using the editor.)

As Table 3-3 (☞ 91) shows, Emacs' flavor of regular expressions is heavily laden with backslashes. For example, ⌈\<\([a-z]+\)\([\n \t]\|<[^>]+>\)+\1\>⌋ is an expression for finding doubled words, similar to the problem in the first chapter. We couldn't use this regex directly, however, because the Emacs regex engine doesn't understand \t and \n. Emacs double-quoted strings, however, do, and convert them to the tab and newline values we desire before the regex engine ever sees them. This is a notable benefit of using normal strings to provide regular expressions. One drawback, particularly with *elisp*'s regex flavor's propensity for backslashes, is that regular expressions can end up looking like a row of scattered toothpicks. Here's a small function for finding the next doubled word:

```
(defun FindNextDbl ()
  "move to next doubled word, ignoring < > tags"    (interactive)
  (re-search-forward "\\<\\([a-z]+\\)\\([\n \t]\\|<[^>]+>\\)+\\1\\>")
)
```

Combine that with **(define-key global-map "\C-x\C-d" 'FindNextDbl)** and you can use the "Control-x Control-d" sequence to quickly search for doubled words.

Care and Handling: Summary

As you can see, there's a wide range of functionalities and mechanics for achieving them. If you are new to these languages, it might be quite confusing at this point. But, never fear! When trying to learn any one particular tool, it is a simple matter to learn its mechanisms.

Strings, Character Encodings, and Modes

Before getting into the various type of metacharacters generally available, there are a number of global issues to understand: regular expressions as strings, character encodings, and match modes.

These are simple concepts, in theory, and in practice, some indeed are. With most, though, the small details, subtleties, and inconsistencies among the various implementations sometimes makes it hard to pin down exactly how they work in practice. The next sections cover some of the common and sometimes complex issues you'll face.

Strings as Regular Expressions

The concept is simple: in most languages except Perl, awk, and sed, the regex engine accepts regular expressions as normal strings — strings that are often provided as string literals like `"^From:(.*)"`. What confuses many, especially early on, is the need to deal with the language's own string-literal metacharacters when composing a string to be used as a regular expression.

Each language's string literals have their own set of metacharacters, and some languages even have more than one type of string literal, so there's no one rule that works everywhere, but the concepts are all the same. Many languages' string literals recognize escape sequences like `\t`, `\\`, and `\x2A`, which are interpreted while the string's value is being composed. The most common regex-related aspect of this is that each backslash in a regex requires two backslashes in the corresponding string literal. For example, `"\\n"` is required to get the regex ⌜\n⌟.

If you forgot the extra backslash for the string literal and used `"\n"`, with many languages you'd then get ⬚, which just happens to do exactly the same thing as ⌜\n⌟. Well, actually, if the regex is in an `/x` type of free-spacing mode, ⬚ becomes empty, while ⌜\n⌟ remains a regex to match a newline. So, you can get bitten if you forget. Table 3-4 on the next page shows a few examples involving `\t` and `\x2A` (2A is the ASCII code for '*'.) The second pair of examples in the table show the unintended results when the string-literal metacharacters aren't taken into account.

Every language's string literals are different, but some are quite different in that '\' is not a metacharacter. For example. VB.NET's string literals have only one

Table 3-4: A Few String-Literal Examples

String literal	`"[\t\x2A]"`	`"[\\t\\x2A]"`	`"\t\x2A"`	`"\\t\\x2A"`
String value	`'[▯*]'`	`'[\t\x2A]'`	`'▯*'`	`'\t\x2A'`
As regex	`⌈[▯*]⌋`	`⌈[\t\x2A]⌋`	`⌈▯*⌋`	`⌈\t\x2A⌋`
Matches	tab or star	tab or star	any number tabs	tab followed by star
In **/x** mode	tab or star	tab or star	*error*	tab followed by star

metacharacter, a double quote. The next sections look at the details of several common languages' string literals. Whatever the individual string-literal rules, the question on your mind when using them should be "what will the regular expression engine see after the language's string processing is done?"

Strings in Java

Java string literals are like those presented in the introduction, in that they are delimited by double quotes, and backslash is a metacharacter. Common combinations such as '\t' (tab), '\n' (newline), '\\' (literal backslash), etc. are supported. Using a backslash in a sequence not explicitly supported by literal strings results in an error.

Strings in VB.NET

String literals in VB.NET are also delimited by double quotes, but otherwise are quite different from Java's. VB.NET strings recognize only one metasequence: a pair of double quotes in the string literal add one double quote into the string's value. For example, `"he said ""hi""\."` results in ⌈he said "hi"\.⌋

Strings in C#

Although all the languages of Microsoft's .NET Framework share the same regular expression engine internally, each has its own rules about the strings used to create the regular-expression arguments. We just saw Visual Basic's simple string literals. In contrast, Microsoft's C# language has two types of string literals.

C# supports the common double-quoted string similar to the kind discussed in this section's introduction, except that `""` rather than `\"` adds a double quote into the string's value. However, C# also supports "verbatim strings," which look like `@"⋯"`. Verbatim strings recognize no backslash sequences, but instead, just one special sequence: a pair of double quotes inserts one double quote into the target value. This means that you can use `"\\t\\x2A"` or `@"\t\x2A"` to create the ⌈\t\x2A⌋ example. Because of this simpler interface, one would tend to use these `@"⋯"` verbatim strings for most regular expressions.

Strings in PHP

PHP also offers two types of strings, yet both differ from either of C#'s types. With PHP's double-quoted strings, you get the common backslash sequences like '\n', but you also get variable interpolation as we've seen with Perl (☞ 77), and also the special sequence {···} which inserts into the string the result of executing the code between the braces.

These extra features of PHP double-quoted strings mean that you'll tend to insert extra backslashes into regular expressions, but there's one additional feature that helps mitigate that need. With Java and C# string literals, a backslash sequence that isn't explicitly recognized as special within strings results in an error, but with PHP double-quoted strings, such sequences are simply passed through to the string's value. PHP strings recognize \t, so you still need "\\t" to get ⌈\t⌉, but if you use "\w", you'll get ⌈\w⌉ because \w is not among the sequences that PHP double-quoted strings recognize. This extra feature, while handy at times, does add yet another level of complexity to PHP double-quoted strings, so PHP also offers its simpler single-quoted strings.

PHP single-quoted strings offer uncluttered strings on the order of VB.NET's strings, or C#'s @"···" strings, but in a slightly different way. Within a PHP single-quoted string, the sequence \' includes one single quote in the target value, and a \\ at the end of the string allows the target value to end with a backslash. Any other character (including any other backslash) is not considered special, and is copied to the target value verbatim. This means that '\t\x2A' creates ⌈\t\x2A⌉. Because of this simplicity, single-quoted strings are the most convenient for PHP regular expressions.

Strings in Python

Python offers a number of string-literal types. You can use either single quotes or double quotes to create strings, but unlike PHP, there is no difference between the two. Python also offers "triple-quoted" strings of the form ''' ''' and """···""", which are different in that they may contain unescaped newlines. All four types offer the common backslash sequences such as \n, but have the same twist that PHP has in that unrecognized sequences are left in the string verbatim. Contrast this with Java and C# strings, for which unrecognized sequences cause an error.

Like PHP and C#, Python offers a more literal type of string, its "raw string." Similar to C#'s @"···" notation, Python uses an 'r' before the opening quote of any of the four quote types. For example, r"\t\x2A" yields ⌈\t\x2A⌉. Unlike the other languages, though, with Python's raw strings, *all* backslashes are kept in the string, including those that escape a double quote (so that the double quote can be included within the string): r"he said \"hi\"\." results in ⌈he said \"hi\"\.⌉. This isn't really a problem when using strings for regular expressions, since

Python's regex flavor treats ⌈\"⌋ as ⌈"⌋, but if you like, you can bypass the issue by using one of the other types of raw quoting: **r'he said "hi"\.'**

Strings in Tcl

Tcl is different from anything else in that it doesn't really have string literals at all. Rather, command lines are broken into "words," which Tcl commands can then consider as strings, variable names, regular expressions, or anything else as appropriate to the command. While a line is being parsed into words, common backslash sequences like \n are recognized and converted, and backslashes in unknown combinations are simply dropped. You can put double quotes around the word if you like, but they aren't required unless the word has whitespace in it.

Tcl also has a raw literal type of quoting similar to Python's raw strings, but Tcl uses braces, {⋯}, instead of r'⋯'. Within the braces, everything except a backslash-newline combination is kept as-is, so you can use **{\t\x2A}** to get ⌈\t\x2A⌋.

Within the braces, you can have additional sets of braces so long as they nest. Those that don't nest must be escaped with a backslash, although the backslash *does* remain in the string's value.

Regex literals in Perl

In the Perl examples we've seen so far in this book, regular expressions have been provided as literals ("regular-expression literals"). As it turns out, you can also provide them as strings. For example:

```
$str =~ m/(\w+)/;
```

can also be written as:

```
$regex = '(\w+)';
$str =~ $regex;
```

or perhaps:

```
$regex = "(\\w+)";
$str =~ $regex;
```

(although using a regex literal can be much more efficient ☞ 242, 348).

When a regex is provided as a literal, Perl provides extra features that the regular-expression engine itself does not, including:

- The interpolation of variables (incorporating the contents of a variable as part of the regular expression).

- Support for a literal-text mode via ⌈\Q⋯\E⌋ (☞ 112).

- Optional support for a \N{*name*} construct, which allows you to specify characters via their official Unicode names. For example, you can match '¡Hola!' with ⌈\N{INVERTED EXCLAMATION MARK}Hola!⌋.

In Perl, a regex literal is parsed like a very special kind of string. In fact, these features are also available with Perl double-quoted strings. The point to be aware of is that these features are *not* provided by the regular-expression engine. Since the vast majority of regular expressions used within Perl are as regex literals, most think that ⌜\Q ··· \E⌝ is part of Perl's regex language, but if you ever use regular expressions read from a configuration file (or from the command line, etc.), it's important to know exactly what features are provided by which aspect of the language.

More details are available in Chapter 7, starting on page 288.

Character-Encoding Issues

A character encoding is merely an explicit agreement on how bytes with various values should be interpreted. A byte with the decimal value 110 is interpreted as the character 'n' with the ASCII encoding, but as '>' with EBCDIC. Why? Because that's what someone decided — there's nothing intrinsic about those values and characters that makes one encoding better than the other. The byte is the same; only the interpretation changes.

ASCII defines characters for only half the values that a byte can hold. The encoding *ISO-8859-1* (commonly called *Latin-1*) fills in the blank spots with accented characters and special symbols, making an encoding usable by a larger set of languages. With this encoding, a byte with a decimal value of 234 is to be interpreted as ê, instead of being undefined as it is with ASCII.

The important question for us is this: when we *intend* for a certain set of bytes to be *considered* in the light of a particular encoding, does the program actually treat them that way? For example, if we have four bytes with the values 234, 116, 101, and 115 that we intend to be considered as Latin-1 (representing the French word "êtes"), we'd like the regex ⌜^\w+$⌝ or ⌜^\b⌝ to match. This happens if the program's \w and \b know to treat those bytes as Latin-1 characters, and probably doesn't happen otherwise.

Richness of encoding-related support

There are many encodings. When you're concerned with a particular one, important questions you should ask include:

* Does the program understand this encoding?
* How does it know to treat this data as being of that encoding?
* How rich is the regex support for this encoding?

The richness of an encoding's support has several important issues, including:

- Are characters that are encoded with multiple bytes recognized as such? Do expressions like dot and [^x] match single *characters*, or single *bytes*?

- Do \w, \d, \s, \b, etc., properly understand all the characters in the encoding? For example, even if ê is known to be a letter, do \w and \b treat it as such?

- Does the program try to extend the interpretation of class ranges? Is ê matched by [a-z]?

- Does case-insensitive matching work properly with all the characters? For example, are ê and Ê equal?

Sometimes things are not as simple as they might seem. For example, the \b of Sun's `java.util.regex` package properly understands all the word-related characters of Unicode, but its \w does not (it understands only basic ASCII). We'll see more examples of this later in the chapter.

Unicode

There seems to be a lot of misunderstanding about just what "Unicode" is. At the most basic level, Unicode is a *character set* or a *conceptual encoding*—a logical mapping between a number and a character. For example, the Korean character 화 is mapped to the number 49,333. The number, called a *code point*, is normally shown in hexadecimal, with "U+" prepended. 49,333 in hex is C0B5, so 화 is referred to as U+C0B5. Included as part of the Unicode concept is a set of attributes for many characters, such as "3 is a digit" and "É is an uppercase letter whose lowercase equivalent is é."

At this level, nothing is yet said about just how these numbers are actually encoded as data on a computer. There are a variety of ways to do so, including the *UCS-2* encoding (all characters encoded with two bytes), the *UCS-4* encoding (all characters encoded with four bytes), *UTF-16* (most characters encoded with two bytes, but some with four), and the *UTF-8* encoding (characters encoded with one to six bytes). Exactly which (if any) of these encodings a particular program uses internally is usually not a concern to the user of the program. The user's concern is usually limited to how to convert external data (such as data read from a file) from a known encoding (ASCII, Latin-1, UTF-8, etc.) to whatever the program uses. Programs that work with Unicode usually supply various encoding and decoding routines for doing the conversion.

Regular expressions for programs that work with Unicode often support a \u*num* metasequence that can be used to match a specific Unicode character (☞ 116). The number is usually given as a four-digit hexadecimal number, so \uC0B5 matches 화. It's important to realize that \uC0B5 is saying "match the Unicode character U+C0B5," and says nothing about what actual bytes are to be compared, which is dependent on the particular encoding used internally to represent Unicode code points. If the program happens to use UTF-8 internally, that character happens to be represented with three bytes. But you, as someone using the Unicode-enabled program, don't really need to care.

But, there are some related issues that you may need to be aware of…

Characters versus combining-character sequences. What a person considers a "character" doesn't always agree with what Unicode or a Unicode-enabled program (or regex engine) considers to be a character. For example, most would consider à to be a single character, but in Unicode, it's composed of two code points, U+0061 (a) combined with the grave accent U+0300 (`). Unicode offers a number of *combining characters* that are intended to follow (and be combined with) a base character. This makes things a bit more complex for the regular-expression engine — for example, should dot match just one code point, or the entire U+0061 plus U+0300 combination?

In practice, it seems that many programs treat "character" and "code point" as synonymous, which means that dot matches each code point individually, whether it is base character or one of the combining characters. Thus, à (U+0061 plus U+0300) is matched by ⌜^..$⌝, and not by ⌜^.$⌝.

Perl happens to support the \X metasequence, which fulfills what many might expect from dot ("match one *character*") in that it matches a base character followed by any number of combining characters. See more on page 125.

It's important to keep combining characters in mind when using a Unicode-enabled editor to input Unicode characters directly into regular-expressions. If an accented character, say Å, ends up in a regular expression as 'A' plus '˚', it likely can't match a string containing the single code point version of Å (single code point versions are discussed in the next section). Also, it appears as two distinct characters to the regular-expression engine itself, so specifying ⌜[···Å···]⌝ adds the two characters to the class, just as the explicit ⌜[···A˚···]⌝ does. If followed by a quantifier, such an Å has the quantifier applying only to the accent, just as with an explicit ⌜A˚+⌝.

Multiple code points for the same character. In theory, Unicode is supposed to be a one-to-one mapping between code points and characters, but there are many situations where one character can have multiple representations. In the previous section I note that à is U+0061 followed by U+0300. It is, however, *also* encoded separately as the single code point U+00E0. Why is it encoded twice? To maintain easier conversion between Unicode and Latin-1. If you have Latin-1 text that you convert to Unicode, à will likely be converted to U+00E0. But, it could well be converted to a U+0061, U+0300 combination. Often, there's nothing you can do to automatically allow for these different ways of expressing characters, but Sun's `java.util.regex` package provides a special match option, CANON_EQ, which causes characters that are "canonically equivalent" to match the same, even if their representations in Unicode differ (☞ 380).

Somewhat related is that different characters can look virtually the same, which could account for some confusion at times among those creating the text you're tasked to check. For example, the Roman letter I (U+0049) could be confused with I, the Greek letter Iota (U+0399). Add *dialytika* to that to get Ï or Ï, and it can be encoded four different ways (U+00CF; U+03AA; U+0049 U+0308; U+0399 U+0308). This means that you might have to manually allow for these four possibilities when constructing a regular expression to match Ï. There are many examples like this.

Also plentiful are single characters that appear to be more than one character. For example, Unicode defines a character called "SQUARE HZ" (U+3390), which appears as Hz. This looks very similar to the two normal characters Hz (U+0048 U+U007A).

Although the use of special characters like Hz is minimal now, their adoption over the coming years will increase the complexity of programs that scan text, so those working with Unicode would do well to keep these issues in the back of their mind. Along those lines, one might already expect, for example, the need to allow for both normal spaces (U+0020) and no-break spaces (U+00A0), and perhaps also any of the dozen or so other types of spaces that Unicode defines.

Unicode 3.1+ and code points beyond U+FFFF. With the release of Unicode Version 3.1 in mid 2001, characters with code points beyond U+FFFF were added. (Previous versions of Unicode had built in a way to allow for characters at those code points, but until Version 3.1, none were actually defined.) For example, there is a character for musical symbol C Clef defined at U+1D121. Older programs built to handle only code points U+FFFF and below won't be able to handle this. Most programs' \u*num* indeed allow only a four-digit hexadecimal number.

One program that can handle characters at these new code points is Perl. Rather than \u*num*, it has \x{*num*} where the number can be any number of digits. You can then use \x{1D121} to match the C Clef character.

Unicode line terminator. Unicode defines a number of characters (and one sequence of two characters) that are to be considered *line terminators,* shown in Table 3-5.

When fully supported, line terminators influence how lines are read from a file (including, in scripting languages, the file the program is being read from). With regular expressions, they can influence both what dot matches (☞ 110), and where ⌜^⌟, ⌜$⌟, and ⌜\z⌟ match (☞ 111).

Table 3-5: Unicode Line Terminators

Characters		Description
LF	U+000A	ASCII Line Feed
VT	U+000B	ASCII Vertical Tab
FF	U+000C	ASCII Form Feed
CR	U+000D	ASCII Carriage Return
CR/LF	U+000D U+000A	ASCII Carriage Return / Line Feed sequence
NEL	U+0085	Unicode NEXT LINE
LS	U+2028	Unicode LINE SEPARATOR
PS	U+2029	Unicode PARAGRAPH SEPARATOR

Regex Modes and Match Modes

Most regex engines support a number of different modes for how a regular expression is interpreted or applied. We've seen an example of each with Perl's /x modifier (regex mode that allows free whitespace and comments ☞72) and /i modifier (match mode for case-insensitive matching ☞47).

Modes can generally be applied globally to the whole regex, or in many modern flavors, partially, to specific subexpressions of the regex. The global application is achieved through modifiers or options, such as Perl's /i or java.util.regex's Pattern.CASE_INSENSITIVE flag (☞98). If supported, the partial application of a mode is achieved with a regex construct that looks like ⌜(?i)⌝ to turn on case-insensitive matching, or ⌜(?-i)⌝ to turn it off. Some flavors also support ⌜(?i:⋯)⌝ and ⌜(?-i:⋯)⌝, which turn on and off case-insensitive matching for the subexpression enclosed.

How these modes are invoked within a regex is discussed later in this chapter (☞133). In this section, we'll merely review some of the modes commonly available in most systems.

Case-insensitive match mode

The almost ubiquitous case-insensitive match mode ignores letter case during matching, so that ⌜b⌝ matches both 'b' and 'B'. This feature relies upon proper character encoding support, so all the cautions mentioned earlier apply.

Historically, case-insensitive matching support has been surprisingly fraught with bugs. Most have been fixed over the years, but some still linger. As we saw in the first chapter, GNU *egrep*'s case-insensitive matching doesn't apply to backreferences. Ruby's case-insensitive matching doesn't apply to octal and hex escapes.

There are special Unicode-related issues with case-insensitive matching (which Unicode calls "loose matching"). For starters, not all alphabets have the concept of upper and lower case, and some have an additional *title case* used only at the start of a word. Sometimes there's not a straight one-to-one mapping between upper and lower case. A common example is that a Greek Sigma, Σ, has two lowercase versions, ς and σ; all three should mutually match in case-insensitive mode. (Of the systems I've tested, only Perl does this correctly.)

Another issue is that sometimes a single character maps to a sequence of multiple characters. One well known example is that the uppercase version of ß is the two-character combination "SS". There are also Unicode-manufactured problems. One example is that while there's a single character ǰ (U+01F0), it has no single-character uppercase version. Rather, J̌ requires a combining sequence (☞ 107), U+006A and U+030C. Yet, ǰ and J̌ should match in a case-insensitive mode. There are even examples like this that involve one-to-three mappings. Luckily, most of these do not involve commonly-used characters.

Free-spacing and comments regex mode

In this mode, whitespace outside of character classes is mostly ignored. Whitespace within a character class still counts (except in `java.util.regex`), and comments are allowed between # and a newline. We've already seen examples of this for Perl (☞ 72), Java (☞ 98), and VB.NET (☞ 99).

It's not quite true that *all* whitespace outside of classes is ignored. It's more as if whitespace is turned into a do-nothing metacharacter. The distinction is important with something like ⌜\12●3⌟, which in this mode is taken as ⌜\12⌟ followed by ⌜3⌟, and not ⌜\123⌟, as some might expect.

Of course, just what is and isn't "whitespace" is subject to the character encoding in effect, and its fullness of support. Most programs recognize only ASCII whitespace.

Dot-matches-all match mode (a.k.a., "single-line mode")

Usually, dot does not match a newline. The original Unix regex tools worked on a line-by-line basis, so the thought of matching a newline wasn't even an issue until the advent of sed and *lex*. By that time, ⌜.*⌟ had become a common idiom to match "the rest of the line," so the new languages disallowed it from crossing line boundaries in order to keep it familiar.[†] Thus, tools that could work with multiple lines (such as a text editor) generally disallow dot from matching a newline.

For modern programming languages, a mode in which dot matches a newline can be as useful as one where dot doesn't. Which of these is most convenient for a particular situation depends, well, on the situation. Many programs now offer ways for the mode to be selected on a per-regex basis.

---

† As Ken Thompson (*ed*'s author) explained it to me, it kept ⌜.*⌟ from becoming "too unwieldy."

There are a few exceptions to the common standard. Unicode-enabled systems, such as Sun's Java regex package, may expand what dot normally does not match to include any of the single-character Unicode line terminators (☞ 108). Tcl's normal state is that its dot matches everything, but in its special "newline-sensitive" and "partial newline-sensitive" matching modes, both dot *and* a negated character class are prohibited from matching a newline.

An unfortunate name. When first introduced by Perl with its /s modifier, this mode was called "single-line mode." This unfortunate name continues to cause no end of confusion because it has nothing whatsoever to do with ⌜^⌟ and ⌜$⌟, which are influenced by the "multiline mode" discussed in the next section. "Single-line mode" merely means that dot has no restrictions and can match any character.

Enhanced line-anchor match mode (a.k.a., "multiline mode")

An enhanced line-anchor match mode influences where the line anchors, ⌜^⌟ and ⌜$⌟, match. The anchor ⌜^⌟ normally does not match at embedded newlines, but rather only at the start of the string that the regex is being applied to. However, in enhanced mode, it can also match after an embedded newline, effectively having ⌜^⌟ treat the string as multiple logical lines if the string contains newlines in the middle. We saw this in action in the previous chapter (☞ 69) while developing a Perl program to converting text to HTML. The entire text document was within a single string, so we could use the search-and-replace **s/^$/<p>/mg** to convert "... tags.◲◲It's ..." to "... tags.◲<p>◲It's ..." The substitution replaces empty "lines" with paragraph tags.

It's much the same for ⌜$⌟, although the basic rules about when ⌜$⌟ can normally match can be a bit more complex to begin with (☞ 127). However, as far as this section is concerned, enhanced mode simply includes locations before an embedded newline as one of the places that ⌜$⌟ can match.

Programs that offer this mode often offer ⌜\A⌟ and ⌜\Z⌟, which normally behave the same as ⌜^⌟ and ⌜$⌟ except they are *not* modified by this mode. This means that ⌜\A⌟ and ⌜\Z⌟ never match at embedded newlines. Some implementations also allow ⌜$⌟ and ⌜\Z⌟ to match before a string-ending newline. Such implementations often offer ⌜\z⌟, which disregards all newlines and matches *only* at the very end of the string. See page 127 for details.

As with dot, there are exceptions to the common standard. A text editor like GNU Emacs normally lets the line anchors match at embedded newlines, since that makes the most sense for an editor. On the other hand, *lex* has its ⌜$⌟ match only before a newline (while its ⌜^⌟ maintains the common meaning.)

Unicode-enabled systems, such as Sun's `java.util.regex`, may allow the line anchors in this mode to match at any line terminator (☞ 108). Ruby's line anchors normally *do* match at any embedded newline, and Python's ⌈\Z⌉ behaves like its ⌈\z⌉, rather than its normal ⌈$⌉.

Traditionally, this mode has been called "multiline mode." Although it is unrelated to "single-line mode," the names confusingly imply a relation. One simply modifies how dot matches, while the other modifies how ⌈^⌉ and ⌈$⌉ match. Another problem is that they approach newlines from different views. The first changes the concept of how dot treats a newline from "special" to "not special," while the other does the opposite and changes the concept of how ⌈^⌉ and ⌈$⌉ treat newlines from "not special" to "special." [†]

Literal-text regex mode

A "literal text" mode is one that doesn't recognize most or all regex metacharacters. For example, a literal-text mode version of ⌈[a-z]*⌉ matches the string '[a-z]*'. A fully literal search is the same as a simple string search ("find this string" as opposed to "find a match for this regex"), and programs that offer regex support also tend to offer separate support for simple string searches. A regex literal-text mode becomes more interesting when it can be applied to just part of a regular expression. For example, Perl regex literals offer the special sequence \Q···\E, the contents of which have all metacharacters ignored (except the \E itself, of course).

Common Metacharacters and Features

The following overview of current regex metacharacters covers common items and concepts. It doesn't discuss every issue, and no one tool includes everything presented here. In one respect, this is just a summary of much of what you've seen in the first two chapters, but in light of the wider, more complex world presented at the beginning of this chapter. During your first pass through this section, a light glance should allow you to continue on to the next chapters. You can come back here to pick up details as you need them.

Some tools add a lot of new and rich functionality and some gratuitously change common notations to suit their whim or special needs. Although I'll sometimes comment about specific utilities, I won't address too many tool-specific concerns here. Rather, in this section I'll just try to cover some common metacharacters and their uses, and some concerns to be aware of. I encourage you to follow along with the manual of your favorite utility.

---

† Tcl normally lets its dot match everything, so in one sense it's more straightforward than other languages. In Tcl regular expressions, newlines are not normally treated specially in any way (neither to dot nor to the line anchors), but by using match modes, they become special. However, since other systems have always done it another way, Tcl could be considered confusing to those used to those other ways.

The following is an outline of the constructs covered in this section, with pointers to the page where each sub-section starts:

Character Representations

This group of metacharacters provides visually pleasing ways to match specific characters that are otherwise difficult to represent.

Character shorthands

Many utilities provide metacharacters to represent certain control characters that are sometimes machine-dependent, and which would otherwise be difficult to input or to visualize:

\a **Alert** (e.g., to sound the bell when "printed") Usually maps to the ASCII <BEL> character, 007 octal.

\b **Backspace** Usually maps to the ASCII <BS> character, 010 octal. (Note ⌐\b⌐ often is a word-boundary metacharacter instead, as we'll see later.)

\e **Escape character** Usually maps to the ASCII <ESC> character, 033 octal.

\f **Form feed** Usually maps to the ASCII <FF> character, 014 octal.

\n **Newline** On most platforms (including Unix and DOS/Windows), usually maps to the ASCII <LF> character, 012 octal. On MacOS systems, usually maps to the ASCII <CR> character, 015 octal. With Java or any .NET language, always the ASCII <LF> character regardless of platform.

\r **Carriage return** Usually maps to the ASCII <CR> character. On MacOS systems, usually maps to the ASCII <LF> character. With Java or any .NET language, always the ASCII <CR> character regardless of platform.

\t **Normal (horizontal) tab** Usually maps to the ASCII <HT> character, 011 octal.

\v **Vertical tab** Usually maps to the ASCII <VT> character, 013 octal.

Table 3-6 lists a few common tools and some of the control shorthands they provide. As discussed earlier, some languages also provide many of the same shorthands for the string literals they support. Be sure to review that section (☞ 101) for some of the associated pitfalls.

These are machine dependent?

As noted in the list, \n and \r are operating-system dependent in many tools,[†] so, it's best to choose carefully when you use them. When you need, for example, "a

---

† If the tool itself is written in C or C++, and converts its regex backslash escapes into C backslash escapes, the resulting value is dependent upon the compiler used, since the C standard leaves the actual values to the discretion of the compiler vendor. In practice, compilers for any particular platform are standardized around newline support, so it's safe to view these as *operating-system dependent*. Furthermore, it seems that only \n and \r vary across operating systems , so the others can be considered standard across all systems.

Table 3-6: A Few Utilities and Some of the Shorthand Metacharacters They Provide

Program	\b (word boundary)	\b (backspace)	\a (alarm)	\e (ASCII escape)	\f (form feed)	\n (newline)	\r (carriage return)	\t (tab)	\v (vertical tab)
		Character shorthands							
Python	✓	✓c	✓		✓	✓	✓	✓	✓
Tcl	as \y	✓	✓	✓	✓	✓	✓	✓	✓
Perl	✓	✓c	✓	✓	✓	✓	✓	✓	
Java	✓x	✓x	✓	✓	✓SR	✓SR	✓SR	✓SR	✓
GNU awk		✓	✓		✓	✓	✓	✓	✓
GNU sed	✓					✓			
GNU Emacs	✓	✓s	✓s	✓s	✓s	✓s	✓s	✓s	✓s
.NET	✓	✓c	✓	✓	✓	✓	✓	✓	✓
PHP	✓	✓c	✓	✓	✓	✓	✓	✓	
MySQL									
GNU grep/egrep	✓								
flex		✓	✓		✓	✓	✓	✓	✓
Ruby	✓	✓c	✓	✓	✓	✓	✓	✓	✓

✓ supported ✓c supported in class only   See page 91 for version information
✓SR supported (also supported by string literals)
✓x supported (but string literals have a different meaning for the same sequence)
✓x not supported (but string literals have a different meaning for the same sequence)
✓s not supported (but supported by string literals)
This table assumes the most regex-friendly type of string per application (☞ 101)

newline" for whatever system your script will happen to run on, use \n. When you need a character with a specific value, such as when writing code for a defined protocol like HTTP, use \012 or whatever the standard calls for. (\012 is an octal escape.) If you wish to match DOS line-ending characters, use ⌈\015\012⌉. To match either DOS or Unix line-ending characters, use ⌈\015?\012⌉. (These actually match the line-ending characters—to match *at* the start or end of a line, use a line anchor ☞ 127).

Octal escape — \num

Implementations supporting octal (base 8) escapes generally allow two- and three-digit octal escapes to be used to indicate a byte or character with a particular value. For example, ⌈\015\012⌉ matches an ASCII CR/LF sequence. Octal escapes can be convenient for inserting hard-to-type characters into an expression. In Perl, for instance, you can use ⌜\e⌟ for the ASCII escape character, but you can't in awk. Since awk does support octal escapes, you can use the ASCII code for the escape character directly: ⌜\033⌟.

Table 3-7 shows the octal escapes some tools support.

Some implementations, as a special case, allow ⌜\0⌟ to match a null byte. Some allow all one-digit octal escapes, but usually don't if backreferences such as ⌜\1⌟ are supported. When there's a conflict, backreferences generally take precedence over octal escapes. Some allow four-digit octal escapes, usually to support a requirement that any octal escape begin with a zero (such as with java.util.regex).

You might wonder what happens with out-of-range values like \565 (8-bit octal values range from \000 to \377). It seems that half the implementations leave it as a larger-than-byte value (which may match a Unicode character if Unicode is supported), while the other half strip it to a byte. In general, it's best to limit octal escapes to \377 and below.

Hex and Unicode escapes: \x*num*, \x{*num*}, \u*num*, \U*num*, ...

Similar to octal escapes, many utilities allow a hexadecimal (base 16) value to be entered using \x, \u, or sometimes \U. If allowed with \x, for example, ⌜\x0D\x0A⌟ matches the CR/LF sequence. Table 3-7 shows the hex escapes that some tools support.

Besides the question of which escape is used, you must also know how many digits they recognize, and if braces may be (or must be) used around the digits. These are also indicated in Table 3-7.

Control characters: \c*char*

Many flavors offer the ⌜\c*char*⌟ sequence to match *control characters* with encoding values less than 32 (some allow a wider range). For example, ⌜\cH⌟ matches a Control-H, which represents a backspace in ASCII, while ⌜\cJ⌟ matches an ASCII linefeed (which is often also matched by ⌜\n⌟, but sometimes by ⌜\r⌟, depending on the platform ☞ 114).

Details aren't uniform among systems that offer this construct. You'll always be safe using uppercase English letters as in the examples. With most implementations, you can use lowercase letters as well, but Sun's Java regex package, for example, does not support them. And what exactly happens with non-alphabetics is very flavor-dependent, so I recommend using only uppercase letters with \c.

Related Note: GNU Emacs supports this functionality, but with the rather ungainly metasequence ⌜?\^*char*⌟ (e.g., ⌜?\^H⌟ to match an ASCII backspace).

Table 3-7: A Few Utilities and the Octal and Hex Regex Escapes Their Regexes Support

	Back-references	Octal escapes	Hex escapes
Python	✓	\0, \07, \377	\xFF
Tcl	✓	\0, \77, \777	\x⋯ \uFFFF; \UFFFFFFFF
Perl	✓	\0, \77, \377	\xFF; \x{⋯}
Java	✓	\07, \077, \0377	\xFF; \uFFFF
GNU awk		\7, \77, \377	\x⋯
GNU sed	✓		
GNU Emacs	✓		
.NET	✓	\0, \77, \377	\xFF, \uFFFF
PHP	✓	\77, \377	\xF, \xFF
MySQL			
GNU egrep	✓		
GNU grep			
flex		\7, \77, \377	\xF, \xFF
Ruby	✓	\0, \77, \377, \0377	\xF, \xFF

\0 – ⌈\0⌋ matches a null byte, but other one-digit octal escapes are not supported
\7, \77 – one- and two- digit octal escapes are supported
\07 – two-digit octal escapes are supported if leading digit is a zero
\077 – three-digit octal escapes are supported if leading digit is a zero
\377 – three-digit octal escapes are supported, until \377
\0377 – four-digit octal escapes are supported, until \0377
\777 – three-digit octal escapes are supported, until \777
\x⋯ – \x allows any number of digits
\x{⋯} – \x{⋯} allows any number of digits
\xF, \xFF – one- and two- digit hex escape is allowed with \x
\uFFFF – four-digit hex escape allowed with \u
\UFFFF – four-digit hex escape allowed with \U
\UFFFFFFFF – eight-digit hex escape allowed with \U   (See page 91 for version information.)

Character Classes and Class-Like Constructs

Modern flavors provide a number of ways to specify a set of characters allowed at a particular point in the regex, but the simple character class is ubiquitous.

Normal classes: [a-z] and [^a-z]

The basic concept of a character class has already been well covered, but let me emphasize again that the metacharacter rules change depending on whether you're in a character class or not. For example, ⌈*⌋ is never a metacharacter within a class, while ⌈-⌋ usually is. Some metasequences, such as ⌈\b⌋, sometimes have a different meaning within a class than outside of one (☞ 115).

With most systems, the order that characters are listed in a class makes no difference, and using ranges instead of listing characters is irrelevant to the execution speed (e.g., [0-9] should be no different from [9081726354]). However, some implementations don't completely optimize classes (Sun's Java regex package comes to mind), so it's usually best to use ranges, which tend to be faster, wherever possible.

A character class is always a *positive assertion*. In other words, it must always match a character to be successful. A negated class must still match a character, but one *not* listed. It might be convenient to consider a negated character class to be a "class to match characters not listed." (Be sure to see the warning about dot and negated character classes, in the next section.) It used to be true that something like ⌈[^LMNOP]⌋ was the same as ⌈[\x00-KQ-\xFF]⌋. In strictly eight-bit systems, it still is, but in a system such as Unicode where character ordinals go beyond 255 (\xFF), a negated class like ⌈[^LMNOP]⌋ suddenly includes all the tens of thousands of characters in the encoding—all except L, M, N, O, and P.

Be sure to understand the underlying character set when using ranges. For example, ⌈[a-Z]⌋ is likely an error, and in any case certainly isn't "alphabetics." One specification for alphabetics is ⌈[a-zA-Z]⌋, at least for the ASCII encoding. (See \p{L} in "Unicode properties" ☞ 119.) Of course, when dealing with binary data, ranges like ⌈\x80-\xFF⌋ make perfect sense.

Almost any character: dot

In some tools, dot is a shorthand for a character class that can match any character, while in most others, it is a shorthand to match any character *except a newline*. It's a subtle difference that is important when working with tools that allow target text to contain multiple logical lines (or to span logical lines, such as in a text editor). Concerns about dot include:

- In some Unicode-enabled systems, such as Sun's Java regex package, dot normally does not match a Unicode line terminator (☞ 108).

- A match mode (☞ 110) can change the meaning of what dot matches.

- The POSIX standard dictates that dot not match a null (a character with the value zero), although all the major scripting languages allow nulls in their text (and dot matches them).

Dot versus a negated character class

When working with tools that allow multiline text to be searched, take care to note that dot usually does not match a newline, while a negated class like ⌈[^"]⌋ usually does. This could yield surprises when changing from something such as ⌈".*"⌋ to ⌈"[^"]*"⌋. The matching qualities of dot can often be changed by a match mode—see "Dot-matches-all match mode" on page 110.

Class shorthands: \w, \d, \s, \W, \D, \S

Support for the following shorthands is quite common:

\d   **Digit**   Generally the same as ⌈[0-9]⌋ or, in some Unicode-enabled tools, all Unicode digits.

\D   **Non-digit**   Generally the same as ⌈[^\d]⌋

\w   **Part-of-word character**   Often the same as ⌈[a-zA-Z0-9_]⌋, although some tools omit the underscore, while others include all the extra alphanumerics characters in the *locale* (☞87). If Unicode is supported, ⌈\w⌋ usually refers to all alphanumerics (notable exception: Sun's Java regex package, whose ⌈\w⌋ is exactly ⌈[a-zA-Z0-9_]⌋).

\W   **Non-word character**   Generally the same as ⌈[^\w]⌋.

\s   **Whitespace character**   On ASCII-only systems, this is often the same as ⌈[\f\n\r\t\v]⌋. Unicode-enabled systems sometimes also include the Unicode "next line" control character U+0085, and sometimes the "whitespace" property ⌈\p{Z}⌋ (described in the next section).

\S   **Non-whitespace character**   Generally the same as ⌈[^\s]⌋.

As described on page 87, a POSIX locale could influence the meaning of these shorthands (in particular, ⌈\w⌋). Unicode-enabled programs likely have ⌈\w⌋ match a much wider scope of characters, such as ⌈\p{L}⌋ (discussed in the next section) plus an underscore.

Unicode properties, scripts, and blocks: \p{Prop}, \P{Prop}

On its surface, Unicode is a mapping (☞106), but the Unicode Standard offers much more. It also defines qualities about each character, such as "this character is a lowercase letter," "this character is meant to be written right-to-left," "this character is a mark that's meant to be combined with another character," etc.

Regular-expression support for these qualities varies, but many Unicode-enabled programs support matching via at least some of them with ⌈\p{*quality*}⌋ (matches characters that have the quality) and ⌈\P{*quality*}⌋ (matches characters without it). One example is ⌈\p{L}⌋, where 'L' is the quality meaning "letter" (as opposed to number, punctuation, accents, etc.). ⌈\p{L}⌋ is an example of a *general property* (also called a *category*). We'll soon see other "qualities" that can be tested by ⌈\p{⋯}⌋ and ⌈\P{⋯}⌋, but the most commonly supported are the general properties.

The general properties are shown in Table 3-8. Each character (each code point actually, which includes those that have no characters defined) can be matched by just one general property. The general property names are one character ('L' for Letter, 'S' for symbol, etc.), but some systems support a more descriptive synonym ('Letter', 'Symbol', etc.) as well. Perl, for example, supports these.

Table 3-8: Basic Unicode Properties

Class	Synonym and description
\p{L}	\p{**Letter**} – Things considered letters.
\p{M}	\p{**Mark**} – Various characters that are not meant to appear by themselves, but with other base characters (accent marks, enclosing boxes, …).
\p{Z}	\p{**Separator**} – Characters that separate things, but have no visual representation (various kinds of spaces…).
\p{S}	\p{**Symbol**} – Various types of Dingbats and symbols.
\p{N}	\p{**Number**} – Any kind of numeric character.
\p{P}	\p{**Punctuation**} – Punctuation characters.
\p{C}	\p{**Other**} – Catch-all for everything else (rarely used for normal characters).

With some systems, single-letter property names may be referenced without the curly braces (e.g., using ⌈\pL⌋ instead of ⌈\p{L}⌋). Some systems may require (or simply allow) 'In' or 'Is' to prefix the letter (e.g., ⌈\p{IsL}⌋). As we look at additional qualities, we'll see examples of where an Is/In prefix is required.[†]

Each one-letter general Unicode property can be further subdivided into a set of two-letter sub-properties, as shown in Table 3-9. Additionally, some implementations support a special composite sub-property, ⌈\p{L&}⌋, which is a shorthand for all "cased" letters: ⌈[\p{Lu}\p{Ll}\p{Lt}]⌋.

Also shown are the full-length synonyms (e.g., "Lowercase_Letter" instead of "Ll"), which may be supported by some implementations. The standard suggests that a variety of forms be accepted ('LowercaseLetter', 'LOWERCASE_LETTER', 'Lowercase⋅Letter', 'lowercase-letter', etc.), but I recommend, for consistency, always using the form shown in Table 3-9.

Scripts. Some systems have support for matching via a *script* (writing system) name with ⌈\p{···}⌋. For example, if supported, ⌈\p{Hebrew}⌋ matches characters that are specifically part of the Hebrew writing system. (A script does not match common characters that might be used by other writing systems as well, such as spaces and punctuation.)

Some scripts are language-based (such as Gujarati, Thai, Cherokee, …). Some span multiple languages (e.g., Latin, Cyrillic), while some languages are composed of multiple scripts, such as Japanese, which uses characters from the Hiragana, Katakana, Han ("Chinese Characters"), and Latin scripts. See your system's documentation for the full list.

---

† As we'll see (and is illustrated in the table on page 123), the whole Is/In prefix business is somewhat of a mess. Previous versions of Unicode recommend one thing, while early implementations often did another. During Perl 5.8's development, I worked with the development group to simplify things for Perl. The rule in Perl now is simply "You don't need to use 'Is' or 'In' unless you specifically want a Unicode Block (☞ 122), in which case you must prepend 'In'."

Table 3-9: Basic Unicode Sub-Properties

Property	Synonym and description
\p{Ll}	\p{**Lowercase_Letter**} – Lowercase letters.
\p{Lu}	\p{**Uppercase_Letter**} – Uppercase letters.
\p{Lt}	\p{**Titlecase_Letter**} – Letters that appear at the start of a word (e.g., the character Dž is the title case of the lowercase dž and of the uppercase DŽ).
\p{L&}	A composite shorthand matching all \p{**Ll**}, \p{**Lu**}, and \p{**Lt**} characters.
\p{Lm}	\p{**Modifier_Letter**} – A small set of letter-like special-use characters.
\p{Lo}	\p{**Other_Letter**} – Letters that have no case, and aren't modifiers, including letters from Hebrew, Arabic, Bengali, Tibetan, Japanese, ...
\p{Mn}	\p{**Non_Spacing_Mark**} – "characters" that modify other characters, such as accents, umlauts, certain "vowel signs," and tone marks.
\p{Mc}	\p{**Spacing_Combining_Mark**} – modification characters that take up space of their own (mostly "vowel signs" in languages that have them, including Bengali, Gujarati, Tamil, Telugu, Kannada, Malayalam, Sinhala, Myanmar, and Khmer).
\p{Me}	\p{**Enclosing_Mark**} – A small set of marks that can enclose other characters, such as circles, squares, diamonds, and "keycaps."
\p{Zs}	\p{**Space_Separator**} – Various kinds of spacing characters, such as a normal space, non-break space, and various spaces of specific widths.
\p{Zl}	\p{**Line_Separator**} – The LINE SEPARATOR character (U+2028).
\p{Zp}	\p{**Paragraph_Separator**} – The PARAGRAPH SEPARATOR character (U+2029).
\p{Sm}	\p{**Math_Symbol**} – +, ÷, a fraction slash, ⋜, ...
\p{Sc}	\p{**Currency_Symbol**} – $, ¢, ¥, €, ...
\p{Sk}	\p{**Modifier_Symbol**} – Mostly versions of the combining characters, but as full-fledged characters in their own right.
\p{So}	\p{**Other_Symbol**} – Various Dingbats, box-drawing symbols, Braille patterns, non-letter Chinese characters, ...
\p{Nd}	\p{**Decimal_Digit_Number**} – zero through nine, in various scripts (not including Chinese, Japanese, and Korean).
\p{Nl}	\p{**Letter_Number**} – mostly Roman numerals.
\p{No}	\p{**Other_Number**} – Numbers as superscripts or symbols; characters representing numbers that aren't digits (Chinese, Japanese, and Korean not included).
\p{Pd}	\p{**Dash_Punctuation**} – Hyphens and dashes of all sorts.
\p{Ps}	\p{**Open_Punctuation**} – Characters like (, ⩰, and ⟪, ...
\p{Pe}	\p{**Close_Punctuation**} – Characters like), ⩰, ⟫ , ...
\p{Pi}	\p{**Initial_Punctuation**} – Characters like «, ", ‹, ...
\p{Pf}	\p{**Final_Punctuation**} – Characters like », ', ›, ...
\p{Pc}	\p{**Connector_Punctuation**} – A few punctuation characters with special linguistic meaning, such as an underscore.
\p{Po}	\p{**Other_Punctuation**} – Catch-all for other punctuation: !, &, ·, :, ¡, ...
\p{Cc}	\p{**Control**} – The ASCII and Latin-1 control characters (TAB, LF, CR, ...)
\p{Cf}	\p{**Format**} – Non-visible characters intended to indicate some basic formatting (*zero width joiner, activate Arabic form shaping,* ...)
\p{Co}	\p{**Private_Use**} – Code points allocated for private use (company logos, etc.).
\p{Cn}	\p{**Not_Assigned**} – Code points that have no characters assigned.

A script does not include all characters used by the particular writing system, but rather, all characters used only (or predominantly) by that writing system. Common characters, such as spacing and punctuation marks, are not included within any script, but rather are included as part of the catch-all pseudo-script `IsCommon`, matched by ⌜`\p{IsCommon}`⌟. A second pseudo-script, `Inherited`, is composed of certain combining characters that inherit the script from the base character that they follow.

Blocks.   Similar (but inferior) to scripts, *blocks* refer to ranges of code points on the Unicode character map. For example, the `Tibetan` block refers to the 256 code points from `U+0F00` through `U+0FFF`. Characters in this block are matched with `\p{InTibetan}` in Perl and `java.util.regex`, and with `\p{IsTibetan}` in .NET. (More on this in a bit.)

There are many blocks, including blocks for most systems of writing (`Hebrew`, `Tamil`, `Basic_Latin`, `Hangul_Jamo`, `Cyrillic`, `Katakana`, …), and for special character types (`Currency`, `Arrows`, `Box_Drawing`, `Dingbats`, …).

`Tibetan` is one of the better examples of a block, since all characters in the block that are defined relate to the Tibetan language, and there are no Tibetan-specific characters outside the block. Block qualities, however, are inferior to script qualities for a number of reasons:

- Blocks can contain unassigned code points. For example, about 25% of the code points in the `Tibetan` block have no characters assigned to them.

- Not all characters that would seem related to a block are actually part of that block. For example, the `Currency` block does not contain the universal currency symbol '¤', nor such notable currency symbols as $, ¢, £, €, and ¥. (Luckily, in this case, you can use the currency property, `\p{Sc}`, in its place.)

- Blocks often have unrelated characters in them. For example, ¥ (Yen symbol) is found in the `Latin_1_Supplement` block.

- What might be considered one *script* may be included within multiple *blocks*. For example, characters used in Greek can be found in both the `Greek` and `Greek_Extended` blocks.

Support for block qualities is more common than for script qualities. There is ample room for getting the two confused because there is a lot of overlap in the naming (for example, Unicode provides for both a Tibetan script and a Tibetan block).

Furthermore, as Table 3-10 on the facing page shows, the nomenclature has not yet been standardized. With Perl and `java.util.regex`, the Tibetan block is ⌜`\p{InTibetan}`⌟, but in the .NET Framework, it's ⌜`\p{IsTibetan}`⌟ (which, to add to the confusion, Perl allows as an alternate representation for the Tibetan *script*).

Other properties/qualities. Not everything talked about so far is universally supported. Table 3-10 gives a few details about what's been covered so far.

Additionally, Unicode defines many other qualities that might be accessible via the ⌈\p{⋯}⌋ construct, including ones related to how a character is written (left-to-right, right-to-left, etc.), vowel sounds associated with characters, and more. Some implementations even allow you to create your own properties on the fly. See your program's documentation for details on what's supported.

Table 3-10: Property/Script/Block Features

	Feature	Perl	Java	.NET
✓	Basic Properties like \p{L}	✓	✓	✓
✓	Basic Properties shorthand like \pL	✓	✓	
	Basic Properties longhand like \p{IsL}	✓	✓	
✓	Basic Properties full like \p{Letter}	✓		
✓	Composite \p{L&}	✓		
✓	Script like \p{Greek}	✓		
	Script longhand like \p{**IsGreek**}	✓		
✓	Block like \p{Cyrillic}	if no script	✓	
✓	Block longhand like \p{**In**Cyrillic}	✓	✓	
	Block longhand like \p{**Is**Cyrillic}			✓
✓	Negated \P{⋯}	✓	✓	✓
	Negated \p{^⋯}	✓		
✓	\p{Any}	✓	as \p{all}	
✓	\p{Assigned}	✓	as \P{Cn}	as \P{Cn}
✓	\p{Unassigned}	✓	as \p{Cn}	as \p{Cn}

Lefthand checkmarks are recommended for new implementations.   (See page 91 for version information)

Class set operations: [[a-z]&&[^aeiou]]

Sun's Java regex package supports set operations within character classes. For example, you can match all non-vowel English letters with "[a-z] minus [aeiou]". The nomenclature for this may seem a bit odd a first — it's written as [[a-z]&&[^aeiou]], and read aloud as "this **and** not that." Before looking at that in more detail, let's look at the two basic class set operations, OR and AND.

OR allows you to add characters to the class by including what looks like an embedded class within the class: [abcxyz] can also be written as [[abc][xyz]], [abc[xyz]], or [[abc]xyz], among others. OR combines sets, creating a new set that is the sum of the argument sets. Conceptually, it's similar to the "bitwise or" operator that many languages have via a '|' or 'or' operator. In character classes, OR is mostly a notational convenience, although the ability to include *negated classes* can be useful in some situations.

AND does a conceptual "bitwise AND" of two sets, keeping only those characters found in both sets. It is achieved by inserting the special class metasequence `&&` between two sets of characters. For example, `[\p{InThai}&&\P{Cn}]` matches all *assigned* code points in the `Thai` block. It does this by taking the intersection between (i.e., keeping only characters in both) `\p{InThai}` and `\P{Cn}`. Remember, `\P{···}` with a capital 'P', matches everything *not* part of the quality, so `\P{Cn}` matches everything *not un*assigned, which in other words, means *is assigned.* (Had Sun supported the `Assigned` quality, I could have used `\p{Assigned}` instead of `\P{Cn}` in this example.)

Be careful not to confuse OR and AND. How intuitive these names feel depends on your point of view. For example, `[[this][that]]` in normally read "accept characters that match `[this]` *or* `[that]`," yet it is equally true if read "the list of characters to allow is `[this]` *and* `[that]`." Two points of view for the same thing.

AND is less confusing in that `[\p{InThai}&&\P{Cn}]` is normally read as "match only characters matchable by `\p{InThai}` *and* `\P{Cn}`," although it is sometimes read as "the list of allowed characters is the *intersection* of `\p{InThai}` and `\P{Cn}`."

These differing points of view can make talking about this confusing: what I call OR and AND, some might choose to call AND and INTERSECTION.

Class subtraction. Thinking further about the `[\p{InThai}&&\P{Cn}]` example, it's useful to realize that `\P{Cn}` is the same as `[^\p{Cn}]`, so the whole thing can be rewritten as the somewhat more complex looking `[\p{InThai}&&[^\p{Cn}]]`. Furthermore, matching "assigned characters in the `Thai` block" is the same as "characters in the `Thai` block, *minus un*assigned characters." The double negative makes it a bit confusing, but it shows that `[\p{InThai}&&[^\p{Cn}]]` means "`\p{InThai}` *minus* `\p{Cn}`."

This brings us back to the `[[a-z]&&[^aeiou]]` example from the start of the section, and shows how to do *class subtraction.* The pattern is that `[this&&[^that]]` means "`[this]` minus `[that]`." I find that the double negatives of `&&` and `[^···]` tend to make my head swim, so I just remember the `[··· && [^···]]` pattern.

Mimicking class set operations with lookaround. If your program doesn't support class set operations, but does support lookaround (☞ 132), you can mimic the set operations. With lookahead, `[\p{InThai}&&[^\p{Cn}]]` can be rewritten as `(?!\p{Cn})\p{InThai}`.[†] Although not as efficient as well-implemented class

---

† Actually, in Perl, this particular example could probably be written simply as `\p{Thai}`, since in Perl `\p{Thai}` is a *script,* which never contains unassigned characters. Other differences between the `Thai` script and block are subtle. It's beneficial to have the documentation as to what is actually covered by any particular script or block. In this case, the script is actually missing a few special characters that are in the block.

set operations, using lookaround can be quite flexible. This example can be written four different ways (substituting `IsThai` for `InThai` in .NET ☞ 123):

```
(?!\p{Cn})\p{InThai}
(?=\P{Cn})\p{InThai}
\p{InThai}(?<!\p{Cn})
\p{InThai}(?<=\P{Cn})
```

Unicode combining character sequence: \X

Perl supports ⌈\X⌋ as a shorthand for ⌈\P{M}\p{M}*⌋, which is like an extended ⌈.⌋ (dot). It matches a *base character* (anything not ⌈\p{M}⌋, followed by any number (including none) of *combining characters* (anything that is ⌈\p{M}⌋).

As discussed earlier (☞ 107), Unicode uses a system of base and combining characters which, in combination, create what look like single, accented characters like à ('a' U+0061 combined with the grave accent '`' U+0300). You can use more than one combining character if that's what you need to create the final result. For example, if for some reason you need 'c̯̆', that would be 'c' followed by a combining cedilla ',' and a combining breve '˘' (U+0063 followed by U+0327 and U+0306).

If you wanted to match either "francais" or "français," it wouldn't be safe to just use ⌈fran.ais⌋ or ⌈fran[cç]ais⌋, as those assume that the 'ç' is rendered with the single Unicode code point U+00C7, rather than 'c' followed by the cedilla (U+0063 followed by U+0327). You could perhaps use ⌈fran(c.?|ç)ais⌋ if you needed to be very specific, but in this case, ⌈fran\Xais⌋ is a good substitute for ⌈fran.ais⌋.

Besides the fact that ⌈\X⌋ matches trailing combining characters, there are two differences between it and dot. One is that ⌈\X⌋ always matches a newline and other Unicode line terminators (☞ 108), while dot is subject to dot-matches-all match-mode (☞ 110), and perhaps other match modes depending on the tool. Another difference is that a dot-matches-all dot is guaranteed to match all characters at all times, while ⌈\X⌋ doesn't match a leading combining character.

POSIX bracket-expression "character class": [[:alpha:]]

What we normally call a *character class*, the POSIX standard calls a *bracket expression*. POSIX uses the term "character class" for a special feature used *within* a bracket expression[†] that we might consider to be the precursor to Unicode's character properties.

A POSIX character class is one of several special metasequences for use within a POSIX bracket expression. An example is `[:lower:]`, which represents any lowercase letter within the current locale (☞ 87). For English text, `[:lower:]` is

---

† In general, this book uses "character class" and "POSIX bracket expression" as synonyms to refer to the entire construct, while "POSIX character class" refers to the special range-like class feature described here.

comparable to a-z. Since this entire sequence is valid only *within* a bracket expression, the full class comparable to ⌈a-z⌉ is ⌈[[:lower:]]⌉. Yes, it's that ugly. But, it has the advantage over ⌈[a-z]⌉ of including other characters, such as ö, ñ, and the like if the locale actually indicates that they are "lowercase letters."

The exact list of POSIX character classes is locale dependent, but the following are usually supported:

[:alnum:]	alphabetic characters and numeric character
[:alpha:]	alphabetic characters
[:blank:]	space and tab
[:cntrl:]	control characters
[:digit:]	digits
[:graph:]	non-blank characters (not spaces, control characters, or the like)
[:lower:]	lowercase alphabetics
[:print:]	like [:graph:], but includes the space character
[:punct:]	punctuation characters
[:space:]	all whitespace characters ([:blank:], newline, carriage return, and the like)
[:upper:]	uppercase alphabetics
[:xdigit:]	digits allowed in a hexadecimal number (i.e., 0-9a-fA-F).

Systems that support Unicode properties (☞ 119) may or may not extend that Unicode support to these POSIX constructs. The Unicode property constructs are more powerful, so those should generally be used if available.

POSIX bracket-expression "collating sequences": [[.span-ll.]]

A locale can have *collating sequences* to describe how certain characters or sets of characters should be ordered. For example, in Spanish, the two characters ll (as in *tortilla*) traditionally sort as if it were one logical character between l and m, and the German ß is a character that falls between s and t, but sorts as if it were the two characters ss. These rules might be manifested in collating sequences named, for example, span-ll and eszet.

A collating sequence that maps multiple physical characters to a single logical character, such as the span-ll example, is considered "one character" to a fully compliant POSIX regex engine. This means that something like ⌈[^abc]⌉ matches the '11' sequence.

A collating sequence element is included within a bracket expression using a [.···.] notation: ⌈torti[[.span-ll.]]a⌉ matches tortilla. A collating sequence allows you to match against those characters that are made up of combinations of other characters. It also creates a situation where a bracket expression can match more than one physical character.

POSIX bracket-expression "character equivalents": [[=n=]]

Some locales define *character equivalents* to indicate that certain characters should be considered identical for sorting and such. For example, a locale might define an equivalence class 'n' as containing n and ñ, or perhaps one named 'a' as containing a, à, and á. Using a notation similar to [:⋯:], but with '=' instead of a colon, you can reference these equivalence classes within a bracket expression: ⌈[[=n=][=a=]]⌋ matches any of the characters just mentioned.

If a character equivalence with a single-letter name is used but not defined in the locale, it defaults to the collating sequence of the same name. Locales normally include normal characters as collating sequences — [.a.], [.b.], [.c.], and so on—so in the absence of special equivalents, ⌈[[=n=][=a=]]⌋ defaults to ⌈[na]⌋.

Emacs syntax classes

GNU Emacs doesn't support the traditional ⌈\w⌋, ⌈\s⌋, etc.; rather, it uses special sequences to reference "syntax classes":

 \s*char* matches characters in the Emacs syntax class as described by *char*

 \S*char* matches characters not in the Emacs syntax class

⌈\sw⌋ matches a "word constituent" character, and ⌈\s-⌋ matches a "whitespace character." These would be written as ⌈\w⌋ and ⌈\s⌋ in many other systems.

Emacs is special because the choice of which characters fall into these classes can be modified on the fly, so, for example, the concept of which characters are word constituents can be changed depending upon the kind of text being edited.

Anchors and Other "Zero-Width Assertions"

Anchors and other "zero-width assertions" don't match actual text, but rather *positions* in the text.

Start of line/string: ˆ, \A

Caret ⌈^⌋ matches at the beginning of the text being searched, and, if in an enhanced line-anchor match mode (☞ 111), after any newline. In some systems, an enhanced-mode ⌈^⌋ can match after Unicode line terminators, as well (☞ 108).

When supported, ⌈\A⌋ always matches only at the start of the text being searched, regardless of any match mode.

End of line/string: $, \Z, \z

As Table 3-11 on the next page shows, the concept of "end of line" can be a bit more complex than its start-of-line counterpart. ⌈$⌋ has a variety of meanings among different tools, but the most common meaning is that it matches at the end of the target string, and before a *string-ending* newline, as well. The latter is common, to allow an expression like ⌈s$⌋ (ostensibly, to match "a line ending with s") to match '⋯s◨', a line ending with s that's capped with an ending newline.

Two other common meanings for ⌈$⌋ are to match only at the end of the target text, and to match after any newline. In some Unicode systems, the special meaning of newline in these rules are replaced by Unicode line terminators (☞ 108).

A match mode (☞ 111) can change the meaning of ⌈$⌋ to match before any embedded newline (or Unicode line terminator as well).

When supported, ⌈\Z⌋ usually matches what the "unmoded" ⌈$⌋ matches, which often means to match at the end of the string, or before a string-ending newline. To complement these, ⌈\z⌋ matches only at the end of the string, period, without regard to any newline. See Table 3-11 for a few exceptions.

Table 3-11: Line Anchors for Some Scripting Languages

Concern	Java	Perl	PHP	Python	Ruby	Tcl	.NET
Normally . . .							
^ matches at start of string	✓	✓	✓	✓	✓	✓	✓
^ matches after any newline					✓₂		
$ matches at end of string	✓	✓	✓	✓	✓	✓	✓
$ matches before string-ending newline	✓₁	✓	✓	✓	✓		✓
$ matches before *any* newline					✓₂		
Has enhanced line-anchor mode (☞111)	✓	✓	✓	✓		✓	✓
In enhanced line-anchor mode . . .							
^ matches at start of string	✓	✓	✓	✓	N/A	✓	✓
^ matches after any newline	✓₁	✓	✓	✓	N/A	✓	✓
$ matches at end of string	✓	✓	✓	✓	N/A	✓	✓
$ matches before *any* newline	✓₁	✓	✓	✓	N/A	✓	✓
\A always matches like normal ^	✓	✓	✓	✓	•₄	✓	✓
\Z always matches like normal $	✓₁	✓	✓	•₃	•₅	✓	✓
\z always matches only at end of string	✓	✓	✓	N/A	N/A	✓	✓

Notes: 1. Sun's Java regex package supports Unicode's *line terminator* (☞ 108) in these cases.
    2. Ruby's $ and ^ match at embedded newlines, but its \A and \Z do not.
    3. Python's \Z matches only at the end of the string.
    4. Ruby's \A, unlike its ^, matches only at the start of the string.
    5. Ruby's \Z, unlike its $, matches at the end of the string, or before a string-ending newline.
                                    (See page 91 for version information.)

Start of match (or end of previous match): \G

⌈\G⌋ was first introduced by Perl to be useful when doing iterative matching with /g (☞ 51), and ostensibly matches the location where the previous match left off. On the first iteration, ⌈\G⌋ matches only at the beginning of the string, just like ⌈\A⌋.

If a match is not successful, the location at which ⌈\G⌋ matches is reset back to the beginning of the string. Thus, when a regex is applied repeatedly, as with Perl's ⌈s/···/···/**g**⌋ or other's "match all" function, The failure that causes the "match all" to fail also resets the location for ⌈\G⌋ for the next time a match of some sort is applied.

Perl's ⌈\G⌋ has three unique aspects that I find quite interesting and useful:

- The location associated with ⌈\G⌋ is an attribute of *each target string*, not of the regexes that are setting that location. This means that multiple regexes can match against a string, in turn, each using ⌈\G⌋ to ensure that they pick up exactly where one of the others left off.

- Perl's regex operators have an option (Perl's /c modifier ☞ 315) that indicates a failing match should *not* reset the ⌈\G⌋ location, but rather to leave it where it was. This works well with the first point to allow tests with a variety of expressions to be performed at one point in the target string, advancing only when there's a match.

- That location associated with ⌈\G⌋ can be inspected and modified by non-regex constructs (Perl's pos function ☞ 313). One might want to explicitly set the location to "prime" a match to start at a particular location, and match only at that location. Also, if the language supports this point, the functionality of the previous point can be mimicked with this feature, if it's not already supported directly.

See the sidebar on the next page for an example of these features in action. Despite these convenient features, Perl's ⌈\G⌋ does have a problem in that it works reliably only when it's the first thing in the regex. Luckily, that's where it's most-naturally used.

End of previous match, or start of the current match?

One detail that differs among implementations is whether ⌈\G⌋ actually matches the "start of the current match" or "end of the previous match." In the vast majority of cases, the two meanings are the same, so it's a non-issue most of the time. Uncommonly, they can differ. There is a realistic example of how this might arise on page 215, but the issue is easiest to understand with a contrived example: consider applying ⌈x?⌋ to 'abcde'. The regex can match successfully at 'abcde', but doesn't actually match any text. In a global search-and-replace situation, where the regex is applied repeatedly, picking up each time from where it left off, unless the transmission does something special, the "where it left off" will always be the same as where it started. To avoid an infinite loop, the transmission forcefully bumps along to the next character when it recognizes this situation. You can see this by applying s/x?/!/g to 'abcde', yielding '!a!b!c!d!e!'.

Advanced Use of \G *with Perl*

Here's the outline of a snippet that performs simple validation on the HTML in the variable $html, ensuring that it contains constructs from among only a very limited subset of HTML (simple <IMG> and <A> tags are allowed, as well as simple entities like >). I've used this method at Yahoo!, for example, to validate that a user's HTML submission met certain guidelines.

This code relies heavily on the behavior of Perl's m/⋯/gc match operator, which applies the regular expression to the target string once, picking up from where the last successful match left off, but *not* resetting that position if it fails (☞ 315).

Using this feature, the various expressions used below all "tag team" to work their way through the string. It's similar in theory to having one big alternation with all the expressions, but this approach allows program code to be executed with each match, and to include or exclude expressions on the fly.

```
my $need_close_anchor = 0;  # True if we've seen <A>, but not its closing </A>.

while (not $html =~ m/\G\z/gc) # While we haven't worked our way to the end . . .
{
  if ($html =~ m/\G(\w+)/gc) {
      . . . have a word or number in $1 -- can now check for profanity, for example . . .
  } elsif ($html =~ m/\G[^<>&\w]+/gc) {
      # Other non-HTML stuff -- simply allow it.
  } elsif ($html =~ m/\G<img\s+([^>]+)>/gci) {
      . . . have an image tag -- can check that it's appropriate . . .
            ⋮
  } elsif (not $need_close_anchor and $html =~ m/\G<A\s+([^>]+)>/gci) {
      . . . have a link anchor — can validate it . . .
            ⋮
      $need_close_anchor = 1; # Note that we now need </A>
  } elsif ($need_close_anchor and $html =~ m{\G</A>}gci) {
      $need_close_anchor = 0; # Got what we needed; don't allow again
  } elsif ($html =~ m/\G&(#\d+|\w+);/gc) {
      # Allow entities like &gt; and &#123;
  } else {
      # Nothing matched at this point, so it must be an error. Grab a dozen or so characters from the
      # HTML so that we can issue an informative error message.
      my ($badstuff) = $html =~ m/\G(.{1,12})/g;
      my $location = pos($html); # Note where the unexpected HTML starts.
      die "Unexpected HTML at position $location: $badstuff\n";
  }
}

# Make sure there's no dangling <A>
if ($need_close_anchor) {
   die "Missing final </A>"
}
```

One side effect of the transmission having to step in this way is that the "end of the previous match" then differs from "the start of the current match." When this happens, the question becomes: which of the two locations does ⌈\G⌋ match? In Perl, actually applying s/\G x?/!/g to 'abcde' yields just '!abcde', so in Perl, ⌈\G⌋ really does match only the end of the previous match. If the transmission does the artificial bump-along, Perl's ⌈\G⌋ is guaranteed to fail.

On the other hand, applying the same search-and-replace with some other tools yields the original '!a!b!c!d!e!', showing that their ⌈\G⌋ matches successfully at the start of each current match, as decided *after* the artificial bump-along.

You can't always rely on the documentation that comes with a tool to tell you which is which, as I've found that both Microsoft's .NET and Sun's Java documentation are incorrect. My testing has shown that java.util.regex and Ruby have ⌈\G⌋ match at the start of the current match, while Perl and the .NET languages have it match at the end of the previous match. (Sun tells me that the next release of java.util.regex will have its ⌈\G⌋ behavior match the documentation.)

Word boundaries: \b, \B, \<, \>, ...

Like line anchors, word-boundary anchors match a location in the string. There are two distinct approaches. One provides separate metasequences for *start-* and *end-of-word* boundaries (often \< and \>), while the other provides ones catch-all *word boundary* metasequence (often \b). Either generally provides a *not-word-boundary* metasequence as well (often \B). Table 3-12 shows a few examples. Tools that don't provide separate start- and end-of-word anchors, but do support lookaround, can mimic word-boundary anchors with the lookaround. In the table, I've filled in the otherwise empty spots that way, wherever practical.

A word boundary is generally defined as a location where there is a "word character" on one side, and not on the other. Each tool has its own idea of what constitutes a "word character," as far as word boundaries go. It would make sense if the word boundaries agree with \w, but that's not always the case. With Sun's Java regex package, for example, \w applies only to ASCII and not the full Unicode that Java supports, so in the table I've used lookaround with the Unicode letter property \pL (which is a shorthand for ⌈\p{L}⌋ ☞ 119).

Whatever the word boundaries consider to be "word characters," word boundary tests are always a simple test of adjoining characters. No regex engine actually does linguistic analysis to decide about words: all consider "NE14AD8" to be a word, but not "M.I.T."

Table 3-12: A Few Utilities and Their Word Boundary Metacharacters

Program	Start-of-word ... End-of-word	Word boundary	Not word-boundary
GNU *egrep*	\< ... \>	\b	\B
GNU Emacs	\< ... \>	\b	\B
GNU awk	\< ... \>	\y	\B
MySQL	[[:<:]] ... [[:>:]]	[[:<:]]|[[:>:]]	
Perl	(?<!\w)(?=\w) ... (?<=\w)(?!\w)	\b	\B
PHP	(?<!\w)(?=\w) ... (?<=\w)(?!\w)	\b	\B
Python	(?<!\w)(?=\w) ... (?<=\w)(?!\w)	\b	\B
Ruby		\b	\B
GNU sed	\< ... \>	\b	\B
Java	(?<!\pL)(?=\pL) ... (?<=\pL)(?!\pL)	\b	\B
Tcl	\m ... \M	\y	\Y
.NET	(?<!\w)(?=\w) ... (?<=\w)(?!\w)	\b	\B

Lookahead (?=···), (?!···); Lookbehind, (?<=···), (?<!···)

Lookahead and lookbehind constructs (collectively, *lookaround*) are discussed with an extended example in the previous chapter's "Adding Commas to a Number with Lookaround" (☞ 59). One important issue not discussed there relates to what kind of expression can appear within either of the lookbehind constructs. Most implementations have restrictions about the length of text matchable within lookbehind (but not within lookahead, which is unrestricted).

The most restrictive rule exists in Perl and Python, where the lookbehind can match only fixed-length strings. For example, (?<!\w) and (?<!this|that) are allowed, but (?<!books?) and (?<!^\w+) are not, as they can match a variable amount of text. In some cases, such as with (?<!books?), you can accomplish the same thing by rewriting the expression, as with ⌈(?<!book)(?<!books)⌋, although that's certainly not easy to read at first glance.

The next level of support allows alternatives of different lengths within the lookbehind, so (?<!books?) can be written as (?<!book|books). PCRE (and the pcre routines in PHP) allows this.

The next level allows for regular expressions that match a variable amount of text, but only if it's of a finite length. This allows (?<!books?) directly, but still disallows (?<!^\w+) since the \w+ is open-ended. Sun's Java regex package supports this level.

When it comes down to it, these first three levels of support are really equivalent, since they can all be expressed, although perhaps somewhat clumsily, with the most restrictive fixed-length matching level of support. The intermediate levels are just "syntactic sugar" to allow you to express the same thing in a more pleasing way. The fourth level, however, allows the subexpression within lookbehind to match any amount of text, including the `(?<!^\w+:)` example. This level, supported by Microsoft's .NET languages, is truly superior to the others, but does carry a potentially huge efficiency penalty if used unwisely. (When faced with lookbehind that can match any amount of text, the engine is forced to check the lookbehind subexpression from the start of the string, which may mean a *lot* of wasted effort when requested from near the end of a long string.)

Comments and Mode Modifiers

With many flavors, the regex modes and match modes described earlier (☞ 109) can be modified within the regex (on the fly, so to speak) by the following constructs.

Mode modifier: (?modifier), such as (?i) or (?-i)

Many flavors now allow some of the regex and match modes (☞ 109) to be set within the regular expression itself. A common example is the special notation ⌜(?i)⌟, which turns on case-insensitive matching, and ⌜(?-i)⌟, which turns it off. For example, ⌜<B>(?i)very(?-i)</B>⌟ has the ⌜very⌟ part match with case insensitivity, while still keeping the tag names case-sensitive. This matches '<B>VERY</B>' and '<B>Very</B>', for example, but not 'Very'.

This example works with most systems that support ⌜(?i)⌟, including Perl, `java.util.regex`, Ruby, and the .NET languages. But, some systems have different semantics. With Python, for example, the appearance of ⌜(?i)⌟ anywhere in the regex turns on case-insensitive matching for the entire regex, and Python doesn't support turning it off with ⌜(?-i)⌟. Tcl's case-insensitive matching is also all-or-nothing, but Tcl requires the ⌜(?i)⌟ to be at the beginning of the regex—anywhere else is an error. Ruby has a bug whereby sometimes ⌜(?i)⌟ doesn't apply to ⌜|⌟-separated alternatives that are lowercase (but does if they're uppercase). PHP has the special case that if ⌜(?i)⌟ is used outside of all parentheses, it applies to the entire regex. So, in PHP, we'd have to write our example with an extra set of "constraining" parentheses: ⌜<B>(?:(?i)very(?-i))</B>⌟.

Actually, that last PHP example can be simplified a bit because with many implementations (including PHP's), when ⌜(?i)⌟ is used within any type of parentheses, its effects are limited by the parentheses (i.e., turn off at the closing parentheses). So, the ⌜(?-i)⌟ can simply be eliminated: ⌜<B>(?:(?i)very)</B>⌟.

The mode-modifier constructs support more than just 'i'. With most systems, you can use at least those shown in Table 3-13.

Table 3-13: Common Mode Modifiers

Letter	Mode
i	case-insensitivity match mode (☞109)
x	free-spacing and comments regex mode (☞110)
s	dot-matches-all match mode (☞110)
m	enhanced line-anchor match mode (☞111)

Some systems have additional letters for additional functions. Tcl has a number of different letters for turning its various modes on and off — see its documentation for the complete list.

Mode-modified span: (?modifier: ⋯), such as (?i: ⋯)

The example from the previous section can be made even simpler for systems that support a mode-modified span. Using a syntax like ⌈(?i: ⋯)⌉, a mode-modified span turns on the mode only for what's matched within the parentheses. Using this, the ⌈<B>(?:(?i)very)</B>⌉ example is simplified to ⌈<B>(?i:very)</B>⌉.

When supported, this form generally works for all mode-modifier letters the system supports. Tcl and Python are two examples that support the ⌈(?i)⌉ form, but not the mode-modified span ⌈(?i: ⋯)⌉ form.

Comments: (?# ⋯) and # ⋯

Some flavors support comments via ⌈(?# ⋯)⌉. In practice, this is rarely used, in favor of the free-spacing and comments regex mode (☞110). However, this type of comment is particularly useful in languages for which it's difficult to get a newline into a string literal, such as VB.NET (☞99, 414).

Literal-text span: \Q ⋯ \E

First introduced with Perl, the special sequence \Q ⋯ \E turns off all regex metacharacters between them, except for \E itself. (If the \E is omitted, they are turned off until the end of the regex.) It allows what would otherwise be taken as normal metacharacters to be treated as literal text. This is especially useful when including the contents of a variable while building a regular expression.

For example, to respond to a web search, you might accept what the user types as $query, and search for it with m/$query/i. As it is, this would certainly have unexpected results if $query were to contain, say, 'C:\WINDOWS\', which results in a run-time error because the search term contains something that isn't a valid regular expression (the trailing lone backslash). To get around this, you could use `m/\Q$query\E/i`, which effectively turns 'C:\WINDOWS\' into 'C:\\WINDOWS\\', resulting in a search that finds 'C:\WINDOWS\' as the user expects.

This kind of feature is less useful in systems with procedural and object-oriented handling (☞ 95), as they accept normal strings. While building the string to be used as a regular expression, it's fairly easy to call a function to make the value from the variable "safe" for use in a regular expression. In VB, for example, one would use the `Regex.Escape` method.

Currently, the only regex engine I know of that fully supports ⌈`\Q`⋯`\E`⌋ is Sun's `java.util.regex` engine. Considering that I just mentioned that this was introduced with Perl (and I gave an example in Perl), you might wonder why I don't include Perl in that statement. Perl supports `\Q`⋯`\E` within regex *literals* (regular expressions typed directly in the program), but not within the contents of variables that might be interpolated into them. See Chapter 7 (☞ 290) for details.

Grouping, Capturing, Conditionals, and Control

Capturing/Grouping Parentheses: (⋯) and \1, \2, ...

Common, unadorned parentheses generally perform two functions, grouping and capturing. Common parentheses are almost always of the form ⌈`(`⋯`)`⌋, but a few flavors use ⌈`\(`⋯`\)`⌋. These include GNU Emacs, sed, *vi*, and *grep*.

Capturing parentheses are numbered by counting their opening parentheses from the left, as shown in figures on pages 41, 43, and 57. If *backreferences* are available, the text matched via an enclosed subexpression can itself be matched later in the same regular expression with ⌈`\1`⌋, ⌈`\2`⌋, etc.

One of the most common uses of parentheses is to pluck data from a string. The text matched by a parenthesized subexpression (also called "the text matched by the parentheses") is made available after the match in different ways by different programs, such as Perl's `$1`, `$2`, etc. (A common mistake is to try to use the ⌈`\1`⌋ syntax *outside* the regular expression; something allowed only with sed and *vi*.)

Table 3-14 on the next page shows how a number of programs make the captured text available after a match. It shows how to access the text matched by the whole expression, and the text matched by a set of capturing parentheses.

Table 3-14: A Few Utilities and Their Access to Captured Text

Program		Entire match	First set of parentheses
GNU *egrep*		N/A	N/A
GNU Emacs		(match-string 0)	(match-string 1)
GNU awk		substr(*$text*, RSTART, RLENGTH)	N/A
MySQL		N/A	N/A
Perl	☞ 41	$&	$1
PHP		*$Matches*[0]	*$Matches*[1]
Python	☞ 97	*MatchObj*.group(0)	*MatchObj*.group(1)
Ruby		$&	$1
GNU sed		\& (in replacement only)	\1 (in replacement only)
Java	☞ 95	*MatcherObj*.group()	*MatcherObj*.group(1)
Tcl		set to user-selected variables via regexp command	
VB.NET	☞ 96	*MatchObj*.Groups(0)	*MatchObj*.Groups(1)
C#		*MatchObj*.Groups[0]	*MatchObj*.Groups[1]
vi		&	\1
		(See page 91 for version information.)	

Grouping-only parentheses: (?: ···)

Now supported by many common flavors, grouping-only parentheses ⌈(?:···)⌋ don't capture, but just group regex components for alternation and the application of quantifiers. Grouping-only parentheses are not counted as part of $1, $2, etc. After a successful match of ⌈(1|one)(?:and|or)(2|two)⌋, for example, $1 contains '1' or 'one', while $2 contains '2' or 'two'. Grouping-only parentheses are also called *non-capturing* parentheses.

Non-capturing parentheses are useful for a number of reasons. They can help make the use of a complex regex more clear in that the reader doesn't need to wonder if what's matched by what they group is accessed elsewhere by $1 or the like. They can also be more efficient — if the regex engine doesn't need to keep track of the text matched for capturing purposes, it can work faster and use less memory. (Efficiency is covered in detail in Chapter 6.)

Non-capturing parentheses are useful when building up a regex from parts. Recall the example from page 76, where the variable $HostnameRegex holds a regex to match a hostname. Imagine now using that to pluck out the whitespace around a hostname, as in the Perl snippet **m/**(\s*)$HostnameRegex(\s*)**/**. After this, you might expect $1 to hold any leading whitespace, and $2 to hold trailing white-space, but that's not the case: the trailing whitespace is actually in $4 because the definition of $HostnameRegex uses two sets of *capturing* parentheses:

```
$HostnameRegex = qr/[-a-z0-9]+(\.[-a-z0-9]+)*\.(com|edu|info)/i;
```

Were those sets of parentheses non-capturing instead, $HostnameRegex could be used without generating this surprise:

```
$HostnameRegex = qr/[-a-z0-9]+(?:\.[-a-z0-9]+)*\.(?:com|edu|info)/i;
```

Another way to avoid the surprise, although not available in Perl, is to use named capture, discussed next.

Named capture: (?<Name>···)

Python and .NET languages support captures to named locations. Python uses the syntax ⌜(?P<*name*>···)⌟, while the .NET languages offer a syntax that I prefer, ⌜(?<*name*>···)⌟. Here's an example:

⌜\b(?<**Area**>\d\d\d\)-(?<**Exch**>\d\d\d)-(?<**Num**>\d\d\d\d)\b⌟

This "fills the names" *Area, Exch,* and *Num* with the components of a phone number. The program can then refer to each matched substring through its name, for example, *RegexObj*.Groups("Area") in VB.NET and most other .NET languages, *RegexObj*.Groups["Area"] in C#, and *RegexObj*.group("Area") in Python. The result is clearer code.

Within the regular expression itself, the captured text is available via ⌜\k<Month>⌟ with .NET, and ⌜(?P=Month)⌟ in Python.

You can use the same name more than once within the same expression. For example, to match an area code that looks like '(###)' as well as '###-', you might use ⌜···(?:\((?<Area>\d\d\d)\)|(?<Area>\d\d\d)-)···⌟. When either matches, the three-digit code is saved to the name *Area.*

Atomic grouping: (?>···)

Atomic grouping, ⌜(?>···)⌟, will be very easy to explain once the important details of how the regex engine carries out its work is understood (☞ 169). Here, I'll just say that once the parenthesized subexpression matches, what it matches is fixed (becomes atomic, unchangeable) for the rest of the match, unless it turns out that the whole set of atomic parentheses needs to be abandoned or revisited. A simple example helps to illustrate this indivisible, "atomic" nature of text matched by these parentheses.

The regex ⌜¡.*!⌟ matches '¡Hola!', but that string is *not* matched if the ⌜.*⌟ is wrapped with atomic grouping, ⌜¡(?>.*)!⌟. In either case, the ⌜.*⌟ first internally matches as much as it can ('¡<u>Hola!</u>'), but in the first case, the ending ⌜!⌟ forces the

⌜.*⌟ to give up some of what it had matched (the final '!') to complete the overall match. In the second case, the ⌜.*⌟ is inside atomic grouping (which never "give up" anything once the matching leaves them), so nothing is left for the final ⌜!⌟, and it can never match.

This example gives no hint to the usefulness of atomic grouping, but atomic grouping has important uses. In particular, they can help make matching more efficient (☞ 171), and can be used to finely control what can and can't be matched (☞ 269).

Alternation: ⋯ | ⋯ | ⋯

Alternation allows several subexpressions to be tested at a given point. Each subexpression is called an *alternative*. The ⌜|⌟ symbol is called various things, but *or* and *bar* seem popular. Some flavors use ⌜\|⌟ instead.

Alternation is a high-level construct (one that has very low precedence) in almost all regex flavors. This means that ⌜this and|or that⌟ has the same meaning as ⌜(this and)|(or that)⌟, and not ⌜this (and|or) that⌟, even though visually, the and|or looks like a unit.

Most flavors allow an empty alternative, like with ⌜(this|that|)⌟. The empty subexpression means to always match, so this example is logically comparable to ⌜(this|that)?⌟.[†] The POSIX standard disallows an empty alternative, as does *lex* and most versions of awk. I think it's useful for its notational convenience or clarity. As Larry Wall explained to me once, "It's like having a zero in your numbering system."

Conditional: (?if then | else)

This construct allows you to express an if/then/else within a regex. The *if* part is a special kind of conditional expression discussed in a moment. Both the *then* and *else* parts are normal regex subexpressions. If the *if* part tests true, the *then* expression is attempted. Otherwise, the *else* part is attempted. (The *else* part my be omitted, and if so, the '|' before it may be omitted as well.)

The kinds of *if* tests available are flavor-dependent, but most implementations allow at least special references to capturing subexpressions and lookaround.

[†] Actually, to be pedantic, ⌜(this|that|)⌟ is logically comparable to ⌜((?:this|that)?)⌟. With either of these, the subexpression within the capturing parentheses is always able to match (although it may match nothingness, but that's the whole point of the empty alternative or the question mark quantifier). On the other hand, with ⌜(this|that)?⌟, it may be that the whole set of capturing parentheses does not match. The difference may seem minor, but some languages provide a way to find out if a certain set of capturing parentheses participated in the match, and with ⌜(this|that|)⌟ the answer is always yes, but with ⌜(this|that)?⌟, the answer could be no.

Using a special reference to capturing parentheses as the test. If the *if* part is a number in parentheses, it evaluates to "true" if that numbered set of capturing parentheses has participated in the match to this point. Here's an example that matches an `<IMG>` HTML tag, either alone, or surrounded by `<A>`···`</A>` link tags. It's shown in a free-spacing mode with comments, and the conditional construct (which in this example has no *else* part) is bold:

```
( <A\s+[^>]+> \s* )?    # Match leading <A> tag, if there.
<IMG\s+[^>]+>           # Match <IMG> tag.
(?(1)\s*</A>)           # Match a closing </A>, if we'd matched an <A> before.
```

The `(1)` in ⌜`(?(1)`···`)`⌟ tests whether the first set of capturing parentheses participated in the match. "Participating in the match" is very different from "actually matched some text," as a simple example illustrates...

Consider these two approaches to matching a word optionally wrapped in "< ···>": ⌜`(<)?\w+(?(1)>)`⌟ works, but ⌜`(<?)\w+(?(1)>)`⌟ does not. The only difference between them is the location of the first question mark. In the first (correct) approach, the question mark governs the capturing parentheses, so the parentheses (and all they contain) are optional. In the flawed second approach, the capturing parentheses are not optional — only the ⌜`<`⌟ matched *within* them is, so they "participate in the match" regardless of a '<' being matched or not. This means that the *if* part of ⌜`(?(1)`···`)`⌟ always tests "true."

If named capture (☞ 137) is supported, you can generally use the name in parentheses instead of the number.

Using lookaround as the test. A full lookaround construct, such as ⌜`(?=`···`)`⌟ and ⌜`(?<=`···`)`⌟, can used as the *if* test. If the lookaround matches, it evaluates to "true," and so the *then* part is attempted. Otherwise, the *else* part is attempted. A somewhat contrived example that illustrates this is ⌜`(?`<u>`(?<=NUM:)`</u>`\d+|\w+)`⌟, which attempts ⌜`\d+`⌟ at positions just after ⌜`NUM:`⌟, but attempts ⌜`\w+`⌟ at other positions. The lookbehind conditional is underlined.

Other tests for the conditional. Perl adds an interesting twist to this conditional construct by allowing arbitrary Perl code to be executed as the test. The return value of the code is the test's value, indicating whether the *then* or *else* part should be attempted. This is covered in Chapter 7, on page 327.

Greedy quantifiers: *, +, ?, {num,num}

The quantifiers (star, plus, question mark, and intervals—metacharacters that affect the *quantity* of what they govern) have already been discussed extensively. However, note that in some tools, ⌜`\+`⌟ and ⌜`\?`⌟ are used instead of ⌜`+`⌟ and ⌜`?`⌟. Also, with some older tools, quantifiers can't be applied to a backreference or to a set of parentheses.

Intervals — *{min,max}* or \ *{min,max}* \ *}*

Intervals can be considered a "counting quantifier" because you specify exactly the minimum number of matches you wish to *require*, and the maximum number of matches you wish to *allow*. If only a single number is given (such as in ⌈[a-z]{3}⌋ or ⌈[a-z]\{3\}⌋, depending upon the flavor), it matches exactly that many of the item. This example is the same as ⌈[a-z][a-z][a-z]⌋ (although one may be more or less efficient than the other ☞ 251).

One caution: don't think you can use something like ⌈x{0,0}⌋ to mean "there must not be an x here." ⌈x{0,0}⌋ is a meaningless expression because it means "no *requirement* to match ⌈x⌋, and, in fact, don't even bother trying to match any. Period." It's the same as if the whole ⌈x{0,0}⌋ wasn't there at all — if there is an x present, it could still be matched by something later in the expression, so your intended purpose is defeated.[†] Use negative lookahead for a true "must not be here" construct.

Lazy quantifiers: *∗?, +?, ??, {num,num}?*

Some tools offer the rather ungainly looking *?, +?, ??, and *{min,max}*?. These are the *lazy* versions of the quantifiers. (They are also called *minimal matching, non-greedy,* and *ungreedy*.) Quantifiers are normally "greedy," and try to match as much as possible. Conversely, these non-greedy versions match as little as possible, just the bare minimum needed to satisfy the match. The difference has far-reaching implications, covered in detail in the next chapter (☞ 159).

Possessive quantifiers: *∗+, ++, ?+, {num,num}+*

Currently supported only by `java.util.regex`, but likely to gain popularity, *possessive quantifiers* are like normally greedy quantifiers, but once they match something, they never "give it up." Like the atomic grouping to which they're related, understanding possessive quantifiers is much easier once the underlying match process is understood (which is the subject of the next chapter).

In one sense, possessive quantifiers are just syntactic sugar, as they can be mimicked with atomic grouping. Something like ⌈.++⌋ has exactly the same result as ⌈(?>.+)⌋, although a smart implementation can optimize possessive quantifiers more than atomic grouping (☞ 250).

---

† In theory, what I say about {0,0} is correct. In practice, what actually happens is even worse — it's almost random! In many programs (including GNU awk, GNU grep, and older versions of Perl) it seems that {0,0} means the same as *, while in many others (including most versions of sed that I've seen, and some versions of *grep*) it means the same as ?. Crazy!

Guide to the Advanced Chapters

Now that we're familiar with metacharacters, flavors, syntactic packaging, and the like, it's time to start getting into the nitty-gritty details of the third concern raised at the start of this chapter, the specifics of how a tool's regex engine goes about applying a regex to some text. In Chapter 4, *The Mechanics of Expression Processing*, we see how the implementation of the match engine influences *whether* a match is achieved, *which* text is matched, and *how much time* the whole thing takes. We'll look at all the details. As a byproduct of this knowledge, you'll find it much easier to craft complex expressions with confidence. Chapter 5, *Practical Regex Techniques* helps to solidify that knowledge with extended examples.

That brings us to Chapter 6, *Crafting an Efficient Expression*. Once you know the basics about how an engine works, you can learn techniques to take full advantage of that knowledge. Chapter 6 looks at regex pitfalls that often lead to unwelcome surprises, and turns the tables to put them to use for us.

Chapters 4, 5, and 6 are the central core of this book. These first three chapters merely lead up to them, and the discussions in the tool-specific chapters that follow rely on them. They're not necessarily what you would call "light reading," but I've taken great care to stay away from math, algebra, and all that stuff that's just mumbo-jumbo to most of us. As with any large amount of new information, it likely takes time to sink in and internalize.

4

The Mechanics of Expression Processing

The previous chapter started with an analogy between cars and regular expressions. The bulk of the chapter discussed features, regex flavors, and other "glossy brochure" issues of regular expressions. This chapter continues with that analogy, talking about the all-important regular-expression engine, and how it goes about its work.

Why would you care how it works? As we'll see, there are several types of regex engines, and the type most commonly used—the type used by Perl, Tcl, Python, the .NET languages, Ruby, PHP, all Java packages I've seen, and more—works in such a way that *how* you craft your expression can influence *whether* it can match a particular string, *where* in the string it matches, and *how quickly* it finds the match or reports the failure. If these issues are important to you, this chapter is for you.

Start Your Engines!

Let's see how much I can milk this engine analogy. The whole point of having an engine is so that you can get from Point A to Point B without doing much work. The engine does the work for you so you can relax and enjoy the sound system. The engine's primary task is to turn the wheels, and how it does that isn't really a concern of yours. Or is it?

Two Kinds of Engines

Well, what if you had an electric car? They've been around for a long time, but they aren't as common as gas cars because they're hard to design well. If you had one, though, you would have to remember not to put gas in it. If you had a gasoline engine, well, watch out for sparks! An electric engine more or less just runs, but a gas engine might need some babysitting. You can get much better performance just by changing little things like your spark plug gaps, air filter, or brand of gas. Do it wrong and the engine's performance deteriorates, or, worse yet, it stalls.

Each engine might do its work differently, but the end result is that the wheels turn. You still have to steer properly if you want to get anywhere, but that's an entirely different issue.

New Standards

Let's stoke the fire by adding another variable: the California Emissions Standards.[†] Some engines adhere to California's strict pollution standards, and some engines don't. These aren't really different kinds of engines, just new variations on what's already around. The standard regulates a result of the engine's work, the emissions, but doesn't say anything about how the engine should go about achieving those cleaner results. So, our two classes of engine are divided into four types: electric (adhering and non-adhering) and gasoline (adhering and non-adhering).

Come to think of it, I bet that an electric engine can qualify for the standard without much change—the standard just "blesses" the clean results that are already par for the course. The gas engine, on the other hand, needs some major tweaking and a bit of re-tooling before it can qualify. Owners of this kind of engine need to pay particular care to what they feed it—use the wrong kind of gas and you're in big trouble.

The impact of standards

Better pollution standards are a good thing, but they require that the driver exercise more thought and foresight (well, at least for gas engines). Frankly, however, the standard doesn't impact most people since all the other states still do their own thing and don't follow California's standard.

So, you realize that these four types of engines can be classified into three groups (the two kinds for gas, and electric in general). You know about the differences, and that in the end they all still turn the wheels. What you don't know is what the heck this has to do with regular expressions! More than you might imagine.

---

† California has rather strict standards regulating the amount of pollution a car can produce. Because of this, many cars sold in America come in "California" and "non-California" models.

Regex Engine Types

There are two fundamentally different types of regex engines: one called "DFA" (the electric engine of our story) and one called "NFA" (the gas engine). The details of what NFA and DFA mean follow shortly (☞156), but for now just consider them names, like Bill and Ted. Or electric and gas.

Both engine types have been around for a long time, but like its gasoline counterpart, the NFA type seems to be used more often. Tools that use an NFA engine include the .NET languages, Ruby, Perl, Python, GNU Emacs, *ed*, sed, PHP, *vi*, most versions of *grep*, and even a few versions of *egrep* and awk. On the other hand, a DFA engine is found in almost all versions of *egrep* and awk, as well as *lex* and *flex*. Some systems have a multi-engine hybrid system, using the most appropriate engine for the job (or even one that swaps between engines for different parts of the same regex, as needed to get the best combination of features and speed). Table 4-1 lists a few common programs and the regex engine that most versions use. If your favorite program is not in the list, the section "Testing the Engine Type" on the next page can help you find out which it is.

Table 4-1: Some Tools and Their Regex Engines

Engine type	Programs
DFA	awk (most versions), *egrep* (most versions), flex, lex, MySQL, Procmail
Traditional NFA	GNU Emacs, Java, *grep* (most versions), *less*, *more*, .NET languages, PCRE library, Perl, PHP (pcre routines), Python, Ruby, sed (most versions), *vi*
POSIX NFA	*mawk*, Mortice Kern Systems' utilities, GNU Emacs (when requested)
Hybrid NFA/DFA	GNU awk, GNU *grep/egrep*, Tcl

As Chapter 3 illustrated, 20 years of development with both DFAs and NFAs resulted in a lot of needless variety. Things were dirty. The POSIX standard came in to clean things up by clearly specifying not only which metacharacters and features an engine should support, as mentioned in the previous chapter, but also *exactly the results you could expect from them*. Superficial details aside, the DFAs (our electric engines) were already well suited to adhere to this new standard, but the kind of results an NFA traditionally provided were different, so changes were needed. As a result, broadly speaking, there are three types of regex engines:

- DFA (POSIX or not—similar either way)
- Traditional NFA (most common: Perl, .NET, Java, Python, ...)
- POSIX NFA

Here, we use "POSIX" to refer to the match *semantics*—the expected operation of a regex that the POSIX standard specifies (which we'll get to later in this chapter). Don't confuse this use of "POSIX" with uses surrounding regex *features* introduced in that same standard (☞ 125). Many programs support the features without supporting the full match semantics.

Old (and minimally featured) programs like *egrep*, awk, and *lex* were normally implemented with the electric DFA engine, so the new standard primarily just confirmed the status quo — no big changes. However, there *were* some gas-powered versions of these programs which had to be changed if they wanted to be POSIX-compliant. The gas engines that passed the California Emission Standards tests (POSIX NFA) were fine in that they produced results according to the standard, but the necessary changes only increased how fickle they were to proper tuning. Where before you might get by with slightly misaligned spark plugs, you now have absolutely no tolerance. Gasoline that used to be "good enough" now causes knocks and pings. But, so long as you know how to maintain your baby, the engine runs smoothly and cleanly.

From the Department of Redundancy Department

At this point, I'll ask you to go back and review the story about engines. Every sentence there rings with some truth about regular expressions. A second reading should raise some questions. Particularly, what does it mean that an electric DFA regex engine more or less "just runs?" What affects a gas-powered NFA? How can I tune my regular expressions to run as I want on an NFA? What special concerns does an emissions-controlled POSIX NFA have? What's a "stalled engine" in the regex world?

Testing the Engine Type

Because the type of engine used in a tool influences the type of features it can offer, and how those features appear to work, we can often learn the type of engine a tool has merely by checking to see how it handles a few test expressions. (After all, if you can't tell the difference, the difference doesn't matter.) At this point in the book, I wouldn't expect you to understand why the following test results indicate what they do, but I want to offer these tests now so that if your favorite tool is not listed in Table 4-1, you can investigate before continuing with this and the subsequent chapters.

Traditional NFA or not?

The most commonly used engine is a Traditional NFA, and spotting it is easy. First, are lazy quantifiers (☞ 140) supported? If so, it's almost certainly a Traditional NFA. As we'll see, lazy quantifiers are not possible with a DFA, nor would they make any sense with a POSIX NFA. However, to make sure, simply apply the regex ˹nfa|nfa·not˼ to the string 'nfa·not' — if only 'nfa' matches, it's a Traditional NFA. If the entire 'nfa·not' matches, it's either a POSIX NFA or a DFA.

DFA or POSIX NFA?

Differentiating between a POSIX NFA and a DFA is sometimes just as simple. Capturing parentheses and backreferences are not supported by a DFA, so that can be one hint, but there are systems that are a hybrid mix between the two engine types, and so may end up using a DFA if there are no capturing parentheses.

Here's a simple test that can tell you a lot. Apply ⌈X(.+)+X⌋ to a string like '=XX====================', as with this *egrep* command:

```
echo =XX======================================== | egrep 'X(.+)+X'
```

If it takes a long time to finish, it's an NFA (and if not a Traditional NFA as per the test in the previous section, it must be a POSIX NFA). If it finishes quickly, it's either a DFA or an NFA with some advanced optimization. Does it display a warning message about a stack overflow or long match aborted? If so, it's an NFA.

Match Basics

Before looking at the differences among these engine types, let's first look at their similarities. Certain aspects of the drive train are the same (or for all practical purposes appear to be the same), so these examples can cover all engine types.

About the Examples

This chapter is primarily concerned with a generic, full-function regex engine, so some tools won't support exactly everything presented. In my examples, the dipstick might be to the left of the oil filter, while under your hood it might be behind the distributor cap. Your goal is to understand the concepts so that you can drive and maintain your favorite regex package (and ones you find interest in later).

I'll continue to use Perl's notation for most of the examples, although I'll occasionally show others to remind you that the *notation* is superficial and that the issues under discussion transcend any one tool or flavor. To cut down on wordiness here, I'll rely on you to check Chapter 3 (☞ 113) if I use an unfamiliar construct.

This chapter details the practical effects of how a match is carried out. It would be nice if everything could be distilled down to a few simple rules that could be memorized without needing to understand what is going on. Unfortunately, that's not the case. In fact, with all this chapter offers, I identify only two all-encompassing rules:

1. The match that begins earliest (leftmost) wins.
2. The standard quantifiers (⌈*⌋, ⌈+⌋, ⌈?⌋, and ⌈{m,n}⌋) are greedy.

We'll look at these rules, their effects, and much more throughout this chapter. Let's start by diving into the details of the first rule.

Rule 1: The Match That Begins Earliest Wins

This rule says that any match that begins earlier (leftmost) in the string is always preferred over any plausible match that begins later. This rule doesn't say anything about how long the winning match might be (we'll get into that shortly), merely that among all the matches possible anywhere in the string, the one that begins leftmost in the string is chosen. Actually, since more than one plausible match can start at the same earliest point, perhaps the rule should read "*a* match..." instead of "*the* match...," but that sounds odd.

Here's how the rule comes about: the match is first attempted at the very beginning of the string to be searched (just before the first character). "Attempted" means that every permutation of the entire (perhaps complex) regex is tested starting right at that spot. If all possibilities are exhausted and a match is not found, the complete expression is re-tried starting from just before the second character. This full retry occurs at each position in the string until a match is found. A "no match" result is reported only if no match is found after the full retry has been attempted at each position all the way to the end of the string (just after the last character).

Thus, when trying to match ⌈ORA⌋ against FLORAL, the first attempt at the start of the string fails (since ⌈ORA⌋ can't match FLO). The attempt starting at the second character also fails (it doesn't match LOR either). The attempt starting at the third position, however, does match, so the engine stops and reports the match: FL<u>ORA</u>L.

If you didn't know this rule, results might sometimes surprise you. For example, when matching ⌈cat⌋ against

        The dragging belly indicates your cat is too fat

the match is in indi<u>cat</u>es, not at the word cat that appears later in the line. This word cat *could* match, but the cat in indi**cat**es appears earlier in the string, so it is the one matched. For an application like *egrep*, the distinction is irrelevant because it cares only *whether* there is a match, not *where* the match might be. For other uses, such as with a search-and-replace, the distinction becomes paramount.

Here's a (hopefully simple) quiz: where does ⌈fat|cat|belly|your⌋ match in the string 'The dragging belly indicates your cat is too fat'? ❖ Turn the page to check your answer.

The "transmission" and the bump-along

It might help to think of this rule as the car's transmission, connecting the engine to the drive train while adjusting for the gear you're in. The engine itself does the real work (turning the crank); the transmission transfers this work to the wheels.

The transmission's main work: the bump-along

If the engine can't find a match starting at the beginning of the string, it's the transmission that bumps the regex engine along to attempt a match at the next position in the string, and the next, and the next, and so on. Usually. For instance, if a regex begins with a start-of-string anchor, the transmission can realize that any bump-along would be futile, for only the attempt at the start of the string could possibly be successful. This and other internal optimizations are discussed in Chapter 6.

Engine Pieces and Parts

An engine is made up of parts of various types and sizes. You can't possibly hope to truly understand how the whole thing works if you don't know much about the individual parts. In a regex, these parts are the individual units — literal characters, quantifiers (star and friends), character classes, parentheses, and so on, as described in Chapter 3 (☞ 113). The combination of these parts (and the engine's treatment of them) makes a regex what it is, so looking at ways they can be combined and how they interact is our primary interest. First, let's take a look at some of the individual parts:

Literal text (e.g.,   a   *   !   枝 ...)

> With a literal, non-metacharacter like ⌜z⌟ or ⌜!⌟, the match attempt is simply "Does this literal character match the current text character?" If your regex is only literal text, such as ⌜usa⌟, it is treated as "⌜u⌟ and then ⌜s⌟ and then ⌜a⌟." It's a bit more complicated if you have the engine do a case-insensitive match, where ⌜b⌟ matches B and vice-versa, but it's still pretty straightforward. (With Unicode, there are a few additional twists ☞ 109.)

Character classes, dot, Unicode properties, and the like

> Matching dot, character classes, Unicode properties, and the like (☞ 117) is usually a simple matter: regardless of the length of the character class, it still matches just one character.[†]

> Dot is just a shorthand for a large character class that matches almost any character (☞ 110), so its actions are simple, as are the other shorthand conveniences such as ⌜\w⌟, ⌜\W⌟, and ⌜\d⌟.

Capturing parentheses

> Parentheses used only for capturing text (as opposed to those used for grouping) don't change how the match is carried out.

[†] Actually, as we saw in the previous chapter (☞ 126), a POSIX collating sequence *can* match multiple characters, but this is not common. Also, certain Unicode characters can match multiple characters when applied in a case-insensitive manner (☞ 109), although most implementations do not support this.

Quiz Answer

❖ *Answer to the question on page 148.*

Remember, the regex is tried *completely* each time, so ⌈fat|cat|belly|your⌉ matches 'The dragging `belly` indicates your cat is too fat' rather than fat, even though ⌈fat⌉ is listed first among the alternatives.

Sure, the regex could conceivably match fat and the other alternatives, but since they are not the *earliest* possible match (the match starting furthest to the left), they are not the one chosen. The entire regex is attempted completely from one spot before moving along the string to try again from the next spot, and in this case that means trying each alternative ⌈fat⌉, ⌈cat⌉, ⌈belly⌉, and ⌈your⌉ at each position before moving on.

Anchors (e.g., ⌈^⌉ ⌈\Z⌉ ⌈(?<=\d)⌉ ...)

There are two basic types of anchors: simple ones (^, $, \G, \b, ... ☞ 127) and complex ones (lookahead and lookbehind ☞ 132). The simple ones are indeed simple in that they test either the quality of a particular location in the target string (^, \z, ...), or compare two adjacent characters (\<, \b, ...). On the other hand, the lookaround constructs can contain arbitrary sub-expressions, and so can be arbitrarily complex.

No "electric" parentheses, backreferences, or lazy quantifiers

I'd like to concentrate here on the similarities among the engines, but as foreshadowing of what's to come in this chapter, I'll point out a few interesting differences. Capturing parentheses (and the associated backreferences and $1 type functionality) are like a gas additive — they affect a gasoline (NFA) engine, but are irrelevant to an electric (DFA) engine. The same thing applies to lazy quantifiers. The way a DFA engine works completely precludes these concepts.[†] This explains why tools developed with DFAs don't provide these features. You'll notice that awk, *lex*, and *egrep* don't have backreferences or any $1 type functionality.

You might, however, notice that GNU's version of *egrep* **does** support backreferences. It does so by having two complete engines under the hood! It first uses a DFA engine to see whether a match is likely, and then uses an NFA engine (which supports the full flavor, including backreferences) to confirm the match. Later in this chapter, we'll see why a DFA engine can't deal with backreferences or capturing, and why anyone ever would want to use such an engine at all. (It has some major advantages, such as being able to match very quickly.)

[†] This does not mean that there can't be some mixing of technologies to try to get the best of both worlds. This is discussed in a sidebar on page 183.

Rule 2: The Standard Quantifiers Are Greedy

So far, we have seen features that are quite straightforward. They are also rather boring—you can't *do* much without involving more-powerful metacharacters such as star, plus, alternation, and so on. Their added power requires more information to understand them fully.

First, you need to know that the standard quantifiers (?, *, +, and {*min*,*max*}) are *greedy*. When one of these governs a subexpression, such as ⌈a⌋ in ⌈a?⌋, the ⌈(*expr*)⌋ in ⌈(*expr*)*⌋, or ⌈[0-9]⌋ in ⌈[0-9]+⌋, there is a minimum number of matches that are required before it can be considered successful, and a maximum number that it will ever attempt to match. This has been mentioned in earlier chapters—what's new here concerns the rule that they always attempt to match as much as possible. (Some flavors provide other types of quantifiers, but this section is concerned only with the standard, greedy ones.)

To be clear, the standard quantifiers settle for something less than the maximum number of allowed matches *if they have to*, but they always attempt to match as many times as they can, up to that maximum allowed. The only time they settle for anything less than their maximum allowed is when matching too much ends up causing some later part of the regex to fail. A simple example is using ⌈\b\w+s\b⌋ to match words ending with an 's', such as 'regexes'. The ⌈\w+⌋ alone is happy to match the entire word, but if it does, it leaves nothing for the ⌈s⌋ to match. To achieve the overall match, the ⌈\w+⌋ must settle for matching only 'regexe<u>s</u>', thereby allowing ⌈s\b⌋ (and thus the full regex) to match.

If it turns out that the only way the rest of the regex can succeed is when the greedy construct in question matches nothing, well, that's perfectly fine, if zero matches are allowed (as with star, question, and {0,*max*} intervals). However, it turns out this way only if the requirements of some later subexpression force the issue. It's because the greedy quantifiers always (or, at least, try to) take more than they minimally need that they are called greedy.

Greediness has many useful (but sometimes troublesome) implications. It explains, for example, why ⌈[0-9]+⌋ matches the full number in March 1998. Once the '1' has been matched, the plus has fulfilled its minimum requirement, but it's greedy, so it doesn't stop. So, it continues, and matches the '998' before being forced to stop by the end of the string. (Since ⌈[0-9]⌋ can't match the nothingness at the end of the string, the plus finally stops.)

A subjective example

Of course, this method of grabbing things is useful for more than just numbers. Let's say you have a line from an email header and want to check whether it is the subject line. As we saw in earlier chapters (☞ 55), you simply use ⌈^Subject:⌋.

However, if you use ⌈^Subject:•(.*)⌉, you can later access the text of the subject itself via the tool's after-the-fact parenthesis memory (for example, $1 in Perl).†

Before looking at why ⌈.*⌉ matches the entire subject, be sure to understand that once the ⌈^Subject:•⌉ part matches, you're guaranteed that the entire regular expression will eventually match. You know this because there's nothing after ⌈^Subject:•⌉ that could cause the expression to fail; ⌈.*⌉ can *never* fail, since the worst case of "no matches" is still considered successful for star.

So, why do we even bother adding ⌈.*⌉? Well, we know that because star is greedy, it attempts to match dot as many times as possible, so we use it to "fill" $1. In fact, the parentheses add nothing to the logic of what the regular expression matches—in this case we use them simply to capture the text matched by ⌈.*⌉.

Once ⌈.*⌉ hits the end of the string, the dot isn't able to match, so the star finally stops and lets the next item in the regular expression attempt to match (for even though the starred dot could match no further, perhaps a subexpression later in the regex could). Ah, but since it turns out that there is no next item, we reach the end of the regex and we know that we have a successful match.

Being too greedy

Let's get back to the concept of a greedy quantifier being as greedy as it can be. Consider how the matching and results would change if we add another ⌈.*⌉: ⌈^Subject:•(.*).*⌉. The answer is: nothing would change. The initial ⌈.*⌉ (inside the parentheses) is so greedy that it matches all the subject text, never leaving anything for the second ⌈.*⌉ to match. Again, the failure of the second ⌈.*⌉ to match something is not a problem, since the star does not require a match to be successful. Were the second ⌈.*⌉ in parentheses as well, the resulting $2 would always be empty.

Does this mean that after ⌈.*⌉, a regular expression can never have anything that is expected to actually match? No, of course not. As we saw with the ⌈\w+s⌉ example, it is possible for something later in the regex to *force* something previously greedy to give back (that is, relinquish or conceptually "unmatch") if that's what is necessary to achieve an overall match.

Let's consider the possibly useful ⌈^.*([0-9][0-9])⌉, which finds the *last* two digits on a line, wherever they might be, and saves them to $1. Here's how it works: at first, ⌈.*⌉ matches the entire line. Because the following ⌈([0-9][0-9])⌉ is *required*, its initial failure to match at the end of the line, in effect, tells ⌈.*⌉ "Hey, you took too much! Give me back something so that I can have a chance to

---

† This example uses capturing as a forum for presenting greediness, so the example itself is appropriate only for NFAs (because only NFAs support capturing). The lessons on greediness, however, apply to all engines, including the non-capturing DFA.

match." Greedy components first try to take as much as they can, but they always defer to the greater need to achieve an overall match. They're just stubborn about it, and only do so when forced. Of course, they'll never give up something that hadn't been optional in the first place, such as a plus quantifier's first match.

With this in mind, let's apply ⌜^.*([0-9][0-9])⌟ to 'about•24•characters•long'. Once ⌜.*⌟ matches the whole string, the requirement for the first ⌜[0-9]⌟ to match forces ⌜.*⌟ to give up 'g' (the last thing it had matched). That doesn't, however, allow ⌜[0-9]⌟ to match, so ⌜.*⌟ is again forced to relinquish something, this time the 'n'. This cycle continues 15 more times until ⌜.*⌟ finally gets around to giving up '4'.

Unfortunately, even though the first ⌜[0-9]⌟ can then match that '4', the second still cannot. So, ⌜.*⌟ is forced to relinquish once more in an attempt fo find an overall match. This time ⌜.*⌟ gives up the '2', which the first ⌜[0-9]⌟ can then match. Now, the '4' is free for the second ⌜[0-9]⌟ to match, and so the entire expression matches 'about•24•char···', with $1 getting '24'.

First come, first served

Consider now using ⌜^.*([0-9]+)⌟, ostensibly to match not just the last two digits, but the last whole number, however long it might be. When this regex is applied to 'Copyright 2003.', what is captured? ❖ Turn the page to check your answer.

Getting down to the details

I should clear up a few things here. Phrases like "the ⌜.*⌟ *gives up...*" and "the ⌜[0-9]⌟ *forces...*" are slightly misleading. I used these terms because they're easy to grasp, and the end result appears to be the same as reality. However, what really happens behind the scenes depends on the basic engine type, DFA or NFA. So, it's time to see what these really are.

Regex-Directed Versus Text-Directed

The two basic engine types reflect a fundamental difference in algorithms available for applying a regular expression to a string. I call the gasoline-driven NFA engine "regex-directed," and the electric-driven DFA "text-directed."

NFA Engine: Regex-Directed

Let's consider one way an engine might match ⌜to(nite|knight|night)⌟ against the text '···tonight···'. Starting with the ⌜t⌟, the regular expression is examined one component at a time, and the "current text" is checked to see whether it is matched by the current component of the regex. If it does, the next component is checked, and so on, until all components have matched, indicating that an overall match has been achieved.

Quiz Answer

❖ *Answer to the question on page 153.*

When ⌜^.*([0-9]+)⌝ is applied to '`Copyright 2003.`', what is captured by the parentheses?

The desire is to get the last whole number, but it doesn't work. As before, ⌜.*⌝ is forced to relinquish some of what it had matched because the subsequent ⌜[0-9]+⌝ requires a match to be successful. In this example, that means unmatching the final period and '3', which then allows ⌜[0-9]⌝ to match. That's governed by ⌜+⌝, so matching just once fulfills its minimum, and now facing '.' in the string, it finds nothing else to match.

Unlike before, though, there's then nothing further that *must* match, so ⌜.*⌝ is not forced to give up the 0 or any other digits it might have matched. Were ⌜.*⌝ to do so, the ⌜[0-9]+⌝ would certainly be a grateful and greedy recipient, but nope, first come first served. Greedy constructs give up something they've matched only when forced. In the end, $1 gets only '3'.

If this feels counter-intuitive, realize that ⌜[0-9]+⌝ is at most one match away from ⌜[0-9]*⌝, which is in the same league as ⌜.*⌝. Substituting that into ⌜^.*([0-9]+)⌝, we get ⌜^.*(.*)⌝ as our regex, which looks suspiciously like the ⌜^Subject: (.*).*⌝ example from page 152, where the second ⌜.*⌝ was guaranteed to match nothing.

With the ⌜to(nite|knight|night)⌝ example, the first component is ⌜t⌝, which repeatedly fails until a 't' is reached in the target string. Once that happens, the ⌜o⌝ is checked against the next character, and if it matches, control moves to the next component. In this case, the "next component" is ⌜(nite|knight|night)⌝ which really means "⌜nite⌝ or ⌜knight⌝ or ⌜night⌝." Faced with three possibilities, the engine just tries each in turn. We (humans with advanced neural nets between our ears) can see that if we're matching `tonight`, the third alternative is the one that leads to a match. Despite their brainy origins (☞ 85), a regex-directed engine can't come to that conclusion until actually going through the motions to check.

Attempting the first alternative, ⌜nite⌝, involves the same component-at-a-time treatment as before: "Try to match ⌜n⌝, then ⌜i⌝, then ⌜t⌝, and finally ⌜e⌝." If this fails, as it eventually does, the engine tries another alternative, and so on until it achieves a match or must report failure. Control moves within the regex from component to component, so I call it "regex-directed."

The control benefits of an NFA engine

In essence, each subexpression of a regex in a regex-directed match is checked independently of the others. Other than backreferences, there's no interrelation among subexpressions, except for the relation implied by virtue of being thrown together to make a larger expression. The layout of the subexpressions and regex control structures (e.g., alternation, parentheses, and quantifiers) controls an engine's overall movement through a match.

Since the regex directs the NFA engine, the driver (the writer of the regular expression) has considerable opportunity to craft just what he or she wants to happen. (Chapters 5 and 6 show how to put this to use to get a job done correctly and efficiently.) What this really means may seem vague now, but it will all be spelled out soon.

DFA Engine: Text-Directed

Contrast the regex-directed NFA engine with an engine that, while scanning the string, keeps track of all matches "currently in the works." In the `tonight` example, the moment the engine hits `t`, it adds a potential match to its list of those currently in progress:

in string	in regex
after ··t͟onight···	possible matches: ⌜t͟o(nite|knight|night)⌟

Each subsequent character scanned updates the list of possible matches. After a few more characters are matched, the situation becomes

in string	in regex
after ··tonight···	possible matches: ⌜to(ni͟te|knight|nig͟ht)⌟

with two possible matches in the works (and one alternative, `knight`, ruled out). With the `g` that follows, only the third alternative remains viable. Once the `h` and `t` are scanned as well, the engine realizes it has a complete match and can return success.

I call this "text-directed" matching because each character scanned from the text controls the engine. As in the example, a partial match might be the start of any number of different, yet possible, matches. Matches that are no longer viable are pruned as subsequent characters are scanned. There are even situations where a "partial match in progress" is also a full match. If the regex were ⌜to(···)?⌟, for example, the parenthesized expression becomes optional, but it's still greedy, so it's always attempted. All the time that a partial match is in progress inside those parentheses, a full match (of 'to') is already confirmed and in reserve in case the longer matches don't pan out.

If the engine reaches a character in the text that invalidates all the matches in the works, it must revert to one of the full matches in reserve. If there are none, it must declare that there are no matches at the current attempt's starting point.

First Thoughts: NFA and DFA in Comparison

If you compare these two engines based only on what I've mentioned so far, you might conclude that the text-directed DFA engine is generally faster. The regex-directed NFA engine might waste time attempting to match different subexpressions against the same text (such as the three alternatives in the example).

You would be right. During the course of an NFA match, the same character of the target might be checked by many different parts of the regex (or even by the same part, over and over). Even if a subexpression can match, it might have to be applied again (and again and again) as it works in concert with the rest of the regex to find a match. A local subexpression can fail or match, but you just never know about the overall match until you eventually work your way to the end of the regex. (If I could find a way to include "It's not over until the fat lady sings." in this paragraph, I would.) On the other hand, a DFA engine is *deterministic*—each character in the target is checked once (at most). When a character matches, you don't know yet if it will be part of the final match (it could be part of a possible match that doesn't pan out), but since the engine keeps track of all possible matches in parallel, it needs to be checked only once, period.

The two basic technologies behind regular-expression engines have the somewhat imposing names *Nondeterministic Finite Automaton* (NFA) and *Deterministic Finite Automaton* (DFA). With mouthfuls like this, you see why I stick to just "NFA" and "DFA." We won't be seeing these phrases spelled out again.[†]

Consequences to us as users

Because of the regex-directed nature of an NFA, the details of how the engine attempts a match are very important. As I said before, the writer can exercise a fair amount of control simply by changing how the regex is written. With the `tonight` example, perhaps less work would have been wasted had the regex been written differently, such as in one of the following ways:

- ⌈`to(ni(ght|te)|knight)`⌋
- ⌈`tonite|toknight|tonight`⌋
- ⌈`to(k?night|nite)`⌋

---

† I suppose I could explain the underlying theory that goes into these names, if I only knew it! As I hinted, the word *deterministic* is pretty important, but for the most part the theory is not relevant, so long as we understand the practical effects. By the end of this chapter, we will.

With any given text, these all end up matching exactly the same thing, but in doing so direct the engine in different ways. At this point, we don't know enough to judge which of these, if any, are better than the others, but that's coming soon.

It's the exact opposite with a DFA — since the engine keeps track of all matches simultaneously, none of these differences in representation matter so long as in the end they all represent the same set of possible matches. There could be a hundred different ways to achieve the same result, but since the DFA keeps track of them all simultaneously (almost magically — more on this later), it doesn't matter which form the regex takes. To a pure DFA, even expressions that appear as different as ⌈abc⌉ and ⌈[aa-a](b|b{1}|b)c⌉ are utterly indistinguishable.

Three things come to my mind when describing a DFA engine:

- DFA matching is very fast.
- DFA matching is very consistent.
- Talking about DFA matching is very boring.

I'll eventually expand on all these points.

The regex-directed nature of an NFA makes it interesting to talk about. NFAs provide plenty of room for creative juices to flow. There are great benefits in crafting an expression well, and even greater penalties for doing it poorly. A gasoline engine is not the only engine that can stall and conk out completely. To get to the bottom of this, we need to look at the essence of an NFA engine: *backtracking*.

Backtracking

The essence of an NFA engine is this: it considers each subexpression or component in turn, and whenever it needs to decide between two equally viable options, it selects one and remembers the other to return to later if need be.

Situations where it has to decide among courses of action include anything with a quantifier (decide whether to try another match), and alternation (decide which alternative to try, and which to leave for later).

Whichever course of action is attempted, if it's successful and the rest of the regex is also successful, the match is finished. If anything in the rest of the regex eventually causes failure, the regex engine knows it can *backtrack* to where it chose the first option, and can continue with the match by trying the other option. This way, it eventually tries all possible permutations of the regex (or at least as many as needed until a match is found).

A Really Crummy Analogy

Backtracking is like leaving a pile of bread crumbs at every fork in the road. If the path you choose turns out to be a dead end, you can retrace your steps, giving up ground until you come across a pile of crumbs that indicates an untried path. Should that path, too, turn out to be a dead end, you can backtrack further, retracing your steps to the next pile of crumbs, and so on, until you eventually find a path that leads to your goal, or until you run out of untried paths.

There are various situations when the regex engine needs to choose between two (or more) options — the alternation we saw earlier is only one example. Another example is that upon reaching ⌜···x?···⌟, the engine must decide whether it should attempt ⌜x⌟. Upon reaching ⌜···x+···⌟, however, there is no question about trying to match ⌜x⌟ at least once — the plus requires at least one match, and that's non-negotiable. Once the first ⌜x⌟ has been matched, though, the *requirement* is lifted and it then must decide to match another ⌜x⌟. If it decides to match, it must decide if it will then attempt to match yet another... and another... and so on. At each of these many decision points, a virtual "pile of crumbs" is left behind as a reminder that another option (to match or not to match, whichever wasn't chosen at each point) remains viable at that point.

A crummy little example

Let's look at a full example using our earlier ⌜to(nite|knight|night)⌟ regex on the string 'hot•tonic•tonight!' (silly, yes, but a good example). The first component, ⌜t⌟, is attempted at the start of the string. It fails to match h, so the entire regex fails at that point. The engine's transmission then bumps along to retry the regex from the second position (which also fails), and again at the third. This time the ⌜t⌟ matches, but the subsequent ⌜o⌟ fails to match because the text we're at is now a space. So, again, the whole attempt fails.

The attempt that eventually starts at ···tonic··· is more interesting. Once the to has been matched, the three alternatives become three available options. The regex engine picks one to try, remembering the others ("leaving some bread crumbs") in case the first fails. For the purposes of discussion, let's say that the engine first chooses ⌜nite⌟. That expression breaks down to "⌜n⌟ + ⌜i⌟ + ⌜t⌟ ...," which gets to ···tonic··· before failing. Unlike the earlier failures, this failure doesn't mean the end of the overall attempt because other options — the as-of-yet untried alternatives — still remain. (In our analogy, we still have piles of breadcrumbs we can return to.) The engine chooses one, we'll say ⌜knight⌟, but it fails right away because ⌜k⌟ doesn't match 'n'. That leaves one final option, ⌜night⌟, but it too eventually fails. Since that was the final untried option, its failure means the failure of the entire attempt starting at ···tonic···, so the transmission kicks in again.

Once the engine works its way to attempt the match starting at ·· ‚tonight!, it gets interesting again. This time, the [night] alternative successfully matches to the end (which means an overall match, so the engine can report success at that point).

Two Important Points on Backtracking

The general idea of how backtracking works is fairly simple, but some of the details are quite important for real-world use. Specifically, when faced with multiple choices, which choice should be tried first? Secondly, when forced to backtrack, which saved choice should the engine use? The answer to that first question is this important principle:

> In situations where the decision is between "make an attempt" and "skip an attempt," as with items governed by quantifiers, the engine always chooses to first *make* the attempt for *greedy* quantifiers, and to first *skip* the attempt for *lazy* (non-greedy) ones.

This has far-reaching repercussions. For starters, it helps explain why the greedy quantifiers are greedy, but it doesn't explain it completely. To complete the picture, we need to know which (among possibly many) saved options to use when we backtrack. Simply put:

> The most recently saved option is the one returned to when a local failure forces backtracking. They're used LIFO (last in first out).

This is easily understood in the crummy analogy — if your path becomes blocked, you simply retrace your steps until you come back across a pile of bread crumbs. The first you'll return to is the one most recently laid. The traditional analogy for describing LIFO also holds: like stacking and unstacking dishes, the most-recently stacked will be the first unstacked.

Saved States

In NFA regular expression nomenclature, the piles of bread crumbs are known as saved *states*. A state indicates where matching can restart from, if need be. It reflects both the position in the regex and the point in the string where an untried option begins. Because this is the basis for NFA matching, let me show the implications of what I've already said with some simple but verbose examples. If you're comfortable with the discussion so far, feel free to skip ahead.

A match without backtracking

Let's look a simple example, matching ⌈ab?c⌉ against abc. Once the ⌈a⌉ has matched, the *current state* of the match is reflected by:

| at 'a͜bc' | matching ⌈a͜b?c⌉ |

However, now that ⌈b?⌉ is up to match, the regex engine has a decision to make: should it attempt the ⌈b⌉, or skip it?. Well, since ? is greedy, it attempts the match. But, so that it can recover if that attempt fails or eventually leads to failure, it adds

| at 'a͜bc' | matching ⌈ab?͜c⌉ |

to its otherwise empty list of saved states. This indicates that the engine can later pick up the match in the regex just *after* the ⌈b?⌉, picking up in the text from just before the b (that is, where it is now). Thus, in effect, skipping the ⌈b⌉ as the question mark allows.

Once the engine carefully places that pile of crumbs, it goes ahead and checks the ⌈b⌉. With the example text, it matches, so the new current state becomes:

| at 'ab͜c' | matching ⌈ab?͜c⌉ |

The final ⌈c⌉ matches as well, so we have an overall match. The one saved state is no longer needed, so it is simply forgotten.

A match after backtracking

Now, if 'ac' had been the text to match, everything would have been the same until the ⌈b⌉ attempt was made. Of course, this time it wouldn't match. This means that the path that resulted from actually attempting the ⌈···?⌉ failed. Since there is a saved state available to return to, this "local failure" does not mean overall failure. The engine backtracks, meaning that it takes the most recently saved state as its new current state. In this case, that would be the

| at 'a͜c' | matching ⌈ab?͜c⌉ |

state that had been saved as the untried option before the ⌈b⌉ had been attempted. This time, the ⌈c⌉ and c match up, so the overall match is achieved.

A non-match

Now let's look at the same expression, but against 'abX'. Before the ⌈b⌉ is attempted, the question mark causes this state to be saved:

| at 'a͜bX' | matching ⌈ab?͜c⌉ |

The ⌜b⌟ matches, but that avenue later turns out to be a dead end because the ⌜c⌟ fails to match X. The failure results in a backtrack to the saved state. The engine next tests ⌜c⌟ against the b that the backtrack effectively "unmatched." Obviously, this test fails, too. If there were other saved states, another backtrack would occur, but since there aren't any, the overall match at the current starting position is deemed a failure.

Are we done? Nope. The engine's transmission still does its "bump along the string and retry the regex," which might be thought of as a pseudo-backtrack. The match restarts at:

at 'a͟bX'	matching ⌜ab?c⌟

The whole match is attempted again from the new spot, and like before, all paths lead to failure. After the next two attempts (from ab͟X and abX͟) similarly fail, overall failure is finally reported.

A lazy match

Let's look at the original example, but with a lazy quantifier, matching ⌜ab??c⌟ against 'abc'. Once the ⌜a⌟ has matched, the state of the match is reflected by:

at 'a͟bc'	matching ⌜a**b??**c⌟

Now that ⌜b??⌟ is next to be applied, the regex engine has a decision to make: attempt the ⌜b⌟ or skip it? Well, since ?? is lazy, it specifically chooses to first skip the attempt, but, so that it can recover if that attempt fails or eventually leads to failure, it adds

at 'a͟bc'	matching ⌜a͟bc⌟

to its otherwise empty list of saved states. This indicates that the engine can later pick up the match by making the attempt of ⌜b⌟, in the text from just before the b. (We know it will match, but the regex engine doesn't yet know that, or even know if it will ever need to get as far as making the attempt.) Once the state has been saved, it goes ahead and continues from after its skip-the-attempt decision:

at 'a͟bc'	matching ⌜ab??c͟⌟

The ⌜c⌟ fails to match 'b', so indeed the engine must backtrack to its one saved state:

at 'a͟bc'	matching ⌜ab͟c⌟

Of course, it matches this time, and the subsequent ⌜c⌟ matches 'c'. The same final match we got with the greedy ⌜ab?c⌟ is achieved, although via a different path.

Backtracking and Greediness

For tools that use this NFA regex-directed backtracking engine, understanding how backtracking works with your regular expression is the key to writing expressions that accomplish what you want, and accomplish it quickly. We've seen how ⌈?⌋ greediness and ⌈??⌋ laziness works, so now let's look at star and plus.

Star, plus, and their backtracking

If you consider ⌈x*⌋ to be more or less the same as ⌈x?x?x?x?x?x? ···⌋ (or, more appropriately, ⌈(x(x(x(x···?)?)?)?)?⌋,† it's not too different from what we have already seen. Before checking the item quantified by the star, the engine saves a state indicating that if the check fails (or leads to failure), the match can pick up after the star. This is done repeatedly, until an attempt via the star actually does fail.

Thus, when matching ⌈[0-9]+⌋ against 'a·1234·num', once ⌈[0-9]⌋ fails to match the space after the 4, there are four saved states corresponding to locations to which the plus can backtrack:

```
a 1234 num
a 1234 num
a 1234 num
a 1234 num
```

These represent the fact that the attempt of ⌈[0-9]⌋ had been optional at each of these positions. When ⌈[0-9]⌋ fails to match the space, the engine backtracks to the most recently saved state (the last one listed), picking up at 'a·1234·num' in the text and at ⌈[0-9]+⌋ in the regex. Well, that's at the end of the regex. Now that we're actually there and notice it, we realize that we have an overall match.

Note that 'a·1234·num' is not in the list of positions, because the first match using the plus quantifier is required, not optional. Would it have been in the list had the regex been ⌈[0-9]*⌋? *(hint: it's a trick question)* ❖ Turn the page to check your answer.

Revisiting a fuller example

With our more detailed understanding, let's revisit the ⌈^.*([0-9][0-9])⌋ example from page 152. This time, instead of just pointing to "greediness" to explain why the match turns out as it does, we can use our knowledge of NFA mechanics to explain why in precise terms.

I'll use 'CA·95472,·USA' as an example. Once the ⌈.*⌋ has successfully matched to the end of the string, there are a dozen saved states accumulated from the star-

---

† Just for comparison, remember that a DFA doesn't care much about the form you use to express which matches are possible; the three examples *are* identical to a DFA.

governed dot matching 12 things that are (if need be) optional. These states note that the match can pick up in the regex at ⌜^.*ₗ([0-9][0-9])⌟, and in the string at each point where a state was created.

Now that we've reached the end of the string and pass control to the first ⌜[0-9]⌟, the match obviously fails. No problem: we have a saved state to try (a baker's dozen of them, actually). We backtrack, resetting the current state to the one most recently saved, to just before where ⌜.*⌟ matched the final A. Skipping that match (or "unmatching" it, if you like) gives us the opportunity to try that A against the first ⌜[0-9]⌟. But, it fails.

This backtrack-and-test cycle continues until the engine effectively unmatches the 2, at which point the first ⌜[0-9]⌟ can match. The second can't, however, so we must continue to backtrack. It's now irrelevant that the first ⌜[0-9]⌟ matched during the previous attempt; the backtrack resets the current state to before the first ⌜[0-9]⌟. As it turns out, the same backtrack resets the string position to just before the 7, so the first ⌜[0-9]⌟ can match again. This time, so can the second (matching the 2). Thus, we have a match: 'CA·95472,·USA', with $1 getting '72'.

A few observations: first, backtracking entails not only recalculating our position within the regex and the text, but also maintaining the status of the text being matched by the subexpression within parentheses. Each backtrack caused the match to be picked up before the parentheses, at ⌜^.*ₗ([0-9][0-9])⌟. As far as the simple match attempt is concerned, this is the same as ⌜^.*ₗ[0-9][0-9]⌟, so I used phrases such as "picks up before the first ⌜[0-9]⌟." However, moving in and out of the parentheses involves updating the status of what $1 should be, which also has an impact on efficiency.

One final observation that may already be clear to you: something governed by star (or any of the greedy quantifiers) first matches as much as it can *without regard to what might follow in the regex*. In our example, the ⌜.*⌟ does not magically know to stop at the first digit, or the second to the last digit, or any other place until what's governed by the greedy quantifier — the dot — finally fails. We saw this earlier when looking at how ⌜^.*([0-9]+)⌟ would never have more than a single digit matched by the ⌜[0-9]+⌟ part (☞ 153).

More About Greediness
and Backtracking

Many concerns (and benefits) of greediness are shared by both an NFA and a DFA. (A DFA doesn't support laziness, which is why we've concentrated on greediness up to this point.) I'd like to look at some ramifications of greediness for both, but with examples explained in terms of an NFA. The lessons apply to a DFA just as well, but not for the same reasons. A DFA is greedy, period, and there's not much

---

Quiz Answer

❖ *Answer to the question on page 162.*

When matching ⌈[0-9]*⌋ against 'a·1234·num', would 'a͜1234·num' be part of a saved state?

The answer is "no." I posed this question because the mistake is commonly made. Remember, a component that has star applied can *always* match. If that's the entire regex, it can always match anywhere. This certainly includes the attempt when the transmission applies the engine the first time, at the start of the string. In this case, the regex matches at 'a͜1234·num' and that's the end of it—it never even gets as far the digits.

In case you missed this, there's still a chance for partial credit. Had there been something in the regex after the ⌈[0-9]*⌋ that kept an overall match from happening before the engine got to:

at 'a·1234···'	matching ⌈[0-9]*···⌋

then indeed, the attempt of the '1' also creates the state:

at 'a·1234···'	matching ⌈[0-9]*···⌋

---

more to say after that. It's very easy to use, but pretty boring to talk about. An NFA, however, is interesting because of the creative outlet its regex-directed nature provides. Besides lazy quantifiers, there are a variety of extra features an NFA can support, including lookaround, conditionals, backreferences, and atomic grouping. And on top of these, an NFA affords the regex author direct control over how a match is carried out, which can be a benefit when used properly, but it does create some efficiency-related pitfalls (discussed in Chapter 6.)

Despite these differences, the match results are often similar. For the next few pages, I'll talk of both engine types, but describe effects in terms of the regex-directed NFA. By the end of this chapter, you'll have a firm grasp of just when the results might differ, as well as exactly why.

Problems of Greediness

As we saw with the last example, ⌈.*⌋ always marches to the end of the line.[†] This is because ⌈.*⌋ just thinks of itself and grabs what it can, only later giving up something if it is required to achieve an overall match.

---

† With a tool or mode where a dot can match a newline, ⌈.*⌋ applied to strings that contain multiline data matches through all the logical lines to the end of the whole string.

Sometimes this can be a real pain. Consider a regex to match text wrapped in double quotes. At first, you might want to write ⌜".*"⌟, but knowing what we know about ⌜.*⌟, guess where it matches in:

```
The name "McDonald's" is said "makudonarudo" in Japanese
```

Actually, since we understand the mechanics of matching, we don't need to guess, because we *know*. Once the initial quote matches, ⌜.*⌟ is free to match, and immediately does so all the way to the end of the string. It backs off (or, perhaps more appropriately, *is backed off* by the regex engine) only as much as is needed until the final quote can match. In the end, it matches

```
The name "McDonald's" is said "makudonarudo" in Japanese
```

which is obviously not the double-quoted string that was intended. This is one reason why I caution against the overuse of ⌜.*⌟, as it can often lead to surprising results if you don't pay careful attention to greediness.

So, how can we have it match "McDonald's" only? The key is to realize that we don't want "anything" between the quotes, but rather "anything except a quote." If we use ⌜[^"]*⌟ rather than ⌜.*⌟, it won't overshoot the closing quote.

The regex engine's basic approach with ⌜"[^"]*"⌟ is exactly the same as before. Once the initial double quote matches, ⌜[^"]*⌟ gets a shot at matching as much as it can. In this case, that's up to the double quote after McDonald's, at which point it finally stops because ⌜[^"]⌟ can't match the quote. At that point, control moves to the closing ⌜"⌟. It happily matches, resulting in overall success:

```
The name "McDonald's" is said "makudonarudo" in Japanese
```

Actually, there's could be one unexpected change, and that's because in most flavors, ⌜[^"]⌟ can match a newline, while dot doesn't. If you want to keep the regex from crossing lines, use ⌜[^"\n]⌟.

Multi-Character "Quotes"

In the first chapter, I talked a bit about matching HTML tags, such as the sequence <B>very</B> that renders the "very" in bold if the browser can do so. Attempting to match a <B>···</B> sequence seems similar to matching a quoted string, except the "quotes" in this case are the multi-character sequences <B> and </B>. Like the quoted string example, multiple sets of "quotes" cause problems if we use ⌜.*⌟:

```
···<B>Billions</B> and <B>Zillions</B> of suns···
```

With ⌜<B>.*</B>⌟, the greedy ⌜.*⌟ causes the match in progress to zip to the end of the line, backtracking only far enough to allow the ⌜</B>⌟ to match, matching the last </B> on the line instead of the one corresponding to the opening ⌜<B>⌟ at the start of the match.

Unfortunately, since the closing delimiter is more than one character, we can't solve the problem with a negated class as we did with double-quoted strings. We can't expect something like ⌜`<B>[^</B>]*</B>`⌝ to work. A character class represents only one character and not the full `</B>` sequence that we want. Don't let the apparent structure of ⌜`[^</B>]`⌟ fool you. It is just a class to match one character—any one except <, >, /, and B. It is the same as, say ⌜`[^/<>B]`⌟, and certainly doesn't work as an "anything not `</B>`" construct. (With lookahead, you can insist that ⌜`</B>`⌝ not match at a particular point; we'll see this in action in the next section.)

Using Lazy Quantifiers

These problems arise because the standard quantifiers are greedy. Some NFAs support lazy quantifiers (☞ 140), with `*?` being the lazy version of `*`. With that in mind, let's apply ⌜`<B>.*?</B>`⌝ to:

    ···<B>Billions</B> and <B>Zillions</B> of suns···

After the initial ⌜`<B>`⌝ has matched, ⌜`.*?`⌟ immediately decides that since it doesn't require any matches, it lazily doesn't bother trying to perform any. So, it immediately passes control to the following ⌜`<`⌟:

at '···`<B>`B̲`illions`···'	matching ⌜`<B>.*?`</B>⌝

The ⌜`<`⌟ doesn't match at that point, so control returns back to ⌜`.*?`⌟ where it still has its untried option to attempt a match (to attempt multiple matches, actually). It begrudgingly does so, with the dot matching the underlined B in ···`<B>`B̲`illions`···. Again, the `*?` has the option to match more, or to stop. It's lazy, so it first tries stopping. The subsequent ⌜`<`⌟ still fails, so ⌜`.*?`⌟ has to again exercise its untried match option. After eight cycles, ⌜`.*?`⌟ eventually matches `Billions`, at which point the subsequent ⌜`<`⌟ (and the whole ⌜`</B>`⌝ subexpression) is finally able to match:

    ···`<B>Billions</B>` and <B>Zillions</B> of suns···

So, as we've seen, the greediness of star and friends can be a real boon at times, while troublesome at others. Having non-greedy, lazy versions is wonderful, as they allow you to do things that are otherwise very difficult (or even impossible). Still, I've often seen inexperienced programmers use lazy quantifiers in inappropriate situations. In fact, what we've just done may not be appropriate. Consider applying ⌜`<B>.*?</B>`⌝ to:

    ···`<B>Billions and <B>Zillions</B>` of suns···

It matches as shown, and while I suppose it depends on the exact needs of the situation, I would think that in this case that match is not desired. However, there's nothing about ⌜`.*?`⌟ to stop it from marching right past the Zillion's `<B>` to its `</B>`.

This is an excellent example of why a lazy quantifier is often not a good replacement for a negated class. In the ⌜".*"⌝ example, using ⌜[^"]⌝ as a replacement for the dot specifically disallows it from marching past a delimiter—a quality we wish our current regex had.

However, if *negative lookahead* (☞ 132) is supported, you can use it to create something comparable to a negated class. Alone, ⌜(?!<B>)⌝ is a test that is successful if <B> is not at the current location in the string. Those are the locations that we want the dot of ⌜<B>.*?</B>⌝ to match, so changing that dot to ⌜((?!<B>).)⌝ creates a regex that matches where we want it, but doesn't match where we don't. Assembled all together, the whole thing can become quite confusing, so I'll show it here in a free-spacing mode (☞ 110) with comments:

```
<B>             # Match the opening <B>
(               # Now, only as many of the following as needed . . .
   (?! <B>  )   #     If not <B> . . .
   .            #             . . . any character is okay
)*?             #
</B>            #  . . . until the closing delimiter can match
```

With one adjustment to the lookahead, we can put the quantifier back to a normal greedy one, which may be less confusing to some:

```
<B>              # Match the opening <B>
(                # Now, only as many of the following as needed . . .
   (?! </?B> )   #     If not <B>, and not </B> . . .
   .             #             . . . any character is okay
)*               #
</B>             #  . . . until the closing delimiter can match.
```

Now, the lookahead prohibits the main body to match beyond </B> as well as <B>, which eliminates the problem we tried to solve with laziness, so the laziness can be removed. This expression can still be improved; we'll see it again during the discussion on efficiency in Chapter 6 (☞ 270).

Greediness and Laziness Always Favor a Match

Recall the price display example from Chapter 2 (☞ 51). We'll examine this example in detail at a number of points during this chapter, so I'll recap the basic issue: due to floating-point representation problems, values that should have been "1.625" or "3.00" were sometimes coming out like "1.62500000002828" and "3.00000000028822". To fix this, I used

```
$price =~ s/(\.\d\d[1-9]?)\d*/$1/;
```

to lop off all but the first two or three decimal digits from the value stored in the variable $price. The ⌜\.\d\d⌝ matches the first two decimal digits regardless, while the ⌜[1-9]?⌝ matches the third digit only if it is non-zero.

I then noted:

> Anything matched so far is what we want to *keep*, so we wrap it in paren-
> theses to capture to $1. We can then use $1 in the replacement string. If this
> is the only thing that matches, we replace exactly what was matched with
> itself—not very useful. However, we go on to match other items outside the
> $1 parentheses. They don't find their way to the replacement string, so the
> effect is that they're removed. In this case, the "to be removed" text is any
> extra digits, the ⌈\d*⌋ at the end of the regex.

So far so good, but let's consider what happens when the contents of the variable
$price is already well formed. When it is 27.625, the ⌈(\.\d\d[1-9]?)⌋ part
matches the entire decimal part. Since the trailing ⌈\d*⌋ doesn't match anything, the
substitution replaces the '.625' with '.625' — an effective no-op.

This is the desired result, but wouldn't it be just a bit more efficient to do the
replacement only when it would have some real effect (that is, do the replacement
only when ⌈\d*⌋ actually matches something)? Well, we know how to write "at
least one digit"! Simply replace ⌈\d*⌋ with ⌈\d+⌋:

```
$price =~ s/(\.\d\d[1-9]?)\d+/$1/
```

With crazy numbers like "1.62500000002828", it still works as before, but with
something such as "9.43", the trailing ⌈\d+⌋ isn't able to match, so rightly, no substitution occurs. So, this is a great modification, yes? *No!* What happens with a three-
digit decimal value like 27.625? We want this value to be left alone, but that's not
what happens. Stop for a moment to work through the match of 27.625 yourself,
with particular attention to how the '5' interacts with the regex.

In hindsight, the problem is really fairly simple. Picking up in the action once
⌈(\.\d\d[1-9]?)\d+⌋ has matched 27.625, we find that ⌈\d+⌋ can't match. That's
no problem for the overall match, though, since as far as the regex is concerned,
the match of '5' by ⌈[1-9]⌋ was *optional* and there is still a saved state to try. This
state allows ⌈[1-9]?⌋ to match nothing, leaving the 5 to fulfill the must-match-one
requirement of ⌈\d+⌋. Thus, we get the match, but not the right match: .625 is
replaced by .62, and the value becomes incorrect.

What if ⌈[1-9]?⌋ were lazy instead? We'd get the same match, but without the intervening "match the 5 but then give it back" steps, since the lazy ⌈[1-9]??⌋ first skips
the match attempt. So, laziness is not a solution to this problem.

The Essence of Greediness, Laziness, and Backtracking

The lesson of the preceding section is that it makes no difference whether there
are greedy or lazy components to a regex; an overall match takes precedence over
an overall non-match. This includes taking from what had been greedy (or giving
to what had been lazy) if that's what is required to achieve a match, because when

a "local failure" is hit, the engine keeps going back to the saved states (retracing steps to the piles of bread crumbs), trying the untested paths. Whether greedily or lazily, *every possible path is tested before the engine admits failure.*

The order that the paths are tested is different between greedy and lazy quantifiers (after all, that's the whole point of having the two!), but in the end, if no match is to be found, it's known only after testing every possible path.

If, on the other hand, there exists just *one* plausible match, both a regex with a greedy quantifier and one with a lazy quantifier find that match, although the series of paths they take to get there may be wildly different. In these cases, selecting greedy or lazy doesn't influence what is matched, but merely how long or short a path the engine takes to get there (which is an efficiency issue, the subject of Chapter 6).

Finally, if there is more than one plausible match, understanding greediness, laziness, and backtracking allows you to know which is selected. The ⌜".*"⌝ example has three plausible matches:

```
The name "McDonald's" is said "makudonarudo" in Japanese
```

We know that ⌜.*⌝, with the greedy star, selects the longest one, and that ⌜".*?"⌝, with the lazy star, selects the shortest.

Possessive Quantifiers and Atomic Grouping

The '.625' example on the facing page shows important insights about NFA matching as we know it, and how with that particular example our naïve intents were thwarted. Some flavors do provide tools to help us here, but before looking at them, it's absolutely essential to fully understand the preceding section, "The Essence of Greediness, Laziness, and Backtracking." Be sure to review it if you have any doubts.

So, continuing with the '.625' example and recalling what we really want to happen, we know that if the matching can successfully get to the marked position in ⌜(\.\d\d[1-9]?)‸\d+⌝, we never want it to go back. That is, we want ⌜[1-9]⌝ to match if possible, but if it does, we don't want that match to be given up. Saying it more forcefully, we would rather have the entire match attempt fail, if need be, before giving up something matched by the ⌜[1-9]⌝. (As you'll recall, the problem before when this regex was applied to '.625' was that it indeed *didn't* fail, but instead went back to try the remaining skip-me alternative.)

Well, what if we could somehow eliminate that skip-me alternative (eliminate the state that ⌜?⌝ saves before it makes the attempt to match ⌜[1-9]⌝)? If there was no state to go back to, a match of ⌜[1-9]⌝ wouldn't be given up. That's what we want! Ah, but if there was no skip-me state to go back to, what would happen if we applied the regex to '.5000'? The ⌜[1-9]⌟ couldn't match, and in this case, we *do* want it to go back and skip the ⌜[1-9]⌟ so that the subsequent ⌜\d+⌟ can match digits to be removed.

It sounds like we have two conflicting desires, but thinking about it, what we really want is to eliminate the skip-me alternative only if the match-me alternative succeeds. That is, if ⌜[1-9]⌟ is indeed able to match, we'd like to get rid of the skip-me saved state so that it is never given up. This *is* possible, with regex flavors that support ⌜(?>⋯)⌟ atomic grouping (☞ 137), or possessive quantifiers like ⌜[1-9]?+⌟ (☞ 140). We'll look at atomic grouping first.

Atomic grouping with ⌜(?>⋯)⌟

In essence, matching within ⌜(?>⋯)⌟ carries on normally, but if and when matching is able to exit the construct (that is, get past its closing parenthesis), all states that had been saved while within it are thrown away. In practice, this means that once the atomic grouping has been exited, whatever text was matched within it is now one unchangeable unit, to be kept or given back only as a whole. All saved states representing untried options within the parentheses are eliminated, so backtracking can never undo any of the decisions made within (at least not once they're "locked in" when the construct is exited).

So, let's consider ⌜(\.\d\d(?>[1-9]?))\d+⌟. Quantifiers work normally within atomic grouping, so if ⌜[1-9]⌟ is not able to match, the regex returns to the skip-me saved state the ⌜?⌟ had left. That allows matching to leave the atomic grouping and continue on to the ⌜\d+⌟. In this case, there are no saved states to flush when control leaves the atomic grouping (that is, there are no saved states remaining that had been created within it).

However, when ⌜[1-9]⌟ *is* able to match, matching can exit the atomic grouping, but this time, the skip-me state is still there. Since it had been created within the atomic grouping we're now exiting, it is thrown away. This would happen when matching against both '.625', and, say, '.625000'. In the latter case, having eliminated the state turns out not to matter, since the ⌜\d+⌟ has the '.625<u>000</u>' to match, after which that regex is done. With '.625' alone, the inability of ⌜\d+⌟ to match has the regex engine wanting to backtrack, but it can't since that skip-me alternative was thrown away. The lack of any state to backtrack to results in the overall match attempt failing, and '.625' is left undisturbed as we wish.

The essence of atomic grouping

The section "The Essence of Greediness, Laziness, and Backtracking," starting on page 168, makes the important point that neither greediness nor laziness influence *which* paths can be checked, but merely the *order* in which they are checked. If no match is found, whether by a greedy or a lazy ordering, in the end, every possible path will have been checked.

Atomic grouping, on the other hand, is fundamentally different because it actually *eliminates possible paths.* Eliminating states can have a number of different consequences, depending on the situation:

- **No Effect** If a match is reached before one of the eliminated states would have been called upon, there is no effect on the match. We saw this a moment ago with the '`.625000`' example. A match was found before the eliminated state would have come into play.

- **Prohibit Match** The elimination of states can mean that a match that would have otherwise been possible now becomes impossible. We saw this with the '`.625`' example.

- **Different Match** In some cases, it's possible to get a *different* match due to the elimination of states.

- **Faster Failure** It's possible for the elimination of states to do nothing more than allow the regex engine, when no match is to be found, report that fact more quickly. This is discussed right after the quiz.

Here's a little quiz: what does the construct ⌈`(?>.*?)`⌋ do? What kind of things do you expect it can match? ❖ Turn the page to check your answer.

Some states may remain. When the engine exits atomic grouping during a match, only states that had been created *while inside the atomic grouping* are eliminated. States that might have been there before still remain after, so the entire text matched by the atomic subexpression may be unmatched, as a whole, if backtracking later reverts to one of those previous states.

Faster failures with atomic grouping. Consider ⌈`^\w+:`⌋ applied to '`Subject`'. We can see, just by looking at it, that it will fail because the text doesn't have a colon in it, but the regex engine won't reach that conclusion until it actually goes through the motions of checking.

So, by the time ⌈`:`⌋ is first checked, the ⌈`\w+`⌋ will have marched to the end of the string. This results in a lot of states—one "skip me" state for each match of ⌈`\w`⌋ by the plus (except the first, since plus requires one match). When then checked at the end of the string, ⌈`:`⌋ fails, so the regex engine backtracks to the most recently saved state:

at '`Subject`'	matching ⌈`^\w+:`⌋

at which point the ⌈`:`⌋ fails again, this time trying to match '`t`'. This backtrack-test-fail cycle happens all the way back to the oldest state:

at '`Subject`'	matching ⌈`^\w+:`⌋

After the attempt from the final state fails, overall failure can finally be announced.

Quiz Answer

❖ *Answer to the question on page 171.*

What does ⌜(?>.*?)⌝ **match?**

It can never match, anything. At best, it's a fairly complex way to accomplish nothing! ⌜*?⌝ is the lazy ⌜*⌝, and governs a dot, so the first path it attempts is the skip-the-dot path, saving the try-the-dot state for later, if required. But the moment that state has been saved, it's thrown away because matching exits the atomic grouping, so the skip-the-dot path is the only one ever taken. If something is always skipped, it's as if it's not there at all.

All that backtracking is a lot of work that after just a glance we know to be unnecessary. If the colon can't match after the last letter, it certainly can't match one of the letters the ⌜+⌝ is forced to give up!

So, knowing that none of the states left by ⌜\w+⌝, once it's finished, could possibly lead to a match, we can save the regex engine the trouble of checking them: ⌜^(?>\w+):⌝ By adding the atomic grouping, we use our global knowledge of the regex to enhance the local working of ⌜\w+⌝ by having its saved states (which we know to be useless) thrown away. If there *is* a match, the atomic grouping won't have mattered, but if there's not to be a match, having thrown away the useless states lets the regex come to that conclusion more quickly. (An advanced implementation may be able to apply this optimization for you automatically ☞ 251.)

As we'll see in the Chapter 6 (☞ 269), this technique shows a very valuable use of atomic grouping, and I suspect it will become the most common use as well.

Possessive Quantifiers, ?+, *+, ++, and* {m,n}+

Possessive quantifiers are much like greedy quantifiers, but they never give up a partial amount of what they've been able to match. Once a plus, for example, finishes its run, it has created quite a few saved states, as we saw with the ⌜^\w+⌝ example. A *possessive* plus simply throws those states away (or, more likely, doesn't bother creating them in the first place).

As you might guess, possessive quantifiers are closely related to atomic grouping. Something possessive like ⌜\w++⌝ appears to match in the same way as ⌜(?>\w+)⌝; one is just a notational convenience for the other.[†] With possessive quantifiers, ⌜^(?>\w+):⌝ can be rewritten as ⌜^\w++:⌝, and ⌜(\.\d\d(?>[1-9]?))\d+⌝ can be rewritten as ⌜(\.\d\d[1-9]?+)\d+⌝.

[†] A smart implementation may be able to make the possessive version a bit more efficient than its atomic-grouping counterpart (☞ 250).

Be sure to understand the difference between ⌜(?>M)+⌟ and ⌜(?>M+)⌟. The first one throws away unused states created by ⌜M⌟, which is not very useful since ⌜M⌟ doesn't create any states. The second one throws away unused states created by ⌜M+⌟, which certainly can be useful.

When phrased as a comparison between ⌜(?>M)+⌟ and ⌜(?>M+)⌟, it's perhaps clear that the second one is the one comparable to ⌜M++⌟, but when converting something more complex like ⌜(\\"|[^"])*+⌟ from possessive quantifiers to atomic grouping, it's tempting to just add '?>' to the parentheses that are already there: ⌜(?>\\"|[^"])*+⌟. The new expression might happen to achieve your goal, but be clear that is *not* comparable to the original possessive-quantifier version; it's as if changing ⌜M++⌟ to ⌜(?>M)+⌟. Rather, to be comparable, remove the possessive plus, and then wrap what remains in atomic grouping: ⌜(?>(\\"|[^"])*)⌟.

The Backtracking of Lookaround

It might not be apparent at first, but lookaround (introduced in Chapter 2 ☞ 59) is closely related to atomic grouping and possessive quantifiers. There are four types of lookaround: positive and negative flavors of lookahead and lookbehind. They simply test whether their subexpression can and can't match starting at the current location (lookahead), or ending at the current location (lookbehind).

Looking a bit deeper, how does lookaround work in our NFA world of saved states and backtracking? As a subexpression within one of the lookaround constructs is being tested, it's as if it's in its own little world. It saves states as needed, and backtracks as necessary. If the entire subexpression is able to match successfully, what happens? With *positive* lookaround, the construct, as a whole, is considered a success, and with *negative* lookaround, it's considered a failure. In either case, since the only concern is whether there's a match (and we just found out that, yes, there's a match), the "little world" of the match attempt, including any saved states that might have been left over from that attempt, is thrown away.

What about when the subexpression within the lookaround can't match? Since it's being applied in its "own little world," only states created within the current lookaround construct are available. That is, if the regex finds that it needs to backtrack further, beyond where the lookaround construct started, it's found that the current subexpression can not match. For positive lookahead, this means failure, while for negative lookahead, it means success. In either case, there are no saved states left over (had there been, the subexpression match would not have finished), so there's no "little world" left to throw away.

So, we've seen that in all cases, once the lookaround construct has finished, there are no saved states left over from its application. Any states that might have been left over, such as in the case of successful positive lookahead, are thrown away.

Well, where else have we seen states being thrown away? With atomic grouping and possessive quantifiers, of course.

Mimicking atomic grouping with positive lookahead

It's perhaps mostly academic for flavors that support atomic grouping, but can be quite useful for those that don't: *if* you have positive lookahead, and *if* it supports capturing parentheses within the lookahead (most flavors do, but Tcl's lookahead, for example, does not), you can mimic atomic grouping and possessive quanti-fiers. `(?>regex)` can be mimicked with `(?=(regex))\1`. For example, compare `^(?>\w+):` with `^(?=(\w+))\1:`.

The lookahead version has `\w+` greedily match as much as it can, capturing an entire word. Because it's within lookahead, the intermediate states are thrown away when it's finished (just as if, incidentally, it had been within atomic group-ing). Unlike atomic grouping, the matched word is not included as part of the match (that's the whole point of lookahead), but the word does remain captured. That's a key point because it means that when `\1` is applied, it's actually being applied to the very text that filled it, and it's certain to succeed. This extra step of applying `\1` is simply to move the regex past the matched word.

This technique is a bit less efficient than real atomic grouping because of the extra time required to rematch the text via `\1`. But, since states are thrown away, it fails more quickly than a raw `\w+:` when the `:` can't match.

Is Alternation Greedy?

How alternation works is an important point because it can work in fundamentally different ways with different regex engines. When alternation is reached, any num-ber of the alternatives might be able to match at that point, but which will? Put another way, if more than one can match, which will? If it's always the one that matches the most text, one might say that alternation is greedy. If it's always the shortest amount of text, one might say it's lazy? Which (if either) is it?

Let's look at the Traditional NFA engine used in Perl, Java packages, .NET lan-guages, and many others (☞ 145). When faced with alternation, each alternative is checked in the right-to-left order given in the expression. With the example regex of `^(Subject|Date):`, when the `Subject|Date` alternation is reached, the first alternative, `Subject`, is attempted. If it matches, the rest of the regex (the subse-quent `:`) is given a chance. If it turns out that it can't match, and if other alterna-tives remain (in this case, `Date`), the regex engine backtracks to try them. *This is just another case of the regex engine backtracking to a point where untried options are still available.* This continues until an overall match is achieved, or until all options (in this case, all alternatives) are exhausted.

So, with that common Traditional NFA engine, what text is actually matched by ⌜tour|to|tournament⌟ when applied to the string 'three·tournaments·won'? All the alternatives are attempted (and fail) during attempts starting at each character position until the transmission starts the attempt at 'three·tournaments·won'. This time, the first alternative, ⌜tour⌟, matches. Since the alternation is the last thing in the regex, the moment the ⌜tour⌟ matches, the whole regex is done. The other alternatives are not even tried again.

So, we see that alternation is neither greedy nor lazy, but *ordered*, at least for a Traditional NFA. This is more powerful than greedy alternation because it allows more control over just how a match is attempted — it allows the regex author to express "try this, then that, and finally try that, until you get a match."

Not all flavors have ordered alternation. DFAs and POSIX NFAs do have greedy alternation, always matching with the alternative that matches the most text (⌜tournament⌟ in this case). But, if you're using Perl, a .NET language, virtually any Java regex package, or any other system with a Traditional NFA engine (list ☞ 145), your alternation is *ordered*.

Taking Advantage of Ordered Alternation

Let's revisit the ⌜(\.\d\d[1-9]?)\d*⌟ example from page 167. If we realize that ⌜\.\d\d[1-9]?⌟, in effect, says "allow either ⌜\.\d\d⌟ or ⌜\.\d\d[1-9]⌟," we can rewrite the entire expression as ⌜(\.\d\d|\.\d\d[1-9])\d*⌟. (There is no compelling reason to make this change — it's merely a handy example.) Is this *really* the same as the original? If alternation is truly greedy, then it is, but the two are quite different with ordered alternation.

Let's consider it as ordered for the moment. The first alternative is selected and tested, and if it matches, control passes to the ⌜\d*⌟ that follows the alternation. If there are digits remaining, the ⌜\d*⌟ matches them, including any initial non-zero digit that was the root of the original example's problem (if you'll recall the original problem, that's a digit we want to match only within the parentheses, not by the ⌜\d*⌟ after the parentheses). Also, realize that if the first alternative can't match, the second alternative will certainly not be able to, as it begins with a copy of the entire first alternative. If the first alternative doesn't match, though, the regex engine nevertheless expends the effort for the futile attempt of the second.

Interestingly, if we swap the alternatives and use ⌜(\.\d\d[1-9]|\.\d\d)\d*⌟, we do effectively get a replica of the original greedy ⌜(\.\d\d[1-9]?)\d*⌟. The alternation has meaning in this case because if the first alternative fails due to the trailing ⌜[1-9]⌟, the second alternative still stands a chance. It's still ordered alternation, but now we've selected the order to result in a greedy-type match.

When first distributing the ⌈[1-9]?⌋ to two alternatives, in placing the shorter one first, we fashioned a non-greedy ⌈?⌋ of sorts. It ends up being meaningless in this particular example because there is nothing that could ever allow the second alternative to match if the first fails. I see this kind of faux-alternation often, and it is invariably a mistake. In one book I've read, ⌈a*((ab)*|b*)⌋ is used as an example in explaining something about regex parentheses. It's a pointless example because the first alternative, ⌈(ab)*⌋, can never fail, so any other alternatives are utterly meaningless. You could add

⌈a*((ab)*|b*|.*|partridge·in·a·pear·tree|[a-z])⌋

and it wouldn't change the meaning a bit. The moral is that with ordered alternation, when more than one alternative can potentially match the same text, care must be taken when selecting the order of the alternatives.

Ordered alternation pitfalls

Ordered alternation can be put to your advantage by allowing you to craft just the match you want, but it can also lead to unexpected pitfalls for the unaware. Consider matching a January date of the form 'Jan 31'. We need something more sophisticated than, say, ⌈Jan·[0123][0-9]⌋, as that allows "dates" such as 'Jan·00', 'Jan·39', and disallows, 'Jan·7'.

One way to match the date part is to attack it in sections. To match from the first through the ninth, using ⌈0?[1-9]⌋ allows a leading zero. Adding ⌈[12][0-9]⌋ allows for the tenth through the 29th, and ⌈3[01]⌋ rounds it out. Putting it all together, we get ⌈Jan·(0?[1-9]|[12][0-9]|3[01])⌋.

Where do you think this matches in 'Jan 31 is Dad's birthday'? We want it to match 'Jan 31', of course, but ordered alternation actually matches only 'Jan 3'. Surprised? During the match of the first alternative, ⌈0?[1-9]⌋, the leading ⌈0?⌋ fails, but the alternative matches because the subsequent ⌈[1-9]⌋ has no trouble matching the 3. Since that's the end of the expression, the match is complete.

When the order of the alternatives is adjusted so that the alternative that can potentially match a shorter amount of text is placed last, the problem goes away. This works: ⌈Jan·([12][0-9]|3[01]|0?[1-9])⌋.

Another approach is ⌈Jan·(31|[123]0|[012]?[1-9])⌋. Like the first solution, this requires careful arrangement of the alternatives to avoid the problem. Yet, a third approach is ⌈Jan·(0[1-9]|[12][0-9]?|3[01]?|[4-9])⌋, which works properly regardless of the ordering. Comparing and contrasting these three expressions can prove quite interesting (an exercise I'll leave for your free time, although the sidebar on the facing page should be helpful).

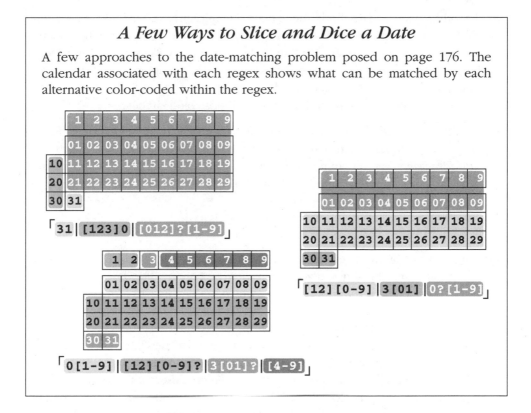

A Few Ways to Slice and Dice a Date

A few approaches to the date-matching problem posed on page 176. The calendar associated with each regex shows what can be matched by each alternative color-coded within the regex.

NFA, DFA, and POSIX

"The Longest-Leftmost"

Let me repeat what I've said before: when the transmission starts a DFA engine from some particular point in the string, and there exists a match or matches to be found at that position, the DFA finds the longest possible match, period. Since it's the longest from among all possible matches that start equally furthest to the left, it's the "longest-leftmost" match.

Really, the longest

Issues of which match is longest aren't confined to alternation. Consider how an NFA matches the (horribly contrived) ⌜one(self)?(selfsufficient)?⌟ against the string oneselfsufficient. An NFA first matches ⌜one⌟ and then the greedy ⌜(self)?⌟, leaving ⌜(selfsufficient)?⌟ left to try against sufficient. It doesn't match, but that's okay since it is optional. So, the Traditional NFA returns <u>oneself</u>sufficient and discards the untried states. (A POSIX NFA is another story that we'll get to shortly.)

On the other hand, a DFA finds the longer <u>oneselfsufficient</u>. An NFA would also find that match if the initial ⌈(self)?⌉ were to somehow go unmatched, as that would leave ⌈(selfsufficient)?⌉ then able to match. A Traditional NFA doesn't do that, but the DFA finds it nevertheless, since it's the longest possible match available to the current attempt. It can do this because it keeps track of all matches simultaneously, and knows at all times about all possible matches.

I chose this silly example because it's easy to talk about, but I want you to realize that this issue is important in real life. For example, consider trying to match *continuation lines*. It's not uncommon for a data specification to allow one logical line to extend across multiple real lines if the real lines end with a backslash before the newline. As an example, consider the following:

```
SRC=array.c builtin.c eval.c field.c gawkmisc.c io.c main.c \
      missing.c msg.c node.c re.c version.c
```

You might normally want to use ⌈^\w+=.*⌉ to match this kind of "var = value" assignment line, but this regex doesn't consider the continuation lines. (I'm assuming for the example that the tool's dot won't match a newline.) To match continuation lines, you might consider appending ⌈(\\\n.*)*⌉ to the regex, yielding ⌈^\w+=.*<u>(\\\n.*)*</u>⌉. Ostensibly, this says that any number of additional logical lines are allowed so long as they each follow an escaped newline. This seems reasonable, but it will never work with a traditional NFA. By the time the original ⌈.*⌉ has reached the newline, *it has already passed the backslash*, and nothing in what was added forces it to backtrack (☞ 152). Yet, a DFA finds the longer multiline match if available, simply because it is, indeed, the longest.

If you have lazy quantifiers available, you might consider using them, such as with ⌈^\w+=.*?(\\\n.*?)*⌉. This allows the escaped newline part to be tested each time before the first dot actually matches anything, so the thought is that the ⌈\\⌉ then gets to match the backslash before the newline. Again, this won't work. A lazy quantifier actually ends up matching something optional only when forced to do so, but in this case, everything after the ⌈=⌉ is optional, so there's nothing to force the lazy quantifiers to match anything. Our lazy example matches only 'SRC=', so it's certainly not the answer.

There are other approaches to solving this problem; we'll continue with this example in the next chapter (☞ 186).

POSIX and the Longest-Leftmost Rule

The POSIX standard requires that if you have multiple possible matches that start at the same position, the one matching the most text must be the one returned.

The POSIX standard document uses the phrase "longest of the leftmost." It doesn't say you have to use a DFA, so if you want to use an NFA when creating a POSIX tool, what's a programmer to do? If you want to implement a POSIX NFA, you'd have to find the full `oneselfsufficient` and all the continuation lines, despite these results being "unnatural" to your NFA.

A Traditional NFA engine stops with the first match it finds, but what if it were to continue to try options (states) that might remain? Each time it reached the end of the regex, it would have another plausible match. By the time *all* options are exhausted, it could simply report the longest of the plausible matches it had found. Thus, a POSIX NFA.

An NFA applied to the first example would, in matching ⌈(self)?⌋, have saved an option noting that it could pick up matching ⌈one(self)?⌆(selfsufficient)?⌋ at oneselfsufficient. Even after finding the `oneselfsufficient` that a Traditional NFA stops at, a POSIX NFA continues to exhaustively check the remaining options, eventually realizing that yes, there is a way to match the longer (and in fact, longest) `oneselfsufficient`.

In Chapter 7, we'll see a method to trick Perl into mimicking POSIX semantics, having it report the longest match (☞ 335).

Speed and Efficiency

If efficiency is an issue with a Traditional NFA (and with backtracking, believe me, it can be), it is doubly so with a POSIX NFA since there can be so much more backtracking. A POSIX NFA engine really does have to try every possible permutation of the regex, every time. Examples in Chapter 6 show that poorly written regexes can suffer extremely severe performance penalties.

DFA efficiency

The text-directed DFA is a really fantastic way around all the inefficiency of backtracking. It gets its matching speed by keeping track of all possible ongoing matches at once. How does it achieve this magic?

The DFA engine spends extra time and memory when it first sees the regular expression, before any match attempts are made, to analyze the regular expression more thoroughly (and in a different way) from an NFA. Once it starts actually attempting a match, it has an internal map describing "If I read such-and-such a character now, it will be part of this-and-that possible match." As each character of the string is checked, the engine simply follows the map.

Building that map can sometimes take a fair amount of time and memory, but once it is done for any particular regular expression, the results can be applied to an unlimited amount of text. It's sort of like charging the batteries of your electric car. First, your car sits in the garage for a while, plugged into the wall, but when you actually use it, you get consistent, clean power.

NFA: *Theory Versus Reality*

The true mathematical and computational meaning of "NFA" is different from what is commonly called an "NFA regex engine." In theory, NFA and DFA engines should match exactly the same text and have exactly the same features. In practice, the desire for richer, more expressive regular expressions has caused their semantics to diverge. An example is the support for backreferences.

The design of a DFA engine precludes backreferences, but it's a relatively small task to add backreference support to a true (mathematically speaking) NFA engine. In doing so, you create a more powerful tool, but you also make it decidedly *nonregular* (mathematically speaking). What does this mean? At most, that you should probably stop calling it an NFA, and start using the phrase "nonregular expressions," since that describes (mathematically speaking) the new situation. No one has actually done this, so the *name* "NFA" has lingered, even though the implementation is no longer (mathematically speaking) an NFA.

What does all this mean to you, as a user? Absolutely nothing. As a user, you don't care if it's regular, nonregular, unregular, irregular, or incontinent. So long as you know what you can expect from it (something this chapter shows you), you know all you need to care about.

For those wishing to learn more about the theory of regular expressions, the classic computer-science text is chapter 3 of Aho, Sethi, and Ullman's *Compilers— Principles, Techniques, and Tools* (Addison-Wesley, 1986), commonly called "The Dragon Book" due to the cover design. More specifically, this is the "red dragon." The "green dragon" is its predecessor, Aho and Ullman's *Principles of Compiler Design*.

The work done when a regex is first seen (the once-per-regex overhead) is called *compiling the regex*. The map-building is what a DFA does. An NFA also builds an internal representation of the regex, but an NFA's representation is like a mini program that the engine then executes.

Summary: NFA and DFA in Comparison

Both DFA and NFA engines have their good and bad points.

DFA versus NFA: *Differences in the pre-use compile*

Before applying a regex to a search, both types of engines compile the regex to an internal form suited to their respective match algorithms. An NFA compile is generally faster, and requires less memory. There's no real difference between a Traditional and POSIX NFA compile.

DFA versus NFA: Differences in match speed

For simple literal-match tests in "normal" situations, both types match at about the same rate. A DFA's match speed is generally unrelated to the particular regex, but an NFA's is directly related.

A Traditional NFA must try every possible permutation of the regex before it can conclude that there's no match. This is why I spend an entire chapter (Chapter 6) on techniques to write NFA expressions that match quickly. As we'll see, an NFA match can sometimes take forever. If it's a Traditional NFA, it can at least stop if and when it finds a match.

A POSIX NFA, on the other hand, must always try every possible permutation of the regex to ensure that it has found the longest possible match, so it generally takes the same (possibly very long) amount of time to complete a successful match as it does to confirm a failure. Writing efficient expressions is doubly important for a POSIX NFA.

In one sense, I speak a bit too strongly, since optimizations can often reduce the work needed to return an answer. We've already seen that an optimized engine doesn't try ⌜^⌟-anchored regexes beyond the start of the string (☞ 149), and we'll see many more optimizations in Chapter 6.

The need for optimizations is less pressing with a DFA since its matching is so fast to begin with, but for the most part, the extra work done during the DFA's pre-use compile affords better optimizations than most NFA engines take the trouble to do.

Modern DFA engines often try to reduce the time and memory used during the compile by postponing some work until a match is attempted. Often, much of the compile-time work goes unused because of the nature of the text actually checked. A fair amount of time and memory can sometimes be saved by postponing the work until it's actually needed during the match. (The technobabble term for this is *lazy evaluation*.) It does, however, create cases where there can be a relationship among the regex, the text being checked, and the match speed.

DFA versus NFA: Differences in what is matched

A DFA (or anything POSIX) finds the longest leftmost match. A Traditional NFA might also, or it might find something else. Any individual engine always treats the same regex/text combination in the same way, so in that sense, it's not "random," but other NFA engines may decide to do slightly different things. Virtually all Traditional NFA engines I've seen work exactly the way I've described here, but it's not something absolutely guaranteed by any standard.

DFA versus NFA: *Differences in capabilities*

An NFA engine can support many things that a DFA cannot. Among them are:

- Capturing text matched by a parenthesized subexpression. Related features are backreferences and after-match information saying *where* in the matched text each parenthesized subexpression matched.

- Lookaround, and other complex zero-width assertions[†] (☞ 132).

- Non-greedy quantifiers and ordered alternation. A DFA could easily support a guaranteed shortest overall match (although for whatever reason, this option never seems to be made available to the user), but it cannot implement the local laziness and ordered alternation that we've talked about.

- Possessive quantifiers (☞ 140) and atomic grouping (☞ 137).

DFA versus NFA: *Differences in ease of implementation*

Although they have limitations, simple versions of DFA and NFA engines are easy enough to understand and to implement. The desire for efficiency (both in time and memory) and enhanced features drives the implementation to greater and greater complexity.

With code length as a metric, consider that the NFA regex support in the Version 7 (January 1979) edition of *ed* was less than 350 lines of C code. (For that matter, the *entire* source for *grep* was a scant 478 lines.) Henry Spencer's 1986 freely available implementation of the Version 8 regex routines was almost 1,900 lines of C, and Tom Lord's 1992 POSIX NFA package `rx` (used in GNU sed, among other tools) is a stunning 9,700 lines.

For DFA implementations, the Version 7 *egrep* regex engine was a bit over 400 lines long, while Henry Spencer's 1992 full-featured POSIX DFA package is over 4,500 lines long.

To provide the best of both worlds, GNU *egrep* Version 2.4.2 utilizes two fully functional engines (about 8,900 lines of code), and Tcl's hybrid DFA/NFA engine (see the sidebar on the facing page) is about 9,500 lines of code.

Some implementations are simple, but that doesn't necessarily mean they are short on features. I once wanted to use regular expressions for some text processing in Pascal. I hadn't used Pascal since college, but it still didn't take long to write a simple NFA regex engine. It didn't have a lot of bells and whistles, and wasn't built for maximum speed, but the flavor was relatively full-featured and was quite useful.

---

† *lex* has *trailing context*, which is exactly the same thing as zero-width positive lookahead at the end of the regex, but it can't be generalized and put to use for embedded lookahead.

DFA Speed with NFA Capabilities: Regex Nirvana?

I've said several times that a DFA can't provide capturing parentheses or backreferences. This is quite true, but it certainly doesn't preclude hybrid approaches that mix technologies in an attempt to reach regex nirvana. The sidebar on page 180 told how NFAs have diverged from the theoretical straight and narrow in search of more power, and it's only natural that the same happens with DFAs. A DFA's construction makes it more difficult, but that doesn't mean impossible.

GNU *grep* takes a simple but effective approach. It uses a DFA when possible, reverting to an NFA when backreferences are used. GNU awk does something similar—it uses GNU *grep*'s fast shortest-leftmost DFA engine for simple "does it match" checks, and reverts to a different engine for checks where the actual extent of the match must be known. Since that other engine is an NFA, GNU awk can conveniently offer capturing parentheses, and it does via its special `gensub` function.

Tcl's regex engine is a true hybrid, custom built by Henry Spencer (whom you may remember having played an important part in the early development and popularization of regular expressions ☞88). The Tcl engine sometimes appears to be an NFA—it has lookaround, capturing parentheses, backreferences, and lazy quantifiers. Yet, it has true POSIX longest-leftmost match (☞177), and doesn't suffer from some of the NFA problems that we'll see in Chapter 6. It really seems quite wonderful.

Currently, this engine is available only to Tcl, but Henry tells me that it's on his to-do list to break it out into a separate package that can be used by others.

Summary

If you understood everything in this chapter the first time you read it, you probably didn't need to read it in the first place. It's heady stuff, to say the least. It took me quite a while to understand it, and then longer still to *understand* it. I hope this one concise presentation makes it easier for you. I've tried to keep the explanation simple without falling into the trap of oversimplification (an unfortunately all-too-common occurrence which hinders true understanding). This chapter has a lot in it, so I've included a lot of page references in the following summary, for when you'd like to quickly check back on something.

There are two underlying technologies commonly used to implement a regex match engine, "regex-directed NFA" (☞153) and "text-directed DFA" (☞155). The abbreviations are spelled out on page 156.

Combine the two technologies with the POSIX standard (☞ 178), and for practical purposes, there are three types of engines:

- Traditional NFA   (gas-guzzling, power-on-demand)
- POSIX NFA   (gas-guzzling, standard-compliant)
- DFA (POSIX or not)   (electric, steady-as-she-goes)

To get the most out of a utility, you need to understand which type of engine it uses, and craft your regular expressions appropriately. The most common type is the Traditional NFA, followed by the DFA. Table 4-1 (☞ 145) lists a few common tools and their engine types, and the section "Testing the Engine Type" (☞ 146) shows how you can test the type yourself.

One overriding rule regardless of engine type: matches starting sooner take precedence over matches starting later. This is due to how the engine's "transmission" tests the regex at each point in the string (☞ 148).

For the match attempt starting at any given spot:

DFA Text-Directed Engines

Find the longest possible match, period. That's it. End of discussion (☞ 177). Consistent, very fast (☞ 179), and boring to talk about.

NFA Regex-Directed Engines

Must "work through" a match. The soul of NFA matching is *backtracking* (☞ 157, 162). The metacharacters control the match: the standard quantifiers (star and friends) are *greedy* (☞ 151), while others may be lazy or possessive (☞ 169). Alternation is ordered (☞ 174) in a traditional NFA, but greedy with a POSIX NFA.

POSIX NFA Must find the longest match, period. But, it's not boring, as you must worry about efficiency (the subject of Chapter 6).

Traditional NFA Is the most expressive type of regex engine, since you can use the regex-directed nature of the engine to craft exactly the match you want.

Understanding the concepts and practices covered in this chapter is the foundation for writing correct and efficient regular expressions, which just happens to be the subject of the next two chapters.

5

Practical Regex Techniques

Now that we've covered the basic mechanics of writing regular expressions, I'd like to put that understanding to work in handling situations more complex than those in earlier chapters. Every regex strikes a balance between matching what you want, but not matching what you don't want. We've already seen plenty of examples where greediness can be your friend if used skillfully, and how it can lead to pitfalls if you're not careful, and we'll see plenty more in this chapter.

For an NFA engine, another part of the balance, discussed primarily in the next chapter, is efficiency. A poorly designed regex—even one that would otherwise be considered correct—can cripple an engine.

This chapter is comprised mostly of examples, as I lead you through my thought processes in solving a number of problems. I encourage you to read through them even if a particular example seems to offer nothing toward your immediate needs.

For instance, even if you don't work with HTML, I encourage you to absorb the examples that deal with HTML. This is because writing a good regular expression is more than a skill—it's an art. One doesn't teach or learn this art with lists or rules, but rather, through experience, so I've written these examples to illustrate for you some of the insight that experience has given me over the years.

You'll still need your own experience to internalize that insight, but spending time with the examples in this chapter is a good first step.

Regex Balancing Act

Writing a good regex involves striking a balance among several concerns:

- Matching what you want, but only what you want

- Keeping the regex manageable and understandable

- For an NFA, being efficient (creating a regex that leads the engine quickly to a match or a non-match, as the case may be)

These concerns are often context-dependent. If I'm working on the command line and just want to *grep* something quickly, I probably don't care if I match a bit more than I need, and I won't usually be too concerned to craft just the right regex for it. I'll allow myself to be sloppy in the interest of time, since I can quickly peruse the output for what I want. However, when I'm working on an important program, it's worth the time and effort to get it right: a complex regular expression is okay if that's what it takes. There is a balance among all these issues.

Efficiency is context-dependent, even in a program. For example, with an NFA, something long like ⌜`^-(display|geometry|cemap|` ⋯ `|quick24|random|raw)$`⌟ to check command-line arguments is inefficient because of all that alternation, but since it is only checking command-line arguments (something done perhaps a few times at the start of the program) it wouldn't matter if it took 100 times longer than needed. It's just not an important place to worry much about efficiency. Were it used to check each line of a potentially large file, the inefficiency would penalize you for the duration of the program.

A Few Short Examples

Continuing with Continuation Lines

With the continuation-line example from the previous chapter (☞ 178), we found that ⌜`^\w+=.*(\\\n.*)*`⌟ applied with a Traditional NFA doesn't properly match both lines of:

```
SRC=array.c builtin.c eval.c field.c gawkmisc.c io.c main.c \
        missing.c msg.c node.c re.c version.c
```

The problem is that the first ⌜`.*`⌟ matches past the backslash, pulling it out from under the ⌜`(\\\n.*)*`⌟ that we want it to be matched by. Well, here's the first lesson of the chapter: if we don't want to match past the backslash, we should say that in the regex. We can do this by changing each dot to ⌜`[^\n\\]`⌟. (Notice how I've made sure to include \n in the negated class? You'll remember that one of the assumptions of the original regex was that dot didn't match a newline, and we don't want its replacement to match a newline either ☞ 118.)

Making that change, we get:

⌜^\w+=[^\n\\]*(\\\n[^\n\\]*)*⌟

This now works, properly matching continuation lines, but in solving one problem, we have perhaps introduced another: we've now disallowed backslashes other than those at the end of lines. This is a problem if the data to which it will be applied could possibly have other backslashes. We'll assume it could, so we need to accommodate the regex to handle them.

So far, our approaches have been along the lines of "match the line, then try to match a continuation line if there." Let's change that approach to one that I find often works in general: concentrate on what is really allowed to match at any particular point. As we match the line, we want either normal (non-backslash, non-newline) characters, or a backslash-anything combination. If we use ⌜\\.⌟ for the backslash-anything combination, and apply it in a dot-matches-all mode, it also can match the backslash-newline combination.

So, the expression becomes ⌜^\w+=([^\n\\]|\\.)*⌟ in a dot-matches-all mode. Due to the leading ⌜^⌟, an enhanced line anchor match mode (☞ 111) may be useful as well, depending on how this expression is used.

But, we're not quite done with this example yet—we'll pick it up again in the next chapter where we work on its efficiency (☞ 270).

Matching an IP Address

As another example that we'll take much further, let's match an IP (Internet Protocol) address: four numbers separated by periods, such as 1.2.3.4. Often, the numbers are padded to three digits, as in 001.002.003.004. If you want to check a string for one of these, you could use ⌜[0-9]*\.[0-9]*\.[0-9]*\.[0-9]*⌟, but that's so vague that it even matches 'and then.....?'. Look at the regex: it doesn't even *require* any numbers—its only requirements are three periods (with nothing but digits, *if anything*, between).

To fix this regex, we first change the star to a plus, since we know that each number must have at least one digit. To ensure that the entire string is only the IP address, we wrap the regex with ⌜^···$⌟. This gives us:

⌜^[0-9]+\.[0-9]+\.[0-9]+\.[0-9]+$⌟

Using ⌜\d⌟ instead of ⌜[0-9]⌟, it becomes ⌜^\d+\.\d+\.\d+\.\d+$⌟, which you may find to be more easily readable,[†] but it still matches things that aren't IP addresses,

---

† Or maybe not—it depends on what you are used to. In a complex regex, I find ⌜\d⌟ more readable than ⌜[0-9]⌟, but note that on some systems, the two might not be exactly the same. Systems that support Unicode, for example, may have their ⌜\d⌟ match non-ASCII digits as well (☞ 119).

like ⌜1234.5678.9101112.131415⌝. (IP addresses have each number in the range
of 0–255.) As a start, you can enforce that each number be three digits long, with
⌜^\d\d\d\.\d\d\d\.\d\d\d\.\d\d\d$⌝, but now we are *too* specific. We still
need to allow one- and two-digit numbers (as in 1.234.5.67). If the flavor supports {*min,max*}, you can use ⌜^\d{1,3}\.\d{1,3}\.\d{1,3}\.\d{1,3}$⌝. If not,
you can always use ⌜\d\d?\d?⌝ or ⌜\d(\d\d?)?⌝ for each part. These allow one to
three digits, each in a slightly different way.

Depending on your needs, you might be happy with some of the various degrees
of vagueness in the expressions so far. If you really want to be strict, you have to
worry that ⌜\d{1,3}⌝ can match 999, which is above 255, and thus an invalid component of an IP address.

Several approaches would ensure that only numbers from 0 to 255 appear. One
silly approach is ⌜0|1|2|3|⋯253|254|255⌝. Actually, this doesn't allow the zero-
padding that is allowed, so you really need ⌜0|00|000|1|01|001|⋯⌝, whose length
becomes even more ridiculous. For a DFA engine, it is ridiculous only in that it's so
long and verbose — it still matches just as fast as any regex describing the same
text. For an NFA, however, all the alternation kills efficiency.

A realistic approach concentrates on which digits are allowed in a number, and
where. If a number is only one or two digits long, there is no worry as to whether
the value is within range, so ⌜\d|\d\d⌝ takes care of it. There's also no worry about
the value for a three-digit number beginning with a 0 or 1, since such a number is
in the range 000–199 and is perfectly valid. This lets us add ⌜[01]\d\d⌝, leaving us
with ⌜\d|\d\d|[01]\d\d⌝. You might recognize this as being similar to the time
example in Chapter 1 (☞ 28), and date example of the previous chapter (☞ 177).

Continuing with our regular expression, a three-digit number beginning with a 2 is
allowed if the number is 255 or less, so a second digit less than 5 means the number is valid. If the second digit *is* 5, the third must be less than 6. This can all be
expressed as ⌜2[0-4]\d|25[0-5]⌝.

This may seem confusing at first, but the approach should make sense upon
reflection. The result is ⌜\d|\d\d|[01]\d\d|2[0-4]\d|25[0-5]⌝. Actually, we can
combine the first three alternatives to yield ⌜[01]?\d\d?|2[0-4]\d|25[0-5]⌝.
Doing so is more efficient for an NFA, since any alternative that fails results in a
backtrack. Note that using ⌜\d\d?⌝ in the first alternative, rather than ⌜\d?\d⌝, allows
an NFA to fail just a bit more quickly when there is no digit at all. I'll leave the
analysis to you — walking through a simple test case with both should illustrate the
difference. We could do other things to make this part of the expression more efficient, but I'll leave that for the next chapter.

Now that we have a subexpression to match a single number from 0 through 255, we can wrap it in parentheses and insert it in place of each ⌜\d{1,3}⌟ in the earlier regex. This gives us (broken across lines to fit the width of the page):

⌜^([01]?\d\d?|2[0-4]\d|25[0-5])\.([01]?\d\d?|2[0-4]\d|25[0-5])\.
([01]?\d\d?|2[0-4]\d|25[0-5])\.([01]?\d\d?|2[0-4]\d|25[0-5])$⌟

Quite a mouthful! Was it worth the trouble? You have to decide for yourself based upon your own needs. It matches only syntactically correct IP addresses, but it can still match *semantically* incorrect ones, such as 0.0.0.0 (invalid because all the digits are zero). With lookahead (☞ 132), you can disallow that specific case by putting ⌜(?!0+\.0+\.0+\.0+$)⌟ after ⌜^⌟, but at some point, you have to decide when being too specific causes the cost/benefit ratio to suffer from diminishing returns. Sometimes it's better to take some of the work out of the regex. For example, if you go back to ⌜^\d{1,3}\.\d{1,3}\.\d{1,3}\.\d{1,3}$⌟ and wrap each component in parentheses to stuff the numbers into the program's version of $1, $2, $3, and $4, you can then validate them by other programming constructs.

Know your context

It's important to realize that the two anchors, ⌜^⌟ and ⌜$⌟, are required to make this regex work. Without them, it can match ip=72<u>123.3.21.99</u>3, or for a Traditional NFA, even ip=<u>123.3.21.223</u>.

In that second case, the expression does not even fully match the final 223 that should have been allowed. Well, it is *allowed*, but there's nothing (such as a separating period, or the trailing anchor) to force that match. The final group's first alternative, ⌜[01]?\d\d?⌟, matched the first two digits, and without the trailing ⌜$⌟, that's the end of the regex. As with the date-matching problem in the previous chapter (☞ 176), we can arrange the order of the alternatives to achieve the desired result. In this case, we would put the alternatives matching three digits first, so any proper three-digit number is matched in full before the two-digit-okay alternative is given a chance. (DFAs and POSIX NFAs don't require the reordering, of course, since they choose the longest match, regardless.)

Rearranged or not, that first mistaken match is still a problem. "Ah!" you might think, "I can use word boundary anchors to solve this problem." Unfortunately, that's probably not enough, since such a regex could still match <u>1.2.3.4</u>.5.6. To disallow embedded matches, you must ensure that the surrounding context has at least no alphanumerics or periods. If you have lookaround, you can wrap the regex in ⌜(?<![\w.])⋯(?![\w.])⌟ to disallow matches that follow just after (or end just before) where ⌜[\w.]⌟ can match. If you don't have lookaround, simply wrapping it in ⌜(^|•)⋯(•|$)⌟ might be satisfactory for some situations.

Working with Filenames

Working with file and path names, like /usr/local/bin/perl on Unix, or perhaps something like \Program Files\Yahoo!\Messenger on Windows, can provide many good regular-expression examples. Since "using" is more interesting
than "reading," I'll sprinkle in a few examples coded in Perl, Java, and VB.NET. If
you're not interested in these particular languages, feel free to skip the code snippets—it's the regex concepts used in them that are important.

Removing the leading path from a filename

As a first example, let's remove the leading path from a filename, turning
/usr/local/bin/gcc, for instance, into gcc. Stating problems in a way that
makes solutions amenable is half of the battle. In this case, we want to remove
anything up to (and including) the final slash (backslash for Windows pathnames).
If there is no slash, it's fine as is, and nothing needs to be done. I've said a number of times that ⌈.*⌋ is often overused, but its greediness is desired here. With
⌈^.*/⌋, the ⌈.*⌋ consumes the whole line, but then backs off (that is, backtracks) to
the last slash to achieve the match.

Here's code to do it in our three test languages, ensuring that a filename in the
variable f has no leading path. First, for Unix filenames:

Language	Code Snippet
Perl	`$f =~ s{^.*/}{};`
java.util.regex	`f = f.replaceFirst("^.*/", "");`
VB.NET	`f = Regex.Replace(f, "^.*/", "")`

The regular expression (or string to be interpreted as a regular expression) is
underlined, and regex components are bold.

For comparison, here they are for Windows filenames:

Language	Code Snippet
Perl	`$f =~ s/^.*\\//;`
java.util.regex	`f = f.replaceFirst("^.*\\\\", "");`
VB.NET	`f = Regex.Replace(f, "^.*\\", "")`

It's interesting to compare the differences needed for each language when going
from one example to the other, particularly the quadruple backslashes needed in
Java (☞ 101).

Please keep in mind this key point: always consider what will happen if there is
no match. In this case, if there is no slash in the string, no substitution is done and
the string is left unchanged. That's just what we want.

For efficiency's sake, it's important to remember how the regex engine goes about its work, if it is NFA-based. Let's consider what happens if we omit the leading caret (something that's easy to forget) and match against a string that doesn't happen to have a slash. As always, the regex engine starts the search at the beginning of the string. The ⌜.*⌟ races to the end of the string, but must back off to find a match for the slash or backslash. It eventually backs off everything that ⌜.*⌟ had gobbled up, yet there's still no match. So, the regex engine decides that there is no possible match *when starting from the beginning of the string*, but it's not done yet!

The transmission kicks in and retries the whole regex from the second character position. In fact, it needs (in theory) to go through the whole scan-and-backtrack routine for each possible starting position in the string. Filenames tend to be short, so it's probably not such a big deal in this case, but the principle applies to many situations. Were the string long, there's a potential for a lot of backtracking. (A DFA has no such problem, of course.)

In practice, a reasonably optimized transmission realizes that almost any regex starting with ⌜.*⌟ that fails at the beginning of the string can never match when started from anywhere else, so it can shift gears and attempt the regex only the one time, at the start of the string (☞ 246). Still, it's smarter to write that into our regex in the first place, as we originally did.

Accessing the filename from a path

Another approach is to bypass the path and simply match the trailing filename part without the path. The final filename is everything at the end that's not a slash: ⌜[^/]*$⌟. This time, the anchor is not just an optimization; we really do need dollar at the end. We can now do something like this, shown with Perl:

```
$WholePath =~ m{ ([^/]*)$ };  # Check variable $WholePath with regex.
$FileName = $1;               # Note text matched
```

You'll notice that I don't check to see whether the regex actually matches, because I *know* it will match every time. The only *requirement* of that expression is that the string has an end to match dollar, and even an empty string has an end. Thus, when I use $1 to reference the text matched within the parenthetical subexpression, I'm assured it will have some value (although that value will be empty when the filename ends with a slash).

Another comment on efficiency: with an NFA, ⌜[^/]*$⌟ is very inefficient. Carefully run through how the NFA engine attempts the match and you see that it can involve a lot of backtracking. Even the short sample '/usr/local/bin/perl' backtracks over 40 times before finally matching. Consider the attempt that starts at ⋯local/⋯. Once ⌜[^/]*⌟ matches through to the second 1 and fails on the slash, the ⌜$⌟ is tried (and fails) for each 1, a, c, o, 1 saved state. If that's not enough, most of it is repeated with the attempt that starts at ⋯local/⋯, and then again ⋯local/⋯, and so on.

It shouldn't concern us too much with this particular example, as filenames tend to be short. (And 40 backtracks is nothing — 40 million is when they really matter!) Again, it's important to be aware of the issues so the general lessons here can be applied to your specific needs.

This is a good time to point out that even in a book about regular expressions, regular expressions aren't always The Best Answer. For example, most programming languages provide non-regex routines for dealing with filenames. But, for the sake of discussion, I'll forge ahead.

Both leading path and filename

The next logical step is to pick apart a full path into both its leading path and filename component. There are many ways to do this, depending on what we want. Initially, you might want to use ⌜^(.*)/(.*)$⌟ to fill $1 and $2 with the requisite parts. It looks like a nicely balanced regular expression, but knowing how greediness works, we are guaranteed that the first ⌜.*⌟ does what we want, never leaving anything with a slash for $2. The only reason the first ⌜.*⌟ leaves anything at all is due to the backtracking done in trying to match the slash that follows. This leaves only that "backtracked" part for the later ⌜.*⌟. Thus, $1 is the full leading path and $2 the trailing filename.

One thing to note: we are relying on the initial ⌜(.*)/⌟ to ensure that the second ⌜(.*)⌟ does not capture any slash. We understand greediness, so this is okay. Still I like to be specific when I can, so I'd rather use ⌜[^/]*⌟ for the filename part. That gives us ⌜^(.*)/([^/]*)$⌟. Since it shows exactly what we want, it acts as documentation as well.

One big problem is that this regex requires at least one slash in the string, so if we try it on something like file.txt, there's no match, and thus no information. This can be a feature if we deal with it properly:

```
if ( $WholePath =~ m!^(.*)/([^/]*)$! ) {
    # Have a match -- $1 and $2 are valid
    $LeadingPath = $1;
    $FileName = $2;
} else {
    # No match, so there's no '/' in the filename
    $LeadingPath = "."; # so "file.txt" looks like "./file.txt" ("." is the current directory)
    $FileName = $WholePath;
}
```

Matching Balanced Sets of Parentheses

Matching balanced sets of parentheses, brackets, and the like presents a special difficulty. Wanting to match balanced parentheses is quite common when parsing many kinds of configuration files, programs, and such. Imagine, for example, that you want to do some processing on all of a function's arguments when parsing a language like C. Function arguments are wrapped in parentheses following the function name, and may themselves contain parentheses resulting from nested function calls or math grouping. At first, ignoring that they may be nested, you might be tempted to use ⌜\bfoo\([^)]*\)⌟, but it won't work.

In hallowed C tradition, I use foo as the example function name. The marked part of the expression is ostensibly meant to match the function's arguments. With examples such as foo(2, 4.0) and foo(somevar, 3.7), it works as expected. Unfortunately, it also matches foo(bar(somevar), 3.7), which is not as we want. This calls for something a bit "smarter" than ⌜[^)]*⌟.

To match the parenthesized expression part, you might consider the following regular expressions, among others:

1.   \(.*\)   literal parentheses with anything in between
2.   \([^)]*\)   from an opening parenthesis to the next closing parenthesis
3.   \([^()]*\)   from an opening parenthesis to the next closing parenthesis, but no other opening parentheses allowed in between

Figure 5-1 illustrates where these match against a sample line of code.

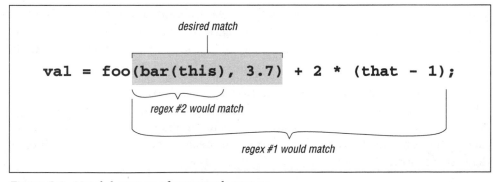

Figure 5-1: Match locations of our sample regexes

We see that regex #1 matches too much,[†] and regex #2 matches too little. Regex #3 doesn't even match successfully. In isolation, #3 would match '(this)', but because it must come immediately after the foo, it fails. So, none of these work.

---

† The use of ⌜.*⌟ should set off warning alarms. Always pay particular attention to decide whether dot is really what you want to apply star to. Sometimes that is exactly what you need, but ⌜.*⌟ is often used inappropriately.

The real problem is that on the vast majority of systems, *you simply can't match arbitrarily nested constructs with regular expressions*. For a long time, this was universally true, but recently, both Perl and .NET offer constructs that make it possible. (See pages 328 and 430, respectively.) But, even without these special constructs, you can still build a regex to match things nested *to a certain depth*, but not to an *arbitrary level* of nesting. Just one level of nesting requires

```
⌜\([^()]*(\([^()]*\)[^()]*)*\)⌟
```

so the thought of having to worry about further levels of nesting is frightening. But, here's a little Perl snippet that, given a $depth, creates a regex to match up to that many levels of parentheses beyond the first. It uses Perl's "*string* x *count*" operator, which replicates *string* by *count* times:

```
$regex = '\(' . '(?:[^()]|\(' x $depth . '[^()]*' . '\))*' x $depth . '\)';
```

I'll leave the analysis for your free time.

Watching Out for Unwanted Matches

It's easy to forget what happens if the text is not formed just as you expect. Let's say you are writing a filter to convert a text file to HTML, and you want to replace a line of hyphens by <HR>, which represent a horizontal rule (a line across the page). If you used a s/-*/<HR>/ search-and-replace command, it would replace the sequences you wanted, but only when they're at the beginning of the line. Surprised? In fact, s/-*/<HR>/ adds <HR> to the beginning of *every* line, whether they begin with a sequence of hyphens or not!

Remember, anything that isn't required is always considered successful. The first time ⌜-*⌟ is attempted at the start of the string, it matches any hyphens that might be there. However, if there aren't any, it is still happy to successfully match nothing. That's what star is all about.

Let's look at a similar example I once saw in a book by a respected author, in which he describes a regular expression to match a number, either integer or floating-point. As his expression is constructed, such a number has an optional leading minus sign, any number of digits, an optional decimal point, and any number of digits that follow. His regex is ⌜-?[0-9]*\.?[0-9]*⌟.

Indeed, this matches such examples as 1, -272.37, 129238843., .191919, and even something like -.0. This is all good, and as expected.

However, how do you think it matches in a string like 'this␣has␣no␣number', 'nothing␣here', or even an empty string? Look at the regex closely—*everything* is optional. *If* a number is there, and *if* it is at the beginning of the string, it is matched, but *nothing is required*. This regex can match all three non-number examples, matching the nothingness at the beginning of the string each time. In fact, it even matches nothingness at the beginning of an example like 'num•123', since that nothingness matches earlier than the number would.

So, it's important to say what you really mean. A floating-point number *must* have at least one digit in it, or it's not a number(!). To construct our regex, let's first assume there is at least one digit before the decimal point. (We'll remove this requirement later.) If so, we need to use plus for those digits: ⌈-?[0-9]+⌋.

Writing the subexpression to match an optional decimal point (and subsequent digits) hinges on the realization that any numbers after the decimal point are contingent upon there being a decimal point in the first place. If we use something naïve like ⌈\.?[0-9]*⌋, the ⌈[0-9]*⌋ gets a chance to match regardless of the decimal point's presence.

The solution is, again, to say what we mean. A decimal point (and subsequent digits, if any) is optional: ⌈(\.[0-9]*)?⌋. Here, the question mark no longer quantifies (that is, governs or controls) only the decimal point, but instead the entire combination of the decimal point plus any following digits. *Within* that combination, the decimal point is required; if it is not there, ⌈[0-9]*⌋ is not even reached.

Putting this all together, we have ⌈-?[0-9]+(\.[0-9]*)?⌋. This still doesn't allow something like '.007', since our regex requires at least one digit before the decimal point. If we change that part to allow zero digits, we have to change the other so it doesn't, since we can't allow *all* digits to be optional (the problem we are trying to correct in the first place).

The solution is to add an alternative that allows for the uncovered situation: ⌈-?[0-9]+(\.[0-9]*)?|-?\.[0-9]+⌋. This now also allows just a decimal point followed by (this time not optional) digits. Details, details. Did you notice that I allowed for the optional leading minus in the second alternative as well? That's easy to forget. Of course, you could instead bring the ⌈-?⌋ out of the alternation, as in ⌈-?([0-9]+(\.[0-9]*)?|\.[0-9]+)⌋.

Although this is an improvement on the original, it's still more than happy to match at '2003.04.12'. Knowing the context in which a regex is intended to be used is an important part of striking the balance between matching what you want, and not matching what you don't want. Our regex for floating-point numbers requires that it be constrained somehow by being part of a larger regex, such as being wrapped by ⌈^···$⌋, or perhaps ⌈num\s*=\s*···$⌋.

Matching Delimited Text

Matching a double-quoted string and matching an IP address are just two examples of a whole class of matching problem that often arises: the desire to match text delimited (or perhaps separated) by some other text. Other examples include:

- Matching a C comment, which is surrounded by '/*' and '*/'.

- Matching an HTML tag, which is text wrapped by <···>, such as <CODE>.

- Extracting items *between* HTML tags, such as the 'super exciting' of the HTML 'a <I>super exciting</I> offer!'

- Matching a line in a *.mailrc* file. This file gives email aliases, where each line is in the form of

    alias   *shorthand   full-address*

  such as 'alias jeff jfriedl@regex.info'. (Here, the delimiters are the whitespace between each item, as well as the ends of the line.)

- Matching a quoted string, but allowing it to contain quotes if they are escaped, as in 'a passport needs a "2\"x3\" likeness" of the holder.'

- Parsing CSV (comma-separated values) files.

In general, the requirements for such tasks can be phrased along the lines of:

1. Match the opening delimiter

2. Match the main text
    (which is really "match anything that is not the closing delimiter")

3. Match the closing delimiter

As I mentioned earlier, the "match anything not the closing delimiter" can become complicated when the closing delimiter is more than one character, or in situations where it can appear within the main text.

Allowing escaped quotes in double-quoted strings

Let's look at the **2\"x3\"** example, where the closing delimiter is a quote, yet can appear within the main part if escaped. It's easy enough to match the opening and closing quotes; the trick is to match the main text without overshooting the closing quote. Thinking clearly about which items the main text allows, we know that if a character is not a double quote (in other words, if it's ⌈[^"]⌋), it is certainly okay. However, if it *is* a double quote, it is okay if preceded by a backslash. Translating that literally, using lookbehind (☞ 132) for the "if preceded" part, it becomes ⌈"([^"]|(?<=\\)")*"⌋, which indeed properly matches our **2\"x3\"** example.

This is a perfect example to show how unintended matches can sneak into a seemingly proper regex, because as much as it seems to be correct, it doesn't always work. We want it to match the marked part of this silly example:

```
Darth Symbol: "/-|-\\" or "[^-^]"
```

but it actually matches:

```
Darth Symbol: "/-|-\\" or "[^-^]"
```

This is because the final quote of the first string indeed has a backslash before it. That backslash is itself escaped, so it *doesn't* escape the quote that follows (which means the quote that follows *does* end the string). Our lookbehind doesn't recognize that the preceding backslash has been itself escaped, and considering that there may be any number of preceding '\\' sequences, it's a can of worms to try to solve this with lookbehind. The real problem is that a backslash that escapes a quote is not being recognized as an escaping backslash when we first process it, so let's try a different approach that tackles it from that angle.

Concentrating again at what kinds of things we want to match between the opening and closing delimiter, we know that something escaped is okay (「\\.」), as well as anything else other than the closing quote (「[^"]」). This yields 「"(\\.|[^"])*"」. Wonderful, we've solved the problem! Unfortunately, not yet. Unwanted matches can still creep in, such as with this example for which we expect no match because the closing quote has been forgotten:

```
"You need a 2\"3\" photo.
```

Why does it match? Recall the lessons from "Greediness and Laziness Always Favor a Match" (☞ 167). Even though our regex initially matches past that last quote, as we want, it still backtracks after it finds that there is no ending quote, to:

at '…2\"3\"•…'	matching 「(\\.|₍[^"])」

From that point, the 「[^"]」 matches the backslash, leaving us at what the regex can consider an ending quote.

An important lesson to take from this example is:

> When backtracking can cause undesired matches in relation to alternation, it's likely a sign that any success is just a happenstance due to the ordering of the alternatives.

In fact, had our original regex had its alternatives reversed, it would match incorrectly in *every* string containing an escaped double quote. The problem is that one alternative can match something that is supposed to be handled by the other.

So, how can we fix it? Well, just as in the continuation-lines example on page 186, we must make sure that there's no other way for that backslash to be matched, which means changing 「[^"]」ⱼ to 「[^\\"]」ⱼ . This recognizes that both a double quote and a backslash are "special" in this context, and must be handled accordingly. The result is ⌜`"(\\.|[^\\"])*"`⌟, which works just fine. (Although this regex now works, it can still be improved so that it is much more efficient for NFA engines; we'll see this example quite a bit in the next chapter ☞ 222.)

This example shows a particularly important moral:

> Always consider the "odd" cases in which you *don't* want a regex to match, such as with "bad" data.

Our fix is the right one, but it's interesting to note that if you have possessive quantifiers (☞ 140) or atomic grouping (☞ 137), this regex can be written as ⌜`"(\\.|[^"])*+"`⌟ and ⌜`"(?>(\\.|[^"])*)"`⌟ respectively. They don't really fix the problem so much as hide it, disallowing the engine from backtracking back to where the problem could show itself. Either way, they get the job done well.

Understanding how possessive quantifiers and atomic grouping help in this situation is extremely valuable, but I would still go ahead and make the previous fix anyway, as it is more descriptive to the reader. Actually, in this case, I would want to use possessive quantifiers or atomic grouping *as well*—not to solve the previous problem, but for efficiency, so that a failure fails more quickly.

Knowing Your Data and Making Assumptions

This is an opportune time to highlight a general point about constructing and using regular expressions that I've briefly mentioned a few times. It is important to be aware of the assumptions made about the kind of data with which, and situations in which, a regular expression will be used. Even something as simple as ⌜`a`⌟ assumes that the target data is in the same character encoding (☞ 105) as the author intends. This is pretty much common sense, which is why I haven't been too picky about saying these things.

However, many assumptions that might seem obvious to one person are not necessarily obvious to another. For example, the solution in the previous section assumes that escaped newlines shouldn't be matched, or that it will be applied in a dot-matches-all mode (☞ 110). If we really want to ensure that dot can match a newline, we should write that by using ⌜`(?s:.)`⌟, if supported by the flavor.

Another assumption made in the previous section is the type of data to which the regex will be applied, as it makes no provisions for any other uses of double quotes in the data. If you apply it to source code from almost any programming language, for example, you'll find that it breaks because there can be double quotes within comments.

There is nothing wrong with making assumptions about your data, or how you intend a regex to be used. The problems, if any, usually lie in overly optimistic assumptions and in misunderstandings between the author's intentions and how the regex is eventually used. Documenting the assumptions can help.

Stripping Leading and Trailing Whitespace

Removing leading and trailing whitespace from a line is not a challenging problem, but it's one that seems to come up often. By far the best all-around solution is the simple use of two substitutions:

```
s/^\s+//;
s/\s+$//;
```

As a measure of efficiency, these use ⌜+⌟ instead of ⌜*⌟, since there's no benefit to doing the substitution unless there is actually whitespace to remove.

For some reason, it seems to be popular to try to find a way to do it all in one expression, so I'll offer a few methods for comparison. I don't recommend them, but it's educational to understand why they work, and why they're not desirable.

```
s/\s*(.*?)\s*$/$1/s
```

This used to be given as a great example of lazy quantifiers, but not any more, because people now realize that it's so much slower than the simple approach. (In Perl, it's about 5× slower). The lack of speed is due to the need to check ⌜\s*$⌟ before *each* application of the lazy-quantified dot. That requires a lot of backtracking.

```
s/^\s*((?:.*\S)?)\s*$/$1/s
```

This one looks more complex than the previous example, but its matching is more straightforward, and is only twice as slow as the simple approach. After the initial ⌜^\s*⌟ has bypassed any leading whitespace, the ⌜.*⌟ in the middle matches all the way to the end of the text. The ⌜\s⌟ that follows forces it to backtrack to the last non-whitespace in the text, thereby leaving the trailing whitespace matched by the final ⌜\s*$⌟, outside of the capturing parentheses.

The question mark is needed so that this expression works properly on a line that has only whitespace. Without it, it would fail to match, leaving the whitespace-filled line unchanged.

```
s/^\s+|\s+$//g
```

This is a commonly thought-up solution that, while not incorrect (none of these are incorrect), it has top-level alternation that removes many optimizations (covered in the next chapter) that might otherwise be possible.

The /g modifier is required to allow each alternative to match, to remove both leading *and* trailing whitespace. It seems a waste to use /g when we know we intend at most two matches, and each with a different subexpression. This is about 4× slower than the simple approach.

I've mentioned the relative speeds as I tested them, but in practice, the actual relative speeds are dependent upon the tool and the data. For example, if the target text is very, very long, but has relatively little whitespace on either end, the middle approach can be somewhat faster than the simple approach. Still, in my programs, I use the language's equivalent of

```
s/^\s+//;
s/\s+$//;
```

because it's almost always fastest, and is certainly the easiest to understand.

HTML-Related Examples

In Chapter 2, we saw an extended example that converted raw text to HTML (☞ 67), including regular expressions to pluck out email addresses and `http` URLs from the text. In this section, we'll do a few other HTML-related tasks.

Matching an HTML Tag

It's common to see ⌜`<[^>]+>`⌝ used to match an HTML tag. It usually works fine, such as in this snippet of Perl that strips tags:

```
$html =~ s/<[^>]+>//g;
```

However, it matches improperly if the tag has '>' within it, as with this perfectly valid HTML: `<input name=dir value=">">`. Although it's not common or recommended, HTML allows a raw '<' and '>' to appear within a quoted tag attribute. Our simple ⌜`<[^>]+>`⌝ doesn't allow for that, so, we must make it smarter.

Allowed within the '< ··· >' are quoted sequences, and "other stuff" characters that may appear unquoted. This includes everything except '>' and quotes. HTML allows both single- and double-quoted strings. It doesn't allow embedded quotes to be escaped, which allows us to use simple regexes ⌜`"[^"]*"`⌝ and ⌜`'[^']*'`⌝ to match them.

Putting these together with the "other stuff" regex ⌜`[^'">]`⌝, we get:

⌜`<("[^"]*"|'[^']*'|[^'">])*>`⌝

That may be a bit confusing, so how about the same thing shown with comments in a free-spacing mode:

```
<                    #  Opening "<"
  (                  #     Any amount of . . .
    "[^"]*"          #        double-quoted string,
    |                #        or . . .
    '[^']*'          #        single-quoted string,
    |                #        or . . .
    [^'">]           #        "other stuff"
  ) *                #
  >                  #  Closing ">"
```

The overall approach is quite elegant, as it treats each quoted part as a unit, and clearly indicates what is allowed at any point in the match. Nothing can be matched by more than one part of the regex, so there's no ambiguity, and hence no worry about unintended matches "sneaking in," as with some earlier examples.

Notice that ⌜*⌝ rather than ⌜+⌝ is used within the quotes of the first two alternatives? A quoted string may be empty (e.g., '**alt=""**'), so ⌜*⌝ is used within each pair of quotes to reflect that. But don't use ⌜*⌝ or ⌜+⌝ in the third alternative, as the ⌜[^'">]⌝ is already directly subject to a quantifier via the wrapping ⌜(⋯)*⌝. Adding another quantifier, yielding an effective ⌜([^'">]+)*⌝, could case a very rude surprise that I don't expect you to understand at this point; it's discussed in great detail in the next chapter (☞ 226).

One thought about efficiency when used with an NFA engine: since we don't use the text captured by the parentheses, we can change them to non-capturing parentheses (☞ 136). And since there is indeed no ambiguity among the alternatives, if it turns out that the final ⌜>⌝ can't match when it's tried, there's no benefit going back and trying the remaining alternatives. Where one of the alternatives matched before, no other alternative can match now from the same spot. So, it's okay to throw away any saved states, and doing so affords a faster failure when no match can be had. This can be done by using ⌜(?>⋯)⌝ atomic grouping instead of the non-capturing parentheses (or a possessive star to quantify whichever parentheses are used).

Matching an HTML Link

Let's say that now we want to match sets of URL and link text from a document, such as pulling the marked items from:

```
⋯<a href="http://www.oreilly.com">O'Reilly And Associates</a>⋯
```

Because the contents of an <A> tag can be fairly complex, I would approach this task in two parts. The first is to pluck out the "guts" of the <A> tag, along with the link text, and then pluck the URL itself from those <A> guts.

A simplistic approach to the first part is a case-insensitive, dot-matches-all application of ⌜<a\b([^>]+)>(.*?)</a>⌝, which features the lazy star quantifier. This puts the <A> guts into $1 and the link text into $2. Of course, as earlier, instead of ⌜[^>]+⌝ I should use what we developed in the previous section. Having said that, I'll continue with this simpler version, for the sake of keeping that part of the regex shorter and cleaner for the discussion.

Once we have the <A> guts in a string, we can inspect them with a separate regex. In them, the URL is the value for the href=*value* attribute. HTML allows spaces on either side of the equal sign, and the value can be quoted or not, as described in the previous section. A solution is shown as part of this Perl snippet to report on links in the variable $Html:

```
# Note: the regex in the while(...) is overly simplistic— see text for discussion
while ($Html =~ m{<a\b([^>]+)>(.*?)</a>}ig)
{
    my $Guts = $1;  # Save results from the match above, to their own . . .
    my $Link = $2;  #  . . . named variables, for clarity below.

    if ($Guts =~ m{
                    \b HREF        # "href" attribute
                    \s* = \s*      # "=" may have whitespace on either side
                    (?:            # Value is
                      "([^"]*)"    #    double-quoted string,
                      |            #    or
                      '([^']*)'    #    single-quoted string,
                      |            #    or
                      ([^'">\s]+)  #    "other stuff"
                    )              #
                  }xi)
    {
        my $Url = $+;  # Gives the highest-numbered actually-filled $1, $2, etc.
        print "$Url with link text: $Link\n";
    }
}
```

Some notes about this:

- This time, I added parentheses to each value-matching alternative, to capture the exact value matched.

- Because I'm using some of the parentheses to capture, I've used non-capturing parentheses where I don't need to capture, both for clarity and efficiency.

- This time, the "other stuff" component excludes whitespace in addition to quotes and '>', as whitespace separates "attribute=value" pairs.

- This time, I do use ⌜+⌟ in the "other stuff" alternative, as it's needed to capture the whole href value. Does this cause the same "rude surprise" as if we used ⌜+⌟ in the "other stuff" alternative on page 200? No, because there's no outer quantifier that directly influences the class being repeated. Again, this is covered in detail in the next chapter.

Depending on the text, the actual URL may end up in $1, $2, or $3. The others will be empty or undefined. Perl happens to support a special variable $+ which is the value of the highest-numbered $1, $2, etc. that actually captured text. In this case, that's exactly what we want as our URL.

Using $+ is convenient in Perl, but other languages offer other ways to isolate the captured URL. Normal programming constructs can always be used to inspect the captured groups, using the one that has a value. If supported, named capturing (☞ 137) is perfect for this, as shown in the VB.NET example on page 204. (It's good that .NET offers named capture, because its $+ is broken ☞ 418.)

Examining an HTTP URL

Now that we've got a URL, let's see if it's an `http` URL, and if so, pluck it apart into its hostname and path components. Since we know we have something intended to be a URL, our task is made much simpler than if we had to *identify* a URL from among random text. That much more difficult task is investigated a bit later in this chapter.

So, given a URL, we merely need to be able to recognize the parts. The hostname is everything after ⌜`^http://`⌟ but before the next slash (if there is another slash), and the path is everything else: ⌜`^http://([^/]+)(/.*)?$`⌟

Actually, a URL may have an optional port number between the hostname and the path, with a leading colon: ⌜`^http://([^/:]+(:(\d+))?)(/.*)?$`⌟

Here's a Perl snippet to report about a URL:

```perl
if ($url =~ m{^http://([^/:]+(:(\d+))?)(/.*)?$}i)
{
  my $host = $1;
  my $port = $3 || 80;   # Use $3 if it exists; otherwise default to 80.
  my $path = $4 || "/";  # Use $4 if it exists; otherwise default to "/".
  print "host: $host\n";
  print "port: $port\n";
  print "path: $path\n";
} else {
  print "not an http url\n";
}
```

Validating a Hostname

In the previous example, we used ⌜`[^/:]+`⌟ to match a hostname. Yet, in Chapter 2 (☞ 76), we used the more complex ⌜`[-a-z]+(\.[-a-z]+)*\.(com|edu|⋯|info)`⌟. Why the difference in complexity for finding ostensibly the same thing?

Well, even though both are used to "match a hostname," they're used quite differently. It's one thing to pluck out something from a known quantity (e.g., from something you know to be a URL), but it's quite another to accurately and unambiguously pluck out that same type of something from among random text. Specifically, in the previous example, we made the assumption that what comes after the 'http://' is a hostname, so the use of ⌜`[^/:]+`⌟ merely to fetch it is reasonable. But in the Chapter 2 example, we use a regex to find a hostname in random text, so it must be much more specific.

Now, for a third angle on matching a hostname, we can consider validating hostnames with regular expressions. In this case, we want to check whether a string is a well-formed, syntactically correct hostname. Officially, a hostname is made up of dot-separated parts, where each part can have ASCII letters, digits, and hyphens, but a part can't begin or end with a hyphen. Thus, one part can be matched with

Link Checker in VB.NET

This Program reports on links within the HTML in the variable *Html*:

```
Imports System.Text.RegularExpressions
   ⋮
' Set up the regular expressions we'll use in the loop
Dim A_Regex as Regex = New Regex(                                 _
             "<a\b(?<guts>[^>]+)>(?<Link>.*?)</a>",              _
             RegexOptions.IgnoreCase)

Dim GutsRegex as Regex = New Regex(  _
    "\b HREF                    (?#  'href' attribute            )" & _
    "\s* = \s*                  (?#  '=' with optional whitespace )" & _
    "(?:                        (?#  Value is ...                )" & _
    "   ""(?<url>[^""]*)""      (?#     double-quoted string,    )" & _
    "   |                       (?#     or ...                   )" & _
    "   '(?<url>[^']*)'         (?#     single-quoted string,    )" & _
    "   |                       (?#     or ...                   )" & _
    "   (?<url>[^'"">\s]+)      (?#     'other stuff'            )" & _
    ")                          (?#                              )",  _
    RegexOptions.IgnoreCase OR RegexOptions.IgnorePatternWhitespace)

' Now check the 'Html' Variable . . .
Dim CheckA as Match = A_Regex.Match(Html)

' For each match within . . .
While CheckA.Success
    ' We matched an <a> tag, so now check for the URL.
    Dim UrlCheck as Match = _
       GutsRegex.Match(CheckA.Groups("guts").Value)
    If UrlCheck.Success
        ' We've got a match, so have a URL/link pair
        Console.WriteLine("Url " & UrlCheck.Groups("url").Value & _
                          " WITH LINK " & CheckA.Groups("Link").Value)
    End If
    CheckA = CheckA.NextMatch
End While
```

A few things to notice:

- VB.NET programs using regular expressions require that first `Imports` line to tell the compiler what object libraries to use.

- I've used ⌈`(?#···)`⌋ style comments because it's inconvenient to get a new-line into a VB.NET string, and normal '#' comments carry on until the next newline or the end of the string (which means that the first one would make the entire rest of the regex a comment). To use normal ⌈`#···`⌋ comments, add `&chr(10)` at the end of each line (☞ 414).

- Each double quote in the regex requires '`""`' in the literal string (☞ 102).

- Named capturing is used in both expressions, allowing the more descriptive `Groups("url")` instead of `Groups(1)`, `Groups(2)`, etc.

a case-insensitive application of ⌈[a-z0-9] | [a-z0-9] [-a-z0-9]*[-a-z0-9]⌉. The final suffix part ('com', 'edu', 'uk', etc.) has a limited set of possibilities, mentioned in passing in the Chapter 2 example. Using that here, we're left with the following regex to match a syntactically valid hostname:

```
(?:i)  # apply this regex in a case-insensitive manner.
# One or more dot-separated parts
(?: [a-z0-9]\. | [a-z0-9][-a-z0-9]*[-a-z0-9]\. )+
# Followed by the final suffix part
(?: com|edu|gov|int|mil|net|org|biz|info|name|museum|coop|aero|[a-z][a-z] )
$
```

Something matching this regex isn't necessarily valid quite yet, as there's a length limitation: individual parts may be no longer than 63 characters. That means that the ⌈[-a-z0-9]*⌉ in there should be ⌈[-a-z0-9]{0,61}⌉.

There's one final change, just to be official. Officially, a name consisting of only one of the suffixes (e.g., 'com', 'edu', etc.) is also syntactically valid. Current practice seems to be that these "names" don't actually have a computer answer to them, but that doesn't always seem to be the case for the two-letter country suffixes. For example, Anguilla's top-level domain 'ai' has a web server: http://ai/ shows a page. A few others like this that I've seen include cc, co, dk, mm, ph, tj, tv, and tw.

So, if you wish to allow for these special cases, change the central ⌈(?:···)+⌉ to ⌈(?:···)*⌉. These changes leave us with:

```
(?:i)  # apply this regex in a case-insensitive manner.
# One or more dot-separated parts
(?: [a-z0-9]\. | [a-z0-9][-a-z0-9]{0,61}[-a-z0-9]\. )*
# Followed by the final suffix part
(?: com|edu|gov|int|mil|net|org|biz|info|name|museum|coop|aero|[a-z][a-z] )
$
```

This now works just dandy to validate a string containing a hostname. Since this is the most specific of the three hostname-related regexes we've developed, you might think that if you remove the anchors, it could be better than the regex we came up with earlier for plucking out hostnames from random text. That's not the case. This regex matches any two-letter word, which is why the less-specific regex from Chapter 2 is better in practice. But, it still might not be good enough for some purposes, as the next section shows.

Plucking Out a URL in the Real World

Working for Yahoo! Finance, I write programs that process incoming financial news and data feeds. News articles are usually provided to us in raw text, and my programs convert them to HTML for a pleasing presentation. (Read financial news at `http://finance.yahoo.com` and see how I've done.) It's often a daunting task due to the random "formatting" (or lack thereof) of the data we receive, and because it's much more difficult to *recognize* things like hostnames and URLs in raw text than it is to *validate* them once you've got them. The previous section alluded to this; in this section, I'll show you code we actually use at Yahoo! to solve the issues we've faced.

We look for several types of URLs to pluck from the text—`mailto`, `http`, `https`, and `ftp` URLs. If we find '`http://`' in the text, we're pretty certain that's the start of a URL, so we can use something simple like ⌈`http://[-\w]+(\.\w[-\w]*)+`⌋ to match up through the hostname part. We're using the knowledge of the text (raw English text provided as ASCII) to realize that it's probably okay to use ⌈`-\w`⌋ instead of ⌈`[-a-z0-9]`⌋. ⌈`\w`⌋ also matches an underscore, and in some systems also matches the whole of Unicode letters, but we know that neither of these really matter to us in this particular situation.

However, often, a URL is given without the `http://` or `mailto:` prefix, such as:

> `visit us at www.oreilly.com or mail to orders@oreilly.com.`

In this case, we need to be much more careful. What we use is quite similar to the regex from the previous section, but it differs in a few ways:

```
(?i: [a-z0-9] (?:[-a-z0-9]*[a-z0-9])? \.●)+ # sub domains
# Now ending .com, etc. For these, we require lowercase
(?-i: com\b
    | edu\b
    | biz\b
    | org\b
    | gov\b
    | in(?:t|fo)\b # .int or .info
    | mil\b
    | net\b
    | name\b
    | museum\b
    | coop\b
    | aero\b
    | [a-z][a-z]\b # two-letter country codes
)
```

In this regex, ⌈`(?i:⋯)`⌋ and ⌈`(?-i:⋯)`⌋ are used to explicitly enable and disable case-insensitivity for specific parts of the regex (☞ 134). We want to match a URL like '`www.OReilly.com`', but not a stock symbol like '`NT.TO`' (the stock symbol for Nortel Networks on the Toronto Stock Exchange—remember, we process financial news and data, which has a lot of stock symbols). Officially, the ending part of a URL (e.g., '`.com`') may be upper case, but we simply won't recognize those. That's the balance we've struck among matching what we want (pretty much every URL we're likely to see), not matching what we don't want (stock symbols), and simplicity. I suppose we could move the ⌈`(?-i:⋯)`⌋ to wrap only the country codes part, but in practice, we just don't get uppercased URLs, so we've left this as it is.

Here's a framework for finding URLs in raw text, into which we can insert the subexpression to match a hostname:

```
\b
# Match the leading part (proto://hostname, or just hostname)
(

    # ftp://, http://, or https:// leading part
    (ftp|https?)://[-\w]+(\.\w[-\w]*)+
  |
    # or, try to find a hostname with our more specific sub-expression
    full-hostname-regex
)

# Allow an optional port number
( : \d+ )?

# The rest of the URL is optional, and begins with / . . .
(
    / path-part
)?
```

I haven't talked yet about the path part of the regex, which comes after the hostname (e.g., the underlined part of `http://www.oreilly.com/catalog/regex/`). The path part turns out to be the most difficult text to match properly, as it requires some guessing to do a good job. As discussed in Chapter 2, what often comes *after* a URL in the text is also allowed as part of a URL. For example, with

```
Read his comments at http://www.oreilly.com/ask_tim/index.html. He ...
```

we can look and realize that the period after 'index.html' is English punctuation and should not be considered part of the URL, yet the period *within* 'index.html' *is* part of the URL.

Although it's easy for us humans to differentiate between the two, it's quite difficult for a program, so we've got to come up with some heuristics that get the job done as best we can. The approach taken with the Chapter 2 example is to use negative lookbehind to ensure that a URL can't end with sentence-ending punctuation characters. What we've been using at Yahoo! Finance was originally written before negative lookbehind was available, and so is more complex than the Chapter 2 approach, but in the end it has the same effect. It's shown in the listing on the next page. The approach taken for the path part is different in a number of respects, and the comparison with the Chapter 2 example on page 75 should be interesting. In particular, the Java version of this regex in the sidebar on page 209 provides some insight as to how it was built.

In practice, I doubt I'd actually write out a full monster like this, but instead I'd build up a "library" of regular expressions and use them as needed. A simple example of this is shown with the use of `$HostnameRegex` on page 76, and also in the sidebar on page 209.

Regex to pluck a URL from financial news

```
\b
#  Match the leading part (proto://bostname, or just bostname)
(
    #  ftp://, http://, or https:// leading part
    (ftp|https?)://[-\w]+(\.\w[-\w]*)+
  |
    #  or, try to find a hostname with our more specific sub-expression
    (?i: [a-z0-9] (?:[-a-z0-9]*[a-z0-9])? \. )+  #  sub domains
    #  Now ending .com, etc. For these, require lowercase
    (?-i: com\b
        | edu\b
        | biz\b
        | gov\b
        | in(?:t|fo)\b #  .int or .info
        | mil\b
        | net\b
        | org\b
        | [a-z][a-z]\b #  two-letter country codes
    )
)

#  Allow an optional port number
( : \d+ )?

#  The rest of the URL is optional, and begins with / ...
(
    /
    #  The rest are heuristics for what seems to work well
    [^;"'<>()\[\]{}\s\x7F-\xFF]*
    (?:
        [.,?]+  [^;"'<>()\[\]{}\s\x7F-\xFF]+
    )*
)?
```

Extended Examples

The next few examples illustrate some important techniques about regular expressions. The discussions are longer, and show more of the thought processes and mistaken paths that eventually lead to a working conclusion.

Keeping in Sync with Your Data

Let's look at a lengthy example that might seem a bit contrived, but which illustrates some excellent points on why it's important to keep in sync with what you're trying to match (and provides some methods to do so).

Let's say that your data is a series of five-digit US postal codes (ZIP codes) that are run together, and that you need to retrieve all that begin with, say, 44. Here is a sample line of data, with the codes we want to retrieve in bold:

0382453144941161521344182950354427275201021744323 5

Building Up a Regex Through Variables in Java

```
String SubDomain  = "(?i:[a-z0-9]|[a-z0-9][-a-z0-9]*[a-z0-9])";
String TopDomains = "(?x-i:com\\b          \n" +
                    "       |edu\\b          \n" +
                    "       |biz\\b          \n" +
                    "       |in(?:t|fo)\\b  \n" +
                    "       |mil\\b          \n" +
                    "       |net\\b          \n" +
                    "       |org\\b          \n" +
                    "       |[a-z][a-z]\\b  \n" + // country codes
                    ")                       \n";
String Hostname = "(?:" + SubDomain + "\\.)+" + TopDomains;

String NOT_IN   = ";\"'<>()\\[\\]\\{\\}\\s\\x7F-\\xFF";
String NOT_END  = ".,?";
String ANYWHERE = "[^" + NOT_IN + NOT_END + "]";
String EMBEDDED = "[" + NOT_END + "]";
String UrlPath  = "/"+ANYWHERE + "*("+EMBEDDED+"+"+ANYWHERE+"+)*";

String Url =
 "(?x:                                                \n"+
 "  \\b                                               \n"+
 "  ## match the hostname part                        \n"+
 "  (                                                 \n"+
 "     (?: ftp | http s? ): // [-\\w]+(\\.\\w[-\\w]*)+ \n"+
 "  |                                                 \n"+
 "     " + Hostname + "                               \n"+
 "  )                                                 \n"+
 "  # allow optional port                             \n"+
 "  (?: \\d+ )?                                       \n"+
 "                                                    \n"+
 "  # rest of url is optional, and begins with /      \n"+
 "  (?: " + UrlPath + ")?                             \n"+
 ")";

// Now convert string we've built up into a real regex object
Pattern UrlRegex = Pattern.compile(Url);
// Now ready to apply to raw text to find urls . . .
    ⋮
```

As a starting point, consider that ⌈\d\d\d\d\d⌋ can be used repeatedly to match all the ZIP codes. In Perl, this is as simple as **@zips = m/\d\d\d\d\d/g;** to create a list with one ZIP code per element. (To keep these examples less cluttered, they assume the text to be matched is in Perl's default target variable **$_** ☞ 79.) With other languages, it's usually a simple matter to call the regex "find" method in a loop. I'd like to concentrate on the regular expression rather than that mechanics particular to each language, so will continue to use Perl to show the examples.

Back to ⌈\d\d\d\d\d⌋. Here's a point whose importance will soon become apparent: the regex never fails until the entire list has been parsed—there are absolutely no bump-and-retries by the transmission. (I'm assuming we'll have only proper data, an assumption that is very situation specific.)

So, it should be apparent that changing ⌜\d\d\d\d\d⌝ to ⌜44\d\d\d⌝ in an attempt to find only ZIP codes starting with 44 is silly — once a match attempt fails, the transmission bumps along one character, thus putting the match for the ⌜44···⌝ out of sync with the start of each ZIP code. Using ⌜44\d\d\d⌝ incorrectly finds a match at '···531**4494**116···'.

You could, of course, put a caret or ⌜\A⌝ at the head of the regex, but they allow a target ZIP code to match only if it's the first in the string. We need to keep the regex engine in sync manually by writing our regex to pass over undesired ZIP codes as needed. The key here is that it must pass over full ZIP codes, not single characters as with the automatic bump-along.

Keeping the match in sync with expectations

The following are a few ways to pass over undesired ZIP codes. Inserting them before what we want (⌜(44\d\d\d)⌝) achieves the desired effect. Non-capturing ⌜(?:···)⌝ parentheses are used to match undesired ZIP codes, effectively allowing us to pass them over on the way toward matching a desired ZIP code within the $1 capturing parentheses:

⌜**(?:[^4]\d\d\d\d|\d[^4]\d\d\d)***···⌝

This brute-force method actively skips ZIP codes that start with something other than 44. (Well, it's probably better to use ⌜[1235-9]⌝ instead of ⌜[^4]⌝, but as I said earlier, I am assuming properly formatted data.) By the way, we can't use ⌜(?:[^4][^4]\d\d\d)*⌝, as it does not match (and thus does not pass over) undesired ZIP codes like 43210.

⌜**(?:(?!44)\d\d\d\d\d)***···⌝

This method, which uses negative lookahead, actively skips ZIP codes that do not start with 44. This English description sounds virtually identical to the previous one, but when rendered into a regular expression looks quite different. Compare the two descriptions and related expressions. In this case, a desired ZIP code (beginning with 44) causes ⌜(?!44)⌝ to fail, thus causing the skipping to stop.

⌜**(?:\d\d\d\d\d)*?**···⌝

This method uses a lazy quantifier to skip ZIP codes only when needed. We use it before a subexpression matching what we *do* want, so that if that subexpression fails, this one matches a ZIP. It's the laziness of ⌜(···)*?⌝ that allows this to happen. Because of the lazy quantifier, ⌜(?:\d\d\d\d\d)⌝ is not even attempted until whatever follows has failed. The star assures that it is repeatedly attempted until whatever follows finally does match, thus effectively skipping only what we want to skip.

Combining this last method with ⌜(44\d\d\d)⌟ gives us

```
@zips = m/(?:\d\d\d\d\d)*?(44\d\d\d)/g;
```

and picks out the desired '44*xxx*' codes, actively skipping undesired ones that intervene. (In this "**@array = m/···/g**" situation, Perl fills the array with what's matched by capturing parentheses during each match attempt ☞ 311.) This regex can work repeatedly on the string because we know each match always leaves the "current match position" at the start of the next ZIP code, thereby priming the next match to start at the beginning of a ZIP code as the regex expects.

Maintaining sync after a non-match as well

Have we *really* ensured that the regex is always applied only at the start of a ZIP code? *No!* We have manually skipped *intervening* undesired ZIP codes, but once there are no more desired ones, the regex finally fails. As always, the bump-along-and-retry happens, thereby starting the match from a position *within* a ZIP code—something our approach relies on never happening.

Let's look at our sample data again:

03824531449411615213**44182**9503544272752010217**443235**

Here, the matched codes are bold (the third of which is undesired), the codes we actively skipped are underlined, and characters skipped via bump-along-and-retry are marked. After the match of 44272, no more target codes are able to be matched, so the subsequent attempt fails. Does the whole match attempt end? Of course not. The transmission bumps along to apply the regex at the next character, putting us out of sync with the real ZIP codes. After the fourth such bump-along, the regex skips 10217 as it matches 44323, reporting it falsely as a desired code.

Any of our three expressions work smoothly so long as they are applied at the start of a ZIP code, but the transmission's bump-along defeats them. This can be solved by ensuring that the transmission doesn't bump along, or that a bump-along doesn't cause problems.

One way to ensure that the transmission doesn't bump along, at least for the first two methods, is to make ⌜(44\d\d\d\)⌟ greedily optional by appending ⌜?⌟. This plays off the knowledge that the prepended ⌜(?:(?!44)\d\d\d\d\d)*···⌟ or ⌜(?:[^4]\d\d\d\d|\d[^4]\d\d\d)*···⌟ finish only when at a desired code, or when there are no more codes (which is why it can't be used for the third, non-greedy method.) Thus, ⌜(44\d\d\d)?⌟ matches the desired ZIP code if it's there, but doesn't force a backtrack if it's not.

There are some problems with this solution. One is that because we can now have a regex match even when we don't have a target ZIP code, the handling code must be a bit more complex. However, to its benefit, it is fast, since it doesn't involve much backtracking, nor any bump-alongs by the transmission.

Maintaining sync with \G

A more general approach is to simply prepend ⌈\G⌋ (☞ 128) to any of the three methods' expressions. Because we crafted each to explicitly end on a ZIP code boundary, we're assured that any subsequent match that has had no intervening bump-along begins on that same ZIP boundary. And if there *has* been a bump-along, the leading ⌈\G⌋ fails immediately, because with most flavors, it's successful only when there's been no intervening bump-along. (This is not true for Ruby and other flavors whose ⌈\G⌋ means "start of the current match" instead of "end of the previous match" ☞ 129.)

So, using the second expression, we end up with

```
@zips = m/\G(?:(?!44)\d\d\d\d\d)*(44\d\d\d\d)/g;
```

without the need for any special after-match checking.

This example in perspective

I'll be the first to admit that this example is contrived, but nevertheless, it shows a number of valuable lessons about how to keep a regex in sync with the data. Still, were I really to need to do this in real life, I would probably not try to solve it completely with regular expressions. I would simply use ⌈\d\d\d\d\d⌋ to grab each ZIP code, then discard it if it doesn't begin with '44'. In Perl, this looks like:

```
@zips = ( ); # Ensure the array is empty

while (m/(\d\d\d\d\d)/) {
    $zip = $1;
    if (substr($zip, 0, 2) eq "44") {
        push @zips, $zip;
    }
}
```

Also, see the sidebar on page 130 for a particularly interesting use of ⌈\G⌋, although one available at the time of this writing only in Perl.

Parsing CSV Files

As anyone who's ever tried to parse a CSV (Comma Separated Values) file can tell you, it can be a bit tricky. The biggest problem is that it seems every program that produces a CSV file has a different idea of just what the format should be. In this section, I'll start off with methods to parse the kind of CSV file that Microsoft Excel generates, and we'll move from there to look at some other format permutations.[†]

Luckily, the Microsoft format is one of the simplest. The values, separated by commas, are either "raw" (just sitting there between the commas), or within double

---

† The final code for processing the Microsoft style CSV files is presented in Chapter 6 (☞ 271) after the efficiency issues discussed in that chapter are taken into consideration.

quotes (and within the double quotes, a double quote itself is represented by a pair of double quotes in a row).

Here's an example:

```
Ten Thousand,10000, 2710 ,,"10,000","It's ""10 Grand"", baby",10K
```

This row represents seven fields:

```
Ten Thousand
10000
 2710
```
an empty field
```
10,000
It's "10 Grand", baby
10K
```

So, to parse out the fields from a line, we need an expression to cover each of two field types. The non-quoted ones are easy—they contain anything except commas and quotes, so they are matched by ⌈`[^",]+`⌋.

A double-quoted field can contain commas, spaces, and in fact anything except a double quote. It can also contain the two quotes in a row that represent one quote in the final value. So, a double-quoted field is matched by any number of ⌈`[^"]|""`⌋ between ⌈`"···"`⌋, which gives us ⌈`"(?:[^"]|"")*"`⌋. (Actually, for efficiency, I can use atomic grouping, ⌈`(?>···)`⌋ instead of ⌈`(?:···)`⌋, but I'll leave that discussion until the next chapter; ☞ 259.)

Putting this all together results in ⌈`[^",]+|"(?:[^"]|"")*"`⌋ to match a single field. That might be getting a bit hard to read, so I'll rewrite it in a free-spacing mode (☞ 110):

```
# Either some non-quote/non-comma text . . .
[^",]+
#  . . . or . . .
 |
#  . . . a double-quoted field (inside, paired double quotes are allowed)
"  # field's opening quote
(?: [^"] | "" )*
"  # field's closing quote
```

Now, to use this in practice, we can apply it repeatedly to a string containing a CSV row, but if we want to actually do anything productive with the results of the match, we should know which alternative matched. If it's the double-quoted field, we need to remove the outer quotes and replace internal paired double quotes with one double quote to yield the original data.

I can think of two approaches to this. One is to just look at the text matched and see whether the first character is a double quote. If so, we know that we must strip the first and last characters (the double quotes) and replace any internal '""' by '"'. That's simple enough, but it's even simpler if we are clever with capturing parentheses. If we put capturing parentheses around each of the subexpressions that match actual field data, we can inspect them after the match to see which group has a value:

```
#  Either some non-quote/non-comma text . . .
(  [^",]+  )
#   . . . or . . .
  |
#  . . . a double-quoted field (inside, paired double quotes are allowed)
"  # field's opening quote
  (    (?:  [^"]  |  ""  )*    )
"  # field's closing quote
```

Now, if we see that the first group captured, we can just use the value as is. If the second group captured, we merely need to replace any '""' with '"' and we can use the value.

I'll show the example now in Perl, and a bit later (after we flush out some bugs) in Java and VB.NET. Here's the snippet in Perl, assuming our line is in `$html` and has had any newline removed from the end (we don't want the newline to be part of the last field!):

```
while ($line =~ m{
              # Either some non-quote/non-comma text . . .
              (  [^",]+  )
              #  . . , or . . .
                |
              #  . . . a double-quoted field ("" allowed inside)
              "  # field's opening quote
                (    (?:  [^"]  |  ""  )*    )
              "  # field's closing quote
          }gx)
{
    if (defined $1) {
        $field = $1;
    } else {
        $field = $2;
        $field =~ s/""/"/g;
    }
    print "[$field]"; # print the field, for debugging
    Can work with $field now . . .
}
```

Applying this against our test data, the output is:

```
[Ten Thousand][10000][ 2710 ][10,000][It's "10 Grand", baby][10K]
```

This looks mostly good, but unfortunately doesn't give us anything for that empty fourth field. If the program's "work with `$field`" is to save the field value to an array, once we're all done, we'd want access to the fifth element of the array to yield the fifth field ("10,000"). That won't work if we don't fill an element of the array with an empty value for each empty field.

The first idea that might come to mind for matching an empty field is to change `[^",]+` to `[^",]*`. Well, that may seem obvious, but does it really work?

Let's test it. Here's the output:

```
[Ten Thousand][][10000][][ 2710 ][][][][10,000][][][It's "10 Grand",...
```

Oops, we somehow got a bunch of extra fields! Well, in retrospect, we shouldn't be surprised. By using `( ⋯ )*` to match a field, we don't actually require anything to match. That works to our advantage when we have an empty field, but consider after having matched the first field, the next application of the regex starts at 'Ten Thousand, 10000 ⋯'. If nothing in the regex can match that raw comma (as is the case), yet an empty match is considered successful, the empty match will indeed be successful *at that point.* In fact, it could be successful an infinite number of times at that point if the regex engine doesn't realize, as modern ones do, that it's in such a situation and force a bump-along so that two zero-width matches don't happen in a row (☞ 129). That's why there's one empty match between each valid match (and although not shown, there's an empty match at the end).

Distrusting the bump-along

The problem here stems from us having relied on the transmission's bump-along to get us past the separating commas. To solve it, we need to take that control into our own hands. Two approaches come to mind:

1. We could try to match the commas ourselves. If we take this approach, we must be sure to match a comma as part of matching a regular field, using it to "pace ourselves" through the string.

2. We could check to be sure that each match start is consistent with locations that we know can start a field. A field starts either at the beginning of the line, or after a comma.

Perhaps even better, we can combine the two. Starting with the first approach (matching the commas ourselves), we can simply require a comma before each field except the first. Alternatively, we can require a comma after each field except the last. We can do this by prepending `^|,` or appending `$|,` to our regex, with appropriate parentheses to control the scope. Let's try prepending, which gives us:

```
(?:^|,)
(?:
    # Either some non-quote/non-comma text....
    ( [^",]* )
  # ⋯ or ⋯
  |
    # ⋯ a double-quoted field (inside, paired double quotes are allowed)
    " # field's opening quote
    ( (?: [^"] | "" )*  )
    " # field's closing quote
)
```

This really sounds like it should work, but plugging it into our test program, the result is disappointing:

```
[Ten Thousand][10000][ 2710 ][][][000][][ baby][10K]
```

Remember, we're expecting:

```
[Ten Thousand][10000][ 2710 ][][10,000][It's "10 Grand", baby][10K]
```

Why didn't this one work? It seems that the double-quoted fields didn't come out right, so the problem must be with the part that matches a double-quoted field, right? No, the problem is before that. Perhaps the moral from page 176 can help: *when more than one alternative can potentially match from the same point, care must be taken when selecting the order of the alternatives.* Since the first alternative, ⌜[^",]*⌟, requires nothing to be successful, the second alternative never gets a chance to match unless forced by something that must match later in the regex. Our regex doesn't have anything after these alternatives, so as it's written, the second alternative is never even reached. Doh!

Wow, you've really got to keep your wits about you. Okay, let's swap the alternatives and try again:

```
(?:^|,)
(?:  # Now, match either a double-quoted field (inside, paired double quotes are allowed) . . .
        "  #  (double-quoted field's opening quote)
        (     (?: [^"] | "" )*     )
        "  #  (double-quoted field's closing quote)
    |
        #  . . . or, some non-quote/non-comma text . . .
        ( [^",]* )
)
```

Now, it works! Well, at least for our test data. Could it fail with other data? This section is named "Distrusting the bump-along," and while nothing takes the place of some thought backed up with good testing, we can use ⌜\G⌟ to ensure that each match begins exactly at the point that the previous match ended. We believe that should be true already because of how we've constructed and apply our regex. If we start out the regex with ⌜\G⌟, we disallow any match after the engine's transmission is forced to bump along. We hope it will never matter, but doing so may make an error more apparent. Had we done this with our previously-failing regex that had given us

```
[Ten Thousand][10000][ 2710 ][][][000][][ baby][10K]
```

we would have gotten

```
[Ten Thousand][10000][ 2710 ][][]
```

instead. This perhaps would have made the error more apparent, had we missed it the first time.

CSV Processing in Java

Here's the CSV example with Sun's `java.util.regex`. This is designed to be clear and simple—a more efficient version is given in Chapter 8 (☞ 386).

```
import java.util.regex.*;
    ⋮
Pattern fieldRegex = Pattern.compile(
  "\\G(?:^|,)                              \n"+
  "(?:                                     \n"+
  "   # Either a double-quoted field ...   \n"+
  "   \"  # field's opening quote          \n"+
  "     (  (?: [^\"]++ | \"\" )*+   )       \n"+
  "   \"  # field's closing quote          \n"+
  " #  ... or ...                          \n"+
  " |                                      \n"+
  "   # ... some non-quote/non-comma text ... \n"+
  "   ( [^\",]* )                          \n"+
  " )                          \n", Pattern.COMMENTS);
Pattern quotesRegex = Pattern.compile("\"\"");
    ⋮
// Given the string in 'line', find all the fields ...



Matcher m = fieldRegex.matcher(line);
while (m.find())
{
    String field;
    if (m.group(1) != null) {
        field = quotesRegex.matcher(m.group(1)).replaceAll("\"");
    } else {
        field = m.group(2);
    }
    // We can now work with the field ...
    System.out.println("[" + field + "]");
}
```

Another approach. The beginning of this section noted two approaches to ensuring we stay properly aligned with the fields. The other is to be sure that a match begins only where a field is allowed. On the surface, this is similar to prepending ⌜^|,⌟, except using lookbehind as with ⌜(?<=^|,)⌟.

Unfortunately, as the section in the previous chapter (☞ 132) explains, even if lookbehind is supported, variable-length lookbehind sometimes isn't, so this approach may not work. If the variable length is the issue, we could replace ⌜(?<=^|,)⌟ with ⌜(?:^|(?<=,))⌟, but this seems overly complex considering that we already have the first approach working. Also, it reverts to relying on the transmission's bump-along to bypass the commas, so if we've made a mistake elsewhere, it could allow a match to begin at a location like '⋯"10,000"⋯'. All in all, it just seems safer to use the first approach.

However, we can use a twist on this approach—requiring a match to *end* before a comma (or before the end of the line). Adding ⌈(?=$|,)⌉ to the end of our regex adds yet another assurance that it won't match where we don't want it to. In practice, would I do add this? Well, frankly, I feel pretty comfortable with what we came up with before, so I'd probably not add it in this exact situation, but it's a good technique to have on hand when you need it.

One change for the sake of efficiency

Although I don't concentrate on efficiency until the next chapter, I'd like to make one efficiency-related change now, for systems that support atomic grouping (☞ 137). If supported, I'd change the part that matches the values of double-quoted fields from ⌈(?:[^"]|"")*⌉ to ⌈(?>[^"]+|"")*⌉. The VB.NET example in the sidebar below shows this.

```
                           CSV Processing in VB.NET
    Imports System.Text.RegularExpressions
      ⋮
    Dim FieldRegex as Regex = New Regex( _
          "(?:^|,)                                            " & _
          "(?:                                                " & _
          "    (?# Either a doublequoted field ...)           " & _
          "    ""   (?# field's opening quote )               " & _
          "    (    (?> [^""]+ | """" )*   )                  " & _
          "    ""   (?# field's closing quote )               " & _
          "  (?# ... or ...)                                  " & _
          "  |                                                " & _
          "    (?# ... some non-quote/non-comma text ...)     " & _
          "    ( [^"",]* )                                    " & _
          "  )", RegexOptions.IgnorePatternWhitespace)

    Dim QuotesRegex as Regex = New Regex(" """" ")  'A string with two double quotes
      ⋮
    Dim FieldMatch as Match = FieldRegex.Match(Line)
    While FieldMatch.Success
       Dim Field as String
       If FieldMatch.Groups(1).Success
         Field = QuotesRegex.Replace(FieldMatch.Groups(1).Value, """")
       Else
         Field = FieldMatch.Groups(2).Value
       End If

       Console.WriteLine("[" & Field & "]")
       ' Can now work with 'Field'. ⋯

       FieldMatch = FieldMatch.NextMatch
    End While
```

If possessive quantifiers (☞ 140) are supported, as they are with Sun's Java regex package, they can be used instead. The sidebar with the Java CSV code shows this.

The reasoning behind these changes is discussed in the next chapter, and eventually we end up with a particularly efficient version, shown on page 271.

Other CSV formats

Microsoft's CSV format is popular because it's Microsoft's CSV format, but it's not necessarily what other programs use. Here are some twists I've seen:

- Using another character, such as '*;*' or a tab, as the separator (which makes one wonder why the format is still called "*comma*-separated values").

- Allowing spaces after the separators, but not counting them as part of the value.

- Using backslashes to escape quotes (e.g., using '\"' rather than '""' to include a quote within the value). This usually means that a backslash is allowed (and ignored) before any character.

These changes are easily accommodated. Do the first by replacing each comma in the regex with the desired separator; the second by adding ⌜\s*⌟ after the first separator, e.g., starting out with ⌜(?:^|,\s*)⌟.

For the third, we can use what we developed earlier (☞ 198), replacing ⌜[^"]+|""⌟ with ⌜[^"\\]+|\\.⌟. Of course, we'd also have to change the subsequent **s/""/"/g** to the more general **s/\\(.)/$1/g**, or our target language's equivalent.

6

Crafting an Efficient Expression

With the regex-directed nature of an NFA engine, as is found in Perl, Java packages, the .NET languages, Python, and PHP (just to name a few; see the table on page 145 for more), subtle changes in an expression can have major effects on what or how it matches. Issues that don't matter with a DFA engine become paramount. The fine control an NFA engine affords allows you to really *craft* an expression, although it can sometimes be a source of confusion to the unaware. This chapter helps you learn this art.

At stake are both correctness and efficiency: matching just what you want and no more, and doing it quickly. Chapters 4 and 5 examined correctness; here we'll look at the efficiency-related issues of NFA engines, and how to make them work to our advantage. (DFA-related issues are mentioned when appropriate, but this chapter is primarily concerned with NFA-based engines.) In a nutshell, the key is to understand the full implications of backtracking, and to learn techniques to avoid it where possible. Armed with the detailed understanding of the processing mechanics, not only will you maximize the speed of matches, you will also be able to write more complex expressions with confidence.

In This Chapter   To arm you well, this chapter first illustrates just how important these issues can be, then prepares you for some of the more advanced techniques presented later by reviewing the basic backtracking described in the previous chapters with a strong emphasis on efficiency and backtracking's global ramifications. Then we'll look at some of the common internal optimizations that can have a fairly substantial impact on efficiency, and on how expressions are best written for implementations that employ them. Finally, I bring it all together with some killer techniques to construct lightning-fast NFA regexes.

Tests and Backtracks

The examples we'll see here illustrate common situations you might meet when using regular expressions. When examining a particular example's efficiency, I'll sometimes report the number of individual tests that the regex engine does during the course of a match. For example, in matching ⌈marty⌉ against smarty, there are six individual tests — the initial attempt of ⌈m⌉ against s (which fails), then the matching of ⌈m⌉ against m, ⌈a⌉ against a, and so on. I also often report the number of backtracks (zero in this example, although the implicit backtrack by the regex engine's transmission to retry the regex at the second character position could be counted as one).

I use these exact numbers not because the precision is important, but rather to be more concrete than words such as "lots," "few," "many," "better," "not too much," and so forth. I don't want to imply that using regular expressions with an NFA is an exercise in counting tests or backtracks; I just want to acquaint you with the relative qualities of the examples.

Another important thing to realize is that these "precise" numbers probably differ from tool to tool. It's the basic relative performance of the examples that I hope will stay with you. One important variation among tools is the optimizations they might employ. A smart enough implementation completely bypasses the application of a particular regex if it can decide beforehand that the target string cannot possibly match (in cases, for instance, when the string lacks a particular character that the engine knows beforehand must be there for any match to be successful). I discuss these important optimizations in this chapter, but the overall lessons are generally more important than the specific special cases.

Traditional NFA versus POSIX NFA

It's important to keep in mind the target tool's engine type, Traditional NFA or POSIX NFA, when analyzing efficiency. As we'll see in the next section, some concerns matter to one but not the other. Sometimes a change that has no effect on one has a great effect on the other. Again, understanding the basics allows you to judge each situation as it arises.

A Sobering Example

Let's start with an example that really shows how important a concern backtracking and efficiency can be. On page 198, we came up with ⌈" (\\. | [^"\\])* "⌉ to match a quoted string, with internal quotes allowed if escaped. This regex works, but if it's used with an NFA engine, the alternation applied at each character is very inefficient. With every "normal" (non-escape, non-quote) character in the string, the engine has to test ⌈\\.⌉, fail, and backtrack to finally match with ⌈[^"\\]⌉. If used where efficiency matters, we would certainly like to be able to speed this regex up a bit.

A Simple Change—Placing Your Best Foot Forward

Since the average double-quoted string has more normal characters than escaped ones, one simple change is to swap the order of the alternatives, putting ⌈[^"\\]⌋ first and ⌈\\.⌋ second. By placing ⌈[^"\\]⌋ first, alternation backtracking need be done only when there actually is an escaped item in the string (and once for when the star fails, of course, since all alternatives must fail for the alternation as a whole to stop). Figure 6-1 illustrates this difference visually. The reduction of arrows in the bottom half represents the increased number of times when the first alternative matches. That means less backtracking.

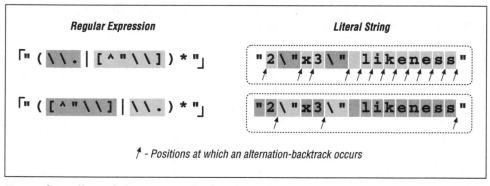

Figure 6-1: Effects of alternative order (Traditional NFA)

In evaluating this change, consider:

- Does this change benefit a Traditional NFA, POSIX NFA, or both?

- Does this change offer the most benefit when the text matches, when the match fails, or at all times?

❖ Consider these questions and flip the page to check your answers. Make sure that you have a good grasp of the answers (and reasons) before continuing on to the next section.

Efficiency Verses Correctness

The most important question to ask when making any change for efficiency's sake is whether the change affects the correctness of a match. Reordering alternatives, as we did earlier, is okay only if the ordering is not relevant to the success of a match. Consider ⌈"(\\.|[^"])*"⌋, which is an earlier (☞ 197) but flawed version of the regex in the previous section. It's missing the backslash in the negated character class, and so can match data that should not be matched. If the regex is only ever applied to valid data that *should* be matched, you'd never know of the prob-

Effects of a Simple Change

❖ *Answers to the questions on page 223.*

Effect for which type of engine? The change has virtually no effect whatsoever for a POSIX NFA engine. Since it must eventually try every permutation of the regex anyway, the order in which the alternatives are tried is irrelevant. For a Traditional NFA, however, ordering the alternatives in such a way that quickly leads to a match is a benefit because the engine stops once the first match is found.

Effect during which kind of result? The change results in a faster match only when there *is* a match. An NFA can fail only after trying all possible permutations of the match (and again, the POSIX NFA tries them all anyway). So if indeed it ends up failing, every permutation must have been attempted, so the order does not matter.

The following table shows the number of tests ("tests") and backtracks ("b.t.") for several cases (smaller numbers are better):

Sample string	Traditional NFA				POSIX NFA	
	`⌜"(\\.|[^"\\])*"⌟`		`⌜"([^"\\]|\\.)*"⌟`		*either*	
	tests	b.t.	tests	b.t.	tests	b.t.
`"2\"x3\" likeness"`	32	14	22	4	48	30
`"makudonarudo"`	28	14	16	2	40	26
`"very…99 more chars…long"`	218	109	111	2	325	216
`"No \"match\" here`	124	86	124	86	124	86

As you can see, the POSIX NFA results are the same with both expressions, while the Traditional NFA's performance increases (backtracks decrease) with the new expression. Indeed, in a non-match situation (the last example in the table), since both engine types must evaluate all possible permutations, all results are the same.

lem. Thinking that the regex is good and reordering alternatives now to gain more efficiency, we'd be in real trouble. Swapping the alternatives so that `⌜[^"]⌟` is first actually ensures that it matches incorrectly every time the target has an escaped quote:

    "You need a 2\"3\" photo."

So, be sure that you're comfortable with the correctness of a match before you worry too much about efficiency.

Advancing Further—Localizing the Greediness

Figure 6-1 makes it clear that in either expression, the star must iterate (or cycle, if you like) for each normal character, entering and leaving the alternation (and the parentheses) over and over. These actions involve overhead, which means extra work—extra work that we'd like to eliminate if possible.

Once while working on a similar expression, I realized that I could optimize it by taking into account that since ⌜[^"\\]⌝ matches the "normal" (non-quote, non-backslash) case, using ⌜[^"\\]+⌝ instead allows one iteration of (⋯)* to read as many normal characters as there are in a row. For strings without any escapes, this would be the entire string. This allows a match with almost no backtracking, and also reduces the star iteration to a bare minimum. I was very pleased with myself for making this discovery.

We'll look at this example in more depth later in this chapter, but a quick look at some statistics clearly shows the benefit. Figure 6-2 looks at this example for a Traditional NFA. In comparison to the original ⌜"(\\.|[^"\\])*"⌝ (the top of the upper pair of Figure 6-2), alternation-related backtracks and star iterations are both reduced. The lower pair in Figure 6-2 illustrates that performance is enhanced even further when this change is combined with our previous reordering.

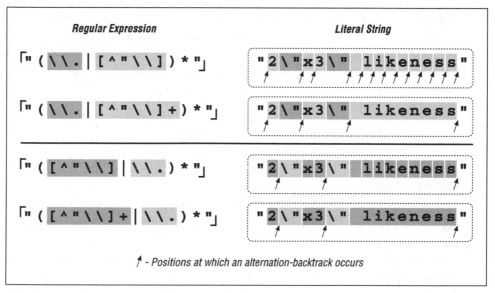

Figure 6-2: Effects of an added plus (Traditional NFA)

The big gain with the addition of plus is the resulting reduction in the number of alternation backtracks, and, in turn, the number of iterations by the star. The star quantifies a parenthesized subexpression, and each iteration entails some amount of overhead as the parentheses are entered and exited, because the engine needs to keep tabs on what text is matched by the enclosed subexpression. (This is discussed in depth later in this chapter.)

Table 6-1 is similar to the one in the answer block on page 224, but with different expressions and has information about the number of iterations required by star. In each case, the number of individual tests and backtracks increases ever so slightly, but the number of cycles is drastically reduced. This is a big savings.

Table 6-1: Match Efficiency for a Traditional NFA

Sample String	⌈"([^"\\]│\\.)*"⌋			⌈"([^"\\]+│\\.)*"⌋		
	tests	b.t.	*-cycles	tests	b.t.	*-cycles
`"makudonarudo"`	16	2	13	17	3	2
`"2\"x3\" likeness"`	22	4	15	25	7	6
`"very…99 more chars…long"`	111	2	108	112	3	2

Reality Check

Yes, I was quite pleased with myself for this discovery. However, as wonderful as this "enhancement" might seem, it is really a disaster waiting to happen. You'll notice that when extolling its virtues, I didn't give statistics for a POSIX NFA engine. If I had, you might have been surprised to find the `"very…long"` example requires over *three hundred thousand million billion trillion* backtracks (for the record, the actual count would be 324,518,553,658,426,726,783,156,020,576,256, or about 325 nonillion). Putting it mildly, that is a LOT of work. This would take well over 50 *quintillion* years, take or leave a few hundred trillion millennia.[†]

Quite surprising indeed! So, why does this happen? Briefly, it's because something in the regex is subject to both an immediate plus and an enclosing star, with nothing to differentiate which is in control of any particular target character. The resulting nondeterminism is the killer. The next section explains a bit more.

"Exponential" matches

Before adding the plus, ⌈[^"\\]⌋ was subject to only the star, and the number of possible ways for the effective ⌈([^"\\])*⌋ to divvy up the line was limited. It matched one character, then another, and so forth, until each character in the target text had been matched at most one time. It may not have matched everything in the target, but at worst, the number of characters matched was directly proportional to the length of the target string. The possible amount of work rose in step with the length of the target string.

---

† The reported time is an estimation based on other benchmarks; I did not actually run the test that long.

With the new regex's effective ⌜([^"\\]+) *⌟, the number of ways that the plus and star might divvy up the string explodes exponentially. If the target string is makudonarudo, should it be considered 12 iterations of the star, where each internal ⌜[^"\\]+⌟ matches just one character (as might be shown by 'makudonarudo')? Or perhaps one iteration of the star, where the internal ⌜[^"\\]+⌟ matches everything ('makudonarudo')? Or, perhaps 3 iterations of the star, where the internal ⌜[^"\\]+⌟ matches 5, 3, and 4 characters respectively ('makudonarudo'). Or perhaps 2, 2, 5, and 3 characters respectively ('makudonarudo'). Or, perhaps...

Well, you get the idea — there are a lot of possibilities (4,096 in this 12-character example). For each extra character in the string, the number of possible combinations doubles, and the POSIX NFA must try them all before returning its answer. That's why these are called "exponential matches." Another appealing phrase I've heard for these types of matches is *super-linear*.

However called, it means backtracking, and lots of it![†] Twelve characters' 4,096 combinations doesn't take long, but 20 characters' million-plus combinations take more than a few seconds. By 30 characters, the billion-plus combinations take hours, and by 40, it's well over a year. Obviously, this is not good.

"Ah," you might think, "but a POSIX NFA is not all that common. I know my tool uses a Traditional NFA, so I'm okay." Well, the major difference between a POSIX and Traditional NFA is that the latter stops at the first full match. If there is no full match to be had, even a Traditional NFA must test every possible combination before it finds that out. Even in the short "No \"match\" ·here example from the previous answer block, 8,192 combinations must be tested before the failure can be reported.

When the regex engine crunches away on one of these neverending matches, the tool just seems to "lock up." The first time I experienced this, I thought I'd discovered a bug in the tool, but now that I understand it, this kind of expression is part of my regular-expression benchmark suite, used to indicate the type of engine a tool implements:

- If one of these regexes is fast even with a non-match, it's likely a DFA.

- If it's fast only when there's a match, it's a Traditional NFA.

- If it's slow all the time, it's a POSIX NFA.

I used "likely" in the first bullet point because NFAs with advanced optimizations can detect and avoid these exponentially-painful neverending matches. (More on this later in this chapter ☞ 250.) Also, we'll see a number of ways to augment or rewrite this expression such that it's fast for both matches and failures alike.

---

† For readers into such things, the number of backtracks done on a string of length n is 2^{n+1}. The number of individual tests is $2^{n+1} + 2^n$.

As the previous list indicates, at least in the absence of certain advanced optimizations, the relative performance of a regex like can tell you about the type of regex engine. That's why a form of this regex is used in the "Testing the Engine Type" section in Chapter 4 (☞ 146).

Certainly, not every little change has the disastrous effects we've seen with this example, but unless you know the work going on behind an expression, you will simply never know until you run into the problem. Toward that end, this chapter looks at the efficiency concerns and ramifications of a variety of examples. As with most things, a firm grasp of the underlying basic concepts is essential to an understanding of more advanced ideas, so before looking at ways to get around exponential matches, I'd like to review backtracking in explicit detail.

A Global View of Backtracking

On a local level, backtracking is simply the return to attempt an untried option. That's simple enough to understand, but the global implications of backtracking are not as easily grasped. In this section, we'll take an explicit look at the details of backtracking, both during a match and during a non-match, and we'll try to make some sense out of the patterns we see emerge.

Let's start by looking closely at some examples from the previous chapters. From page 165, if we apply ⌜".*"⌝ to

    The name "McDonald's" is said "makudonarudo" in Japanese

we can visualize the matching action as shown in Figure 6-3.

The regex is attempted starting at each string position in turn, but because the initial quote fails immediately, nothing interesting happens until the attempt starting at the location marked **A**. At this point, the rest of the expression is attempted, but the transmission (☞ 148) knows that if the attempt turns out to be a dead end, the full regex can still be tried at the next position.

The ⌜.*⌝ then matches to the end of the string, where the dot is unable to match the nothingness at the end of the string and so the star finally stops. None of the 46 characters matched by ⌜.*⌝ is required, so while matching them, the engine accumulated 46 more situations to where it can backtrack if it turns out that it matched too much. Now that ⌜.*⌝ has stopped, the engine backtracks to the last of those saved states, the " try ⌜".*"⌝ at ···**anese**ˌ" state.

This means that we try to match the closing quote at the end of the string. Well, a quote can match nothingness no better than dot, so this fails too. The engine backtracks again, this time trying to match the closing quote at ···Japaneseˌ, which also fails.

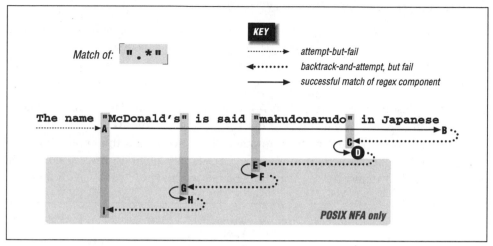

Figure 6-3: Successful match of ⌜"."⌝*

The remembered states accumulated while matching from **A** to **B** are tried in reverse (latest first) order as we move from **B** to **C**. After trying only about a dozen of them, the state that represents "try ⌜".*"⌝ at ···**arudo"**·**in**·**Japa**···" is reached, point **C**. This *can* match, bringing us to **D** and an overall match:

> The name <u>"McDonald's" is said "makudonarudo"</u> in Japanese

If this is a Traditional NFA, the remaining unused states are simply discarded and the successful match is reported.

More Work for a POSIX NFA

For POSIX NFA, the match noted earlier is remembered as "the longest match we've seen so far," but all remaining states must still be explored to see whether they could come up with a longer match. We know this won't happen in this case, but the regex engine must find that out for itself.

So, the states are tried and immediately discarded except for the remaining two situations where there is a quote in the string available to match the final quote. Thus, the sequences **D-E-F** and **F-G-H** are similar to **B-C-D**, except the matches at **F** and **H** are discarded as being shorter than a previously found match at **D**

By **I**, the only remaining backtrack is the "bump along and retry" one. However, since the attempt starting at **A** *was* able to find a match (three in fact), the POSIX NFA engine is finally done and the match at **D** is reported.

Work Required During a Non-Match

We still need to look at what happens when there is no match. Let's look at
⌈".*"!⌋. We know this won't match our example text, but it comes close on a number of occasions throughout the match attempt. As we'll see, that results in much
more work.

Figure 6-4 illustrates this work. The **A-I** sequence looks similar to that in Figure
6-3. One difference is that this time it does not match at point **D** (because the ending exclamation point can't match). Another difference is that the entire sequence
in Figure 6-4 applies to both Traditional and POSIX NFA engines: finding no match,
the Traditional NFA must try as many possibilities as the POSIX NFA—all of them.

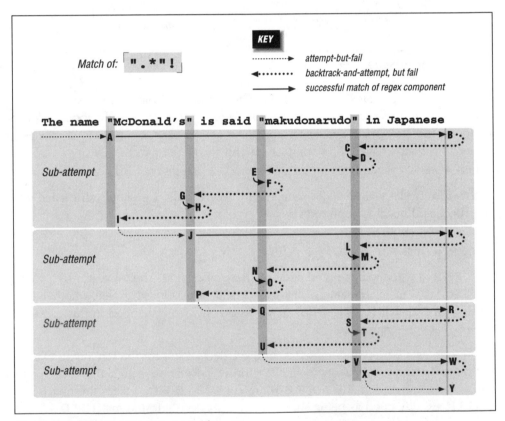

Figure 6-4: Failing attempt to match ⌈".*"!⌋

Since there is no match from the overall attempt starting at **A** and ending at **I**, the
transmission bumps along to retry the match. Attempts eventually starting at points
J, **Q**, and **V** look promising, but fail similarly to the attempt at **A**. Finally at **Y**, there
are no more positions for the transmission to try from, so the overall attempt fails.
As Figure 6-4 shows, it took a fair amount of work to find this out.

Being More Specific

As a comparison, let's replace the dot with ⌈[^"]⌋. As discussed in the previous chapter, this gives less surprising results because it is more specific, and the end result is that with it, the new regex is more efficient to boot. With ⌈"[^"]*"!⌋, the ⌈[^"]*⌋ can't get past the closing quote, eliminating much matching and subsequent backtracking.

Figure 6-5 shows the failing attempt (compare to Figure 6-4). As you can see, much less backtracking is needed. If the different results suit your needs, the reduced backtracking is a welcome side effect.

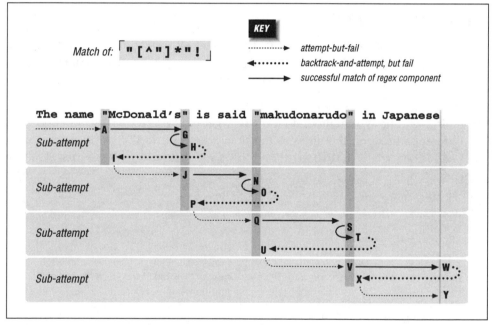

Figure 6 5: Failing attempt to match ⌈"[^"]*"!⌋

Alternation Can Be Expensive

Alternation can be a leading cause of backtracking. As a simple example, let's use our makudonarudo test string to compare how ⌈u|v|w|x|y|z⌋ and ⌈[uvwxyz]⌋ go about matching. A character class is usually a simple test,[†] so ⌈[uvwxyz]⌋ suffers only the bump-along backtracks (34 of them) until we match at:

```
The name "McDonald's" is said "makudonarudo" in Japanese
```

---

† Some implementations are not as efficient as others, but it's safe to assume that a class is always faster than the equivalent alternation.

With ⌜u|v|w|x|y|z⌟, however, six backtracks are required at each starting position, eventually totaling 204 before we achieve the same match. Obviously, not every alternation is replaceable, and even when it is, it's not necessarily as easily as with this example. In some situations, however, certain techniques that we'll look at later can greatly reduce the amount of alternation-related backtracking required for a match.

Understanding backtracking is perhaps the most important facet of NFA efficiency, but it's still only part of the equation. A regex engine's optimizations can *greatly* improve efficiency. Later in this chapter, we'll look in detail at what a regex engine needs to do, and how it can optimize its performance.

Benchmarking

Because this chapter talks a lot about speed and efficiency, and I often mention benchmarks I've done, I'd like to mention a few principles of benchmarking. I'll also show simple ways to benchmark in a few languages.

Basic benchmarking is simply timing how long it takes to do some work. To do the timing, get the system time, do the work, get the system time again, and report the difference between the times as the time it took to do the work. As an example, let's compare ⌜^(a|b|c|d|e|f|g)+$⌟ with ⌜^[a-g]+$⌟. We'll first look at benchmarking in Perl, but will see it in other languages in a bit. Here's a simple (but as we'll see, somewhat lacking) Perl script:

```
use Time::HiRes 'time'; # So time() gives a high-resolution value.

$StartTime = time();
"abababdedfg" =~ m/^(a|b|c|d|e|f|g)+$/;
$EndTime = time();
printf("Alternation takes %.3f seconds.\n", $EndTime - $StartTime);

$StartTime = time();
"abababdedfg" =~ m/^[a-g]+$/;
$EndTime = time();
printf("Character class takes %.3f seconds.\n", $EndTime - $StartTime);
```

It looks (and is) simple, but there are some important points to keep in mind while constructing a test for benchmarking:

- **Time only "interesting" work**   Time as much of the "work" as possible, but as little "non-work" as possible. If there is some initialization or other setup that must done, do it before the starting time is taken. If there's cleanup, do it after the ending time is taken.

- **Do "enough" work**   Often, the time it takes to do what you want to test is very short, and a computer's clock doesn't have enough granularity to give meaning to the timing.

When I run the simple Perl test on my system, I get

```
Alternation takes 0.000 seconds.
Character class takes 0.000 seconds.
```

which really doesn't tell me anything other than both are faster than the short-est time that can be measured. So, if something is fast, do it twice, or 10 times, or even 10,000,000 times—whatever is required to make "enough" work. What is "enough" depends on the granularity of the system clock, but most systems now have clocks accurate down to 1/100th of a second, and in such cases, tim-ing even half a second of work may be sufficient for meaningful results.

- **Do the "right" work** Doing a very fast operation ten million times involves the overhead of ten million updates of a counter variable in the block being timed. If possible, it's best to increase the amount of *real* work being done in a way that doesn't increase the *overhead* work. In our Perl example, the regu-lar expressions are being applied to fairly short strings: if applied to much longer strings, they'd do more "real" work each time.

So, taking these into account, here's another version:

```perl
use Time::HiRes 'time';  # So time() gives a high-resolution value.
$TimesToDo = 1000;                # Simple setup
$TestString = "abababdedfg" x 1000; # Makes a huge string

$Count = $TimesToDo;
$StartTime = time();
while (--$Count > 0) {
    $TestString =~ m/^(a|b|c|d|e|f|g)+$/;
}
$EndTime = time();
printf("Alternation takes %.3f seconds.\n", $EndTime - $StartTime);

$Count = $TimesToDo;
$StartTime = time();
while (--$Count > 0) {
    $TestString =~ m/^[a-g]+$/;
}
$EndTime = time();
printf("Character class takes %.3f seconds.\n", $EndTime - $StartTime);
```

Notice how the $TestString and $Count are initialized before the timing starts? ($TestString is initialized with Perl's convenient x operator, which replicates the string on its left as many times as the number on its right.) On my system, with Perl 5.8, this prints:

```
Alternation takes 7.276 seconds.
Character class takes 0.333 seconds.
```

So, with this test case, one is about 11× faster than the other. The benchmark should be executed a few times, with the fastest times taken, to lessen the impact of sporadic background system activity.

Know What You're Measuring

It might be interesting to see what happens when the initialization is changed to:

```
my $TimesToDo = 1000000;
my $TestString = "abababdedfg";
```

Now, the test string is 1,000 times shorter, but the test is done 1,000× more times. Conceptually, the amount of "work" should be the same, but the results are quite different:

```
Alternation takes 18.167 seconds.
Character class takes 5.231 seconds.
```

Both are slower than before, but the difference between the two is now a factor of only 3.5×. Why the relative difference ? After the change, there's more "non-work" overhead than before. That is, the update and testing of $Count, and the setup of the regex engine, now happen 1,000× more than before.

These tests are about 5.3 and 4.1 seconds slower than the first tests. Most of the extra time is probably the overhead of working with $Count. The fact that `^(a|b|c|d|e|f|g)+$` is hit relatively harder (5.3 seconds slower than the first time, rather than 4.1 seconds slower) may reflect additional pre-match (or early-match) setup by the regex engine before getting into the main part of the match.

In any case, the point of this change is to illustrate that the results are strongly influenced by how much real work vs. non-work overtime is part of the timing.

Benchmarking with Java

Benchmarking Java can be a slippery science, for a number of reasons. Let's first look at a somewhat naïve example, and then look at why it's naïve, and at what can be done to make it less so. The listing on the facing page shows the benchmark example with Java, using Sun's `java.util.regex`.

Notice how the regular expressions are compiled in the initialization part of the program? We want to benchmark the matching speed, not the compile speed.

Speed is dependent upon which virtual machine (VM) is used. Sun standard JRE[†] comes with two virtual machines, a *client* VM optimized for fast startup, and a *server* VM optimized for heavy-duty long-haul work.

---

† I had to use a shorter string for this test to run on my Linux system, as a longer string somehow tickles a problem with the VM, causing the test to abort. Engineers at Sun tell me it's due to an unexpected interaction between the aggressively optimizing C compiler used to build the VM (gcc), and an overly conservative use of Linux's stack-monitoring hooks. It may be fixed as early as Java 1.4.1. To compensate for the shortened string in the current test, I've increased the number of times the loop executes the match, so these results should be comparable to the original.

Benchmarking with `java.util.regex`

```java
import java.util.regex.*;
public class JavaBenchmark {
 public static void main(String [] args)
 {
   Matcher regex1 = Pattern.compile("^(a|b|c|d|e|f|g)+$").matcher("");
   Matcher regex2 = Pattern.compile("^[a-g]+$").matcher("");
   long timesToDo = 4000;

   StringBuffer temp = new StringBuffer();
   for (int i = 250; i > 0; i--)
          temp.append("abababdedfg");
   String testString = temp.toString();

   // Time first one . . .
   long count = timesToDo;
   long startTime = System.currentTimeMillis();
   while (--count > 0)
          regex1.reset(testString).find();
   double seconds = (System.currentTimeMillis() - startTime)/1000.0;
   System.out.println("Alternation takes " + seconds + " seconds");

   // Time second one . . .
   count = timesToDo;
   startTime = System.currentTimeMillis();
   while (--count > 0)
          regex2.reset(testString).find();
   seconds = (System.currentTimeMillis() - startTime)/1000.0;
   System.out.println("Character Class takes " + seconds + " seconds");
 }
}
```

On my system, running the benchmark on the client VM produces:

```
Alternation takes 19.318 seconds
Character Class takes 1.685 seconds
```

while the server VM yields:

```
Alternation takes 12.106 seconds
Character Class takes 0.657 seconds
```

What makes benchmarking slippery, and this example somewhat naïve, is that the timing can be highly dependent on how well the automatic pre-execution compiler works, or how the run-time compiler interacts with the code being tested. Some VM have a JIT (Just-In-Time compiler), which compiles code on the fly, just before it's needed.

Sun's Java 1.4 has what I call a BLTN (Better-Late-Than-Never) compiler, which kicks in *during* execution, compiling and optimizing heavily-used code on the fly. The nature of a BLTN is that it doesn't "kick in" until it senses that some code is "hot" (being used a lot). A VM that's been running for a while, such as in a server environment, will be "warmed up," while our simple test ensures a "cold" server (nothing yet optimized by the BLTN).

One way to see "warmed up" times is to run the benchmarked parts in a loop:

```
//  Time first one . . .
for (int i = 4; i > 0; i--)
{
    long count = timesToDo;
    long startTime = System.currentTimeMillis();
    while (--count > 0)
          regex1.reset(testString).find();
    double seconds = (System.currentTimeMillis() - startTime)/1000.0;
    System.out.println("Alternation takes " + seconds + " seconds");
}
```

If the extra loop runs enough times (say, for 10 seconds), the BLTN will have optimized the hot code, leaving the last times reported as representative of a warmed-up system. Testing again with the server VM, these times are indeed a bit faster by about 8% and 25%:

```
Alternation takes 11.151 seconds
Character Class takes 0.483 seconds
```

Another issue that makes Java benchmarking slippery is the unpredictable nature of thread scheduling and garbage collection. Again, running the test long enough helps amortize their unpredictable influence.

Benchmarking with VB.NET

The benchmark example in VB.NET is shown in the listing on the facing page. On my system, it produces:

```
Alternation takes 13.311 seconds
Character Class takes 1.680 seconds
```

The .NET Framework allows a regex to be compiled to an even more efficient form, by providing `RegexOptions.Compiled` as a second argument to each `Regex` constructor (☞ 404). Doing that results in:

```
Alternation takes 5.499 seconds
Character Class takes 1.157 seconds
```

Both tests are faster using the `Compiled` option, but alternation sees a greater relative benefit (its almost 3× faster when `Compiled`, but the class version is only about 1.5× faster), so it seems that alternation benefits from the more efficient compilation relatively more than a character class does.

Benchmarking with VB.NET

```
Option Explicit On
Option Strict On

Imports System.Text.RegularExpressions

Module Benchmark
Sub Main()
   Dim Regex1 as Regex = New Regex("^(a|b|c|d|e|f|g)+$")
   Dim Regex2 as Regex = New Regex("^[a-g]+$")
   Dim TimesToDo as Integer = 1000
   Dim TestString as String = ""
   Dim I as Integer
   For I = 1 to 1000
      TestString = TestString & "abababdedfg"
   Next

   Dim StartTime as Double = Timer()
   For I = 1 to TimesToDo
      Regex1.Match(TestString)
   Next
   Dim Seconds as Double = Math.Round(Timer() - StartTime, 3)
   Console.WriteLine("Alternation takes " & Seconds & " seconds")

   StartTime = Timer()
   For I = 1 to TimesToDo
      Regex2.Match(TestString)
   Next
   Seconds = Math.Round(Timer() - StartTime, 3)
   Console.WriteLine("Character Class takes " & Seconds & " seconds")
End Sub
End Module
```

Benchmarking with Python

The benchmark example in Python is shown in the listing on the next page.

For Python's regex engine, I had to cut the size of the string a bit because the original causes an internal error ("maximum recursion limit exceeded") within the regex engine. To compensate, I increased the number of times the test is done by a proportional amount.

On my system, the benchmark produces:

```
Alternation takes 10.357 seconds
Character Class takes 0.769 seconds
```

Benchmarking with Python

```python
import re
import time
import fpformat

Regex1 = re.compile("^(a|b|c|d|e|f|g)+$")
Regex2 = re.compile("^[a-g]+$")

TimesToDo = 1250;
TestString = ""
for i in range(800):
    TestString += "abababdedfg"

StartTime = time.time()
for i in range(TimesToDo):
   Regex1.search(TestString)
Seconds = time.time() - StartTime
print "Alternation takes " + fpformat.fix(Seconds,3) + " seconds"

StartTime = time.time()
for i in range(TimesToDo):
   Regex2.search(TestString)
Seconds = time.time() - StartTime
print "Character Class takes " + fpformat.fix(Seconds,3) + " seconds"
```

Benchmarking with Ruby

Here's the benchmark example in Ruby:

```ruby
TimesToDo=1000
testString=""
for i in 1..1000
    testString += "abababdedfg"
end

Regex1 = Regexp::new("^(a|b|c|d|e|f|g)+$");
Regex2 = Regexp::new("^[a-g]+$");

startTime = Time.new.to_f
for i in 1..TimesToDo
   Regex1.match(testString)
end
print "Alternation takes .3f seconds\n" % (Time.new.to_f - startTime);

startTime = Time.new.to_f
for i in 1..TimesToDo
    Regex2.match(testString)
end
print "Character Class takes .3f seconds\n" % (Time.new.to_f - startTime);
```

On my system, it produces:

```
Alternation takes 16.311 seconds
Character Class takes 3.479 seconds
```

Benchmarking with Tcl

Here's the benchmark example in Tcl:

```
set TimesToDo 1000
set TestString ""
for {set i 1000} {$i > 0} {incr i -1} {
    append TestString "abababdedfg"
}

set Count $TimesToDo
set StartTime [clock clicks -milliseconds]
for {} {$Count > 0} {incr Count -1} {
    regexp {^(a|b|c|d|e|f|g)+$} $TestString
}
set EndTime [clock clicks -milliseconds]
set Seconds [expr ($EndTime - $StartTime)/1000.0]
puts [format "Alternation takes .3f seconds" $Seconds]

set Count $TimesToDo
set StartTime [clock clicks -milliseconds]
for {} {$Count > 0} {incr Count -1} {
    regexp {^[a-g]+$} $TestString
}
set EndTime [clock clicks -milliseconds]
set Seconds [expr ($EndTime - $StartTime)/1000.0]
puts [format "Character class takes .3f seconds" $Seconds]
```

On my system, this benchmark produces:

```
Alternation takes 0.362 seconds
Character class takes 0.352 seconds
```

Wow, they're both about the same speed! Well, recall from the table on page 145 that Tcl has a hybrid NFA/DFA engine, and these regular expressions are exactly the same to a DFA engine. Most of what this chapter talks about simply does not apply to Tcl. See the sidebar on page 243 for more.

Common Optimizations

A smart regex implementation has many ways to optimize how quickly it produces the results you ask of it. Optimizations usually fall into two classes:

- **Doing something faster**   Some types of operations, such as ⌜\d+⌟, are so common that the engine might have special-case handling set up to execute them faster than the general engine mechanics would.

- **Avoiding work**   If the engine can decide that some particular operation is unneeded in producing a correct result, or perhaps that some operation can be applied to less text than originally thought, skipping those operations can result in a time savings. For example, a regex beginning with ⌜\A⌟ (start-of-line) can match only when started at the beginning of the string, so if no match is found there, the transmission need not bother checking from other positions.

Over the next dozen or so pages, we'll look at many of the different and ingenious optimizations that I've seen. No one language or tool has them all, or even the same mix as another language or tool, and I'm sure that there are plenty of other optimizations that I've not yet seen, but this chapter should leave you much more empowered to take advantage of whatever optimizations your tool offers.

No Free Lunch

Optimizations often result in a savings, but not always. There's a benefit only if the amount of time saved is more than the extra time spent checking to see whether the optimization is applicable in the first place. In fact, if the engine checks to see if an optimization is applicable and the answer is "no," the overall result is *slower* because it includes the fruitless check on top of the subsequent normal application of the regex. So, there's a balance among how much time an optimization takes, how much time it saves, and importantly, how likely it is to be invoked.

Let's look at an example. The expression ⌜\b\B⌟ (*word boundary* at the same location as a *non-word boundary*) can't possibly match. If an engine were to realize that a regex contained ⌜\b\B⌟ in such a way that it was required for any match, the engine would know that the overall regex could never match, and hence never have to actually apply that regex. Rather, it could always immediately report failure. If applied to long strings, the savings could be substantial.

Yet, no engine that I know of actually uses this optimization. Why not? Well, first of all, it's not necessarily easy to decide whether it applies to a particular regex. It's certainly possible for a regex to have ⌜\b\B⌟ somewhere in it, yet still match,[†] so the engine has to do extra work ahead of time to be absolutely certain. Still, the savings could be truly substantial, so it could be worth doing the extra work if ⌜\b\B⌟ was expected to be common. But, it's not common (I think it's silly!), so even though the savings could be huge, it's not worth slowing every other regex by the extra overhead required to do the check.

Everyone's Lunch is Different

Keep this in mind when looking at the various kinds of optimizations that this chapter discusses. Even though I've tried to pick simple, clean names for each one, it may well be that every engine that implements it does so in a different way. A seemingly innocuous change in a regex can cause it to become substantially faster with one implementation, but substantially slower with another.

---

† I've used ⌜\b\B⌟ before to cause one part of a larger expression to fail, during testing. For example, I might insert in at the marked point of ⌜ (this ⁀| this other) ⌟ to guaranteed failure of the first alternative. These days, when I need a "must fail" component, I use ⌜(?!)⌟. You can see an interesting Perl-specific example of this on page 333.

The Mechanics of Regex Application

Before looking at the ways advanced systems optimize their regex performance, and ways we can take advantage of those optimizations, it's important to first understand the basics of regex application. We've already covered the details about backtracking, but in this short section, we'll step back a bit to look at the broader picture.

Here are the main steps taken in applying a regular expression to a target string:

1. **Regex Compilation** The regex is inspected for errors, and if valid, compiled into an internal form.

2. **Transmission Begins** The transmission "positions" the engine at the start of the target string.

3. **Component Tests** The engine works through the regex and the text, moving from component to component in the regex, as described in Chapter 4. We've already covered backtracking for NFAs in great detail, but there are a few additional points to mention:

   - With components next to each other, as with the ⌈s⌋, ⌈u⌋, ⌈b⌋, ⌈j⌋, ⌈e⌋..., of ⌈Subject⌋, each component is tried in turn, stopping only if one fails.

   - With quantifiers, control jumps between the quantifier (to see whether the quantifier should continue to make additional attempts) and the component quantified (to test whether it matches).

   - There is some overhead when control enters or exits a set of capturing parentheses. The actual text matched by the parentheses must be remembered so that $1 and the like are supported. Since a set of parentheses may be "backtracked out of," the state of the parentheses is part of the states used for backtracking, so entering and exiting capturing parentheses requires some modification of that state.

4. **Finding a Match** If a match is found, a Traditional NFA "locks in" the current state and reports overall success. On the other hand, a POSIX NFA merely remembers the possible match if it is the longest seen so far, and continues with any saved states still available. Once no more states are left, the longest match that was seen is the one reported.

5. **Transmission Bump-Along** If no match is found, the transmission bumps the engine along to the next character in the text, and the engine applies the regex all over again (going back to step 3).

6. **Overall Failure** If no match is found after having applied the engine at every character in the target string (and after the last character as well), overall failure must be reported.

The next few sections discuss the many ways this work can be reduced by smart implementations, and taken advantage of by smart users.

Pre-Application Optimizations

A good regex engine implementation can reduce the amount of work that needs to be done before the actual application of a regex, and sometimes can even decide quickly beforehand that the regex can never match, thereby avoiding the need to even apply the regex in the first place.

Compile caching

Recall the mini mail program from Chapter 2 (☞ 57). The skeleton of the main loop, which processes every line of the header, looks like:

```
while (···) {
    if ($line =~ m/^\s*$/ )  ···
    if ($line =~ m/^Subject: (.*)/)  ···
    if ($line =~ m/^Date: (.*)/)  ···
    if ($line =~ m/^Reply-To: (\S+)/) ···
    if ($line =~ m/^From: (\S+) \(([^()]*)\)/) ···
       ⋮
}
```

The first thing that must be done before a regular expression can be used is that it must be inspected for errors, and compiled into an internal form. Once compiled, that internal form can be used in checking many strings, but will it? It would certainly be a waste of time to recompile each regex each time through the loop. Rather, it is much more time efficient (at the cost of some memory) to save, or *cache*, the internal form after it's first compiled, and then use that same internal form for each subsequent application during the loop.

The extent to which this can be done depends on the type of regular-expression handling the application offers. As described starting on page 93, the three types of handling are *integrated, procedural*, and *object-oriented*.

Compile caching in the integrated approach

An integrated approach, like Perl's and awk's, allows compile caching to be done with ease. Internally, each regex is associated with a particular part of the code, and the compiled form can be associated with the code the first time it's executed, and merely referenced subsequent times. This provides for the maximum optimization of speed at the cost of the memory needed to hold all the cached expressions.

The ability to interpolate variables into the regex operand (that is, use the contents of a variable as part of the regular expression) throws somewhat of a monkey wrench into the caching plan. When variables are interpolated, as with something like `m/^Subject: \Q$DesiredSubject\E\s*$/`, the actual regular expression

DFAs, Tcl, and Hand-Tuning Regular Expressions

For the most part, the optimizations described in this chapter simply don't apply to DFAs. The *compile caching* optimization, discussed on page 242, does apply to all types of engines, but none of the techniques for hand-tuning discussed throughout this chapter apply to DFAs. As Chapter 4 makes clear (☞ 157), expressions that are logically equivalent — ⌐this|that⌐ and ⌐th(is|at)⌐, for example — *are* equivalent to a DFA. It's because they're not necessarily equivalent to an NFA that this chapter exists.

But what about Tcl, which has a hybrid DFA/NFA engine? Tcl's regex engine was custom built for Tcl by regular-expression legend Henry Spencer (☞ 88), who has done a fantastic job blending the best of both DFA and NFA worlds. Henry noted himself in an April 2000 Usenet posting:

> In general, the Tcl RE-matching engine is much less sensitive to the exact form of the RE than traditional matching engines. Things that it does quickly will be fast no matter how you write them; things that it does slowly will be slow no matter how you write them. The old folklore about hand-optimizing your REs simply does not apply.

Henry's Tcl regex engine is an important step forward. If this technology were more widespread, much of this chapter would not be needed.

---

may change from iteration to iteration because it depends on the value in the variable, which can change from iteration to iteration. If it changes every time, the regex must be compiled every time, so nothing can be reused.

Well, the regular expression *might* change with each iteration, but that doesn't mean it needs to be recompiled each time. An intermediate optimization is to check the results of the interpolation (the actual value to be used as the regular expression), and recompile only if it's different from the previous time. If the value actually changes each time, there's no optimization, as the regex indeed must be recompiled each time. But, if it changes only sporadically, the regular expression need only be checked (but not compiled) most times, yielding a handsome optimization.

Compile caching in the procedural approach

With an integrated approach, regex use is associated with a particular location in a program, so the compiled version of the regex can be cached and used the next time that location in the program is executed. But, with a procedural approach, there is just a general "apply this regex" function that is called as needed. This means that there's no location in a program with which to associate the compiled form, so the next time the function is called, the regex must be compiled from scratch again. That's how it works in theory, but in practice, it's much too inefficient to abandon all attempts at caching. Rather, what's often done is that a mapping of recently used regex patterns is maintained, linking each pattern to its resulting compiled form.

When the apply-this-regex function is called, it compares the pattern argument with those in the cache of saved regular expressions, and uses the cached version if it's there. If it's not, it goes ahead and compiles the regex, saving it to the cache (and perhaps flushing an old one out, if the cache has a size limit). When the cache has become full and a compiled form must be thrown out, it's usually the least recently used one.

GNU Emacs keeps a cache of 20 expressions, while Tcl keeps 30. A large cache size is important because if more regular expressions are used within a loop than the size of the cache, by the time the loop restarts, the first regex will have been flushed from the cache, guaranteeing that every expression will have to be compiled from scratch every time.

Compile caching in the object-oriented approach

The object-oriented approach puts control of when a regex is compiled directly into the programmer's hands. Compilation of the regex is exposed to the user via object constructors such as **New Regex**, **re.compile**, and **Pattern.compile** (which are from .NET, Python, and java.util.regex). In the simple examples from Chapter 3 where these are introduced (starting on page 95), the compilation is done just before the regex is actually used, but there's no reason that they can't be done earlier (such as sometime before a loop, or even at program initialization) and then used freely as needed. This is done, in the benchmarking examples on pages 234, 236, and 237.

The object-oriented approach also affords the programmer control over when a compiled form is thrown away, via the object's destructor. Being able to immediately throw away compiled forms that will no longer be needed saves memory.

Pre-check of required character/substring optimization

Searching a string for a particular character (or perhaps some literal substring) is a much "lighter" operation than applying a full NFA regular expression, so some systems do extra analysis of the regex during compilation to determine if there are any characters or substrings that are *required* to exist in the target for a possible match. Then, before actually applying the regex to a string, the string is quickly checked for the required character or string—if it's not found, the entire application of the regex can be bypassed.

For example, with `^Subject: (.*)`, the string 'Subject:' is required. A program can look for the entire string, perhaps using the *Boyer-Moore* search algorithm (which is fast way to search for literal strings within text—the longer the literal string, the more efficient the search). A program not wishing to implement the Boyer-Moore algorithm can still gain a benefit by picking a required character and just checking every character in the target text. Picking a character less likely to be found in the target (such as picking ':' over 't' from our 'Subject: •' example) is likely to yield better results.

While it's trivial for a regex engine to realize what part of ⌈^Subject: •(.*)⌋ is a fixed literal string required for any match, it's more work to recognize that 'th' is required for any match of ⌈this|that|other⌋, and most don't do it. It's not exactly black and white — an implementation not realizing that 'th' is required may well still be able to easily realize that 'h' and 't' are required, so at least do a one-character check.

There is a great variety in how well different applications can recognize required characters and strings. Most are thwarted by the use of alternation. With such systems, using ⌈th(is|at)⌋ can provide an improvement over ⌈this|that⌋. Also, be sure to see the related section "Initial character/class/substring discrimination" on the next page.

Length-cognizance optimization

⌈^Subject: •(.*)⌋ can match arbitrarily long text, but any match is certainly at least nine characters long. Therefore, the engine need not be started up and applied to strings shorter than that length. Of course, the benefit is more pronounced with a regex with a longer required length, such as ⌈:\d{79}:⌋ (81 characters in any match).

Also see the *length-cognizance transmission* optimization on page 247.

Optimizations with the Transmission

If the regex engine can't decide ahead of time that a particular string can never match, it may still be able to reduce the number of locations that the transmission actually has to apply the regex.

Start of string/line anchor optimization

This optimization recognizes that any regex that begins with ⌈^⌋ can match only when applied where ⌈^⌋ can match, and so need be applied at those locations only.

The comments in the "Pre-check of required character/substring" section on the facing page about the ability of the regex engine to derive just when the optimization is applicable to a regex is also valid here. Any implementation attempting this optimization should be able to recognize that ⌈^(this|that)⌋ can match starting only at locations where ⌜^⌝ can match, but many won't come to the same realization with ⌜^this|^that⌝. In such situations, writing ⌜^(this|that)⌝ or (even better) ⌜^(?:this|that)⌝ can allow a match to be performed much faster.

Similar optimizations involves ⌜\A⌝, and for repeated matches, ⌜\G⌝.

Implicit-anchor optimization

An engine with this optimization realizes that if a regex begins with ⌜.*⌝ or ⌜.+⌝, and has no global alternation, an implicit ⌜^⌝ can be prepended to the regex. This allows the *start of string/line anchor* optimization of the previous section to be used, which can provide a lot of savings.

More advanced systems may realize that the same optimization can also be applied when the leading ⌜.*⌝ or ⌜.+⌝ is within parentheses, but care must be taken when the parentheses are capturing. For example, the regex ⌜(.+)X\1⌝ finds locations where a string is repeated on either side of 'X', and an implicit leading ⌜^⌝ causes it to improperly not match '1234X2345'.[†]

End of string/line anchor optimization

This optimization recognizes that some regexes ending with ⌜$⌝ or other end anchors (☞ 127) have matches that start within a certain number of bytes from the end of the string. For example, with ⌜regex(es)?$⌝, any match must start no more than eight[‡] characters from the end of the string, so the transmission can jump directly to that spot, potentially bypassing many positions if the target string is long.

Initial character/class/substring discrimination optimization

A more generalized version of the *pre-check of required character/string* optimization, this optimization uses the same information (that any match by the regex must begin with a specific character or literal substring) to let the transmission use a fast substring check so that it need apply the regex only at appropriate spots in the string. For example ⌜this|that|other⌝ can match only at locations beginning with ⌜[ot]⌝, so having the transmission pre-check each character in the string and applying the regex only at matching positions can afford a huge savings. The longer the substring that can be pre-checked, the fewer "false starts" are likely.

---

† It's interesting to note that Perl had this over-optimization bug unnoticed for over 10 years until Perl developer Jeff Pinyan discovered (and fixed) it in early 2002. Apparently, regular expressions like ⌜(.+)X\1⌝ aren't used often, or the bug would have been discovered sooner. Most regex engines don't have this bug because they don't have this optimization, but some still do have the bug. These include Ruby, PCRE, and tools that use PCRE, such as PHP.

‡ I say eight characters rather than seven because in many flavors, ⌜$⌝ can match before a string-ending newline (☞ 127).

Embedded literal string check optimization

This is almost exactly like the *initial string discrimination* optimization, but is more advanced in that it works for literal strings embedded a known distance into any match. ⌈\b(perl|java)\.regex\.info\b⌋, for example, has '.regex.info' four characters into any match, so a smart transmission can use a fast Boyer-Moore literal-string check to find '.regex.info', and then actually apply the regex starting four characters before.

In general, this works only when the literal string is embedded a fixed distance into any match. It doesn't apply to ⌈\b(vb|java)\.regex\.info\b⌋, which does have a literal string, but one that's embedded either two or four characters into any match. It also doesn't apply to ⌈\b(\w+)\.regex\.info\b⌋, whose literal string is embedded any number of characters into any match.

Length-cognizance transmission optimization

Directly related to the *Length-cognizance optimization* on page 245, this optimization allows the transmission to abandon the attempt if it's gotten too close to the end of the string for a match to be possible.

Optimizations of the Regex Itself

Literal string concatenation optimization

Perhaps the most basic optimization is that ⌈abc⌋ can be treated by the engine as "one part," rather than the three parts "⌈a⌋ then ⌈b⌋ then ⌈c⌋." If this is done, the one part can be applied by one iteration of the engine mechanics, avoiding the overhead of three separate iterations.

Simple quantifier optimization

Uses of start, plus, and friends that apply to simple items, such as literal characters and character classes, are often optimized such that much of the step-by-step overhead of a normal NFA engine is removed. The main control loop inside a regex engine must be general enough to deal with all the constructs the engine supports. In programming, "general" often means "slow," so this important optimization makes simple quantifiers like ⌈.*⌋ into one "part," replacing the general engine mechanics of quantifier processing with fast, specialized processing. Thus, the general engine is short-circuited for these tests.

For example, ⌈.*⌋ and ⌈(?:.)*⌋ are logically identical, but for systems with this optimization, the simple ⌈.*⌋ is substantially faster than ⌈(?:.)*⌋. A few examples: with Sun's Java regex package, it's about 10% faster, but with Ruby and the .NET languages, it's about two and a half times faster. With Python, it's about 50 times faster, and with PCRE/PHP, it's about 150 times faster. Because Perl has the optimization discussed in the next section, both ⌜.*⌟ and ⌜(?:.)*⌟ are the same speed. (Be sure to see the sidebar below for a discussion on how to interpret these numbers.)

Needless parentheses elimination

If an implementation can realize that ⌜(?:.)*⌟ is exactly the same as ⌜.*⌟, it opens up the latter to the previous optimization.

Understanding Benchmarks in This Chapter

For the most part, benchmarks in this chapter are reported as relative ratios for a given language. For example, on page 247, I note that a certain optimized construct is 10% faster than the unoptimized construct, at least with Sun's Java regex package. In the .NET Framework, the optimized and unoptimized constructs differ by a factor of two and a half, but in PCRE, it's a factor of about whopping 150×. In Perl, it's a factor of one (i.e., they are the same speed—no difference).

From this, what can you infer about the speed of one language compared to another? Absolutely nothing. The 150× speedup for the optimization in PCRE may mean that the optimization has been implemented particularly well, relative to the other languages, or it may mean that the unoptimized version is particularly slow. For the most part, I report very little timing information about how languages compare against each other, since that's of interest mostly for bragging rights among language developers.

But, for what it's worth, it may be interesting to see the details behind such different results as Java's 10% speedup and PCRE's 150× speedup. It turns out that PCRE's unoptimized ⌜(?:.)*⌟ is about 11 times *slower* than Java's, but its optimized ⌜.*⌟ is about 13 times *faster*. Java's and Ruby's optimized versions are about the same speed, but Ruby's unoptimized version is about 2.5 times slower than Java's unoptimized version. Ruby's unoptimized version is only about 10% slower than Python's unoptimized version, but Python's optimized version is about 20 times faster than Ruby's optimized version.

All of these are slower than Perl's. Both Perl's optimized and unoptimized versions are 10% faster than Python's fastest. Note that each language has its own strong points, and these numbers are for only one specific test case.

For an example of a head-to-head comparison, see "Warning: Benchmark results can cause drowsiness!" in Chapter 8 (☞ 376).

Needless character class elimination

A character class with a single character in it is a bit silly because it invokes the processing overhead of a character class, but without any benefits of one. So, a smarter implementation internally converts something like ⌈[.]⌋ to ⌈\.⌋.

Character following lazy quantifier optimization

With a lazy quantifier, as in ⌈"(.*?)"⌋, the engine normally must jump between checking what the quantifier controls (the dot) with checking what comes after (⌈"⌋). For this and other reasons, lazy quantifiers are generally much slower than greedy ones, especially for greedy ones that are optimized with the *simple quantifier* optimization discussed two sections ago. Another factor is that if the lazy quantifier is inside capturing parentheses, control must repeatedly jump in and out of the capturing, which causes additional overhead.

So, this optimization involves the realization that if a literal character follows the lazy quantifier, the lazy quantifier can act like a normal greedy quantifier so long as the engine is not at that literal character. Thus, implementations with this optimization switch to specialized lazy quantifier processing for use in these situations, which quickly checks the target text for the literal character, bypassing the normal "skip this attempt" if the target text is not at that special literal character.

Variations on this optimization might include the ability to pre-check for a class of characters, rather than just a specific literal character (for instance, a pre-check for ⌈['"]⌋ with ⌈['"](.*?)["']⌋, which is similar to the *initial character discrimination* optimization discussed on page 246).

"Excessive" backtracking detection

The problem revealed with the "Reality Check" on page 226 is that certain combinations of quantifiers, such as ⌈(.+)*⌋, can create an exponential amount of backtracking. One simple way to avoid this is to keep a count of the backtracking, and abort the match when there's "too much." This is certainly useful in the reality-check situation, but it puts an artificial limit on the amount of text that some regular expressions can be used with.

For example, if the limit is 10,000 backtracks, ⌈.*?⌋ can never match text longer than 10,000 characters, since each character matched involves a backtrack. Working with these amounts of text is not all that uncommon, particularly when working with, say, web pages, so the limitation is unfortunate.

For different reasons, some implementations have a limit on the size of the backtrack stack (on how many saved states there can be at any one time). For example, Python allows at most 10,000. Like a backtrack limit, it limits the length of text some regular-expressions can work with.

This issue made constructing some of the benchmarks used while researching this book rather difficult. To get the best results, the timed portion of a benchmark should do as much of the target work as possible, so I created huge strings and compared the time it took to execute, say, ⌜`"(.*)"`⌟, ⌜`"(.)*"`⌟, ⌜`"(.)*?"`⌟, and ⌜`"([^"])*?"`⌟. To keep meaningful results, I had to limit the length of the strings so as not to trip the backtrack-count or stack-size limitations. You can see an example on page 237.

Exponential (a.k.a, super-liner) short-circuiting

A better solution to avoid matching forever on an exponential match is to detect when the match attempt has gone super-linear. You can then make the extra effort to keep track of the position at which each quantifier's subexpression has been attempted, and short-circuit repeat attempts.

It's actually fairly easy to detect when a match has gone super-linear. A quantifier should rarely "iterate" (loop) more times than there are characters in the target string. If it does, it's a good sign that it may be an exponential match. Having been given this clue that matching may go on forever, it's a more complex issue to detect and eliminate redundant matches, but since the alternative is matching for a very, very long time, it's probably a good investment.

One negative side effect of detecting a super-linear match and returning a quick failure is that a truly inefficient regex now has its inefficiency mostly hidden. Even with exponential short-circuiting, these matches are much slower than they need to be, but no longer slow enough to be easily detected by a human (instead of finishing long after the sun has gone dormant, it may take $1/100$ of a second—quick to us, but still an eternity in computer time).

Still, the overall benefit is probably worth it. There are many people who don't care about regex efficiency—they're scared of regular expressions and just want the thing to work, and don't care how. (You may have been this way before, but I hope reading this book emboldens you, like the title says, to master the use of regular expressions.)

State-suppression with possessive quantifiers

After something with a normal quantifier has matched, a number of "try the non-match option" states have been created (one state per iteration of the quantifier). Possessive quantifiers (☞ 140) don't leave those states around. This can be accomplished by removing the extra states after the quantifier has run its course, or, it can be done more efficiently by removing the previous iteration's state while adding the current iteration's. (During the matching, one state is always required so that the regex can continue once the quantified item can no longer match.)

The reason the on-the-fly removal is more efficient is because it takes less memory. Applying ⌈.*⌉ leaves one state per character matched, which could consume a vast amount of memory if the string is long.

Automatic "Possessification"

Recall the example from Chapter 4 (☞ 171) where ⌈^\w+:⌉ is applied to 'Subject'. Once ⌈\w+⌉ matches to the end of the string, the subsequent colon can't match, and the engine must waste the effort of trying ⌈:⌉ at each position where backtracking forces ⌈\w+⌉ to give up a character. The example then concluded that we could have the engine avoid that extra work by using atomic grouping, ⌈^(?>\w+):⌉, or possessive quantifiers, ⌈^\w++>:⌉.

A smart implementation should be able to do this for you. When the regex is first compiled, the engine can see that what *follows the quantifier* can't be matched by what *is quantified*, so the quantifier can be automatically turned into a possessive one.

Although I know of no system that currently has this optimization, I include it here to encourage developers to consider it, for I believe it can have a substantial positive impact.

Small quantifier equivalence

Some people like to write ⌈\d\d\d\d⌉ directly, while some like to use a small quantifier and write ⌈\d{4}⌉. Is one more efficient than the other? For an NFA, the answer is almost certainly "yes," but which is faster depends on the tool. If the tool's quantifier has been optimized, the ⌈\d{4}⌉ version is likely faster unless the version without the quantifier can somehow be optimized more. Sound a bit confusing? It is.

My tests show that with Perl, Python, PCRE, and .NET, ⌈\d{4}⌉ is faster by as much as 20%. On the other hand, with Ruby and Sun's Java regex package, ⌈\d\d\d\d⌉ is faster — sometimes several times faster. So, this seems to make it clear that the small quantifier is better for some, but worse for others. But, it can be more complex than that.

Compare ⌈====⌉ with ⌈={4}⌉. This is a quite different example because this time, the subject of the repetition is a literal character, and perhaps using ⌈====⌉ directly makes it easier for the regex engine to recognize the literal substring. If it can, the highly effective *initial character/substring discrimination* optimization (☞ 246) can kick in, if supported. This is exactly the case for Python and Sun's Java regex package, for whom the ⌈====⌉ version can be up to 100× faster than ⌈={4}⌉.

More advanced still, Perl, Ruby, and .NET recognize this optimization with *either* ⌜====⌟ or ⌜={4}⌟, and as such, both are equally fast (and in either case, can be hundreds or thousands of times faster than the ⌜\d\d\d\d⌟ and ⌜\d{4}⌟ counterparts). On the other hand, PCRE *doesn't* recognize it in either case.

Need cognizance

One simple optimization is if the engine realizes that some aspect of the match result isn't needed (say, the capturing aspect of capturing parentheses), it can eliminate the work to support them. The ability to detect such a thing is very language dependent, but this optimization can be gained as easily as allowing an extra match-time option to disable various high-cost features.

One example of a system that has this optimization is Tcl. Its capturing parentheses don't actually capture unless you explicitly ask. Conversely, the .NET Framework regular expressions have an option that allows the programmer to indicate that capturing parentheses shouldn't capture.

Techniques for Faster Expressions

The previous pages list the kinds of optimizations that I've seen implemented in Traditional NFA engines. No one program has them all, and whichever ones your favorite program happens to have now, they're certain to change sometime in the future. But, just understanding the kinds of optimizations that can be done gives you an edge in writing more efficient expressions. Combined with the understanding of how a Traditional NFA engine works, this knowledge can be applied in three powerful ways:

- **Write to the optimizations** Compose expressions such that known optimizations (or ones that might be added in the future) can kick in. For example, using ⌜xx*⌟ instead of ⌜x+⌟ can allow a variety of optimizations to more readily kick in, such as the check of a required character or string (☞ 244), or initial-character discrimination (☞ 246).

- **Mimic the optimizations** There are situations where you know your program doesn't have a particular optimization, but by mimicking the optimization yourself, you can potentially see a huge savings. As an example that we'll expand on soon, consider adding ⌜(?=t)⌟ to the start of ⌜this|that⌟, to somewhat mimic the initial-character discrimination (☞ 246) in systems that don't already determine from the regex that any match must begin with 't'.

- **Lead the engine to a match** Use your knowledge of how a Traditional NFA engine works to lead the engine to a match more quickly. Consider the ⌜this|that⌟ example. Each alternative begins with ⌜th⌟; if the first's alternative can't match its ⌜th⌟, the second alternative's ⌜th⌟ certainly can't match, so the

attempt to do so is wasted. To avert that, you can use ⌜th(?:is|at)⌟ instead.
That way, the ⌜th⌟ is tested only once, and the relatively expensive alternation
is avoided until it's actually needed. And as a bonus, the leading raw-text ⌜th⌟
of ⌜th(?:is|at)⌟ is exposed, potentially allowing a number of other optimiza-
tions to kick in.

It's important to realize that efficiency and optimizations can sometimes be touchy.
There are a number of issues to keep in mind as you read through the rest of this
section:

- Making a change that would seem to be certainly helpful can, in some situations, slow things down because you've just untweaked some other optimization that you didn't know was being applied.

- If you add something to mimic an optimization that you know doesn't exist, it
  may well turn out that the work required to process what you added actually
  takes more time than it saves.

- If you add something to mimic an optimization that you know doesn't currently exist, it may defeat or duplicate the real optimization if it's later added
  when the tool is upgraded.

- Along the same lines, contorting an expression to try to pique one kind of
  optimization today may prohibit some future, more advantageous optimization
  from kicking in when the tool is upgraded.

- Contorting an expression for the sake of efficiency may make the expression
  more difficult to understand and maintain.

- The magnitude of the benefit (or harm) a particular change can have is almost
  certainly strongly dependent on the data it's applied to. A change that is beneficial with one set of data may actually be harmful with another type of data.

Let me give a somewhat crazy example: you find ⌜(000|999)$⌟ in a Perl script, and
decide to turn those capturing parentheses into non-capturing parentheses. This
should make things a bit faster, you think, since the overhead of capturing can
now be eliminated. But surprise, this small and seemingly beneficial change can
slow this regex down by *several orders of magnitude* (thousands and thousands of
times slower). *What!?* It turns out that a number of factors come together just right
in this example to cause the *end of string/line anchor* optimization (☞ 246) to be
turned off when non-capturing parentheses are used. I don't want to dissuade you
from using non-capturing parentheses with Perl—their use is beneficial in the vast
majority of cases—but in this particular case, it's a disaster.

So, testing and benchmarking with the kind of data you expect to use in practice
can help tell you how beneficial or harmful any change will be, but you've still got
to weigh all the issues for yourself. That being said, I'll touch on some techniques
that can be used toward squeezing out the last bit of efficiency out of an engine.

Common Sense Techniques

Some of the most beneficial things you can do require only common sense.

Avoid recompiling

Compile or define the regular expression as few times as possible. With object-oriented handling (☞ 95), you have the explicit control to do this. If, for example, you want to apply a regex in a loop, create the regex object *outside* of the loop, then *use* it repeatedly inside the loop.

With a procedural approach, as with GNU Emacs and Tcl, try to keep the number of regular expressions used within a loop below the cached threshold of the tool (☞ 243).

With an integrated approach like Perl, try not to use variable interpolation within a regex inside a loop, because at a minimum, it causes the regex value to be reevaluated at each iteration, even if you know the value never changes. (Perl does, however, provide efficient ways around the problem ☞ 348.)

Use non-capturing parentheses

If you don't use the capturing aspect of capturing parentheses, use non-capturing ⌈(?:⋯)⌋ parentheses (☞ 45). Besides the direct savings of not having to capture, there can be residual savings because it can make the state needed for backtracking less complex, and hence faster. It can also open up additional optimizations, such as needless-parentheses elimination (☞ 248).

Don't add superfluous parentheses

Use parentheses as you need them, but adding them otherwise can prohibit optimizations from kicking in. Unless you need to know the last character matched by ⌈.*⌋, don't use ⌈(.)*⌋. This may seem obvious, but after all, this is the "common sense techniques" section.

Don't use superfluous character classes

This may seem to be overly obvious as well, but I've often seen expressions like ⌈^.*[:]⌋ from novice programmers. I'm not sure why one would ever use a class with a single character in it — it incurs the processing overhead of a class without gaining any multi-character matching benefits of a class. I suppose that when the character is a metacharacter, such as ⌈[.]⌋ and ⌈[*]⌋, it's probably because the author didn't know about escaping, as with ⌈\.⌋ and ⌈*⌋. I see this most often with white-space in a free-spacing mode (☞ 110).

Somewhat related, users of Perl that read the first edition of this book may sometimes write something like ⌜^[Ff][Rr][Oo][Mm]:⌟ instead of a case-insensitive use of ⌜^from:⌟. Old versions of Perl were very inefficient with their case-insensitive matching, so I recommended the use of classes like this in some cases. That recommendation has been lifted, as the case-insensitive inefficiency has been fixed for some years now.

Use leading anchors

Except in the most rare cases, any regex that begins with ⌜.*⌟ should probably have ⌜^⌟ or ⌜\A⌟ (☞ 127) added to the front. If such a regex can't match when applied at the beginning of the string, it won't be able to match any better when the bump-along applies it starting at the second character, third character, and so on. Adding the anchor (either explicitly, or auto-added via an optimization ☞ 246) allows the common start-of-line anchor optimization to kick in, saving a lot of wasted effort.

Expose Literal Text

Many of the native optimizations we've seen in this chapter hinge on the regex engine's ability to recognize that there is some span of literal text that must be part of any successful match. Some engines are better at figuring this out than others, so here are some hand-optimization techniques that help "expose" literal text, increasing the chances that an engine can recognize more of it, allowing the various literal-text optimizations to kick in.

"Factor out" required components from quantifiers

Using ⌜xx*⌟ instead of ⌜x+⌟ exposes 'x' as being required. The same logic applies to the rewriting of ⌜-{5,7}⌟ as ⌜------{0,2}⌟.

"Factor out" required components from the front of alternation

Using ⌜th(?:is|at)⌟ rather than ⌜(?:this|that)⌟ exposes that ⌜th⌟ is required. You can also "factor out" on the right side, when the common text follows the differing text: ⌜(?:optim|standard)ization⌟. As the next section describes, these can be particularly important when what is being factored out includes an anchor.

Expose Anchors

Some of the most fruitful internal regex optimizations are those that take advantage of anchors (like ⌜^⌟, ⌜$⌟, and ⌜\G⌟) that tie the expression to one end of the target string or another. Some engines are not as good as others at understanding when such an optimization can take place, but there are techniques you can use to help.

Expose ˆ and \G at the front of expressions

⌜ˆabc|ˆ123⌟ and ⌜ˆ(?:abc|123)⌟ are logically the same expression, but many more regex engines can apply the *Start of string/line anchor* optimization (☞ 245) with the first than the second. So, choosing to write it the first way can make it much more efficient. PCRE (and tools that use it) is efficient with either, but most other NFA tools are much more efficient with the exposed version.

Another difference can be seen by comparing ⌜(ˆabc)⌟ and ⌜ˆ(abc)⌟. The former doesn't have many redeeming qualities, as it both "hides" the anchor, and causes the capturing parentheses to be entered before the anchor is even checked, which can be inefficient with some systems. Some systems (PCRE, Perl, the .NET languages) are efficient with either, but others (Ruby and Sun's Java regex library) recognize the optimization only with the exposed version.

Python doesn't seem to have the anchor optimization, so these techniques don't currently matter for it. Of course, most optimizations in this chapter don't apply to Tcl (☞ 243).

Expose $ at the end of expressions

This is conceptually very similar to the previous section, where ⌜abc$|123$⌟ and ⌜(?:abc|123)$⌟ are logically the same expression, but can be treated differently by the optimizers. Currently, there is a difference only for Perl, as only Perl currently has the *End of string/line anchor* optimization (☞ 246). The optimization kicks in with ⌜(⋯|⋯)$⌟ but not with ⌜(⋯$|⋯$)⌟.

Lazy Versus Greedy: Be Specific

Usually, the choice between lazy and greedy quantifiers is dictated by the specific needs of the regex. For example, ⌜ˆ.*:⌟ differs substantially from ⌜ˆ.*?:⌟ in that the former one matches until the final colon, while the latter one matches until the first. But, suppose that you knew that your target data had exactly one colon on it. If that's the case, the semantics of both are the same ("match until the colon"), so it's probably smart to pick the one that will run fastest.

It's not always obvious which is best, but as a rule of thumb when the target strings are long, if you expect the colon to generally be near the start of the string, using the lazy quantifier allows the engine to find the colon sooner. Use the greedy quantifier if you expect the colon to be toward the end of the string. If the data is random, and you have no idea which will be more likely, use a greedy quantifier, as they are generally optimized a bit better than non-greedy quantifier, especially when what follows in the regex disallows the *character following lazy quantifier* optimization (☞ 249).

When the strings to be tested are short, it becomes even less clear. When it comes down to it, either way is pretty fast, but if you need every last bit of speed, benchmark against representative data.

A somewhat related issue is in situations where either a lazy quantifier or a negated class can be used (such as ⌜`.*?:`⌟ vs. ⌜`[^:]*:`⌟), which should be used? Again, this is dependent on the data and the language, but with most engines, using a negated class is much more efficient than a lazy quantifier. One exception is Perl, because it has that *character following lazy quantifier* optimization.

Split Into Multiple Regular Expressions

There are cases where it's much faster to apply many small regular expressions instead of one large one. For a somewhat contrived example, if you wanted to check a large string to see if it had any of the month names, it would probably be much faster to use separate checks of ⌜`January`⌟, ⌜`February`⌟, ⌜`March`⌟, etc., than to use one ⌜`January|February|March|···`⌟. With the latter, there's no literal text known to be required for any match, so an *embedded literal string check* optimization (☞ 247) is not possible. With the all-in-one regex, the mechanics of testing each subexpression at each point in the text can be quite slow.

Here's an interesting situation I ran into at about the same time that I was writing this section. When working with a Perl data-handling module, I realized that I had a bug with my client program that caused it to sent bogus data that looked like '`HASH(0x80f60ac)`' instead of the actual data. So, I thought I'd augment the module to look for that kind of bogus data and report an error. The straightforward regex for what I wanted is ⌜`\b(?:SCALAR|ARRAY|···|HASH)\(0x[0-9a-fA-F]+\)`⌟.

This was a situation where efficiency was extremely important. Would this be fast? Perl has a debugging mode that can tell you about some of the optimizations it uses with any particular regex (☞ 361), so I checked. I hoped to find that the *precheck of required string* optimization (☞ 244) would kick in, since an advanced enough engine should be able to figure out that '`(0x`' is required in any match. Knowing the data that I'd apply this to would almost never have '`(0x`', I knew that such a pre-check would eliminate virtually every line. Unfortunately, Perl didn't pick this out, so I was left with a regex that would entail a lot of alternation at every character of every target string. That's slower than I wanted.

Since I was in the middle of researching and writing about optimizations, I thought hard about how I could rewrite the regex to garner some of the better optimizations. One thought I had was to rewrite it along the form of the somewhat complex ⌜`\(0x(?<=(?:SCALAR|···|HASH)\(0x)[0-9a-fA-F]+\)`⌟. The approach here is that once ⌜`\(0x`⌟ has matched, the negative lookahead (underlined for clarity) makes sure that what came before is allowed, and then checks that what comes after is expected as well. The whole reason to go through these regex gymnastics is to get the regex to lead with non-optional literal text ⌈\(0x⌋, which allows a lot of good optimizations to kick in. In particular, I'd expect that *pre-check of required string* optimization to kick in, as well as the *initial character/substring discrimination* optimization (☞ 246). I'm sure that these would have made it very fast, but Perl doesn't allow variable-length lookbehind (☞ 132), so I was back to square one.

However, I realized that since Perl wasn't doing the pre-check for ⌈\(0x⌋ for me, I could just do it myself:

```
if ($data =~ m/\(0x/
    and
    $data =~ m/(?:SCALAR|ARRAY| … |HASH)\(0x[0-9a-fA-F]+\)/)
{
    # warn about bogus data…
}
```

The check of ⌈\(0x⌋ eliminates virtually every line, so this leaves the check of the relatively slow full regex for only when the likelihood of a match is high. This created a wonderful balance of efficiency (very high) and readability (very high).[†]

Mimic Initial-Character Discrimination

If the *initial-character discrimination* optimization (☞ 246) its not done by your implementation, you can mimic it yourself by adding appropriate lookahead (☞ 132) to the start of the regex. The lookahead can "pre-check" that you're at an appropriate starting character before you let the rest of the regex match. For example, for ⌈Jan|Feb| … |Dec⌋, use ⌈**(?=[JFMASOND])**(?:Jan|Feb| … |Dec)⌋. The leading ⌈[JFMASOND]⌋ represents letters that can begin the month names in English. This must be done with care, though, because the added overhead of the lookahead may overshadow the savings. In this particular example, where the lookahead is pre-checking for many alternatives that are likely to fail, it is beneficial for most systems I've tested (Java, Perl, Python, Ruby, .NET languages, and PCRE), none of which apparently are able to derive ⌈[JFMASOND]⌋ from ⌈Jan|Feb| … |Dec⌋ themselves. (Tcl, of course, can do it perfectly ☞ 243.)

A behind-the-scenes check of ⌈[JFMASOND]⌋ by an engine's native optimization is certainly faster than the same check explicitly added by us to the regex proper. Is there a way we can modify the regex so that the engine will check natively? Well, with many systems, you can by using the horribly contorted:

⌈[JFMASOND]**(?:**(?<=J)an|(?<=F)eb| … |(?<=D)ec)⌋

---

† You can see this in action for yourself. The module in question, DBIx::DWIW, is available on CPAN. It's a module that allows very easy access to a MySQL database. Jeremy Zawodny and I developed it at Yahoo!.

I don't expect you to be able to understand that regex at first sight, but taking the time to understand what it does, and how, is a good exercise. The simple class leading the expression can be picked up by most systems' *initial-character dis-crimination* optimization, thereby allowing the transmission itself to effectively pre-check ⌜[JFMASOND]⌝. If the target string has few matching characters, the result can be substantially faster than the ⌜Jan| ··· |Dec⌝ original, or our prepended-look-ahead. But, if the target string has many first-character matches, the extra overhead of all the added lookbehind can actually make things slower. On top of this worry, it's certainly a *much* less readable regular expression. But, the exercise is interesting and instructive nevertheless.

Don't do this with Tcl

The previous example shows how hand tweaking has the potential to really make things worse. The sidebar on page 243 notes that regular expressions in Tcl are mostly immune to the form of the expression, so for the most part attempts to hand optimize are meaningless. Well, here's an example where it *does* matter. Adding the explicit ⌜(?=[JFMASOND])⌝ pre-check causes Tcl to slow down by a factor of about 100× in my tests.

Use Atomic Grouping and Possessive Quantifiers

There are many cases when atomic grouping (☞ 137) and possessive quantifiers (☞ 140) can greatly increase the match speed, even though they don't change the kind of matches that are possible. For example, if ⌜^[^:]+:⌝ can't match the first time the colon is attempted, it certainly can't match after backtracking back into the ⌜[^:]+⌝, since any character "given up" by that backtracking, by definition, can't match a colon. The use of atomic grouping ⌜^(?>[^:]+):⌝ or a possessive quantifier ⌜^[^:]++:⌝ causes the states from the plus to be thrown away, or not created in the first place. Since this leaves nothing for the engine to backtrack to, it ensures that it doesn't backtrack unfruitfully. (The sidebar on page 251 suggests that this can be done automatically by a smart enough engine.)

However, I must stress that misusing either of these constructs can inadvertently change what kind of matches are allowed, so great care must be taken. For example, using them with ⌜^.*:⌝, as with ⌜^(?>.*):⌝, guarantees failure. The entire line is matched by ⌜.*⌝, and this includes any colon that the later ⌜:⌝ needs. The atomic grouping removes the ability for the backtracking required to let ⌜:⌝ match, so failure is guaranteed.

Lead the Engine to a Match

One concept that goes a long way toward more efficient NFA regular expressions is pushing "control" issues as far back in the matching process as possible. One example we've seen already is the use of ⌜th(?:is|at)⌟ instead of ⌜this|that⌟. With the latter, the alternation is a top-level control issue, but with the former, the relatively expensive alternation is not considered until ⌜th⌟ has been matched.

The next section, "Unrolling the Loop," is an advanced form of this, but there are a few simple techniques I can mention here.

Put the most likely alternative first

Throughout the book, we've seen a number of situations where the order in which alternatives are presented matters greatly (☞ 28, 176, 189, 216). In such situations, the correctness of the match take precedence over optimization, but otherwise, if the order doesn't matter to the correctness, you can gain some efficiency by placing the most-likely alternatives first.

For example, when building a regex to match a hostname (☞ 205) and listing the final domain parts, some might find it appealing to list them in alphabetical order, as with ⌜(?:aero|biz|com|coop|⋯)⌟. However, some of those early in the list are new and not currently popular, so why waste the time to check for them first when you know they will likely fail most of the time? An arrangement with the more popular first, such as ⌜(?:com|edu|org|net|⋯)⌟, is likely to lead to a match more quickly, more often.

Of course, this matters only for a Traditional NFA engine, and then, only for when there *is* a match. With a POSIX NFA, or with a failure, all alternatives must be checked and so the ordering doesn't matter.

Distribute into the end of alternation

Continuing with a convenient example, compare ⌜**(?:**com|edu|⋯|[a-z][a-z]**)\b**⌟ with ⌜com**\b**|edu**\b**|⋯**\b**|[a-z][a-z]**\b**⌟. In the latter, the ⌜\b⌟ after the alternation has been distributed onto the end of each alternative. The possible benefit is that it may allow an alternative that matches, but whose match would have been undone by the ⌜\b⌟ after the alternation, to fail a bit quicker, inside the alternation. This allows the failure to be recognized before the overhead of exiting the alternation is needed.

This is perhaps not the best example to show the value of this technique, since it shows promise only for the specific situation when an alternative is likely to match, but what comes right after is likely to fail. We'll see a better example of this concept later in this chapter—look for the discussion of $OTHER* on page 280.

This optimization can be dangerous. One very important concern in applying this hand optimization is that you take care not to defeat more profitable native optimizations. For example, if the "distributed" subexpression is literal text, as with the distribution of the colon from ⌜(?:this|that):)⌝ to ⌜this:|that:⌝, you're directly conflicting with some of the ideas in the "Expose Literal Text" section (☞ 255). All things being equal, I think that those optimizations would be much more fruitful, so be careful not to defeat them in favor of this one.

A similar warning applies to distributing a regex-ending ⌜$⌝ on systems that benefit from an exposed end-anchor (☞ 256). On such systems, ⌜(?:com|edu|⋯)$⌝ is much faster than the distributed ⌜com$|edu$|⋯$⌝. (Among the many systems I tested, only Perl currently supports this.)

Unrolling the Loop

Regardless of what native optimizations a system may support, perhaps the most important gains are to be had by understanding the basics of how the engine works, and writing expressions that help lead the engine to a match. So, now that we've reviewed the basics in excruciating detail, let's step up to the big leagues with a technique I call "unrolling the loop." It's effective for speeding up certain common expressions. Using it, for example, to transform the neverending match from near the start of this chapter (☞ 226) results in an expression that actually finishes a non-match in our lifetime, and as a bonus is faster with a match as well.

The "loop" in the name is the implicit loop imparted by the star in an expression that fits a ⌜(*this*|*that*|⋯)*⌝ pattern. Indeed, our earlier ⌜"(\\.|[^"\\]+)*"⌝ neverending match fits this pattern. Considering that it takes approximately forever to report a non-match, it's a good example to try to speed up!

There are two competing roads one can take to arrive at this technique:

1. We can examine which parts of ⌜(\\.|[^"\\]+)*⌝ actually succeed during a variety of sample matches, leaving a trail of used subexpressions in its wake. We can then reconstruct an efficient expression based upon the patterns we see emerge. The (perhaps far-fetched) mental image I have is that of a big ball, representing a ⌜(⋯)*⌝ regex, being rolled over some text. The parts inside (⋯) that are actually used then stick to the text they match, leaving a trail of subexpressions behind like a dirty ball rolling across the carpet.

2. Another approach takes a higher-level look at the construct we want to match. We'll make an informed assumption about the likely target strings, allowing us to take advantage of what we believe will be the common situation. Using this point of view, we can construct an efficient expression.

Either way, the resulting expressions are identical. I'll begin from the "unrolling" point of view, and then converge on the same result from the higher-level view.

To keep the examples as uncluttered and as widely usable as possible, I'll use ⌜(···)⌟ for all parentheses. If ⌜(?:···)⌟ non-capturing parentheses are supported, their use imparts a further efficiency benefit. Later, we'll also look at using atomic grouping (☞ 137) and possessive quantifiers (☞ 140).

Method 1: Building a Regex From Past Experiences

In analyzing ⌜"(\\.|[^"\\]+)*"⌟, it's instructive to look at some matching strings to see exactly which subexpressions are used during the overall match. For example, with '"hi"', the expression effectively used is just ⌜"[^"\\]+"⌟. This illustrates that the overall match used the initial ⌜"⌟, one application of the alternative ⌜[^"\\]+⌟, and the closing ⌜"⌟. With

    "he said \"hi there\" and left"

it is ⌜"[^"\\]+ \\.[^"\\]+ \\.[^"\\]+"⌟. In this example, as well as in Table 6-2, I've marked the expressions to make the patterns apparent. It would be nice if we could construct a specific regex for each particular input string. That's not possible, but we can still identify common patterns to construct a more efficient, yet still general, regular expression.

Table 6-2: Unrolling-the-Loop Example Cases

Target String	Effective Expression
"hi there"	"[^"\\]+"
"just one \" here"	"[^"\\]+ \\.[^"\\]+"
"some \"quoted\" things"	"[^"\\]+ \\.[^"\\]+ \\"[^"\\]+"
"with \"a\" and \"b\"."	"[^"\\]+ \\.[^"\\]+ \\.[^"\\]+ \\.[^"\\]+ \\.[^"\\]+"
"\"ok\"\n"	"\\.[^"\\]+ \\.\\."
"empty \"\" quote"	"[^"\\]+ \\.\\.[^"\\]+"

For the moment, let's concentrate on the first four examples in Table 6-2. I've underlined the portions that refer to "an escaped item, followed by further normal characters." This is the key point: in each case, the expression between the quotes begins with ⌜[^"\\]+⌟ and is followed by some number of ⌜\\.[^"\\]+⌟ sequences. Rephrasing this as a regular expression, we get ⌜[^"\\]+(\\.[^"\\]+)*⌟. This is a specific example of a general pattern that can be used for constructing many useful expressions.

Constructing a general "unrolling-the-loop" pattern

In matching the double-quoted string, the quote itself and the escape are "special" —the quote because it can end the string, and the escape because it means that whatever follows won't end the string. Everything else, ⌜[^"\\]⌟, is "normal." Looking at how these were combined to create ⌜[^"\\]+(\\.[^"\\]+)*⌟, we can see that it fits the general pattern ⌜*normal*+ (*special normal*+)*⌟.

Adding in the opening and closing quote, we get ⌈`" [^"\\]+ (\\. [^"\\]+) * "`⌋. Unfortunately, this won't match the last two examples in Table 6-2. The problem, essentially, is that our current expression's two ⌈`[^"\\]+`⌋ *require* a normal character at the start of the string and after any special character. As the examples show, that's not always appropriate—the string might start or end with an escaped item, or there might be two escaped items in a row.

We could try changing the two pluses to stars: ⌈`" [^"\\]* (\\. [^"\\]*) * "`⌋. Does this have the desired effect? More importantly, does it have any undesirable effects?

As far as desirable effects, it is easy to see that all the examples now match. In fact, even a string such as `"\"\"\""` now matches. This is good. However, we can't make such a major change without being quite sure there are no undesirable effects. Could anything other than a legal double-quoted string match? Can a legal double-quoted string not match? What about efficiency?

Let's look at ⌈`" [^"\\]* (\\. [^"\\]*) * "`⌋ carefully. The leading ⌈`" [^"\\]*`⌋ is applied only once and doesn't seem dangerous: it matches the required opening quote and any normal characters that might follow. No danger there. The subsequent ⌈`(\\. [^"\\]*) *`⌋ is wrapped by `(···) *`, so is allowed to match zero times. That means that removing it should still leave a valid expression. Doing so, we get ⌈`" [^"\\]* "`⌋, which is certainly fine — it represents the common situation where there are no escaped items.

On the other hand, if ⌈`(\\. [^"\\]*) *`⌋ matches once, we have an effective ⌈`" [^"\\]* \\. [^"\\]* "`⌋. Even if the trailing ⌈`[^"\\]*`⌋ matches nothing (making it an effective ⌈`" [^"\\]* \\. "`⌋), there are no problems. Continuing the analysis in a similar way (if I can remember my high school algebra, it's "by induction"), we find that there are, indeed, no problems with the proposed changes.

So, that leaves us with the final expression to match a double-quoted string with escaped double quotes inside:

⌈`" [^"\\]* (\\. [^"\\]*) * "`⌋

The Real "Unrolling-the-Loop" Pattern

Putting it all together, then, our expression to match a double-quoted string with escaped-items is ⌈`" [^"\\]* (\\. [^"\\]*) * "`⌋. This matches exactly the same strings as our alternation version, and it fails on the same strings that the alternation version fails on. But, this unrolled version has the added benefit of finishing in our lifetime because it is much more efficient and avoids the neverending-match problem.

The general pattern for unrolling the loop is:

⌜*opening normal*＊ (*special* *normal*＊)＊ *closing*⌟

Avoiding the neverending match

Three extremely important points prevent ⌜" [^"\\]＊(\\.[^"\\]＊)＊"⌟ from becoming a neverending match:

The start of special and normal must never intersect

The *special* and *normal* subexpressions must be written such that they can never match at the same point. With our ongoing example, where *normal* is ⌜[^"\\]⌟ and *special* is ⌜\\.⌟, it's clear that they can never begin a match at the same character since the latter one requires a leading backslash, while the former one explicitly disallows a leading backslash.

On the other hand, ⌜\\.⌟ and ⌜[^"]⌟ can both match starting at '"Hello\n"', so they are inappropriate as *special* or *normal*. If there is a way they can match starting at the same location, it's not clear which should be used at such a point, and the non-determinism creates a neverending match. The 'makudonarudo' example illustrates this graphically (☞ 227). A failing match (or any kind of match attempt with POSIX NFA engines) has to test all these possibilities and permutations. That's too bad, since the whole reason to re-engineer in the first place was to avoid this.

If we ensure that *special* and *normal* can never match at the same point, *special* acts to checkpoint the nondeterminism that would arise when multiple applications of *normal* could, by different iterations of the ⌜(···)＊⌟ loop, match the same text. If we ensure that *special* and *normal* can never match at the same point, there is exactly one "sequence" of *specials* and *normals* in which a particular target string matches. Testing this one sequence is much faster than testing a hundred million of them, and thus a neverending match is avoided.

Special must not match nothingness

The second important point is that *special* must always match at least one character if it matches anything at all. If it were able to match without consuming characters, adjacent normal characters would be able to be matched by different iterations of ⌜(*special normal*＊)＊⌟, bringing us right back to the basic (···)＊ problem.

For example, choosing a *special* of ⌜(\\.)＊⌟ violates this point. In trying to match the ill-fated ⌜" [^"\\]＊((\\.)＊[^"\\]＊)＊"⌟ against '"Tubby' (which fails), the engine must try every permutation of how multiple ⌜[^"\\]＊⌟ might match 'Tubby' before concluding that the match is a failure. Since *special* can match nothingness, it doesn't act as the checkpoint it purports to be.

Special must be atomic

Text matched by one application of special must not be able to be matched by multiple applications of special. Consider matching a string of optional Pascal { ⋯ } comments and spaces. A regex to match the comment part is ⌜\{[^}]*\}⌟, so the whole (neverending) expression becomes ⌜(\{[^}]*\}|␣+)*⌟. With this regex, you might consider *special* and *normal* to be:

special	normal
⌜␣+⌟	⌜\{[^}]*\}⌟

Plugging this into the ⌜*normal** (*special normal**) *⌟ pattern we've developed, we get: ⌜(\{[^}]*\})* (␣+ (\{[^}]*\})*) *⌟. Now, let's look at a string:

{comment}␣␣␣{another}␣␣

A sequence of multiple spaces could be matched by a single ⌜␣+⌟, by many ⌜␣+⌟ (each matching a single space), or by various combinations of ⌜␣+⌟ matching differing numbers of spaces. This is directly analogous to our 'makudonarudo' problem.

The root of the problem is that *special* is able to match a smaller amount of text *within* a larger amount that it could also match, and is able to do so multiple times thanks to (⋯)*. The nondeterminism opens up the "many ways to match the same text" can of worms.

If there is an overall match, it is likely that only the all-at-once ⌜␣+⌟ will happen just once, but if no match is possible (such as might happen if this is used as a subexpression of a larger regex that could possibly fail), the engine must work through each permutation of the effective ⌜(␣+)*⌟ to each series of multiple spaces. That takes time, but without any hope for a match. Since *special* is supposed to act as the checkpoint, there is nothing to check *its* nondeterminism in this situation.

The solution is to ensure that *special* can match only a fixed number of spaces. Since it must match at least one, but could match more, we simply choose ⌜␣⌟ and let multiple applications of *special* match multiple spaces via the enclosing ⌜(⋯) *⌟.

This example is useful for discussion, but in real-life use, it's probably more efficient to swap the *normal* and *special* expressions to come up with

⌜␣* (\{[^}]*\} ␣*) *⌟

because I would suspect that a Pascal program has more spaces than comments, and it's more efficient to have *normal* be the most common case.

General things to look out for

Once you internalize these rules (which might take several readings and some practical experience), you can generalize them into guidelines to help identify regular expressions susceptible to a neverending match. Having multiple levels of quantifiers, such as ⌜(···*)*⌟, is an important warning sign, but many such expressions are perfectly valid. Examples include:

- ⌜(Re:·*)*⌟, to match any number of 'Re:' sequences (such as might be used to clean up a 'Subject:·Re:·Re:·Re:·hey' subject line).

- ⌜(·*\$[0-9]+)*⌟, to match dollar amounts, possibly space-separated.

- ⌜(.*\n)+⌟, to match one or more lines. (Actually, if dot can match a newline, and if there is anything following this subexpression that could cause it to fail, this would become a quintessential neverending match.)

These are okay because each has something to checkpoint the match, keeping a lid on the "many ways to match the same text" can of worms. In the first, it's ⌜Re:⌟, in the second it's ⌜\$⌟, and in the third (when dot doesn't match newline), it's ⌜\n⌟.

Method 2: A Top-Down View

Recall that I said that there were two paths to the same "unrolling the loop" expression. In this second path, we start by matching only what's most common in the target, then adding what's needed to handle the rare cases. Let's consider what the neverending ⌜(\\.|[^"\\]+)*⌟ attempts to accomplish and where it will likely be used. Normally, I would think, a quoted string would have more regular characters than escaped items, so ⌜[^"\\]+⌟ does the bulk of the work. The ⌜\\.⌟ is needed only to take care of the occasional escaped item. Using alternation to allow either makes a useful regex, but it's too bad that we need to compromise the efficiency of the whole match for the sake of a few (or more commonly, no) escaped characters.

If we think that ⌜[^"\\]+⌟ will normally match most of the body of the string, we know that once it finishes we can expect either the closing quote or an escaped item. If we have an escape, we want to allow one more character (whatever it might be), and then match more of the bulk with another ⌜[^"\\]+⌟. Every time ⌜[^"\\]+⌟ ends, we are in the same position we were before: expecting either the closing quote or another escape.

Expressing this naturally as a single expression, we arrive at the same expression we had early in Method 1: ⌜" [^"\\]+ (\\.[^"\\]+)*"⌟. Each time the matching reaches the point marked by ↟, we know that we're expecting either a backslash or a closing quote. If the backslash can match, we take it, the character that follows, and more text until the next "expecting a quote or backslash" point.

As in the previous method, we need to allow for when the initial non-quote segment, or inter-quote segments, are empty. We can do this by changing the two pluses to stars, which results in the same expression as we ended up with on page 263.

Method 3: An Internet Hostname

I promised two methods to arrive at the *unrolling-the-loop* technique, but I'd like to present something that can be considered a third. It struck me while working with a regex to match a hostname such as www.yahoo.com. A hostname is essentially dot-separated lists of subdomain names, and exactly what's allowed for one subdomain name is fairly complex to match (☞ 203), so to keep this example less cluttered, we'll just use ⌜[a-z]+⌟ to match a subdomain.

If a subdomain is ⌜[a-z]+⌟ and we want a dot-separated list of them, we need to match one subdomain first. After that, further subdomains require a leading period. Expressing this literally, we get: ⌜[a-z]+(\.[a-z]+)*⌟. Now, if I add an underline and some gray, ⌜[a-z]+(\.[a-z]+)*⌟, it sure looks like it almost fits a very familiar pattern, doesn't it!

To illustrate the similarity, let's try to map this to our double-quoted string example. If we consider a string to be sequences of our *normal* ⌜[^\\"]⌟, separated by *special* ⌜\\.⌟, all within '"…"', we can plug them into our unrolling-the-loop pattern to form ⌜"[^\\"]+(\\.[^\\"]+)*"⌟, which is exactly what we had at one point while discussing Method 1. This means that conceptually, we can take the view we used with a hostname—stuff separated by separators—and apply it to double-quoted strings, to give us "sequences of non-escaped stuff separated by escaped items." This might not seem intuitive, but it yields an interesting path to what we've already seen.

The similarity is interesting, but so are the differences. With Method 1, we went on to change the regex to allow empty spans of *normal* before and after each *special*, but we don't want to do that here because a subdomain part cannot be empty. So, even though this example isn't exactly the same as the previous ones, it's in the same class, showing that the unrolling technique is powerful *and* flexible.

There are two differences between this and the subdomain example:

- Domain names don't have delimiters at their start and end.

- The *normal* part of a subdomain can never be empty (meaning two periods are not allowed in a row, and can neither start nor end the match). With a double-quoted string, there is no requirement that there be any *normal* parts at all, even though they are likely, given our assumptions about the data. That's why we were able to change the ⌜[^\\"]+⌟ to ⌜[^\\"]*⌟. We can't do that with the subdomain example because *special* represents a *separator*, which is required.

Observations

Recapping the double-quoted string example, I see many benefits to our expression, ⌜`" [^"\\] * ( \\. [^"\\] * ) * "`⌟, and few pitfalls.

Pitfalls:

- **Readability** The biggest pitfall is that the original ⌜`" ( [^"\\] | \\.)* "`⌟ is probably easier to understand at first glance. We've traded a bit of readability for efficiency.

- **Maintainability** Maintaining ⌜`" [^"\\] * ( \\. [^"\\] * ) * "`⌟ might be more difficult, since the two copies of ⌜`[^"\\]`⌟ must be kept identical across any changes. We've traded a bit of maintainability for efficiency.

Benefits:

- **Speed** The new regex doesn't buckle under when no match is possible, or when used with a POSIX NFA. By carefully crafting the expression to allow only one way for any particular span of text to be matched, the engine quickly comes to the conclusion that non-matching text indeed does not match.

- **More speed** The regex "flows" well, a subject taken up in "The Freeflowing Regex" (☞ 277). In my benchmarks with a Traditional NFA, the unrolled version is consistently faster than the old alternation version. This is true even for successful matches, where the old version did not suffer the lockup problem.

Using Atomic Grouping and Possessive Quantifiers

The problem with our original neverending match regex, ⌜`" (\\. | [^"\\]+) * "`⌟, is that it bogs down when there is no match. When there *is* a match, though, it's quite fast. It's quick to find the match because the ⌜`[^"\\]+`⌟ component is what matches most of the target string (the *normal* in the previous discussion). Because ⌜`[⋯]+`⌟ is usually optimized for speed (☞ 247), and because this one component handles most of the characters, the overhead of the alternation and the outer ⌜`(⋯) *`⌟ quantifier is greatly reduced.

So, the problem with ⌜`" (\\. | [^"\\]+) * "`⌟, is that it bogs down on a non-match, backtracking over and over to what we know will always be unfruitful states. We know they're unfruitful because they're just testing different permutations of the same thing. (If ⌜abc⌟ doesn't match 'foo', neither will ⌜abc⌟ or ⌜abc⌟ (or ⌜abc⌟, ⌜abc⌟, or ⌜abc⌟, for that matter). So, if we could throw those states away, this regex would report the non-match quickly.

There are two ways to actually throw away (or otherwise ignor) states: atomic grouping (☞ 137) and possessive quantifiers (☞ 140). At the time of this writing, only Sun's regex package for Java supports possessive quantifiers, but I believe they'll gain popularity soon, so I'll cover them here.

Before I get into the elimination of the backtracking, I'd like to swap the order of the alternatives from ⌜`" ( \\ . | [ ^ " \ \ ] + ) * "`⌝ to ⌜`" ( [ ^ " \ \ ] + | \ \ . ) * "`⌝, as this places the component matching "normal" text first. As has been noted a few times in the last several chapters, when two or more alternatives can potentially match at the same location, care must be taken when selecting their order, as that order can influence what exactly is matched. But if, as in this case, all alternatives are mutually exclusive (none can match at a point where another can match), the order doesn't matter from a correctness point of view, so the order can be chosen for clarity or efficiency.

Making a neverending match safe with possessive quantifiers

Our neverending regex ⌜`" ( [ ^ " \ \ ] + | \ \ . ) * "`⌝ has two quantifiers. We can make one possessive, the other possessive, or both possessive. Does it matter? Well, most of the backtracking troubles were due to the states left by the ⌜`[ ⋯ ] +`⌝, so making that possessive is my first thought. Doing so yields a regex that's pretty fast, even when there's no match. However, making the outer ⌜`( ⋯ ) *`⌝ possessive throws away all the states from inside the parentheses, which includes both those of ⌜`[ ⋯ ] +`⌝ and of the alternation, so if I had to pick one, I'd pick that one.

But I don't have to pick one because I can make both possessive. Which of the three situations is fastest probably depends a lot on how optimized possessive quantifiers are. Currently, they are supported only by Sun's Java regex package, so my testing has been limited, but I've run all three combinations through tests with it, and found examples where one combination or the other is faster. I would expect the situation where both are possessive could be the fastest, so these results tend to make me believe that Sun hasn't yet optimized them to their fullest.

Making a neverending match safe with atomic grouping

Looking to add atomic grouping to ⌜`" ( [ ^ " \ \ ] + | \ \ . ) * "`⌝, it's tempting to replace the normal parentheses with atomic ones: ⌜`" (?> [ ^ " \ \ ] + | \ \ . ) * "`⌝. It's important to realize that ⌜`(?> ⋯ | ⋯ ) *`⌝ is very different from the possessive ⌜`( ⋯ | ⋯ ) *+`⌝ in the previous section when it comes to the states that are thrown away.

The possessive ⌜`( ⋯ | ⋯ ) *+`⌝ leaves no states when it's done. On the other hand, the atomic grouping in ⌜`(?> ⋯ | ⋯ ) *`⌝ merely eliminates any states left by each alternative, and by the alternation itself. The star is *outside* the atomic grouping, so is unaffected by it and still leaves all its "can try skipping this match" states. That means that the individual matches can still be undone via backtracking. We want to eliminate the outer quantifier's states as well, so we need an outer set of atomic grouping. That's why ⌜`(?> ( ⋯ | ⋯ ) *)`⌝ is needed to mimic the possessive ⌜`( ⋯ | ⋯ ) *+`⌝.

⌈(···|···)*+⌋ and ⌈(?>···|···)*⌋ are both certainly helpful in solving the neverending match, but which states are thrown away, and when, are different. (For more on the difference between the two, see page 173.)

Short Unrolling Examples

Now that we've got the basic idea of unrolling under our belt, let's look at some examples from earlier in the book, and see how unrolling applies to them.

Unrolling "multi-character" quotes

In Chapter 4 on page 167, we saw this example:

```
<B>                       # Match the opening <B>
(                         # Now, only as many of the following as needed . . .
   (?! </?B>   )          #     If not <B>, and not </B> . . .
   .                      #           . . . any character is okay
) *                       #
</B>                      #   . . . until the closing delimiter can match.
```

With a *normal* of ⌈[^<]⌋ and a *special* of ⌈(?! </?B>) <⌋, here's the unrolled version:

```
<B>                       # Match the opening <B>
  (?> [^<] * )            # Now match any "normal" . . .
  (?>                     # Any amount of . . .
      (?! </?B> ) #          if not at <B> or </B>,
      <                  #          match one "special"
      [^<] *             #          and then any amount of "normal"
  ) *                     #
</B>                      # And finally the closing </B>
```

The use of atomic grouping is not required, but does make the expression faster when there's only a partial match.

Unrolling the continuation-line example

The continuation-line example from the start of the previous chapter (☞ 186) left off with ⌈^\w+ = ([^\n\\] | \\ .)*⌋. Well, that certainly looks ripe for unrolling:

```
^ \w+ =                        # leading field name and '='
# Now read (and capture) the value . . .
(
    (?> [^\n\\] * )            # "normal"*
    (?> \\. [^\n\\] * ) * # ( "special" "normal"* )*
)
```

As with earlier examples of unrolling, the atomic grouping is not required for this to work, but helps to allow the engine to announce a failure more quickly.

Unrolling the CSV regex

Chapter 5 has a long discussion of CSV processing, which finally worked its way to this snippet, from page 216:

```
(?:^|,)
(?:  # Now, match either a double-quoted field (inside, paired double quotes are allowed) . . .
       "  #  (double-quoted field's opening quote)
           (    (?: [^"]  |  "" )*    )
       "  #  (double-quoted field's closing quote)
   |
       #  . . . or, some non-quote/non-comma text . . .
           (  [^",]*  )
)
```

The text then went on to suggest adding ⌜\G⌟ to the front, just to be sure that the bump-along didn't get us in trouble as it had throughout the example, and some other efficiency suggestions. Now that we know about unrolling, let's see where in this example we can apply it.

Well, the part to match a Microsoft CSV string, ⌜(?: [^"] | "")*⌟, certainly looks inviting. In fact, the way it's presented already has our *normal* and *special* picked out for us: ⌜[^"]⌟ and ⌜""⌟. Here's how it looks with that part unrolled, plugged back into the original Perl snippet to process each field:

```perl
while ($line =~ m{
          \G(?:^|,)
          (?:
              # Either a double-quoted field (with "" for each ")...
              " # field's opening quote
              ( (?> [^"]* ) (?> "" [^"]* )*  )
              " # field's closing quote
          # ..or...
          |
              # ... some non-quote/non-comma text....
              ( [^",]* )
          )
     }gx)
{
   if (defined $2) {
       $field = $2;
   } else {
       $field = $1;
       $field =~ s/""/"/g;
   }
   print "[$field]"; # print the field, for debugging
   Can work with $field now . . .
}
```

As with the other examples, the atomic grouping is not required, but may help with efficiency.

Unrolling C Comments

I'd like to give an example of unrolling the loop with a somewhat more complex target. In the C language, comments begin with **/***, end with ***/**, and can span across lines, but can't be nested. (C++, Java, and C# also allow this type of comment.) An expression to match such a comment might be useful in a variety of situations, such as in constructing a filter to remove them. It was when working on this problem that I first came up with my unrolling technique, and the technique has since become a staple in my regex arsenal.

To unroll or to not unroll . . .

I originally developed the regex that is the subject of this section back in the early 1990s. Prior to that, matching C comments with a regular expression was considered difficult at best, if not impossible, so when I developed something that worked, it became the standard way to match C comments. But, when Perl introduced lazy quantifiers, a much simpler approach became evident: a dot-matches-all application of ⌈/* .*?*/⌋.

Had lazy quantifiers been around when I first developed the unrolling technique, I might not have bothered to do so, for the need wouldn't have been so apparent. Yet, such a solution was still valuable because with that first version of Perl supporting lazy quantifiers, the unrolled version is faster than the lazy-quantifier version by a significant amount (in the variety of tests I've done, anywhere from about 50% faster, to 3.6× faster).

Yet, with today's Perl and its different mix of optimizations, those numbers go the other way, with the lazy-quantifier version running anywhere from about 50% faster to 5.5× faster. So, with modern versions of Perl, I'd just use ⌈/* .*?*/⌋ to match C comments and be done with it.

Does this mean that the unrolling-the-loop technique is no longer useful for matching C comments? Well, if an engine doesn't support lazy quantifiers, the ability to use the unrolling technique certainly becomes appealing. And not all regex engines have the same mix of optimizations: the unrolling technique is faster with every other language I've tested—in my tests, up to 60 times faster! The unrolling technique is definitely useful, so the remainder of this example explores how to apply it to matching C comments.

Since there are no escapes to be recognized within a C comment the way \" must be recognized within a double-quoted string, one might think that this should make things simpler, but actually, it's much more complex. This is because ***/**, the "ending quote," is more than one character long. The simple ⌈/*[^*]**/⌋ might look good, but that doesn't match **/** some comment here **/** because it has a '*****' within. It should be matched, so we need a new approach.

Avoiding regex headaches

You might find that ⌜/*[^*]**/⌟ is a bit difficult to read, even with the subtle easy-on-the-eyes spacing I've used in typesetting this book. It is unfortunate for our eyes that one of the comment's delimiting characters, '*', is also a regex meta-character. The resulting backslashes are enough to give me a headache. To make things more readable during this example, we'll consider /x⋯x/, rather than /*⋯*/, to be our target comment. This superficial cosmetic change allows ⌜/*[^*]**/⌟ to be written as the more readable ⌜/x[^x]*x/⌟. As we work through the example and the expression becomes more complex, our eyes will thank us for the reprieve.

A direct approach

In Chapter 5 (☞ 196), I gave a standard formula for matching delimited text:

1. Match the opening delimiter
2. Match the main text: really "match anything that is not the ending delimiter"
3. Match the ending delimiter

Our pseudo comments, with /x and x/ as our opening and closing delimiters, appear to fit into this pattern. Our difficulties begin when we try to match "anything that is not the ending delimiter." When the ending delimiter is a single character, we can use a negated character class to match all characters except that delimiter. A character class can't be used for multi-character subexpressions, but if you have negative lookahead, you can use something like ⌜(?:(?!x/).)*⌟. This is essentially ⌜(*anything not* x/)*⌟.

Using that, we get ⌜/x(?:(?!x/).)*x/⌟ to match comments. It works perfectly well, but it can be quite slow (in some of my tests, hundreds of times slower than what we'll develop later in this section). This approach can be useful, but it's of little use in this particular case because any flavor that supports lookahead almost certainly supports lazy quantifiers, so if efficiency is not an issue, you can just use ⌜/x.*?x/⌟ and be done with it.

So, continuing with the direct, three-step approach, is there another way to match until the first x/? Two ideas might come to mind. One method is to consider x to be the start of the ending delimiter. That means we'd match anything not x, and allow an x if it is followed by something other than a slash. This makes the "anything that is not the ending delimiter" one of:

- Anything that is not x: ⌜[^x]⌟
- x, so long as not followed by a slash: ⌜x[^/]⌟

This yields ⌜([^x]|x[^/])*⌟ to match the main text, and ⌜/x([^x]|x[^/])*x/⌟ to match the entire pseudo comment. As we'll see, this doesn't work.

Another approach is to consider a slash as the ending delimiter, but only if preceded by x. This makes the "anything not the ending delimiter" one of:

- Anything that is not a slash: ⌜[^/]⌟
- A slash, so long as not preceded by x: ⌜[^x]/⌟

This yields ⌜([^/] | [^x] /) *⌟ to match the main text, and ⌜/x ([^/] | [^x] /) * x/⌟ to match the whole comment.

Unfortunately, it also doesn't work.

For ⌜/x ([^x] | x[^/]) * x/⌟, consider '/xx·foo·xx/' — after matching 'foo', the first closing x is matched by ⌜x[^/]⌟, which is fine. But then, ⌜x[^/]⌟ matches x**x**/, which is the x that should be ending the comment. This opens the door for the next iteration's ⌜[^x]⌟ to match the slash, thereby errantly matching past the closing x/.

As for ⌜/x ([^/] | [^x] /) * x/⌟, it can't match '/**x**/·foo·/**x**/' (the whole of which is a comment and should be matched). In other cases, it can march past the end of a comment that has a slash immediately after its end (in a way similar to the other method). In such a case, the backtracking involved is perhaps a bit confusing, so it should be instructive to understand why ⌜/x ([^/] | [^x] /) * x/⌟ matches

```
    years = days /x divide x//365; /x assume non-leap year x/
```

as it does (an investigation I'll leave for your free time).

Making it work

Let's try to fix these regexes. With the first one, where ⌜x[^/]⌟ inadvertently matches the comment-ending ···xx/, consider ⌜/x ([^x] | x+[^/]) * x/⌟. The added plus will, we think, have ⌜x+[^/]⌟ match a row of x's ending with something other than a slash. Indeed it will, but due to backtracking, that "something other than a slash" can still be x. At first, the greedy ⌜x+⌟ matches that extra x as we want, but backtracking will reclaim an x if needed to secure an overall match. So, it still matches too much of:

```
    /xx A xx/ foo() /xx B xx/
```

The solution comes back to something I've said before: *say what you mean*. If we want "some x, if not followed by a slash" to imply that the non-slash also doesn't include an x, we should write exactly that: ⌜x+[^/x]⌟. As we want, this stops it from eating '···xxx/', the final x of a row of x that ends the comment. In fact, it has the added effect of not matching *any* comment-ending x, so it leaves us at '···xxx/' to match the ending delimiter. Since the ending delimiter part had been expecting just the one x, it won't match until we insert ⌜x+/⌟ to allow this final case.

Translating Between English and Regex

On page 273, when discussing two ways one might consider the C comment "anything that is not the ending delimiter," I presented one idea as
"x, so long as not followed by a slash: ⌈x[^/]⌋"
and another as:
"a slash, so long as not preceded by x: ⌈[^x]/⌋"

In doing so, I was being informal—the English descriptions are actually quite different from the regexes. Do you see how?

To see the difference, consider the first case with the string 'regex'—it certainly has an x not followed by a slash, but it would *not* be matched by match ⌈x[^/]⌋. The character class requires a character to match, and although that character can't be a slash, it still must be *something*, and there's nothing after the x in 'regex'. The second situation is analogous. As it turns out, what I need at that point in the discussion are those specific expressions, so it's the English that is in error.

If you have lookahead, "x, so long as not followed by a slash" is simply ⌈x(?!/)⌋. If you don't, you might try to get by with ⌈x([^/]|$)⌋. It still matches a character after the x, but can also match at the end of the line. If you have lookbehind, "slash, so long as not preceded by x" becomes ⌈(?<!x)/⌋. If you don't have it, you have to make due with ⌈(^|[^x])/⌋.

We won't use any of these while working with C comments, but it's good to understand the issue.

This leaves us with: ⌈/x([^x]|x+[^/x])*x+/⌋ to match our pseudo comments.

Phew! Somewhat confusing, isn't it? Real comments (with * instead of x) require ⌈/*([^*]|*+[^/*])**+/⌋ which is even more confusing. It's not easy to read; just remember to keep your wits about you as you carefully parse complex expressions in your mind.

Unrolling the C loop

For efficiency's sake, let's look at unrolling this regex. Table 6-3 on the next page shows the expressions we can plug in to our unrolling-the-loop pattern.

Like the subdomain example, the ⌈normal*⌋ is not actually free to match nothingness. With subdomains, it was because the normal part was not allowed to be empty. In this case, it's due to how we handle the two-character ending delimiter. We ensure that any *normal* sequence ends with the first character of the ending delimiter, allowing *special* to pick up the ball only if the following character does not complete the ending.

Table 6-3: Unrolling-the-Loop Components for C Comments

⌈opening normal* (`special` normal*) * closing⌋		
Item	**What We Want**	**Regex**
opening	start of comment	`/x`
normal*	comment text up to, and including, one or more 'x'	`[^x]*x+`
special	something other than the ending slash (and also not 'x')	`[^/x]`
closing	trailing slash	`/`

So, plugging these in to the general unrolling pattern, we get:

⌈`/x[^x]*x+(`╷`[^/x] [^x]*x+)*/`⌋.

Notice the spot marked with ╷ ? The regex engine might work to that spot in two ways (just like the expression on page 266). The first is by progressing to it after the leading ⌈`/x[^x]*x+`⌋. The second is by looping due to the `(···)*`. Via either path, once we're at that spot we know we've matched x and are at a pivotal point, possibly on the brink of the comment's end. If the next character is a slash, we're done. If it's anything else (but an x, of course), we know the x was a false alarm and we're back to matching normal stuff, again waiting for the next x. Once we find it, we're right back on the brink of excitement at the marked spot.

Return to reality

⌈`/x[^x]*x+([^/x] [^x]*x+)*/`⌋ is not quite ready to be used. First, of course, comments are `/*···*/` and not `/x···x/`. This is easily fixed by substituting each x with `\*` (or, within character classes, each x with `*`):

⌈`/\*[^*]*\*+([^/*] [^*]*\*+)*/`⌋

A use-related issue is that comments often span across lines. If the text being matched contains the entire multiline comment, this expression should work. With a strictly line-oriented tool such as *egrep*, though, there is no way to apply a regex to the full comment. With most utilities mentioned in this book, you can, and this expression might be useful for, say, removing comments.

In practical use, a larger problem arises. This regex understands C comments, but does not understand other important aspects of C syntax. For example, it can falsely match where there is no comment:

```
const char *cstart = "/*", *cend = "*/";
```

We'll develop this example further, right in the next section.

The Freeflowing Regex

We just spent some time constructing a regex to match a C comment, but left off with the problem of how to stop comment-like items within strings from being matched. Using Perl, we might mistakenly try to remove comments with:

```
$prog =~ s{/\*[^*]*\*+(?:[^/*][^*]*\*+)*/}{}g;  # remove C comments (and more!)
```

Text in the variable `$prog` that is matched by our regex is removed (that is, replaced by nothing). The problem with this is that there's nothing to stop a match from starting *within* a string, as in this C snippet:

```
char *CommentStart = "/*";   /* start of comment */
char *CommentEnd   = "*/";   /* end of comment */
```

Here, the underlined portions are what the regex finds, but the bold portions are what we *wish* to be found. When the engine is searching for a match, it tries to match the expression at each point in the target. Since it is successful only from where a comment begins (or where it looks like one begins), it doesn't match at most locations, so the transmission bump-along bumps us right into the double-quoted string, whose contents look like the start of a comment. It would be nice if we could tell the regex engine that when it hits a double-quoted string, it should zip right on past it. Well, we can.

A Helping Hand to Guide the Match

Consider:

```
$COMMENT = qr{/\*[^*]*\*+(?:[^/*][^*]*\*+)*/};   # regex to match a comment
$DOUBLE = qr{"(?:\\.|[^"\\])*"};                  # regex to match double-quoted string
$text =~ s/$DOUBLE|$COMMENT//g;
```

There are two new things here. One is that this time the regex operand, `$DOUBLE|$COMMENT`, is made up of two variables, each of which is constructed with Perl's special `qr/···/` regex-style "double-quoted string" operator. As discussed at length in Chapter 3 (☞ 101), one must be careful when using strings that are meant to be interpreted as regular expressions. Perl alleviates this problem by providing the `qr/···/` operator, which treats its operand as a regular expression, but doesn't actually apply it. Rather, it returns a "regex object" value that can later be used to build up a larger regular expression. It's extremely convenient, as we saw briefly in Chapter 2 (☞ 76). Like `m/···/` and `s/···/···/`, you can pick delimiters to suit your needs (☞ 71), as we've done here using braces.

The other new thing here is the matching of double-quoted strings via the `$DOUBLE` portion. When the transmission has brought us to a position where the `$DOUBLE` part can match, it will do so, thereby bypassing the whole string in one fell swoop. It's possible to have both alternatives because they're entirely unambiguous with respect to each other. When applied to a string, as you read from the beginning, any point you that the text is:

- Matchable by the comment part, thereby skipping immediately to the end of the comment, or...

- Matchable by the double-quoted string part, thereby skipping immediately to the end of the string, or...

- Not matchable by either, causing the attempt to fail. This means that the normal bump-along will skip only the one, uninteresting character.

This way, the regex will never be *started* from *within* a string or comment, the key to its success. Well, actually, right now it isn't helpful yet, since it removes the strings as well as the comments, but a slight change puts us back on track.

Consider:

```
$COMMENT = qr{/\*[^*]*\*+(?:[^/*][^*]*\*+)*/};  # regex to match a comment
$DOUBLE  = qr{"(?:\\.|[^"\\])*"};               # Regex to match double-quoted string
$text =~ s/($DOUBLE)|$COMMENT/$1/g;
```

The only differences are that we've:

- Added the parentheses to fill $1 if the match is via the string alternative. If the match is via the comment alternative, $1 is left empty.

- Made the replacement value that same $1. The effect is that if a double-quoted string is matched, the replacement is that same double-quoted string — the string is not removed and the substitute becomes an effective no-op (but has the side effect of getting us past the string, which is the reason to add it in the first place). On the other hand, if the comment alternative is the one that matches, the $1 is empty, so the comment is replaced by nothingness just as we want.[†]

Finally, we need to take care of single-quoted C constants such as '\t' and the like. This is easy—we simply add another alternative inside the parentheses. If we would like to removeC++ /Java/C# style // comments too, that's as simple as adding `//[^\n]*` as a fourth alternative, outside the parentheses:

```
$COMMENT  = qr{/\*[^*]*\*+(?:[^/*][^*]*\*+)*/};  # regex to match a comment
$COMMENT2 = qr{//[^\n]*};                        # regex to match a C++ // comment
$DOUBLE   = qr{"(?:\\.|[^"\\])*"};               # regex to match double-quoted string
$SINGLE   = qr{'(?:\\.|[^'\\])*'};               # regex to match single-quoted string

$text =~ s/($DOUBLE|$SINGLE)|$COMMENT|$COMMENT2/$1/g;
```

[†] In Perl, if $1 is not filled during the match, it's given a special "no value" value "undef". When used in the replacement value, undef is treated as an empty string, so it works as we want. But, if you have Perl warnings turned on (as every good programmer should), the use of an undef value in this way causes a warning to be printed. To avoid this, you can use the 'no warnings;' pragma before the regular expression is used, or use this special Perl form of the substitute operator:

```
$text =~ s/($DOUBLE)|$COMMENT/defined($1) ? $1 : ""/ge;
```

The basic premise is quite slick: when the engine checks the text, it quickly grabs (and if appropriate, removes) these special constructs. On my system, this Perl snippet took about 16.4 seconds to remove all the comments from a 16-megabyte, 500,000-line test file. This is fast, but we'll speed it up considerably.

A Well-Guided Regex is a Fast Regex

With just a little hand holding, we can help direct the flow of the regex engine's attention to match much faster. Let's consider the long spans of normal C code between the comments and strings. For each such character, the regex engine has to try each of the four alternatives to see whether it's something that should be gobbled up, and only if all four fail does it bump-along to bypass the character as uninteresting. This is a lot of work that we really don't need to do.

We know, for example, that for any of the alternatives to have a chance at matching, the lead character must be a slash, a single quote, or a double quote. One of these doesn't guarantee a match, but *not* being one does guarantee a non-match. So, rather than letting the engine figure this out the slow and painful way, let's just tell it directly by adding ⌈[^'"/]⌋ as an alternative. In fact, any number of such characters in a row can be scooped right up, so let's use ⌈[^'"/]+⌋ instead. If you remember the neverending match, you might feel worried about the added plus. Indeed, it could be of great concern if it were within some kind of (⋯) ＊ loop, but in this stand-alone case it's quite fine (there's nothing that follows that could force it to backtrack at all). So, adding:

```
$OTHER = qr{[^"'/]};   # Stuff that couldn't possibly begin one of the other alternatives
   ⋮
$text =~ s/( $DOUBLE | $SINGLE | $OTHER+) | $COMMENT | $COMMENT2/$1/g;
```

For reasons that will become apparent after a bit, I've put the plus quantifier after $OTHER, rather than part of the contents of $OTHER.

So, I retry my benchmarks, and wow, this one change cuts the time by over 75%! We've crafted the regex to remove most of the overhead of having to try all the alternatives so often. There are still a few cases where none of the alternatives can match (such as at 'c ⌄/ 3.14'), and at such times, we'll have to be content with the bump-along to get us by.

However, we're not done yet—we can still help the engine flow to a faster match:

* In most cases, the most popular alternative will be ⌈$OTHER+⌋, so let's put that first inside the parentheses. This isn't an issue for a POSIX NFA engine because it must always check all alternatives anyway, but for a Traditional NFA, which stops once a match has been found, why make it check for relatively rare matches before checking the one we believe will match most often?

- After one of the quoted items matches, it will likely be followed by some
  $OTHER before another string or a comment is found. If we add ⌈$OTHER*⌋ after
  each item, we tell the engine that it can immediately flow right into matching
  $OTHER without bothering with the /g looping. This is similar to the unrolling-
  the-loop technique. In fact, unrolling the loop gains much of its speed from
  the way it leads the regex engine to a match, using our global knowledge to
  create the local optimizations that feed the engine just what it needs to work
  quickly.

  Note that it is *very* important that this $OTHER, added after each string-match-
  ing subexpression, be quantified with star, while the previous $OTHER (the one
  we moved to the head of the alternation) be quantified by plus. If it's not
  clear, consider what could happen if the appended $OTHER had plus and there
  were, say, two double-quoted strings right in a row. Also, if the leading
  $OTHER used star, it would always match!

These changes yield

⌈($OTHER+|$DOUBLE $OTHER*|$SINGLE $OTHER*)|$COMMENT|$COMMENT2⌋

as the regex, and further cuts the time by an additional five percent.

Let's step back and think about these last two changes. If we go to the trouble of
scooping up $OTHER* after each quoted string, there are only two situations in
which the original $OTHER+ (which we moved to be the first alternative) can
match: 1> at the very start of the whole s/···/···/g, before any of the quoted strings
get a chance to match, and 2) after any comment. You might be tempted to think
"Hey, to take care of point #2, let's just add $OTHER* after the comments as well!"
This would be nice, except everything we want to keep must be inside that first
set of parentheses—putting it after the comments would throw out the baby code
with the comment bathwater.

So, if the original $OTHER+ is useful primarily only after a comment, do we really
want to put it first? I guess that depends on the data—if there are more comments
than quoted strings, then yes, placing it first makes sense. Otherwise, I'd place it
later. As it turns out with my test data, placing it first yields better results. Placing it
later takes away about half the gains we achieved in the last step.

Wrapup

We're not quite done yet. Don't forget, each of the quoted-string subexpressions is
ripe for unrolling — heck, we spent a long section of this chapter on that very
topic. So, as a final change, let's replace the two string subexpressions with:

```
$DOUBLE = qr{"[^"\\]*(?:\\.[^"\\]*)*"};
$SINGLE = qr{'[^'\\]*(?:\\.[^'\\]*)*'};
```

This change yields yet another 15 percent gain. Just a few changes has sped things up from 16.4 seconds to 2.3 seconds—a speedup of over 7×.

This last change also shows how convenient a technique it can be to use variables to build up a regular expression. Individual components, such as $DOUBLE, can be considered in relative isolation, and can be changed without having to wade into the full expression. There are still some overall issues (the counting of capturing parentheses, among others) that must be kept in mind, but it's a wonderful technique.

One of the features that makes it so convenient in this case is Perl's qr/⋯/ operator, which acts like a regex-related type of "string." Other languages don't have this exact functionality, but many languages do have string types that are amenable to building regular expressions. See "Strings as Regular Expressions" starting on page 101.

You'll particularly appreciate the building up of regular expressions this way when you see the raw regex. Here it is, broken across lines to fit the page:

```
([^"\'/]+|"[^"\\]*(?:\\.[^"\\]*)*"[^"\'/]*|'[^'\\]*
(?:\\.[^'\\]*)*'[^"\'/]*)|/\*[^*]*\*+(?:[^/*][^*]*\*+)*/|//[^\n]*
```

In Summary: Think!

I'd like to end this chapter with a story that illustrates just how much benefit a little thought can go when using NFA regular expressions. Once when using GNU Emacs, I wanted a regex to find certain kinds of contractions such as "don't," "I'm," "we'll," and so on, but to ignore other situations where a single quote might be next to a word. I came up with a regex to match a word, ⌜\<\w+⌟, followed by the Emacs equivalent of ⌜'([tdm]|re|ll|ve)⌟. It worked, but I realized that using ⌜\<\w+⌟ was silly when I needed only \w. You see, if there is a \w immediately before the apostrophe, \w+ is certainly there too, so having the regex check for something we know is there doesn't add any new information unless I want the exact extent of the match (which I didn't, I merely wanted to get to the area). Using \w alone made the regex more than 10 times faster.

Yes, a little thought can go a long way. I hope this chapter has given you a little to think about.

7

Perl

Perl has been featured prominently in this book, and with good reason. It is popular, extremely rich with regular expressions, freely and readily obtainable, easily approachable by the beginner, and available for a remarkably wide variety of platforms, including pretty much all flavors of Windows, Unix, and the Mac.

Some of Perl's programming constructs superficially resemble those of C or other traditional programming languages, but the resemblance stops there. The way you wield Perl to solve a problem — *The Perl Way* — is different from traditional languages. The overall layout of a Perl program often uses traditional structured and object-oriented concepts, but data processing often relies heavily on regular expressions. In fact, I believe it is safe to say that **regular expressions play a key role in virtually all Perl programs**. This includes everything from huge 100,000-line systems, right down to simple one-liners, like

```
% perl -pi -e 's{([-+]?\d+(\.\d*)?)F\b}{sprintf "%.0fC",($1-32)*5/9}eg' *.txt
```

which goes through *.txt files and replaces Fahrenheit values with Celsius ones (reminiscent of the first example from Chapter 2).

In This Chapter
This chapter looks at everything regex about Perl,[†] including details of its regex flavor and the operators that put them to use. This chapter presents the regex-relevant details from the ground up, but I assume that you have at least a basic familiarity with Perl. (If you've read Chapter 2, you're already familiar enough to at least start using this chapter.) I'll often use, in passing, concepts that have not yet been examined in detail, and I won't dwell much on non-regex aspects of the language. It might be a good idea to keep the Perl documentation handy, or perhaps O'Reilly's *Programming Perl*.

---

† This book covers features of Perl as of Version 5.8.

Perhaps more important than your current knowledge of Perl is your *desire to understand more*. This chapter is not light reading by any measure. Because it's not my aim to teach Perl from scratch, I am afforded a luxury that general books about Perl do not have: I don't have to omit important details in favor of weaving one coherent story that progresses unbroken through the whole chapter. Some of the issues are complex, and the details thick; don't be worried if you can't take it all in at once. I recommend first reading the chapter through to get the overall picture, and returning in the future to use it as a reference as needed.

To help guide your way, here's a quick rundown of how this chapter is organized:

- "Perl's Regex Flavor" (☞ 286) looks at the rich set of metacharacters supported by Perl regular expressions, along with additional features afforded to raw regex literals.

- "Regex Related Perlisms" (☞ 293) looks at some aspects of Perl that are of particular interest when using regular expressions. *Dynamic scoping* and *expression context* are covered in detail, with a strong bent toward explaining their relationship with regular expressions.

- Regular expressions are not useful without a way to apply them, so the following sections provide all the details to Perl's sometimes magical regex controls:
    "The qr/···/ Operator and Regex Objects" (☞ 303)
    "The Match Operator" (☞ 306)
    "The Substitution Operator" (☞ 318)
    "The Split Operator" (☞ 321)

- "Fun with Perl Enhancements" (☞ 326) goes over a few Perl-only enhancements to Perl's regular-expression repertoire, including the ability to execute arbitrary Perl code during the application of a regular expression.

- "Perl Efficiency Issues" (☞ 347) delves into an area close to every Perl programmer's heart. Perl uses a Traditional NFA match engine, so you can feel free to start using all the techniques from Chapter 6 right away. There are, of course, Perl-specific issues that can greatly affect in what way, and how quickly, Perl applies your regexes. We'll look at them here.

Perl in Earlier Chapters
Perl is touched on throughout most of this book:

- **Chapter 2** contains an introduction to Perl, with many regex examples.

- **Chapter 3** contains a section on Perl history (☞ 88), and touches on numerous regex-related issues that apply to Perl, such as character-encoding issues (including Unicode ☞ 105), match modes (☞ 109), and a long overview of metacharacters (☞ 112).

- **Chapter** 4 is a key chapter that demystifies the Traditional NFA match engine found in Perl. Chapter 4 is extremely important to Perl users.

- **Chapter** 5 contains many examples, discussed in the light of Chapter 4. Many of the examples are in Perl, but even those not presented in Perl apply to Perl.

- **Chapter** 6 is an important chapter to the user of Perl interested in efficiency.

In the interest of clarity for those not familiar with Perl, I often simplified Perl examples in these earlier chapters, writing in as much of a self-documenting pseudo-code style as possible. In this chapter, I'll try to present examples in a more Perlish style of Perl.

Regular Expressions as a Language Component

An attractive feature of Perl is that regex support is so deftly built in as part of the language. Rather than providing stand-alone functions for applying regular expressions, Perl provides regular-expression *operators* that are meshed well with the rich set of other operators and constructs that make up the Perl language.

With as much regex-wielding power as Perl has, one might think that it's overflowing with different operators and such, but actually, Perl provides only four regex-related operators, and a small handful of related items, shown in Table 7-1.

Table 7-1: Overview of Perl's Regex-Related Items

Regex-Related Operators		Modifiers	Modify How ...
m/*regex*/*mods* (☞ 306)		/x /o	regex is interpreted (☞ 292, 348)
s/*regex*/*replacement*/*mods* (☞ 318)		/s /m /i	engine considers target text (☞ 292)
qr/*regex*/*mods* (☞ 303)		/g /c /e	other (☞ 311, 315, 319)
split(···) (☞ 321)		**After-Match Variables** (☞ 299)	
Related Pragmas		$1, $2, etc.	captured text
use charnames 'full'; (☞ 290)		$^N $+	latest/highest filled $1, $2, ...
use overload; (☞ 341)		@- @+	arrays of indices into target
use re 'eval'; (☞ 337)		$` $& $'	text before, of, and after match
use re 'debug'; (☞ 361)			(best to avoid—see "Perl Efficiency Issues" ☞ 356)
Related Functions		**Related Variables**	
lc lcfirst uc ucfirst (☞ 290)		$_	default search target (☞ 308)
pos (☞ 313) quotemeta (☞ 290)		$^R	embedded-code result (☞ 302)
reset (☞ 308) study (☞ 359)			

Perl is extremely powerful, but all that power in such a small set of operators can be a dual-edged sword.

Perl's Greatest Strength

The richness of variety and options among Perl's operators and functions is perhaps its greatest feature. They can change their behavior depending on the context in which they're used, often doing just what the author naturally intends in each differing situation. In fact, O'Reilly's *Programming Perl* goes so far as to boldly state "In general, Perl operators do exactly what you want...." The regex match operator m/*regex*/, for example, offers an amazing variety of different functionality depending upon where, how, and with which modifiers it is used.

Perl's Greatest Weakness

This concentrated richness in expressive power is also one of Perl's least-attractive features. There are innumerable special cases, conditions, and contexts that seem to change out from under you without warning when you make a subtle change in your code—you've just hit another special case you weren't aware of.[†] The *Programming Perl* quote in the previous paragraph continues "...unless you want consistency." Certainly, when it comes to computer science, there is a certain appreciation to boring, consistent, dependable interfaces. Perl's power can be a devastating weapon in the hands of a skilled user, but it sometimes seems with Perl, you become skilled by repeatedly shooting yourself in the foot.

Perl's Regex Flavor

Table 7-2 on the facing page summarizes Perl's regex flavor. It used to be that Perl had many metacharacters that no other system supported, but over the years, other systems have adopted many of Perl's innovations. These common features are covered by the overview in Chapter 3, but there are a few Perl-specific items discussed later in this chapter. (Table 7-2 has references to where each item is discussed.)

The following notes supplement the table:

- ⌈\b⌋ matches a backspace only in class; otherwise, it's a word boundary.

- Octal escapes accept two- and three-digit numbers.

- The ⌈\x*num*⌋ hex escape accepts two-digit numbers (and one-digit numbers, but with a warning if warnings are turned on). The ⌈\x{*num*}⌋ syntax accepts a hexadecimal number of any length.

---

† That they're innumerable doesn't stop this chapter from trying to cover them all!

Table 7-2: Overview of Perl's Regular-Expression Flavor

Character Shorthands		
☞ 114	(c)	`\a \b \e \f \n \r \t` `\`*octal* `\x`*hex* `\x{`*hex`}` `\c`*char*
Character Classes and Class-Like Constructs		
☞ 117		Classes: `[⋯]` `[^⋯]` (may contain POSIX-like `[:alpha:]` notation)
☞ 118		Any character except newline: *dot* (with `/s`, any character at all)
☞ 328		Forced match of single byte (can be dangerous): `\C`
☞ 125		Unicode combining sequence: `\X`
☞ 119	(c)	Class shorthands: `\w \d \s \W \D \S`
☞ 119	(c)	Unicode properties, scripts, and blocks: `\p{`*Prop`}` `\P{`*Prop`}`
Anchors and other Zero-Width Tests		
☞ 127		Start of line/string: `^` `\A`
☞ 127		End of line/string: `$` `\z` `\Z`
☞ 315		End of previous match: `\G`
☞ 131		Word boundary: `\b` `\B`
☞ 132		Lookaround: `(?=⋯)` `(?!⋯)` `(?<=⋯)` `(?<!⋯)`
Comments and Mode Modifiers		
☞ 133		Mode modifiers: `(?`*mods*`-`*mods*`)` Modifiers allowed: `x s m i` (☞ 292)
☞ 134		Mode-modified spans: `(?`*mods*`-`*mods*`:⋯)`
☞ 134		Comments: `(?#⋯)` `#⋯` (from '#' until newline, or end of regex)
Grouping, Capturing, Conditional, and Control		
☞ 135		Capturing parentheses: `(⋯)` `\1 \2 ...`
☞ 136		Grouping-only parentheses: `(?:⋯)`
☞ 137		Atomic grouping: `(?>⋯)`
☞ 138		Alternation: `|`
☞ 139		Greedy quantifiers: `*` `+` `?` `{n}` `{n,}` `{x,y}`
☞ 140		Lazy quantifiers: `*?` `+?` `??` `{n}?` `{n,}?` `{x,y}?`
☞ 138		Conditional: `(?`*if then*`|`*else*`)` – "if" can be embedded code, lookaround, or `(`*num*`)`
☞ 327		Embedded code: `(?{⋯})`
☞ 327		Dynamic regex: `(??{⋯})`
In Regex Literals Only		
☞ 289	(c)	Variable interpolation: `$`*name* `@`*name*
☞ 290	(c)	Fold next character's case: `\l` `\u`
☞ 290	(c)	Case-folding span: `\U` `\L` `...` `\E`
☞ 290	(c)	Literal-text span: `\Q` `...` `\E`
☞ 290	(c)	Named Unicode character: `\N{`*name`}` – optional; see page 290

(c) – may be used within a character class

- Perl's Unicode support is for Unicode Version 3.2.

- *dot* treats Unicode combining characters as separate characters (☞ 107). Also see ⌈\X⌋ (☞ 125).

- ⌈\w⌋, ⌈\d⌋, and ⌈\s⌋ fully support Unicode.

- Perl's ⌈\s⌋ does not match an ASCII vertical tab character (☞ 114).

- Unicode Scripts are supported. Script and property names may have the 'Is' prefix, but they don't require it (☞ 123). Block names may have the 'In' prefix, but require it only when a block name conflicts with a script name.

  The ⌈\p{L&}⌋ pseudo-property is supported, as well as ⌈\p{Any}⌋, ⌈\p{All}⌋, ⌈\p{Assigned}⌋, and ⌈\p{UNASSIGNED}⌋.

  The long property names like ⌈\p{Letter}⌋ are supported. Names may have a space, underscore, or nothing between the word parts of a name (for example ⌈\p{Lowercase_Letter}⌋ may also be written as ⌈\p{LowercaseLetter}⌋ or ⌈\p{Lowercase•Letter}⌋.) For consistency, I recommend using the long names as shown in the table on page 121.

- ⌈\p{^···}⌋ is the same as ⌈\P{···}⌋.

- Word boundaries fully support Unicode.

- Lookaround may have capturing parentheses.

- Lookbehind is limited to subexpressions that always match fixed-width text.

- The /x modifier recognizes only ASCII whitespace. The /m modifier affects only newlines, and not the full list of Unicode line terminators.

Not all metacharacters are created equal. Some "regex metacharacters" are not even supported by the regex engine, but by the preprocessing Perl gives to regex literals.

Regex Operands and Regex Literals

The final items in Table 7-1 are marked "regex literals only." A *regex literal* is the "*regex*" part of **m/*regex*/**, and while casual conversation refers to that as "the regular expression," the part between the '/' delimiters is actually parsed using its own unique rules. In Perl jargon, a regex literal is treated as a "regex-aware double-quoted string," and it's the result of that processing that's passed to the regex engine. This regex-literal processing offers special functionality in building the regular expression.

For example, a regex literal offers *variable interpolation*. If the variable $num contains 20, the code m/:.{$num}:/ produces the regex ⌈:.{20}:⌋. This way, you can build regular expressions on the fly. Another service given to regex literals is automatic case folding, as with \U···\E to ensure letters are uppercased. As a silly example, m/abc\Uxyz\E/ creates the regex ⌈abcXYZ⌉. This example is silly because if someone wanted ⌈abcXYZ⌉ they could just type m/abcXYZ/ directly, but its value becomes apparent when combined with variable interpolation: if the variable $tag contains the string "title", the code m{</\U$tag\E>} produces ⌈</TITLE>⌉.

What's the opposite of a regex literal? You can also use a string (or any expression) as a regex operand. For example:

```
$MatchField = "^Subject:"; # Normal string assignment
   ⋮
if ($text =~ $MatchField) {
   ⋮
```

When $MatchField is used as an operand of =~, its contents are interpreted as a regular expression. That "interpretation" is as a plain vanilla regex, so variable interpolation and things like \Q···\E are not supported as they would be for a regex literal.

Here's something interesting: if you replace

```
$text =~ $MatchField
```

with

```
$text =~ m/$MatchField/
```

the result is exactly the same. In this case, there's a regex literal, but it's composed of just one thing—the interpolation of the variable $MatchField. The *contents* of a variable interpolated by a regex literal are *not* treated as a regex literal, and so things like \U···\E and $*var* within the value interpolated are *not* recognized. (Details on exactly how regex literals are processed are covered on page 292.)

If used more than once during the execution of a program, there are important efficiency issues with regex operands that are raw strings, or that use variable interpolation. These are discussed starting on page 348.

Features supported by regex literals

The following features are offered by regex literals:

- **Variable Interpolation** Variable references beginning with $ and @ are interpolated into the value to use for the regex. Those beginning with $ insert a simple scalar value. Those beginning with @ insert an array or array slice into the value, with elements separated by spaces (actually, by the contents of the $" variable, which defaults to a space).

  In Perl, '%' introduces a hash variable, but inserting a hash into a string doesn't make much sense, so interpolation via % is not supported.

- **Named Unicode Characters**   If you have "**use charnames ':full';**" in the program, you can refer to Unicode characters by name using the \N{*name*} sequence. For instance, \N{LATIN SMALL LETTER SHARP S} matches "ß". The list of Unicode characters that Perl understands can be found in Perl's *unicore* directory, in the file *UnicodeData.txt*. This snippet shows the file's location:

  ```
  use Config;
  print "$Config{privlib}/unicore/UnicodeData.txt\n";
  ```

  It's easy to forget "**use charnames ':full';**", or the colon before 'full', but if you do, \N{···} won't work. Also, \N{···} doesn't work if you use regex overloading, described later in this list.

- **Case-Folding Prefix**   The special sequences **\l** and **\u** cause the character that follows to be made lowercase and uppercase, respectively. This is usually used just before variable interpolation to force the case on the first character brought in from the variable. For example, if the variable $title contains "mr.", the code m/···\u$title···/ creates the regex ⌈···Mr.···⌋. The same functionality is provided by the Perl functions lcfirst() and ucfirst().

- **Case-Folding Span**   The special sequences **\L** and **\U** cause characters that follow to be made lowercase and uppercase, respectively, until the end of the regex literal, or until the special sequence **\E**. For example, with the same $title as before, the code m/···\U$title\E···/ creates the regex ⌈···MR.···⌋. The same functionality is provided by the Perl functions lc() and uc().

  You can combine a case-folding prefix with a case-folding span: the code m/···\L\u$title\E···/ ensures ⌈···Mr.···⌋ regardless of the original capitalization.

- **Literal-Text Span**   The sequence **\Q** "quotes" *regex* metacharacters (i.e., puts a backslash in front of them) until the end of the string, or until a **\E** sequence. It quotes *regex* metacharacters, but not quote *regex-literal* items like variable interpolation, **\U**, and, of course, the **\E** itself. Oddly, it also does not quote backslashes that are part of an unknown sequence, such as in \F or \&. Even with \Q···\E, such sequences still produce "unrecognized escape" warnings.

  In practice, these restrictions are not that big a drawback, as \Q···\E is normally used to quote interpolated text, where it properly quotes *all* metacharacters. For example, if $title contains "Mr.", the code m/···\Q$title\E···/ creates the regex ⌈···Mr\.···⌋, which is what you'd want if you wanted to match the *text* in $title, rather than the *regex* in $title.

  This is particularly useful if you want to incorporate user input into a regex. For example, m/\Q$UserInput\E/i does a case-insensitive search for the characters (as a string, not a regex) in $UserInput.

  The \Q···\E functionality is also provided by the Perl function quotemeta().

- **Overloading** You can pre-process the literal parts of a regex literal in any way you like with *overloading*. It's an interesting concept, but one with severe limitations as currently implemented. Overloading is covered in detail, starting on page 341.

Picking your own regex delimiters

One of the most bizarre (yet, most useful) aspects of Perl's syntax is that you can pick your own delimiters for regex literals. The traditional delimiter is a forward slash, as with m/···/, s/···/···/, and qr/···/, but you can actually pick any non-alphanumeric, non-whitespace character. Some commonly used examples include:

```
m!···!          m{···}
m,···,          m<···>
s|···|···|      m[···]
qr#···#         m(···)
```

The four on the right are among the special-case delimiters:

- The four examples on the right side of the list above have different opening and closing delimiters, and may be nested (that is, may contain copies of the delimiters so long as the opens and closes pair up properly). Because parentheses and square brackets are so prevalent in regular expressions, m(···) and m[···] are probably not as appealing as the others. In particular, with the /x modifier, something such as the following becomes possible:

```
m{
    regex  # comments
    here   # here
}x;
```

If one of these pairs is used for the regex part of a substitute, another pair (the same as the first, or, if you like, different) is used for the replacement string. Examples include:

```
s{···}{···}
s{···}!···!
s<···>(···)
s[···]/···/
```

If this is done, you can put whitespace and comments between the two pairs of delimiters. More on the substitution operator's replacement string operand can be found on page 319.

- For the match operator only, a question mark as a delimiter has a little-used special meaning (suppress additional matches) discussed in the section on the match operator (☞ 308).

- As mentioned on page 288, a regex literal is parsed like to a "regex-aware double-quoted string." If a single quote is used as the delimiter, however, those features are inhibited. With `m'⋯'`, variables are *not* interpolated, and the constructs that modify text on the fly (e.g., `\Q⋯\E`) do not work, nor does the `\N{⋯}` construct. `m'⋯'` might be convenient for a regex that has many @, to save having to escape them.

For the match operator only, the `m` may be omitted if the delimiter is a slash or a question mark. That is,

```
$text =~ m/⋯/;
$text =~  /⋯/;
```

are the same. My preference is to always explicitly use the `m`.

How Regex Literals Are Parsed

For the most part, one "just uses" the regex-literal features just discussed, without the need to understand the exact details of how Perl converts them to a raw regular expression. Perl is very good at being intuitive in this respect, but there are times when a more detailed understanding can help. The following lists the order in which processing appears to happen:

1. The closing delimiter is found, and the modifiers (such as `/i`, etc.) are read. The rest of the processing then knows if it's in `/x` mode.

2. Variables are interpolated.

3. If regex overloading is in effect, each part of the literal is given to the overload routine for processing. Parts are separated by interpolated variables; the values interpolated are not made available to overloading.

   If regex overloading is not in effect, `\N{⋯}` sequences are processed.

4. Case-folding constructs (e.g., `\Q⋯\E`) are applied.

5. The result is presented to the regex engine.

This describes how the processing appears to the programmer, but in reality, the internal processing done by Perl is quite complicated. Even step #2 must understand the regular-expression metacharacters, so as not to, for example, treat the underlined portion of ⌈this$|that$⌋ as a variable reference.

Regex Modifiers

Perl's regex operands allow *regex modifiers*, placed after the closing delimiter of the regex literal (like the `i` in `m/⋯/i`, `s/⋯/⋯/i`, or `qr/⋯/i`). There are five core modifiers that all regex operands support, shown in Table 7-3.

The first four, described in Chapter 3, can also be used within a regex itself as a mode-modifier (☞ 133) or mode-modified span (☞ 134). When used both within

Table 7-3: The Core Modifiers Available to All Regex Operators

/i	☞109	Ignore letter case during match
/x	☞110	Free-spacing and comments regex mode
/s	☞110	Dot-matches-all match mode
/m	☞111	Enhanced line anchor match mode
/o	☞348	Compile only once

the regex, and as part of one of the match operators, the in-regex versions take precedence for the part of the regex they control. (Another way to look at it is that once a modifier has been applied to some part of a regex, nothing can "unmodify" that part of a regex.)

The fifth core modifier, /o, has mostly to do with efficiency. It is discussed later in this chapter, starting on page 348.

If you need more than one modifier, group the letters together and place them in any order after the closing delimiter, whatever it might be.[†] Keep in mind that the slash is not part of the modifier—you can write **m/<title>/i** as **m|<title>|i**, or perhaps **m{<title>}i**, or even **m<<title>>i**. Nevertheless, when discussing modifiers, it's common to always write them with a slash, e.g., "the /i modifier."

Regex-Related Perlisms

A variety of general Perl concepts pertain to our study of regular expressions. The next few sections discuss:

- **Context**　An important concept in Perl is that many functions and operators respond to the *context* they're used in. For example, Perl expects a scalar value as the conditional of a while loop, but a list of values as the arguments to a print statement. Since Perl allows expressions to "respond" to the context in which they're in, identical expressions in each case might produce wildly different results.

- **Dynamic Scope**　Most programming languages support the concept of local and global variables, but Perl provides an additional twist with something known as *dynamic scoping*. Dynamic scoping temporarily "protects" a global variable by saving a copy of its value and automatically restoring it later. It's an intriguing concept that's important for us because it affects $1 and other match-related variables.

---

† Because modifiers can appear in any order, a large portion of a programmer's time is spent adjusting the order to achieve maximum cuteness. For example, learn/by/osmosis is valid code (assuming you have a function called learn). The osmosis are the modifiers. Repeating modifiers is allowed, but meaningless (except for the substitution-operator's /e modifier, discussed later).

Expression Context

The notion of *context* is important throughout Perl, and in particular, to the match operator. An expression might find itself in one of three contexts, *list*, *scalar*, or *void*, indicating the type of value expected from the expression. Not surprisingly, a *list context* is one where a list of values is expected of an expression. A *scalar context* is one where a single value is expected. These two are very common and of great interest to our use of regular expressions. *Void context* is one in which no value is expected.

Consider the two assignments:

```
$s = expression one;
@a = expression two;
```

Because `$s` is a simple scalar variable (it holds a single value, not a list), it expects a simple scalar value, so the first expression, whatever it may be, finds itself in a scalar context. Similarly, because `@a` is an array variable and expects a list of values, the second expression finds itself in a list context. Even though the two expressions might be exactly the same, they might return completely different values, and cause completely different side effects while they're at it. Exactly what happens depends on each expression.

For example, the `localtime` function, if used in a list context, returns a list of values representing the current year, month, date, hour, etc. But if used in a scalar context, it returns a textual version of the current time along the lines of 'Mon Jan 20 22:05:15 2003'.

As another example, an I/O operator such as `<MYDATA>` returns the next line of the file in a scalar context, but returns a list of all (remaining) lines in a list context.

Like `localtime` and the I/O operator, many Perl constructs respond to their context. The regex operators do as well — the match operator `m/···/`, for example, sometimes returns a simple true/false value, and sometimes a list of certain match results. All the details are found later in this chapter.

Contorting an expression

Not all expressions are natively context-sensitive, so Perl has rules about what happens when a general expression is used in a context that doesn't exactly match the type of value the expression normally returns. To make the square peg fit into a round hole, Perl "contorts" the value to make it fit. If a scalar value is returned in a list context, Perl makes a list containing the single value on the fly. Thus, `@a = 42` is the same as `@a = (42)`.

On the other hand, there's no general rule for converting a list to a scalar. If a literal list is given, such as with

```
$var = ($this, &is, 0xA, 'list');
```

the comma-operator returns the last element, `'list'`, for $var. If an array is given, as with **$var = @array**, the length of the array is returned.

Some words used to describe how other languages deal with this issue are *cast*, *promote*, *coerce*, and *convert*, but I feel they are a bit too consistent (boring?) to describe Perl's attitude in this respect, so I use "contort."

Dynamic Scope and Regex Match Effects

Perl's two types of storage (global and private variables) and its concept of *dynamic scoping* are important to understand in their own right, but are of particular interest to our study of regular expressions because of how after-match information is made available to the rest of the program. The next sections describe these concepts, and their relation to regular expressions.

Global and private variables

On a broad scale, Perl offers two types of variables: global and private. Private variables are declared using my(⋯). Global variables are not declared, but just pop into existence when you use them. Global variables are always visible from anywhere and everywhere within the program, while private variables are visible, lexically, only to the end of their enclosing block. That is, the only Perl code that can directly access the private variable is the code that falls between the my declaration and the end of the block of code that encloses the my.

The use of global variables is normally discouraged, except for special cases, such as the myriad of special variables like $1, $_, and @ARGV. Regular user variables are global unless declared with my, even if they might "look" private. Perl allows the names of global variables to be partitioned into groups called *packages*, but the variables are still global. A global variable $Debug within the package Acme::Widget has a *fully qualified name* of $Acme::Widget::Debug, but no matter how it's referenced, it's still the same global variable. If you **use strict;**, all (non-special) globals must either be referenced via fully-qualified names, or via a name declared with our (our declares a *name*, not a new variable—see the Perl documentation for details).

Dynamically scoped values

Dynamic scoping is an interesting concept that few programming languages provide. We'll see the relevance to regular expressions soon, but in a nutshell, you can have Perl save a copy of the value of a global variable that you intend to modify within a block, and restore the original copy automatically at the time when the block ends. Saving a copy is called *creating a new dynamic scope,* or *localizing.*

One reason that you might want to do this is to temporarily update some kind of global state that's maintained in a global variable. Let's say that you're using a package, Acme::Widget, and it provides a debugging flag via the global variable $Acme::Widget::Debug. You can temporarily ensure that debugging is turned on with code like:

```
    ⋮
  {
      local($Acme::Widget::Debug) = 1;  # Ensure it's turned on
      # work with Acme::Widget while debugging is on
          ⋮
  }
  # $Acme::Widget::Debug is now back to whatever it had been before
    ⋮
```

It's that extremely ill-named function local that creates a new dynamic scope. Let me say up front that *the call to local does not create a new variable.* local is an action, not a declaration. Given a global variable, local does three things:

1. Saves an internal copy of the variable's value

2. Copies a new value into the variable (either undef, or a value assigned to the local)

3. Slates the variable to have its original value restored when execution runs off the end of the block enclosing the local

This means that "local" refers only to how long any changes to the variable will last. The localized value lasts as long as the enclosing block is executing. Even if a subroutine is called from within that block, the localized value is seen. (After all, the variable is still a global variable.) The only difference from a non-localized global variable is that when execution of the enclosing block finally ends, the previous value is automatically restored.

An automatic save and restore of a global variable's value is pretty much all there is to local. For all the misunderstanding that has accompanied local, it's no more complex than the snippet on the right of Table 7-4 illustrates.

As a matter of convenience, you can assign a value to local($SomeVar), which is exactly the same as assigning to $SomeVar in place of the undef assignment. Also, the parentheses can be omitted to force a scalar context.

As a practical example, consider having to call a function in a poorly written library that generates a lot of "Use of uninitialized value" warnings. You use Perl's -w option, as all good Perl programmers should, but the library author apparently didn't. You are exceedingly annoyed by the warnings, but if you can't change the

Table 7-4: The Meaning of local

Normal Perl	Equivalent Meaning

{
 	
    local($SomeVar); # *save copy*
 	
    $SomeVar = 'My Value';
        •
        •
        •
} # *Value automatically restored*
	{
	
	    my $TempCopy = $SomeVar;
	    $SomeVar = undef;
	
	    $SomeVar = 'My Value';
	        •
	        •
	    $SomeVar = $TempCopy;
	}

library, what can you do short of stop using -w altogether? Well, you could set a
local value of $^W, the in-code debugging flag (the variable name ^W can be
either the two characters, caret and 'W', or an actual control-W character):

```
{
    local $^W = 0;  # Ensure warnings are off.
    UnrulyFunction(⋯);
}
# Exiting the block restores the original value of $^W.
```

The call to local saves an internal copy of the value of the global variable $^W,
whatever it might be. Then that same $^W receives the new value of zero that we
immediately scribble in. When UnrulyFunction is executing, Perl checks $^W and
sees the zero we wrote, so doesn't issue warnings. When the function returns, our
value of zero is still in effect.

So far, everything appears to work just as if local isn't used. However, when the
block is exited right after the subroutine returns, the original value of $^W is
restored. Your change of the value was local, in *time*, to the life of the block.
You'd get the same effect by making and restoring a copy yourself, as in Table 7-4,
but local conveniently takes care of it for you.

For completeness, let's consider what happens if I use my instead of local.[†] Using
my creates a *new variable* with an initially undefined value. It is visible only within
the lexical block it is declared in (that is, visible only by the code written between
the my and the end of the enclosing block). It does not change, modify, or in any
other way refer to or affect other variables, including any global variable of the
same name that might exist. The newly created variable is not visible elsewhere in
the program, including from within UnrulyFunction. In our example snippet, the
new $^W is immediately set to zero but is never again used or referenced, so it's
pretty much a waste of effort. (While executing UnrulyFunction and deciding
whether to issue warnings, Perl checks the unrelated global variable $^W.)

---

† Perl doesn't allow the use of my with this special variable name, so the comparison is only academic.

A better analogy: clear transparencies

A useful analogy for `local` is that it provides a clear transparency (like used with an overhead projector) over a variable on which you scribble your own changes. You (and anyone else that happens to look, such as subroutines and signal handlers) will see the new values. They shadow the previous value until the point in time that the block is finally exited. At that point, the transparency is automatically removed, in effect, removing any changes that might have been made since the `local`.

This analogy is actually much closer to reality than saying "an internal copy is made." Using `local` doesn't actually make a copy, but instead puts your new value earlier in the list of those checked whenever a variable's value is accessed (that is, it shadows the original). Exiting a block removes any shadowing values added since the block started. Values are added manually, with `local`, but here's the whole reason we've been looking localization: **regex side-effect variables have their values dynamically scoped automatically**.

Regex side effects and dynamic scoping

What does dynamic scoping have to do with regular expressions? A lot. A number of variables like `$&` (refers to the text matched) and `$1` (refers to the text matched by the first parenthesized subexpression) are automatically set as a side effect of a successful match. They are discussed in detail in the next section. These variables have their value dynamically scoped *automatically* upon entry to every block.

To see the benefit of this design choice, realize that each call to a subroutine involves starting a new block, which means a new dynamic scope is created for these variables. Because the values before the block are restored when the block exits (that is, when the subroutine returns), the subroutine can't change the values that the caller sees.

As an example, consider:

```
if (m/(···)/)
{
    DoSomeOtherStuff();
    print "the matched text was $1.\n";
}
```

Because the value of `$1` is dynamically scoped automatically upon entering each block, this code snippet neither cares, nor needs to care, whether the function `DoSomeOtherStuff` changes the value of `$1` or not. Any changes to `$1` by the function are contained within the block that the function defines, or perhaps within a sub-block of the function. Therefore, they can't affect the value this snippet sees with the `print` after the function returns.

The automatic dynamic scoping is helpful even when not so apparent:

```
if ($result =~ m/ERROR=(.*)/) {
    warn "Hey, tell $Config{perladmin} about $1!\n";
}
```

The standard library module `Config` defines an associative array `%Config`, of which the member `$Config{perladmin}` holds the email address of the local Perlmaster. This code could be very surprising if `$1` were not automatically dynamically scoped, because `%Config` is actually a *tied* variable. That means any reference to it involves a behind-the-scenes subroutine call, and the subroutine within `Config` that fetches the appropriate value when `$Config{···}` is used invokes a regex match. That match lies between your match and your use of `$1`, so if `$1` were not dynamically scoped, it would be destroyed before you used it. As it is, any changes in `$1` during the `$Config{···}` processing are safely hidden by dynamic scoping.

Dynamic scoping versus lexical scoping

Dynamic scoping provides many rewards if used effectively, but haphazard dynamic scoping with `local` can create a maintenance nightmare, as readers of a program find it difficult to understand the increasingly complex interactions among the lexically disperse `local`, subroutine calls, and references to localized variables.

As I mentioned, the `my(···)` declaration creates a private variable with *lexical scope*. A private variable's lexical scope is the opposite of a global variable's global scope, but it has little to do with dynamic scoping (except that you can't `local` the value of a `my` variable). Remember, `local` is just an *action*, while `my` is both an action *and*, importantly, a declaration.

Special Variables Modified by a Match

A successful match or substitution sets a variety of global, read-only variables that are always automatically dynamically scoped. These values *never* change if a match attempt is unsuccessful, and are *always* set when a match is successful. When appropriate, they are set to the empty string (a string with no characters in it), or undefined (a "no value" value, similar to, yet testably distinct from, an empty string). Table 7-5 shows examples.

In more detail, here are the variables set after a match:

$&   A copy of the text successfully matched by the regex. This variable (along with `$'` and `$'`, described next) is best avoided for performance reasons. (See the discussion on page 356.) `$&` is never undefined after a successful match, although it can be an empty string.

Table 7-5: Example Showing After-Match Special Variables

After the match of

```
              1 2                        2 3    4      4 31
"Pi is 3.14159, roughly" =~ m/\b((tasty|fattening)|(\d+(\.\d*)?))\b/;
```

the following special variables are given the values shown.

Variable	Meaning	Value
$`	Text before match	Pi·is·
$&	Text matched	3.14159
$'	Text after match	,·roughly
$1	Text matched within 1st set of parentheses	3.14159
$2	Text matched within 2nd set of parentheses	*undef*
$3	Text matched within 3rd set of parentheses	3.14159
$4	Text matched within 4th set of parentheses	.14159
$+	Text from highest-numbered $1, $2, etc.	.14159
$^N	Text from most recently closed $1, $2, etc.	3.14159
@-	Array of match-start indices into target text	(6, 6, undef, 6, 7)
@+	Array of match-end indices into target text	(13, 13, undef, 13, 13)

**$`**    A copy of the target text in front of (to the left of) the match's start. When used in conjunction with the /g modifier, you might wish $` to be the text from start of the *match attempt*, but it's the text from the start of the whole string, each time. $` is never undefined after a successful match.

$'   A copy of the target text after (to the right of) the successfully matched text. $' is never undefined after a successful match. After a successful match, the string "$`$&$'" is always a copy of the original target text.[†]

$1, $2, $3, etc.

The text matched by the 1st, 2nd, 3rd, etc., set of capturing parentheses. (Note that $0 is not included here—it is a copy of the script name and not related to regular expressions.) These are guaranteed to be undefined if they refer to a set of parentheses that doesn't exist in the regex, or to a set that wasn't actually involved in the match.

These variables are available after a match, including in the replacement operand of s/···/···/. They can also be used within the *code* parts of an embedded-code or dynamic-regex construct (☞327). Otherwise, it makes little sense to use them within the regex itself. (That's what ⌐\1⌐ and friends are for.) See "Using $1 Within a Regex?" on page 303.

The difference between ⌐(\w+)⌐ and ⌐(\w)+⌐ can be seen in how $1 is set. Both regexes match exactly the same text, but they differ in what

---

† Actually, if the original target is undefined, but the match successful (unlikely, but possible), "$`$&$'" would be an empty string, not undefined. This is the only situation where the two differ.

subexpression falls within the parentheses. Matching against the string 'tubby', the first one results in $1 having the full 'tubby', while the latter one results in it having only 'y': with ⌈(\w)+⌋, the plus is outside the parentheses, so each iteration causes them to start capturing anew, leaving only the last character in $1.

Also, note the difference between ⌈(x)?⌋ and ⌈(x?)⌋. With the former, the parentheses and what they enclose are optional, so $1 would be either 'x' or undefined. But with ⌈(x?)⌋, the parentheses enclose a match — what is optional are the contents. If the overall regex matches, the contents matches something, although that something might be the nothingness ⌊x?⌋ allows. Thus, with ⌈(x?)⌋ the possible values of $1 are 'x' and an empty string. The following table shows some examples:

Sample Match	Resulting $1	Sample Match	Resulting $1
"::" =~ m/:(A?):/	empty string	"::" =~ m/:(\w*):/	empty string
"::" =~ m/:(A)?:/	undefined	"::" =~ m/:(\w)*:/	undefined
":A:" =~ m/:(A?):/	A	":Word:" =~ m/:(\w*):/	Word
":A:" =~ m/:(A)?:/	A	":Word:" =~ m/:(\w)*:/	d

When adding parentheses just for capturing, as was done here, the decision of which to use is dependent only upon the semantics you want. In these examples, since the added parentheses have no affect on the overall match (they all match the same text), the only differences among them is in the side effect of how $1 is set.

$+ This is a copy of the highest numbered $1, $2, etc. explicitly set during the match. This might be useful after something like

```
$url =~ m{
    href \s* = \s*          # Match the "href = " part, then the value . . .
    (?: "([^"]*)"           # a double-quoted value, or . . .
      | '([^']*)'           # a single-quoted value, or . . .
      | ([^'"<>]+) )  # an unquoted value.
}ix;
```

to access the value of the href. Without $+, you would have to check each of $1, $2, and $3 and use the one that's not undefined.

If there are no capturing parentheses in the regex (or none are used during the match), it becomes undefined.

$^N A copy of the most-recently-closed $1, $2, etc. explicitly set during the match (i.e., the $1, $2, etc., associated with the final closing parenthesis). If there are no capturing parentheses in the regex (or none used during the match), it becomes undefined. A good example of its use is given starting on page 344.

@- and **@+**

These are arrays of starting and ending offsets (string indices) into the target text. They might be a bit confusing to work with, due to their odd names. The first element of each refers to the overall match. That is, the first element of @-, accessed with $-[0], is the offset from the beginning of the target string to where the match started. Thus, after

```
$text = "Version 6 coming soon?";
    ⋮
$text =~ m/\d+/;
```

the value of $-[0] is 8, indicating that the match started eight characters into the target string. (In Perl, indices are counted started at zero.)

The first element of @+, accessed with $+[0], is the offset to the end of the match. With this example, it contains 9, indicating that the overall match ended nine characters from the start of the string. So, using them together, **substr($text, $-[0], $+[0] - $-[0])** is the same as $& if $text has not been modified, but doesn't have the performance penalty that $& has (☞ 356). Here's an example showing a simple use of @-:

```
1 while $line =~ s/\t/' ' x (8 - $-[0] % 8)/e;
```

Given a line of text, it replaces tabs with the appropriate number of spaces.[†]

Subsequent elements of each array are the starting and ending offsets for captured groups. The pair $-[1] and $+[1] are the offsets into the target text where $1 was taken, $-[2] and $+[2] for $2, and so on.

$^R   This variable is useful only within the *code* parts of embedded-code and dynamic-regex constructs (☞ 327), and has no value outside of a regex. It is the resulting value of the most recently executed embedded-code construct, except that an embedded-code construct used as the *if* of a ⌈**(?** *if* *then* **|** *else***)**⌋ conditional (☞ 138) does not set $^R. It is automatically localized to each part of the match, so values of $^R set by code that gets "unmatched" due to backtracking are properly forgotten. Put another way, it has the "most recent" value with respect to the match path that got the engine to the current location.

When a regex is applied repeatedly with the /g modifier, each iteration sets these variables afresh. That's why, for instance, you can use $1 within the replacement operand of s/⋯/⋯/g and have it represent a new slice of text with each match.

---

† This tab-replacement snippet has the limitation that it works only with "traditional" western text. It doesn't produce correct results with wide characters like 枝, which is one character but takes up two spaces, nor some Unicode renditions of accented characters like à (☞ 107).

Using $1 within a regex?

The Perl man page makes a concerted effort to point out that ⌜\1⌟ is not available as a backreference outside of a regex. (Use the variable $1 instead.) The variable $1 refers to a string of static text matched during some previously completed successful match. On the other hand, ⌜\1⌟ is a true regex metacharacter that matches text similar to that matched within the first parenthesized subexpression *at the time that the regex-directed NFA reaches the* ⌜\1⌟. What it matches might change over the course of an attempt as the NFA tracks and backtracks in search of a match.

The opposite question is whether $1 and other after-match variables are available within a regex operand. They are commonly used within the *code* parts of embedded-code and dynamic-regex constructs (☞ 327), but otherwise make little sense within a regex. A $1 appearing in the "regex part" of a regex operand is treated exactly like any other variable: its value is interpolated before the match or substitution operation even begins. Thus, as far as the regex is concerned, the value of $1 has nothing to do with the current match, but rather is left over from some previous match.

The qr/···/ *Operator and Regex Objects*

Introduced briefly in Chapter 2 and Chapter 6 (☞ 76; 277), qr/···/ is a unary operator that takes a regex operand and returns a *regex object*. The returned object can then be used as a regex operand of a later match, substitution, or split, or can be used as a sub-part of a larger regex.

Regex objects are used primarily to encapsulate a regex into a unit that can be used to build larger expressions, and for efficiency (to gain control over exactly when a regex is compiled, discussed later).

As described on page 291, you can pick your own delimiters, such as qr{···} or qr!···!. It supports the core modifiers /i, /x, /s, /m, and /o.

Building and Using Regex Objects

Consider the following, with expressions adapted from Chapter 2 (☞ 76):

```
my $HostnameRegex = qr/[-a-z0-9]+(?:\.[-a-z0-9]+)*\.(?:com|edu|info)/i;

my $HttpUrl = qr{
    http:// $HostnameRegex \b   # Hostname
    (?:
            / [-a-z0-9_:\@&?=+,.!/~*'%\$]*  # Optional path
              (?<![.,?!])  # Not allowed to end with [.,?!]
    )?
}ix;
```

The first line encapsulates our simplistic hostname-matching regex into a regular-expression object, and saves it to the variable $HostnameRegex. The next lines then use that in building a regex object to match an HTTP URL, saved to the variable $HttpUrl. Once constructed, they can be used in a variety of ways, such as

```
if ($text =~ $HttpUrl) {
    print "There is a URL\n";
}
```

to merely inspect, or perhaps

```
while ($text =~ m/($HttpUrl)/g) {
    print "Found URL: $1\n";
}
```

to find and display all HTTP URLs.

Now, consider changing the definition of $HostnameRegex to this, derived from Chapter 5 (☞ 205):

```
my $HostnameRegex = qr{
    # One or more dot-separated parts⋯
    (?: [a-z0-9]\.  |  [a-z0-9][-a-z0-9]{0,61}[-a-z0-9]\. )*
    # Followed by the final suffix part⋯
    (?: com|edu|gov|int|mil|net|org|biz|info|⋯|aero|[a-z][a-z] )
}xi;
```

This is intended to be used in the same way as our previous version (for example, it doesn't have a leading ⌜^⌟ and trailing ⌜$⌟, and has no capturing parentheses), so we're free to use it as a drop-in replacement. Doing so gives us a stronger $HttpUrl.

Match modes (or lack thereof) are very sticky

qr/⋯/ supports the core modifiers described on page 292. Once a regex object is built, the match modes of the regex it represents can't be changed, even if that regex object is used inside a subsequent m/⋯/ that has its own modifiers. For example, the following **does not** work:

```
my $WordRegex = qr/\b \w+ \b/;  # Oops, missing the /x modifier!
    ⋮
if ($text =~ m/^($WordRegex)/x) {
    print "found word at start of text: $1\n";
}
```

The /x modifiers are used here ostensibly to modify how $WordObject is *applied*, but this does not work because the modifiers (or lack thereof) are locked in by the qr/⋯/ when $WordObject is *created*. So, the appropriate modifiers must be used at that time.

Here's a working version of the previous example:

```
my $WordRegex = qr/\b \w+ \b/x;   # This works!
    ⋮
if ($text =~ m/^($WordRegex)/) {
    print "found word at start of text: $1\n";
}
```

Now, contrast the original snippet with the following:

```
my $WordRegex = '\b \w+ \b';   # Normal string assignment
    ⋮
if ($text =~ m/^($WordRegex)/x) {
    print "found word at start of text: $1\n";
}
```

Unlike the original, this one works even though no modifiers are associated with $WordRegex when it is created. That's because in this case, $WordRegex is a normal variable holding a simple string that is interpolated into the m/···/ regex literal. Building up a regex in a string is much less convenient than using regex objects, for a variety of reasons, including the problem in this case of having to remember that this $WordRegex must be applied with /x to be useful.

Actually, you can solve that problem even when using strings by putting the regex into a *mode-modified span* (☞ 134) when creating the string:

```
my $WordRegex = '(?x:\b \w+ \b)';   # Normal string assignment
    ⋮
if ($text =~ m/^($WordRegex)/) {
    print "found word at start of text: $1\n";
}
```

In this case, after the m/···/ regex literal interpolates the string, the regex engine is presented with ⌜^((?x:\b·\w+·\b))⌟, which works the way we want.

In fact, this is what logically happens when a regex object is created, except that a regex object always explicitly defines the "on" or "off" for each of the /i, /x, /m, and /s modes. Using **qr/\b \w+ \b/x** creates ⌜(?x-ism:\b·\w+·\b)⌟. Notice how the mode-modified span, ⌜(?x-ism:···)⌟, has /x turned on, while /i, /s, and /m are turned off. Thus, qr/···/ always "locks in" each mode, whether given a modifier or not.

Viewing Regex Objects

The previous paragraph talks about how regex objects logically wrap their regular expression with mode-modified spans like ⌜(?x-ism:···)⌟. You can actually see this for yourself, because if you use a regex object where Perl expects a string, Perl kindly gives a textual representation of the regex it represents. For example:

```
% perl -e 'print qr/\b \w+ \b/x, "\n"'
(?ix-sm:\b \w+ \b)
```

Here's what we get when we `print` the `$HttpUrl` from page 304:

```
(?ix-sm:
  http:// (?ix-sm:
  # One or more dot-separated parts
  (?: [a-z0-9]\. | [a-z0-9][-a-z0-9]{0,61}[-a-z0-9]\. )*
  # Followed by the final suffix part
  (?: com|edu|gov|int|mil|net|org|biz|info| |aero|[a-z][a-z] )
) \b          # hostname
(?:
      / [-a-z0-9_:\@&?=+,.!/~*'%\$]* # Optional path
        (?<![.,?!]) # Not allowed to end with [.,?!]
)?
)
```

The ability to turn a regex object into a string is very useful for debugging.

Using Regex Objects for Efficiency

One of the main reasons to use regex objects is to gain control, for efficiency reasons, of exactly when Perl compiles a regex to an internal form. The general issue of regex compilation was discussed briefly in Chapter 6, but the more complex Perl-related issues, including regex objects, are discussed in "Regex Compilation, the /o Modifier, qr/···/, and Efficiency" (☞ 348).

The Match Operator

The basic match

```
$text =~ m/regex/
```

is the core of Perl regular-expression use. In Perl, a regular-expression match is an *operator* that takes two *operands*, a target string operand and a regex operand, and returns a value.

How the match is carried out, and what kind of value is returned, depend on the context the match is used in (☞ 294), and other factors. The match operator is quite flexible—it can be used to test a regular expression against a string, to pluck data from a string, and even to parse a string part by part in conjunction with other match operators. While powerful, this flexibility can make mastering it more complex. Some areas of concern include:

- How to specify the regex operand
- How to specify match modifiers, and what they mean
- How to specify the target string to match against
- A match's side effects
- The value returned by a match
- Outside influences that affect the match

The general form of a match is:

```
StringOperand =~ RegexOperand
```

There are various shorthand forms, and it's interesting to note that each part is optional in one shorthand form or another. We'll see examples of all forms throughout this section.

Match's Regex Operand

The regex operand can be a regex literal or a regex object. (Actually, it can be a string or any arbitrary expression, but there is little benefit to that.) If a regex literal is used, match modifiers may also be specified.

Using a regex literal

The regex operand is most often a regex literal within m/···/ or just /···/. The leading m is optional if the delimiters for the regex literal are forward slashes or question marks (delimiters of question marks are special, discussed in a bit). For consistency, I prefer to always use the m, even when it's not required. As described earlier, you can choose your own delimiters if the m is present (☞ 291).

When using a regex literal, you can use any of the core modifiers described on page 292. The match operator also supports two additional modifiers, /g and /c, discussed in a bit.

Using a regex object

The regex operand can also be a regex object, created with qr/···/. For example:

```
my $regex = qr/regex/;
    ⋮
if ($text =~ $regex) {
    ⋮
```

You can use m/···/ with a regex object. As a special case, if the *only* thing within the "regex literal" is the interpolation of a regex object, it's exactly the same as using the regex object alone. This example's if can be written as:

```
if ($text =~ m/$regex/) {
    ⋮
```

This is convenient because it perhaps looks more familiar, and also allows you to use the /g modifier with a regex object. (You can use the other modifiers that m/···/ supports as well, but they're meaningless in this case because they can never override the modes locked in a regex object ☞ 304.)

The default regex

If no regex is given, such as with m// (or with m/$SomeVar/ where the variable $SomeVar is empty or undefined), Perl reuses the regular expression *most recently used successfully within the enclosing dynamic scope.* This used to be useful for efficiency reasons, but is now obsolete with the advent of regex objects (☞ 303).

Special match-once ?···?

In addition to the special cases for the regex-literal delimiters described earlier, the match operator treats the question mark as a special delimiter. The use of a question mark as the delimiter (as with m?···?) enables a rather esoteric feature such that after the successfully m?···? matches once, it cannot match again until the function `reset` is called in the same package. Quoting from the Perl Version 1 manual page, this features was "a useful optimization when you only want to see the first occurrence of something in each of a set of files," but for whatever reason, I have never seen it used in modern Perl.

The question mark delimiters are a special case like the forward slash delimiters, in that the m is optional: ?···? by itself is treated as m?···?.

Specifying the Match Target Operand

The normal way to indicate "this is the string to search" is using =~, as with **$text =~ m/···/**. Remember that =~ is *not* an assignment operator, nor is it a comparison operator. It is merely a funny-looking way of linking the match operator with one of its operands. (The notation was adapted from awk.)

Since the whole "*expr* =~ **m/···/**" is an expression itself, you can use it wherever an expression is allowed. Some examples (each separated by a wavy line):

```
$text =~ m/···/;    # Just do it, presumably, for the side effects.
```

```
if ($text =~ m/···/) {
    # Do code if match is successful
    ⋮
```

```
$result = ( $text =~ m/···/ ); # Set $result to result of match against $text
$result =   $text =~ m/···/   ; # Same thing; =~ has higher precedence than =
```

```
    $copy = $text;              # Copy $text to $result ...
    $copy          =~ m/···/;   # ... and perform match on $result
  ( $copy = $text ) =~ m/···/;   # Same thing in one expression
```

The default target

If the target string is the variable $_, you can omit the "**$_** =~" parts altogether. In other words, the default target operand is $_.

Something like

```
$text =~ m/regex/;
```

means "Apply *regex* to the text in $text, ignoring the return value but doing the side effects." If you forget the '~', the resulting

```
$text = m/regex/;
```

becomes "Apply *regex* to the text in $_, do the side effects, and return a true or false value that is then assigned to $text." In other words, the following are the same:

```
$text =        m/regex/;
$text = ($_ =~ m/regex/);
```

Using the default target string can be convenient when combined with other constructs that have the same default (as many do). For example, this is a common idiom:

```
while (<>)
{
   if (m/⋯/) {
      ⋮
   } elsif (m/⋯/) {
      ⋮
```

In general, though, relying on default operands can make your code less approachable by less experienced programmers.

Negating the sense of the match

You can also use !~ instead of =~ to logically negate the sense of the return value. (Return values and side effects are discussed soon, but with !~, the return value is always a simple true or false value.) The following are identical:

```
if ($text !~ m/⋯/)

if (not $text =~ m/⋯/)

unless ($text =~ m/⋯/)
```

Personally, I prefer the middle form. With any of them, the normal side effects, such as the setting of $1 and the like, still happen. !~ is merely a convenience in an "if this doesn't match" situation.

Different Uses of the Match Operator

You can always use the match operator as if it returns a simple true/false indicating the success of the match, but there are ways you can get additional information about a successful match, and to work in conjunction with other match operators. How the match operator works depends primarily on the *context* in which it's used (☞ 294), and whether the /g modifier has been applied.

Normal "does this match?"—scalar context without /g

In a scalar context, such as the test of an `if`, the match operator returns a simple true or false:

```
if ($target =~ m/…/) {
    #  …processing after successful match …
    ⋮
} else {
    #  …processing after unsuccessful match …
    ⋮
}
```

You can also assign the result to a scalar for inspection later:

```
my $success  =  $target =~ m/…/;
⋮
if ($success) {
⋮
}
```

Normal "pluck data from a string"—list context, without /g

A list context without /g is the normal way to pluck information from a string. The return value is a list with an element for each set of capturing parentheses in the regex. A simple example is processing a date of the form `69/8/31`, using:

```
my ($year, $month, $day)  =  $date =~ m{^ (\d+) / (\d+) / (\d+) $}x;
```

The three matched numbers are then available in the three variables (and $1, $2, and $3 as well). There is one element in the return-value list for each set of capturing parentheses, or an empty list upon failure.

It is possible for a set of capturing parentheses to not participate in the final success of a match. For example, one of the sets in **m/**(this)|(that)**/** is guaranteed not to be part of the match. Such sets return the undefined value `undef`. If there are no sets of capturing parentheses to begin with, a successful list-context match without /g returns the list `(1)`.

A list context can be provided in a number of ways, including assigning the results to an array, as with:

```
my @parts  =  $text =~ m/^(\d+)-(\d+)-(\d+)$/;
```

If you're assigning to just one scalar variable, take care to provide a list context to the match if you want the captured parts instead of just a Boolean indicating the success. Compare the following tests:

```
my ($word)   =  $text =~ m/(\w+)/;
my $success  =  $text =~ m/(\w+)/;
```

The parentheses around the variable in the first example cause its my to provide a list context to the assignment (in this case, to the match). The lack of parentheses in the second example provides a scalar context to the match, so `$success` merely gets a true/false result.

This example shows a convenient idiom:

```
if ( my ($year, $month, $day) = $date =~ m{^ (\d+) / (\d+) / (\d+) $}x ) {
    # Process for when we have a match: $year and such are available
} else {
    # here if no match . . .
}
```

The match is in a list context (provided by the "`my` (...) `=`"), so the list of variables is assigned their respective `$1`, `$2`, etc., if the match is successful. However, once that's done, since the whole combination is in the scalar context provided by the `while` conditional, Perl must contort the list to a scalar. To do that, it takes the number of items in the list, which is conveniently zero if the match wasn't successful, and non-zero (i.e., true) if it was.

"Pluck all matches"—list context, with the /g modifier

This useful construct returns a list of all text matched within capturing parentheses (or if there are no capturing parentheses, the text matched by the whole expression), not only for one match, as in the previous section, but for all matches in the string.

A simple example is the following, to fetch all integers in a string:

```
my @nums  =  $text =~ m/\d+/g;
```

If `$text` contains an IP address like '64.156.215.240', `@nums` then receives four elements, '64', '156', '215', and '240'. Combined with other constructs, here's an easy way to turn an IP address into an eight-digit hexadecimal number such as '409cd7f0', which might be convenient for creating compact log files:

```
my $hex_ip = join '', map { sprintf("%02x", $_) } $ip =~ m/\d+/g;
```

You can convert it back with a similar technique:

```
my $ip = join '.', map { hex($_) } $hex_ip =~ m/../g
```

As another example, to match all floating-point numbers on a line, you might use:

```
my @nums  =  $text =~ m/\d+(?:.\d+)?|\.\d+/g;
```

The use of non-capturing parentheses here is very important, since adding capturing ones changes what is returned. Here's an example showing how one set of capturing parentheses can be useful:

```
my @Tags  =  $Html =~ m/<(\w+)/g;
```

This sets `@Tags` to the list of HTML tags, in order, found in `$Html`, assuming it contains no stray '<' characters.

Here's an example with multiple sets of capturing parentheses: consider having the entire text of a Unix mailbox alias file in a single string, where logical lines look like:

```
alias   Jeff        jfriedl@regex.info
alias   Perlbug     perl5-porters@perl.org
alias   Prez        president@whitehouse.gov
```

To pluck an alias and full address from one of the logical lines, you can use **m/^alias\s+(\S+)\s+(.+)/m** (without /g). In a list context, this returns a list of two elements, such as **('Jeff', 'jfriedl@regex.info')**. Now, to match all such sets, add /g. This returns a list like:

```
( 'Jeff', 'jfriedl@regex.info', 'Perlbug',
   'perl5-porters@perl.org', 'Prez', 'president@whitehouse.gov' )
```

If the list happens to fit a key/value pair pattern as in this example, you can actually assign it directly to an associative array. After running

```
my %alias  = $text =~ m/^alias\s+(\S+)\s+(.+)/mg;
```

you can access the full address of 'Jeff' with $alias{Jeff}.

Iterative Matching: Scalar Context, with /g

A scalar-context m/⋯/g is a special construct quite different from the others. Like a normal m/⋯/, it does just one match, but like a list-context m/⋯/g, it pays attention to where previous matches occurred. Each time a scalar-context m/⋯/g is reached, such as in a loop, it finds the "next" match. If it fails, it resets the "current position," causing the next application to start again at the beginning of the string.

Here's a simple example:

```
$text = "WOW! This is a SILLY test.";

$text =~ m/\b([a-z]+\b)/g;
print "The first all-lowercase word: $1\n";

$text =~ m/\b([A-Z]+\b)/g;
print "The subsequent all-uppercase word: $1\n";
```

With both scalar matches using the /g modifier, it results in:

```
The first all-lowercase word: is
The subsequent all-uppercase word: SILLY
```

The two scalar-/g matches work together: the first sets the "current position" to just after the matched lowercase word, and the second picks up from there to find the first uppercase word *that follows*. The /g is required for either match to pay attention to the "current position," so if *either* didn't have /g, the second line would refer to 'WOW'.

A scalar context /g match is quite convenient as the conditional of a while loop. Consider:

```
while ($ConfigData =~ m/^(\w+)=(.*)/mg) {
    my($key, $value) = ($1, $2);
      ⋮
}
```

All matches are eventually found, but the body of the while loop is executed between the matches (well, *after* each match). Once an attempt fails, the result is false and the while loop finishes. Also, upon failure, the /g state is reset, which means that the next /g match starts over at the start of the string.

Compare

```
while ($text =~ m/(\d+)/) { # dangerous!
    print "found: $1\n";
}
```

and:

```
while ($text =~ m/(\d+)/g) {
    print "found: $1\n";
}
```

The only difference is /g, but it's a huge difference. If $text contained, say, our earlier IP example, the second prints what we want:

```
found: 64
found: 156
found: 215
found: 240
```

The first, however, prints "found: 64" over and over, forever. Without the /g, the match is simply "find the first ⌈(\d+)⌋ in $text," which is '64' no matter how many times it's checked. Adding the /g to the scalar-context match turns it into "find the *next* ⌈(\d+)⌋ in $text," which finds each number in turn.

The "current match location" and the pos() function

Every string in Perl has associated with it a "current match location" at which the transmission first attempts the match. It's a property of the string, and not associated with any particular regular expression. When a string is created or modified, the "current match location" starts out at the beginning of the string, but when a /g match is successful, it's left at the location where the match ended. The next time a /g match is applied to the string, the match begins inspecting the string at that same "current match location."

You have access to the target string's "current match location" via the pos(⋯) function. For example:

```
my $ip = "64.156.215.240";
while ($ip =~ m/(\d+)/g) {
    printf "found '$1' ending at location %d\n", pos($ip);
}
```

This produces:

```
found '64' ending at location 2
found '156' ending at location 6
found '215' ending at location 10
found '240' ending at location 14
```

(Remember, string indices are zero-based, so "location 2" is just before the 3rd character into the string.) After a successful /g match, $+[0] (the first element of @+ ☞ 302) is the same as the pos of the target string.

The default argument to the pos() function is the same default argument for the match operator: the $_ variable.

Pre-setting a string's pos

The real power of pos() is that you can write to it, to tell the regex engine where to start the next match (if that next match uses /g, of course). For example, the web server logs I work with at Yahoo! are in a custom format that contains 32 bytes of fixed-width data, followed by the page being requested, followed by other information. One way to pick out the page is to use ⌈^.{32}⌋ to skip over the fixed-width data:

```
if ($logline =~ m/^.{32}(\S+)/) {
    $RequestedPage = $1;
}
```

This brute-force method isn't elegant, and forces the regex engine to work to skip the first 32 bytes. That's less efficient and less clear than doing it explicitly ourself:

```
pos($logline) = 32;  # The page starts at the 32nd character, so start the next match there . . .
if ($logline =~ m/(\S+)/g) {
    $RequestedPage = $1;
}
```

This is better, but isn't quite the same. It has the regex *start* where we want it to start, but doesn't require a match *at that position* the way the original does. If for some reason the 32nd character can't be matched by ⌈\S⌋, the original version correctly fails, but the new version, without anything to anchor it to a particular position in the string, is subject to the transmission's bump-along. Thus, it could return, in error, a match of ⌈\S+⌋ from later in the string. Luckily, the next section shows that this is an easy problem to fix.

Using ⌈\G⌉

⌈\G⌉ is the "anchor to where the previous match ended" metacharacter. It's exactly what we need to solve the problem in the previous section:

```
pos($logline) = 32;  # The page starts at the 32nd character, so start the next match there ...
if ($logline =~ m/\G(\S+)/g) {
    $RequestedPage = $1;
}
```

⌈\G⌉ tells the transmission "don't bump-along with this regex — if you can't match successfully right away, fail."

There are discussions of ⌈\G⌉ in previous chapters: see the general discussion in Chapter 3 (☞ 128), and the extended example in Chapter 5 (☞ 212).

Note that Perl's ⌈\G⌉ is restricted in that it works predictably only when it is the first thing in the regex, and there is no top-level alternation. For example, in Chapter 6 when the CSV example is being optimized (☞ 271), the regex begins with ⌈\G(?:^|,) ···⌉. Because there's no need to check for ⌈\G⌉ if the more restrictive ⌈^⌉ matches, you might be tempted to change this to ⌈(?:^|\G,) ···⌉. Unfortunately, this doesn't work in Perl; the results are unpredictable.†

"Tag-team" matching with /gc

Normally, a failing m/···/g match attempt resets the target string's pos to the start of the string, but adding the /c modifier to /g introduces a special twist, causing a failing match to *not* reset the target's pos. (/c is never used without /g, so I tend to refer to it as /gc.)

m/···/gc is most commonly used in conjunction with ⌈\G⌉ to create a "lexer" that tokenizes a string into its component parts. Here's a simple example to tokenize the HTML in variable $html:

```
while (not $html =~ m/\G\z/gc) # While we haven't worked to the end ...
{
    if     ($html =~ m/\G( <[^>]+>    )/xgc) { print "TAG: $1\n"            }
    elsif  ($html =~ m/\G( &\w+;      )/xgc) { print "NAMED ENTITY: $1\n"   }
    elsif  ($html =~ m/\G( &\#\d+;    )/xgc) { print "NUMERIC ENTITY: $1\n" }
    elsif  ($html =~ m/\G( [^<>&\n]+ )/xgc) { print "TEXT: $1\n"           }
    elsif  ($html =~ m/\G \n          /xgc) { print "NEWLINE\n"             }
    elsif  ($html =~ m/\G( .          )/xgc) { print "ILLEGAL CHAR: $1\n"   }
    else {
        die "$0: oops, this shouldn't happen!";
    }
}
```

---

† This *would* work with most other flavors that support ⌈\G⌉, but even so, I would generally not recommend using it, as the optimization gains by having ⌈\G⌉ at the start of the regex usually outweigh the small gain by not testing ⌈\G⌉ an extra time (☞ 245).

The bold part of each regex matches one type of HTML construct. Each is checked in turn starting from the current position (due to /gc), but can match *only* at the current position (due to ⌈\G⌉). The regexes are checked in order until the construct at that current position has been found and reported. This leaves $html's pos at the start of the next token, which is found during the next iteration of the loop.

The loop ends when m/\G\z/gc is able to match, which is when the current position (⌈\G⌉) has worked its way to the very end of the string (⌈\z⌉).

An important aspect of this approach is that one of the tests *must* match each time through the loop. If one doesn't (and if we don't abort), there would be an infinite loop, since nothing would be advancing or resetting $html's pos. This example has a final *else* clause that will never be invoked as the program stands now, but if we were to edit the program (as we will soon), we could perhaps introduce a mistake, so keeping the *else* clause is prudent. As it is now, if the data contains a sequence we haven't planned for (such as '<>'), it generates one warning message per unexpected character.

Another important aspect of this approach is the ordering of the checks, such as the placement of ⌈\G(.)⌉ as the last check. Or, consider extending this application to recognize <script> blocks with:

```
$html =~ m/\G ( <script[^>]*>.*?</script> )/xgcsi
```

(Wow, we've used five modifiers!) To work properly, this must be inserted into the program *before* the currently-first ⌈<[^>]+>⌉. Otherwise, ⌈<[^>]+>⌉ would match the opening <script> tag "out from under" us.

There's a somewhat more advanced example of /gc in Chapter 3 (☞ 130).

Pos-related summary

Here's a summary of how the match operator interacts with the target string's pos:

Type of match	Where match starts	pos upon success	pos upon failure
m/⋯/	start of string (pos ignored)	reset to undef	reset to undef
m/⋯/g	starts at target's pos	set to end of match	reset to undef
m/⋯/gc	starts at target's pos	set to end of match	left unchanged

Also, modifying a string in any way causes its pos to be reset to undef (which is the initial value, meaning the start of the string).

The Match Operator's Environmental Relations

The following sections summarize what we've seen about how the match operator influences the Perl environment, and vice versa.

The match operator's side effects

Often, the side effects of a successful match are more important than the actual return value. In fact, it is quite common to use the match operator in a void context (i.e., in such a way that the return value isn't even inspected), just to obtain the side effects. (In such a case, it acts as if given a scalar context.) The following summarizes the side effects of a *successful* match attempt:

- After-match variables like $1 and @+ are set for the remainder of the current scope (☞ 299).

- The *default regex* is set for the remainder of the current scope (☞ 308).

- If m?···? matches, it (the specific m?···? operator) is marked as unmatchable, at least until the next call of reset in the same package (☞ 308).

Again, these side effects occur only with a match that is successful—an unsuccessful match attempt has no influence on them. However, the following side effects happen with *any* match attempt:

- pos is set or reset for the target string (☞ 313).

- If /o is used, the regex is "fused" to the operator so that re-evaluation does not occur (☞ 352).

Outside influences on the match operator

What a match operator does is influenced by more than just its operands and modifiers. This list summarizes the outside influences on the match operator:

context
: The context that a match operator is applied in (scalar, array, or void) has a large influence on how the match is performed, as well as on its return value and side effects.

pos(···)
: The pos of the target string (set explicitly or implicitly by a previous match) indicates where in the string the next /g-governed match should begin. It is also where ⌈\G⌋ matches.

default regex
: The default regex is used if the provided regex is empty (☞ 308).

study
: It has no effect on what is matched or returned, but if the target string has been studied, the match might be faster (or slower). See "The Study Function" (☞ 359).

m?···? and reset
: The invisible "has/hasn't matched" status of m?···? operators is set when m?···? matches or reset is called (☞ 308).

Keeping your mind in context (and context in mind)

Before leaving the match operator, I'll put a question to you. Particularly when changing among the `while`, `if`, and `foreach` control constructs, you really need to keep your wits about you. What do you expect the following to print?

```
while ("Larry Curly Moe" =~ m/\w+/g) {
    print "WHILE stooge is $&.\n";
}
print "\n";

if ("Larry Curly Moe" =~ m/\w+/g) {
    print "IF stooge is $&.\n";
}
print "\n";

foreach ("Larry Curly Moe" =~ m/\w+/g) {
    print "FOREACH stooge is $&.\n";
}
```

It's a bit tricky. ❖ Turn the page to check your answer.

The Substitution Operator

Perl's substitution operator **s/**···**/**···**/** extends a match to a full match-and-replace. The general form is:

```
$text =~ s/regex/replacement/modifiers
```

In short, the text first matched by the regex operand is replaced by the value of the replacement operand. If the `/g` modifier is used, the regex is repeatedly applied to the text following the match, with additional matched text replaced as well.

As with the match operator, the target text operand and the connecting `=~` are optional if the target is the variable `$_`. But unlike the match operator's `m`, the substitution's `s` is never optional.

We've seen that the match operator is fairly complex—how it works, and what it returns, is dependent upon the context it's called in, the target string's `pos`, and the modifiers used. In contrast, the substitution operator is simple: it always returns the same information (an indication of the number of substitutions done), and the modifiers that influence how it works are easy to understand.

You can use any of the core modifiers described on page 292, but the substitution operator also supports two additional modifiers: `/g` and, described in a bit, `/e`.

The Replacement Operand

With the normal `s/···/···/`, the replacement operand immediately follows the regex operand, using a total of three instances of the delimiter rather than the two of `m/···/`. If the regex uses balanced delimiters (such as `<···>`), the replacement operand then has its own independent pair of delimiters (yielding a total of four). For example, `s{···}{···}` and `s[···]/···/` and `s<···>'···'` are all valid. In such cases, the two sets may be separated by whitespace, and if so, by comments as well. Balanced delimiters are commonly used with `/x` or `/e`:

```
$text =~ s{
    ...some big regex here, with lots of comments and such...
} {
    ...a Perl code snippet to be evaluated to produce the replacement text...
}ex;
```

Take care to separate in your mind the regex and replacement operands. The regex operand is parsed in a special regex-specific way, with its own set of special delimiters (☞ 291). The replacement operand is parsed and evaluated as a normal double-quoted string. The evaluation happens after the match (and with `/g`, after each match), so `$1` and the like are available to refer to the proper match slice.

There are two situations where the replacement operand is not parsed as a double-quoted string:

* When the replacement operand's delimiters are single quotes, it is parsed as a single-quoted string, which means that no variable interpolation is done.

* If the `/e` modifier (discussed in the next section) is used, the replacement operand is parsed like a little Perl script instead of like a double-quoted string. The little Perl script is executed after each match, with its result being used as the replacement.

The /e Modifier

The `/e` modifier causes the replacement operand to be evaluated as a Perl code snippet, as if with **eval {···}**. The code snippet's syntax is checked to ensure it's valid Perl when the script is loaded, but the code is evaluated afresh after each match. After each match, the replacement operand is evaluated in a scalar context, and the result of the code is used as the replacement. Here's a simple example:

```
$text =~ s/-time-/localtime/ge;
```

This replaces occurrences of ⌐-time-¬ with the results of calling Perl's `localtime` function in a scalar context (which returns a textual representation of the current time, such as "Wed Sep 25 18:36:51 2002").

Since the evaluation is done after each match, you can refer to the text just matched with the after-match variables like `$1`. For example, special characters

---

Quiz Answer

❖ *Answer to the question on page 318.*

The question snippets on page 318 produce:

```
WHILE stooge is Larry.
WHILE stooge is Curly.
WHILE stooge is Moe.

IF stooge is Larry.

FOREACH stooge is Moe.
FOREACH stooge is Moe.
FOREACH stooge is Moe.
```

Note that if the `print` within the `foreach` loop had referred to `$_` rather than `$&`, its results would have been the same as the `while`'s. In this `foreach` case, however, the result returned by the `m/···/g`, (`'Larry'`, `'Curly'`, `'Moe'`), goes unused. Rather, the side effect `$&` is used, which almost certainly indicates a programming mistake, as the side effects of a list-context `m/···/g` are not often useful.

---

that might not otherwise be allowed in a URL can be encoded using `%` followed by their two-digit hexadecimal representation. To encode all non-alphanumerics this way, you can use

```
$url =~ s/([^a-zA-Z0-9])/sprintf('%%02x', ord($1))/ge;
```

and to decode back to the original, you can use:

```
$url =~ s/%([0-9a-f][0-9a-f])/pack("C", hex($1))/ige;
```

In short, `sprintf('%%02x', ord(`*character*`))` converts characters to their numeric URL representation, while `pack("C", `*value*`)` does the opposite; consult your favorite Perl documentation for more information.

Multiple uses of /e

Normally, repeating a modifier with an operator doesn't hurt (except perhaps to confuse the reader), but repeating the `/e` modifier actually changes how the replacement is done. Normally, the replacement operator is evaluated once, but if more than one 'e' is given, the results of the evaluation are themselves evaluated as Perl, over and over, for as many extra 'e' as are provided. This is perhaps useful mostly for an Obfuscated Perl Contest.

Still, it can be useful. Consider interpolating variables into a string manually (such as if the string is read from a configuration file). That is, you have a string that looks like '··· $var ···' and you want to replace the substring '$var' with the value of the variable $var.

A simple approach uses:

```
$data =~ s/(\$[a-zA-Z_]\w*)/$1/eeg;
```

Without any /e, this would simply replace the matched '$var' with itself, which is not very useful. With one /e, it evaluates the code $1, yielding '$var', which again, effectively replaces the matched text with itself (which is again, not very useful). But with two /e, that '$var' is itself evaluated, yielding its contents. Thus, this mimics the interpolation of variables.

Context and Return Value

Recall that the match operator returns different values based upon the particular combination of context and /g. The substitution operator, however, has none of these complexities—it always returns either the number of substitutions performed or, if none were done, an empty string.

Conveniently, when interpreted as a Boolean (such as for the conditional of an if), the return value is taken as true if any substitutions are done, false if not.

The Split Operator

The multifaceted split operator (often called a *function* in casual conversation) is commonly used as the converse of a list-context m/···/g (☞ 311). The latter returns text matched by the regex, while a split with the same regex returns text *separated* by matches. The normal match **$text =~ m/:/g** applied against a $text of '**IO.SYS:225558:95-10-03:-a-sh:optional**', returns the four-element list

```
(':', ':', ':', ':')
```

which doesn't seem useful. On the other hand, **split(/:/, $text)** returns the five-element list:

```
('IO.SYS', '225558', '95-10-03', '-a-sh', 'optional')
```

Both examples reflect that ⌈:⌉ matches four times. With split, those four matches partition a copy of the target into five chunks, which are returned as a list of five strings.

That example splits the target string on a single character, but it you can split on any arbitrary regular expression. For example,

```
@Paragraphs = split(m/\s*<p>\s*/i, $html);
```

splits the HTML in $html into chunks, at <p> or <P>, surrounded by optional whitespace. You can even split on locations, as with

```
@Lines = split(m/^/m, $lines);
```

to break a string into its logical lines.

In its most simple form with simple data like this, split is as easy to understand as it is useful. However, there are many options, special cases, and special situations that complicate things. Before getting into the details, let me show two particularly useful special cases:

- The special match operand **//** causes the target string to be split into its component characters. Thus, **split(//, "short test")** returns a list of ten elements: **("s", "h", "o", ⋯, "s", "t")**.

- The special match operand **" "** (a normal string with a single space) causes the target string to be split on whitespace, similar to using m/\s+/ as the operand, except that any leading and trailing whitespace are ignored. Thus, **split(" ", "···a·short···test···")** returns the strings 'a', 'short', and 'test'.

These and other special cases are discussed a bit later, but first, the next sections go over the basics.

Basic Split

split is an operator that looks like a function, and takes up to three operands:

```
split(match operand, target string, chunk-limit operand)
```

The parentheses are optional. Default values (discussed later in this section) are provided for operands left off the end.

split is always used in a list context. Common usage patterns include:

```
($var1, $var2, $var3, ⋯) = split(⋯);

@array = split(⋯);

for my $item (split(⋯)) {
    ⋮
}
```

Basic match operand

The match operand has several special-case situations, but it is normally the same as the regex operand of the match operator. That means that you can use /⋯/ and m{⋯} and the like, a regex object, or any expression that can evaluate to a string. Only the core modifiers described on page 292 are supported.

If you need parentheses for grouping, be sure to use the ⌈(?:⋯)⌋ non-capturing kind. As we'll see in a few pages, the use of capturing parentheses with split turns on a very special feature.

Target string operand

The target string is inspected, but is never modified by split. The content of $_ is the default if no target string is provided.

Basic chunk-limit operand

In its primary role, the chunk-limit operand specifies a limit to the number of chunks that `split` partitions the string into. With the sample data from the first example, **split(/:/, $text, 3)** returns:

```
( 'IO.SYS', '225558', '95-10-03:-a-sh:optional' )
```

This shows that `split` stopped after `/:/` matched twice, resulting in the requested three-chunk partition. It could have matched additional times, but that's irrelevant because of this example's chunk limit. The limit is an upper bound, so no more than that many elements will ever be returned (unless the regex has capturing parentheses, which is covered in a later section). You may still get fewer elements than the chunk limit; if the data can't be partitioned enough to begin with, nothing extra is produced to "fill the count." With our example data, **split(/:/, $text, <u>99</u>)** still returns only a five-element list. However, there is an important difference between **split(/:/, $text)** and **split(/:/, $text, <u>99</u>)** which does not manifest itself with this example — keep this in mind when the details are discussed later.

Remember that the *chunk*-limit operand refers to the *chunks* between the matches, not to the number of matches themselves. If the limit were to refer to the matches themselves, the previous example with a limit of three would produce

```
('IO.SYS', '225558', '95-10-03', '-a-sh:optional')
```

which is not what actually happens.

One comment on efficiency: let's say you intended to fetch only the first few fields, such as with:

```
($filename, $size, $date) = split(/:/, $text);
```

As a performance enhancement, Perl stops splitting after the fields you've requested have been filled. It does this by automatically providing a chunk limit of one more than the number of items in the list.

Advanced split

`split` can be simple to use, as with the examples we've seen so far, but it has three special issues that can make it somewhat complex in practice:

- Returning empty elements
- Special regex operands
- A regex with capturing parentheses

The next sections cover these in detail.

Returning Empty Elements

The basic premise of `split` is that it returns the text separated by matches, but there are times when that returned text is an empty string (a string of length zero, e.g., `""`). For example, consider

```
@nums = split(m/:/, "12:34::78");
```

This returns

```
("12", "34", "", "78")
```

The regex ⌈:⌋ matches three times, so four elements are returned. The empty third element reflects that the regex matched twice in a row, with no text in between.

Trailing empty elements

Normally, trailing empty elements are *not* returned. For example,

```
@nums = split(m/:/, "12:34::78:::");
```

sets `@nums` to the same four elements

```
("12", "34", "", "78")
```

as the previous example, even though the regex was able to match a few extra times at the end of the string. By default, `split` does not return empty elements at the end of the list. However, you can have `split` return all trailing elements by using an appropriate chunk-limit operand...

The chunk-limit operand's second job

In addition to possibly limiting the number of chunks, any non-zero chunk-limit operand also preserves trailing empty items. (A chunk limit given as zero is exactly the same as if no chunk limit is given at all.) If you don't want to limit the number of chunks returned, but do want to leave trailing empty elements intact, simply choose a very large limit. Or, better yet, use -1, because a negative chunk limit is taken as an arbitrarily large limit: **split(/:/, $text, -1)** returns all elements, including any trailing empty ones.

At the other extreme, if you want to remove *all* empty items, you could put **grep {length}** before the `split`. This use of grep lets pass only list elements with non-zero lengths (in other words, elements that aren't empty):

```
my @NonEmpty = grep { length } split(/:/, $text);
```

Special matches at the ends of the string

A match at the very beginning normally produces an empty element:

```
@nums = split(m/:/, ":12:34::78");
```

That sets @nums to:

```
("", "12", "34", "", "78")
```

The initial empty element reflects the fact that the regex matched at the beginning of the string. However, as a special case, if the regex doesn't actually match any text when it matches at the start or end of the string, leading and/or trailing empty elements are *not* produced. A simple example is **split(/\b/, "a simple test")**, which can match at the six marked locations in 'a⌄simple⌄test'. Even though it matches six times, it doesn't return seven elements, but rather only the five elements: **("a", "", "simple", "", "test")**. Actually, we've already seen this special case, with the **@Lines = split(m/^/m, $lines)** example on page 321.

Split's Special Regex Operands

split's match operand is normally a regex literal or a regex object, as with the match operator, but there are some special cases:

- An empty regex for split does not mean "Use the current default regex," but to split the target string into a list of characters. We saw this before at the start of the split discussion, noting that **split(//, "short test")** returns a list of ten elements: **("s", "h", "o", &bigmidddot, "s", "t")**.

- A match operand that is a *string* (**not** a regex) consisting of exactly one space is a special case. It's almost the same as /\s+/, except that leading whitespace is skipped. Trailing whitespace is ignored as well if an appropriately large (or negative) chunk-limit operand is given. This is all meant to simulate the default input-record-separator splitting that awk does with its input, although it can certainly be quite useful for general use.

  If you'd like to keep leading whitespace, just use m/\s+/ directly. If you'd like to keep trailing whitespace, use −1 as the chunk-limit operand.

- If no regex operand is given, a string consisting of one space (the special case in the previous point) is used as the default. Thus, a raw split without any operands is the same as **split(' ', $_, 0)**.

- If the regex ⌈^⌉ is used, the /m modifier (for the enhanced line-anchor match mode) is automatically supplied for you. (For some reason, this does not happen for ⌈$⌉.) Since it's so easy to just use m/^/**m** explicitly, I would recommend doing so, for clarity. Splitting on m/^/m is an easy way to break a multiline string into individual lines.

Split has no side effects

Note that a split match operand often *looks* like a match operator, but it has none of the side effects of one. The use of a regex with split doesn't affect the default regex for later match or substitution operators. The variables $&, $', $1, and so on are not set or otherwise affected by a split. A split is completely isolated from the rest of the program with respect to side effects.[†]

Split's Match Operand with Capturing Parentheses

Capturing parentheses change the whole face of split. When they are used, the returned list has additional, independent elements interjected for the item(s) captured by the parentheses. This means that some or all text normally *not* returned by split is now included in the returned list.

For example, as part of HTML processing, split(/(<[^>]*>)/) turns

```
···and·<B>very·<FONT·color=red>very</FONT>·much</B>·effort···
```

into:

```
( '...·and ', '<B>', 'very·', '<FONT·color=red>',
  'very', '</FONT>', '·much', '</B>', '·effort...' )
```

With the capturing parentheses removed, split(/<[^>]*>/) returns:

```
( '...·and ', 'very·', 'very', '·much', '·effort...' )
```

The added elements do not count against a chunk limit. (The chunk limit limits the chunks that the original string is partitioned into, not the number of elements returned.)

If there are multiple sets of capturing parentheses, multiple items are added to the list with each match. If there are sets of capturing parentheses that don't contribute to a match, undef elements are inserted for them.

Fun with Perl Enhancements

Many regular-expression concepts that are now available in other languages were first made available only in Perl. Examples include non-capturing parentheses, lookahead, (and later, lookbehind), free-spacing mode, (most modes, actually — and with them comes ⌜\A⌟, ⌜\z⌟, and ⌜\Z⌟), atomic grouping, ⌜\G⌟, and the conditional construct. However, these are no longer Perl specific, so they are all covered in the main chapters of this book.

Still, Perl developers remain innovative, so there are some major concepts available at this time only in Perl. One of the most interesting is the ability to execute arbitrary code *during the match attempt.* Perl has long featured strong integration of regular expressions into code, but this brings integration to a whole new level.

---

† Actually, there is one side effect remaining from a feature that has been deprecated for many years, but has not actually been removed from the language yet. If split is used in a scalar context, it writes its results to the @_ variable (which is also the variable used to pass function arguments, so be careful not to use split in a scalar context by accident). **use warnings** or the -w command-line argument will warn you if split is used in a scalar context.

We'll continue with a short overview about this and other innovations available currently only in Perl, followed by the details.

The *dynamic regex* construct ⌈**(??{** *perl code* **})**⌋

Each time this construct is reached during the application of the regex in which it's found, the *perl code* is executed. The result of that execution (either a regex object or a string that's then interpreted as a regex) is applied right then, as part of the current match.

This simple example ⌈**^(\d)(??{** **"X{$1}"** **})$**⌋ is shown with the dynamic regex construct underlined. Overall, this regex matches a number at the beginning of the line, followed by exactly that many 'X' until the end of the line. It matches '3XXX' and '12XXXXXXXXXXXX', for example, but not '3X' or '7XXXX'. If we trace though the '3XXX' example, the leading ⌈**(\d+)**⌋ part matches '3XXX', setting $1 to '3'. The regex engine then reaches the dynamic regex construct, which executes the code **"X{$1}"**, resulting in the value 'X{3}'. This is then interpreted as ⌈X{3}⌋, and applied as part of the current regex (matching the '3XXX'). Once that's done, the trailing ⌈$⌋ then matches at '3XXX', resulting in an overall match.

As we'll see in the examples that follow, a dynamic regex is particularly useful for matching arbitrarily nested constructs.

The *embedded-code* construct ⌈**(?{** *arbitrary perl code* **})**⌋

Like the dynamic regex construct, this construct also executes the Perl code each time it's reached during the application of a regex, but this construct is more general in that the code doesn't need to return any specific result. Usually, the return value is not even used. (But in case it is needed later in the same regex, the return value is available in the $^R variable ☞ 302).

There's one case where the value produced by the code is used: when an embedded-code construct is used as the *if* of an ⌈**(?** *if* *then* **|** *else* **)**⌋ conditional (☞ 138). In this case, the result is interpreted as a Boolean value, upon which either the *then* or *else* part will be applied.

Embedded code can be used for many things, but it's particularly useful for debugging. Here's a simple example that displays a message every time the regex is actually applied, with the embedded-code construct underlined:

```
"have a nice day" =~ m{
  (?{ print "Starting match.\n" })
  \b(?: the | an | a )\b
}x;
```

The regex matches fully just once in this test, but the message is shown six times, reflecting that the regex was at least partially applied by the transmission at the five character positions prior to the sixth time, at which point it matches fully.

Regex-literal overloading

Regex-literal overloading lets you add your own custom pre-processing of regex literals, before they're given to the regex engine. You can use this to effectively add features to Perl's regex flavor. For example, Perl doesn't have separate start-of-word and end-of-word metacharacters (it has a catch-all \b word boundary), but you might want to have it recognize \< and \>, converting these constructs behind the scenes to ones Perl does know.

Regex overloading has some important limitations that severely restrict its usefulness. We'll look at this, as well as examples like the \< and \> idea, later in this section.

Force match of single byte

One other feature I should mention in this list is that the ⌈\c⌋ metacharacter matches one *byte*, even if that byte is just one of several that might encode a single *character*. This is dangerous — its misuse can cause internal errors, so it shouldn't be used unless you really know what you're doing. I can't think of a good use for it, so I won't mention it further.

When working with Perl code embedded within a regex (either in a dynamic regex construct or an embedded-code construct), it's best to use only global variables until you understand the important issue related to my variables discussed starting on page 338.

Using a Dynamic Regex to Match Nested Pairs

A dynamic regex's main use is to allow a regex to match arbitrarily nested constructs (something long thought to be impossible with regular expressions). Its quintessential example is to match content with arbitrarily nested parentheses. To see how a dynamic regex is useful for this, let's first look at why it's not possible with traditional constructs.

This simple regex matches a parenthesized run of text: ⌈\(([^()])* \)⌋. It doesn't allow parentheses within the outer parentheses, so it doesn't allow any nesting (that is, it supports zero levels of nesting). We can put it into a regex object and use it like this:

```
my $Level0 = qr/ \( ( [^()] )* \) /x;  # Parenthesized text
    ⋮
if ($text =~ m/\b( \w+$Level0 )/x) {
   print "found function call: $1\n";
}
```

This would match "substr($str, 0, 3)", but not "substr($str, 0, (3+2))" because it has nested parentheses. Let's expand our regex to handle it. That means accommodating one level of nesting.

Allowing one level of nesting means allowing parenthesized text within the outer parentheses. So, we need to expand on the subexpression that matches between them, which is currently ⌈[^()]⌉, by adding a subexpression that matches parenthesized text. Well, we just created that: $Level0 holds such a regex. Using it, we can create the next level:

```
my $Level0 = qr/ \(  ( [^()]              )* \) /x; # Parenthesized text
my $Level1 = qr/ \(  ( [^()]| $Level0 )* \) /x; # One level of nesting
```

The $Level0 here is the same as before; what's new is its use in building $Level1, which matches its own set of parentheses, *plus* those of $Level0. That's one level of nesting.

To match another level, we can use the same approach, creating a $Level2 that uses $Level1 (which still uses $Level0):

```
my $Level0 = qr/ \(  ( [^()]            )* \) /x; # Parenthesized text
my $Level1 = qr/ \(  ( [^()] | $Level0 )* \) /x; # One level of nesting
my $Level2 = qr/ \(  ( [^()] | $Level1 )* \) /x; # Two levels of nesting
```

We can continue this indefinitely:

```
my $Level3 = qr/ \(  ( [^()] | $Level2 )* \) /x; # Three levels of nesting
my $Level4 = qr/ \(  ( [^()] | $Level3 )* \) /x; # Four levels of nesting
my $Level5 = qr/ \(  ( [^()] | $Level4 )* \) /x; # Five levels of nesting
    ⋮
```

Figure 7-1 shows the first few levels graphically.

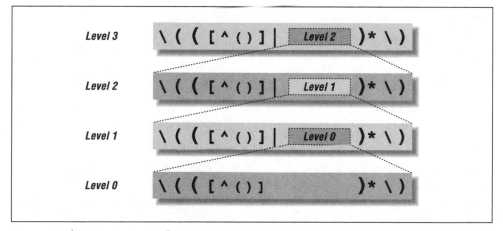

Figure 7-1: Capturing parentheses

It's interesting to see the result of all those levels. Here's what $Level3 boils down to:

```
\((([^()]|\((([^()]|\((([^()]|\((([^()])*\))*\))*\))*\)
```

Wow, that's ugly.

Luckily, we don't have to interpret it directly (that's the regex engine's job). The approach with the `Level` variables is easy enough to work with, but its drawback is that nesting is limited to however many `$Level` variables we build. This approach doesn't allow us to match to an *arbitrary level.* (Murphy's Law being what it is, if we happen to pick *X* levels to support, we'll run into data with *X+1* levels of nesting.)

Luckily, we can use a dynamic regex to handle nesting to an arbitrary level. To get there, realize that each of the `$Level` variables beyond the first is constructed identically: when it needs to match an addition level of nesting, it includes the `$Level` variable below it. But if the `$Level` variables are all the same, it could just as well include the `$Level` above it. In fact, if they're all the same, it could just include *itself.* If it could somehow include itself when it wanted to match another level of nesting, it would recursively handle *any* level of nesting.

And that's just what we can do with a dynamic regex. If we create a regex object comparable to one of the `$Level` variables, we can refer to it from within a dynamic regex. (A dynamic-regex construct can contain arbitrary Perl code, so long as its results can be interpreted as a regular expression; Perl code that merely returns a pre-existing regex object certainly fits the bill.) If we put our `$Level`-like regex object into `$LevelN`, we can refer to it with ⌜`(??{ $LevelN })`⌟, like this:

```
my $LevelN;  # This must be predeclared because it's used in its own definition.
$LevelN = qr/ \(( [^()] | (??{ $LevelN }) )* \) /x;
```

This matches arbitrarily nested parenthesized text, and can be used just like `$Level0` was used earlier:

```
if ($text =~ m/\b( \w+$LevelN )/x) {
   print "found function call: $1\n";
}
```

Phew! It's not necessarily easy to wrap one's brain around this, but once it "clicks," it's a valuable tool.

Now that we have the basic approach worked out, I'd like to make a few tweaks for efficiency's sake. I'll replace the capturing parentheses with atomic grouping (there's no need to capture, nor to backtrack), and once that's done, I can change ⌜`[^()]`⌟ to ⌜`[^()]+`⌟ for added efficiency. (Don't make this change without using atomic grouping, or you'll set yourself up for a neverending match ☞ 226.)

Finally, I'd like to move the ⌜`\(`⌟ and ⌜`\)`⌟ so that they directly surround the dynamic regex. This way, the dynamic regex construct isn't invoked by the engine until it's sure that there's something for it to match. Here's the revised version:

```
$LevelN = qr/ (?> [^()]+ | \( (??{ $LevelN }) \)  )* /x;
```

Since this no longer has outer ⌜`\(`⋯`\)`⌟, we need to include them ourselves when invoking `$LevelN`.

As a side effect of that, we have the flexibility to apply it where there *may* be sets of parentheses, not just where there *are* sets of parentheses:

```
if ($text =~ m/\b( \w+ \( $LevelN \) )/x) {
    print "found function call: $1\n";
}
```

```
if (not $text =~ m/^ $LevelN $/x) {
    print "mismatched parentheses!\n";
}
```

You can see another example of `$LevelN` in action on page 343;

Using the Embedded-Code Construct

The embedded-code construct is particularly useful for regex debugging, and for accumulating information about a match while it's happening. The next few pages walk through a series of examples that eventually lead to a method for mimicking POSIX match semantics. The journey there is perhaps more interesting than the actual destination (unless you need POSIX match semantics, of course) because of the useful techniques and insight we gain along the way.

We'll start with some simple regex debugging techniques.

Using embedded code to display match-time information

This code:

```
"abcdefgh" =~ m{
    (?{ print "starting match at [$`|$']\n" })
    (?:d|e|f)
}x;
```

produces:

```
starting match at [|abcdefgh]
starting match at [a|bcdefgh]
starting match at [ab|cdefgh]
starting match at [abc|defgh]
```

The embedded-code construct is the first thing in the regex, and so executes

```
print "starting match at [$`|$']\n"
```

whenever the regex starts a new match attempt. The displayed string uses the `$`` and `$'` variables (☞ 300)[†] to print the target text being matched, with '|' inserted to mark the current location in the match (which in this case is where the match attempt is starting). From the result, you can tell that the regex was applied four times by the transmission (☞ 148) before it was successful.

---

† Normally, I recommend against using the special match variables `$``, `$&`, and `$'`, as they can inflict a major efficiency penalty on the entire program (☞ 356), but they're fine for temporary debugging.

In fact, if we were to add

```
(?{ print "matched at [$`<$&>$']\n" })
```

just before the end of the regex, it would show the match:

```
matched at [abc<d>efgh]
```

Now, compare the first example with the following, which is identical except that the "main" regex is now ⌈[def]⌉ rather than ⌈(?:d|e|f)⌉:

```
"abcdefgh" =~ m{
  (?{  print "starting match at [$`|$']\n" })
  [def]
}x;
```

In theory, the results should be identical, yet this produces only:

```
starting match at [abc|defgh]
```

Why the difference? Perl is smart enough to apply the *initial class discrimination* optimization (☞ 246) to the regex with ⌈[def]⌉, thereby allowing the transmission to bypass attempts it felt were obviously destined to fail. As it turns out, it was able to bypass all attempts except the one that resulted in a match, and the embedded-code construct allows us to see that happen.

---

panic: top_env

If you're working with embedded code or a dynamic regex, and your program suddenly ends with an unceremonial

```
panic: top_env
```

it is likely due to a syntax error in the code part of the regex. Perl currently doesn't handle certain kinds of broken syntax well, and the panic is the result. The solution, of course, is to correct the syntax.

Using embedded code to see all matches

Perl has a Traditional NFA engine, so it stops the moment a match is found, even though there may be additional possible matches. With the clever use of embedded code, we can trick Perl into showing us *all* possible matches. To see how, let's revisit the silly 'oneself' example from page 177:

```
"oneselfsufficient" =~ m{
    one(self)?(selfsufficient)?
   (?{ print "matched at [$`<$&>$']\n" })
}x;
```

As might be expected, this displays

```
matched at [<oneself>sufficient]
```

indicating that 'oneselfsufficient' had been matched at that point in the regex.

It's important to realize that despite the "matched" in the message, the print is not actually showing "the match," but rather the match *to that point*. The distinction is academic with this example because the embedded-code construct is the last thing in the regex. We know that the regex does indeed finish the moment the embedded-code construct has finished, reporting that same result as the actual match.

What if we added ⌈(?!)⌉ just after the embedded-code construct? ⌈(?!)⌉ is a negative lookahead that always fails. When it fails just after the embedded code is processed (just after a "matched" message is printed), it forces the engine to backtrack in search of a (new) match. The failure is forced after every "match" is printed, so we end up exploring every path to a match, and thus see all possible matches:

```
matched at [<oneself>sufficient]
matched at [<oneselfsufficient>]
matched at [<one>selfsufficient]
```

What we've done ensures that the overall match attempt actually fails, but in doing so we've got the regex engine to report all the possible matches. Without the ⌈(?!)⌉, Perl returns the first match found, but with it, we can see the remaining permutations.

With that in mind, what do you think the following prints?

```
"123" =~ m{
   \d+
   (?{ print "matched at [$`<$&>$']\n" })
   (?!)
}x;
```

It displays:

```
matched at [<123>]
matched at [<12>3]
matched at [<1>23]
matched at [1<23>]
matched at [1<2>3]
matched at [12<3>]
```

Hopefully at least the first three were expected, but the rest might be unexpected if you're not on your toes. The (?!) forces backtracking and the eventual appearance of the 2nd and 3rd lines. When the attempt at the start of the line fails, the transmission reapplies the regex again starting just before the 2nd character. (Chapter 4 explains this in great detail.) The 4th and 5th lines shown are from that second attempt, and the last line shown is from the third attempt.

So, adding the (?!) really does cause it to show *all* possible matches, not just all of them from a particular starting point. It may be useful to see only the possible matches from a particular starting point; we'll look into that in a bit.

Finding the longest match

Now, instead of showing all the matches, let's find and save the longest match. We can do this by using a variable to keep track of the longest match seen so far and comparing each new "almost match" against it. Here is the solution with the 'oneself' example:

```
$longest_match = undef;  # We'll keep track of the longest match here

"oneselfsufficient" =~ m{
   one(self)?(selfsufficient)?
   (?{
       # Check to see if the current match ($&) is the longest so far
       if (not defined($longest_match)
           or
           length($&) > length($longest_match))
       {
           $longest_match = $&;
       }
   })
   (?!)  # Force failure so we'll backtrack to find further "matches"
}x;

# Now report the accumulated result, if any
if (defined($longest_match)) {
   print "longest match=[$longest_match]\n";
} else {
   print "no match\n";
}
```

Not surprisingly, this shows 'longest match=[oneselfsufficient]'. That bit of embedded code is pretty long, and something we'll likely use in the future, so let's encapsulate it and the ⌜(?!)⌟ into their own regex object:

```
my $RecordPossibleMatch = qr{
   (?{
       # Check to see if the current match ($&) is the longest so far
       if (not defined($longest_match)
           or
           length($&) > length($longest_match))
       {
           $longest_match = $&;
       }
   })
   (?!)  # Force failure so we'll backtrack to find further "matches"
}x;
```

Here's a simple example that uses finds '9938', the longest match *overall*:

```
$longest_match = undef; # We'll keep track of the longest match here
"800-998-9938" =~ m{ \d+ $RecordPossibleMatch }x;
# Now report the accumulated result, if any
if (defined($longest_match)) {
    print "longest match=[$longest_match]\n";
} else {
    print "no match\n";
}
```

Finding the longest-leftmost match

Now that we know how to find the longest match overall, let's restrict it to finding the longest-*leftmost* match. That just happens to be the match that a POSIX NFA would find (☞ 177). To accomplish this, we need to disable the transmission's bump-ahead *if* we've seen a match so far. That way, once we find the first match, normal backtracking still brings us to any other matches available from the same starting location (allowing us to keep track of the longest match), but the disabled bump-ahead inhibits the finding of matches that start later in the string.

Perl doesn't give us direct hooks into the transmission, so we can't disable the bump-ahead directly, but we can get the same effect by not allowing the regex to proceed past the start if $longest_match is already defined. The test for that is `(?{ defined $longest_match})`, but that alone not enough, since it's just a test. The key to using the results of the test lies in a *conditional.*

Using embedded code in a conditional

To have the regex engine respond to the results of our test, we use the test as the *if* of an `(? if then | else)` conditional (☞ 138). Since we want the regex to stop if the test is true, we use a fail-now (?!) as the *then* part. (We don't need an *else* part, so we just omit it.) Here's a regex object that encapsulates the conditional:

```
my $BailIfAnyMatch = qr/(?(?{ defined $longest_match})(?!))/;
```

The *if* part is underlined, and the *then* part is shown in bold. Here it is in action, combined with the $RecordPossibleMatch defined on the facing page:

```
"800-998-9938" =~ m{ $BailIfAnyMatch \d+ $RecordPossibleMatch }x;
```

This finds '800', the POSIX "longest of all leftmost matches" match.

Using `local` in an Embedded-Code Construct

The use of `local` within an embedded-code construct takes on special meaning. Understanding it requires a good understanding of *dynamic scoping* (☞ 295) and of the "crummy analogy" from the Chapter 4's discussion of how a regex-directed NFA engine goes about its work (☞ 158). The following contrived (and, as we'll see, flawed) example helps to illustrate why, without a lot of extraneous clutter. It checks to see if a line is composed of only ⌈\w+⌋ and ⌈\s+⌋, but counts how many of the ⌈\w+⌋ are really ⌈\d+\b⌋:

```
my $Count = 0;

$text =~ m{
   ^ (?> \d+ (?{ $Count++ }) \b | \w+ | \s+ )* $
}x;
```

When this is matched against a string like '123 abc 73 9271 xyz', the $Count variable is left with a value of three. However, when applied to '123 abc 73xyz' it's left with a value of two, even though it should be left with a value of just one. The problem is that $Count is updated after matching '73', something that is matched by ⌈\d+⌋ but later "unmatched" via backtracking because the subsequent ⌈\b⌋ can't match. The problem arises because the code executed via the embedded-code construct is not somehow "unexecuted" when its part of the regex is "unmatched" via backtracking.

In case you have any confusion with the use of ⌈(?>···)⌋ atomic grouping (☞ 137) and the backtracking going on here, I'll mention that the atomic grouping is used to prevent a neverending-match (☞ 269), and does not affect backtracking *within* the construct, only backtracking *back into* the construct after it's been exited. So the ⌈\d+⌋ is free to be "unmatched" if the subsequent ⌈\b⌋ cannot match.

The easy solution for this contrived example is to put the ⌈\b⌋ before incrementing $Count, to ensure that it is incremented only when it won't be undone. However, I'd like to show a solution using `local`, to illustrate its effect within Perl executed during the application of a regex. With that in mind, consider this new version:

```
our $Count = 0;

$text =~ m{
   ^ (?> \d+ (?{ local($Count) = $Count + 1 }) \b | \w+ | \s+ )* $
}x;
```

The first change to notice is that $Count changed from a `my` variable to a global one (if you **use strict**, as I always recommend, you can't use an unqualified global variable unless you "declare" it with Perl's `our` declarator).

The other change is that the increment of $Count has been localized. Here's the key behavior: *when a variable is localized within a regex, the original value is replaced (the new value is lost) if the code with the `local` is "unmatched" because of backtracking.* So, even though `local($Count) = $Count + 1` is executed after '73' is matched by ⌈\d+⌋, changing $Count from one to two, that change is "localized to the success of the path" that the regex is on when `local` is called. When the ⌈\b⌋ fails, the regex engine logically backtracks to before the `local`, and $Count reverts to its original value of one. And that's the value it ends up having when the end of the regex is eventually reached.

Interpolating Embedded Perl

As a security measure, Perl doesn't normally allow an embedded-code construct ⌜(?{···})⌟ or a dynamic-subexpression construct ⌜(??{···})⌟ to be interpolated into the regex from a string variable. (They are allowed, though, from a regex object, as with $RecordPossibleMatch on page 334.) That is,

```
m{   (?{ print "starting\n" })   some regex···   }x;
```

is allowed, but

```
my $ShowStart = '(?{ print "starting\n" })';
   ⋮
m{ $ShowStart some regex···   }x;
```

is not. This limitation is imposed because it has long been common to include user input as part of a regex, and the introduction of these constructs suddenly allowing such a regex to run arbitrary code creates a huge security hole. So, the default is that it's disallowed.

If you'd like to allow this kind of interpolation, the declaration:

```
use re 'eval';
```

lifts the restriction. (With different arguments, the use re pragma can also be used for debugging; ☞ 361.)

Sanitizing user input for interpolation

If you use this and do allow user input to be interpolated, be sure that it has no embedded-Perl or dynamic-regex constructs. You can do this by checking against ⌜\(\s*\?+[p{]⌟. If this matches the input, it's not safe to use in a regex. The ⌜\s+⌟ is needed because the /x modifier allows spaces after the opening parentheses. (I'd think that they shouldn't be allowed there, but they are.) The plus quantifies ⌜\?⌟ so that both constructs are recognized. Finally, the p is included to catch the now-deprecated ⌜(?p{···})⌟ construct, the forerunner of ⌜(??{···})⌟.

I think it would be useful if Perl supported a modifier of some sort that allowed or prohibited embedded code on a per-regex or subexpression basis, but until one is introduced, you'll have to check for it yourself, as described above.

So, local is required to keep $Count consistent until the end of the regex. If we were to put ⌜(?{ print "Final count is $Count.\n" })⌟ at the end of the regex, it would report the proper count. Since we want to use $Count after the match, we need to save it to a non-localized variable at some point before the match officially ends. This is because all values that had been localized during the match are lost when the match finishes.

Here's an example:

```
my $Count = undef;
our $TmpCount = 0;

$text =~ m{
  ^ (?> \d+ (?{ local($TmpCount) = $TmpCount + 1 }) \b | \w+ | \s+ )* $
  (?{ $Count = $TmpCount }) # Save the "ending" $Count to a non-localized variable
}x;
if (defined $Count) {
    print "Count is $Count.\n";
} else {
    print "no match\n";
}
```

This seems like a lot of work for something so simple, but again, this is a contrived example designed just to show the mechanics of localized variables within a regex. We'll see practical use in "Mimicking Named Capture" on page 344.

A Warning About Embedded Code and my Variables

If you have a my variable declared *outside* a regex, but refer to it from *inside* regex embedded code, you must be very careful about a subtle issue with Perl's variable binding that has a very unsubtle impact. Before describing the issue, I'll note up front that if you use only global variables within regex embedded code, you don't have to worry about this issue, and you can safely skip this section. Warning: this section is not light reading.

This contrived example illustrates the problem:

```
sub CheckOptimizer
{
    my $text  = shift; # The first argument is the text to check.
    my $start = undef; # We'll note here where the regex is first applied.

    my $match = $text =~ m{
      (?{ $start = $-[0] if not defined $start}) # Save the first starting position
      \d # This is the regex being tested
    }x;

    if (not defined $start) {
        print "The whole match was optimized away.\n";
        if ($match) {
            # This can't possibly happen!
            print "Whoa, but it matched! How can this happen!?\n";
        }
    } elsif ($start == 0) {
        print "The match start was not optimized.\n";
    } else {
        print "The optimizer started the match at character $start.\n"
    }
}
```

This code has three my variables, but only one, $start, is related to this issue (the others are not referenced from within embedded code, so are not at issue). It works by first setting `$start` to the undefined value, then applying a match in which the leading component is an embedded-code construct that sets `$start` to the starting location of the attempt, but only if it hasn't already been set. The "starting location of the attempt" is derived from `$-[0]` (the first element of `@-` ☞ 302).

So, when this function is called with

```
CheckOptimizer("test 123");
```

the result is:

```
The optimizer started the match at character 5.
```

That's okay, but if we invoke the exact same call again, the second time shows:

```
The whole match was optimized away.
Whoa, but it matched! How can this happen!?
```

Even though the text checked by the regex is the same (as is the regex itself, for that matter), the result is different, and seems to be wrong. Why? The problem is that the second time through, the `$start` that the embedded code is updating is the one that existed the first time through, when the regex was compiled. The `$start` that the rest of the function uses is actually a new variable created afresh when the `my` is executed at the start of each function call.

The key to this issue is that `my` variables in embedded code are "locked in" (*bound*, in programming terminology) to *the specific instance* of the `my` variable that is active *at the time* the regex is compiled. (Regex compilation is discussed in detail starting on page 348.) Each time `CheckOptimizer` is called, a *new instance* of `$start` is created, but for esoteric reasons, the `$start` inside the embedded code still refers to the first instance that is now long gone. Thus, the instance of `$start` that the rest of the function uses doesn't receive the value ostensibly written to it within the regex.

This type of instance binding is called a *closure*, and books like *Programming Perl* and *Object Oriented Perl* show discuss why it's a valuable feature of the language. There is debate in the Perl community, however, as to just how much of a "feature" it is in this case. To most people, it's very unintuitive.

The solution is to not refer to `my` variables from within a regex unless you know that the regex literal will be compiled at least as often as the `my` instances are refreshed. For example, the `my` variable `$NestedStuffRegex` is used within the `SimpleConvert` subroutine in the listing on page 346, but we know this is not a problem because there's only ever one instance of `$NestedStuffRegex`. Its `my` is not in a function or a loop, so it's created just once when the script is loaded, with that same instance existing until the program ends.

Matching Nested Constructs with Embedded Code

The example on page 328 shows how to match arbitrarily nested pairs using a dynamic regex. That's generally the easiest way to do it, but it's instructive to see a method using only embedded-code constructs, so I'd like to show it to you here.

The approach is simply this: keep a count of how many open parentheses we've seen that have not yet been closed, and allow a closing parenthesis only if there are outstanding opens. We'll use embedded code to keep track of the count as we match through the text, but before looking at that, let's look at a (not yet working) skeleton the expression:

```
my $NestedGuts = qr{
  (?>
    (?:
        # Stuff not parenthesis
        [^()]+
        # An opening parenthesis
      |   \(
        # A closing parenthesis
      |   \)
    )*
  )
}x;
```

The atomic grouping is required for efficiency, to keep the ⌜([···]+ | ···)*⌟ from becoming a neverending match (☞ 226) if $NestedGuts is used as part of some larger expression that could cause backtracking. For example, if we used it as part of m/^\($NestedGuts \)$/x and applied it to '(this·is·missing·the·close', it would track and backtrack for a long time if atomic grouping didn't prune the redundant states.

To incorporate the counting, we need these four steps:

❶ Before beginning, the count must be initialized to zero:

```
(?{ local $OpenParens = 0 })
```

❷ When an open parenthesis is seen, we increment the count to indicate that one more set of parentheses has yet to balance.

```
(?{ $OpenParens++ })
```

❸ When a close parenthesis is seen, we check the count, and if it's currently positive, we decrement the count to recognize that one less set remains unbalanced. On the other hand, if the count is zero, we can't allow the match to continue (because the close parenthesis does not balance with an open), so we apply ⌜(?!)⌟ to force failure:

```
(?(?{ $OpenParens }) (?{ $OpenParens-- }) | (?!) )
```

This uses an ⌜(? *if* *then* | *else*)⌟ conditional (☞ 138), with an embedded-code construct checking the count as the *if*.

❹ Finally, once matching has completed, we check the count to be sure it's zero. If it's not, there weren't enough close parentheses to balance the opens, so we should fail:

```
(?(?{ $OpenParens != 0 })(?!))
```

Adding these items to skeleton expression gives us:

```
my $NestedGuts = qr{
    (?{ local $OpenParens = 0 })  # ❶ Counts the number of nested opens waiting to close.
    (?>  # atomic-grouping for efficiency
        (?:
            # Stuff not parenthesis
            [^()]+
            # ❷ An opening parenthesis
        |   \(    (?{ $OpenParens++ })
            # ❸ Allow a closing parenthesis, if we're expecting any
        |   \)  (?(?{ $OpenParens != 0 }) (?{ $OpenParens-- }) | (?!) )
        )*
    )
    (?(?{ $OpenParens != 0 })(?!))  # ❹ If there are any open parens left, don't finish
}x;
```

This can now be used just like `$LevelN` on page 330.

The `local` is used as a precaution to isolate this regex's use of `$OpenParens` from any other use the global variable might have within the program. Unlike `local`'s use in the previous section, it's not needed for backtracking protection because the atomic grouping in the regex ensures that once an alternative has been matched, it can't ever be "unmatched." In this case, the atomic grouping is used for both efficiency and to absolutely ensure that the text matched near one of the embedded-code constructs can't be unmatched by backtracking (which would break the sync between the value of `$OpenParens` and the number of parentheses actually matched).

Overloading Regex Literals

You can pre-process the literal parts of a regex literal in any way you like with *overloading*. The next sections show examples.

Adding start- and end-of-word metacharacters

Perl doesn't support ⌈\<⌋ and ⌈\>⌋ as start- and end-of-word metacharacters, and that's probably because it's rare that ⌈\b⌋ doesn't suffice. However, if we wish to have them, we can support them ourselves using overloading to replace '\<' and '\>' in a regex by ⌈(?<!\w)(?=\w)⌋ and ⌈(?<=\w)(?!\w)⌋, respectively.

First, we'll create a function, say, `MungeRegexLiteral`, that does the desired preprocessing:

```
sub MungeRegexLiteral($)
{
    my ($RegexLiteral) = @_; # Argument is a string
    $RegexLiteral =~ s/\\</(?<!\\w)(?=\\w)/g; # Mimic \< as start-of-word boundary
    $RegexLiteral =~ s/\\>/(?<=\\w)(?!\\w)/g; # Mimic \> as end-of-word boundary
    return $RegexLiteral; # Return possibly-modified string
}
```

When this function is passed a string like '···\<···', it converts it and returns the string '···(?<!\w)(?=\w)···'. Remember, because the replacement part of a substitution is like a double-quoted string, it needs '\\w' to get '\w' into the value.

Now, to install this so that it gets called automatically on each literal part of a regex literal, we put it into a file, say *MyRegexStuff.pm*, with the Perl mechanics for overloading:

```
package MyRegexStuff; # Best to call the package something unique
use strict;    # Good practice to always use this
use warnings; # Good practice to always use this
use overload; # Allows us to invoke Perl's overloading mechanism
# Have our regex handler installed when we're use'd ....
sub import { overload::constant qr => \&MungeRegexLiteral }

sub MungeRegexLiteral($)
{
    my ($RegexLiteral) = @_; # Argument is a string
    $RegexLiteral =~ s/\\</(?<!\\w)(?=\\w)/g; # Mimic \< as start-of-word boundary
    $RegexLiteral =~ s/\\>/(?<=\\w)(?!\\w)/g; # Mimic \> as end-of-word boundary
    return $RegexLiteral; # Return possibly-modified string
}

1; # Standard idiom so that a 'use' of this file returns something true
```

If we place *MyRegexStuff.pm* in the Perl library path (see PERLLIB in the Perl documentation), we can then invoke it from Perl script files in which we want the new features made available. For testing, though, we can just leave it in the same directory as the test script, invoking it with:

```
use lib '.';      # Look for library files in the current directory
use MyRegexStuff; # We now have our new functionality available!
    ⋮
$text =~ s/\s+\</ /g; # Normalize any type of whitespace before a word to a single space
    ⋮
```

We must use `MyRegexStuff` in any file in which we want this added support for regex literals, but the hard work of building *MyRegexStuff.pm* need be done only once. (The new support isn't available in *MyRegexStuff.pm* itself because it doesn't **use MyRegexStuff** — something you wouldn't want to do.)

Adding support for possessive quantifiers

Let's extend *MyRegexStuff.pm* to add support for possessive quantifiers like ⌈x++⌉ (☞ 140). Possessive quantifiers work like normal greedy quantifiers, except they never give up (never "unmatch") what they've matched. They can be mimicked with atomic grouping by simply removing the final '+' and wrapping everything in atomic quotes, e.g., by changing ⌈regex*+⌉ to ⌈(?> regex*)⌉ (☞ 173).

The *regex* part can be a parenthesized expression, a metasequence like ⌈\w⌉ or ⌈\x{1234}⌉, or even just a normal character. Handling all possible cases is difficult, so to keep the example simple for the moment, let's concentrate on ?+, *+, or ++ quantifying only a parenthesized expression. Using $LevelN from page 330, we can add

```
$RegexLiteral =~ s/(  \( $LevelN \) [*+?] )\+/(?>$1)/gx;
```

to the MungeRegexLiteral function.

That's it. Now, with it part of our overloaded package, we can use a regex literal with possessive quantifiers, like this example from page 198:

```
$text =~ s/"(\\.|[^"])*+"//; # Remove double-quoted strings
```

Extending this beyond just parenthesized expressions is tricky because of the variety of things that can be in a regular expression. Here's one attempt:

```
$RegexLiteral =~ s{
  (
    # Match something that can be quantified ...
    (?:  \\[\\abCdDefnrsStwWX] # \n, \w, etc.
      |  \\c. # \cA
      |  \\x[\da-fA-F]{1,2}     # \xFF
      |  \\x\{[\da-fA-F]*\}     # \x{1234}
      |  \\[pP]\{[^{}]+\}       # \p{Letter}
      |  \[\]?[^]]+\]           # "poor man's" class
      |  \\W                    # \*
      |  \( $LevelN \)          # (···)
      |  [^()*+?\\]             # almost anything else
    )
    # ... and is quantified ...
    (?: [*+?] | \{\d+(?:,\d*)?\} )
  )
  \+ # ... and has an extra '+' after the quantifier.
}{(?>$1)}gx;
```

The general form of this regex is the same as before: match something quantified possessively, remove the '+', and wrap the result in ⌈(?>···)⌉. It's only a half-hearted attempt to recognize the complex syntax of Perl regular expressions. The part to match a class is particularly needy, in that it doesn't recognize escapes within the class. Even worse, the basic approach is flawed because it doesn't understand every aspect of Perl regular expressions. For example, if faced with '\(blah\)++', it doesn't properly ignore the opening literal parenthesis, so it thinks the ⌈++⌉ is applied to more than just ⌈\)⌉.

These problems can be overcome with great effort, perhaps using a technique that carefully walks through the regex from start to finish (similar to the approach shown in the sidebar on page ☞ 130). I'd like to enhance the part that matches a character class, but in the end, I don't feel it's worth it to address the other issues, for two reasons. The first is that the situations in which it doesn't already work well are fairly contrived, so just fixing the character class part is probably enough to make it acceptable in practice. But in the end, Perl's regex overloading currently has a fatal flaw, discussed in the next section, which renders it much less useful than it might otherwise be.

Problems with Regex-Literal Overloading

Regex-literal overloading can be extremely powerful, at least in theory, but unfortunately, it's not very useful in practice. The problem is that it applies to only the *literal* part of a regex literal, and not the parts that are interpolated. For example, with the code **m/($MyStuff)*+//** our `MungeRegexLiteral` function is called twice, once with the literal part of the regex before the variable interpolation ("**(**"), and once with the part after ("**)*+**"). (It's never even given the contents of `$MyStuff`.) Since our function requires both parts at the same time, variable interpolation effectively disables it.

This is less of an issue with the support for \< and \> we added earlier, since they're not likely to be broken up by variable interpolation. But since overloading doesn't affect the contents of an interpolated variable, a string or regex object containing '\<' or '\>' would not be processed by overloading. Also, as the previous section touched on, when a regex literal is processed by overloading, it's not easy to be complete and accurate every time. Even something as simple as our support for \> gets in the way when given '\\>', ostensibly to match a '\' followed by '>'.

Another problem is that there's no way for the overload processing to know about the modifiers that the regex was applied with. In particular, it may be crucial to know whether /x was specified, but there's currently no way to know that.

Finally, be warned that using overloading disables the ability to include characters by their Unicode name (⌈\N{*name*}⌋ ☞ 290).

Mimicking Named Capture

Despite the shortcomings of overloading, I think it's instructive to see a complex example bringing together many special constructs. Perl doesn't offer named capture (☞ 137), but it can be mimicked with capturing parentheses and the $^N variable (☞ 301), which references the text matched by the most-recently-closed set of capturing parentheses. (I put on the hat of a Perl developer and added $^N support to Perl expressly to allow named-capture to be mimicked.)

As a simple example, consider:

```
⌈href\s*=\s*($HttpUrl)(?{ $url = $^N })⌋
```

This uses the `$HttpUrl` regex object developed on page 303. The underlined part is an embedded-code construct that saves the text matched by `$HttpUrl` to the variable `$url`. In this simple situation, it seems overkill to use `$^N` instead of `$1`, or to even use the embedded-code construct in the first place, since it seems so easy to just use `$1` after the match. But consider encapsulating part of that into a regex object, and then using it multiple times:

```
my $SaveUrl = qr{
    ($HttpUrl)              # Match an HTTP URL . . .
    (?{ $url = $^N })       #  . . . and save to $url
}x;
$text =~ m{
    http \s*=\s* ($SaveUrl)
  | src  \s*=\s* ($SaveUrl)
}xi;
```

Regardless of which matches, `$url` is set to the URL that matched. Again, in this particular use, you could use other means (such as the `$+` variable ☞ 301), but as `$SaveUrl` is used in more complex situations, the other solutions become more difficult to maintain, so saving to a named variable can be much more convenient.

One problem with this example is that values written to `$url` are not "unwritten" when the construct that wrote to them is unmatched via backtracking. So, we need to modify a localized temporary variable during the initial match, writing to the "real" variable only after an overall match has been confirmed, just as we did in the example on page 338.

The listing on the next page shows one way to solve this. From the user's point of view, after using ⌈(?<Num>**\d+**)⌋, the number matched by ⌈\d+⌋ is available in the global hash `%^N`, as `$^N{`**Num**`}`. Although future versions of Perl could decide to turn `%^N` into a special system variable of some sort, it's not currently special, so we're free to use it.

I could have chosen a name like `%NamedCapture`, but instead chose `%^N` for a few reasons. One is that it's similar to `$^N`. Another is that it's not required to be pre-declared with `our` when used under `use strict`. Finally, it's my hope that Perl will eventually add named capture natively, and I think adding it via `%^N` would be a fine idea. If that happens, `%^N` would likely be automatically dynamically scoped like the rest of the regex-related special variables (☞ 299). But as of now, it's a normal global variable, so is not dynamically scoped automatically.

Again, even this more-involved approach suffers from the same problems as anything using regex-literal overloading, such as an incompatibility with interpolated variables.

Mimicking Named Capture

```perl
package MyRegexStuff;
use strict;
use warnings;
use overload;
sub import { overload::constant('qr' => \&MungeRegexLiteral) }

my $NestedStuffRegex;  # This should be predeclared, because it's used in its own definition.
$NestedStuffRegex = qr{
  (?>
    (?:   # Stuff not parens, not '#', and not an escape . . .
        [^()\#\\]+
        # Escaped stuff . . .
      | (?s: \\. )
        # Regex comment . . .
      | \#.*\n
        # Matching parens, with more nested stuff inside . . .
      | \(  (??{ $NestedStuffRegex })   \)
    )*
  )
}x;

sub SimpleConvert($);   # This must be predeclared, as it's used recursively
sub SimpleConvert($)
{
  my $re = shift;   # Regex to mangle
  $re =~ s{
    \(\?  #    "(?"
        <  ( (?>\w+) ) >       #       < $1 >  $1 is an identifier
        ( $NestedStuffRegex )  #       $2 - possibly-nested stuff
      \)                       #    ")"
  }{
    my $id   = $1;
    my $guts = SimpleConvert($2);
    # We change
    #     (?<id>guts)
    # to
    #     (?: (guts)   # match the guts
    #            (?{
    #                local($^N{$id}) = $guts  # Save to a localized element of %^T
    #            })
    #        )
    "(?:($guts)(?{ local(\$^T{'$id'}) = \$^N }))"
  }xeog;
  return $re;   # Return mangled regex
}

sub MungeRegexLiteral($)
{
  my ($RegexLiteral) = @_;   # Argument is a string
  # print "BEFORE: $RegexLiteral\n";   # Uncomment this for debugging
  my $new = SimpleConvert($RegexLiteral);
  if ($new ne $RegexLiteral)
  {
    my $before = q/(?{ local(%^T) = () })/;   # Localize temporary hash
    my $after  = q/(?{ %^N = %^T        })/;   # Copy temp to "real" hash
    $RegexLiteral = "$before(?:$new)$after";
  }
  # print "AFTER:  $RegexLiteral\n";   # Uncomment this for debugging
  return $RegexLiteral;
}

1;
```

Perl Efficiency Issues

For the most part, efficiency with Perl regular expressions is achieved in the same way as with any tool that uses a Traditional NFA. Use the techniques discussed in Chapter 6 — the internal optimizations, the unrolling methods, the "Think" section — all apply to Perl.

There are, of course, Perl-specific issues as well, and in this section, we'll look at the following topics:

- **There's More Than One Way To Do It**   Perl is a toolbox offering many approaches to a solution. Knowing which problems are nails comes with understanding *The Perl Way*, and knowing which hammer to use for any particular nail goes a long way toward making more efficient and more understandable programs. Sometimes efficiency and understandability seem to be mutually exclusive, but a better understanding allows you to make better choices.

- **Regex Compilation, `qr/⋯/`, the `/o` Modifier, and Efficiency**   The interpolation and compilation of regex operands are fertile ground for saving time. The `/o` modifier, which I haven't discussed much yet, along with regex objects (`qr/⋯/`), gives you some control over when the costly re-compilation takes place.

- **The `$&` Penalty**   The three match side effect variables, `$``, `$&`, and `$'`, can be convenient, but there's a hidden efficiency *gotcha* waiting in store for any script that uses them, even once, anywhere. Heck, you don't even have to *use* them — the entire script is penalized if one of these variables even *appears* in the script.

- **The Study Function**   Since ages past, Perl has provided the `study(⋯)` function. Using it supposedly makes regexes faster, but it seems that no one really understands if it does, or why. We'll see whether we can figure it out.

- **Benchmarking**   When it comes down to it, the fastest program is the one that finishes first. (You can quote me on that.) Whether a small routine, a major function, or a whole program working with live data, benchmarking is the final word on speed. Benchmarking is easy and painless with Perl, although there are various ways to go about it. I'll show you the way I do it, a simple method that has served me well for the hundreds of benchmarks I've done while preparing this book.

- **Perl's Regex Debugging**   Perl's regex-debug flag can tell you about some of the optimizations the regex engine and transmission do, or don't do, with your regexes. We'll look at how to do this and see what secrets Perl gives up.

"There's More Than One Way to Do It"

There are often many ways to go about solving any particular problem, so there's no substitute for really knowing all that Perl has to offer when balancing efficiency and readability. Let's look at the simple problem of padding an IP address like '18.181.0.24' such that each of the four parts becomes exactly three digits: '018.181.000.024'. One simple and readable solution is:

```
$ip = sprintf("%03d.%03d.%03d.%03d", split(/\./, $ip));
```

This is a fine solution, but there are certainly other ways to do the job. In the interest of comparison, Table 7-6 examines various ways to achieve the same goal, and their relative efficiency (they're listed from the most efficient to the least). This example's goal is simple and not very interesting in and of itself, yet it represents a common text-handling task, so I encourage you to spend some time understanding the various approaches. You may even see some Perl techniques that are new to you.

Each approach produces the same result when given a correct IP address, but fails in different ways if given something else. If there is any chance that the data will be malformed, you'll need more care than any of these solutions provide. That aside, the practical differences lie in efficiency and readability. As for readability, #1 and #13 seem the most straightforward (although it's interesting to see the wide gap in efficiency). Also straightforward are #3 and #4 (similar to #1) and #8 (similar to #13). The rest all suffer from varying degrees of crypticness.

So, what about efficiency? Why are some less efficient than others? It's the interactions among how an NFA works (Chapter 4), Perl's many regex optimizations (Chapter 6), and the speed of other Perl constructs (such as sprintf, and the mechanics of the substitution operator). The substitution operator's /e modifier, while indispensable at times, does seem to be mostly at the bottom of the list.

It's interesting to compare two pairs, #3/#4 and #8/#14. The two regexes of each pair differ only in their use of parentheses — the one without the parentheses is just a bit faster than the one with. But #8's use of $& as a way to avoid parentheses comes at a high cost not shown by these benchmarks (☞ 355).

Regex Compilation, the /o Modifier, qr/···/, and Efficiency

An important aspect of Perl's regex-related efficiency relates to the setup work Perl must do behind the scenes when program execution reaches a regex operator, before actually applying the regular expression. The precise setup depends on the

Table 7-6: A Few Ways to Pad an IP Address

Rank	Time	Approach
1.	1.0×	`$ip = sprintf("%03d.%03d.%03d.%03d", split(m/\./, $ip));`

2.	1.3×	`substr($ip,  0, 0) = '0' if substr($ip,  1, 1) eq '.';`
		`substr($ip,  0, 0) = '0' if substr($ip,  2, 1) eq '.';`
		`substr($ip,  4, 0) = '0' if substr($ip,  5, 1) eq '.';`
		`substr($ip,  4, 0) = '0' if substr($ip,  6, 1) eq '.';`
		`substr($ip,  8, 0) = '0' if substr($ip,  9, 1) eq '.';`
		`substr($ip,  8, 0) = '0' if substr($ip, 10, 1) eq '.';`
		`substr($ip, 12, 0) = '0' while length($ip) < 15;`

3.	1.6×	`$ip = sprintf("%03d.%03d.%03d.%03d", $ip =~ m/\d+/g);`
4.	1.8×	`$ip = sprintf("%03d.%03d.%03d.%03d", $ip =~ m/(\d+)/g);`
5.	1.8×	`$ip = sprintf("%03d.%03d.%03d.%03d",` `             $ip =~ m/^(\d+)\.(\d+)\.(\d+)\.(\d+)$/);`
6.	2.3×	`$ip =~ s/\b(?=\d\b)/00/g;` `$ip =~ s/\b(?=\d\d\b)/0/g;`
7.	3.0×	`$ip =~ s/\b(\d(\d?)\b)/$2 eq '' ? "00$1" : "0$1"/eg;`
8.	3.3×	`$ip =~ s/\d+/sprintf("%03d", $&)/eg;`
9.	3.4×	`$ip =~ s/(?:(?<=\.)|^)(?=\d\b)/00/g;` `$ip =~ s/(?:(?<=\.)|^)(?=\d\d\b)/0/g;`
10.	3.4×	`$ip =~ s/\b(\d\d?\b)/'0' x (3-length($1)) . $1/eg;`
11.	3.4×	`$ip =~ s/\b(\d\b)/00$1/g;` `$ip =~ s/\b(\d\d\b)/0$1/g;`
12.	3.4×	`$ip =~ s/\b(\d\d?\b)/sprintf("%03d", $1)/eg;`
13.	3.5×	`$ip =~ s/\b(\d{1,2}\b)/sprintf("%03d", $1)/eg;`
14.	3.5×	`$ip =~ s/(\d+)/sprintf("%03d", $1)/eg;`
15.	3.6×	`$ip =~ s/\b(\d\d?(?!\d))/sprintf("%03d", $1)/eg;`
16.	4.0×	`$ip =~ s/(?:(?<=\.)|^)(\d\d?(?!\d))/sprintf("%03d", $1)/eg;`

type of regex operand. In the most common situation, the regex operand is a regex literal, as with m/···/ or s/···/···/ or qr/···/. For these, Perl has to do a few different things behind the scenes, each taking some time we'd like to avoid, if possible. First, let's look at what needs to be done, and then at ways we might avoid it.

The internal mechanics of preparing a regex

The behind-the-scenes work done to prepare a regex operand is discussed generally in Chapter 6 (☞ 241), but Perl has its unique twists.

Perl's pre-processing of regex operands happens in two general phases.

1. **Regex-literal processing** If the operand is a regex literal, it's processed as described in "How Regex Literals Are Parsed" (☞ 292). One of the benefits provided by this stage is variable interpolation.

2. **Regex Compilation** The regex is inspected, and if valid, compiled into an internal form appropriate for its actual application by the regex engine. (If invalid, the error is reported to the user.)

Once Perl has a compiled regex in hand, it can actually apply it to the target string, as per Chapters 4-6.

All that pre-processing doesn't necessarily need be done every time each regex operator is used. It must always be done the *first* time a regex literal is used in a program, but if execution reaches the same regex literal more than once (such as in a loop, or in a function that's called more than once), Perl can sometimes re-use some of the previously-done work. The next sections show when and how Perl might do this, and additional techniques available to the programmer to further increase efficiency.

Perl steps to reduce regex compilation

In the next sections, we'll look at two ways in which Perl avoids some of the pre-processing associated with regex literals: *unconditional caching* and *on-demand recompilation*.

Unconditional caching

If a regex literal has no variable interpolation, Perl knows that the regex can't change from use to use, so after the regex is compiled once, that compiled form is saved ("cached") for use whenever execution again reaches the same code. The regex is examined and compiled just once, no matter how often it's used during the program's execution. Most regular expressions shown in this book have no variable interpolation, and so are perfectly efficient in this respect.

Variables within embedded code and dynamic regex constructs don't count, as they're not *interpolated* into the value of the regex, but rather part of the unchanging code the regex executes. When my variables are referenced from within embedded code, there may be times that you wish it were interpreted every time: see the warning on page 338.

Just to be clear, caching lasts only as long as the program executes — nothing is cached from one run to the next.

On-demand recompilation

Not all regex operands can be cached. Consider this snippet:

```
my $today = (qw<Sun Mon Tue Wed Thu Fri Sat>)[(localtime)[6]];
# $today now holds the day ("Mon", "Tue", etc., as appropriate)

while (<LOGFILE>) {
    if (m/^$today:/i) {
    ⋮
```

The regex in m/^$today:/ requires interpolation, but the way it's used in the loop ensures that the result of that interpolation will be the same every time. It would be inefficient to recompile the same thing over and over each time through the loop, so Perl automatically does a simple string check, comparing the result of the interpolation against the result the last time through. If they're the same, the cached regex that was used the previous time is used again this time, eliminating the need to recompile. But if the result of the interpolation turns out to be different, the regex is recompiled. So, for the price of having to redo the interpolation and check the result with the cached value, the relatively expensive compile is avoided whenever possible.

How much do these features actually save? Quite a lot. As an example, I benchmarked the cost of pre-processing three forms of the $HttpUrl example from page 303 (using the extended $HostnameRegex). I designed the benchmarks to show the overhead of regex pre-processing (the interpolation, string check, compilation, and other background tasks), not the actual application of the regex, which is the same regardless of how you get there.

The results are pretty interesting. I ran a version that has no interpolation (the entire regex manually spelled out within m/···/), and used that as the basis of comparison. The interpolation and check, if the regex doesn't change each time, takes about 25× longer. The full pre-processing (which adds the recompilation of the regex each time) takes about 1,000× longer! Wow.

Just to put these numbers into context, realize that even the full pre-processing, despite being over 1,000× slower than the static regex literal pre-processing, still takes only about 0.00026 seconds on my system. (It benchmarked at a rate of about 3,846 per second; on the other hand, the static regex literal's pre-processing benchmarked at a rate of about 3.7 million per second.) Still, the savings of not having to do the interpolation are impressive, and the savings of not having to recompile are down right fantastic. In the next sections, we'll look at how you can take action to enjoy these savings in even more cases.

The "compile once" /o modifier

Put simply, if you use the /o modifier with a regex literal operand, the regex literal will be inspected and compiled just once, regardless of whether it uses interpolation. If there's no interpolation, adding /o doesn't buy you anything because expressions without interpolation are always cached automatically. If there *is* interpolation, the first time execution arrives at the regex literal, the normal full preprocessing happens, but because of /o, the internal form is cached. If execution comes back again to the same regex operator, that cached form is used directly.

Here's the example from the previous page, with the addition of /o:

```
my $today = (qw<Sun Mon Tue Wed Thu Fri Sat>)[(localtime)[6]];

while (<LOGFILE>) {
    if (m/^$today:/io) {
        ⋮
```

This is now much more efficient because the regex ignores $today on all but the first iteration through the loop. Not having to interpolate or otherwise pre-process and compile the regex every time represents a real savings that Perl couldn't do for us automatically because of the variable interpolation: $today *might* change, so Perl must play it safe and reinspect it each time. By using /o, we tell Perl to "lock in" the regex after the regex literal is first pre-processed and compiled. It's safe to do this when we know that the variables interpolated into a regex literal won't change, or when we don't want Perl to use the new values even if they do change.

Potential "gotchas" of /o

There's an important "gotcha" to watch out for with /o. Consider putting our example into a function:

```
sub CheckLogfileForToday()
{
    my $today = (qw<Sun Mon Tue Wed Thu Fri Sat>)[(localtime)[6]];

    while (<LOGFILE>) {
        if (m/^$today:/io) {  #dangerous -- has a gotcha
            ⋮
        }
    }
}
```

Remember, /o indicates that the regex operand should be compiled *once*. The first time CheckLogfileForToday() is called, a regex operand representing the current day is locked in. If the function is called again some time later, even though $today may change, it will not be not inspected again; the original locked-in regex is used every time for the duration of execution.

This is a major shortcoming, but as we'll see in the next section, regex objects provide a best-of-both-worlds way around it.

Using regex objects for efficiency

All the discussion of pre-processing we've seen so far applies to regex *literals*. The goal has been to end up with a compiled regex with as little work as possible. Another approach to the same end is to use a regex *object*, which is basically a ready-to-use compiled regex encapsulated into a variable. They're created with the qr/…/ operator (☞303).

Here's a version of our example using a regex object:

```
sub CheckLogfileForToday()
{
    my $today = (qw<Sun Mon Tue Wed Thu Fri Sat>)[(localtime)[6]];

    my $RegexObj = qr/^$today:/i; # compiles once per function call

    while (<LOGFILE>) {
        if ($_ =~ $RegexObj) {
                 ⋮
        }
    }
}
```

Here, a new regex object is created each time the function is called, but it is then used directly for each line of the log file. When a regex object is used as an operand, it undergoes none of the pre-processing discussed throughout this section. The pre-processing is done when the regex object is *created*, not when it's later *used*. You can think of a regex object, then, as a "floating regex cache," a ready-to-use compiled regex that you can apply whenever you like.

This solution has the best of both worlds: it's efficient, since only one regex is compiled during each function call (not with each line in the log file), but, unlike the previous example where /o was used inappropriately, this example actually works correctly with multiple calls to CheckLogfileForToday().

Be sure to realize that there are two regex operands in this example. The regex operand of the qr/…/ is *not* a regex object, but a regex literal supplied to qr/…/ to *create* a regex object. The object is then used as the regex operand for the =~ match operator in the loop.

Using m/…/ with regex objects

The use of the regex object,

```
    if ($_ =~ $RegexObj) {
```

can also be written as:

```
    if (m/$RegexObj/) {
```

This is not a normal regex literal, even though it looks like one. When the only thing in the "regex literal" is a regex object, it's just the same as using a regex object. This is useful for several reasons. One is simply that the m/···/ notation may be more familiar, and perhaps more comfortable to work with. It also relieves you from explicitly stating the target string $_, which makes things look better in conjunction with other operators that use the same default. Finally, it allows you to use the /g modifier with regex objects.

Using /o with qr/···/

The /o modifier can be used with qr/···/, but you'd certainly not want to in this example. Just as when /o is used with any of the other regex operators, qr/···/o locks in the regex the first time it's used, so if used here, $RegexObj would get the same regex object each time the function is called, regardless of the value of $today. That would be the same mistake as when we used m/···/o on page 352.

Using the default regex for efficiency

The default regex (☞ 308) feature of regex operators can be used for efficiency, although the need for it has mostly been eliminated with the advent of regex objects. Still, I'll describe it quickly. Consider:

```
sub CheckLogfileForToday()
{
    my $today = (qw<Sun Mon Tue Wed Thu Fri Sat>)[(localtime)[6]];

    # Keep trying until one matches, so the default regex is set.
    "Sun:" =~ m/^$today:/i or
    "Mon:" =~ m/^$today:/i or
    "Tue:" =~ m/^$today:/i or
    "Wed:" =~ m/^$today:/i or
    "Thu:" =~ m/^$today:/i or
    "Fri:" =~ m/^$today:/i or
    "Sat:" =~ m/^$today:/i;

    while (<LOGFILE>) {
        if (m//) { # Now use the default regex
            ⋮
        }
    }
}
```

The key to using the default regex is that a match must be successful for it to be set, which is why this example goes to such trouble to get a match after $today has been set. As you can see, it's fairly kludgey, and I wouldn't recommend it.

Understanding the "Pre-Match" Copy

While doing matches and substitutions, Perl sometimes must spend extra time and memory to make a pre-match copy of the target text. As we'll see, sometimes this copy is used in support of important features, but sometimes it's not. When the copy is made but not used, the wasted effort is an inefficiency we'd like to avoid, especially in situations where the target text is very long, or speed particularly important.

In the next sections, we'll look at when and why Perl might make a pre-match copy of the target text, when the copy is actually used, and how we might avoid the copy when efficiency is at a premium.

Pre-match copy supports $1, $&, $´, $+, …

Perl makes a pre-match copy of the original target text of a match or substitution to support $1, $&, and the other after-match variables that actually hold text (☞ 299). After each match, Perl doesn't actually create each of these variables because many (or all) may never be used by the program. Rather, Perl just files away a copy of the original text, remembers *where* in that original string the various matches happened, and then refers to that if and when $1 or the like is actually used. This requires less work up-front, which is good, because often, some or all of these after-match variables are not even used. This is a form of "lazy evaluation," and successfully avoids a lot of unneeded work.

Although Perl saves work by not creating $1 and the like until they're used, it still has to do the work of saving the extra copy of the target text. But why does this really need to be done? Why can't Perl just refer to that original text to begin with? Well, consider:

```
$Subject =~ s/^(?:Re:\s*)+//;
```

After this, $& properly refers to the text that was removed from $Subject, but since it was *removed* from $Subject, Perl can't refer to $Subject itself when providing for a subsequent use of $&. The same logic applies for something like:

```
if ($Subject =~ m/^SPAM:(.+)/i) {
    $Subject = "-- spam subject removed --";
    $SpamCount{$1}++;
}
```

By the time $1 is referenced, the original $Subject has been erased. Thus, Perl must make an internal pre-match copy.

The pre-match copy is not always needed

In practice, the primary "users" of the pre-match copy are $1, $2, $3, and the like. But what if a regex doesn't even have capturing parentheses? If it doesn't, there's no need to even worry about $1, so any work needed to support it can be bypassed. So, at least those regexes that don't have capturing parentheses can avoid the costly copy? Not always . . .

The variables $`, $&, and $' are naughty

The three variables $`, $&, and $' aren't related to capturing parentheses. As the text before, of, and after the match, they can potentially apply to *every* match and substitution. Since it's impossible for Perl to tell which match any particular use of one of these variables refers to, Perl must make the pre-match copy *every time*.

It might sound like there's no opportunity to avoid the copy, but Perl is smart enough to realize that if these variables do not appear in the program, *anywhere* (including in any library that might be used) the blind copying to support them is no longer needed. **Thus, ensuring that you don't use $`, $&, and $' allows all matches without capturing parentheses to dispense with the pre-match copy — a handsome optimization!** Having even one $`, $&, or $' anywhere in the program means the optimization is lost. How unsociable! For this reason, I call these three variables "naughty."

How expensive is the pre-match copy?

I ran a simple benchmark, checking m/c/ against each of the 130,000 lines of C that make up the main Perl source. The benchmark noted whether a 'c' appeared on each line, but didn't do anything further, since the goal was to determine the effect of the behind-the-scenes copying. I ran the test two different ways: once where I made sure not to trigger the pre-match copy, and once where I made sure to do so. The only difference, therefore, was in the extra copy overhead.

The run with the pre-match copying consistently took over 40 percent longer than the one without. This represents an "average worst case," so to speak, since the benchmark didn't do any "real work," whose time would reduce the relative relevance of (and perhaps overshadow) the extra overhead.

On the other hand, in true worst-case scenarios, the extra copy might truly be an overwhelming portion of the work. I ran the same test on the same data, but this time as *one huge line* incorporating the more than 3.5 megabytes of data, rather than the 50,000 or so reasonably sized lines. Thus, the relative performance of a single match can be checked. The match without the pre-match copy returned almost immediately, since it was sure to find a 'c' somewhere near the start of the string. Once it did, it was finished. The test *with* the pre-match copy is the same except that it had to make a copy of the huge string first. It took over 7,000 times longer! Knowing the ramifications, therefore, of certain constructs allows you to tweak your code for better efficiently.

Avoiding the pre-match copy

It would be nice if Perl knew the programmer's intentions and made the copy only as necessary. But remember, the copies are not "bad" — Perl's handling of these bookkeeping drudgeries behind the scenes is why we use it and not, say, C or assembly language. Indeed, Perl was first developed in part to free users from the mechanics of bit fiddling so they could concentrate on creating solutions to problems.

Never use naughty variables. Still, it's nice to avoid the extra work if possible. Foremost, of course, is to never use `$``, `$&`, or `$'` *anywhere* in your code. Often, `$&` is easy to eliminate by wrapping the regex with capturing parentheses, and using `$1` instead. For example, rather than using `s/<\w+>/\L$&\E/g` to lowercase certain HTML tags, use `s/(<\w+>)/\L$1\E/g` instead.

`$`` and `$'` can often be easily mimicked if you still have an unmodified copy of the original target string. After a match against a given *target*, the following shows valid replacements:

Variable	Mimicked with
`$``	`substr(`*target*`, 0, $-[0])`
`$&`	`substr(`*target*`, $-[0], $+[0] - $-[0])`
`$'`	`substr(`*target*`, $+[0])`

Since `@-` and `@+` (☞ 302) are arrays of *positions* in the original target string, rather than actual *text* in it, they can be safely used without an efficiency penalty.

I've included a substitute for `$&` in there as well. This may be a better alternative to wrapping with capturing parentheses and using `$1`, as it may allow you to eliminate capturing parentheses altogether. Remember, the whole point of avoiding `$&` and friends is to avoid the copy for matches that have no capturing parentheses. If you make changes to your program to eliminate `$&`, but end up adding capturing parentheses to every match, you haven't saved anything.

Don't use naughty modules. Of course, part of not using `$``, `$&`, or `$'` is to not use modules that use them. The core modules that come with Perl do not use them, except for the `English` module. If you wish to use that module, you can have it not apply to these three variables by invoking it as:

```
use English '-no_match_vars';
```

This makes it safe. If you download modules from CPAN or elsewhere, you may wish to check to see if they use the variables. See the sidebar on the next page for a technique to check to see if your program is infected with any of these variables.

How to Check Whether Your Code is Tainted by $&

It's not always easy to notice whether your program is naughty (references $&, $`, or $'), especially with the use of libraries, but there are several ways to find out. The easiest is perhaps to use the **-c** and **-Mre=debug** command-line arguments (☞ 361) and look toward the end of the output for either '`Enabling $` $& $' support`' or '`Omitting $` $& $' support`'. If it's enabled, the code is tainted.

It's possible (but unlikely) that the code could be tainted by the use of a naughty variable within an eval that's not known to Perl until it's executed. One option to catch those as well is to install the `Devel::SawAmpersand` package from CPAN (`http://www.cpan.org`):

```
END {
    require Devel::SawAmpersand;
    if (Devel::SawAmpersand::sawampersand) {
        print "Naughty variable was used!\n";
    }
}
```

Included with `Devel::SawAmpersand` comes `Devel::FindAmpersand`, a package that purportedly shows you where the offending variable is located. Unfortunately, it doesn't work reliably with the latest versions of Perl. Also, they both have some installation issues, so your mileage may vary. (Check `http://regex.info/` for possible updates.)

Also, it may be interesting to see how you can check for naughtiness by just checking for the performance penalty:

```
use Time::HiRes;
sub CheckNaughtiness()
{
    my $text = 'x' x 10_000; # Create some non-small amount of data.

    # Calculate the overhead of a do-nothing loop.
    my $start = Time::HiRes::time();
    for (my $i = 0; $i < 5_000; $i++)  {  }
    my $overhead = Time::HiRes::time() - $start;

    # Now calculate the time for the same number of simple matches.
    $start = Time::HiRes::time();
    for (my $i = 0; $i < 5_000; $i++)  { $text =~ m/^/  }
    my $delta = Time::HiRes::time() - $start;

    # A differential of 5 is just a heuristic.
    printf "It seems your code is %s (overhead=%.2f, delta=%.2f)\n",
        ($delta > $overhead*5) ? "naughty" : "clean", $overhead, $delta;
}
```

The Study Function

In contrast to optimizing the regex itself, study(⋯) optimizes certain kinds of searches of a *string*. After studying a string, a regex (or multiple regexes) can benefit from the cached knowledge when applied to the string. It's generally used like this:

```
while (<>)
{
    study($_); # Study the default target $_ before doing lots of matches on it
    if (m/regex 1/) { ⋯ }
    if (m/regex 2/) { ⋯ }
    if (m/regex 3/) { ⋯ }
    if (m/regex 4/) { ⋯ }
}
```

What study does is simple, but understanding when it's a benefit can be quite difficult. It has no effect whatsoever on any values or results of a program—the only effects are that Perl uses more memory, and that overall execution time might increase, stay the same, or (here's the goal) decrease.

When a string is studied, Perl takes some time and memory to build a list of places in the string that each character is found. On most systems, the memory required is four times the size of the string). study's benefit can be realized with each subsequent regex match against the string, but only until the string is modified. Any modification of the string invalidates the study list, as does studying a different string.

How helpful it is to have the target string studyied is highly dependent on the regex matching against it, and the optimizations that Perl is able to apply. For example, searching for literal text with m/foo/ can see a huge speedup due to study (with large strings, speedups of 10,000× are possible). But, if /i is used, that speedup evaporates, as /i currently removes the benefit of study (as well as some other optimizations).

When not to use study

- Don't use study on strings you intend to check only with /i, or when all literal text is governed by ⌜(?i)⌟ or ⌜(?i:⋯)⌟, as these disable the benefits of study.

- Don't use study when the target string is short. In such cases, the normal fixed-string cognizance optimization should suffice (☞ 247). How short is "short"? String length is just one part of a large, hard-to-pin-down mix, so when it comes down to it, only benchmarking *your* expressions on *your* data will tell you if study is a benefit. But for what it's worth, I generally don't even consider study unless the strings are at least several kilobytes long.

- Don't use `study` when you plan only a few matches against the target string before it's modified, or before you `study` a different string. An overall speedup is more likely if the time spent to `study` a string is amortized over many matches. With just a few matches, the time spent building the `study` list can overshadow any savings.

- Use `study` only on strings that you intend to search with regular expressions having "exposed" literal text (☞ 255). Without a known character that must appear in any match, `study` is useless. (Along these lines, one might think that `study` would benefit the `index` function, but it doesn't seem to.)

When study can help

`study` is best used when you have a large string you intend to match many times before the string is modified. A good example is a filter I use in the preparation of this book. I write in a home-grown markup that the filter converts to SGML (which is then converted to *troff*, which is then converted to PostScript). Within the filter, an entire chapter eventually ends up within one huge string (for instance, this chapter is about 475KB). Before exiting, I apply a bevy of checks to guard against mistaken markup leaking through. These checks don't modify the string, and they often look for fixed strings, so they're what `study` thrives on.

Benchmarking

If you really care about efficiency, it may be best to try benchmarking. Perl comes standard with the `Benchmark` module, which has fine documentation ("`perldoc Benchmark`"). Perhaps more out of habit than anything else, I tend to write my benchmarks from scratch. After

```
use Time::HiRes 'time';
```

I wrap what I want to test in something simple like:

```
my $start = time;
    ⋮
my $delta = time - $start;
printf "took %.1f seconds\n", $delta;
```

Important issues with benchmarking include making sure to benchmark enough work to show meaningful times, and to benchmark as much of the work you want to measure while benchmarking as little of the work you don't. This is discussed in more detail in Chapter 6 (☞ 232). It might take some time to get used to benchmarking in a reasonable way, but the results can be quite enlightening and rewarding.

Regex Debugging Information

Perl carries out a phenomenal number of optimizations to try to arrive at a match result quickly; some of the less esoteric ones are listed in Chapter 6's "Common Optimizations" (☞ 239), but there are many more. Most optimizations apply to only very specific cases, so any particular regex benefits from only some (or none) of them.

Perl has debugging modes that tell you about some of the optimizations. When a regex is first compiled, Perl figures out which optimizations go with the regex, and the debugging mode reports on some of them. The debugging modes can also tell you a lot about how the engine actually applies that expression. A detailed analysis of this debugging information is beyond the scope of even this book, but I'll provide a short introduction here.

You can turn on the debugging information by putting **use re 'debug';** in your code, and you can turn it back off with **no re 'debug';** but it turns off automatically at the end of the block or file in which the use is placed. (We've seen this use re pragma before, with different arguments, to allow embedded code in interpolated variables ☞ 337.)

Alternatively, if you want to turn it on for the entire script, you can use the -Mre=debug command-line argument. This is particularly useful just for inspecting how a single regex is compiled. Here's an example (edited to remove some lines that are not of interest):

```
❶ % perl -cw -Mre=debug -e 'm/^Subject: (.*)/'
❷ Compiling REx '^Subject: (.*)'
❸ rarest char j at 3
❹     1: BOL(2)
❺     2: EXACT <Subject: >(6)
          ⋮
❻    12: END(0)
❼ anchored 'Subject: ' at 0 (checking anchored) anchored(BOL) minlen 9
❽ Omitting $` $& $' support.
```

At ❶, I invoke *perl* at my shell prompt, using the command-line flags **-c** (which means to check the script, but don't actually execute it), **-w** (issue warnings about things Perl thinks are dubious — always used as a matter of principle), and **-Mre=debug** to turn on regex debugging. The **-e** flag means that the following argument, 'm/^Subject: (.*)/', is actually a mini Perl program to be run or checked.

Line ❸ reports the "rarest" character (the least common, as far as Perl guesses) from among those in the longest fixed substring part of the regex. Perl uses this for some optimizations (such as pre-check of required character/substring ☞ 244).

Lines ❹ through ❻ represents Perl's compiled form of the regex. For the most part, we won't be concerned much about it here. However, in even a casual look, line ❺ sticks out as understandable.

Line ❼ is where most of the action is. Some of the information that might be shown here includes:

`anchored '`*string*`' at` *offset*
> Indicates that any match must have the given *string*, starting *offset* characters from the start of the match. If '$' is shown immediately after '*string*', the *string* also ends the match.

`floating '`*string*`' at` *from..to*
> Indicates that any match must have the given *string*, but that it could start anywhere from *from* characters into the match, to *to* characters. If '$' is shown immediately after '*string*', the *string* also ends the match.

`stclass '`*list*`'`
> Shows the list of characters with which a match can begin.

`anchored(MBOL), anchored(BOL), anchored(SBOL)`
> The regex leads with ⌈^⌋. The MBOL version appears when the /m modifier is used, while BOL and SBOL appear when it's is not used. (The difference between BOL and SBOL is not relevant for modern Perl. SBOL relates to the regex-related $* variable, which has long been deprecated.)

`anchored(GPOS)`
> The regex leads with ⌈\G⌋.

`implicit`
> The `anchored(MBOL)` is an implicit one added by Perl because the regex begins with ⌈.*⌋.

`minlen` *length*
> Any match is at least *length* characters long.

`with eval`
> The regex has ⌈(?{···})⌋ or ⌈(??{···})⌋.

Line ❽ is not related to any particular regex. After loading the whole program, Perl reports if support for $& and friends has been enabled (☞ 356).

Run-time debugging information

We've already seen how we can use embedded code to get information about how a match progresses (☞ 331), but Perl's regex debugging can show much more. If you omit the -c compile-only option, Perl displays quite a lot of information detailing just how each match progresses.

If you see "Match rejected by optimizer," it means that one of the optimizations enabled the transmission to realize that the regex could never match the target text, and so the application is bypassed altogether. Here's an example:

```
% perl -w -Mre=debug -e '"this is a test" =~ m/^Subject:/;'
    ⋮
Did not find anchored substr 'Subject:'
Match rejected by optimizer
```

When debugging is turned on, you'll see the debugging information for any regular expressions that are used, not necessarily just your own. For example

```
% perl -w -Mre=debug -e 'use warnings'
    . . . lots of debugging information . . .
    ⋮
```

does nothing more than load the `warnings` module, but because that module has regular expressions, you see a lot of debugging information.

Other ways to invoke debugging messages

I've mentioned that you can use "`use re 'debug';`" or `-Mre=debug` to turn on regex debug information. However, if you use `debugcolor` instead of `debug` with either of these, and if you are using a terminal that understands ANSI terminal control escape sequences, the information is shown with highlighting that makes the output easier to read.

Another option is that if your perl binary has been compiled with extra debugging support turned on, you can use the `-Dr` command-line flag as a shorthand for `-Mre=debug`.

Final Comments

I'm sure it's obvious that I'm quite enamored with Perl's regular expressions, and as I noted at the start of the chapter, it's with good reason. Larry Wall, Perl's creator, apparently let himself be ruled by common sense and the Mother of Invention. Yes, the implementation has its warts, but I still allow myself to enjoy the delicious richness of the regex language and the integration with the rest of Perl.

However, I'm not a blind fanatic—Perl does not offer features that I wish for. Since several of the features I pined for in the first edition of this book were eventually added, I'll go ahead and wish for more here. The most glaring omission offered by other implementations is named capture (☞ 137). This chapter offers a way to mimic them, but with severe restrictions; it would be much nicer if they were built in. Class set operations (☞ 123) would also be very nice to have, even though with some effort, they can already be mimicked with lookaround (☞ 124).

Then there are possessive quantifiers (☞ 140). Perl has atomic grouping, which offers more overall functionality, but still, possessive quantifiers offer a clearer, more elegant solution in some situations. So, I'd like both notations. In fact, I'd also like two related constructs that no flavor currently offers. One is a simple "cut" operator, say ⌈\v⌋, which would immediately flush any saved states that currently exist (with this, ⌈x+\v⌋ would be the same as the possessive ⌈x++⌋ or the atomic grouping ⌈(?>x+)⌋). The other related construct I'd like would take the additional step of prohibiting any further bump-alongs by the transmission. It would mean "either a match is found from the current path I'm on, or no match will be allowed, period." Perhaps ⌈\V⌋ would be a good notation for that.

Somewhat related to my idea for ⌈\V⌋, I think that it would be useful to somehow have general hooks into the transmission. This would make it easier to do what we did on page 335.

Finally, I as I mentioned on page 337, I think it would be nice to have more control over when embedded code can be interpolated into a regex.

Perl is not the ideal regex-wielding language, but it very close, and is always getting better. In fact, as this book is going to print, Larry Wall is forging ahead on the design of Perl 6, including a recently-released paper describing his radical new ideas for the future of regular expressions. It will still be some while before Perl 6 is a reality, but the future certainly looks exciting.

8

Java

Java didn't come with a regex package until Java 1.4, so early programmers had to do without regular expressions. Over time, many programmers independently developed Java regex packages of varying degrees of quality, functionality, and complexity. With the early-2002 release of Java 1.4, Sun entered the fray with their `java.util.regex` package. In preparing this chapter, I looked at Sun's package, and a few others (detailed starting on page 372). So which one is best? As you'll soon see, there can be many ways to judge that.

In This Chapter Before looking at what's in this chapter, it's important to mention what's *not* in this chapter. In short, this chapter doesn't restate everything from Chapters 1 through 6. I understand that some readers interested only in Java may be inclined to start their reading with this chapter, and I want to encourage them not to miss the benefits of the preface and the earlier chapters: Chapters 1, 2, and 3 introduce basic concepts, features, and techniques involved with regular expressions, while Chapters 4, 5, and 6 offer important keys to regex understanding that directly apply to every Java regex package that I know of.

As for this chapter, it has several distinct parts. The first part, consisting of "Judging a Regex Package" and "Object Models," looks abstractly at some concepts that help you to understand an unfamiliar package more quickly, and to help judge its suitability for your needs. The second part, "Packages, Packages, Packages," moves away from the abstract to say a few words about the specific packages I looked at while researching this book. Finally, we get to the real fun, as the third part talks in specifics about two of the packages, Sun's `java.util.regex` and Jakarta's ORO package.

Judging a Regex Package

The first thing most people look at when judging a regex package is the regex flavor itself, but there are other technical issues as well. On top of that, "political" issues like source code availability and licensing can be important. The next sections give an overview of some points of comparison you might use when selecting a regex package.

Technical Issues

Some of the technical issues to consider are:

- **Engine Type?**   Is the underlying engine an NFA or DFA? If an NFA, is it a POSIX NFA or a Traditional NFA? (See Chapter 4 ☞ 143)

- **Rich Flavor?**   How full-featured is the flavor? How many of the items on page 113 are supported? Are they supported well? Some things are more important than others: lookaround and lazy quantifiers, for example, are more important than possessive quantifiers and atomic grouping, because lookaround and lazy quantifiers can't be mimicked with other constructs, whereas possessive quantifiers and atomic grouping can be mimicked with lookahead that allows capturing parentheses.

- **Unicode Support?**   How well is Unicode supported? Java strings support Unicode intrinsically, but does ⌜\w⌟ know which Unicode characters are "word" characters? What about ⌜\d⌟ and ⌜\s⌟? Does ⌜\b⌟ understand Unicode? (Does its idea of a word character match ⌜\w⌟'s idea of a word character?) Are Unicode properties supported? How about blocks? Scripts? (☞ 119) Which version of Unicode's mappings do they support: Version 3.0? Version 3.1? Version 3.2? Does case-insensitive matching work properly with the full breadth of Unicode characters? For example, does a case-insensitive 'ß' really match 'ss'? (Even in lookbehind?)

- **How Flexible?**   How flexible are the mechanics? Can the regex engine deal only with `String` objects, or the whole breadth of `CharSequence` objects? Is it easy to use in a multi-threaded environment?

- **How Convenient?**   The raw engine may be powerful, but are there extra "convenience functions" that make it easy to do the common things without a lot of cumbersome overhead? Does it, borrowing a quote from Perl, "make the easy things easy, and the hard things possible?"

- **JRE Requirements?**   What version of the JRE does it require? Does it need the latest version, which many may not be using yet, or can it run on even an old (and perhaps more common) JRE?

- **Efficient?** How efficient is it? The length of Chapter 6 tells you how much there is to be said on this subject. How many of the optimizations described there does it do? Is it efficient with memory, or does it bloat over time? Do you have any control over resource utilization? Does it employ lazy evaluation to avoiding computing results that are never actually used?

- **Does it Work?** When it comes down to it, does the package work? Are there a few major bugs that are "deal-breakers?" Are there many little bugs that would drive you crazy as you uncover them? Or is it a bulletproof, rock-solid package that you can rely on?

Of course, this list just the tip of the iceberg—each of these bullet points could be expanded out to a full chapter on its own. We'll touch on them when comparing packages later in this chapter.

Social and Political Issues

Some of the non-technical issues to consider are:

- **Documented?** Does it use Javadoc? Is the documentation complete? Correct? Approachable? Understandable?

- **Maintained?** Is the package still being maintained? What's the turnaround time for bugs to be fixed? Do the maintainers really care about the package? Is it being enhanced?

- **Support and Popularity?** Is there official support, or an active user community you can turn to for reliable support (and that you can provide support to, once you become skilled in its use)?

- **Ubiquity?** Can you assume that the package is available everywhere you go, or do you have to include it whenever you distribute your programs?

- **Licensing?** *May* you redistribute it when you distribute your programs? Are the terms of the license something you can live with? Is the source code available for inspection? *May* you redistribute modified versions of the source code? *Must* you?

Well, there are certainly a lot of questions. Although this book can give you the answers to some of them, it can't answer the most important question: *which is right for you?* I make some recommendations later in this chapter, but only you can decide which is best for you. So, to give you more background upon which to base your decision, let's look at one of the most basic aspects of a regex package: its object model.

Object Models

When looking at different regex packages in Java (or in any object-oriented language, for that matter), it's amazing to see how many different object models are used to achieve essentially the same result. An object model is the set of class structures through which regex functionality is provided, and can be as simple as one object of one class that's used for everything, or as complex as having separate classes and objects for each sub-step along the way. There is not an object model that stands out as the clear, obvious choice for every situation, so a lot of variety has evolved.

A Few Abstract Object Models

Stepping back a bit now to think about object models helps prepare you to more readily grasp an unfamiliar package's model. This section presents several representative object models to give you a feel for the possibilities without getting mired in the details of an actual implementation.

Starting with the most abstract view, here are some tasks that need to be done in using a regular expression:

> **Setup** . . .
> ❶ Accept a string as a regex; compile to an internal form.
> ❷ Associate the regex with the target text.
> **Actually apply the regex** . . .
> ❸ Initiate a match attempt.
> **See the results** . . .
> ❹ Learn whether the match is successful.
> ❺ Gain access to further details of a successful attempt.
> ❻ Query those details (what matched, where it matched, etc.).

These are the steps for just one match attempt; you might repeat them from ❸ to find the next match in the target string.

Now, let's look at a few potential object models from among the infinite variety that one might conjure up. In doing so, we'll look at how they deal with matching ⌜\s+(\d+)⌟ to the string 'May·16, ·1998' to find out that '·16' is matched overall, and '16' matched within the first set of parentheses (within "group one"). Remember, the goal here is to merely get a general feel for some of the issues at hand—we'll see specifics soon.

An "all-in-one" model

In this conceptual model, each regular expression becomes an object that you then use for everything. It's shown visually in Figure 8-1 below, and in pseudo-code here, as it processes all matches in a string:

```
DoEverythingObj myRegex = new DoEverythingObj("\\s+(\\d+)"); // ❶

   ⋮
while (myRegex.findMatch("May 16, 1998")) { // ❷, ❸, ❹
    String matched = myRegex.getMatchedText();  // ❻
    String num     = myRegex.group(1);          // ❻
   ⋮
}
```

As with most models in practice, the compilation of the regex is a separate step, so it can be done ahead of time (perhaps at program startup), and used later, at which point most of the steps are combined together, or are implicit. A twist on this might be to clone the object after a match, in case the results need to be saved for a while.

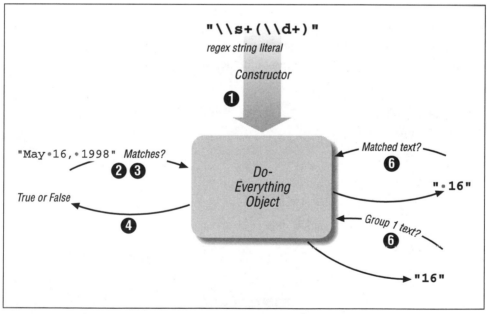

Figure 8-1: An "all-in-one" model

A *"match state" model*

This conceptual model uses two objects, a "Pattern" and a "Matcher." The Pattern object represents a compiled regular expression, while the Matcher object has all of the state associated with applying a Pattern object to a particular string. It's shown visually in Figure 8-2 below, and its use might be described as: "Convert a regex string to a Pattern object. Give a target string to the Pattern object to get a Matcher object that combines the two. Then, instruct the Matcher to find a match, and query the Matcher about the result." Here it is in pseudo-code:

```
PatternObj myPattern = new PatternObj("\\s+(\\d+)"); // ❶
    ⋮
MatcherObj myMatcher = myPattern.MakeMatcherObj("May 16, 1998"); // ❷
while (myMatcher.findMatch()) { // ❸, ❹
    String matched = myMatcher.getMatchedText();   // ❻
    String num     = myMatcher.Group(1);           // ❻
    ⋮
}
```

This might be considered conceptually cleaner, since the compiled regex is in an immutable (unchangeable) object, and all state is in a separate object. However, It's not necessarily clear that the conceptual cleanliness translates to any practical benefit. One twist on this is to allow the Matcher to be reset with a new target string, to avoid having to make a new Matcher with each string checked.

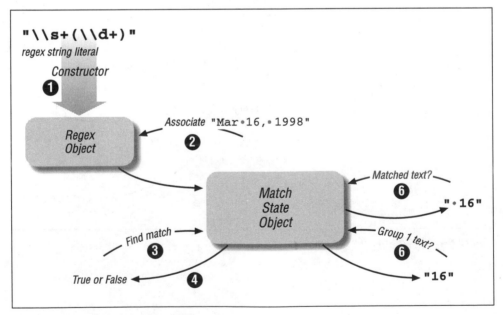

Figure 8-2: A "match state" model

A "match result" model

This conceptual model is similar to the "all-in-one" model, except that the result of a match attempt is not a Boolean, but rather a Result object, which you can then query for the specifics on the match. It's shown visually in Figure 8-3 below, and might be described as: "Convert a regex string to a Pattern object. Give it a target string and receive a Result object upon success. You can then query the Result object for specific." Here's one way it might be expressed it in pseudo-code:

```
PatternObj myPattern = new PatternObj("\\s+(\\d+)"); // ❶
   ⋮
ResultObj myResult = myPattern.findFirst("May 16, 1998"); // ❷, ❸, ❺
while (myResult.wasSuccessful()) { // ❹
    String matched = myResult.getMatchedText(); // ❻
    String num     = myResult.Group(1);         // ❻
   ⋮
    myResult = myPattern.findNext(); ❸, ❺
}
```

This compartmentalizes the results of a match, which might be convenient at times, but results in extra overhead when only a simple true/false result is desired. One twist on this is to have the Pattern object return `null` upon failure, to save the overhead of creating a Result object that just says "no match."

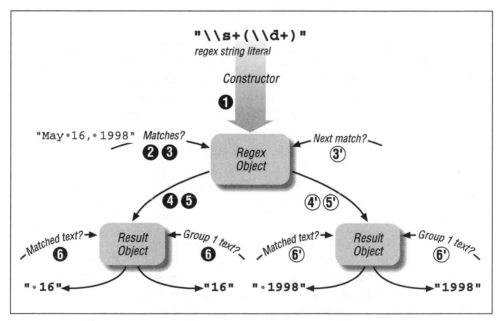

Figure 8-3: A "match result" model

Growing Complexity

These conceptual models are just the tip of the iceberg, but give you a feel for some of the differences you'll run into. They cover only simple matches — when you bring in search-and-replace, or perhaps string splitting (splitting a string into substrings separated by matches of a regex), it can become much more complex.

Thinking about search-and-replace, for example, the first thought may well be that it's a fairly simple task, and indeed, a simple "replace *this* with *that*" interface is easy to design. But what if the "that" needs to depend on what's matched by the "this," as we did many times in examples in Chapter 2 (☞ 67). Or what if you need to execute code upon every match, using the resulting text as the replacement? These, and other practical needs, quickly complicate things, which further increases the variety among the packages.

Packages, Packages, Packages

There are many regex packages for Java; the list that follows has a few words about those that I investigated while researching this book. (See this book's web page, `http://regex.info/`, for links). The table on the facing page gives a superficial overview of some of the differences among their flavors.

Sun

> `java.util.regex`   Sun's own regex package, finally standard as of Java 1.4. It's a solid, actively maintained package that provides a rich Perl-like flavor. It has the best Unicode support of these packages. It provides all the basic functionality you might need, but has only minimal convenience functions. It matches against `CharSequence` objects, and so is extremely flexible in that respect. Its documentation is clear and complete. It is the all-around fastest of the engines listed here. This package is described in detail later in this chapter.
> Version Tested: 1.4.0.
> License: comes as part of Sun's JRE. Source code is available under SCSL (Sun Community Source Licensing)

IBM

> `com.ibm.regex`   This is IBM's commercial regex package (although it's said to be similar to the `org.apache.xerces.utils.regex` package, which I did not investigate). It's actively maintained, and provides a rich Perl-like flavor, although is somewhat buggy in certain areas. It has very good Unicode support. It can match against `char[]`, `CharacterIterator`, and `String`. Overall, not quite as fast as Sun's package, but the only other package that's in the same class.
> Version Tested: 1.0.0.
> License: commercial product

Table 8-1: Superficial Overview of Some Java Package Flavor Differences

Feature	Sun	IBM	ORO	JRegex	Pat	GNU	Regexp
Basic Functionality							
Engine type	NFA	NFA	NFA	NFA	NFA	POSIX NFA	NFA
Deeply-nested parens	✓	✓	✓	✓	✓	✓	
dot doesn't match:	various	various	\n	\n , \r	\n	\r\n	\n
\s includes [\t\r\n\f]	✓	✓	✓			✓	✓
\w includes underscore	✓	✓	✓	✓	✓	✓	
Class set operators	✓	✓(partial)					
POSIX [[:···:]]	✓(partial)	✓(partial)	✓				
Metacharacter Support							
\A,\z,\Z	\A,\Z	\A,\z,\Z	\A,\z,\Z	\A,\z,\Z	\A,\Z	\A,\Z	
\G	✓	✓	✗		✓		
(?#···)		✓	✓	✓	✓	✓	
Octal escapes	✓		✓	✓	✓	✓	
2-, 4-, 6-digit hex escapes	2, 4	2, 4, 6	2	2, 4, 6	2		2, 4
Lazy quantifiers	✓	✓	✓	✓	✓	✓	✓
Atomic grouping		✓		✓			
Possessive quantifiers	✓						
Word boundaries	\b	\b	\b	\< \b \>	\b	\< \>	✗
Non-word boundaries	✓	✓	✓	✓	✗		✗
\Q···\E	✓					✗	
(*if then*| *else*) conditional		✓		✓			
Non-capturing parens	✓	✓	✓	✓	✓	✓	
Lookahead	✓	✓	✓	✓	✓	✓	
Lookbehind	✓	✗		✓	✓(partial)		
(?*mod*)	✓	✗	✓	✓	✓		
(?-*mod*:···)	✓	✗	✓	✓	✗		
(?*mod*:)	✓	✗		✓	✓		
Unicode-Aware Metacharacters							
Unicode properties	✓	✓		✓			
Unicode blocks	✓	✓		✓			
dot, ^, $	✓	✓					
\w		✓	✓	✓		✓	✓
\d		✓	✓	✓		✓	✓
\s		✓	partial	✓		partial	partial
Word boundaries	✓	✓	✓	✓	✗	✓	✓

✓ - supported   ✓- partial support   ✗ - supported, but buggy   (Version info ☞372)

ORO

org.apache.oro.text.regex   The Apache Jakarta project has two unrelated regex packages, one of which is "Jakarta-ORO." It actually contains multiple regex engines, each targeting a different application. I looked at one engine, the very popular Perl5Compiler matcher. It's actively maintained, and solid, although its version of a Perl-like flavor is much less rich than either the Sun or the IBM packages. It has minimal Unicode support. Overall, the regex engine is notably slower than most other packages. Its ⌈\G⌉ is broken. It can match against char[] and String.

One of its strongest points is that it has a vast, modular structure that exposes almost all of the mechanics that surround the engine (the transmission, search-and-replace mechanics, etc.) so advanced users can tune it to suit their needs, but it also comes replete with a fantastic set of convenience functions that makes it one of the easiest packages to work with, particularly for those coming from a Perl background (or for those having read Chapter 2 of this book). This is discussed in more detail later in this chapter.

Version Tested: 2.0.6.

License: ASL (Apache Software License)

JRegex

jregex   Has the same object model as Sun's package, with a fairly rich Perl-like feature set. It has good Unicode support. Its speed places it is in the middle of the pack.

Version Tested: v1.01

License: GNU-like

Pat

com.stevesoft.pat   It has a fairly rich Perl-like flavor, but no Unicode support. Very haphazard interface. It has provisions for modifying the regex flavor on the fly. Its speed puts it on the high end of the middle of the pack.

Version Tested: 1.5.3

License: GNU LGPL (GNU Lesser General Public License)

GNU

gnu.regexp   The more advanced of the two "GNU regex packages" for Java. (The other, gnu.rex, is a very small package providing only the most bare-bones regex flavor and support, and is not covered in this book.) It has some Perl-like features, and minimal Unicode support. It's very slow. It's the only package with a POSIX NFA (although its POSIXness is a bit buggy at times).

Version Tested: 1.1.4

License: GNU LGPL (GNU Lesser General Public License)

Regexp

org.apache.regexp   This is the other regex package under the umbrella of the Apache Jakarta project. It's somewhat popular, but quite buggy. It has the fewest features of the packages listed here. Its overall speed is on par with ORO. Not actively maintained. Minimal Unicode support.
Version Tested: 1.2
License: ASL (Apache Software License)

Why So Many "Perl5" Flavors?

The list mentions "Perl-like" fairly often; the packages themselves advertise "Perl5 support." When version 5 of Perl was released in 1994 (☞ 89), it introduced a new level of regular-expression innovation that others, including Java regex developers, could well appreciate. Perl's regex flavor is powerful, and its adoption by a wide variety of packages and languages has made it somewhat of a de facto standard.

However, of the many packages, programs, and languages that claim to be "Perl5 compliant," none truly are. Even Perl itself differs from version to version as new features are added and bugs are fixed. Some of the innovations new with early 5.x versions of Perl were non-capturing parentheses, lazy quantifiers, lookahead, inline mode modifiers like ⌈(?i)⌉, and the /x free-spacing mode (all discussed in Chapter 3). Packages supporting only these features claim a "Perl5" flavor, but miss out on later innovations, such as lookbehind, atomic grouping, and conditionals.

There are also times when a package doesn't limit itself to only "Perl5" enhancements. Sun's package, for example, supports possessive quantifiers, and both Sun and IBM support character class set operations. Pat offers an innovative way to do lookbehind, and a way to allow matching of simple arbitrarily nested constructs.

Lies, Damn Lies, and Benchmarks

It's probably a common twist on Sam Clemens' famous "lies, damn lies, and statistics" quote, but when I saw its use with "benchmarks" in a paper from Sun while doing research for this chapter, I knew it was an appropriate introduction for this section. In researching these seven packages, I've run literally thousands of benchmarks, but the only fact that's clearly emerged is that there are no clear conclusions.

There are several things that cloud regex benchmarking with Java. First, there are language issues. Recall the benchmarking discussion from Chapter 6 (☞ 234), and the special issues that make benchmarking Java a slippery science at best (primarily, the effects of the Just-In-Time or Better-Late-Than-Never compiler). In doing these benchmarks, I've made sure to use a server VM that was "warmed up" for the benchmark (see "BLTN" ☞ 235), to show the truest results.

Then there are regex issues. Due to the complex interactions of the myriad of optimizations like those discussed in Chapter 6, a seemingly inconsequential change while trying to test one feature might tickle the optimization of an unrelated feature, anonymously skewing the results one way or the other. I did many (many!) very specific tests, usually approaching an issue from multiple directions, and so I believe I've been able to get meaningful results . . . but one never truly knows.

Warning: Benchmark results can cause drowsiness!

Just to show how slippery this all can be, recall that I judged the two Jakarta packages (ORO and Regexp) to be roughly comparable in speed. Indeed, they finished equally in some of the many benchmarks I ran, but for the most part, one generally ran at least twice the speed of the other (sometimes 10× or 20× the speed). But which was "one" and which "the other" changed depending upon the test.

For example, I targeted the speed of greedy and lazy quantifiers by applying ⌈`^.*:`⌉ and ⌈`^.*?:`⌉ to a very long string like '`···xxx:x`'. I expected the greedy one to be faster than the lazy one with this type of string, and indeed, it's that way for every package, program, and language I tested . . . except one. For whatever reason, Jakarta's Regexp's ⌈`^.*:`⌉ performed 70% slower than its ⌈`^.*?:`⌉. I then applied the same expressions to a similarly long string, but this time one like '`x:xxx···`' where the '`:`' is near the beginning. This should give the lazy quantifier an edge, and indeed, with Regexp, the expression with the lazy quantifier finished 670× faster than the greedy. To gain more insight, I applied ⌈`^[^:]*:`⌉ to each string. This should be in the same ballpark, I thought, as the lazy version, but highly contingent upon certain optimizations that may or may not be included in the engine. With Regexp, it finished the test a bit slower than the lazy version, for both strings.

Does the previous paragraph make your eyes glaze over a bit? Well, it discusses just six tests, and for only one regex package — we haven't even started to compare these Regexp results against ORO or any of the other packages. When compared against ORO, it turns out that Regexp is about 10× slower with four of the tests, but about 20× faster with the other two! It's faster with ⌈`^.*?:`⌉ and ⌈`^[^:]*:`⌉ applied to the long string with '`:`' at the front, so it seems that Regexp does poorly (or ORO does well) when the engine must walk through a lot of string, and that the speeds are reversed when the match is found quickly.

Are you eyes completely glazed over yet? Let's try the same set of six tests, but this time on short strings instead of very long ones. It turns out that Regexp is faster — three to ten times faster — than ORO for *all* of them. Okay, so what does this tell us? Perhaps that ORO has a lot of clunky overhead that overshadows the actual match time when the matches are found quickly. Or perhaps it means that Regexp is generally much faster, but has an inefficient mechanism for accessing the target string. Or perhaps it's something else altogether. I don't know.

Another test involved an "exponential match" (☞ 226) on a short string, which tests the basic churning of an engine as it tracks and backtracks. These tests took a long time, yet Regexp tended to finish in half the time of ORO. There just seems to be no rhyme nor reason to the results. Such is often the case when benchmarking something as complex as a regex engine.

And the winner is . . .

The mind-numbing statistics just discussed take into account only a small fraction of the many, varied tests I did. In looking at them all for Regexp and ORO, one package does not stand out as being faster overall. Rather, the good points and bad points seem to be distributed fairly evenly between the two, so I (perhaps somewhat arbitrarily) judge them to be about equal.

Adding the benchmarks from the five other packages into the mix results in a lot of drowsiness for your author, and no obviously clear winner, but overall, Sun's package seems to be the fastest, followed closely by IBM's. Following in a group somewhat behind are Pat, Jregex, Regexp, and ORO. The GNU package is clearly the slowest.

The overall difference between Sun and IBM is not so obviously clear that another equally comprehensive benchmark suite wouldn't show the opposite order if the suite happened to be tweaked slightly differently than mine. Or, for that matter, it's entirely possible that someone looking at all my benchmark data would reach a different conclusion. And, of course, the results could change drastically with the next release of any of the packages or virtual machines (and may well have, by the time you read this). It's a slippery science.

In general, Sun did most things very well, but it's missing a few key optimizations, and some constructs (such as character classes) are much slower than one would expect. Over time, these will likely be addressed by Sun (and in fact, the slowness of character classes is slated to be fixed in Java 1.4.2). The source code is available if you'd like to hack on it as well; I'm sure Sun would appreciate ideas and patches that improve it.

Recommendations

There are many reasons one might choose one package over another, but Sun's `java.util.regex` package—with its high quality, speed, good Unicode support, advanced features, and future ubiquity—is a good recommendation. It comes integrated as part of Java 1.4: `String.matches()`, for example, checks to see whether the string can be completely matched by a given regex.

`java.util.regex`'s strengths lie in its core engine, but it doesn't have a good set of "convenience functions," a layer that hides much of the drudgery of bit-shuffling behind the scenes. ORO, on the other hand, while its core engine isn't as strong, does have a strong support layer. It provides a very convenient set of functions for casual use, as well as the core interface for specialized needs. ORO is designed to allow multiple regex core engines to be plugged in, so the combination of `java.util.regex` with ORO sounds very appealing. I've talked to the ORO developer, and it seems likely that this will happen, so the rest of this chapter looks at Sun's `java.util.regex` and ORO's interface.

Sun's Regex Package

Sun's regex package, `java.util.regex`, comes standard with Java as of Version 1.4. It provides powerful and innovative functionality with an uncluttered (if somewhat simplistic) class interface to its "match state" object model discussed (☞ 370). It has fairly good Unicode support, clear documentation, and good efficiency.

We've seen examples of `java.util.regex` in earlier chapters (☞ 81, 95, 98, 217, 234). We'll see more later in this chapter when we look at its object model and how to actually put it to use, but first, we'll take a look at the regex flavor it supports, and the modifiers that influence that flavor.

Regex Flavor

`java.util.regex` is powered by a Traditional NFA, so the rich set of lessons from Chapters 4, 5, and 6 apply. Table 8-2 on the facing page summarizes its metacharacters. Certain aspects of the flavor are modified by a variety of match modes, turned on via flags to the various functions and factories, or turned on and off via ⌜(?*mods*-*mods*)⌟ and ⌜(?*mods*-*mods*:···)⌟ modifiers embedded within the regular expression itself. The modes are listed in Table 8-3 on page 380.

A regex flavor certainly can't be described with just a tidy little table, so here are some notes to augment Table 8-2:

- The table shows "raw" backslashes, not the doubled backslashes required when regular expressions are provided as Java string literals. For example, ⌜\n⌟ in the table must be written as `"\\n"` as a Java string. See "Strings as Regular Expressions" (☞ 101).

- With the `Pattern.COMMENTS` option (☞ 380), #···◩ sequences are taken as comments. (Don't forget to add newlines to multiline string literals, as in the sidebar on page 386.) Unescaped ASCII whitespace is ignored. **Note:** unlike most implementations that support this type of mode, comments and free whitespace *are* recognized within character classes.

Table 8-2: Overview of Sun's java.util.regex Flavor

Character Shorthands		
☞ 114	(c)	`\a` `\b` `\e` `\f` `\n` `\r` `\t` `\0`*octal* `\x##` `\u####` `\c`*char*

Character Classes and Class-Like Constructs

☞ 117	(c)	Classes: `[`···`]` `[^`···`]` (may contain class set operators ☞ 123)
☞ 118		Almost any character: *dot* (various meanings, changes with modes)
☞ 119	(c)	Class shorthands: `\w` `\d` `\s` `\W` `\D` `\S`
☞ 119	(c)	Unicode properties and blocks `\p{`*Prop*`}` `\P{`*Prop*`}`

Anchors and other Zero-Width Tests

☞ 127		Start of line/string: `^` `\A`
☞ 127		End of line/string: `$` `\z` `\Z`
☞ 128		Start of current match: `\G`
☞ 131		Word boundary: `\b` `\B`
☞ 132		Lookaround: `(?=`···`)` `(?!`···`)` `(?<=`···`)` `(?<!`···`)`

Comments and Mode Modifiers

☞ 133		Mode modifiers: `(?`*mods*-*mods*`)` Modifiers allowed: `x d s m i u`
☞ 134		Mode-modified spans: `(?`*mods*-*mods*`:`···`)`
☞ 112	(c)	Literal-text mode: `\Q`···`\E`

Grouping, Capturing, Conditional, and Control

☞ 135		Capturing parentheses: `(`···`)` `\1` `\2` ...
☞ 136		Grouping-only parentheses: `(?:`···`)`
☞ 137		Atomic grouping: `(?>`···`)`
☞ 138		Alternation: `|`
☞ 139		Greedy quantifiers: `*` `+` `?` `{n}` `{n,}` `{x,y}`
☞ 140		Lazy quantifiers: `*?` `+?` `??` `{n}?` `{n,}?` `{x,y}?`
☞ 140		Possessive quantifiers: `*+` `++` `?+` `{n}+` `{n,}+` `{x,y}?`

(c) – may be used within a character class   (See text for notes on many items)

- `\b` is valid as a backspace only within a character class (outside, it matches a word boundary).

- `\x##` allows exactly two hexadecimal digits, e.g., ⌜`\xFCber`⌝ matches 'über'.

- `\u####` allows exactly four hexadecimal digits, e.g., ⌜`\u00FCber`⌝ matches 'über', and ⌜`\u20AC`⌝ matches '€'.

- `\0`*octal* requires the leading zero, with one to three following octal digits.

- `\c`*char* is *case sensitive*, blindly *xor*ing the ordinal value of the following character with 64. This bizarre behavior means that, unlike any other regex flavor I've ever seen, `\cA` and `\ca` are different. Use uppercase letters to get the traditional meaning of `\x01`. As it happens, `\ca` is the same as `\x21`, matching '!'. (The case sensitivity is scheduled to be fixed in Java 1.4.2.)

Table 8-3: The java.util.regex Match and Regex Modes

Compile-Time Option	(?*mode*)	Description
`Pattern.UNIX_LINES`	d	Changes how *dot* and ⌜^⌟ match (☞ 382)
`Pattern.DOTALL`	s	Causes *dot* to match any character (☞ 110)
`Pattern.MULTILINE`	m	Expands where ⌜^⌟ and ⌜$⌟ can match (☞ 382)
`Pattern.COMMENTS`	x	Free-spacing and comment mode (☞ 72) (Applies even inside character classes)
`Pattern.CASE_INSENSITIVE`	i	Case-insensitive matching for ASCII characters
`Pattern.UNICODE_CASE`	u	Case-insensitive matching for non-ASCII characters
`Pattern.CANON_EQ`		Unicode "canonical equivalence" match mode (different encodings of the same character match as identical ☞ 107)

- **\w**, **\d**, and **\s** (and their uppercase counterparts) match only ASCII characters, and don't include the other alphanumerics, digits, or whitespace in Unicode. That is, \d is exactly the same as [0-9], \w is the same as [0-9a-zA-Z_], and \s is the same as [\t\n\f\r\x0B] (\x0B is the little-used ASCII VT character).

  For full Unicode coverage, you can use Unicode properties (☞ 119): use \p{L} for \w, use \p{Nd} for \d, and use \p{Z} for \s. (Use the \P{⋯} version of each for \W, \D, and \S.)

- **\p{⋯}** and **\P{⋯}** support most standard Unicode properties and blocks. Unicode scripts are not supported. Only the short property names like \p{Lu} are supported—long names like \p{Lowercase_Letter} are not supported. (See the tables on pages 120 and 121.) One-letter property names may omit the braces: \pL is the same as \p{L}. Note, however, that the special composite property \p{L&} is not supported. Also, for some reason, \p{P} does not match characters matched by \p{Pi} and \p{Pf}. \p{C} doesn't match characters matched by \p{Cn}.

  \p{all} is supported, and is equivalent to (?s:.). \p{assigned} and \p{unassigned} are *not* supported: use \P{Cn} and \p{Cn} instead.

- This package understands Unicode blocks as of Unicode Version 3.1. Blocks added to or modified in Unicode since Version 3.1 are not known (☞ 108).

  Block names require the 'In' prefix (see the table on page 123), and only the raw form unadorned with spaces and underscores may be used. For example, \p{In_Greek_Extended} and \p{In Greek Extended} are not allowed; \p{InGreekExtended} is required.

- **$** and **\z** actually match line terminators when they should only match *at* the line terminators (for example, a pattern of `"(.*$)"` actually captures the line terminator). This is scheduled to be fixed in Java 1.4.1.

- **\G** matches the location where the current match started, despite the documentation's claim that it matches at the ending location of the previous match (☞ 128). ⌈\G⌋ is scheduled to be fixed (to agree with the documentation and match at the end of the previous match) in Java 1.4.1.

- The **\b** and **\B** word boundary metacharacters' idea of a "word character" is not the same as \w and \W's. The word boundaries understand the properties of Unicode characters, while \w and \W match only ASCII characters.

- Look*ahead* constructs can employ arbitrary regular expressions, but look*behind* is restricted to subexpressions whose possible matches are finite in length. This means, for example, that ⌈?⌋ is allowed within lookbehind, but ⌈*⌋ and ⌈+⌋ are not. See the description in Chapter 3, starting on page 132.

- At least until Java 1.4.2 is released, character classes with many elements are not optimized, and so are very slow; use ranges when possible (e.g., use `[0-9A-F]` instead of `[0123456789ABCDEF]`), and if there are characters or ranges that are likely to match more often than others, put them earlier in the class's list.

Using java.util.regex

The mechanics of wielding regular expressions with `java.util.regex` are fairly simple. Its object model is the "match state" model discussed on page 370. The functionality is provided with just three classes:

```
java.util.regex.Pattern
java.util.regex.Matcher
java.util.regex.PatternSyntaxException
```

Informally, I'll refer to the first two simply as "`Pattern`" and "`Matcher`". In short, the `Pattern` object is a compiled regular expression that can be applied to any number of strings, and a `Matcher` object is an individual instance of that regex being applied to a specific target string. The third class is the exception thrown upon the attempted compilation of an ill-formed regular expression.

Sun's documentation is sufficiently complete and clear that I refer you to it for the complete list of all methods for these objects (if you don't have the documentation locally, see `http://regex.info` for links). The rest of this section highlights just the main points.

Sun's *java.util.regex* "Line Terminators"

Traditionally, pre-Unicode regex flavors treat a newline specially with respect to *dot*, ⌜^⌟, ⌜$⌟, and ⌜\z⌟. However, the Unicode standard suggests the larger set of "line terminators" discussed in Chapter 3 (☞ 108). Sun's package supports a subset of the these consisting of these five characters and one character sequence:

Character Codes	Nicknames		Description
U+000A	LF	\n	ASCII Line Feed
U+000D	CR	\r	ASCII Carriage Return
U+000D U+000A	CR/LF	\r\n	ASCII Carriage Return / Line Feed
U+0085	NEL		Unicode NEXT LINE
U+2028	LS		Unicode LINE SEPARATOR
U+2029	PS		Unicode PARAGRAPH SEPARATOR

This list is related to the *dot*, ⌜^⌟, ⌜$⌟, and ⌜\z⌟ metacharacters, but the relationships are neither constant (they change with modes), nor consistent (one would expect ⌜^⌟ and ⌜$⌟ to be treated similarly, but they are not).

Both the `Pattern.UNIX_LINES` and `Pattern.DOTALL` match modes (available also via ⌜(?d)⌟ and ⌜(?s)⌟) influence what *dot* matches.

⌜^⌟ can always match at the beginning of the string, but can match elsewhere under the `(?m)` `Pattern.MULTILINE` mode. It also depends upon the ⌜(?d)⌟ `Pattern.UNIX_LINES` mode.

⌜$⌟ and ⌜\z⌟ can always match at the end of the string, but they can also match just before certain string-ending line terminators. With the `Pattern.MULTILINE` mode, ⌜$⌟ can match after certain embedded line terminators as well. With Java 1.4.0, `Pattern.UNIX_LINES` does not influence ⌜$⌟ and ⌜\z⌟ in the same way (but it's slated to be fixed in 1.4.1 such that it does). The following table summarizes the relationships as of 1.4.0.

	LF	CR	CR/LF	NEL	LS	PS
Default action, without modifiers						
dot matches all but:	✔	✓		✓	✓	✓
^ matches at beginning of line only						
$ and \z match before line-ending:	✔	✔	✔		✔	✔
With `Pattern.MULTILINE` or (?m)						
^ matches after any:	✔	✓	✓	✓	✓	✓
$ matches before any:	✔	✔	✔		✔	✔
With `Pattern.DOTALL` or (?s)						
dot matches any character						

✓ — does not apply if `Pattern.UNIX_LINES` or (?d) is in effect

Finally, note that there is a bug in Java 1.4.0 that is slated to be fixed in 1.4.1: ⌜$⌟ and ⌜\z⌟ actually *match* the line terminators, when present, rather than merely matching *at* line terminators.

Here's a complete example showing a simple match:

```
public class SimpleRegexTest {
  public static void main(String[] args)
  {
    String sampleText = "this is the 1st test string";
    String sampleRegex = "\\d+\\w+";
    java.util.regex.Pattern p = java.util.regex.Pattern.compile(sampleRegex);
    java.util.regex.Matcher m = p.matcher(sampleText);

    if (m.find()) {
      String matchedText = m.group();
      int    matchedFrom = m.start();
      int    matchedTo   = m.end();
      System.out.println("matched [" + matchedText + "] from " +
                          matchedFrom + " to " + matchedTo + ".");
    } else {
      System.out.println("didn't match");
    }
  }
}
```

This prints '**matched [1st] from 12 to 15.**'. As with all examples in this chapter, names I've chosen are in italic. Notice the `Matcher` object, after having been created by associating a `Pattern` object and a target string, is used to instigate the actual match (with its `m.find()` method), and to query the results (with `m.group()`, etc.).

The parts shown in bold can be omitted if

```
import java.util.regex.*;
```

or perhaps

```
import java.util.regex.Pattern;
import java.util.regex.Matcher;
```

are inserted at the head of the program, just as with the examples in Chapter 3 (☞ 95). Doing so makes the code more manageable, and is the standard approach. The rest of this chapter assumes the `import` statement is always supplied. A more involved example is shown in the sidebar on page 386.

The `Pattern.compile()` *Factory*

A `Pattern` regular-expression object is created with `Pattern.compile(⋯)`. The first argument is a string to be interpreted as a regular expression (☞ 101). Optionally, compile-time options shown in Table 8-3 on page 380 can be provided as a second argument. Here's a snippet that creates a `Pattern` object from the string in the variable `sampleRegex`, to be matched in a case-insensitive manner:

```
Pattern pat = Pattern.compile(sampleRegex,
                   Pattern.CASE_INSENSITIVE | Pattern.UNICODE_CASE);
```

A call to `Pattern.compile(⋯)` can throw two kinds of exceptions: an invalid regular expression throws `PatternSyntaxException`, and an invalid option value throws `IllegalArgumentException`.

Pattern's `matcher(···)` method

A `Pattern` object offers some convenience methods we'll look at shortly, but for the most part, all the work is done through just one method: `matcher(···)`. It accepts a single argument: the string to search.[†] It doesn't actually apply the regex, but prepares the general `Pattern` object to be applied to a specific string. The `matcher(···)` method returns a `Matcher` object.

The `Matcher` Object

Once you've associated a regular expression with a target string by creating a `Matcher` object, you can instruct it to apply the regex in various ways, and query the results of that application. For example, given a `Matcher` object m, the call `m.find()` actually applies m's regex to its string, returning a Boolean indicating whether a match is found. If a match is found, the call `m.group()` returns a string representing the text actually matched.

The next sections list the various `Matcher` methods that actually apply a regex, followed by those that query the results.

Applying the regex

Here are the main `Matcher` methods for actually applying its regex to its string:

find()

> Applies the object's regex to the object's string, returning a Boolean indicating whether a match is found. If called multiple times, the next match is returned each time.

find(*offset*)

> If `find(···)` is given an integer argument, the match attempt starts from the given *offset* number of characters from the start of the string. It throws `IndexOutOfBoundsException` if the *offset* is negative or beyond the end of the string.

matches()

> This method returns a Boolean indicating whether the object's regex *exactly* matches the object's string. That is, the regex is wrapped with an implied ⌜\A···\z⌟.[‡] This is also available via `String`'s `matches()` method. For example, `"123".matches("\\d+")` is true.

---

† Actually, `matcher`'s argument can be any object implementing the `CharSequence` interface (of which `String`, `StringBuffer`, and `CharBuffer` are examples). This provides the flexibility to apply regular expressions to a wide variety of data, including text that's not even kept in contiguous strings.

‡ Due to the bug with ⌜\z⌟ mentioned at the bottom of page 382, with version 1.4.0, the regex actually appears to be wrapped with an implied ⌜\A···\Z⌟ instead.

lookingAt()

Returns a Boolean indicating whether the object's regex matches the object's string *from its beginning.* That is, the regex is applied with an implied leading ⌜\A⌟. This is also available via String's matches() method. For example, "Subject: spam".lookingAt("^\\w+:") is true.

Querying the results

The following Matcher methods return information about a successful match. They throw IllegalStateException if the object's regex hasn't yet been applied to the object's string, or if the previous application was not successful. The methods that accept a *num* argument (referring to a set of capturing parentheses) throw IndexOutOfBoundsException when an invalid *num* is given.

group()

Returns the text matched by the previous regex application.

groupCount()

Returns the number of sets of capturing parentheses in the object's regex. Numbers up to this value can be used in the group(*num*) method, described next.

group(*num*)

Returns the text matched by the *num*[th] set of capturing parentheses, or null if that set didn't participate in the match. A *num* of zero indicates the entire match, so group(0) is the same as group().

start(*num*)

Returns the offset, in characters, from the start of the string to the start of where the *num*[th] set of capturing parentheses matched. Returns −1 if the set didn't participate in the match.

start()

The offset to the start of the match; this is the same as start(0).

end(*num*)

Returns the offset, in characters, from the start of the string to the end of where the *num*[th] set of capturing parentheses matched. Returns −1 if the set didn't participate in the match.

end()

The offset to the end of the match; this is the same as end(0).

Reusing Matcher objects for efficiency

The whole point of having separate compile and apply steps is to increase efficiency, alleviating the need to recompile a regex with each use (☞ 241). Additional efficiency can be gained by reusing Matcher objects when applying the same regex to new text. This is done with the reset method, described next.

CSV Parsing with java.util.regex

Here's the `java.util.regex` version of the CSV example from Chapter 6
(☞ 271). The regex has been updated to use possessive quantifiers (☞ 140)
for a bit of extra efficiency.

First, we set up `Matcher` objects that we'll use in the actual processing. The
'\n' at the end of each line is needed because we use ⌈#···⌋ comments, which
end at a newline.

```
// Prepare the regexes we'll use

Pattern pCSVmain = Pattern.compile(
    "  \\G(?:^|,)                                             \n"+
    "  (?:                                                    \n"+
    "      # Either a double-quoted field...                  \n"+
    "      \" # field's opening quote                         \n"+
    "        (  (?> [^\"]*+ ) (?> \"\" [^\"]*+ )*+  )         \n"+
    "      \" # field's closing quote                         \n"+
    "    #  ... or ...                                        \n"+
    "    |                                                    \n"+
    "        # ... some non-quote/non-comma text ...          \n"+
    "        ( [^\",]*+ )                                     \n"+
    "  )                                                      \n",
    Pattern.COMMENTS);
Pattern pCSVquote = Pattern.compile("\"\"");
// Now create Matcher objects, with dummy text, that we'll use later.
Matcher mCSVmain  = pCSVmain.matcher("");
Matcher mCSVquote = pCSVquote.matcher("");
```

Then, to parse the string in `csvText` as CSV text, we use those `Matcher`
objects to actually apply the regex and use the results:

```
mCSVmain.reset(csvText); // Tie the target text to the mCSVmain object
while ( mCSVmain.find() )
{
    String field; // We'll fill this in with $1 or $2 . . .
    String first = mCSVmain.group(2);
    if ( first != null )
        field = first;
    else {
        // If $1, must replace paired double-quotes with one double quote
        mCSVquote.reset(mCSVmain.group(1));
        field = mCSVquote.replaceAll("\"");
    }
    // We can now work with field . . .
    System.out.println("Field [" + field + "]");
}
```

This is more efficient than the similar version shown on page 217 for two
reasons: the regex is more efficient (as per the Chapter 6 discussion), and
that one `Matcher` object is reused, rather than creating and disposing of new
ones each time (as per the discussion on page 385).

reset(*text***)**

> This method reinitializes the `Matcher` object with the given `String` (or any object that implements a `CharSequence`), such that the next regex operation will start at the beginning of this text. This is more efficient than creating a new `Matcher` object (☞ 385). You can omit the argument to keep the current text, but to reset the match state to the beginning.

Reusing the `Matcher` object saves the Java mechanics of disposing of the old object and creating a new one, and requires only about one fourth the overhead of creating a new `Matcher` object.

In practice, you usually need only one `Matcher` object per regex, at least if you intend to apply the regex to only one string at a time, as is commonly the case. The sidebar on the facing page shows this in action. Dummy strings are immediately associated with each `Pattern` object to create the `Matcher` objects. It's okay to start with a dummy string because the object's `reset(⋯)` method is called with the real text to match against before the object is used further.

In fact, there's really no need to actually save the `Pattern` objects to variables, since they're not used except to create the `Matcher` objects. The lines:

```
Pattern pCSVquote = Pattern.compile("\"\"");
Matcher mCSVquote = mCSVquote.matcher("");
```

can be replaced by

```
Matcher mCSVquote = Pattern.compile("\"\"").matcher("");
```

thus eliminating the `pCSVquote` variable altogether.

Simple search and replace

You can implement search-and-replace operations using just the methods mentioned so far, but the `Matcher` object offers convenient methods to do simple search-and-replace for you:

replaceAll(*replacement***)**

> The `Matcher` object is reset, and its regex is repeatedly applied to its string. The return value is a copy of the object's string, with any matches replaced by the *replacement* string.

> This is also available via a `String`'s `replaceAll` method:

```
string.replaceAll(regex, replacement);
```

> is equivalent to:

```
Pattern.compile(regex).matcher(string).replaceAll(replacement)
```

replaceFirst(*replacement***)**

> The `Matcher` object is reset, and its regex is applied once to its string. The return value is a copy of the object's string, with the first match (if any) replaced by the *replacement* string.

This is also available via a `String`'s `replaceFirst` method, as just described with `replaceAll`.

With any of these functions, the *replacement* string receives special parsing:

- Instances of '`$1`', '`$2`', etc., within the replacement string are replaced by the text matched by the associated set of capturing parentheses. (`$0` is replaced by the entire text matched.)

    `IllegalArgumentException` is thrown if the character following the '`$`' is not an ASCII digit.

    Only as many digits after the '`$`' as "make sense" are used. For example, if there are three capturing parentheses, '`$25`' in the replacement string is interpreted as `$2` followed by the character '`5`'. However, in the same situation, '`$6`' in the replacement string throws `IndexOutOfBoundsException`.

- A backslash escapes the character that follows, so use '`⋯\$⋯`' in the replacement string to include a dollar sign in it. By the same token, use '`⋯\\⋯`' to get a backslash into the replacement value. (And if you're providing the replacement string as a Java string literal, that means you need "`⋯\\\\⋯`" to get a backslash into the replacement value.) Also, if there are, say, 12 sets of capturing parentheses and you'd like to include the text matched by the first set, followed by '2', you can use a replacement value of '`⋯$1\2⋯`'.

Advanced search and replace

Two additional methods provide raw access to `Matcher`'s search-and-replace mechanics. Together, they build a result in a `StringBuffer` that you provide. The first is called after each match, to fill the result with the replacement string, as well as the text between the matches. The second is called after all matches have been found, to tack on the text remaining after the final match.

appendReplacement(*stringBuffer*, *replacement***)**

Called immediately after a regex has been successfully applied (e.g., with `find`), this method appends two strings to the given *stringBuffer*: first, it copies in the text of the original target string prior to the match. Then it appends the *replacement* string, as per the special processing described in the previous section.

For example, let's say we've got a `Matcher` object m that associates the regex ⌜`\w+`⌟ with the string '`-->one+test<--`'. The first time through this `while` loop:

```
while (m.find())
    m.appendReplacement(sb, "XXX")
```

the `find` matches the underlined portion of '`-->one+test<--`'. The call to `appendReplacement` fills the *stringBuffer* sb with the text before the match,

'-->', then bypasses what matched, instead appending the replacement string, 'XXX', to sb.

The second time through the loop, find matches '-->one+test<--'. The call to appendReplacement appends the text before the match, '+', then again appends the replacement string, 'XXX'.

This leaves sb with '-->XXX+XXX', and the original target string within the m object marked at '-->one+test<--'.

appendTail(*stringBuffer***)**

Called after all matches have been found (or, at least, after the desired matches have been found — you can stop early if you like), this method appends the remaining text. Continuing the previous example,

> *m*.appendTail(*sb*)

appends '<--' to sb. This leaves it with '-->XXX+XXX<--', completing the search and replace.

Here's an example showing how you might implement your own version of replaceAll using these. (Not that you'd want to, but it's illustrative.)

```
public static String replaceAll(Matcher m, String replacement)
{
    m.reset(); // Be sure to start with a fresh Matcher object
    StringBuffer result = new StringBuffer(); // We'll build the updated copy here
    while (m.find())
        m.appendReplacement(result, replacement);
    m.appendTail(result);
    return result.toString(); // Convert to a String and return
}
```

Here's a slightly more involved snippet, which prints a version of the string in the variable Metric, with Celsius temperatures converted to Fahrenheit:

```
// Build a matcher to find numbers followed by "C" within the variable "Metric"
Matcher m = Pattern.compile("(\\d+(?:\\.(\\d+))?)C\\b").matcher(metric);

StringBuffer result = new StringBuffer(); // We'll build the updated copy here
while (m.find()) {
    float celsius = Float.parseFloat(m.group(1));   // Get the number, as a number
    int fahrenheit = (int) (celsius * 9/5 + 32);     // Convert to a Fahrenheit value
    m.appendReplacement(result, fahrenheit + "F");   // Insert it
}
m.appendTail(result);
System.out.println(result.toString()); // Display the result
```

For example, if the variable Metric contains '**from 36.3C to 40.1C.**', it displays '**from 97F to 104F.**'.

Other `Pattern` *Methods*

In addition to the main `compile(···)` factories, the `Pattern` class contains some helper functions and methods that don't add new functionality, but make the current functionality more easily accessible.

`Pattern.matches`(*pattern,* *text*)

> This static function returns a Boolean indicating whether the string *pattern* can match the `CharSequence` (e.g., `String`) *text*. Essentially, this is:
>
> ```
> Pattern.compile(pattern).matcher(text).matches();
> ```
>
> If you need to pass compile options, or need to gain access to more information about the match than whether it was successful, you'll have to use the methods described earlier.

Pattern's split method, with one argument

`split`(*text*)

> This `Pattern` method accepts *text* (a `CharSequence`) and returns an array of strings from *text* that are delimited by matches of the object's regex. This is also available via a `String`'s `split` method.

This trivial example

```
String[] result = Pattern.compile("\\.").split("209.204.146.22");
```

returns the array of four strings ('`209`', '`204`', '`146`', and '`22`') that are separated by the three matches of ⌜`\.`⌟ in the text. This simple example splits on only a single literal character, but you can split on an arbitrary regular expression. For example, you might approximate splitting a string into "words" by splitting on non-alphanumerics:

```
String[] result = Pattern.compile("\\W+").split(Text);
```

When given a string like '`What's␣up,␣␣Doc`' it returns the four strings ('`What`', '`s`', '`up`', and '`Doc`') delimited by the three matches of the regex. (If you had non-ASCII text, you'd probably want to use ⌜`\P{L}+`⌟, or perhaps ⌜`[^\p{L}\p{N}_]`⌟, as the regex, instead of ⌜`\W+`⌟ ☞ 380.)

Empty elements with adjacent matches

If the object's regex can match at the beginning of the *text*, the first string returned by `split` is an empty string (a valid string, but one that contains no characters). Similarly, if the regex can match two or more times in a row, empty strings are returned for the zero-length text "separated" by the adjacent matches. For example,

```
String[] result = Pattern.compile("\\s*,\\s*").split(", one, two , ,, 3");
```

splits on a comma and any surrounding whitespace, returning an array of five strings: an empty string, 'one', 'two', two empty strings, and '3'.

Finally, any empty strings that might appear at the *end* of the list are suppressed:

```
String[] result = Pattern.compile(":").split(":xx:");
```

This produces just two strings: an empty string and 'xx'. To keep trailing empty elements, use the two-argument version of split(⋯), described next.

Pattern's split method, with two arguments

split(*text, limit*)

> This version of split(⋯) provides some control over how many times the Pattern's regex is applied, and what is done with trailing empty elements.

The *limit* argument takes on different meanings depending on whether it's less than zero, zero, or greater than zero.

Split with a limit less than zero

Any *limit* less than zero means to keep trailing empty elements in the array. Thus,

```
String[] result = Pattern.compile(":").split(":xx:", -1);
```

returns an array of three strings (an empty string, 'xx', and another empty string).

Split with a limit of zero

An explicit limit of zero is the same as if there were no limit given, i.e., trailing empty elements arc suppressed.

Split with a limit greater than zero

With a *limit* greater than zero, split(⋯) returns an array of at most *limit* elements. This means that the regex is applied at most *limit*-1 times. (A limit of three, for example, requests *three* strings separated by *two* matches.)

After having matched *limit*-1 times, no further matches are checked, and the entire remainder of the string after the final match is returned as the last string in the array. For example, if you had a string with

```
Friedl,Jeffrey,Eric Francis,America,Ohio,Rootstown
```

and wanted to isolate just the three name components, you'd split the string into four parts (the three name components, and one final "everything else" string):

```
String[] NameInfo = Pattern.compile(",").split(Text, 4);
// NameInfo[0] is the family name
// NameInfo[1] is the given name
// NameInfo[2] is the middle name (or in my case, middle names)
// NameInfo[3] is everything else, which we don't need, so we'll just ignore it.
```

The reason to limit split in this way is for enhanced efficiency — why bother going through the work of finding the rest of the matches, creating new strings, making a larger array, etc., when there's no intention to use the results of that work? Supplying a limit allows just the required work to be done.

A Quick Look at Jakarta-ORO

Jakarta-ORO (from now on, just "ORO") is a vast, modular framework of mostly regex-related text-processing features containing a dizzying eight interfaces and 35+ classes. When first faced with the documentation, you can be intimidated until you realize that you can get an amazing amount of use out of it by knowing just one class, `Perl5Util`, described next.

ORO's `Perl5Util`

This ORO version of the example from page 383 shows how simple `Perl5Util` is to work with:

```
import org.apache.oro.text.perl.Perl5Util;

public class SimpleRegexTest {
  public static void main(String[] args)
  {
      String sampleText = "this is the 1st test string";
      Perl5Util engine = new Perl5Util();

      if (engine.match("/\\d+\\w+/", sampleText)) {
          String matchedText = engine.group(0);
          int    matchedFrom = engine.beginOffset(0);
          int    matchedTo   = engine.endOffset(0);
          System.out.println("matched [" + matchedText + "] from " +
                              matchedFrom + " to " + matchedTo + ".");
      } else {
          System.out.println("didn't match");
      }
  }
}
```

One class hides all the messy details about working with regular expressions behind a simple façade that somewhat mimics regular-expression use in Perl. Where Perl has

```
$input =~ /^([-+]?[0-9]+(\.[0-9]*)?)\s*([CF])$/i
```

(from an example in Chapter 2 ☞ 48), ORO allows:

```
engine.match("/^([-+]?[0-9]+(\\.[0-9]*)?)\\s*([CF])$/i", input)
```

Where Perl then has

```
$InputNum = $1;   # Save to named variables to make the ...
$Type     = $3;   # ... rest of the program easier to read.
```

ORO provides for:

```
inputNum = engine.group(1);   // Save to named variables to make the ...
type     = engine.group(3);   // ... rest of the program easier to read.
```

If you're not familiar with Perl, the /···/i trappings may seem a bit odd, and they can be cumbersome at times, but it lowers the barrier to regex use about as low as it can get in Java.[†] (Unfortunately, not even ORO can get around the extra escaping required to get regex backslashes and double quotes into Java string literals.)

Even substitutions can be simple. An example from Chapter 2 to "commaify" a number (☞ 67) looks like this in Perl:

```
$text =~ s/(\d)(?=(\d\d\d)+(?!\d))/$1,/g;
```

and this with ORO:

```
text = engine.substitute("s/(\\d)(?=(\\d\\d\\d)+(?!\\d))/$1,/g", text);
```

Traditionally, regular-expression use in Java has a class model that involves pre-compiling the regex to some kind of pattern object, and then using that object later when you actually need to apply the regex. The separation is for efficiency, so that repeated uses of a regex doesn't have to suffer the repeated costs of compiling each time.

So, how does `Perl5Util`, with its procedural approach of accepting the raw regex each time, stay reasonably efficient? It *caches* the results of the compile, keeping a behind-the-scenes mapping between a string and the resulting regex object. (See "Compile caching in the procedural approach" in Chapter 6 ☞ 243.)

It's not perfectly efficient, as the argument string must be parsed for the regex delimiters and modifiers each time, so there's some extra overhead, but the caching keeps it reasonable for casual use.

A Mini `Perl5Util` Reference

The ORO suite of text-processing tools at first seems complex because of the raw number of classes and interfaces. Although the documentation is well-written, it's hard to know exactly where to start. The `Perl5Util` part of the documentation, however, is fairly self-contained, so it's the only thing you really need at first. The next sections briefly go over the main methods.

`Perl5Util` basics—initiating a match

match(*expression, target*)

Given a match *expression* in Perl notation, and a *target* string, returns true if the regex can match somewhere in the string:

```
if (engine.match("/^Subject: (.*)/im", emailMessageText))
{
    ⋮
```

As with Perl, you can pick your own delimiters, but unlike Perl, the leading m is not required, and ORO does not support nested delimiters (e.g., m{ ⋯ }).

[†] One further step, I think, would be to remove the Perl trappings and just have separate arguments for the regex and modifier. The whole m/ / bit may be convenient for those coming to Java from a Perl background, but it doesn't seem "natural" in Java.

Modifier letters may be placed after the closing delimiter. The modifiers allowed are:

i (case-insensitive match ☞ 109)

x (free-spacing and comments mode ☞ 110)

s (dot-matches-all ☞ 110)

m (enhanced line anchor mode ☞ 111)

If there's a match, the various methods described in the next section are available for querying additional information about the match.

substitute(_expression, target_**)**

Given a string showing a Perl-like substitute *expression*, apply it to the *target* text, returning a possibly-modified copy:

```
headerLine = engine.substitute("s/\\b(Re:\\s*)*//i", headerLine);
```

The modifiers mentioned for `match` can be placed after the final delimiter, as can **g**, which has the substitution continue after the first match, applying the regex to the rest of the string in looking for subsequent matches to replace.[†]

The substitution part of the *expression* is interpreted specially. Instances of $1, $2, etc. are replaced by the associated text matched by the first, second, etc., set of capturing parentheses. $0 and $& are replaced with the entire matched text. \U···\E and \L···\E cause the text between to be converted to upper- and lowercase, respectively, while \u and \l cause just the next character to be converted. Unicode case conversion is supported.

Here's an example that turns words in all caps to leading-caps:

```
phrase = engine.substitute("s/\\b([A-Z])([A-Z]+)/$1\\L$2\\E/g", phrase);
```

(In Perl this would be better written as s/\b([A-Z]+)/\L\u$1\E/g, but ORO currently doesn't support the combination of \L···\E with \u or \l.)

substitute(_result, expression, target_**)**

This version of the `substitute` method writes the possibly-modified version of the *target* string into a `StringBuffer` result, and returns the number of replacements actually done.

split(_collection, expression, target, limit_**)**

The m/···/ *expression* (formatted in the same way as for the `match` method) is applied to the *target* string, filling *collection* with the text separated by matches. There is no return value.

The *collection* should be an object implementing the `java.util.Collection` interface, such as `java.util.ArrayList` or `java.util.Vector`.

---

† An **o** modifier is also supported. It's not particularly useful, so I don't cover it in this book, but it's important to note that it is completely unrelated to Perl's /o modifier.

The *limit* argument, which is optional, limits the number of times the regex is applied to *limit* minus one. When the regex has no capturing parentheses, this limits the returned collection to at most *limit* elements.

For example, if your input is a string of values separated by simple commas, perhaps with spaces before or after, and you want to isolate just the first two values, you would use a *limit* of three:

```
java.util.ArrayList list = new java.util.ArrayList();
engine.split(list, "m/\\s+ , \\s+/x", input, 3);
```

An input string of **"USA, NY, NYC, Bronx"**, result in a list of three elements, 'USA', 'NY', and 'NYC, Bronx'. Because you want just the first two, you could then eliminate the "everything else" third element.

An omitted *limit* allows all matches to happen, as does a non-positive one.

If the regex has capturing parentheses, *additional* elements associated with each $1, $2, etc., may be inserted for each successful regex application. With ORO's split, they are inserted only if not empty (e.g., empty elements are not created from capturing parentheses.) Also, note that the *limit* limits the number of regex applications, not the number of elements returned, which is dependent upon the number of matches, as well as the number of capturing parentheses that actually capture text.

Perl's split operator has a number of somewhat odd rules as to when it returns leading and trailing empty elements that might result from matches at the beginning and end of the string (☞ 323). As of Version 2.0.6, ORO does not support these, but there is talk among the developers of doing so in a future release.

Here's a simple little program that's convenient for testing split:

```
import org.apache.oro.text.perl.Perl5Util;
import java.util.*;

public class OroSplitTest {
    public static void main(String[] args) {
        Perl5Util engine = new Perl5Util();
        List list = new ArrayList();
        engine.split(list, args[0], args[1], Integer.parseInt(args[2]));
        System.out.println(list);
    }
}
```

The `println` call shows each element within [···], separated by commas. Here are a few examples:

```
% java OroSplitTest  '/\./'  '209.204.146.22'  -1
[209, 204, 146, 22]
% java OroSplitTest  '/\./'  '209.204.146.22'  2
[209, 204.146.22]
% java OroSplitTest  'm|/+|'  '/usr/local/bin//java'  -1
[, usr, local, bin, java]
% java OroSplitTest  'm/(?=(?:\d\d\d)+$)/'  1234567890  -1
[1, 234, 567, 890]
% java OroSplitTest  'm/\s*<BR>\s*/i'  'this<br>that<BR>other'  -1
[this, that, other]
% java OroSplitTest  'm/\s*(<BR>)\s*/i'  'this<br>that<BR>other' -1
[this, <br>, that, <BR>, other]
```

Note that with most shells, you don't need to double the backslashes if you use single quotes to delimit the arguments, as you do when entering the same expressions as Java string literals.

Perl5Util basics—inspecting the results of a match

The following `Perl5Util` methods are available to report on the most recent successful match of a regular expression (an unsuccessful attempt does not reset these). They throw `NullPointerException` if called when there hasn't yet been a successful match.

group(*num* **)**

Returns the text matched by the *num*[th] set of capturing parentheses, or by the whole match if *num* is zero. Returns `null` if there aren't at least *num* sets of capturing parentheses, or if the named set did not participate in the match.

toString()

Returns the text matched—the same as `group(0)`.

length()

Returns the length of the text matched—the same as `group(0).length()`.

beginOffset(*num* **)**

Returns the number of characters from the start of the target string to the start of the text returned by `group(num)`. Returns `-1` in cases where `group(num)` returns `null`.

endOffset(*num* **)**

Returns the number of characters from the start of the target string to the first character after the text returned by `group(num)`. Returns `-1` in cases where `group(num)` returns `null`.

groups()

Returns the number of capturing groups in the regex, plus one (the extra is to account for the virtual group zero of the entire match). All *num* values to the methods just mentioned must be less than this number.

getMatch()

Returns an `org.apache.oro.text.regex.MatchResult` object, which has all the result-querying methods listed so far. It's convenient when you want to save the results of the latest `match` beyond the next use of the `Perl5Util` object. `getMatch()` is valid only after a successful `match`, and not after a `substitute` or `split`.

preMatch()

Returns the part of the target string before (to the left of) the match.

postMatch()

Returns the part of the target string after (to the right of) the match.

Using ORO's Underlying Classes

If you need to do things that `Perl5Util` doesn't allow, but still want to use ORO, you'll need to use the underlying classes (the "vast, modular framework") directly. As an example, here's an ORO version of the CSV-processing script on page 386.

First, we need these 11 classes:

```
import org.apache.oro.text.regex.PatternCompiler;
import org.apache.oro.text.regex.Perl5Compiler;
import org.apache.oro.text.regex.Pattern;
import org.apache.oro.text.regex.PatternMatcher;
import org.apache.oro.text.regex.Perl5Matcher;
import org.apache.oro.text.regex.MatchResult;
import org.apache.oro.text.regex.Substitution;
import org.apache.oro.text.regex.Util;
import org.apache.oro.text.regex.Perl5Substitution;
import org.apache.oro.text.regex.PatternMatcherInput;
import org.apache.oro.text.regex.MalformedPatternException;
```

Then, we prepare the regex engine—this is needed just once per thread:

```
PatternCompiler compiler = new Perl5Compiler();
PatternMatcher  matcher  = new Perl5Matcher();
```

Now we declare the variables for our two regexes, and also initialize an object representing the replacement text for when we change '**""**' to '**"**':

```
Pattern rCSVmain  = null;
Pattern rCSVquote = null;
// When rCSVquote matches, we'll want to replace with one double quote:
Substitution sCSVquote = new Perl5Substitution("\"");
```

Now we create the regex objects. The raw ORO classes require pattern exceptions to always be caught or thrown, even though we know the hand-constructed regex will always work (well, after we've tested it once to make sure we've typed it correctly).

```
try {
   rCSVmain = compiler.compile(
        "   (?:^|,)                                          \n"+
        "   (?:                                              \n"+
        "      # Either a double-quoted field...             \n"+
        "      \" # field's opening quote                    \n"+
        "        (  [^\"]* (?: \"\" [^\"]* )*  )             \n"+
        "      \" # field's closing quote                    \n"+
        "   # ... or ...                                     \n"+
        "   |                                                \n"+
        "      # ... some non-quote/non-comma text ...       \n"+
        "      ( [^\",]* )                                   \n"+
        "   )                                                \n",
        Perl5Compiler.EXTENDED_MASK);
   rCSVquote = compiler.compile("\"\"");
}
catch (MalformedPatternException e) {
   System.err.println("Error parsing regular expression.");
   System.err.println("Error: " + e.getMessage());
   System.exit(1);
}
```

ORO's ⌈\G⌋ doesn't work properly (at least as of Version 2.0.6), so I've removed it. You'll recall from the original discussion in Chapter 5 (☞ 216) that ⌈\G⌋ had been used as a precaution, and wasn't strictly required, so it's okay to remove here.

Finally, this snippet actually does the processing:

```
PatternMatcherInput inputObj = new PatternMatcherInput(inputCSVtext);
while ( matcher.contains(inputObj, rCSVmain) )
{
    String field; // We'll fill this in with $1 or $2
    String first = matcher.getMatch().group(2);
    if ( first != null ) {
        field = first;
    } else {
        field = matcher.getMatch().group(1);
        // If $1, must replace paired double quotes with one double quote
        field = Util.substitute(matcher,        // the matcher to use
                                rCSVquote,       // the pattern to match with it
                                sCSVquote,       // the replacement to be done
                                field,           // the target string
                                Util.SUBSTITUTE_ALL); // do all replacements
    }
    // We can now work with the field . . .
    System.out.println("Field [" + field + "]");
}
```

Phew! Seeing all that's involved certainly helps you to appreciate `Perl5Util`!

9

.NET

Microsoft's .NET Framework, usable with Visual Basic, C#, and C++ (among other languages), offers a shared regular-expression library that unifies regex semantics among the languages. It's a full-featured, powerful engine that allows you the maximum flexibility in balancing speed and convenience.

Each language has a different syntax for handling objects and methods, but those underlying objects and methods are the same regardless of the language, so even complex examples shown in one language directly translate to the other languages of the .NET language suite. Examples in this chapter are shown with Visual Basic.

In This Chapter Before looking at what's in this chapter, it's important to emphasize that this chapter relies heavily on the base material in Chapters 1 through 6. I understand that some readers interested only in .NET may be inclined to start their reading with this chapter, and I want to encourage them not to miss the benefits of the preface (in particular, the typographical conventions) and the earlier chapters: Chapters 1, 2, and 3 introduce basic concepts, features, and techniques involved with regular expressions, while Chapters 4, 5, and 6 offer important keys to regex understanding that directly apply to .NET's regex engine.

This chapter first looks at .NET's regex flavor, including which metacharacters are supported and how,[†] as well as the special issues that await the .NET programmer. Then there's a quick overview of .NET's regex-related object model, and how it's been designed to allow you to wield a regex, followed by a detailed look at each of the core regex-related classes. It all ends with an example of how to build a personal regex library by encapsulating pre-built regular expressions into a shared assembly.

---

† This book covers .NET "Version 2002." While researching this book, I uncovered a few bugs, which Microsoft tells me will be fixed in the 2004 release of .NET.

.NET's Regex Flavor

.NET has been built with a Traditional NFA regex engine, so all the important NFA-related lessons from Chapters 4, 5, and 6 are applicable. Table 9-1 on the facing page summarizes .NET's regex flavor, most of which is discussed in Chapter 3,

Certain aspects of the flavor can be modified by *match modes* (☞ 109), turned on via option flags to the various functions and constructors that accept regular expressions, or in some cases, turned on and off within the regex itself via ⌈(?*mods–mods*)⌋ and ⌈(?*mods–mods*: ⋯)⌋ constructs. The modes are listed in Table 9-2 on page 402.

A regex flavor can't be described with just a simple table or two, so here are some notes to augment Table 9-1:

- In the table, "raw" escapes like ⌈\w⌋ are shown. These can be used directly in VB.NET string literals ("\w"), and in C# verbatim strings (@"\w"). In languages without regex-friendly string literals, such as C++, each backslash in the regex requires two in the string literal ("\\w"). See "Strings as Regular Expressions" (☞ 101).

- **\b** is valid as a backspace only within a character class (outside, it matches a word boundary).

- **\x##** allows exactly two hexadecimal digits, e.g., ⌈\xFCber⌋ matches 'über'.

- **\u####** allows exactly four hexadecimal digits, e.g., ⌈\u00FCber⌋ matches 'über', and ⌈\u20AC⌋ matches '€'.

- **\w**, **\d**, and **\s** (and their uppercase counterparts) normally match the full range of appropriate Unicode characters, but change to an ASCII-only mode with the RegexOptions.ECMAScript option (☞ 406).

- In its default mode, **\w** matches the Unicode properties \p{Ll}, \p{Lu}, \p{Lt}, \p{Lo}, \p{Nd}, and \p{Pc}. Note that this does not include the \p{Lm} property. (See the table on page 121 for the property list.)

- In its default mode, **\s** matches ⌈[\f\n\r\t\v\x85\p{Z}]⌋. U+0085 is the Unicode NEXT LINE control character, and \p{Z} matches Unicode "separator" characters (☞ 120).

- **\p{⋯}** and **\P{⋯}** support most standard Unicode properties and blocks. Unicode scripts are not supported. Only the short property names like \p{Lu} are supported—long names like \p{Lowercase_Letter} are not supported. (See the tables on pages 120 and 121.) Note, however, that the special composite property \p{L&} is not supported, nor, for some reason, are the \p{Pi} and \p{Pf} properties. Single-letter properties *do* require the braces (that is, the \pL shorthand for \p{L} is *not* supported).

Table 9-1: Overview of .NET's Regular-Expression Flavor

Character Shorthands		
☞ 114	(c)	`\a \b \e \f \n \r \t \v` *octal* `\x##` `\u####` `\c`*char*
Character Classes and Class-Like Constructs		
☞ 117		Classes: `[`⋯`]` `[^`⋯`]`
☞ 118		Any character except newline: *dot* (sometimes any character at all)
☞ 119	(c)	Class shorthands: `\w \d \s \W \D \S`
☞ 119	(c)	Unicode properties and blocks: `\p{`*Prop*`}` `\P{`*Prop*`}`
Anchors and other Zero-Width Tests		
☞ 127		Start of line/string: `^` `\A`
☞ 127		End of line/string: `$` `\z` `\Z`
☞ 128		End of previous match: `\G`
☞ 131		Word boundary: `\b` `\B`
☞ 132		Lookaround: `(?=`⋯`)` `(?!`⋯`)` `(?<=`⋯`)` `(?<!`⋯`)`
Comments and Mode Modifiers		
☞ 133		Mode modifiers: `(?`*mods-mods*`)` Modifiers allowed: `x s m i n` (☞ 402)
☞ 134		Mode-modified spans: `(?`*mods-mods*`:`⋯`)`
☞ 134		Comments: `(?#`⋯`)`
Grouping, Capturing, Conditional, and Control		
☞ 135		Capturing parentheses: `(`⋯`)` `\1` `\2` ...
☞ 430		Balanced grouping: `(?<`*name-name*`>`⋯`)`
☞ 137		Named capture, backreference: `(?<`*name*`>`⋯`)` `\k<`*name*`>`
☞ 136		Grouping-only parentheses: `(?:`⋯`)`
☞ 137		Atomic grouping: `(?>`⋯`)`
☞ 138		Alternation: `|`
☞ 139		Greedy quantifiers: `*  +  ?  {n}  {n,}  {x,y}`
☞ 140		Lazy quantifiers: `*?  +?  ??  {n}?  {n,}?  {x,y}?`
☞ 138		Conditional: `(?`*if then*`|`*else*`)` – "if" can be lookaround, `(`*num*`)`, or `(`*name*`)`

(c) – may be used within a character class

Also not supported are the special properties \p{All}, \p{Assigned}, and \p{Unassigned}. Instead, you might use ⌈(?s:.)⌋, ⌈\P{Cn}⌋, and ⌈\p{Cn}⌋, respectively.

- This package understands Unicode blocks as of Unicode Version 3.1. Additions and modifications since Version 3.1 are not known (☞ 108).

Block names require the 'Is' prefix (see the table on page 123), and only the raw form unadorned with spaces and underscores may be used. For example, \p{Is_Greek_Extended} and \p{Is Greek Extended} are not allowed; \p{IsGreekExtended} is required.

- **\G** matches the *end* of the *previous* match, despite the documentation's claim that it matches at the *beginning* of the *current* match (☞ 128).

- Both lookahead *and* lookbehind can employ arbitrary regular expressions. As of this writing, the .NET regex engine is the only one that I know of that allows lookbehind with a subexpression that can match an arbitrary amount of text (☞ 132).

- The `RegexOptions.ExplictCapture` option (also available via the **(?n)** mode modifier) turns off capturing for raw ⌈(⋯)⌋ parentheses. Explicitly-named captures like ⌈**(?<num>**\d+**)**⌋ still work (☞ 137). If you use named captures, this option allows you to use the visually more pleasing ⌈(⋯)⌋ for grouping instead of ⌈(?⋯)⌋.

Table 9-2: The .NET Match and Regex Modes

RegexOptions option	(? *mode*)	Description
.Singleline	s	Causes *dot* to match any character (☞ 110)
.Multiline	m	Expands where ⌈^⌋ and ⌈$⌋ can match (☞ 110)
.IgnorePatternWhitespace	x	Sets free-spacing and comment mode (☞ 72)
.IgnoreCase	i	Turns on case-insensitive matching
.ExplicitCapture	n	Turns capturing off for ⌈(⋯)⌋, so only ⌈(?<*name*>⋯)⌋ capture
.ECMAScript		Restricts ⌈\w⌋, ⌈\s⌋, and ⌈\d⌋ to match ASCII characters only, and more (☞ 406)
.RightToLeft		The transmission applies the regex normally, but in the opposite direction (starting at the *end* of the string and moving toward the start). Unfortunately, buggy. (☞ 405)
.Compiled		Spends extra time up front optimizing the regex so it matches more quickly when applied (☞ 404)

Additional Comments on the Flavor

A few issues merit longer discussion than a bullet point allows.

Named capture

.NET supports named capture (☞ 137), through the ⌈(?<*name*>⋯)⌋ or ⌈(?'*name*'⋯)⌋ syntax. Both syntaxes mean the same thing and you can use either freely, but I prefer the syntax with <⋯>, as I believe it will be more widely used.

You can backreference the text matched by a named capture within the regex with ⌈\k<*name*>⌉ or ⌈\k'*name*'⌉.

After the match (once a `Match` object has been generated; an overview of .NET's object model follows, starting on page 410), the text matched within the named capture is available via the `Match` object's `Groups(`*name*`)` property. (C# requires `Groups[`*name*`]` instead.)

Within a replacement string (☞ 418), the results of named capture are available via a `${`*name*`}` sequence.

In order to allow all groups to be accessed numerically, which may be useful at times, named-capture groups are also given numbers. They receive their numbers *after* all the non-named ones receive theirs:

$$\begin{matrix} 1 & 1\ 3 & 3\ 2 & 2 \\ \ulcorner(\backslash w) & (?<Num>\backslash d+) & (\backslash s+)\urcorner \end{matrix}$$

The text matched by the ⌈\d+⌉ part of this example is available via both `Groups("Num")` and `Groups(3)`. It's still just one group, but with two names.

An unfortunate consequence

It's not recommended to mix normal capturing parentheses and named captures, but if you do, the way the capturing groups are assigned numbers has important consequences that you should be aware of. The ordering becomes important when capturing parentheses are used with `Split` (☞ 419), and for the meaning of '$+' in a replacement string (☞ 418). Both currently have additional, unrelated problems that make them more or less broken anyway (although Microsoft is working on a fix for the 2004 release of .NET).

Conditional tests

The *if* part of an ⌈(? *if then* | *else*)⌉ conditional (☞ 138) can be any type of look-around, or a captured group number or captured group name in parentheses. Plain text (or a plain regex) in this location is automatically treated as positive lookahead (that it, it has an implicit ⌈(?=⋯)⌉ wrapped around it). This can lead to an ambiguity: for instance, the ⌈(Num)⌉ of ⌈⋯(?(Num) *then* | *else*)⋯⌉ is turned into ⌈(?=Num)⌉ (lookahead for 'Num') if there is no ⌈(?<Num>⋯)⌉ named capture elsewhere in the regex. If there is such a named capture, whether it was successful is the result of the *if*.

I recommend not relying on "auto-lookaheadification." Use the explicit ⌈(?=⋯)⌉ to make your intentions clearer to the human reader, and also to avert a surprise if some future version of the regex engine adds additional *if* syntax.

"Compiled" expressions

In earlier chapters, I use the word "compile" to describe the pre-application work any regex system must do to check that a regular expression is valid, and to convert it to an internal form suitable for its actual application to text. For this, .NET regex terminology uses the word "parsing." It uses two versions of "compile" to refer to optimizations of that parsing phase.

Here are the details, in order of increasing optimization:

- **Parsing**   The first time a regex is seen during the run of a program, it must be checked and converted into an internal form suitable for actual application by the regex engine. This process is referred to as "compile" elsewhere in this book (☞ 241).

- **On-the-Fly Compilation**   `RegexOptions.Compiled` is one of the options available when building a regex. Using it tells the regex engine to go further than simply converting to the default internal form, but to *compile* it to low-level MSIL (Microsoft Intermediate Language) code, which itself is then amenable to being optimized even further into even faster native machine code by the JIT ("Just-In-Time" compiler) when the regex is actually applied.

  It takes more time and memory to do this, but it allows the resulting regular expression to work faster. These tradeoffs are discussed later in this section.

- **Pre-Compiled Regexes**   A `Regex` object (or objects) can be encapsulated into an assembly written to disk in a DLL (a Dynamically Loaded Library, i.e., a shared library). This makes it available for general use in other programs. This is called "compiling the assembly." For more, see "Regex Assemblies" (☞ 428).

When considering on-the-fly compilation with `RegexOptions.Compiled`, there are important tradeoffs among initial startup time, ongoing memory usage, and regex match speed:

Metric	Without `RegexOptions.Compiled`	With `RegexOptions.Compiled`
Startup time	Faster	Slower (by 60×)
Memory usage	Low	High (about 5-15k each)
Match speed	Not as fast	Up to 10× faster

The initial regex parsing (the default kind, without `RegexOptions.Compiled`) that must be done the first time each regex is seen in the program is relatively fast. Even on my clunky old 550MHz NT box, I benchmark about 1,500 complex compilations/second. When `RegexOptions.Compiled` is used, that goes down to about 25/second, and increases memory usage by about 10k bytes per regex. More importantly, that memory remains used for the life of the program—there's no way to unload it.

It definitely makes sense to use RegexOptions.Compiled in time-sensitive areas where processing speed is important, particularly for expressions that work with a lot of text. On the other hand, it makes little sense to use it on simple regexes that aren't applied to a lot of text. It's less clear which is best for the multitude of situations in between—you'll just have to weight the benefits and decide on a case-by-case basis.

In some cases, it may make sense to encapsulate an application's compiled expressions into its own DLL, as pre-compiled Regex objects. This uses less memory in the final program (the loading of the whole regex compilation package is bypassed), and allows faster loading (since they're compiled when the DLL is built, you don't have to wait for them to be compiled when you use them). A nice byproduct of this is that the expressions are made available to other programs that might wish to use them, so it's a great way to make a personal regex library. See "Creating Your Own Regex Library With an Assembly" on page 429.

Right-to-left matching

The concept of "backwards" matching (matching from right to left in a string, rather than from left to right) has long intrigued regex developers. Perhaps the biggest issue facing the developer is to define exactly what "right-to-left matching" really means. Is the regex somehow reversed? Is the target text flipped? Or is it just that the regex is applied normally from each position within the target string, with the difference being that the transmission starts at the end of the string instead of at the beginning, and moves backwards with each bump-along rather than forward?

Just to think about it in concrete terms for a moment, consider applying ⌈\d+⌋ to the string '123 and 456'. We know a normal application matches '123', and instinct somehow tells us that a right-to-left application should match '456'. However, if the regex engine uses the semantics described at the end of the previous paragraph, where the only difference is the starting point of the transmission and the direction of the bump-along, the results may be surprising. In these semantics, the regex engine works normally ("looking" to the right from where it's started), so the first attempt of ⌈\d+⌋, at '⋯456', doesn't match. The second attempt, at '⋯456' *does* match, as the bump-along has placed it "looking at" the '6', which certainly matches ⌈\d+⌋. So, we have a final match of only the final '6'.

One of .NET's regex options is RegexOptions.RightToLeft. What are its semantics? The answer is: "that's a good question." The semantics are not documented, and my own tests indicate only that I can't pin them down. In many cases, such as the '123 and 456' example, it acts surprisingly intuitively (it matches '456'). However, it sometimes fails to find *any* match, and at other times finds a match that seems to make no sense when compared with other results.

If you have a need for it, you may find that `RegexOptions.RightToLeft` seems to work exactly as you wish, but in the end, you use it at your own risk. Microsoft is working on pinning down the semantics (to be released in the 2004 or 2005 version of .NET), and so the semantics that you happen to see now may change.

Backlash-digit ambiguities

When a backslash is followed by a number, it's either an octal escape or a backreference. Which of the two it's interpreted as, and how, depends on whether the `RegexOptions.ECMAScript` option has been specified. If you don't want to have to understand the subtle differences, you can always use ⌐\k<*num*>⌐ for a backreference, or start the octal escape with a zero (e.g., ⌐\08⌐) to ensure it's taken as one. These work consistently, regardless of `RegexOptions.ECMAScript` being used or not.

If `RegexOptions.ECMAScript` is *not* used, single-digit escapes from ⌐\1⌐ through ⌐\9⌐ are always backreferences, and an escaped number beginning with zero is always an octal escape (e.g., ⌐\012⌐ matches an ASCII linefeed character). If it's not either of these cases, the number is taken as a backreference if it would "make sense" to do so (i.e., if there are at least that many capturing parentheses in the regex). Otherwise, so long as it has a value between \000 and \377, it's taken as an octal escape. For example, ⌐\12⌐ is taken as a backreference if there are at least 12 sets of capturing parentheses, or an octal escape otherwise.

The semantics for when `RegexOptions.ECMAScript` is specified is described in the next section.

ECMAScript mode

ECMAScript is a standardized version of JavaScript[†] with its own semantics of how regular expressions should be parsed and applied. A .NET regex attempts to mimic those semantics if created with the `RegexOptions.ECMAScript` option. If you don't know what ECMAScript is, or don't need compatibility with it, you can safely ignore this section.

When `RegexOptions.ECMAScript` is in effect, the following apply:

- Only the following may be combined with `RegexOptions.ECMAScript`:

    ```
    RegexOptions.IgnoreCase
    RegexOptions.Multiline
    RegexOptions.Compiled
    ```

- \w, \d, and \s (and \W, \D, and \S) change to ASCII-only matching.

---

† ECMA stands for "European Computer Manufacturers Association," a group formed in 1960 to standardize aspects of the growing field of computers.

- When a backslash-digit sequence is found in a regex, the ambiguity between backreference and octal escape changes to favor a backreference, even if that means having to ignore some of the trailing digits. For example, with ⌈(⋯)\10⌋, the ⌈\10⌋ is taken as a backreference to the first group, followed by a literal '0'.

Using .NET Regular Expressions

.NET regular expressions are powerful, clean, and provided through a complete and easy-to-use class interface. But as wonderful a job that Microsoft did building the package, the documentation is just the opposite—it's horrifically bad. It's woefully incomplete, poorly written, disorganized, and sometimes even wrong. It took me quite a while to figure the package out, so it's my hope that the presentation in this chapter makes the use of .NET regular expressions clear for you.

Regex Quickstart

You can get quite a bit of use out of the .NET regex package without even knowing the details of its regex class model. Knowing the details lets you get more information more efficiently, but the following are examples of how to do simple operations without explicitly creating any classes. These are just examples; all the details follow shortly.

Any program that uses the regex library must have the line

```
Imports System.Text.RegularExpressions
```

at the beginning of the file (☞ 409), so these examples assume that's there.

The following examples all which work with the text in the `String` variable `TestStr`. As with all examples in this chapter, names I've chosen are in italic.

Quickstart: Checking a string for match

This example simply checks to see whether a regex matches a string:

```
If Regex.IsMatch(TestStr, "^\s*$")
    Console.WriteLine("line is empty")
Else
    Console.WriteLine("line is not empty")
End If
```

This example uses a match option:

```
If Regex.IsMatch(TestStr, "^subject:", RegexOptions.IgnoreCase)
    Console.WriteLine("line is a subject line")
Else
    Console.WriteLine("line is not a subject line")
End If
```

Quickstart: Matching and getting the text matched

This example identifies the text actually matched by the regex. If there's no match, TheNum is set to an empty string.

```
Dim TheNum as String = Regex.Match(TestStr, "\d+").Value
If TheNum <> ""
    Console.WriteLine("Number is: " & TheNum)
End If
```

This example uses a match option:

```
Dim ImgTag as String = Regex.Match(TestStr, "<img\b[^>]*>", _
                                    RegexOptions.IgnoreCase).Value
If ImgTag <> ""
    Console.WriteLine("Image tag: " & ImgTag)
End If
```

Quickstart: Matching and getting captured text

This example gets the first captured group (e.g., $1) as a string:

```
Dim Subject as String = _
    Regex.Match(TestStr, "^Subject: (.*)").Groups(1).Value
If Subject <> ""
    Console.WriteLine("Subject is: " & Subject)
End If
```
Note that C# uses Groups[1] instead of Groups(1).

Here's the same thing, using a match option:

```
Dim Subject as String = _
    Regex.Match(TestStr, "^subject: (.*)", _
              RegexOptions.IgnoreCase).Groups(1).Value
If Subject <> ""
    Console.WriteLine("Subject is: " & Subject)
End If
```

This example is the same as the previous, but using named capture:

```
Dim Subject as String = _
    Regex.Match(TestStr, "^subject: (?<Subj>.*)", _
              RegexOptions.IgnoreCase).Groups("Subj").Value
If Subject <> ""
    Console.WriteLine("Subject is: " & Subject)
End If
```

Quickstart: Search and replace

This example makes our test string "safe" to include within HTML, converting characters special to HTML into HTML entities:

```
TestStr = Regex.Replace(TestStr, "&", "&amp;")
TestStr = Regex.Replace(TestStr, "<", "&lt;")
TestStr = Regex.Replace(TestStr, ">", "&gt;")
Console.WriteLine("Now safe in HTML: " & TestStr)
```

The replacement string (the third argument) is interpreted specially, as described in the sidebar on page 418. For example, within the replacement string, '$&' is replaced by the text actually matched by the regex. Here's an example that wraps <B>···</B> around capitalized words:

```
TestStr = Regex.Replace(TestStr, "\b[A-Z]\w*", "<B>$&</B>")
Console.WriteLine("Modified string: " & TestStr)
```

This example replaces <B>···</B> (in a case-insensitive manner) with <I>···</I>:

```
TestStr = Regex.Replace(TestStr, "<b>(.*?)</b>", "<I>$1</I>", _
                        RegexOptions.IgnoreCase)
Console.WriteLine("Modified string: " & TestStr)
```

Package Overview

You can get the most out .NET regular expressions by working with its rich and convenient class structure. To give us an overview, here's a complete console application that shows a simple match using explicit objects:

```
Option Explicit On  ' These are not specifically required to use regexes,
Option Strict On    '  but their use is good general practice.

'  Make regex-related classes easily available.
Imports System.Text.RegularExpressions

Module SimpleTest
Sub Main()
    Dim SampleText as String = "this is the 1st test string"
    Dim R as Regex = New Regex("\d+\w+")  ' Compile the pattern.
    Dim M as Match = R.match(SampleText)  ' Check against a string.
    If not M.Success
        Console.WriteLine("no match")
    Else
        Dim MatchedText as String  = M.Value ' Query the results . . .
        Dim MatchedFrom as Integer = M.Index
        Dim MatchedLen  as Integer = M.Length
        Console.WriteLine("matched [" & MatchedText & "]" & _
                          " from char#" & MatchedFrom.ToString() & _
                          " for " & MatchedLen.ToString() & " chars.")
    End If
End Sub
End Module
```

When executed from a command prompt, it applies ⌜\d+\w+⌟ to the sample text and displays:

```
matched [1st] from char#12 for 3 chars.
```

Importing the regex namespace

Notice the `Imports System.Text.RegularExpressions` line near the top of the program? That's required in any VB program that wishes to access the .NET regex objects, to make them available to the compiler.

The analogous statement in C# is:

```
using System.Text.RegularExpressions;  // This is for C#
```

The example shows the use of the underlying raw regex objects. The two main action lines:

```
Dim R as Regex = New Regex("\d+\w+")   ' Compile the pattern.
Dim M as Match = R.Match(SampleText)   ' Check against a string.
```

can also be combined, as:

```
Dim M as Match = Regex.Match(SampleText, "\d+\w+")   ' Check pattern against string.
```

The combined version is easier to work with, as there's less for the programmer to type, and less objects to keep track of. It does, however, come with at a slight efficiency penalty (☞ 426). Over the coming pages, we'll first look at the raw objects, and then at the "convenience" functions like the `Regex.Match` static function, and when it makes sense to use them.

For brevity's sake, I'll generally not repeat the following lines in examples that are not complete programs:

```
Option Explicit On
Option Strict On
Imports System.Text.RegularExpressions
```

It may also be helpful to look back at some of VB examples earlier in the book, on pages 96, 99, 204, 218, and 236.

Core Object Overview

Before getting into the details, let's first take a step back and look the .NET regex object model. An object model is the set of class structures through which regex functionality is provided. .NET regex functionality is provided through seven highly-interwoven classes, but in practice, you'll generally need to understand only the three shown visually in Figure 9-1 on the facing page, which depicts the repeated application of ⌈\s+(\d+)⌋ to the string 'Mar•16, •1998'.

Regex objects

The first step is to create a `Regex` object, as with:

```
Dim R as Regex = New Regex("\s+(\d+)")
```

Here, we've made a regex object representing ⌈\s+(\d+)⌋ and stored it in the R variable. Once you've got a `Regex` object, you can apply it to text with its `Match(text)` method, which returns information on the first match found:

```
Dim M as Match = R.Match("May 16, 1998")
```

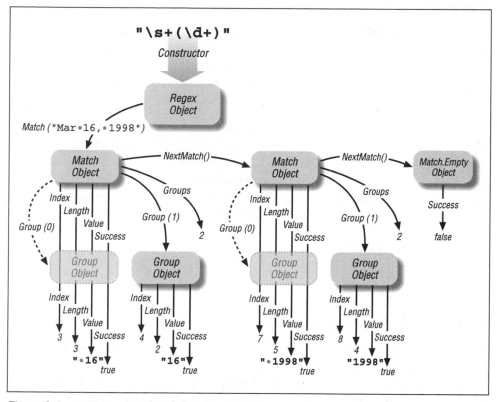

Figure 9-1: .NET's Regex-related object model

Match objects

A `Regex` object's `Match(⋯)` method provides information about a match result by creating and returning a `Match` object. A `Match` object has a number of properties, including `Success` (a Boolean value indicating whether the match was successful) and `Value` (a copy of the text actually matched, if the match was successful). We'll look at the full list of `Match` properties later.

Among the details you can get about a match from a `Match` object is information about the text matched within capturing parentheses. The Perl examples in earlier chapters used Perl's `$1` variable to get the text matched within the first set of capturing parentheses. .NET offers two methods to retrieve this data: to get the raw text, you can index into a `Match` object's `Groups` property, such as with `Groups(1).Value` to get the equivalent of Perl's `$1`. (Note: C# requires a different syntax, `Groups[1].Value`, instead.) Another approach is to use the `Result` method, which is discussed starting on page 423.

Group objects

The `Groups(1)` part in the previous paragraph actually references a `Group` object, and the subsequent `.Value` references *its* `Value` property (the text associated with the group). There is a `Group` object for each set of capturing parentheses, and a "virtual group," numbered zero, which holds the information about the overall match.

Thus, *MatchObj*`.Value` and *MatchObj*`.Groups(0).Value` are the same — a copy of the entire text matched. It's more concise and convenient to use the first, shorter approach, but it's important to know about the zeroth group because *MatchObj*`.Groups.Count` (the number of groups known to the `Match` object) includes it. The *MatchObj*`.Groups.Count` resulting from a successful match with ⌜`\s+(\d+)`⌟ is two (the whole-match "zeroth" group, and the $1 group).

Capture objects

There is also a `Capture` object. It's not used often, but it's discussed starting on page 431.

All results are computed at match time

When a regex is applied to a string, resulting in a `Match` object, all the results (where it matched, what each capturing group matched, etc.) are calculated and encapsulated into the `Match` object. Accessing properties and methods of the `Match` object, including its `Group` objects (and their properties and methods) merely fetches the results that have already been computed.

Core Object Details

Now that we've seen an overview, let's look at the details. First, we'll look at how to create a `Regex` object, followed by how to apply it to a string to yield a `Match` object, and how to work with that object and its `Group` objects.

In practice, you can often avoid having to explicitly create a `Regex` object, but it's good to be comfortable with them, so during this look at the core objects, I'll always explicitly create them. We'll see later what shortcuts .NET provides to make things more convenient.

In the lists that follow, I don't mention little-used methods that are merely inherited from the `Object` class.

Creating Regex Objects

The constructor for creating a `Regex` object is uncomplicated. It accepts either one argument (the regex, as a string), or two arguments (the regex and a set of options). Here's a one-argument example:

```
Dim StripTrailWS = new Regex("\s+$")  ' for removing trailing whitespace
```

This just creates the `Regex` object, preparing it for use; no matching has been done to this point.

Here's a two-argument example:

```
Dim GetSubject = new Regex("^subject: (.*)", RegexOptions.IgnoreCase)
```

That passes one of the `RegexOptions` flags, but you can pass multiple flags if they're OR'd together, as with:

```
Dim GetSubject = new Regex("^subject: (.*)", _
                     RegexOptions.IgnoreCase OR RegexOptions.Multiline)
```

Catching exceptions

An `ArgumentException` error is thrown if a regex with an invalid combination of metacharacters is given. You don't normally need to catch this exception when using regular expressions you know to work, but it's important to catch it if using regular expressions from "outside" the program (e.g., entered by the user, or read from a configuration file). Here's an example:

```
Dim R As Regex
Try
    R = New Regex(SearchRegex)
Catch e As ArgumentException
    Console.WriteLine("*ERROR* bad regex: " & e.ToString)
    Exit Sub
End Try
```

Of course, depending on the application, you may want to do something other than writing to the console upon detection of the exception.

Regex options

The following option flags are allowed when creating a `Regex` object:

RegexOptions.**IgnoreCase**

> This option indicates that when the regex is applied, it should be done in a case-insensitive manner (☞ 109).

RegexOptions.**IgnorePatternWhitespace**

> This option indicates that the regex should be parsed in a free-spacing and comments mode (☞ 110). If you use raw `#` comments, be sure to include a newline at the end of each logical line, or the first raw comment "comments out" the entire rest of the regex.

In VB.NET, this can be achieved with chr(10), as in this example:

```
Dim R as Regex = New Regex( _
    "# Match a floating-point number ...             " & chr(10) & _
    "  \d+(?:\.\d*)? # with a leading digit...        " & chr(10) & _
    "  |              # or ...                         " & chr(10) & _
    "  \.\d+          # with a leading decimal point", _
    RegexOptions.IgnorePatternWhitespace)
```

That's cumbersome; in VB.NET, ⌜(?#···)⌟ comments can be more convenient:

```
Dim R as Regex = New Regex( _
    "(?# Match a floating-point number ...            )" & _
    "  \d+(?:\.\d*)? (?# with a leading digit...       )" & _
    "  |              (?# or ...                        )" & _
    "  \.\d+          (?# with a leading decimal point )", _
    RegexOptions.IgnorePatternWhitespace)
```

RegexOptions.**Multiline**

This option indicates that the regex should be applied in an enhanced line-anchor mode (☞ 111). This allows ⌜^⌟ and ⌜$⌟ to match at embedded newlines in addition to the normal beginning and end of string, respectively.

RegexOptions.**Singleline**

This option indicates that the regex should be applied in a dot-matches-all mode (☞ 110). This allows *dot* to match any character, rather than any character except a newline.

RegexOptions.**ExplicitCapture**

This option indicates that even raw ⌜(···)⌟ parentheses, which are normally capturing parentheses, should not capture, but rather behave like ⌜(?:···)⌟ grouping-only non-capturing parentheses. This leaves named-capture ⌜(?<*name*>···)⌟ parentheses as the only type of capturing parentheses.

If you're using named capture and also want non-capturing parentheses for grouping, it makes sense to use normal ⌜(···)⌟ parentheses and this option, as it keeps the regex more visually clear.

RegexOptions.**RightToLeft**

This option sets the regex to a right-to-left match mode (☞ 405).

RegexOptions.**Compiled**

This option indicates that the regex should be compiled, on the fly, to a highly-optimized format, which generally leads to much faster matching. This comes at the expense of increased compile time the first time it's used, and increased memory use for the duration of the program's execution.

If a regex is going to be used just once, or sparingly, it makes little sense to use RegexOptions.Compiled, since its extra memory remains used even when a Regex object created with it has been disposed of. But if a regex is used in a time-critical area, it's probably advantageous to use this flag.

You can see an example on page 236, where this option cuts the time for one benchmark about in half. Also, see the discussion about compiling to an assembly (☞ 428).

RegexOptions.**ECMAScript**

This option indicates that the regex should be parsed in a way that's compatible with ECMAScript (☞ 406). If you don't know what ECMAScript is, or don't need compatibility with it, you can safely ignore this option.

RegexOptions.**None**

This is a "no extra options" value that's useful for initializing a `RegexOptions` variable, should you need to. As you decide options are required, they can be OR'd in to it.

Using Regex Objects

Just having a regex object is not useful unless you apply it, so the following methods swing it into action.

RegexObj.**IsMatch**(*target*)   Return type: **Boolean**
RegexObj.**IsMatch**(*target*, *offset*)

The `IsMatch` method applies the object's regex to the *target* string, returning a simple `Boolean` indicating whether the attempt is successful. Here's an example:

```
Dim R as RegexObj = New Regex("^\s*$")
    ⋮
If R.IsMatch(Line) Then
   ' Line is blank . . .
        ⋮
Endif
```

If an *offset* (an integer) is provided, that many characters in the target string are bypassed before the regex is first attempted.

RegexObj.**Match**(*target*)   Return type: **Match** object
RegexObj.**Match**(*target*, *offset*)
RegexObj.**Match**(*target*, *offset*, *maxlength*)

The `Match` method applies the object's regex to the *target* string, returning a `Match` object. With this `Match` object, you can query information about the results of the match (whether it was successful, the text matched, etc.), and initiate the "next" match of the same regex in the string. Details of the `Match` object follow, starting on page 421.

If an *offset* (an integer) is provided, that many characters in the target string are bypassed before the regex is first attempted.

If you provide a *maxlength* argument, it puts matching into a special mode where the *maxlength* characters starting *offset* characters into the *target* string are taken as the *entire* target string, as far as the regex engine is concerned. It pretends that characters outside the range don't even exist, so, for example, ⌜^⌟ can match at *offset* characters into the original *target* string, and ⌜$⌟ can match at *maxlength* characters after that. It also means that lookaround can't "see" the characters outside of that range. This is all very different from when only *offset* is provided, as that merely influences where the transmission begins applying the regex — the engine still "sees" the entire target string.

This table shows examples that illustrate the meaning of *offset* and *maxlength* :

Method call	Results when *RegexObj* is built with . . .		
	⌜\d\d⌟	⌜^\d\d⌟	⌜^\d\d$⌟
RegexObj.Match("May 16, 1998")	match '16'	fail	fail
RegexObj.Match("May 16, 1998", 9)	match '99'	fail	fail
RegexObj.Match("May 16, 1998", 9, 2)	match '99'	match '99'	match '99'

RegexObj.**Matches**(*target*)   Return type: **MatchCollection**

RegexObj.**Matches**(*target*,   *offset*)

The Matches method is similar to the Match method, except Matches returns a collection of Match objects representing *all* the matches in the *target*, rather than just one Match object representing the *first* match. The returned object is a MatchCollection.

For example, after this initialization:

```
Dim R as New Regex("\w+")
Dim Target as String = "a few words"
```

this code snippet

```
Dim BunchOfMatches as MatchCollection = R.Matches(Target)
Dim I as Integer
For I = 0 to BunchOfMatches.Count - 1
    Dim MatchObj as Match = BunchOfMatches.Item(I)
    Console.WriteLine("Match: " & MatchObj.Value)
Next
```

produces this output:

```
Match: a
Match: few
Match: words
```

The following example, which produces the same output, shows that you can dispense with the MatchCollection variable altogether:

```
Dim MatchObj as Match
For Each MatchObj in R.Matches(Target)
    Console.WriteLine("Match: " & MatchObj.Value)
Next
```

Finally, as a comparison, here's how you can accomplish the same thing another way, with the `Match` (rather than `Matches`) method:

```
Dim MatchObj as Match = R.Match(Target)
While MatchObj.Success
    Console.WriteLine("Match: " & MatchObj.Value)
    MatchObj = MatchObj.NextMatch()
End While
```

RegexObj.**Replace**(*target, replacement*)   Return type: **String**

RegexObj.**Replace**(*target, replacement, count*)

RegexObj.**Replace**(*target, replacement, count, offset*)

The `Replace` method does a search-and-replace on the *target* string, returning a (possibly changed) copy of it. It applies the `Regex` object's regular expression, but instead of returning a `Match` object, it replaces the matched text. What the matched text is replaced with depends on the *replacement* argument. The replacement argument is overloaded; it can be either a string or a `MatchEvaluator` delegate. If *replacement* is a string, it is interpreted according to the sidebar on the next page. For example,

```
Dim R_CapWord as New Regex("\b[A-Z]\w*")
  ⋮
Text = R_CapWord.Replace(Text, "<B>$1</B>")
```

wraps each capitalized word with `<B>`…`</B>`.

If *count* is given, only that number of replacements is done. (The default is to do all replacements). To replace just the first match found, for example, use a *count* of one. If you know that there will be only one match, using an explicit *count* of one is more efficient than letting the `Replace` mechanics go through the work of trying to find additional matches. A *count* of -1 means "replace all" (which, again, is the default when no *count* is given).

If an *offset* (an integer) is provided, that many characters in the target string are bypassed before the regex is applied. Bypassed characters are copied through to the result unchanged.

For example, this canonicalizes all whitespace (that is, reduces sequences of whitespace down to a single space):

```
Dim AnyWS as New Regex("\s+")
  ⋮
Target = AnyWS.Replace(Target, " ")
```

This converts 'some••••random••••spacing' to 'some•random•spacing'. The following does the same, except it leaves any *leading* whitespace alone:

```
Dim AnyWS     as New Regex("\s+")
Dim LeadingWS as New Regex("^\s+")
  ⋮
Target = AnyWS.Replace(Target, " ", -1, LeadingWS.Match(Target).Length)
```

This converts '••••some•••random••••spacing' to '••••some•random•spacing'. It uses the length of what's matched by `LeadingWS` as the offset (as the count of characters to skip) when doing the search and replace. It uses a convenient feature of the `Match` object, returned here by `LeadingWS.Match(Target)`, that its `Length` property may be used even if the match fails. (Upon failure, the `Length` property has a value of zero, which is exactly what we need to apply `AnyWS` to the entire target.)

Special Per-Match Replacement Sequences

Both the `Regex.Replace` method and the `Match.Result` method accept a "replacement" string that's interpreted specially. Within it, the following sequences are replaced by appropriate text from the match:

Sequence	Replaced by
$&	text matched by the regex (also available as $0)
$1, $2, ...	text matched by the corresponding set of capturing parentheses
${*name*}	text matched by the corresponding named capture
$`	text of the target string *before* the match location
$'	text of the target string *after* the match location
$$	a single '$' character
$_	a copy of the entire original target string
$+	(see text below)

The `$+` sequence is fairly useless as currently implemented. Its origins lie with Perl's useful `$+` variable, which references the highest-numbered set of capturing parentheses that *actually participated* in the match. (There's an example of it in use on page 202.) This .NET replacement-string `$+`, though, merely references the highest-numbered set of capturing parentheses in the regex. It's particularly useless in light of the capturing-parentheses renumbering that's automatically done when named captures are used (☞ 403).

Any uses of '$' in the replacement string in situations other than those described in the table are left unmolested.

Using a replacement delegate

The *replacement* argument isn't limited to a simple string. It can be a *delegate* (basically, a pointer to a function). The delegate function is called after each match to generate the text to use as the replacement. Since the function can do any processing you want, it's an extremely powerful replacement mechanism.

The delegate is of the type `MatchEvaluator`, and is called once per match. The function it refers to should accept the `Match` object for the match, do whatever processing you like, and return the text to be used as the replacement.

As examples for comparison, the following two code snippets produce identical results:

```
Target = R.Replace(Target, "<<$&>>"))
```

```
Function MatchFunc(ByVal M as Match) as String
  return M.Result("<<$&>>")
End Function
Dim Evaluator as MatchEvaluator = New MatchEvaluator(AddressOf MatchFunc)
    ⋮
Target = R.Replace(Target, Evaluator)
```

Both snippets highlight each match by wrapping the matched text in `<< ⋯ >>`. The advantage of using a delegate is that you can include code as complex as you like in computing the replacement. Here's an example that converts Celsius temperatures to Fahrenheit:

```
Function MatchFunc(ByVal M as Match) as String
  ' Get numeric temperature from $1, then convert to Fahrenheit
  Dim Celsius as Double = Double.Parse(M.Groups(1).Value)
  Dim Fahrenheit as Double = Celsius * 9/5 + 32
  Return Fahrenheit & "F"  ' Append an "F", and return
End Function

Dim Evaluator as MatchEvaluator = New MatchEvaluator(AddressOf MatchFunc)
    ⋮
Dim R_Temp as Regex = New Regex("(\d+)C\b", RegexOptions.IgnoreCase)
Target = R_Temp.Replace(Target, Evaluator)
```

Given '`Temp is 37C.`' in `Target`, it replace it with '`Temp is 98.6F.`'.

RegexObj.**Split**(*target*)   Return type: array of **String**

RegexObj.**Split**(*target,* *count*)

RegexObj.**Split**(*target,* *count,* *offset*)

The `Split` method applies the object's regex to the *target* string, returning an array of the strings *separated* by the matches. Here's a trivial example:

```
Dim R as New Regex("\.")
Dim Parts as String() = R.Split("209.204.146.22")
```

The `R.Split` returns the array of four strings ('`209`', '`204`', '`146`', and '`22`') that are separated by the three matches of ⌈`\.`⌋ in the text.

If a *count* is provided, no more than *count* strings will be returned (unless capturing parentheses are used—more on that in a bit). If *count* is not provided, `Split` returns as many strings as are separated by matches. Providing a *count* may mean that the regex stops being applied before the final match, and if so, the last string has the unsplit remainder of the line:

```
Dim R as New Regex("\.")
Dim Parts as String() = R.Split("209.204.146.22", 2)
```

This time, `Parts` receives two strings, '`209`' and '`204.146.22`'.

If an *offset* (an integer) is provided, that many characters in the target string are bypassed before the regex is attempted. The bypassed text becomes part of the first string returned (unless `RegexOptions.RightToLeft` has been specified, in which case the bypassed text becomes part of the *last* string returned).

Using `Split` *with capturing parentheses*

If capturing parentheses of any type are used, additional entries for captured text are *usually* inserted into the array. (We'll see in what cases they might not be inserted in a bit.) As a simple example, to separate a string like '2002-12-31' or '04/12/2003' into its component parts, you might split on ⌈[-/]⌋, like:

```
Dim R as New Regex("[-/]")
Dim Parts as String() = R.Split(MyDate)
```

This returns a list of the three numbers (as strings). However, adding capturing parentheses and using ⌈([-/])⌋ as the regex causes `Split` to return five strings: if `MyDate` contains '2002-12-31', the strings are '2002', '-', '12', '-', and '31'. The extra '-' elements are from the per-capture $1.

If there are multiple sets of capturing parentheses, they are inserted in their numerical ordering (which means that all named captures come after all unnamed captures ☞ 403).

`Split` works consistently with capturing parentheses so long as all sets of capturing parentheses actually participate in the match. However, there's a bug with the current version of .NET such that if there is a set of capturing parentheses that doesn't participate in the match, it and all higher-numbered sets *don't* add an element to the returned list.

As a somewhat contrived example, consider wanting to split on a comma with optional whitespace around it, yet have the whitespace added to the list of elements returned. You might use ⌈(\s+)?,(\s+)?⌋ for this. When applied with `Split` to 'this␣,␣␣that', four strings are returned, 'this', '␣', '␣␣', and 'that'. However, when applied to 'this,␣that', the inability of the first set of capturing parentheses to match inhibits the element for it (and for all sets that follow) from being added to the list, so only two strings are returned, 'this' and 'that'. The inability to know beforehand exactly how many strings will be returned per match is a major shortcoming of the current implementation.

In this particular example, you could get around this problem simply by using ⌈(\s*),(\s*)⌋ (in which both groups are guaranteed to participate in any overall match). However, more complex expressions are not easily rewritten.

RegexObj.**GetGroupNames()**
RegexObj.**GetGroupNumbers()**
RegexObj.**GroupNameFromNumber(** *number* **)**
RegexObj.**GroupNumberFromName(** *name* **)**

These methods allow you to query information about the names (both numeric and, if named capture is used, by name) of capturing groups in the regex. They don't refer to any particular match, but merely to the names and numbers of groups that exist in the regex. The sidebar on the next page shows an example of their use.

RegexObj.**ToString()**
RegexObj.**RightToLeft**
RegexObj.**Options**

These allow you to query information about the `Regex` object itself (as opposed to applying the regex object to a string). The `ToString()` method returns the pattern string originally passed to the regex constructor. The `RightToLeft` property returns a Boolean indicating whether `RegexOptions.RightToLeft` was specified with the regex. The `Options` property returns the `RegexOptions` that are associated with the regex. The following table shows the values of the individual options, which are added together when reported:

0	None	16	Singleline
1	IgnoreCase	32	IgnorePatternWhitespace
2	Multiline	64	RightToLeft
4	ExplicitCapture	256	ECMAScript
8	Compiled		

The missing 128 value is for a Microsoft debugging option not available in the final product.

The sidebar on the next page shows an example these methods in use.

Using Match Objects

`Match` objects are created by a `Regex`'s `Match` method, the `Regex.Match` static function (discussed in a bit), and a `Match` object's own `NextMatch` method. It encapsulates all information relating to a single application of a regex. It has the following properties and methods:

MatchObj.**Success**

This returns a Boolean indicating whether the match was successful. If not, the object is a copy of the static `Match.Empty` object.

Displaying Information about a Regex Object

This displays what's known about the Regex object in the variable R:

```
' Display information known about the Regex object in the variable R
Console.WriteLine("Regex is: " & R.ToString())
Console.WriteLine("Options are: " & R.Options)
If R.RightToLeft
    Console.WriteLine("Is Right-To-Left: True")
Else
    Console.WriteLine("Is Right-To-Left: False")
End If

Dim S as String
For Each S in R.GetGroupNames()
    Console.WriteLine("Name """ & S & """ is Num #" & _
                      R.GroupNumberFromName(S))
Next
Console.WriteLine("---")
Dim I as Integer
For Each I in R.GetGroupNumbers()
    Console.WriteLine("Num #" & I & " is Name """ & _
                      R.GroupNameFromNumber(I) & """")
Next
```

Run twice, once with each of the two Regex objects created with

```
New Regex("^(\w+)://([^/]+)(/\S*)")

New Regex("^(?<proto>\w+)://(?<host>[^/]+)(?<page>/\S*)",
          RegexOptions.Compiled)
```

the following output is produced (with one regex cut off to fit the page):

```
Regex is: ^(\w+)://([^/]+)(/\S*)      Regex is: ^(?<proto>\w+)://(?<host> ···
Option are: 0                         Option are: 8
(Is Right-To-Left: False)             (Is Right-To-Left: False)
Name "0" is Num #0                    Name "0" is Num #0
Name "1" is Num #1                    Name "proto" is Num #1
Name "2" is Num #2                    Name "host" is Num #2
Name "3" is Num #3                    Name "page" is Num #3
---                                   ---
Num #0 is Name "0"                    Num #0 is Name "0"
Num #1 is Name "1"                    Num #1 is Name "proto"
Num #2 is Name "2"                    Num #2 is Name "host"
Num #3 is Name "3"                    Num #3 is Name "page"
```

MatchObj.**Value**

MatchObj.**ToString()**

These return copies of the text actually matched.

MatchObj.**Length**

This returns the length of the text actually matched.

MatchObj.**Index**

This returns an integer indicating the position in the target text where the match was found. It's a zero-based index, so it's the number of characters from the start (left) of the string to the start (left) of the matched text. This is true even if `RegexOptions.RightToLeft` had been used to create the regex that generated this `Match` object.

MatchObj.**Groups**

This property is a `GroupCollection` object, in which a number of `Group` objects are encapsulated. It is a normal collection object, with a `Count` and `Item` properties, but it's most commonly accessed by indexing into it, fetching an individual `Group` object. For example, `M.Groups(3)` is the `Group` object related to the third set of capturing parentheses, and `M.Groups("HostName")` is the group object for the "Hostname" named capture (e.g., after the use of ⌜`(?<HostName>…)`⌟ in a regex).

Note that C# requires `M.Groups[3]` and `M.Groups["HostName"]` instead.

The zeroth group represents the entire match itself. *MatchObj*.`Groups(0).Value`, for example, is the same as *MatchObj*.`Value`.

MatchObj.**NextMatch()**

The `NextMatch()` method re-invokes the original regex to find the next match in the original string, returning a new `Match` object.

MatchObj.**Result(***string***)**

Special sequences in the given *string* are processed as shown in the sidebar on page 418, returning the resulting text. Here's a simple example:

```
Dim M as Match = Regex.Match(SomeString, "\w+")
Console.WriteLine(M.Result("The first word is '$&'"))
```

You can use this to get a copy of the text to the left and right of the match, with

```
M.Result("$`")    ' This is the text to the left of the match
M.Result("$'")    ' This is the text to the right of the match
```

During debugging, it may be helpful to display something along the lines of:

```
M.Result("[$`<$&>$']"))
```

Given a `Match` object created by applying ⌜`\d+`⌟ to the string 'May 16, 1998', it returns 'May <16>, 1998', clearly showing the exact match.

MatchObj.**Synchronized()**

This returns a new `Match` object that's identical to the current one, except that it's safe for multi-threaded use.

MatchObj.**Captures**

The `Captures` property is not used often, but is discussed starting on page 431.

Using Group Objects

A `Group` object contains the match information for one set of capturing parentheses (or, if a zeroth group, for an entire match). It has the following properties and methods:

GroupObj.**Success**

This returns a Boolean indicating whether the group participated in the match. Not all groups necessarily "participate" in a successful overall match. For example, if ⌜(this)|(that)⌟ matches successfully, one of the sets of parentheses is guaranteed to have participated, while the other is guaranteed to have not. See the footnote on page 138 for another example.

GroupObj.**Value**
GroupObj.**ToString()**

These both return a copy of the text captured by this group. If the match hadn't been successful, these return an empty string.

GroupObj.**Length**

This returns the length of the text captured by this group. If the match hadn't been successful, it returns zero.

GroupObj.**Index**

This returns an integer indicating where in the target text the match was found. The return value is a zero-based index, so it's the number of characters from the start (left) of the string to the start (left) of the captured text. (This is true even if `RegexOptions.RightToLeft` had been used to create the regex that generated this `Match` object.)

GroupObj.**Captures**

The `Group` object also has a `Captures` property discussed starting on page 431.

Static "Convenience" Functions

As we saw in the "Regex Quickstart" beginning on page 407, you don't always have to create explicit `Regex` objects. The following static functions allow you to apply with regular expressions directly:

```
Regex.IsMatch(target, pattern)
Regex.IsMatch(target, pattern, options)

Regex.Match(target, pattern)
Regex.Match(target, pattern, options)

Regex.Matches(target, pattern)
Regex.Matches(target, pattern, options)

Regex.Replace(target, pattern, replacement)
Regex.Replace(target, pattern, replacement, options)

Regex.Split(target, pattern)
Regex.Split(target, pattern, options)
```

Internally, these are just wrappers around the core `Regex` constructor and methods we've already seen. They construct a temporary `Regex` object for you, use it to call the method you've requested, and then throw the object away. (Well, they don't actually throw it away—more on this in a bit.)

Here's an example:

```
If Regex.IsMatch(Line, "^\s*$")
  ⋮
```

That's the same as

```
Dim TemporaryRegex = New Regex("^\s*$")
If TemporaryRegex.IsMatch(Line)
  ⋮
```

or, more accurately, as:

```
If New Regex("^\s*$").IsMatch(Line)
  ⋮
```

The advantage of using these convenience functions is that they generally make simple tasks easier and less cumbersome. They allow an object-oriented package to appear to be a procedural one (☞ 95). The disadvantage is that the *pattern* must be reinspected each time.

If the regex is used just once in the course of the whole program's execution, it doesn't matter from an efficiency standpoint whether a convenience function is used. But, if a regex is used multiple times (such as in a loop, or a commonly-called function), there's some overhead involved in preparing the regex each time (☞ 241). The goal of avoiding this usually expensive overhead is the primary reason you'd build a `Regex` object once, and then use it repeatedly later when actually checking text. However, as the next section shows, .NET offers a way to have the best of both worlds: procedural convenience with object-oriented efficiency.

Regex Caching

Having to always build and save a separate `Regex` object for every little regex you'd like to use can be extremely cumbersome and inconvenient, so it's wonderful that the .NET regex package employs *regex caching.* If you use a pattern/option combination that has already been used during the execution of the program, the internal `Regex` object that had been built the first time is reused, saving *you* the drudgery of having to save and manage the `Regex` object.

.NET's regex caching seems to be very efficient, so I would feel comfortable using the convenience functions in most places. There is a small amount of overhead, as the cache must compare the pattern string and its list of options to those it already has, but that's a small tradeoff for the enhanced program readability of the less-complicated approach that convenience functions offer. I'd still opt for building and managing a raw `Regex` object in very time-sensitive situations, such as applying regexes in a tight loop.

Support Functions

Besides the convenience functions described in the previous section, there are a few other static support functions:

Match.Empty

This function returns a `Match` object that represents a failed match. It is perhaps useful for initializing a `Match` object that you may or may not fill in later, but do intend to query later. Here's a simple example:

```
Dim SubMatch as Match = Match.Empty ' Initialize, in case it's not set in the loop below
  ⋮
Dim Line as String
For Each Line in EmailHeaderLines
    ' If this is the subject, save the match info for later . . .
    Dim ThisMatch as Match = Regex.Match(Line, "^Subject:\s*(.*)", _
                                        RegexOptions.IgnoreCase)
    If ThisMatch.Success
       SubMatch = ThisMatch
    End If
    ⋮
Next
  ⋮
If SubMatch.Success
   Console.WriteLine(SubMatch.Result("The subject is: $1"))
Else
   Console.WriteLine("No subject!")
End If
```

If the string array `EmailHeaderLines` actually has no lines (or no `Subject` lines), the loop that iterates through them won't ever set `SubMatch`, so the inspection of

`SubMatch` after the loop would result in a null reference exception if it hadn't somehow been initialized. So, it's convenient to use `Match.Empty` as the initializer in cases like this.

Regex.Escape(*string*)

Given a string, `Match.Escape(···)` returns a copy of the string with regex metacharacters escaped. This makes the original string appropriate for inclusion in a regex as a literal string.

For example, if you have input from the user in the string variable `SearchTerm`, you might use it to build a regex with:

```
Dim UserRegex as Regex = New Regex("^" & Regex.Escape(SearchTerm) & "$", _
                         RegexOptions.IgnoreCase)
```

This allows the search term to contain regular-expression metacharacters without having them treated as such. If not escaped, a `SearchTerm` value of, say, ':-)' would result in an `ArgumentException` being thrown (☞ 413).

Regex.Unescape(*string*)

This odd little function accepts a string, and returns a copy with certain regex character escape sequences interpreted, and other backslashes removed. For example, if it's passed '\:\-\)', it returns ':-)'.

Character shorthands are also decoded. If the original string has '\n', it's actually replaced with a newline in the returned string. Or if it has '\u1234', the corresponding Unicode character will be inserted into the string. All character shorthands listed at the top of page 401 are interpreted.

I can't imagine a good regex-related use for `Regex.Unescape`, but it may be useful as a general tool for endowing VB strings with some knowledge of escapes.

Regex.CompileToAssembly(···)

This allows you to create an assembly encapsulating a `Regex` object—see the next section.

Advanced .NET

The following pages cover a few features that haven't fit into the discussion so far: building a regex library with regex assemblies, using an interesting .NET-only regex feature for matching nested constructs, and a discussion of the `Capture` object.

Regex Assemblies

.NET allows you to encapsulate `Regex` objects into an assembly, which is useful in creating a regex library. The example in the sidebar on the facing page shows how to build one.

When the sidebar example executes, it creates the file *JfriedlsRegexLibrary.DLL* in the project's *bin* directory.

I can then use that assembly in another project, after first adding it as a reference via Visual Studio .NET's *Project > Add Reference* dialog.

To make the classes in the assembly available, I first import them:

```
Imports jfriedl
```

I can then use them just like any other class, as in this example::

```
Dim FieldRegex as CSV.GetField = New CSV.GetField ' This makes a new Regex object
   ⋮
Dim FieldMatch as Match = FieldRegex.Match(Line)  ' Apply the regex to a string . . .
While FieldMatch.Success
  Dim Field as String
  If FieldMatch.Groups(1).Success
    Field = FieldMatch.Groups("QuotedField").Value
    Field = Regex.Replace(Field, """""", """")  ' replace two double quotes with one
  Else
    Field = FieldMatch.Groups("UnquotedField").Value
  End If

  Console.WriteLine("[" & Field & "]")
  ' Can now work with 'Field'....

  FieldMatch = FieldMatch.NextMatch
End While
```

In this example, I chose to import only from the `jfriedl` namespace, but could have just as easily imported from the `jfriedl.CSV` namespace, which then would allow the `Regex` object to be created with:

```
Dim FieldRegex as GetField = New GetField ' This makes a new Regex object
```

The difference is mostly a matter of style. You can also choose to not import anything, but rather use them directly:

```
Dim FieldRegex as jfriedl.CSV.GetField = New jfriedl.CSV.GetField
```

This is a bit more cumbersome, but documents clearly where exactly the object is coming from. Again, it's a matter of style.

Creating Your Own Regex Library With an Assembly

This example builds a small regex library. This complete program builds an assembly (DLL) that holds three pre-built `Regex` constructors I've named `jfriedl.Mail.Subject`, `jfriedl.Mail.From`, and `jfriedl.CSV.GetField`.

The first two are simple examples just to show how it's done, but the complexity of the final one really shows the promise of building your own library. Note that you don't have to give the `RegexOptions.Compiled` flag, as that's implied by the process of building an assembly.

See the text (☞ 428) for how to use the assembly after it's built.

```
Option Explicit On
Option Strict On

Imports System.Text.RegularExpressions
Imports System.Reflection

Module BuildMyLibrary
Sub Main()
  ' The calls to RegexCompilationInfo below provide the pattern, regex options, name within the class,
  ' class name, and a Boolean indicating whether the new class is public. The first class, for example,
  ' will be available to programs that use this assembly as "jfriedl.Mail.Subject", a Regex constructor.
  Dim RCInfo() as RegexCompilationInfo = {
    New RegexCompilationInfo(
      "^Subject:\s*(.*)", RegexOptions.IgnoreCase,
      "Subject", "jfriedl.Mail", true),
    New RegexCompilationInfo(
      "^From:\s*(.*)", RegexOptions.IgnoreCase,
      "From", "jfriedl.Mail", true),
    New RegexCompilationInfo(
      "\G(?:^|,)                                  " &
      "(?:                                        " &
      "  (?# Either a double-quoted field... )    " &
      "  ""  (?# field's opening quote )          " &
      "    (?<QuotedField>  (?> [^""]+ | """" )*   )  " &
      "  ""  (?# field's closing quote )          " &
      "  (?# ...or... )                           " &
      "  |                                        " &
      "  (?# ...some non-quote/non-comma text... ) " &
      "  (?<UnquotedField> [^"",]* )              " &
      "  )",
      RegexOptions.IgnorePatternWhitespace,
      "GetField", "jfriedl.CSV", true)
  }
  ' Now do the heavy lifting to build and write out the whole thing . . .
  Dim AN as AssemblyName = new AssemblyName()
  AN.Name = "JfriedlsRegexLibrary" ' This will be the DLL's filename
  AN.Version = New Version("1.0.0.0")
  Regex.CompileToAssembly(RCInfo, AN) ' Build everything
End Sub
End Module
```

Matching Nested Constructs

Microsoft has included an interesting innovation for matching balanced constructs (historically, something not possible with a regular expression). It's not particularly easy to understand—this section is short, but be warned, it is very dense.

It's easiest to understand with an example, so I'll start with one:

```
Dim R As Regex = New Regex(" \(                    " & _
                  "     (?>                        " & _
                  "         [^()]+                 " & _
                  "       |                        " & _
                  "         \( (?<DEPTH>)           " & _
                  "       |                        " & _
                  "         \) (?<-DEPTH>)          " & _
                  "     )*                          " & _
                  "     (?(DEPTH)(?!))              " & _
                  " \)                              ", _
          RegexOptions.IgnorePatternWhitespace)
```

This matches the first properly-paired nested set of parentheses, such as the under-lined portion of 'before (nope (yes (here) okay) after'. The first parenthesis isn't matched because it has no associated closing parenthesis.

Here's the super-short overview of how it works:

1. With each '(' matched, ⌈(?<DEPTH>)⌉ adds one to the regex's idea of how deep the parentheses are currently nested (at least, nested beyond the initial ⌈\(⌉ at the start of the regex).

2. With each ')' matched, ⌈(?<-DEPTH>)⌉ subtracts one from that depth.

3. ⌈(?(DEPTH)(?!))⌉ ensures that the depth is zero before allowing the final literal ⌈\)⌉ to match.

This works because the engine's backtracking stack keeps track of successfully-matched groupings. ⌈(?<DEPTH>)⌉ is just a named-capture version of ⌈()⌉, which is always successful. Since it has been placed immediately after ⌈\(⌉, its success (which remains on the stack until removed) is used as a marker for counting opening parentheses.

Thus, the number of successful 'DEPTH' groupings matched so far is maintained on the backtracking stack. We want to subtract from that whenever a closing parentheses is found. That's accomplished by .NET's special ⌈(?<-DEPTH>)⌉ construct, which removes the most recent "successful DEPTH" notation from the stack. If it turns out that there aren't any, the ⌈(?<-DEPTH>)⌉ itself fails, thereby disallowing the regex from over-matching an extra closing parenthesis.

Finally, ⌈(?(DEPTH)(?!))⌉ is a normal conditional that applies ⌈(?!)⌉ if the 'DEPTH' grouping is currently successful. If it's still successful by the time we get here, there was an unpaired opening parenthesis whose success had never been subtracted by a balancing ⌜(?<-DEPTH>)⌟. If that's the case, we want to exit the match (we don't want to match an unbalanced sequence), so we apply ⌜(?!)⌟, which is normal negative lookbehind of an empty subexpression, and guaranteed to fail.

Phew! That's how to match nested constructs with .NET regular expressions.

Capture Objects

There's an additional component to .NET's object model, the `Capture` object, which I haven't discussed yet. Depending on your point of view, it either adds an interesting new dimension to the match results, or adds confusion and bloat.

A `Capture` object is almost identical to a `Group` object in that it represents the text matched within a set of capturing parentheses. Like the `Group` object, it has methods for `Value` (the text matched), `Length` (the length of the text matched), and `Index` (the zero-based number of characters into the target string that the match was found).

The main difference between a `Group` object and a `Capture` object is that each `Group` object contains a collection of `Captures` representing all the *intermediary* matches by the group during the match, as well as the final text matched by the group.

Here's an example with ⌜^(..)+⌟ applied to 'abcdefghijk':

```
Dim M as Match = Regex.Match("abcdefghijk", "^(..)+")
```

The regex matches four sets of ⌜(..)⌟, which is most of the string: 'a͟b͟c͟d͟e͟f͟g͟h͟i͟j͟k'. Since the plus is outside of the parentheses, they recapture with each iteration of the plus, and are left with only 'ij' (that is, `M.Groups(1).Value` is 'ij'). However, that `M.Groups(1)` also contains a collection of `Captures` representing the complete 'ab', 'cd', 'ef', 'gh', and 'ij' that ⌜(..)⌟ walked through during the match:

M.`Groups(1).Captures(0).Value` is 'ab'
M.`Groups(1).Captures(1).Value` is 'cd'
M.`Groups(1).Captures(2).Value` is 'ef'
M.`Groups(1).Captures(3).Value` is 'gh'
M.`Groups(1).Captures(4).Value` is 'ij'
M.`Groups(1).Captures.Count` is 5.

You'll notice that the last capture has the same 'ij' value as the overall match, `M.Groups(1).Value`. It turns out that the `Value` of a `Group` is really just a shorthand notation for the group's final capture. `M.Groups(1).Value` is really:

M.Groups(1).Captures(M.Groups(1).Captures.Count - 1 **).Value**

Here are some additional points about captures:

- `M.Groups(1).Captures` is a `CaptureCollection`, which, like any collection, has `Items` and `Count` properties. However, it's common to forego the `Items` property and index directly through the collection to its individual items, as with `M.Groups(1).Captures(3)` (`M.Groups[1].Captures[3]` in C#).

- A `Capture` object does not have a `Success` method; check the `Group`'s `Success` instead.

- So far, we've seen that `Capture` objects are available from a `Group` object. Although it's not particularly useful, a `Match` object *also* has a `Captures` property. `M.Captures` gives direct access to the `Capture` property of the zeroth group (that is, `M.Captures` is the same as `M.Group(0).Captures`). Since the zeroth group represents the entire match, there are no iterations of it "walking through" a match, so the zeroth captured collection always has only one `Capture`. Since they contain exactly the same information as the zeroth `Group`, both `M.Captures` and `M.Group(0).Captures` are not particularly useful.

.NET's `Capture` object is an interesting innovation that appears somewhat more complex and confusing than it really is by the way it's been "overly integrated" into the object model. After getting past the .NET documentation and actually understanding what these objects add, I've got mixed feelings about them. On one hand, it's an interesting innovation that I'd like to get to know. Uses for it don't immediately jump to mind, but that's likely because I've not had the same years of experience with it as I have with traditional regex features.

On the other hand, the construction of all these extra capture groups during a match, and then their encapsulation into objects after the match, seems an efficiency burden that I wouldn't want to pay unless I'd requested the extra information. The extra `Capture` groups won't be used in the vast majority of matches, but as it is, all `Group` and `Capture` objects (and their associated `GroupCollection` and `CaptureCollection` objects) are built when the `Match` object is built. So, you've got them whether you need them or not; if you can find a use for the `Capture` objects, by all means, use them.

Index

About the Author

Jeffrey E. F. Friedl was raised in the countryside of Rootstown, Ohio, and had aspirations of being an astronomer until one day noticing a TRS-80 Model I sitting unused in the corner of the chem lab (bristling with a full 16K of RAM, no less). He eventually began using Unix (and regular expressions) in 1980, and earned degrees in Computer Science from Kent (BS) and the University of New Hampshire (MS). He did kernel development for Omron Corporation in Kyoto, Japan for eight years before moving in 1997 to Silicon Valley to apply his regular-expression know-how to financial news and data for a little-known company called "Yahoo!".

When faced with the daunting task of filling his copious free time, Jeffrey enjoys playing Ultimate Frisbee and basketball with friends at Yahoo!, programming his house, and feeding the squirrels and jays in his back yard. He also enjoys spending time with his wife Fumie, and preparing for the Fall 2002 release of their first "software project" together.

Colophon

Our look is the result of reader comments, our own experimentation, and feedback from distribution channels. Distinctive covers complement our distinctive approach to technical topics, breathing personality and life into potentially dry subjects.

The animals on the cover of *Mastering Regular Expressions*, Second Edition, are owls. There are two families and approximately 180 species of these birds of prey distributed throughout the world, with the exception of Antarctica. Most species of owls are nocturnal hunters, feeding entirely on live animals, ranging in size from insects to hares.

Because they have little ability to move their large, forward-facing eyes, owls must move their entire heads in order to look around. They can rotate their heads up to 270 degrees, and some can turn their heads completely upside down. Among the physical adaptations that enhance owls' effectiveness as hunters is their extreme sensitivity to the frequency and direction of sounds. Many species of owl have asymmetrical ear placement, which enables them to more easily locate their prey in dim or dark light. Once they've pinpointed the location, the owl's soft feathers allow them to fly noiselessly and thus to surprise their prey.

While people have traditionally anthropomorphized birds of prey as evil and cold-blooded creatures, owls are viewed differently in human mythology. Perhaps because their large eyes give them the appearance of intellectual depth, owls have been portrayed in folklore through the ages as wise creatures.

Jeffrey E. F. Friedl was the production editor for *Mastering Regular Expressions*, Second Edition. Sarah Jane Shangraw was the proofreader. Jane Ellin provided quality control.

Edie Freedman designed the cover of this book. The cover image is a 19th-century engraving from the Dover Pictorial Archive. Emma Colby produced the cover layout with QuarkXPress 4.1 using Adobe's ITC Garamond font.

The text was prepared by Jeffrey Friedl in a hybrid markup of his own design, mixing SGML, raw troff, raw PostScript, and his own markup. A home-grown filter translated the latter to the other, lower-level markups, the result of which was processed by a locally-modified version of O'Reilly's SGML tools. That result was then processed by a locally-modified version of James Clark's gtroff, producing camera-ready PostScript for O'Reilly.

Ken Lunde of Adobe Systems provided special font and typesetting help, including custom-designed characters and Japanese characters from Adobe Systems's Heisei Mincho W3 typeface.

The text and heading fonts are ITC Garamond Light and Garamond Book; the code font is Constant Willison. The illustrations that appear in the book were produced by Chris Reilly, Robert Romano, and Jessamyn Read using Macromedia FreeHand 9 and Adobe Photoshop 6.

 # More Titles from O'Reilly

Perl

Learning Perl, 3rd Edition

By Randal Schwartz & Tom Phoenix
3rd Edition July 2001
330 pages, ISBN 0-596-00132-0

Learning Perl is the quintessential tutorial for the Perl programming language. The third edition has not only been updated to Perl Version 5.6, but has also been rewritten from the ground up to reflect the needs of programmers learning Perl today. Other books may teach you to program in Perl, but this book will turn you into a Perl programmer.

Learning Perl on Win32 Systems

By Randal L. Schwartz, Erik Olson &
Tom Christiansen
1st Edition August 1997
306 pages, ISBN 1-56592-324-3

In this carefully paced course, leading Perl trainers and a Windows NT practitioner teach you to program in the language that promises to emerge as the scripting language of choice on NT. Based on the "llama" book, this book features tips for PC users and new NT-specific examples, along with a foreword by Larry Wall, the creator of Perl, and Dick Hardt, the creator of Perl for Win32.

Perl/Tk Pocket Reference

By Stephen Lidie
1st Edition November 1998
103 pages, ISBN 1-56592-517-3

The *Perl/Tk Pocket Reference* is a companion volume to *Learning Perl/Tk*. This handy reference book describes every Perl/Tk graphical element, including general widget and variable information, callbacks, geometry management, bindings, events, and window management, as well as composite widget, font, and image creation and manipulation commands.

Mastering Perl/Tk

By Steve Lidie & Nancy Walsh
1st Edition January 2002
768 pages, ISBN 1-56592-716-8

Beginners and seasoned Perl/Tk programmers alike will find *Mastering Perl/Tk* to be the definitive book on creating graphical user interfaces with Perl/Tk. After a fast-moving tutorial, the book goes into detail on creating custom widgets, working with bindings and callbacks, IPC techniques, and examples using many of the non-standard add-on widgets for Perl/Tk (including Tix widgets). Every Perl/Tk programmer will need this book.

Perl Cookbook

By Tom Christiansen & Nathan Torkington
1st Edition August 1998
794 pages, ISBN 1-56592-243-3

The *Perl Cookbook* is a comprehensive collection of problems, solutions, and practical examples for anyone programming in Perl. You'll find hundreds of rigorously reviewed Perl "recipes" for manipulating strings, numbers, dates, arrays, and hashes; pattern matching and text substitutions; references, data structures, objects, and classes; signals and exceptions; and much more.

O'REILLY®

TO ORDER: **800-998-9938** • **order@oreilly.com** • **www.oreilly.com**
ONLINE EDITIONS OF MOST O'REILLY TITLES ARE AVAILABLE BY SUBSCRIPTION AT **safari.oreilly.com**
ALSO AVAILABLE AT MOST RETAIL AND ONLINE BOOKSTORES

Perl

Perl & LWP

By Sean M. Burke
1st Edition, June 2002
264 pages, 0-596-00178-9

This comprehensive guide to LWP and its applications comes with many practical examples. Topics include programmatically fetching web pages, submitting forms, using various techniques for HTML parsing, handling cookies, and authentication. With the knowledge in Perl & LWP, you can automate any task on the Web, from checking the prices of items at online stores to bidding at auctions automatically.

Perl Graphics Programming

By Shawn Wallace
1st Edition, August 2002 (est.)
504 pages (est.), 0-596-00219-X

This insightful volume focuses on scripting programs that enable programmers to manipulate graphics for the Web. The book also helps demystify the manipulation of graphics formats for web newcomers with a practical, resource-like approach. While most of the examples use Perl as a scripting language, the concepts are applicable to any programming language. The book documents ways to use several powerful Perl modules for generating graphics, including GD, PerlMagick, and GIMP.

Computer Science & Perl Programming: Best of The Perl Journal

Edited by Jon Orwant
1st Edition, November 2002 (est.)
600 pages, ISBN 0-596-00310-2

The first of three volumes from the archives of The Perl Journal that O'Reilly has exclusive rights to distribute, this book is a compilation of the best from TPJ: 71 articles providing a comprehensive tour of how experts implement computer science concepts in the real world, with code walkthroughs, case studies, and explanations of difficult techniques that can't be found in any other book.

Web, Graphics & Perl/Tk: Best of The Perl Journal

Edited by Jon Orwant
1st Edition November 2002 (est.)
504 pages (est.), ISBN 0-596-00311-0

Web, Graphics & Perl/Tk Programming, the second volume of The Perl Journal series, covers topics not included in O'Reilly's other Perl books. Half of the articles in this volume deal with essential issues faced by web developers using Perl, such as CGI scripting, mod_perl programming, and content management with the Apache web server. Remaining articles offer top-to-bottom coverage of how Perl programmers can create graphical applications with Perl/Tk and Gnome. TPJ's archives go back as far as 1996 and the material is still vital today.

Games, Diversions & Perl Culture: Best of the Perl Journal

Edited by Jon Orwant
1st Edition November 2002 (est.)
504 pages (est.), ISBN 0-596-00312-9

Games, Diversions & Perl Culture, focuses on entertaining topics that make Perl users such fanatics about the language. Inside, you will find all of the playful features TPJ offered over the years, including the Obfuscated Perl Contests, Perl Quiz Shows, humor articles, and renowned one-line recipes.

O'REILLY®

TO ORDER: 800-998-9938 • order@oreilly.com • www.oreilly.com
ONLINE EDITIONS OF MOST O'REILLY TITLES ARE AVAILABLE BY SUBSCRIPTION AT safari.oreilly.com
ALSO AVAILABLE AT MOST RETAIL AND ONLINE BOOKSTORES

Microsoft .NET Programming

VB.NET Language in a Nutshell, 2nd Edition

By Steven Roman, Ron Petrusha & Paul Lomax
2nd Edition May 2002
682 pages, ISBN 0-596-00308-0

The documentation that comes with VB typically provides only the bare details for each language element; left out is the valuable inside information that a programmer really needs to know in order to solve programming problems or to use a particular language element effectively. *VB .NET Language in a Nutshell*, 2nd Edition documents the undocumented and presents the kind of wisdom that comes from the authors' many years of experience with the language. Bonus CD ingegrates the book's reference section with Visual Studio .NET.

Programming C#, 2nd Edition

By Jesse Liberty
2nd Edition February 2002
650 pages, ISBN 0-596-00309-9

The first part of *Programming C#*, 2nd Edition introduces C# fundamentals, then goes on to explain the development of desktop and Internet applications, including Windows Forms, ADO.NET, ASP.NET (including Web Forms), and Web Services. Next, this book gets to the heart of the .NET Framework, focusing on attributes and reflection, remoting, threads and synchronization, streams, and finally, it illustrates how to interoperate with COM objects.

Programming Visual Basic .NET

By Dave Grudgeiger
1st Edition December 2001
460 pages, ISBN 0-596-00093-6

Starting with a sample application and a high-level map, *Programming Visual Basic .NET* will give you an idea of where the various parts of .NET fit with VB .NET. Ensuing chapters break down and present the language, the common language runtime, Windows Forms, ASP.NET and Web Forms, Web Services, and ADO.NET. The book then moves into topics on developing transactional applications, internationalization, security, and debugging.

Programming ASP.NET

By Jesse Liberty & Dan Hurwitz
1st Edition February 2002
960 pages, ISBN 0-596-00171-1

Programming ASP.NET is aimed at experienced programmers and web developers, who have the desire to quickly create ASP.NET applications. Rudimentary topics such as language syntax, datatypes, and program control are treated concisely so greater attention can be devoted to applications development. By design, this book features many short examples, rather than a single, unmanageably large application, in order to show the widest range of constructs, both valid and invalid.

C# in a Nutshell

By Peter Drayton & Ben Albarhari
1st Edition March 2002
856 pages, ISBN 0-596-00181-9

C# is likely to become one of the most widely used languages for building .NET applications. *C# in a Nutshell* contains a concise introduction to the language and its syntax, plus brief tutorials used to accomplish common programming tasks. It also includes O'Reilly's classic-style, quick-reference material for all the types and members in core .NET namespaces, including System, System.Text, System.IO, and System.Collections.

ASP.NET in a Nutshell

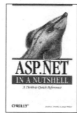

By G. Andrew Duthie & Matthew MacDonald
1st Edition June 2002
816 pages, ISBN 0-596-00116-9

As a quick reference, *ASP.NET in a Nutshell* goes beyond the published documentation by highlighting little-known details, stressing practical uses for particular features, and providing real-world examples. With only a quick introduction, this book then documents application and web service development, the creation of custom controls, data access, security, deployment, and error handling. It also presents an overview of the class libraries and provides information on migration from ASP to ASP.NET.

Microsoft .NET Programming

.NET Framework Essentials, 2nd Edition

By Thuan L. Thai, Hoang Lam
2nd Edition February 2002
320 pages, 0-596-00302-1

.NET Framework Essentials, 2nd Edition is a concise and technical overview of the Microsoft .NET Framework. Covered here are all of the most important topics—from the underlying Common Language Runtime (CLR) to its specialized packages for ASP.NET, Web Forms, Windows Forms, XML and data access (ADO.NET). The authors survey each of the major .NET languages, including Visual Basic .NET, C# and Managed C++.

C# Essentials, 2nd Edition

By Brad Merrill, Peter Drayton & Ben Albahari
2nd Edition January 2002
216 pages, 0-596-00315-3

Concise but thorough, this second edition of *C# Essentials* introduces the Microsoft C# programming language, including the Microsoft .NET Common Language Runtime (CLR) and .NET Framework Class Libraries (FCL) that support it. This book's compact format and terse presentation of key concepts serve as a roadmap to the online documentation included with the Microsoft .NET Framework SDK; the many examples provide much-needed context.

COM and .NET Component Services

By Juval Löwy
1st Edition September 2001
384 pages, 0-596-00103-7

COM & .NET Component Services provides both traditional COM programmers and new .NET component developers with the information they need to begin developing applications that take full advantage of COM+ services. This book focuses on COM+ services, including support for transactions, queued components, events, concurrency management, and security.

VB.NET Framework Class Library in a Nutshell

By Budi Kurniawan
1st Edition May 2002
576 pages, ISBN 0-596-00257-2

With both a fast-paced tutorial and a reference, *VB.NET Framework Class Library* in a Nutshell meets the needs of two primary audiences: programmers who want a quick introduction to using the FCL, and those who want a comprehensive reference to the FCL in book form. This book is a sequel to *VB.NET Language in a Nutshell* in that it covers the classes in the .NET framework using VB syntax. It's a hardworking manual that belongs on every VB developer's bookshelf.

How to stay in touch with O'Reilly

1. Visit our award-winning web site

http://www.oreilly.com/

★ "Top 100 Sites on the Web"—PC Magazine
★ CIO Magazine's Web Business 50 Awards

Our web site contains a library of comprehensive product information (including book excerpts and tables of contents), downloadable software, background articles, interviews with technology leaders, links to relevant sites, book cover art, and more. File us in your bookmarks or favorites!

2. Join our email mailing lists

Sign up to get email announcements of new books and conferences, special offers, and O'Reilly Network technology newsletters at:

http://www.elists.oreilly.com

It's easy to customize your free elists subscription so you'll get exactly the O'Reilly news you want.

3. Get examples from our books

To find example files for a book, go to:

http://www.oreilly.com/catalog

select the book, and follow the "Examples" link.

4. Work with us

Check out our web site for current employment opportunites:

http://jobs.oreilly.com/

5. Register your book

Register your book at:

http://register.oreilly.com

6. Contact us

O'Reilly & Associates, Inc.
1005 Gravenstein Hwy North
Sebastopol, CA 95472 USA
TEL: 707-827-7000 or 800-998-9938
          (6am to 5pm PST)
FAX: 707-829-0104

order@oreilly.com
For answers to problems regarding your order or our products. To place a book order online visit:

http://www.oreilly.com/order_new/

catalog@oreilly.com
To request a copy of our latest catalog.

booktech@oreilly.com
For book content technical questions or corrections.

proposals@oreilly.com
To submit new book proposals to our editors and product managers.

international@oreilly.com
For information about our international distributors or translation queries. For a list of our distributors outside of North America check out:

http://international.oreilly.com/distributors.html